For Reference

Not to be taken from this room

TELEVISION DRAMA
SERIES PROGRAMMING:
A Comprehensive Chronicle,

1947-1959

by

Larry James Gianakos

The Scarecrow Press, Inc.
Metuchen, N.J., & London
1980

Library of Congress Cataloging in Publication Data

Gianakos, Larry James.
   Television drama series programming.

   Includes index.
   1. Television programs--United States.
I. Title.
PN1992.3.U5G48   791.45'75'0202   80-17023
ISBN 0-8108-1330-0

For my grandparents: James and Irene Gianakos, and
Anthony and Arhontoula Mougianis; and all their fellow
immigrants.

... they that were the prophets, poets, the carriers of
traditions and the harbingers of august dreams. In our
seasons of forebearance, they maintained replenishing
souls; not to dust they finally surrendered, but to eternal embers.

ACKNOWLEDGMENTS

Laudation must first be accorded the staff of the Kent State University Trumbull Campus Library--director Mrs. Evelina Smith and librarians Mr. Joseph Molendyke, Mrs. Barbara Bell and Mrs. Irma Fye--who induced a vitality out of somnolent afternoons.

Once again an appreciative note is extended the Warren Public Library reference staff, newly assisted by Ms. Meredith Elliott, Ms. Mona Stevenson, and Ms. Deborah Rinderknecht.

Lastly, I wish to thank Mr. Robert Reed for his timely amplifications.

CONTENTS

PREFACE

In a continuing effort to provide the reader with the most comprehensive coverage of television drama, the present volume contains several new features, added since the publication of its predecessor, Television Drama Series Programming: A Comprehensive Chronicle, 1959-1975.

A new section, "An Overview," seasonally expounds upon programming trends, augmenting critical reviews of selected teleplays, as well as discussing significant specials which would otherwise have been excluded from the series format that the volumes together adhere to.

The "Days and Times" section now includes all non-network programming, drama or otherwise. Situation comedies bear their featured performers in parentheses, while documentaries and interview programs are followed by hosts or hostesses. The reader who searches in vain for a fondly-remembered dramatic teleplay should be cautioned that many anthologies were subsequently telecast under new titles. Thus, by way of the notations provided, it is learned that the 1950 Story Theatre is a syndicated title for the 1949 Your Show Time, while the 1952 Ford Television Theatre alone provides episodes for several summer entries.

Dramatic programming comprehensively covered in Section III includes annotations for those teleplays later filmed, while in almost every case an adapted teleplay is accompanied by its original source. Therefore, segments composing the TV Reader's Digest are not merely followed by original authors, but by the original Reader's Digest issues and the inclusive page numbers in which the articles appear. There is frequent cross-referencing: Gore Vidal's Studio One teleplays "Dark Possession" and "Summer Pavilion" were

vii

subsequently restaged for the Matinee Theatre, for example. Like the last volume, a number of documentaries have also been included in this section. Those drama series commencing after the fall of 1959 but excluded from the previous volume have been restored herein. Once again programming arrangement adheres to the seasonal sequence of the "Days and Times" section.

The "Addenda" restores nearly all episode titles omitted from the last volume as well as providing any additional cast members or writers for teleplays already chronicled.

Syndicated titles for all dramatic series have been alphabetized in the index, bearing appropriate notation. Included are those series initiating previous to the fall of 1959 but chronicled in the second book.

SOURCES AND SELECTED BIBLIOGRAPHY

The chronicle of programming in this volume is essentially a composite of those listings contained in the New York Times (the microfilm edition meticulously researched reel-by-reel completely from 1947), Cue, and TV Guide magazines. To these, once again, has been added material drawn from the author's own viewing of teleplays for casts, literary and technical credits. Also, an excellent summary of television live drama by Worthington Miner appears in The Reader's Encyclopedia of World Drama (Thomas Y. Crowell, 1969).

In addition to the aforementioned periodicals, the author advises consulting the following supplementary materials:

Broadcast Information Bureau--TV Series Source Book (New York City, Semi-Annual Updates)

The Emmy Awards: A Pictorial History (Crown, 1971)

How Sweet It Was (Shorecrest, 1966)

A Pictorial History of Television (Chilton/Bonanza, 1959)

The New York Times Encyclopedia of Television (Quadrangle, 1977)

The Complete Encyclopedia of Television Programs (A. S. Barnes, 1976)

Actors' Television Credits (Scarecrow, 1972; supplemented 1978)

The Motion Picture Film Editor (Scarecrow, 1974)
A Title Guide to the Talkies (Scarecrow, 1965; updated 1977)
An Actor Guide to the Talkies (Scarecrow, 1967; updated 1977)
Drury's Guide to Best Plays (third edition; Scarecrow, 1978)

Again the author would be grateful for any corrections or amplifications on programming in either volume.

Larry Gianakos
1786 Dodge Drive N. W.
Warren, Ohio 44485

September 1, 1979

INTRODUCTION

It is a foregone conclusion that we are never again to witness so splendorous and flourishing a time for drama over American airwaves as once emerged from New York theatre houses in the 1950's. From the moment <u>Kraft Television Theatre</u> presented the original drama "Double Door" on May 7, 1947, unto its concluding teleplay of June 4, 1958, "The Last of the Belles" (James Cavanagh's fine rendering of the F. Scott Fitzgerald classic), a generation was emblematized of class. Now the sun has gone in dramatic programming, irretrievably buried, as it is, beneath banal scrip's produced with alarming speed out of Nielsen-conscious studios.

Nor should we be pleased by occasional network specials-- the much heralded reliefs from the banality. For in Stewart Stern's "Sybil," James Costigan's "Eleanor and Franklin," Herbert Brodkin's "Holocaust" and Steve Allen's continuing "Meeting of Minds," we have the genius of video veterans; creative minds who were the fruit of a less-constricted medium. Having preceded the inhibitory Hollywood practice of contract writing, these literate men sometimes resurface, living bastions of artistry for the home screen. Then, in affirmation of the substantive drama, normally subdued critics euphorically intone that a renaissance is in the making. Television, they proudly affirm, has become "relevant"--a word they indiscriminately apply to programs on dipsomania, aging, incest, poverty, and political scandal. And therein lies the fallacy. For television drama cannot be a substitute for reality; it must, instead, poetically raise that which begins in reality unto an art form. To do so requires creative minds of which contemporary Hollywood has precious few: they who were trained in the days of the live studio product (Stern, Costigan, Brodkin, and Allen), or they who are second- or

third-generation Hollywood, infused with the poetry of their progen-
itors (of which Tracy Keenan Wynn, whose pen distinguished "Tribes"
and "The Autobiography of Miss Jane Pittman," is an example).
Having plummeted from the artistic high of live studio drama, and
now struggling blindly through proliferating situation vehicles, television, indeed, has become symptomatic of a widespread mediocrity.
That brilliant scientific minds, who flourish now more than ever,
may conquer the stars says nothing of advancement in the arts. For
while technology moves forward undaunted, the arts in all areas--
on the stage, in music, in the novel, and most particularly on the
video--are regressing just as rapidly. The result for television will
be an international use of beautifully crafted videodisks--and very little of substance produced in the last decade to utilize them for.

Genuine artistry being a very infrequent commodity, we become the consumers of the incorporeal network amalgam, and this
because nowhere is there a powerful Industry voice for change.
Soap, that most insulting of contraptions--not for its toying with the
taboo, but for its leaving behind no tangible moral thread--is one
example of the dissipation. It cannot be properly called satire, nor
even very black comedy. Instead, it is a screaming Hollywood con-
ception of decadence made fun for everyone. Such, indeed, is the
decline of the medium, that before a huge undiscriminating audience,
personalities, and not actors, emerge as superstars; that trends are
blindly accepted. Even the normally prophetic All in the Family,
which, in its pristine episodes, was a serious social satire indeed,
has contributed to our overflowing can of video banality. For
through it spawned All That Glitters, unredeemed by its singularly
dubious premise that a fascist view of women should emerge funny
if seen as a fascist view of men, and Mary Hartman, Mary Hartman
and progeny, all less improvisational than gutterly conversational.
Unrelieved, the home screen offers a special brand of cacophony,
and grates like the sharpest of squeaking chalk on the human ears.

All of which further serves to call attention to the medium's
limitless potential as cultural inducement. Those who harbor vivid
recollections of Studio One, Kraft Theatre, Philco Playhouse, or

Omnibus, bear testament to the fact that sustained dramatic excellence over airwaves owes much to the anthologized form. For by
allowing a frequent exchange of writers and directors--and so of
material--one accepts the bad with the good, but always in anticipa-
tion of the latter. But with the exodus to the West Coast, ensuring
the Hollywood hierarchical domination of the filmed product in the
mid-fifties, the extended studio anthology could not have survived
the decade.

Yet, in the great migration, an abundance of the better New
York television artists also struck out to make their claim in the
film capital. Urged on by a highly conscientious Federal Communi-
cations Director in the person of Newton Minow, enthusiastic veterans prepared for the coming literary revival. Like a litany,
echoed and re-echoed through studio corridors, the industry an-
swered the Newton Minow chastisement on the "vast wasteland."
Continuing characters emerged more than one dimensional; writers
took their teleplay titles from classical quotations, including those
of Shelley, Hilaire Belloc, Yeats, Ernest Dowson, Wilde, Milton,
Shakespeare and the Bible. Just as Rod Serling had fused poetry
and science fiction to create the Twilight Zone in 1959, so, too,
would playwright Leslie Stevens elicit poetry from those employed
to dwell in The Outer Limits. And let there be no doubting of John
Kennedy's role. Though we may fault it politically, Camelot was,
after all, a gathering of the erudite and artistic. Here are just a
few of the splendid entries between the fall of 1961 and the close
of 1963:

> The Defenders. Herbert Brodkin's and Reginald Rose's
> unexcelled study of the legal process, reflecting the profes-
> sion's pre-Watergate patrician days of glory. Novelist How-
> ard Fast was but one contributor among a galaxy of resur-
> rected live anthology composers. One hundred and thirty-two
> of the most resplendent hours of courtroom folly and human
> rectitude in the medium's thirty years.
> Bus Stop. William Inge's much underrated adaptation of
> his celebrated drama-comedy. Beautifully poetic, its tale of
> nomads through a Colorado town in extremely well-told par-
> ables on human frailty remains a classic. This also accom-
> panied the fervor caused by Ellis Kadison's teleplay of a
> Tom Wicker novel, A Lion Walks Among Us, in which a cap-

italist murders for the stylish urgency it creates in him.
How perfectly discordant a teleplay to an age that prided itself on looking forward with optimism.
Combat! A shattering account on the sins of war. Just
to relate one Robert Altman teleplay will suffice. Protagon-
ist Sergeant Saunders is ordered to escort a seemingly ruth-
less lady journalist through the battlefronts. He finds her
dynamic pursual of story and photo unsettling. Until, she
having gone, Saunders receives the article, filled with eulogy
for the war's unending casualties. "I understand now," she
writes him. "But do you?" he silently responds. All of
this put to the accompaniment of Leonard Rosenman's beautiful musical score.
The Naked City. Mark Hellinger's masterpiece of urban
parable, transformed into a poetic urgency. All sorts of mis-
fits and dreamers fusing to erupt as a polity. So grandly
claustrophobic are the inhabitants it is as if the city were ex-
pressing itself.
East Side, West Side. David Susskind's triumphant tale of
a Manhattan private welfare agency, performed with the greatest of class by George C. Scott, Elizabeth Wilson and Cicely
Tyson as social workers and secretary. Expertly filmed,
even to the cadence of street rumblings.
The Eleventh Hour. The most potent group of psychological
case studies ever strung together for network consumption.
The magnum opus of producer Norman Felton, who later condescended to the espionage of The Man from U.N.C.L.E.

If to a Kennedy era must as well belong the reason for Ian

Fleming's James Bond characters, whose domination of the medium

would immediately follow the shots at Dallas, here credit must be

accorded the quality of these very early entries. So finely satirical,

yet with a foundation in this world, were those first Man from

U.N.C.L.E segments, one is inclined to forgive their deleterious

effect--rationalizing human extermination as they did. But even

artistic vestiges would almost vanish entirely with commercial series

over the coming years.

The emphasis in the secret intelligence series was now upon

the scientific technology utilized, with Mission: Impossible a popular

Cold War continuing adventure. Significantly, writers equated their

teleplays with reality; the aggressive "foreign power" was now given

a definite geographical limit. The intelligence operations, which

then seemed bizarre, were destined to have real-life foundations.

In a time of the Vietnam War and increasing social protest at home,

television remained oblivious to the gathering storm.

Once out of manifest destiny, out of Vietnam, past the Watergate political scandals that left an indelible scar of mistrust on those in power, nullifying the "law and order" thesis, the video merely glossied up its heroes. Satire was seldom understated and never poetic. The choice was either complete fantasy, via comic strip characters, or the "no-nonsense" police detective whose practices, as writers created them, were pretentious in their very exploitation. Rather than counselors, policemen were seen as two-fisted realists, screeching cars through seedy locales. At twenty-two segments a year, and with fifty-two minutes of teleplay, almost every plot now mirrored some other one; cars raced endlessly to no apparent destination; proper English was mutilated by way of the vernacular which, again, served no real topical purpose, but an exploitative one. And variations on The Mary Tyler Moore Show format resulted in stagnant replications as Hollywood looked to its own film classics for source material.

The British, meantime, asserted their mastery over historical drama. Elizabeth R, The Six Wives of Henry VIII, and the most sophisticated of the imports, Jack Pulman's adaptation of Robert Graves' I, Claudius, all were welcomed by academics and, indeed, by much of the video audience. If we had personalities, the British had their actors, and their public enthusiasm over quality drama could not easily be rivaled.

As the use of video recorders proliferates, Hollywood is expected to lose its network domination. For as viewer selectivity becomes a matter of videocassette purchasing, a commercial institution will necessarily yield to new dimensions. Until that time, scholars will continue to offer persuasive arguments on behalf of the medium's role in the literacy decline. But perhaps beyond that time, what will have been made decades ago will yet prove the most artistically satisfying; yesterday's writers having a majesty all their own.

SECTION I

Dramatic Programming, 1947-1959:
An Overview

1947-1959: AN OVERVIEW

Television had been anticipated and heralded, technologically ready, far in advance of the Second World War. It had been used extensively previous to and for the duration of it; but as a carrier of an image or an event. It was there to disseminate to the masses; a camera of far-extending receivers. With radio, drama was merely the logical progression; a total narrative art performed even as a parent might read to a child. Unlike the cinema, which could subvert in darkness, the radio waves could but titillate a singular sense; subversion depended upon a synesthesia in which the impetus was frequently oratory of the most carefully crafted components. But for a medium to stimulate yet another sense--thereby assuming a total potential to influence as art--and that might be institutionalized for the regular performing of art, could not, in the immediate years following the War, yet be comprehended. It was that lack of comprehension that left Hollywood, rich as the cinema bastion, to go forth initially unperturbed. It was that lack that gave to New York, cultural center of the world, the solitary right to let loose a bevy of artists who might explore a cultural resource of unfathomable bounds.

1948-1949 SEASON

Like the vapor out of a primeval bog, drama came to the airwaves anthologized as The Kraft Television Theatre on May 4, 1947, with the five-character "Double Door," to be followed almost consistently for the first few seasons by adaptations of New York plays. Jeffrey Dell's "Payment Deferred" (aired October 1, 1947), A. A. Milne's "The Truth About Blayds" (aired January 7, 1948), and Barry Connor's "Applesauce" (June 16, 1948) were among the second season offerings. Novice playwright hopefuls edited stage successes to fit the less than (allowing for commercials) sixty-minute time slots; a practice in itself artistically deleterious, but the rigidity of which schooled a generation on how to embellish the product for corporate gain. It was, it must be emphasized, initially the medium of the single sponsor who yielded some influence; the name more often than not preceded the drama. It might be thought that this singularity would be heinous to the creator, but, conversely, because one knew to whom he must answer, and because the viewing audience was comparatively a highly literate few, video art would come to flourish by mid-decade.

As if to usher in the excitement, the first Actor's Studio production bowed with the consummate husband and wife acting team of Hume Cronyn and Jessica Tandy; the former directing the latter in an original teleplay by Tennessee Williams. For that series Marlon Brando would make his first--and only (until, that is, the 1979 Roots II performance as a Nazi advocate)--appearance on the medium with the playlet "I'm No Hero" of January 9, 1949.

Then there came a steady stream of live anthologies, always sure to augment the sponsor's role in production. Philco Television Playhouse debuted October 3, 1948, with the Edna Ferber-George S. Kaufman classic "Dinner at Eight" with a stellar cast that also saw producer Fred Coe display his directorial finesse. Like Kraft Theatre, Philco's first few seasons were largely devoted to adaptations; it would take the advent of Goodyear Theatre, regularly displacing Philco in 1951, to bring out the brilliant youthful playwrights Paddy Chayefsky, Rod Serling, N. Richard Nash, J. P. Miller and their circle. Westinghouse Presents Studio One, bowing the Sunday of November 7, 1948, and soon becoming a Monday evening staple, was much distinguished in having the erudite Worthington Miner as overseer. First with the mystery "The Storm," then with Gian-Carlo Menotti's "The Medium," a beautiful modern dress "Julius Caesar" and the S. Ansky "The Dybbuk," it was a first season of enormous sophistication. Here was a testing ground for the likes of Jack Lemmon, Charlton Heston, John Forsythe and the most celebrated video actress of her day, Felicia Montealegre (later Mrs. Leonard Bernstein).

The Ford Motor Company quickly followed with an original teleplay on November 21, 1948, "Joy to the World," for its largely adapted anthology series The Ford Theatre Hour. The Chevrolet Tele-Theatre contrarily opened September 27, 1948, with a series of largely original, if uninspired, playlets. Both Suspense and the Robert L. Ripley Believe It or Not series took to the airwaves, after established time on radio, the following spring. Neither could be called consistently good, but Suspense was far the better, dramatizing well stories by John Collier, Somerset Maugham and Halstead Welles in its six seasons. The filmed, usually ersatz, Hollywood product was destined to arrive with the Fireside Theatre via the National Broadcasting Company as of April 5, 1949, with the married Yul Brynner and Virginia Gilmore (hosts of an early panel show) in "Friend of the Family." Filmed as well was the twenty-six segment anthology of famous short story adaptations, Your Show Time, sponsored by the American Tobacco Company and hosted by Arthur Shields.

The year closed, unabetted by the summer mystery entry Lights Out, having diminished from the high expectation the first fine teleplays induced, yet surviving well the apprehension that greets an unwalked labyrinth. At year's end the television net income was $14,900,000; by no means a corporate paradise, and so much the better for the eager artists.

1949-1950 SEASON

A profusion of anthologies arrived, some filmed (Silver

Theatre, The Boris Karloff Mystery Playhouse), but mostly live
(Video Theatre, Starlight Theatre, The Trap) significant principally
for their introducing Hollywood film and New York stage veterans
to the teleplay. Julie Harris scored well with "Bernice Bobs Her
Hair, " the F. Scott Fitzgerald adaptation for the Starlight Theatre's
second season episode of May 17, 1951. And Eva Gabor, Burgess
Meredith, Vicki Cummings, Glenda Farrell and Ward Bond followed
through as staple figures on the home screen. Bond had the distinction of appearing in the first "filmed" (that is, "non-kinescope")
teleplay with "My Brother's Keeper" on February 20, 1950, for the
Silver Theatre; a drama that also featured the then juvenile Glenn
Corbett.

The long-running (eight seasons) Robert Montgomery Presents
Your Lucky Strike Theatre arrived January 30, 1950, with an adaptation of Somerset Maugham's "The Letter" while for some time
thereafter offering a mixture of famous play, novel, and film scenario video presentations. More important was producer Montgomery's
establishment of repertory companies to do dramas for the summer
hiatus, a practice beginning 1952. Otherwise, Robert Montgomery
Presents was a very uneven omnibus that frequently faltered, even
with the original teleplays of the later seasons.

Not yet imposing enough for most industries (the net income
for the year 1949 was $24, 300, 000), television did however acquire
the ultimate test of audience strength with the Chicago A. C. Nielsen
company's audimeter, displacing the Hooper ratings as of March 12,
1950. The death knell for consistent artistry over the airwaves was
not to come until later in the decade, when the established ratings
fused with a newly transplanted capital (New York to Hollywood) to
leave literacy smouldering.

The summer of 1950 saw the dawn of the documentary-drama
Armstrong Circle Theatre (seemingly obsessed with moralizing over
communism by mid-decade) on June 6; the splendid Masterpiece Playhouse, consisting of seven classics, debuted the twenty-third of July.
The suspense anthology The Web commenced July 4 and paved an
only slightly distinguished path for the duration of its 210 teleplays;
but the fine craftsman Albert McCleery ignited a more majestic
flame with his Cameo Theatre, which included a teleplay by Irwin
Shaw and an excellent three-part adaptation of Ibsen's "Peer Gynt"
in its third season.

1950-1951 SEASON

From radio came the Lux Video Theatre, opening with an
adaptation of Maxwell Anderson's "Saturday's Children" on October
2, 1950, and providing the medium's first seasonally scheduled yuletide drama, Stephen Vincent Benét's "A Child Is Born, " premiering
Christmas Day. While Lux had offered teleplays by Rod Serling
(most notably "Mr. Finchley Versus the Bomb" for the fifty-ninth
telecast) and the prolific Robert Howard Lindsay, it would inevitably
(by the fifth season) become a package of condensed motion picture
scenarios.

Musical Comedy Time, a mere thirteen programs beginning October 2, 1950, did little to sustain audience attention, so pallid seemed the productions alongside their Broadway originals. And Billy Rose's Playbill left one to ponder how the great showman could permit so meager a take-off. But Danger, premiering September 26, 1950, would prove the foremost suspense anthology of its day, what with the splendid supervision of Yul Brynner and Sidney Lumet. Saki, W. F. Harvey, Agatha Christie, Stephen Crane, and Ambrose Bierce were among the sources whose mysteries were credibly realized, even if the musical accompaniment was poorly received.

The Pulitzer Prize Playhouse, the recipient of the 1950 "Emmy" award as the best dramatic series, somewhat confused its viewers by leading them to believe the dramas were based on Pulitzer Prize laureates when, indeed, several of the sources were not even nominees. Rather, the theme seemed to be that the source have some connection to the Prize, even if not a winner. Whichever the case, these were indeed literate versions as hosted by the playwright Elmer Davis. Neither Stars Over Hollywood nor The Nash Airflyte Theatre could accommodate the literary palate; neither lasted out the season.

Meantime, the Prudential Family Playhouse did little to heighten its thirteen stock productions as transposed and edited from the Broadway stage. But the viewers were well-served by the British erudition of Somerset Maugham, host to forty-seven of his adapted stories, collectively referred to as Teller of Tales. Faith Baldwin, having reigned over the domestic drama, could not, needless to say, successfully adapt the same formula by introducing her mid-season Theatre of Romance episodes.

Chiming in the forthcoming spring, as if in celebration of the fact that television had spread to ten million households, was the Richard Rodgers Jubilee Show. In commemoration of the musician's twenty-fifth year in the theatre and featuring the video debut of Mary Martin (assisted by Celeste Holm, Patrice Munsel, Lawrence Tibbett, Jerome Hines, Valerie Bettis, Brian Sullivan, and Vivienne Segal), Jubilee's evening of March 4, 1951, foreshadowed the prime-time "spectaculars" not far away.

1951-1952 SEASON

Once again it was a year of Broadway adaptations dominating air time. Celanese Theatre won a coveted Peabody Award for its twenty-segment anthology of estimable theatre works; O'Neill's Ah, Wilderness!, the first, aired October 3, 1951. The Broadway Television Theatre staged well seventy-four of the more celebrated New York plays; productions were repeated each weeknight so as to be the more accessible. A spring entry, this Television Theatre first presented Bayard Veiller's "The Trial of Mary Dugan" April 4, 1952, and closed three seasons later, January 25, 1954, with Barry Connor's "The Patsy."

As produced by George Schaefer and Mildred Freed Alberg,
The Hallmark Hall of Fame was transposed from radio Christmas
evening of 1951, when the NBC Opera Company presented the debut
of Gian-Carlo Menotti's neo-classic Amahl and the Night Visitors.
Its splendid reception by both critics and the general public made
it a certain candidate for annual holiday revival; it was repeated
for several years thereafter until Menotti withdrew it, only to re-
vise it in 1978. Hallmark then became a regular series of biographical dramas January 6, 1952, with Sarah Churchill (daughter
of Sir Winston) as hostess and occasional star. But the series'
chief distinction was its special presentations, Shakespeare's Hamlet, King Richard II, and Macbeth, and Melville's Moby Dick
among them. By the fall of 1955, the series had completely abandoned the biographies in favor of sometimes superb ninety-minute
productions of established and original plays.

The filmed product continued its proliferation. The flat
twenty-six segment Hollywood originated Gruen Guild Playhouse
arrived September 27, 1951 to be succeeded by the (initially) hour-
long Schlitz Playhouse of the Stars the fifth of October. Schlitz
prodded forth an undistinguished career, but for a few of its (for
the most part) original teleplays: Walter C. Brown's "The Unlighted
Road" with the brooding James Dean was just such an exception. In
later years the anthology would introduce the pilots to two profitable
westerns: Tales of Wells Fargo with Dale Robertson, and The Restless Gun with John Payne.

Tales of Tomorrow, inaugurated August 3, 1951, did little to
augment the poetry of science fiction (that would have to wait until
Rod Serling's Twilight Zone of 1959 and Leslie Stevens' The Outer
Limits of 1963), but it did present well two of the genre's best:
Mary Shelley's Frankenstein and Jules Verne's Twenty Thousand
Leagues Under the Sea. Not any of the remaining spring filmed
entries--The Unexpected, Rebound, Police Story--were cause for
sustained viewing; low-budgeted and stilted, none survived beyond a
second season.

The connoisseur looked to established entries for fine drama.
Michael Dyne's highly acclaimed Pontius Pilate, the basis for his
Broadway play Most Honourable Gentleman, was the April 7, 1952,
offering for Studio One, while Kraft Theatre and Philco Playhouse
were readying for the fall with an array of impressive teleplays.

1952-1953 SEASON

The fall saw the birth of the nacreous Omnibus, the Ford
Foundation's Television Workshop's special assortment for eight
years of literate afternoons. With the sure guidance of producer
William Spier and the urbane commentary of host Alistair Cooke,
Omnibus gracefully mixed the arts and sciences and called on the
expertise of men and women highly regarded in academia. Among
the quintet of features on the opening program, November 9, 1952,
was Maxwell Anderson's own adaptation of his Anne of the Thousand

Days, directed by Alex Segal and featuring the then husband and wife Rex Harrison and Lilli Palmer. Other outstanding first season programs included James Agee's serialized biographical drama "Mr. Lincoln"; William Saroyan's holiday feature "The Christmas Tie"; the Metropolitan Opera Company's premiere television production of Johann Strauss' Die Fledermaus which was succeeded by Puccini's La Boheme; Tennessee Williams' "Lord Byron's Love Letter" and the George Gershwin operetta "135th Street."

As usual the filmed dramas were far inferior. The Ford Television Theatre, after its radio run, arrived October 2, 1952, as a vehicle for the display of guest stars and was sustained through 194 episodes which could be packaged under separate titles for summer program scheduling. The Four Star Playhouse, the video offering of a newly formed independent production team of Charles Boyer, Dick Powell, David Niven and Ida Lupino, hardly ameliorated acting careers. Powell, however, achieved a purely popular triumph as a night club proprietor turned private eye, Willie Dante, of the featured episodes forming Dante's Inferno.

Cavalcade of America came from radio October 1, 1952, to offer four seasons of biographical dramas before taking the sponsor's title and becoming the non-historical Dupont Theatre. Cavalcade's accounts were not the most meticulously researched and its list of subjects was both dubious and desultory. A number of other dramas, The Gulf Playhouse, Your Jeweler's Showcase and the twice weekly, fifteen-minute Short, Short Drama meanwhile passed through the season relatively unnoticed.

Impressive in concept was You Are There, as derived from the radio series, which placed CBS reporters anachronously alongside historical figures, there to comment on destiny's course. Its first re-enactment was "The Landing of the Hindenburg," airing February 1, 1953, to be followed by resurrections of Jesse James, John Dillinger, Joan of Arc and Julius Caesar. Its five seasons of historical commentary earned it critical plaudits while making a family celebrity of its staccato-voiced host, Walter Cronkite. For the more sophisticated mind there was the Peabody award-winning "Victory at Sea," a superbly edited reconstruction of some 60,000,000 feet of government film on World War II naval history. As produced by Henry Salomon Jr., with a celebrated musical score by Richard Rodgers and orchestration by Robert Russell Bennett, it was panegyrized by Harper's as "an epic poem in praise of sea power."

Of the video's first medical entry, The Doctor, with Warner Anderson as general practitioner, it can only be said that it did nothing for medicine or drama. Spring brought The Plymouth Playhouse, no more than a group of introductory films for projected series; Robert Montgomery's short lived and poorly received mystery anthology Eyewitness, and the both filmed and live General Electric Theatre which was seldom worthwhile.

Nobel laureate William Faulkner first attempted the teleplay with his adaptation of his short story "The Brooch" for the Lux Video Theatre episode of April 2, 1953. Critics were not impressed, noting the story's emasculation for the diet of home viewers. Again, Faulkner attempted a teleplay for Lux, this time of his "Shall Not Perish" (aired February 11, 1954) which was made contemporary to the Korean War; again the critical reaction was unfavorable. The Hollywood Screen Test departed from its regular format to present Alton Alexander's and Mort Lewis' poignant drama With Malice Toward None, with Hal Holbrook as the off-stage narrator and Abraham Lincoln voice. As directed by Frederick Carr it pleased the critics who watched February 2, 1953.

A beauteous NBC opera presentation was Leonard Bernstein's Trouble in Tahiti, telecast November 16, 1952, with featured performers Beverly Wolff and David Atkinson, and Seymour Lipkin as pianist. It preceded the Christmas Day restaging of Menotti's Amahl and the Night Visitors which the NBC Opera Company again cast with Rosemary Kuhlmann, William McIver, and Andrew McKinley.

The following summer's new dramatic series induced little intellectual stimulation. First Person Playhouse, The Campbell Television Soundstage, and The Chrysler Medallion Theatre seemed to serve as a respite for the more probing playwrights whose gifts were reserved for the coming season's proven anthologies. The Revlon Mirror Theatre, launched June 23, 1953, did open with a restaging of the William Marik fine Actor's Studio drama "Little Wife"; though its glory days were yet to come, already the new medium was reminiscing.

The multi-talented Jackie Gleason endeared viewers with his "Tawny, " having himself composed the musical score which was choreographed by June Taylor. It was both a personal triumph for Gleason and a plus to the summer, airing as a segment of the Jackie Gleason Show May 30, 1953.

Neither the excitement of the first televised Academy Awards program, airing March 23, 1953, nor the spectacle of the Queen Elizabeth II coronation of June 2, 1953, had quite prepared Americans for Ford Motor Company Fiftieth Anniversary Show, subtitled The American Road and telecast June 15, 1953, via both NBC and CBS networks. To say that the critics were ecstatic would be an understatement. "Terrific!, Terrific!" was the banner attached the Jack Gould review in the New York Times the following day; Gould adding that "seldom has there been such glorious television. "

The American Road, under the production hand of Leland Hayward, drew the utmost from its stellar group of writers, singers, actors and dancers. With choreography by Jerome Robbins, musical accompaniment by Bernard Green, scripts by Frederick Lewis and Agnes Rogers Allen, Howard Teichman and Sidney Olson, costumes by Irene Sharaff, narration by Oscar Hammerstein II and Edward R. Murrow, it was a director's dream. And that Clark Jones guided his procession--Mary Martin, Ethel Merman, Frank Sinatra, Dorothy

Stickney, Rudy Vallee, Eddie Fisher, Wally Cox, Marian Anderson among the crowd--with unabated euphoria there could be no doubt. Two of its most celebrated scenes have been widely imitated but never rivaled. The first involved a fashion show by Miss Martin, satirically modeling changes in period dress; the latter, the most fondly remembered, solitarily set Misses Merman and Martin on stools, the better to heighten the competitive vocalizing of their most famous show tunes. Having reached a jubilant pinnacle, artists apprehensively awaited the coming season.

1953-1954 SEASON

But the cheering died. And not for lack of artistry, but for the suffusion of McCarthyism. A sustained inquisitorial infraction of civil liberties came to the home screen, transplanted from Hollywood House Un-American Activities Committee rooms. Yet somehow obsessed with their believed "infiltration" of the motion picture industry by communists, inquisitors could not prevent, if the West Coast product be mitigated, creative flow out of New York studios. There a noble circle had gone forth undaunted, as if in defiance of the prevailing cesspool.

In the face of demagogues the mass audience had seen reticent witnesses, willing informers and the adamantly conscientious. Among the gifted maligned were Carl Foreman, Dorothy Parker and her husband Alan Campbell, Edward and Jerome Chodorov, Dashiell Hammett, Donald Ogden Stewart, Robert Rosson, and Ring Lardner Jr., John Howard Lawson and Dalton Trumbo of the "Hollywood Ten." The brilliant Lillian Hellman was particularly inspiring in her unfaltering disapproval of McCarthy method. Now so many who had meant so much to the legitimate stage were forced to compose under pseudonym. It would take, however, the McCarthy allegations on infiltration in the sacrosanct American army, as televised with "The Army McCarthy hearings," to bring the long deserved public chastisement.

First, however, came an excoriation by Newton Minow, via his See It Now of March 9, 1954 to which Joseph McCarthy replied vehemently on April 9, 1954. Having watched the contrary addresses, viewers awaited the impending storm. After thirty days of hearings, on April 22, 1954, McCarthy unmercifully attacked one Fred Fisher, once an aide to Army counsel Joseph Welch. Having too long borne witness to the vituperation, the normally quiescent Attorney Welsh cathartically intoned "You have done enough. Have you no sense of decency, sir, at long last? Have you left no sense of decency?" Like a great "Amen," the storm had broken, having surrendered its vitriol.

Against the political winds the fall season of 1953 arrived with the live studio product scoring several notes of triumph. Studio One entered its sixth season with a splendid William Templeton adaptation of George Orwell's 1984, as directed by Paul Nickell and

produced by Felix Jackson for the evening of September 21, 1953.
Reginald Rose triumphed twice for the Studio One season: first with
his allegorical "The Remarkable Incident at Carson Corners" (January 11, 1954), then with a sentimental tale of a veteran's readjust-
ment to civilian life, "The Life and Death of Larry Benson" (May 31,
1954).   Paddy Chayefsky likewise twice enjoyed critical plaudits for
his Philco Playhouse dramas "The Bachelor Party" (October 11,
1953) and "The Mother" (April 4, 1954).   Kraft Theatre entered a
twice weekly format as of October 15, 1953, while giving the young
James Dean his best role yet with "A Long Time Till Dawn" (November 11, 1953).   Omnibus, meanwhile, continued its penchant for
excellence with William Inge's "Glory in the Flower," the second
season opener on October 4, 1953 and with the inimitable Orson
Welles in the title role of a seventy-three minute condensation of
King Lear, which was directed by Peter Brook.

        After a distinguished career on radio The Theatre Guild of the
Air bowed October 27, 1953, with David Davidson's "P. O. W. ," the
first in the twelve seasons of United States Steel Hour productions.
The single season Motorola Television Hour paled by comparison;
a musical adaptation of James Thurber's "The Thirteen Clocks" was
among its few programs of merit.   Of course no literary salvation
could be expected of the several new filmed series; of short duration
were The Pepsi Cola Playhouse, Love Story, and The Playhouse.
Nor could the more discriminating taste be satisfied by the stock
productions of A Letter to Loretta, in which the glamourous Loretta
Young weekly sashayed through doorways, beginning September 20,
1953, and for eight seasons thereafter.

        The spring entry Justice, however, with its dramas based on
Legal Aid files, seemed a fitting edification after the McCarthy fall.
The season's spectacular, The General Foods Twenty-fifth Anniversary Show, heralded the coming of better days having pleased a
huge audience (carried by 245 stations representing all three networks) on March 28, 1954.   Essentially an homage paid the partnership of Richard Rodgers and Oscar Hammerstein II, the General
Foods Anniversary consisted of numbers from the Broadway shows
Oklahoma!, Carousel, State Fair, Allegro, The King and I and Me
and Juliet, with several of the original performers.   Another special,
although not on so grand a scale, was Once Upon an Eastertime,
airing April 18, 1954.   Under the sponsorship of Leon Leonidoff,
this holiday observation showcased the talents of Gwen Verdon,
Doretta Morrow, Bobby Clark, and Pud Flanagan.

1954-1955 SEASON

        Autumn brought forth the regularly scheduled "spectacular"
first taking the form of the dismal Satins and Spurs, an original
musical comedy airing September 12, 1954.   With music and lyrics
by Jay Livingston and Ray Evans, a book by William Friedberg and
Max Liebman (who also produced) and art direction by Frederick
Fox, Satins and Spurs proferred small creative advancement.   Indeed,

with its western theme of the love of a cowgirl (Betty Hutton) for a
contrasting gentlemanly reporter (Kevin McCarthy), Satins seemed
an anemic echo of Annie Get Your Gun. Yet producer Liebman
went forward, offering "spectaculars" every fourth Sunday.

A far more successful enterprise was the monthly Monday
festivity Producer's Showcase, employing a dizzying array of talents.
The first Showcase, Tonight at 8:30, F. Hugh Herbert's collection
of three Noel Coward plays under the production hands of Otto Preminger, joyously entered living rooms the evening of October 18, 1954.
The coming programs successively outdid each other, climaxing in
the most splendid "spectacular" of them all, the melodious "Peter
Pan." Performed with even greater gusto than the Broadway premiere of October 20, 1954, this "Peter Pan" mixed the choreograph-
ic genius of Jerome Robbins, the lyrics of Carolyn Leigh, Betty
Comden and Adolph Green, to the music of Mark Charlap and Jule
Styne to make the evening of March 7, 1955, a clarion to the heart.
Later filmed, and annually repeated, Peter Pan, having Mary Martin sailing on wires and vocalizing octaves, and Cyril Ritchard as
a perfectly perfidious Captain Hook, continually electrifies video
audiences. The Best of Broadway, meantime, highlighted nine
Wednesday evenings commencing with the George S. Kaufman-Edna
Ferber play "The Royal Family," telecast September 15, 1954.

Light's Diamond Jubilee, an all network celebration in honor
of the seventy-fifth anniversary of the electric light, captivated the
evening of October 24, 1954. As produced by David O. Selznick,
with direction by Christian Nyby, King Vidor, William A. Wellman,
Alan Handley, teleplays by Irwin Shaw, John Steinbeck, Arthur Gordon and Max Schulman, and photography by James Wong Howe, the
Jubilee could not have been a more glittering commemorative. Yet
the sketches varied wildly, from Dorothy Dandridge singing to Gershwin, Judith Anderson dramatizing the significance of the Statue of
Liberty and a George Gobel monologue, to historical playlets with
the likes of Helen Hayes, Thomas Mitchell, David Niven and Lauren
Bacall. But the tapestry held together, in any event, with the uni-
fying narration of Joseph Cotten.

Anthologized drama gained a worthy collection with The Elgin
Hour, Appointment with Adventure, Pond's Theatre (essentially Kraft
Theatre under new sponsorship), and the summer entries Front Row
Center and Windows. Elgin Hour provided two especially well-
composed teleplays with Joseph Schull's "The Bridge," and Reginald
Rose's "Crime in the Streets," which was filmed by Allied Artists
in 1956. Appointment with Adventure proved an enjoyable excursion
for composers the calibre of Rod Serling, Jerome Ross, and Mann
Rubin, while Pond's Theatre enabled the former actor Wendell Mayes
to display his literary skill with the westerns "No Riders," "Hang
Up My Guns" and "Death Is a Spanish Dancer." Front Row Center
graced the summer months with notable Broadway adaptations, even
as the five teleplays composing Windows could boast respectable
versions of Ray Bradbury's and Mary E. Wilkins Freeman's short
stories.

But the filmed series again left much to be desired. The
non-network Studio 57, the Hollywood originated Rheingold Theatre
(with thirteen adaptations of Somerset Maugham), The Damon Runyon
Theatre and Stage 7 all merely served to better illustrate the uninhibited way in which a celluloid product could proceed. Producer
Chester Erskine brought TV Reader's Digest from its radio counterpart, to further dramatize favorite articles from the widely read
monthly magazine. Predictably routine, the video Digest occasionally
eschewed communist manifesto in such Frederick Sondern Jr. pieces
as "Comrade Lindemann's Conscience" and "The Brainwashing of
John Hayes." James Moser's meticulously researched Medic, however, unceremoniously diagnosed its medical clientele in the fifty-
nine teleplays beginning September 13, 1954.

Then there was Climax!, which was to alternate with the
monthly Shower of Stars. Initially packaged as a suspense anthology,
Climax! first offered Raymond Chandler's "The Long Goodbye" on
October 7, 1954, and proceeded with Ian Fleming's "Casino Royale,"
Mary Roberts Rinehart's "The After House," William Faulkner's
"An Error in Chemistry," and an uninspired version of the Lucille
Fletcher radio classic "Sorry, Wrong Number." Shower of Stars
gifted the Christmas holiday with a sublime musical "A Christmas
Carol." The Dickens favorite was set to music by Bernard Herr-
mann and had a libretto by the incomparable Maxwell Anderson; the
production was thrice presented as a yuletide feature for Shower of
Stars first on the evening of December 23, 1954. Mid-season arrivals
included Star Tonight (just that--a star's outing), and Truman Bradley's Science Fiction Theatre, the films of which were opened and
closed with factual commentaries.

The real dramatic rewards could be found amid the pre-
existing anthologies. Rod Serling's superb study of clashing business executives, Patterns, was much lauded, initially airing January
12, 1955, and encored February 9, 1955. Among the drama's outstanding players were Everett Sloane, Ed Begley, Richard Kiley,
Joanna Roos and Elizabeth Wilson--each attuned to the directorial
brilliance of Fielder Cook. Basking in the limelight of its Patterns,
Kraft Theatre then offered an exemplary "Emperor Jones," with
Ossie Davis as the principal of the Eugene O'Neill classic. Studio
One entered its seventh season with Reginald Rose's intense drama
of jury room polemic, "Twelve Angry Men," telecast September 26,
1954. Rose followed through with the acclaimed "An Almanac on
Liberty," which was based on the collected essays of Supreme Court
Associate Justice William O. Douglas. And Gore Vidal, whose
"Dark Possession" had been an eminent Studio One program on February 15, 1954, again composed for the same production crew a
penetrating Southern drama, "Summer Pavilion," presented May 2,
1955. Not to be outdone, The Philco Playhouse opened its seventh
season with Paddy Chayefsky's Middle of the Night on September 19,
1954. The Sunday anthology then presented works by Sumner Locke
Elliott, J. P. Miller, Marc Brandel, Tad Mosel and Robert Alan
Aurthur. Finally, Omnibus displayed again its high standards with
historian Allan Nevins' continued analysis of the Adams family whose

lives were dramatized in four parts beginning January 9, 1955.
Other season dramas were condensations of Sophocles' Antigone,
George Bernard Shaw's The Trial of St. Joan, and Gore Vidal's
adaptation of Henry James' The Turn of the Screw. Omnibus also
first featured Leonard Bernstein as lecturer, with his "Analysis of
the First Movement of Beethoven's Fifth Symphony," on November
14, 1954.

Filtering through the quality programming was the smoke of
the McCarthy fire. The anti-communist commentary following the
Producer's Showcase adaptation of Sidney Kingsley's "Darkness at
Noon," as delivered by Vice President Richard Nixon, bewildered
both critics and the general audience. Although it was a time of
falling ideologues, conservatives whispered concern over an increas-
ingly libertarian High Court. Not a summer before, See It Now's
Edward R. Murrow had explored the effects of the Brown decision
with the May 25, 1954, program, "Two Southern Towns Look at the
Supreme Court Decision." To skirt both whispers and solemnity,
the network subterfuge took the form of inducing purely escapist
programming. Thus, Disneyland brought the animator genius of
Walt Disney to the airwaves commencing October 27, 1954 (the
series continues, after an unabated twenty-five years, to this day).
And animated characters might best be used to describe those 205
monetary recipients of the estate of The Millionaire, the escapist
entry beginning January 19, 1955. Even the "spectacular" had ac-
quired a stymied look: the summer's Swengali and the Blonde
(after George du Maurier's Trilby) little accentuated the talents of
Carol Channing, Ethel Barrymore and Basil Rathbone. Still, aes-
thetes awaited their replenishing fall.

1955-56 SEASON

A blaze of glory for the medium, what with Playwrights '56
a superb addition to the dramatic anthology. Playwrights was to
alternate with Armstrong Circle Theatre and would offer, as but one
sublime example, William Faulkner's The Sound and the Fury on
December 6, 1955, with very potent performances by Franchot Tone,
Janice Rule, Lillian Gish, Valerie Bettis, Steven Hill and Ethel
Waters in the faithful William Durkee teleplay. Too long had the
parent film industry patronized; mitigating aesthetic capabilities.
And so it was that this year an overwhelming number of live teleplays, deliberately and justifiably prepossessing, could carry their
own before the Hollywood celluloid. Indeed, New York writers
would soon find themselves firmly implanted on the West Coast,
adapting for the cinema: Robert Alan Aurthur would transpose his
fine "A Man Is Ten Feet Tall" (telecast for Philco Playhouse October 2, 1955) with Edge of the City (1956); Reginald Rose would bring
to Dino (1957) all the poignance of the juvenile's despair as first
conveyed for Studio One January 2, 1956, and Melvin Wald and Jack
Jacobs would augment the crisis of broken home with their Man on
Fire (1957), initially created for The Alcoa Hour of March 4, 1956.

There was further cause for celebration: master film director Alfred Hitchcock would emerge a staple silhouette before television audiences for ten years dispensing a criminal polemic for
which the proverbial flaw not always surfaced. His series would be
a heavily literary omnibus: Francis Didelot, H. G. Wells, John
Collier and Cornell Woolrich novels were well-served alongside original compositions by Ray Bradbury, Robert Bloch, and Roald Dahl.
The latter's "Lamb to the Slaughter" (telecast April 13, 1958) about
a murder weapon (the leg of lamb) served by the murderess and
consumed by detectives, wonderfully illuminated that tongue-in-cheek
style. Such was the magnanimity of Hitchcock's presence that,
freed of the notorious Hollywood hierarchical mold, his 358 aired
teleplays are still syndicated and satisfying; the opening dictums yet
evoke knowing smiles.

But there were seeds of destruction nurturing, taking the
form of the mass-produced studio product, as executives saw fresh
commercial gains. From Warner Brothers there came Cheyenne,
a western saga of a peregrinating Indian-bred hero, a role seemingly created for its actor, Clint Walker. Admittedly a step forward
for the video horse opera, the series was, however, a perfect example of how easily banality emerges from contract writing.

The Twentieth Century-Fox Hour, totalling thirty-six features
(which may still be purchased for syndication), dubiously copied
classics by the film enterprise of the title. Here was Henry Hathaway's Fourteen Hours (1951) re-scripted as "The Man on the Ledge";
William Welman's The Ox-Bow Incident (1943) as "The Lynch Mob";
Noel Coward's Cavalcade (filmed 1933 by Frank Lloyd) as "The
Heart of a Woman"; and Henry King's 1938 In Old Chicago as "City
In Flames." All were rather haphazardly pieced together; forever
unworthy of their parent products. To compound the dissipation,
prevalent were the playlets used to no other apparent end than to
fill air time: Screen Director's Playhouse, Star Stage, Star Tonight, and the didactic Crossroads.

Still the drama flourished, with the occasional Ford Star
Jubilee carrying on the tradition of lavish specials. Here was Herman Wouk's "The Caine Mutiny" directed with great reverence and
with a superlative cast that included Lloyd Nolan, Barry Sullivan
and Frank Lovejoy in leads; here was Maxwell Anderson's "High
Tor" with a vibrant Julie Andrews, Bing Crosby and Hans Conried;
here was the legendary Orson Welles strikingly cast against Betty
Grable in the Ben Hecht/Charles MacArthur "The Twentieth Century."

Then, too, the existing anthologies had their share of ex-
tremely potent dramas. Reginald Rose's masterful tale of vigilante
terror and its ultimate excoriation, "Tragedy in a Temporary Town,"
telecast on The Alcoa Hour of February 19, 1956 trenchantly directed
by Sidney Lumet, brought weighty panegyrics. Jack Gould of the
New York Times assessed its impact as that which made "a viewer's
flesh creep." Marvelous also was Alvin Sapinsley's allegorical

"Even the Weariest River," directed by Robert Mulligan. Beautifully poetic, even to its title (a stanza from Swinburne's Garden of
Proserpine), Jack Gould held it as "one of the season's finest
achievements."

Finally, to carry the torch, there was Matinee Theatre, with
five afternoon dramas per week, intended to offset those dreary
hours before prime-time. The medium still pristine with a creative
force, there would yet be seasons to hold back the impending artistic prostitution.

1956-57 SEASON

It was the year of Playhouse 90, that hour-and-a-half masterpiece of continued production, employing, quite simply, the best
there was. Under the auspices of veterans Martin Manulis, Fred
Coe, John Houseman and Herbert Brodkin; directors the calibre of
John Frankenheimer, George Roy Hill, Alex Segal, Franklin Schaffner, Delbert Mann and Robert Stevens; beautifully realized teleplays
by Horton Foote, Irving Gaynor Neiman, Rod Serling, J. P. Miller,
Stewart Stern, Reginald Rose and Sumner Locke Elliott, it was a
glittering diamond in the sky, there to remind of the medium's potential.

Through Playhouse 90 William Faulkner enthusiast Horton
Foote would emerge the Laureate's foremost video translator. "Old
Man," telecast November 20, 1958, with Sterling Hayden and Geraldine Page in the leads, and "Tomorrow," telecast March 7, 1960,
and featuring Kim Stanley and Richard Boone, gracefully augmented
Faulkner's regional force. J. P. Miller's haunting study of a young
couple's excursion through the dredges of dipsomania fully lived up
to the evocative Ernest Dowson title "The Days of Wine and Roses."
And here was Ernest Hemingway, as well adapted as ever before,
with A. E. Hotchner's two-part "For Whom the Bell Tolls," telecast March 12 and March 19, 1959. There were three memorable
feature films derived from teleplays: Rod Serling's "Requiem for a
Heavyweight" (October 11, 1959; filmed 1962); the Helen Keller autobiography as adapted by William Gibson with "The Miracle Worker"
(February 7, 1957; filmed 1962), and Abby Mann's "Judgment at
Nuremberg" (April 16, 1959; filmed 1961).

Not any of the numerous other dramatic anthologies (most of
them filmed) were particularly noteworthy. The vogue was to capi-
talize on the appeal of a star host: Joseph Cotten introduced the
courtroom drama On Trial; Thomas Mitchell appeared as O. Henry
for The O. Henry Playhouse, a syndicated entry; Errol Flynn, Lilli
Palmer, Ethel Barrymore and George Sanders each had a series of
playlets bearing their name.

Elsewhere, West Point Story was a rather cumbersome tale
of martinets and unruly novices (these were, after all, the days of
military valor); Noah's Ark was a typical Jack Webb exercise in its

adulation of veterinarians; the costume dramas The Buccaneers and The Adventures of Sir Lancelot drifted far from historical record, and the western genre was not ameliorated by the presence of Broken Arrow and Tales of Wells Fargo.

Critics, then, kept their eyes to the continuing live dramas, whose days were surely numbered.

1957-58 SEASON

It was not, surely, a season of dramatic growth. So brilliant, so stylized an anthology as The Alcoa Hour and The Goodyear Playhouse dissipated into the half-hour A Turn of Fate, a prototype of true dramatic series, which for producers meant regular performers and a similarity of themes.   Warner Brothers, inspired by the success of Cheyenne, and as if to echo luminously Roy Huggins' parody Maverick, followed through with an entry on the least likely of western heroes, a discontented lad bound but for the confines of litigatory procedure--Tom Brewster as "Sugarfoot."   And yet the irreverence was welcome; the hero was freer as was the terrain in which he wandered and somehow, the always present commemorative ballad seemed the more apt in the relaxed atmosphere.   Yet the grandest of all western anthologies was Wagon Train, which, in the best of Horace Greeley traditions, evoked a sentimental, quiescent journey through a much romanticized West.   Frequently well-written, Wagon Train had a knack for casting guest performers against type-- as testament: Lou Costello a derelict and John Barrymore Jr. a psychopath.   Man was now married finally to his land; he had kingdoms to cross, and in this great spirit an immense audience would revel.

What it meant was that you were to be larger than life, and, as this had everything to do with ego, narcissism was expected, eagerly anticipated.   And so it was that in 1957 Erle Stanley Gardner's unflinching counselor "Perry Mason, " a panacea for the legally disenfranchised (despite the fact that clientele were noticeably upper-echelon), was born, ushering in a stream of judicial illusions. Against this pandemic desire for pluperfect heroes, whose motives were crystal clear, whose life-style was open to public inspection, there evolved detective heroes the likes of Lieutenant Bill Ballinger (Lee Marvin's role in M Squad) and Mr. McGraw, the lone rebel of Meet McGraw, a vehicle for an especially gruff Frank Lovejoy.

Through the dissipation there remained an original thread, in the form of the anthology Suspicion and in The Seven Lively Arts, John Houseman's mélange of documentaries, dramas and musical programs with an erudite host in the person of John Crosby, critic for the New York Herald Tribune.   Arts was, to say the least, short-lived and soon forgotten.   Suspicion, however, was impressive both critically and in terms of amassing a fair share of audience. Its opening program was a well-adapted (by Francis Cockrell) version of Cornell Woolrich's Four O'Clock, stylishly directed by no less than

Alfred Hitchcock. Among the other fine segments of the anthology were Eric Ambler's own retelling of his "The Eye of Truth" and an inspired adaptation of William Hope Hodgson's eerie classic "The Voice in the Night."

1958-59 SEASON

Still carrying on was the hero-worship--near idolatry--on the part of a less discriminating audience. In the year's great cultish entry, Roy Huggins' 77 Sunset Strip, the basic Cold War values (reverence for the patriarchal figure, deference to the authority to freely perform its function) were not unchanged; it was but the packaging that was glossier. For here again, in piquant verse, in the finger snapping significance of Mack David's theme, a generational blend of detective heroes found plaudits in the consanguinity of law-and-order spirited Americans. The much distorted communist manifesto lingered on.

The anthologies yet condescended to the dissipation. Both Pursuit and the Canadian-produced Encounter were short-lived. Desilu Productions's Desilu Playhouse, alternating with I Love Lucy situation comedies, was seldom a critical success and was perhaps but twice memorable: for Rod Serling's "The Time Element" and for Paul Monash's trend-setting "The Untouchables."

The western genre continued its proliferation. Warner Brothers produced Bronco, whose hero's rudiments were firmly implanted in the Civil War. Elsewhere, the vogue ran the gamut of character types, from the urbane Bat Masterson to the no-nonsense marksman Lucas McCain of The Rifleman.

One half-hour entry, Mark Hellinger's The Naked City, was a brilliant bloom in the vacuity. One could watch it only for its lensing of New York City locale, but its heroes were real and its criminals also quite human. A small but significant maturation for the medium, The Naked City would emerge a brilliant hour entry a couple of years later.

1959-60 SEASON

Television at the fringe of the decade was characterized by action-adventure programming that heralded the primacy of individualism, an esprit epitomized by the detective protagonists of such series as Philip Marlowe (Raymond Chandler's celebrated character), Johnny Staccato (a pianist turned investigator), Five Fingers (the adventures of a United States Intelligence Agent), Richard Diamond (an attempt at glamorizing the detective by way of designing idiosyncrasies for his sexual counterpart: Diamond's girl being a whispering telephone operator), and 77 Sunset Strip which did much to emulate that illusory locale.

Essentially, these series did much to affirm an assortment
of Cold War themes.   Weakness became the paramount vice, for
series characters felt a compulsive need to augment, if rather
frenetically, the image of the investigator as hero.   It was not by
coincidence that the investigator, and not the policeman, was protag-
onist.   Like the spirited investigators of the House Committee on
Un-American Activities, whose Hollywood inquisitions of 1947 and
1951 left artists alternately protesting or tergiversating before Committee demands, the series investigator rationalized his means to
his end.   We often heard, if only in passing, the words "suspicious
characters" used in the episodes.   The term, of course, did not
initiate with the television detective genre, but the frequency of its
usage along with the writers' emphasis on the gruelling, peremptory
nature of the investigator as hero had parallels in the character of
real-life "anti-subversives."   The basic difference between the value
themes of this era's detective vogue and a subsequent (post-1969)
era's police show vogue lies in the law-and-order image conveyed.
In the latter instance, the cop is deified outright; in the former, the
cop is seen in the guise of the investigator and the law-and-order
values are more subtle.

Another vogue of the period was the western series, whose
heroes, by their very nature, emblematized the concept, as far as
the television audience saw it, of strength.   If there was a disparity
to be realized between the sheriff's "getting his man" and his having
to kill indiscriminately to do so, no one much cared.   Like their
motion picture predecessors, these westerns fiercely expounded on
the patriarchal figure and relegated death to the backdrop, subor-
dinate to the action.   What was disturbing about this genre on television was that it saturated air time--in 1959 alone, no less than
twenty-four of the dramatic entries were in the western vein.   This
American faith in the gunmen remained for the duration of the new
decade--a faith finding new physical form in the laconic police hero,
espousing imperialist litanies everywhere.   And, but for occasional
specials, television beyond the artistically vibrant J. F. Kennedy/
Newton Minow years, would be bereft of the creative flow once so
uniquely endemic to the total medium.

SECTION II

Days and Times for Prime Time Programming,
1947-summer, 1959

DAYS AND TIMES

Commercial programming began July 1, 1941, with the establishment of the New York City pilot stations WCBS and WNBT (NBC). The Dumont network, having the New York pilot WABD, was inaugurated June 28, 1942, commercialized the following year, and assumed a daytime format as well on November 7, 1948. Early network programming consisted largely of filmed features, theatrical releases and live telecasts. The Second World War necessarily curtailed program advances, so that regular scheduling initiated with the fall of 1946. The third network, the American Broadcasting Company, proceeded as a result of the purchase of the radio NBC "Blue Network"; New York station WJZ-TV, opening August 10, 1948, became the ABC outlet. The New York based WOR-TV opened Sunday, October 9, 1949, joining existing non-network stations WPIX and WATZ, in addition to the Dumont. The programming below begins with the 1948-1949 season, but notations are provided for earlier season entries.

Key to New York Stations: WCBS (channel 2); WNBT (channel 4); WABD (channel 5); WJZ-TV (channel 7); WOR-TV (channel 9); WPIX-TV (channel 11); WATZ-TV (channel 13)

1948-1949 SEASON

	CBS	NBC	ABC
Saturday			
6:30			The Quizdom Class†
7:00			News and Views
			7:15: films
7:30		Hopalong Cassidy†	sports
			7:45: Three About Town† (9/18)
8:00	music and weather	Hopalong Cassidy	Play the Game† (9/18)
8:30	Rodeo from Madison Square Garden	The Television Screen Magazine† (9/18; Herbert Hoover was guest, 9/25)	theatrical films
9:00	Rodeo from Madison Square Garden	theatrical films	theatrical films
9:30	Rodeo from Madison Square Garden	theatrical flims	theatrical films
Sunday			
5:30	music and weather		

*Indicates that the drama is included in this volume.
†Indicates that the series--whatever the type--was a new entry in the season.

	CBS	NBC	ABC

6:00 Scrapbook Junior
      Meeting† (9/19)

6:30 films [subsequently dis-
      placed by The
      United Nations
      Singers† (12/19)]

7:00 films   Pauline Frederick's
      7:15: The Week In Re-   Guest Book† (9/19)
      view

                         7:20: The Review of
                         the News

7:30 Studio One†* (11/7) The Admiral Five Star films
      alternating with   Review† (10/10)
      The Ford Theatre
      Hour†* (11/21)

8:00 Studio One alternat- Author Meets the   The Hollywood Screen
      ing with The Ford   Critics† (9/19)   Test† (Neil Hamilton,
      Theatre Hour   host) (11/7)

8:30 films   Meet the Press [pre- Actor's Studio†* (9/26)
                          miered November
                          20, 1947]

9:00 The Toast of the   The Philco Television theatrical films
      Town [otherwise   Playhouse†* (10/3)
      known as The Ed
      Sullivan Show] [pre-
      miered June 20,
      1948, at 8-9:00]

9:30 The Toast of the   The Philco Television theatrical films
      Town   Playhouse

7-8:00 WABD The Ted Mack Original Amateur Hour†

Monday

                         5:30-6:00 weekdays The
                         Howdy Doody Show
                         ["Buffalo" Bob Smith,
                         host] [continuing from
                         1947]

      6:30-6:45 weekdays:
      Lucky Pup† [Hope
      and Money Bunin,
      puppeteers] (9/13)

      6:45-7:00 weekdays:
      Sing It Again† [oth-
      erwise known as The
      Bob Howard Show]
      (9/13)

7:00 films   News
      7:15: Places, Please†   7:15: The Fitzgeralds†
      (Barry Wood, host)   (9/13)
      (9/13)

7:30 News, with Douglas   Newsreel Theatre   Kiernan's Corner†
      Edwards   (Walter Kiernan,
                                                 host) (9/13)
      7:45: Make Mine Mu-
      sic† (9/13)

	CBS	NBC	ABC
8:00	Prize Party† (12/6)	The Chevrolet Tele-Theatre†* [otherwise known as The Broadway Playhouse] (9/27)	Quizzing the News† (9/13)
8:30	films	Americana† (Ben Grauer, host) (9/13) [subsequently displaced by The Nature of Things† (Dr. Roy K. Marshall, host) as of 12/13]	theatrical films
9:00	sports	Television Newsreel 9:10: The Village Barn† (9/13)	theatrical films
9:30	sports 9:55: newsreel	Americana [this time as of 12/13]	

6-6:30 weekdays WABD The Small Fry Club† (9/13)
6:30-7:00 weekdays WABD Russ Hodges and the Sports† (9/13)

Tuesday

			News 7:15: films
7:00	films		
7:30	News, with Douglas Edwards 7:45: Face the Music† (9/14) (Johnny Desmond, Sandra Deel) [program subsequently retitled Make Mine Music]	Musical Miniatures† (9/14) 7:50: Newsreel Theatre	Movieland Quiz† (9/12)
8:00	Kobb's Corner† (9/14)	The Texaco Star Theatre† [otherwise known as The Milton Berle Show] (9/14)	films
8:30	films	The Texaco Star Theatre	America's Town Meeting of the Air† (George V. Denny, moderator) (10/5)
9:00	We, the People† (9/14)	The Mary Margaret McBride Show† (9/14)	
9:30	Straws in the Wind† (Lyman Brison, Elmo Roper) (9/14)	wrestling	
10:00	newsreel	wrestling	

7-7:30 WABD The Zero Mostel Show† (with Joey Faye) (9/14)

Wednesday

			News
7:00	films		
7:30	News, with Douglas Edwards	You Are an Artist† (Don Gnagy, host) (9/15)	Critic at Large† (John Mason Brown) (9/15)

	CBS	NBC	ABC
7:45	Face the Music†	7:50: Newsreel Theatre	7:45: The Fitzgeralds†
8:00	To the Queen's Taste† (9/15) [subsequently displaced by Kobb's Corner as of 11/24]	The Kyle MacDonnell Show† [otherwise known as Girl About Town] (9/15)	The Gay Nineties Revue† (9/15)
		8:20: Picture This† (Wendy Barrie, hostess) (9/15)	
8:30	Winner Take All† (Bud Collyer, host) (10/27)	The Ted Steele Show† (9/15) [subsequently displaced by The Phil Silvers Show† (Silvers, Len Hale, Jerry Hauser) (11/24); which alternated with Musical Miniatures† as of 12/1]	Candid Microphone† [forerunner to Candid Camera] (9/15)
			8:45: Three About Town†
9:00	theatrical films / boxing	The Kraft Television Theatre* (9/22) [premiered May 7, 1947 at 7:30-8:30]	wrestling
9:30	theatrical films / boxing 9:55: newsreel	The Kraft Television Theatre	wrestling
10:00		Television Newsreel	wrestling

Thursday

	CBS	NBC	ABC
7:00	sports		News
			7:15: films
7:30	News, with Douglas Edwards	Musical Miniatures†	Club Seven† (Johnny Thompson, host) (9/16)
	7:45: Face the Music†		
8:00	To the Queen's Taste†	7:50: Newsreel Theatre films	Caught in the Act† (9/16)
		8:15: The Nature of Things†	
8:30	Rodeo from Madison Square Garden	The Lanny Ross Show† (9/16)	
9:00	Rodeo from Madison Square Garden	The Road Show†, with Bob Smith (9/16)	
9:30	Rodeo from Madison Square Garden	The Amazing Dunninger† (11/4) alternating with The Paul Winchell Show† (11/11) [the series are collectively referred to as The Bigelow Show]	

CBS	NBC	ABC

Friday

			5:30: Here Comes the Circus† News
7:00	films	films 7:10: Touchdown (sports, with Bob Hall)	
	7:15: Places, Please†		7:15: The Fitzgeralds†
7:30	News, with Douglas Edwards 7:45: Face the Music	The Musical Merry-Go-Round† (9/17)	films
		7:50: Newsreel	
8:00	Sportsman Quiz	films	The Teen-age Book Club† (Margaret Scoggio, hostess) (9/17)
	8:15: What's It Worth?† (Gil Gates, host) (9/17)		
8:30	Captain Billy's Mississippi Music Hall† (Ralph Dumke, Virginia Gibson, Johnny Downs) (10/8)	Stop Me If You've Heard This One† (Cal Tunney, Benny Rubin) (9/17)	That Reminds Me† (interview) (9/17)
9:00	theatrical films	The Ted Steele Show† [this day as of 11/26] 9:25: The Friday Night Fights	films
9:30	theatrical films	The Friday Night Fights	Play the Game† [charades, with Irene Wicker] (9/17)
10:00	The Old Nick Playhouse† (films) (10/8)	The Friday Night Fights	The Gay Nineties Revue† [this day as of 12/24]

1948-49 MIDSEASON

Saturday

7:30	In the First Person (Quincy Howe, host) 7:45: Jeanne Bargy	The Television Screen Magazine	theatrical films
8:00	theatrical films/ sports	The Saturday Night Jamboree† (2/26)	theatrical films
8:30	theatrical films/ sports	The Eddie Condon Floor Show† (2/26)	Jack Carter and Company† (3/11) regularly displaced by Think Fast† (Dr. Mason Gross, host) (3/25)

	CBS	NBC	ABC
9:00	theatrical films/ sports	sports	The Paul Whiteman TV Teen Club† (4/2)
9:30	theatrical films/ sports	sports	The Paul Whiteman TV Teen Club
10:00	theatrical films/ sports	sports	sports
10:30	theatrical films/ sports	sports (to 11:15)	sports

7:45-8:00   WPIX Broadway in Revue† (John Chapman, host and commentator)
8:15-8:30   WPIX Hollywood in New York† (Lois Wilson, hostess)
SPECIAL 6:30-8:00 NBC Arturo Toscanini Conducts Aida† (3/26)

Sunday

5:00			Super Circus† (from Chicago; 2/27)
		5:15: Hopalong Cassidy	
5:30	theatrical films	Hopalong Cassidy	Super Circus
6:00	theatrical films	Hopalong Cassidy	Cartoon Tale-Tales†
6:30	Mr. I Magination† (Paul Tripp)(4/17)	Act It Out† (charades)	The Singing Lady†
7:00	film shorts	The Explorer's Club†	The Shop Reporter†
7:30	Studio One [regular- ly displaced by The Ford Theatre Hour]	The Grace and Paul Hartman Show† (2/27)	The Shop Reporter
			7:45: Sing-co-Pation† (2/27)
8:00	Studio One [regular- ly displaced by The Ford Theatre Hour]	Author Meets the Critics	The Hollywood Screen Test
8:30	Riddle Me This† (quiz, with John Daly, Ilka Chase, Al Capp) (2/27)	The Lamb's Gambol† (variety; 2/27)	Actor's Studio [subse- quently displaced by Celebrity Time† (Conrad Nagel, host) (3/20)]
9:00	The Toast of the Town [subsequent- ly displaced by The Fred Waring Show† (4/17); at which time The Toast of the Town moved to 8:00; Studio One to 7:00]	The Philco Television Playhouse	The Television Players† [2/27; subsequently displaced by Sing-co- Pation (at 9:00 as of 3/20]
9:30	The Toast of the Town [subsequent- ly displaced by The Fred Waring Show]	The Philco Television Playhouse	Music in Velvet
10:00	The Week in Review 10:15: Yesterday's Newsreel	News 10:15: The Kyle MacDonnell and Earl Wrightson Show (songs)	Bowling Headliners
10:30		Who Said That?† (quiz; 12/27/48)	Bowling Headliners

8-9:00   WABD The Ted Mack Original Amateur Hour [continuing]

	CBS	NBC	ABC

Monday

3:30-4:00 weekdays:
Mr. and Mrs.
Yul Brynner
(Brynner, Virginia Gilmore)
Present Theatre
Reviews† (2/7)

5-5:30 weekdays
These Are My
Children† [video's
first soap opera,
composed by Irma
Phillips, was telecast
from Chicago] (1/31)
5:30-6:00 weekdays
Howdy Doody
[continuing]

7:00	Your Sports Special	Kukla, Fran and Ollie†	News and Views
			7:15: The Earl Wrightson Show† (1/31)
7:30	News	Newsreel Theatre	Joe Kiernan's Kaleidoscope† (3/14)
	7:45 The Quadrangle† (3/14)	7:45 News	
8:00	The Goldbergs† (Gertrude Berg, Robert H. Harris, Arlene McQuade, Tom Taylor, Eli Mintz; subsequently Philip Loeb, Larry Robinson) (1/17) [The Preview† (Tex McCrary, Jinx Falkenberg) displaced The Goldbergs this time as of 3/7]	The Nature of Things† [Dr. Roy Marshall, host; 12/13/48, initially at 8:30; this time as of 3/14]	Kiernan's Corner
8:30	Arthur Godfrey's Talent Scouts† (12/6/48)	The Chevrolet Tele-Theatre (formerly at 8:00; this time as of 3/14)	The Barn Dance
9:00	The Goldbergs [this time as of 3/7; subsequently displaced by Through the Crystal Ball† (4/18)]	NBC Presents†* (12/27/48)	Identity† (Bob Elson and guests) (12/27/48)
			9:15: The Skip Farrell Show† (1/17)
9:30	sports	Ben Grauer's Americana	
10:00	sports	Boxing	

CBS	NBC	ABC
10:30 sports	Boxing [previously Who Said That?† with Bob Trout (12/27/48) which was moved to Sunday at 10:30]	

7-7:30 WABD Inside Photoplay† (Wendy Barrie, hostess)

Tuesday

	CBS	NBC	ABC
7:00	Your Sports Special	Kukla, Fran and Ollie†	News
			7:15: A Gift of Life† (1/4)
7:30	News	Musical Miniatures [subsequently displaced by The Maggie McNeills Show† (4/12)]	films
	7:45: Make Mine Music† (Carol Coleman; 3/1)	7:45: News	
8:00	Cross-question† (fictional jury trial; 1/18)	The Texaco Star Theatre	The Ray Knight Revue† (3/15)
8:30	Cross-question	The Texaco Star Theatre	America's Town Meeting
9:00	We, the People	Fireside Theatre†* (4/5)	The Billy Bean Show† (Arnold Stang) (3/22)
9:30	Suspense†* (3/1)	Believe It or Not†* (Robert L. Ripley, host) (3/1)	The Molly Picon House Party† (3/22)
10:00	Backstage† (Barry Wood, host) (3/1) 10:15: Jeanne Bargy	Wrestling	Boxing
10:30		Wrestling	Boxing

8-8:30 CBS regular specials New York University Television Workshop Dramas† (the first being "Obscure Destination") (2/1)
9-9:30 WABD Schoolhouse† (Kenny Delmar, host)

Wednesday

	CBS	NBC	ABC
7:00	Your Sports Special	Kukla, Fran and Ollie† (1/12)	News
			7:15: Child's World† (1/5)
7:30	News	Young Broadway† (1/12)	Lenny and Ginger† (3/16)
	7:45: Masters of Music† (3/8)	7:45: News	7:45: The Fitzgeralds
8:00	The Arthur Godfrey Show	local	At Home and How† (Louise Ulinslow) (3/16)
8:30	The Arthur Godfrey Show	local	Critic at Large (Clifton Fadiman)
9:00	Mary Kay and Johnny† (3/2)	The Kraft Television Theatre	Critic at Large

	CBS	NBC	ABC
9:30	Kobb's Corner [Stan Fritz; this time as of 3/2]	The Kraft Television Theatre	sports
10:00		Meet the Press	sports
10:30		The Village Barn	

7-7:30 WABD The Wendy Barrie Show†

Thursday

	CBS	NBC	ABC
7:00	Your Sports Special 7:15: Manhattan Showcase† (Johnny Downs) (3/3)	Kukla, Fran and Ollie†	News 7:15: The Wren's Nest† (1/6)
7:30	News	You Are an Artist (John Gnagy) (as of 3/31) 7:45: News	films
8:00	Dione Lucas† (cooking) (3/3)	The Phil Silvers Show (as of 3/31)	American Minstrels† (Jack Carter, host) (1/20)
8:30	Winner Take All (as of 3/3)	The Lanny Ross Show	Actor's Studio (as of 3/24)
9:00	sports	The Road Show with Bob Smith	theatrical films
9:30	sports	The Amazing Dunninger alternating with The Paul Winchell Show	theatrical films
10:00	sports	The Candlelight Revue† 10:20: Musical Miniatures (as of 3/31)	On Trial
10:30	sports		

Friday

	CBS	NBC	ABC
7:00	Messing's Prize Party† [as of 1/21; premiered 12/6/48 Mondays 8-8:30]	Kukla, Fran and Ollie†	theatrical films
7:30	News 7:45: Jeanne Bargy	The Joe Kilty Show† (1/21) 7:45: News	theatrical films 7:45: The Fitzgeralds
8:00	Variety Music† (1/21) alternating with Adventures in Jazz† (Bill Williams, Jo Sullivan, Yank Lasso; 11/24/48)	The Admiral Broadway Review† [Sid Caesar, Imogene Coca, Mary McCarty, Marge and Gower Champion; 1/28]	Vaudeo Varieties† (1/21)
8:30	What's It Worth?† (Sigmund Rothchild; 1/21)	The Admiral Broadway Review†	Vaudeo Varieties†
9:00	The Johns Hopkins Science Review† (1/21)	Stop Me If You've Heard This One (Cal Tunney, Benny Rubin)	Break the Bank† (Bert Parks; 1/21)

	CBS	NBC	ABC
9:30	theatrical films	Your Show Time†* (1/21)	The Joe Hasel Sports Review† (1/21) [displaced by Sparring Partners† (Walter Kiernan, host; 4/8)] 9:45: The Seven Branch Ranch† (1/21)
10:00	theatrical films	The Friday Night Fights	
10:30	theatrical films	The Friday Night Fights 11-11:30 The Chesterfield Supper Club with Perry Como† [as of 1/28; premiered 12/24/48 Fridays 7-7:30]	

7-7:30 WABD The Wendy Barrie Show†
7:30-7:45 WPIX Your Lucky Star† (Ralph Bellamy) (4/8)
9-9:30 WABD Front Row Center† (Buddy Lester, host) (3/18)
9:30-10:00 WATZ Respectfully Yours† (Paul Brenner, Rick Mardell) (3/18)

Summer Programming, 1949

Sunday
3-3:30 ABC afternoon American Forum† (5/22)
6-6:30 NBC Guess Who† (adapted from the radio game series; Happy Felton, host) (5/15)
7-7:30 NBC Hold It, Please† (5/8)
7:30-8:00 CBS Wesley (Donald Devlin)† (5/8)
8-9:00 ABC Stop the Music [Bert Parks; this day as of 6/12]

Monday
6-6:30 weekdays WABD The Small Fry Club† [Bob Emery, host; 6/13]
7-7:30 weekdays WABD Captain Video† (6/13)
7:30-7:45 Monday, Wednesday and Friday NBC Morton Downey† (songs) (6/13)
8:30-9:00 CBS It Pays to Be Ignorant† [adapted from the radio series; Tom Howard, Lulu McConnell, Harry McNaughton, George Shelton, panel; 6/6]
8:30-9:00 NBC The Black Robe† [films; 8/15]
8-8:30 NBC Academy Theatre†* (8/1)
9-9:30 NBC Vic and Sade† (Bernadine Flynn, Frank Dane) (7/11)

Tuesday
9-9:30 NBC Lights Out†* (7/19)
9-9:30 ABC Talent Jackpot† (7/19)

Wednesday
9:30-10:00 CBS This Is Show Business† (5/11)
10-11:00 CBS Studio One* (as of 5/11)

Thursday
7:30-8:00 ABC Blind Date† (Arlene Francis, hostess) (5/5)
8-9:00 ABC Stop the Music (Bert Parks) (this day as of 6/2)
8-9:00 CBS The Fifty-fourth Street Revue† (5/5)

CBS	NBC	ABC

Friday

8-8:30 CBS I Remember Mama† [Peggy Wood, Dickie (Richard) Van Patten, Iris Mann, Rosemary Rice, Judson Laire] (7/1)

9-9:30 NBC The Benny Rubin Show† [previously Stop Me If You've Heard This One] (4/29)

9-9:30 NBC Meet Your Congress† (7/1)

9-9:30 ABC Fun for the Money† (Johnny Olsen, host) (6/17)

1949-50 SEASON

Saturday

	CBS	NBC	ABC
7:30	In the First Person	The Nature of Things (as of 9/3)	Hollywood Screen Test (as of 9/3)
	7:45: Jeanne Bargy		
8:00	News	Meet Your Congress [as of 9/3; alternating with theatrical films]	The Paul Whiteman TV Teen Club
8:30	theatrical films	theatrical films	The Paul Whiteman TV Teen Club
		8:45: Studs' Place† (Studs Terkel) (9/3)	
9:00	theatrical films	Who Said That? (9/3)	theatrical films
9:30	theatrical films	Meet the Press (as of 9/3)	theatrical films
10:00	theatrical films	Night Court Drama† (films; 9/3)	
10:30	theatrical films	Night Court Drama	

7-7:45 WOR Apartment 3-C† (John and Barbara Cray) (9/3)

9-10:00 WABD Cavalcade of Stars† (Jerry Lester) (9/3)

Sunday

	CBS	NBC	ABC
4:30	Lamp unto My Feet† (10/2)	The Armed Forces Hour† (9/4)	
5:00	Overseas Press Club† (10/2)	The Armed Forces Hour	Super Circus (9/4)
5:30	The Chuck Wagon† (9/25)	Hopalong Cassidy	Super Circus
6:00	The Chuck Wagon 6:15 Talk, with Burton Holmes (9/25)	Hopalong Cassidy	theatrical films
6:30	Mr. I Magination	Say It with Acting† (formerly Act It Out)	theatrical films
7:00	Tonight on Broadway† (sketches) (10/2)	Leave It to the Girls [panel with Maggi McNellis, Eloise McElhone, Florence Pritchett; this day and time as of 10/16]	The Paul Whiteman Revue† (9/4)

	CBS	NBC	ABC
7:30	This Is Show Business [previously This Is Broadway, with George S. Kaufman, Abe Burrows, Clifton Fadiman, Sam Levenson; 10/2]	The Aldrich Family† [Lois Wilson, House Jameson, Jack Kelk, Robert Casey; subsequently Barbara Robbins, Bobby Ellis, June Dayton and for a time Paul Newman; 10/2]	
8:00	The Toast of the Town [second anniversary, 6/19/49]	The Chesterfield Supper Club (10/16)	
8:30	The Toast of the Town	Video Theatre†* (10/16)	
9:00	The Fred Waring Show (9/25)	The Philco Television Playhouse* (9/4)	theatrical films
9:30	The Fred Waring Show	The Philco Television Playhouse	
10:00	News in Review	Garroway at Large† (9/4)	Celebrity Time (as of 9/4)
10:30	films	Tropic Holiday† (9/4)	Bowling Headliners

Monday

		5:30-6:00 weekdays: Howdy Doody [continuing]	
	6:30-6:45 weekdays: Lucky Pup [Hope and Morey Bunin, puppeteers; continuing] 6:45-7:00 weekdays: The Bob Howard Show [continuing]		
7:00	The Roar of the Rails† (9/5) 7:15: The Paul Arnold Show† (9/5)	Kukla, Fran and Ollie (9/5)	theatrical films
7:30	News 7:45: The Sonny Kendis Show† (9/5) 7:55: The Herb Shriner Show† (9/5)	Morton Downey [Carmen Masters Orchestra; 9/5] 7:45: News Caravan	theatrical films
8:00	Silver Theatre†* (10/3)	The Chevrolet Tele-Theatre* (9/19)	Your Witness† (10/17)
8:30	Arthur Godfrey's Talent Scouts (9/5)	The Voice of Firestone† [Howard Barlow Orchestra; 9/5]	Wendy Barrie Interviews (9/5)
9:00	Candid Camera† (Allen Funt, host; 9/5)	Lights Out* (11/17)	Barn Dance (9/5)

CBS	NBC	ABC
9:30 The Goldbergs (8/29)	Band of America† (10/17)	Dr. Black† [sketches; 9/5]
10:00 Studio One* (9/12)	The Quiz Kids† (Joe Kelly, host; 9/5)	theatrical films
10:30 Studio One	local	theatrical films

7-7:30 weekdays WABD Captain Video [continuing; 9/5]
11-11:15 CBS The Faye Emerson Show† (10/24)

Tuesday
       5-5:30: Vanity Fair†
       (Dorothy Dean;
       9/6)

CBS	NBC	ABC
7:00 Prize Party (as of 9/6)	Kukla, Fran and Ollie	Headline Edition (news)
7:30 News	Roberta Quinlan† (9/6)	Counter Spy† [Don McLaughlin; 9/6]
7:45: The Sonny Kendis Show† 7:55: The Herb Shriner Show†	7:45: News Caravan	
8:00 theatrical films	The Texaco Star Theatre (9/20)	Carnegie Hall (9/6)
8:30 theatrical films	The Texaco Star Theatre	America's Town Meeting
9:00 Actor's Studio* (9/28; 11/1)	Fireside Theatre* (9/6)	America's Town Meeting
9:30 Suspense* (9/6)	The Life of Riley† (Jackie Gleason, Rosemary De Camp; 10/4)	theatrical films
10:00 The Week in Sports	The Ted Mack Original Amateur Hour (network as of 10/4)	
10:30 Pantomine Quiz (10/4)	The Ted Mack Original Amateur Hour	

9-9:30 WABD The O'Neills† (with Vera Allen) (9/6)

Wednesday

CBS	NBC	ABC
7:00 The Kirby Stone Quintet† (9/7)	Kukla, Fran and Ollie	
7:30 News 7:45: The Earl Wrightson Show† (9/7)	Morton Downey 7:45: News Caravan	
8:00 The Arthur Godfrey Show (9/7)	Crisis† (documentaries) (10/5)	Actor's Studio* [9/28; displaced this day by Photoplay Time (Wendy Barrie, hostess) as of 11/1]/
8:30 The Arthur Godfrey Show	The Clock†* (9/7)	
9:00 The Amazing Dunninger (10/5)	The Kraft Television Theatre* (9/21)	The Wendy Barrie Show [9/7; subsequently displaced this time by Photocrime† (Chuck Webster) (11/1)]

CBS	NBC	ABC
9:30 The Wednesday Night Fights	The Kraft Television Theatre	
10:00 The Wednesday Night Fights	Believe It or Not* [9/7; subsequently displaced by Break the Bank (10/5)]	
10:30 The Wednesday Night Fights	Top Views in Sports	

8-8:30 WABD The Plainclothesman† (Ken Lynch) (10/5)
8:30-9:00 WOR What Happens Now?† (9/28)
9:30-10:00 WABD Famous Jury Trials† (10/5)

Thursday
7:00

7:00	Kukla, Fran and Ollie	
		7:15: The Fitzgeralds (9/22)
7:30 News	Roberta Quinlan†	The Lone Ranger† (Clayton Moore, Jay Silverheels) (9/29)
7:45: The Sonny Kendis Show† 7:55: The Herb Shriner Show†	7:45: News Caravan	
8:00 The Front Page† (James Daly, Mark Roberts) (10/6)	Stop the Music [Bert Parks; this network 9/22]	Stop the Music [Bert Parks; 11/9]
8:30 Inside, U.S.A. † (Peter Lind Hayes, Mary Healey, hosts) (9/29) alternating with Theatre of Romance†* (11/3)	Mary Kay and Johnnie (9/22)	Stop the Music
9:00 The Ed Wynn Show† (10/6)	Kay Kyser's College of Musical Knowledge† (12/1)	The Boris Karloff Mystery Playhouse†* (9/22)
9:30 theatrical films	The Glamour-Go-Round† (Ilka Chase) (9/22)	The Ruggles† (Charles Ruggles) (9/22)
10:00 theatrical films	Martin Kane, Private Detective† (William Gargan) (9/1)	Roller Derby from Madison Square Garden
10:30 theatrical films	The Hank McCune Show† (9/1)	Roller Derby from Madison Square Garden

7:30-8:00 WPIX The Truex Family† (Ernest Truex) (10/13)
9-9:30 WABD The Morey Amsterdam Show† (10/6)
9:30-11:00 WABD Boxing

Friday

	6-7:00 Hopalong Cassidy	
7:00 The Kirby Stone Quintet† 7:15: The Paul Arnold Show†	Kukla, Fran and Ollie	The Fitzgeralds

	CBS	NBC	ABC
7:30	News	Morton Downey	Touchdown† (football highlights) (9/23)
	7:45: The Sonny Kendis Show† 7:55: The Herb Shriner Show†	7:45: News Caravan	
8:00	I Remember Mama (10/7)	One Man's Family† (Bert Lytell, Marjorie Gateson, Eva Marie Saint) (11/4)	Majority Rules† (9/23)
8:30	Man Against Crime† (Ralph Bellamy) (10/7)	We, the People (9/9)	Blind Date (Arlene Francis) (9/23)
9:00	The Ford Theatre Hour* (10/7) alternating with The Fifty-fourth Street Revue (10/14)	Versatile Varieties† (9/9)	Auction-Aire Show† (9/30)
9:30	The Ford Theatre Hour* alternating with The Fifty-fourth Street Revue	The Big Story† (9/2) alternating with TV Detective† (12/16)	Fun for the Money (Johnny Olsen) (9/23)
10:00	The People's Platform† (Charles Collingwood, host) (9/9)	The Friday Night Fights	A Couple of Joes† (Variety and music) (9/23)
10:30	The Capitol Cloak Room† (9/9)	The Friday Night Fights	A Couple of Joes

8-8:30 WABD Hands of Murder† (9/30)
8-10:00 WPIX Premiere Theatre† (theatrical films) (9/9)
8:30-9:00 WABD Headline Clues† (9/30)
9-9:30 WABD Fishing and Hunting Club† (9/30)
9:30-10:00 WABD The Case of the Jealous Blonde† (9/30)
10-10:30 WABD Amateur Boxing

1949-50 MIDSEASON

Saturday

7:00			Buck Rogers† (4/29)
7:30	In the First Person 7:45: Jeanne Bargy	The Nature of Things	Hollywood Screen Test
8:00	The Ken Murray Show† (1/14)	The Jack Carter Show† (2/25)	Paul Whiteman TV Teen Club
8:30	The Ken Murray Show	The Jack Carter Show	Paul Whiteman TV Teen Club
9:00	The Trap†* (4/29)	The Saturday Night Revue† (with Sid Caesar and Imogene Coca) (2/25)	theatrical films
9:30	theatrical films	The Saturday Night Revue†	theatrical films
10:00	theatrical films	The Saturday Night Revue	
10:30	theatrical films		

CBS	NBC	ABC

5:30-6:30 WGR Italian Feature Film† (4/29)

Sunday

	CBS	NBC	ABC
4:00		Today with Mrs. Roosevelt† (2/12)	
4:30		The Armed Forces Hour	
5:00	Overseas Press Club	The Armed Forces Hour	Super Circus
5:30	The Chuck Wagon	The Star Spangled Revue† (4/9)	Super Circus
6:00	The Chuck Wagon	The Star Spangled Revue	theatrical films
6:30	Mr. I Magination	Say It with Acting	theatrical films
7:00	Young and Gay† (1/1) followed by Starlight Theatre†* (4/2)	Leave It to the Girls	Paul Whiteman Revue
7:30	This Is Show Business	The Aldrich Family	
8:00	The Toast of the Town	The Chesterfield Supper Club	
8:30	The Toast of the Town	Video Theatre	
9:00	The Fred Waring Show	The Philco Television Playhouse	theatrical films
9:30	The Fred Waring Show	The Philco Television Playhouse	theatrical films
10:00	Celebrity Time (4/2; this network)	Garroway at Large	
10:30	News in Review (4/2; this time)		

Monday

	CBS	NBC	ABC
7:00	The Roar of the Rails 7:15: The Paul Arnold Show	Kukla, Fran and Ollie	theatrical films
7:30	News 7:45: The Sonny Kendis Show 7:55: The Herb Shriner Show	Morton Downey 7:45: News Caravan	theatrical films
8:00	Silver Theatre	The Chevrolet Tele-Theatre	Your Witness
8:30	Arthur Godfrey's Talent Scouts	The Voice of Firestone	Wendy Barrie Interviews
9:00	Candid Camera	Lights Out	Barn Dance
9:30	The Goldbergs	Robert Montgomery Presents†* (1/30) alternating with NBC Opera† (2/7) & specials	Dr. Black
10:00	Studio One	Robert Montgomery Presents alternating with NBC Opera & specials	
10:30	Studio One	local	

	CBS	NBC	ABC
Tuesday			
7:00		Kukla, Fran and Ollie	Headline Edition (news)
7:30	News	Roberta Quinlan	Counter Spy
	7:45: The Sonny Kendis Show 7:55: The Herb Shriner Show	7:45: News Caravan	
8:00	theatrical films	The Texaco Star Theatre	Carnegie Hall
8:30	theatrical films	The Texaco Star Theatre	America's Town Meeting
9:00	Actor's Studio†* [this network as of 11/1/49; subsequently displaced by Stage Door† (Louise Albritton, Scott McKay) (2/7)]	Fireside Theatre	America's Town Meeting
9:30	Suspense	Mr. Cmm† (Charles Korvin) (4/4) followed by Downbeat† (5/9)	
10:00	The Week in Sports	The Ted Mack Original Amateur Hour	
	10:15: Newsreel		
10:30	Pantomine Quiz	The Ted Mack Original Amateur Hour	
Wednesday			
7:00		Kukla, Fran and Ollie	
7:30	News	Morton Downey	
	7:45: Earl Wrightson	7:45: News Caravan	
8:00	The Arthur Godfrey Show	Believe It or Not* (resumed 1/4)	
8:30	The Arthur Godfrey Show	The Clock	
9:00	Abe Burrows Almanac† (1/4) followed by Twin Time† (4/5)	The Kraft Television Theatre	That Wonderful Guy† (Jack Lemmon, Neil Hamilton) (1/4)
9:30	The Wednesday Night Fights	The Kraft Television Theatre	
10:00	The Wednesday Night Fights	Break the Bank	
10:30	The Wednesday Night Fights	Top Views in Sports	
Thursday			
7:00		Kukla, Fran and Ollie	
7:30	News	Roberta Quinlan	The Lone Ranger
	7:45: The Sonny Kendis Show 7:55: The Herb Shriner Show	7:45: News Caravan	
8:00	The Front Page	Studs' Place (resumed 4/13)	
8:30	The Show Goes On† (Robert Q. Lewis) (1/26)	Mary Kay and Johnnie	

	CBS	NBC	ABC
9:00	The Alan Young Show† (4/6)	Kay Kyser's College of Musical Knowledge	The Wendy Barrie Show (resumed 12/22)
9:30	theatrical films	Cameo Theatre†* (5/16)	Holiday Hotel† (Edward Everett Horten) (3/24)
10:00	theatrical films	Martin Kane, Private Detective	
10:30	theatrical films	The Hank McCune Show	

Friday

	CBS	NBC	ABC
		6-7:00: Hopalong Cassidy	
7:00		Kukla, Fran and Ollie	The Fitzgeralds
7:30	News 7:45: The Sonny Kendis Show 7:55: The Herb Shriner Show	Morton Downey 7:45: News Caravan	
8:00	I Remember Mama	One Man's Family	
8:30	Man Against Crime	We, the People	That Wonderful Guy (resumed 4/7) followed by My True Story† (5/5)
9:00	The Ford Theatre Hour alternating with The Play's the Thing†* (3/3)	Versatile Varieties	
9:30	The Ford Theatre Hour alternating with The Play's the Thing†	Life Begins at 80† (1/13) alternating with The Big Story in turn alternating with The Clock (4/7)	The Tin Pan Alley Show† (Johnny Desmond) (4/28)
10:00	The People's Platform	Friday Night Fights	
10:30	The Capitol Cloakroom	Friday Night Fights	

Summer Programming, 1950

Saturday
7-8:00 CBS The Big Top† (Jack Sterling) (7/1)

Sunday
7-7:30 CBS For Women Only† (Beatrice Kay) (7/2)
8:30-9:00 NBC The Hank McCune Show (resumed 7/2)
9-10:00 NBC Masterpiece Playhouse†* (7/23)
10:30-11:00 CBS What's My Line?† (Louis Untermeyer, Dorothy Kilgallen, Hal Block, Arlene Francis) (6/4)

Monday
8-8:30 CBS Twilight Theatre†* (7/3)
8-8:30 NBC The Magnificent Menasha† (Menasha Skulnick) (7/3)
8:30-9:00 CBS Prize Performance† (Cedric Adams) (7/3)
9-9:30 NBC Your Hit Parade† (Snooky Lanson, Dorothy Collins, Eileen Wilson and the Raymond Scott Orchestra) (7/10)

CBS	NBC	ABC

Tuesday
7:30-7:45 Tuesday and Thursday CBS The Wendy Barrie Show (resumed, 6/6)
7:30-7:45 Tuesday and Thursday NBC The Little Show† (John Conte)
9-9:30 NBC Lights, Camera, Action† (7/4)
9:30-10:00 NBC The Armstrong Circle Theatre†* (6/6)
9:30-10:00 CBS The Web* (7/4)
9:30-10:00 NBC Cameo Theatre†* (5/16)

Wednesday
8-8:30 NBC The Pinky Lee Show† (5/17)
8:30-9:00 NBC Cameo Theatre* (this day as of 6/7)
9:30-10:00 CBS Stage 13†* (5/3)

Thursday
8-8:30 NBC Believe It or Not* (this day as of 5/18)
9-9:30 CBS Starlight Theatre* (this day as of 7/20)
9:30-9:45 CBS The Ilka Chase Show† (6/6)
9:45-10:00 CBS Winner Take All† (6/6)

Friday
8:30-9:00 CBS The Detective's Wife† (Lynn Bari, Donald Curtis) (7/7)
9-10:00 CBS Songs for Sale† (Johnny Johnston, Rosemary Clooney) (7/7)
8-8:30 NBC The Magic Slate† (6/2)

1950-51 SEASON

Saturday

	CBS	NBC	ABC
6:30	Big Top	Smilin' Ed McConnell and His Buster Brown Gang (9/9)	Hollywood Theatre (films)
7:00	Big Top	The Hank McCune Show (9/9)	Hollywood Theatre (films)
7:30	News	One Man's Family (9/9)	The Trouble with Father† (The Stu Edwin Show) (10/14)
	7:45: The Faye Emerson Show		
8:00	The Ken Murray Show (10/7)	The Jack Carter Show (9/9)	Paul Whiteman TV Teen Club (10/7)
8:30	The Ken Murray Show (10/7)	The Jack Carter Show (9/9)	Saturday Night Sports† (10/7)
9:00	The Frank Sinatra Show† (10/7)	Your Show of Shows (9/9)	Saturday Night Sports
9:30	The Frank Sinatra Show	Your Show of Shows	Saturday Night Sports
10:00	Sing It Again† (10/7)	Your Show of Shows	Saturday Night Sports
10:30	Sing It Again	Your Hit Parade† (8/19)	Saturday Night Sports (to 11:15)
	11-12:00 Songs for Sale (10/7)		11:15-11:30: Song Time† (10/7)

Sunday

	CBS	NBC	ABC
		3:30-4:00: Mrs. Roosevelt Meets the Public (10/1)	

	CBS	NBC	ABC
5:00	The Capitol Cloak Room (10/1)	The Gabby Hayes Show† (9/10)	Super Circus (from 4:30)
5:30	The People's Platform (10/1)	Watch the Word† (9/10)	Captain Glenn's Bandwagon†
6:00	The Chuck Wagon (10/1)	Hopalong Cassidy	Cowboys 'n' Injuns† (theatrical films)
6:30	Mr. I Magination	Hopalong Cassidy	The Ruggles (10/1)
7:00	The Gene Autry Show† (9/10)	Leave It to the Girls (9/10)	The Paul Whiteman Revue
7:30	This Is Show Business (10/1)	The Aldrich Family (9/10)	Showtime, U.S.A. † (10/1)
8:00	The Toast of the Town	The Colgate Comedy Hour† (9/10) (Eddie Cantor, Fred Allen, Donald O'Connor, Martin & Lewis)	theatrical films
8:30	The Toast of the Town	The Colgate Comedy Hour	theatrical films
9:00	The Fred Waring Show	The Philco Television Playhouse* (9/10)	Soap Box Theatre† (films)
9:30	The Fred Waring Show	The Philco Television Playhouse	Soap Box Theatre (films)
10:00	Celebrity Time (Conrad Nagel) (10/1)	Garroway at Large	Old Fashioned Meeting
10:30	What's My Line?	Take a Chance† (Don Ameche) (10/1)	Youth on the March† (10/1)

Monday

	CBS	NBC	ABC
		4-5:00 weekdays: The Kate Smith Show† (9/25)	
	6:45-7:00 weekdays: Tom Corbett, Space Cadet† (9/25)		
7:00	The Stork Club† (9/25)	Kukla, Fran and Ollie (8/28)	News/Club Seven
			7:25: Gordon Frazer† (9/4)
7:30	News	Roberta Quinlan Show (8/28)	Hollywood Screen Test
	7:45: The Perry Como Show† (10/2)	7:45: News Caravan	
8:00	The Lux Video Theatre†* (10/2)	The Paul Winchell Show† (9/18)	Treasury Men in Action† (9/4)
8:30	Arthur Godfrey's Talent Scouts (9/25)	The Voice of Firestone (Howard Barlowe Orchestra)	Author Meets the Critics† (8/28)
9:00	The Horace Heidt Show† (10/2)	Lights Out* (8/28)	The College Bowl† (10/2)
9:30	The Goldbergs (9/25)	Robert Montgomery Presents* (9/11) alternating with Musical Comedy Time†* (10/2)	On Trial† (discussion) (10/2)

	CBS	NBC	ABC
10:00	Studio One* (8/28)	Robert Montgomery Presents alternating with Musical Comedy Time	theatrical films
10:30	Studio One	Talent Search (8/28) 11-12:00 weeknights: Broadway Open House† (Morey Amsterdam, Jerry Lester, and Dagmar) (8/28)	theatrical films

7-7:30 WABD weekdays Captain Video

Tuesday

	CBS	NBC	ABC
7:00	The Stock Club†	Kukla, Fran and Ollie	News/Club Seven 7:25: Gordon Frazer
7:30	News	John Conte's Little Show	Beulah† (Ethel Waters, Butterfly McQueen) (10/3)
	7:45: The Faye Emerson Show (10/3)	7:45: News Caravan	
8:00	Sure As Fate†* (9/5) alternating with The Prudential Family Playhouse†* (10/10)	The Texaco Star Theatre (9/19)	Football Game of the Week
8:30	Sure As Fate alternating with The Prudential Family Playhouse	The Texaco Star Theatre	Buck Rogers (10/3)
9:00	The Vaughn Monroe Show† (8/29)	Fireside Theatre* (8/29)	Billy Rose's Playbill†* (10/3)
9:30	Suspense* (8/29)	The Armstrong Circle Theatre* (8/29)	Can You Top This?† (10/3)
10:00	Danger†* (10/3)	The Ted Mack Original Amateur Hour	Life Begins at 80 (10/3)
10:30	Tales of the Black Cat† (films with James Monks) (9/5)	The Ted Mack Original Amateur Hour	Roller Derby

8:30-9:00 WABD The Johns Hopkins Science Review† (10/13)

Wednesday

	CBS	NBC	ABC
7:00	The Stork Club†	Kukla, Fran and Ollie	News/Club Seven 7:25: Gordon Frazer†
7:30	News	Roberta Quinlan Show	Chance of a Lifetime† (9/13)
	7:45: The Perry Como Show†	7:45: News Caravan	
8:00	Arthur Godfrey and His Friends (8/29)	Four Star Revue† (Ed Wynn, Danny Thomas, Jimmy Durante) (10/4)	First Nighter† (theatrical films)

	CBS	NBC	ABC
8:30	Arthur Godfrey and His Friends	Four Star Revue†	First Nighter (theatrical films)
9:00	Somerset Maugham Theatre† (a. k. a. Teller of Tales†)* (10/18)	The Kraft Television Theatre* (9/27)	Don McNeill's TV Club† (9/13)
9:30	The Web* (8/30)	The Kraft Television Theatre	Don McNeill's TV Club
10:00	Wednesday Night Fights	Break the Bank (Bert Parks) (9/27)	Wrestling (from Chicago)
10:30	Wednesday Night Fights	Stars Over Hollywood†* (9/27)	Wrestling (from Chicago)

Thursday

7:00	The Stork Club†	Kukla, Fran and Ollie	News/Club Seven 7:25: Gordon Frazer†
7:30	News	John Conte's Little Show	The Lone Ranger (9/14)
	7:45: The Faye Emerson Show	7:45: News Caravan	
8:00	The Burns and Allen Show† (10/12) alternating with Starlight Theatre* (resumed 11/16)	You Bet Your Life† (Groucho Marx) (10/5)	Stop the Music (9/14)
8:30	The Show Goes On† (9/21)	The Peter Lind Hayes Show† (9/7)	Stop the Music
9:00	The Allan Young Show (9/14)	Kay Kyser's College of Musical Knowledge (10/5)	Holiday Hotel (Don Ameche) (9/14)
9:30	Big Town† (10/5)	Kay Kyser's College of Musical Knowledge	Blind Date (8/31)
10:00	Truth or Consequences† (9/14)	Martin Kane, Private Detective (9/7)	I Cover Times Square† (Harold Huber) (10/5)
10:30	The Nash Airflyte Theatre†* (9/21)	Quick on the Draw† (charades) (9/7)	Roller Derby

Friday

7:00	The Stork Club†	Kukla, Fran and Ollie	News/Club Seven 7:25: Gordon Frazer†
7:30	News	Roberta Quinlan Show	Life with Linkletter† (10/6)
	7:45: The Perry Como Show†	7:45: News Caravan	
8:00	I Remember Mama (8/4)	The Quiz Kids (9/8)	The Eva Gabor Show† (interview) (9/15)
8:30	Man Against Crime (9/8)	We, the People (9/8)	Football Interview
9:00	The Ford Theatre Hour* (9/8) alternating with Charlie Wilde, Private Detective† (12/22)	Versatile Varieties (9/8)	The Pulitzer Prize Playhouse†* (10/6)

	CBS	NBC	ABC
9:30	The Ford Theatre Hour* (9/8) alternating with Charlie Wilde, Private Detective	The Clock* (9/8) alternating with The Big Story (9/1)	The Pulitzer Prize Playhouse
10:00	Star of the Family† (Morton Downey) (9/22)	Friday Night Fights	Penthouse Party† (Betty Furness) (9/15)
10:30	Beat the Clock† (Bud Collyer) (9/15)	Friday Night Fights 10:45-11:00: Greatest Fights of the Century†	Studs' Place (9/15)

8-8:30 WABD Story Theatre† [repeats of Your Show Time] (12/8)
10-11:00 WABD Cavalcade of Stars† (Jackie Gleason) (9/8)

1950-51 MIDSEASON

Saturday

	CBS	NBC	ABC
			11-11:30 A.M. Faith Baldwin Playhouse†* (1/20) alternating with The Kay Westfall Show† (2/24)
6:30	Kid Gloves Boxing	Mr. Wizard† (1/6)	theatrical films
7:00	The Sam Levene Show† (1/6)	America at Mid-Century† (1/6)	theatrical films
7:30	Beat the Clock	One Man's Family	The Trouble with Father
8:00	The Ken Murray Show	The Jack Carter Show	Paul Whiteman's TV Teen Club
8:30	The Ken Murray Show	The Jack Carter Show	Paul Whiteman's TV Teen Club
9:00	The Frank Sinatra Show	Your Show of Shows	Sports [including Girls' Baseball (5/26]
9:30	The Frank Sinatra Show	Your Show of Shows	Sports
10:00	Sing It Again	Your Show of Shows	Sports
10:30	Sing It Again 11:00-11:15: The Florian Zabach Show† (3/10)	Your Hit Parade	Sports

Sunday

	CBS	NBC	ABC
5:00	The Facts We Know† (1/28)	The Gabby Hayes Show	Super Circus
5:30	The People's Platform	The Magic Slate† (1/14)	Super Circus
6:00	The Bigelow-Sanford Theatre† [repeats of Silver Theatre] (1/28)	Hopalong Cassidy	The Ted Mack Family Hour† (1/7)
6:30	Mr. I Magination	Hopalong Cassidy	The Ted Mack Family Hour

	CBS	NBC	ABC
7:00	The Gene Autry Show	Leave It to the Girls	Paul Whiteman Revue
7:30	This Is Show Business alternating with The Jack Benny Show† (1/28)	The Aldrich Family	Showtime, U.S.A.
8:00	The Toast of the Town	The Colgate Comedy [Abbott and Costello debut 1/7] Hour	theatrical films
8:30	The Toast of the Town	The Colgate Comedy Hour	theatrical films
9:00	The Fred Waring Show	The Philco Television Playhouse	film documentaries
9:30	The Fred Waring Show	The Philco Television Playhouse	film documentaries
10:00	Celebrity Time	Garroway at Large	The Search (as of 1/8)
10:30	What's My Line?	Star Night† (audience participation) (1/14)	Youth on the March

6-6:30 WPIX Opera Cameos (2/18)

Monday
<u> </u>
11:30-Noon weekdays
Strike It Rich†
(Warren Hall) (5/7)

	CBS	NBC	ABC
			Noon-12:30 The Joe Franklin Show† (weekdays) (4/12)
	1:30-2:00 weekdays The Garry Moore Show†		
7:00	The Early Show† (films)	Kukla, Fran and Ollie	News/Club Seven
			7:15: The Faye Emerson Show
7:30	News 7:45: The Perry Como Show	Roberta Quinlan Show 7:45: News Caravan	Hollywood Screen Test
8:00	The Lux Video Theatre	The Paul Winchell Show	Can You Top This? (resumed 1/22)
8:30	Arthur Godfrey's Talent Scouts	The Voice of Firestone	The Bill Gwinn Show† (1/22)
9:00	The Horace Heidt Show	Lights Out	The Arthur Murray Party† (1/22)
9:30	The Goldbergs	Robert Montgomery Presents alternating with Musical Comedy Time; subsequently Somerset Maugham Theatre (4/2)	On Trial
10:00	Studio One	Robert Montgomery Presents alternating with Musical Comedy Time; Somerset Maugham Theatre	theatrical films
10:30	Studio One	The Arthur Murray Party† [this network (4/2)]	theatrical films
			11-11:30 The Circuit Rider† (3/5)

CBS	NBC	ABC

NBC weekdays Miss Susan† (Susan Peters, Mark Roberts) (3/5)

Tuesday

	CBS	NBC	ABC
7:00	The Steve Allen Show† (1/23)	Kukla, Fran and Ollie	News/Club Seven
			7:15: Going Places† (Betty Betz) (2/20)
7:30	News	John Conte's Little Show	Beulah
	7:45: The Stork Club	7:45: News Caravan	
8:00	The Prudential Family Playhouse alternating with Sure As Fate; replaced by Film Theatre of the Air† (4/17)	The Texaco Star Theatre	mystery films
8:30	The Prudential Family Playhouse alternating with Sure As Fate; replaced by Film Theatre of the Air†	The Texaco Star Theatre	mystery films
9:00	The Vaughn Monroe Show	Fireside Theatre	The Q. E. D. Quiz Show† (4/3)
9:30	Suspense	The Armstrong Circle Theatre	Life Begins at 80
10:00	Danger	The Ted Mack Original Amateur Hour	Roller Derby
10:30	Tales of the Black Cat	The Ted Mack Original Amateur Hour	Roller Derby

Wednesday

	CBS	NBC	ABC
7:00	The Early Show† (films)	Kukla, Fran and Ollie	News/Club Seven
			7:15: The Faye Emerson Show
7:30	News	Roberta Quinlan Show	Chance of a Lifetime
	7:45: The Perry Como Show	7:45: News Caravan	
8:00	Arthur Godfrey and His Friends	Four Star Revue	local
8:30	Arthur Godfrey and His Friends	Four Star Revue	The Bandstand† (3/27)
9:00	Charlie Wild, Private Detective (this time as of 4/4)	The Kraft Television Theatre	Don McNeill's TV Club
9:30	The Web	The Kraft Television Theatre	Wrestling (from Chicago)
10:00	Wednesday Night Fights	Break the Bank	Wrestling
10:30	Wednesday Night Fights	Stars Over Hollywood	Wrestling

9:30-10:00 WABD The Plainclothesman (resumed 1/24)
10-10:30 WABD Ladies Before Gentlemen† (discussion) (2/21)

	CBS	NBC	ABC
Thursday			
7:00	The Early Show† (films)	Kukla, Fran and Ollie	News/Club Seven
			7:15: The Andy and Della Russell Show† (4/5)
7:30	News	John Conte's Little Show	The Lone Ranger
	7:45: The Stork Club	7:45: News Caravan	
8:00	The Burns and Allen Show alternating with Starlight Theatre	You Bet Your Life	Stop the Music (with Phil Silvers)
8:30	The Show Goes On	Treasury Men In Action (as of 4/5)	Stop the Music
9:00	The Allan Young Show	The James Melton Ford Festival† (4/5)	Holiday Hotel
9:30	Big Town	The James Melton Ford Festival	Blind Date
10:00	Truth Or Consequences	Martin Kane, Private Detective	Roller Derby
10:30	Crime Photographer† (Darren McGavin) (5/3) following the documentary Crisis in Korea†	Quick on the Draw	Roller Derby
Friday			
7:00	The Early Show†	Kukla, Fran and Ollie	News/Club Seven 7:15: The Andy and Della Russell Show†
7:30	News	Roberta Quinlan Show	Life With Linkletter
	7:45: The Perry Como Show	7:45: News Caravan	
8:00	I Remember Mama	The Quiz Kids	The Wendy Barrie Show
8:30	Man Against Crime	We, the People	Penthouse Party
9:00	The Ford Theatre Hour alternating with Live Like a Millionaire† (4/13)	The Big Story	Pulitzer Prize Playhouse
9:30	The Ford Theatre Hour alternating with The Edgar Bergen/Charlie McCarthy Show† (4/27)	The Henry Morgan Talent Show† (1/26)	Pulitzer Prize Playhouse
10:00	Star of the Family	Friday Night Fights	The March of Time† (3/2)
10:30	We Take Your Word† (Abe Burrows) (4/27)	Friday Night Fights	Video Venus† (3/2)

7:45-8:00 WABD Not for Publication† (4/27)
8:30-9:00 WABD You Asked for It† (Art Baker) (1/19)
9:30-10:00 WABD Front Page Detective† (Edmund Lowe) (3/16)

CBS	NBC	ABC

Summer Programming, 1951

Saturday
5:30-6:00 CBS Red Cross Training Film† (13 episodes, hosted by Joan Bennett) (5/19)
7:30-8:00 NBC The Art Ford Show† (8/4)
10-10:30 NBC The Doodles Weaver Show (resumed, from 1946) (6/2)
11:30-12:00 A Date with Judy† (6/2)

Sunday
7:30-8:00 CBS Comedy Quiz† (Jan Murray) (7/15)
9-10:00 CBS Guest House† (Oscar Levant) (7/1)

Monday
7:30-8:00 ABC Music in Velvet (7/8)
7:45-8:00 CBS weeknights TV's Top Tunes† (Peggy Lee, Mel Tormé) (7/2)
5-5:30 NBC Uncle Lumpy's Secret Cabin† (Hugh Branum) (8/20)
8-8:30 CBS Pantomine Quiz† (Mike Stokey, host) (7/2)
8-8:30 ABC The Jerry Colonna Show† (5/28)
8-8:30 ABC The March of Time (resumed 5/14)
8-8:30 NBC Cameo Theatre* (resumed 6/18)
8-8:30 NBC Tag the Gag† (Hal Block) (8/13)
9:30-10:00 CBS Who's Whose† (6/25)
10-10:30 NBC The Arthur Murray Party† (from 6/25)

Tuesday
12:30-1:00 ABC afternoon Jessie's TV Notebook† (6/19)
6:30-7:00 ABC Wild Bill Hickok† (Guy Madison, Andy Devine) (6/26)

Wednesday
8-9:00 ABC The Paul Dixon Show† (8/8)
9:30-10:00 WABD Shadow of the Cloak† (6/13)

Thursday
8-8:30 NBC It Pays to Be Ignorant† (Lulu McConnell, Tom Howard) (7/5)
9-9:30 ABC Musical Playhouse† (Don Ameche, Betty Brewer) (7/5)
9:30-10:00 WABD Royal Playhouse† [repeats of Fireside Theatre] (5/10)

Friday
10:05-11:00 CBS Meet Corliss Archer† (Freda Inescort, Eugene Sanders, Bobby Ellis, Fred Shields) (7/13)
8:30-9:00 NBC The Clock* (resumed 7/6)
9-9:30 NBC The Door with No Name† (7/13)

1951-52 SEASON

Saturday

Noon-12:30: Betty Crocker Star Matinee† (11/3)
10:30-11:00 A.M.: Hollywood Junior Circus† (9/8)

	CBS	NBC	ABC
			11-11:30: Foudini the Great† (9/1)
			12:30-1:00 P.M.: I Cover Times Square (9/1) alternating with The Faith Baldwin Playhouse; subsequently displaced by City Hospital† (11/3) alternating with Personal Appearance Theatre† (11/10)
7:00	The Sammy Kaye Show† (9/8)	American Youth Forum† (9/8)	Hollywood Theatre Time† (films)
7:30	News	One Man's Family (9/22)	The Jerry Colonna Show
	7:45: Beat the Clock (Bill Hart) (9/8)		
8:00	The Ken Murray Show (9/8)	The All-Star Revue† (Jimmy Durante, Olsen and Johnson, et al.) (9/8)	The Paul Whiteman TV Teen Club
8:30	The Ken Murray Show	The All-Star Revue	The Paul Whiteman TV Teen Club
9:00	Faye Emerson's Wonderful Town† (9/8)	Your Show of Shows	Lesson in Safety† (films)
9:30	The Show Goes On (9/8)	Your Show of Shows	America's Health† (films)
10:00	Songs for Sale (Steve Allen) (9/8)	Your Show of Shows	Harness Racing (from Chicago)
10:30	Songs for Sale	Your Hit Parade (9/8)	Harness Racing

Sunday

		3:30-4:00: See It Now† (Edward R. Murrow) (11/18)	
4:00	Lamp unto My Feet (9/9)	Meet the Press (8/26)	
4:30	What in the World?† (panel show) (9/9)	Zoo Parade† (8/26)	Space Patrol† (9/9)
5:00	The Man of the Week† (9/9)	The Gabby Hayes Show (8/26)	Super Circus
5:30	News	Sky King Theatre† (Kirby Grant) (10/14)	Super Circus
	5:45: The Sarah Churchill Hallmark Show† (10/7)		
6:00	The Big Question† (9/9)	Hopalong Cassidy	The Ted Mack Family Hour
6:30	Star of the Family (Peter Lind Hayes) (9/9)	Hopalong Cassidy	The Ted Mack Family Hour
7:00	The Gene Autry Show (9/9)	Sound-Off Time† (Fred Allen) (10/7)	The Paul Whiteman Revue

CBS	NBC	ABC
7:30 This Is Show Business (9/9) alternating with The Jack Benny Show (9/16)	Young Mr. Bobbin† (Jackie Kelk) (8/26)	Music in Velvet; subsequently By-Line† (Betty Furness) (10/14)
8:00 The Toast of the Town	The Colgate Comedy Hour (9/2)	Admission Free† (theatrical films)
8:30 The Toast of the Town	The Colgate Comedy Hour	Admission Free† (theatrical films)
9:00 The Fred Waring Show (9/9)	The Philco Television Playhouse* alternating with The Goodyear Theatre†* (10/14)	films
9:30 The Fred Waring Show	The Philco Television Playhouse alternating with The Goodyear Theatre†	films
10:00 Celebrity Time (9/9)	The Red Skelton Show† (9/30) alternating with American Forum	Billy Graham Crusade
10:30 What's My Line?	Author Meets the Critics (9/16)	Youth on the March (9/16)

Monday

Noon-12:30 weekdays: The Egg and I† (Patricia Kirkland) (9/3)		Noon-1:00 weekdays: The Frances Langford-Don Ameche Show† (9/10)
1:30-2:00 weekdays: The Garry Moore Show (continuing)		
	4-5:00 weekdays: The Kate Smith Hour (9/10)	
7:00 local	Kukla, Fran and Ollie (8/27)	Candid Camera† (8/27)
	7:15: The Bob and Ray Show† (11/26)	7:15: Sports with Russ Hodges (10/1) and John Daly World News† (10/22)
7:30 News	Those Two† (Pinky Lee, Vivian Blaine) (11/26), following Roberta Quinlan (9/3)	Hollywood Screen Test
7:45: The Perry Como Show (8/27)	7:45: Camel News Caravan	
8:00 The Lux Video Theatre* (8/27)	The Paul Winchell Show (9/17)	The Amazing Mr. Malone† (Lee Tracy) (9/24) alternating with Mr. District Attorney (Jay Jostyn) (10/1)
8:30 Arthur Godfrey's Talent Scouts (9/24)	The Voice of Firestone	Life Begins at 80

CBS	NBC	ABC
9:00 I Love Lucy† (10/15) following its pilot episode (10/1)	Lights Out* (8/27)	The Paul Dixon Show†
9:30 Its News to Me† (John Daly) (9/17)	Robert Montgomery Presents* (9/10) alternating with Somerset Maugham Theatre* (9/17)	The Paul Dixon Show
10:00 Studio One* (9/17)	Robert Montgomery Presents* alternating with Somerset Maugham Theatre	The Bill Gwinn Show
10:30 Studio One	The Boston Blackie† (Kent Taylor, Lois Collier) (9/10)	Studs' Place (10/1)

8:30-9:00 WABD The Gallery of Mme. Liu-Tsong†* (8/27)

Tuesday

	CBS	NBC	ABC
			6:30-7:00 weeknights: Wild Bill Hickok (9/4)
7:00	local	Kukla, Fran and Ollie 7:15: local	Sports with Russ Hodges† 7:15: The Carmel Myers Show† (9/4) alternating with Dining Out with Dana† (10/16)
7:30	News	John Conte's Little Show (8/28) followed by The Dinah Shore Show† (11/27)	Beulah (9/4)
	7:45: The Stork Club	7:45: Camel News Caravan	
8:00	The Frank Sinatra Show (10/9)	The Texaco Star Theatre (9/18)	Charlie Wild, Private Detective (9/11)
8:30	The Frank Sinatra Show	The Texaco Star Theatre	How Did You Get That Way? (10/16)
9:00	Crime Syndicated† (with Rudolph Halley) (9/18)	Fireside Theatre* (6/26)	United Or Not? (films)
9:30	Suspense* (9/18)	The Armstrong Circle Theatre* (9/18)	On Trial
10:00	Danger* (9/18)	The Ted Mack Original Amateur Hour	Actors' Hotel† (Carie Cellini) (9/25)
10:30	local	The Ted Mack Original Amateur Hour	Chicago Symphony Orchestra† (9/25)

9-10:00 WABD Cosmopolitan Theatre†* (10/2)
10-10:30 WABD Hands of Destiny† (9/11)

Wednesday

	CBS	NBC	ABC
7:00	local	Kukla, Fran and Ollie	Sports with Russ Hodges and John Daly World News†
		7:15: The Bob and Ray Show†	7:15: Candid Camera

	CBS	NBC	ABC
7:30	News	Those Two† (following Roberta Quinlan)	Chance of a Lifetime
	7:45: The Perry Como Show	7:45: Camel News Caravan	
8:00	The Arthur Godfrey Show (9/26)	The Four Star Revue (Kate Smith, et al.) (9/19)	Frosty Frolics† (films) (9/19)
8:30	The Arthur Godfrey Show	The Four Star Revue	Frosty Frolics (films)
9:00	Strike It Rich† (9/12)	The Kraft Television Theatre* (9/12)	Don McNeill's TV Club (9/12) alternating with The Arthur Murray Party (9/19)
9:30	The Web* (9/26)	The Kraft Television Theatre	The Clock* (10/17)
10:00	Blue Ribbon Bouts (boxing)	Break the Bank (9/12)	Celanese Theatre†* (10/3) alternating with Crossroads† (films); subsequently Pulitzer Prize Playhouse* (12/19)
10:30	Blue Ribbon Bouts (boxing)	The Freddy Martin Show† (9/12)	Celanese Theatre† alternating with Crossroads† (films); subsequently Pulitzer Prize Playhouse 11-11:15: Short Story Theatre† (films, with Milo Boulton, host) (10/3)

Thursday

7:00	local	Kukla, Fran and Ollie	Sports with Russ Hodges and John Daly World News†
		7:15: local	7:15: The Eva Gabor Show (10/4)
7:30	News	John Conte's Little Show followed by The Dinah Shore Show†	The Lone Ranger (9/13)
	7:45: The Stork Club	7:45: Camel News Caravan	
8:00	The George Burns-Gracie Allen Show (10/11) alternating with The Garry Moore Show† (10/18)	You Bet Your Life (10/4)	Stop the Music (Bert Parks) (9/13)
8:30	Amos 'n' Andy† (Spencer Williams, Tim Moore) (6/28)	Treasury Men in Action (10/4)	Stop the Music
9:00	The Alan Young Show (9/27)	The James Melton Show (10/4)	The Herb Shriner Show (10/4)
9:30	Big Town (9/27)	The James Melton Show	Gruen Guild Playhouse†* (9/27)

	CBS	NBC	ABC
10:00	Racket Squad† (Reed Hadley) (9/27)	Martin Kane, Private Eye† (Lloyd Nolan) (8/30)	The Paul Dixon Show (9/27)
10:30	Crime Photographer (9/27)	Foreign Intrigue† (Jerome Thor) (10/4)	The At Home Show† (Earl Wrightson) (8/30)

9-9:30 WABD The Adventures of Ellery Queen† (Lee Bowman) (9/13)
9:30-10:00 WABD The Public Prosecutor† (Warren Hull) (9/6)
10-10:30 WABD The Bigelow-Sanford Theatre [repeats of Silver Theater] (9/6)

Friday

7:00	local	Kukla, Fran and Ollie	Sports with Russ Hodges and John Daly World News†
		7:15: The Bob and Ray Show	7:15: Candid Camera
7:30	News	Those Two† (following Roberta Quinlan)	Life with Linkletter (8/31) alternating with Say It with Acting (9/7)
	7:45: The Perry Como Show	7:45: Camel News Caravan	
8:00	I Remember Mama (9/7)	The Quiz Kids (9/7) followed by The Ezio Pinza Show† (11/25)	The Mark Saber Mystery Theatre† (Tom Conway) (10/5)
8:30	Man Against Crime (8/10)	We, the People (Dan Seymour) (9/7)	The Trouble with Father (10/5)
9:00	The Schlitz Playhouse of the Stars†* (10/5)	The Big Story (8/31)	Crime with Father† (Rusty Lane and Reggy Gobbin) (8/31)
9:30	The Schlitz Playhouse of the Stars†	The Aldrich Family (9/7)	Tales of Tomorrow†* (8/31) alternating with Versatile Varieties (9/21)
10:00	Live Like a Millionaire† (John Nelson) (9/4)	Madison Square Garden Friday Night Fights (9/7)	At Home Gardener† (Phil Alampi) (8/31)
10:30	Hollywood Opening Night† [repeats of Stars Over Hollywood] (9/4)	Madison Square Garden Friday Night Fights	America in View† (films) (8/31)

10-11:00 WABD Cavalcade of Stars (Jackie Gleason) [continuing]

1951-52 MIDSEASON

Saturday

7:00	The Sammy Kaye Show	American Youth Forum	local
7:30	News 7:45: Beat the Clock	One Man's Family	The Jerry Colonna Show
8:00	The Ken Murray Show	The All-Star Revue	The Paul Whiteman TV Teen Club

CBS	NBC	ABC
8:30 The Ken Murray Show	The All-Star Revue	The Paul Whiteman TV Teen Club
9:00 Faye Emerson's Wonderful Town	Your Show of Shows	films
9:30 The Show Goes On	Your Show of Shows	films
10:00 Songs for Sale	Your Show of Shows	Sports
10:30 Songs for Sale	Your Hit Parade	Sports

Sunday

CBS	NBC	ABC
3:00 The Quiz Kids (resumed 1/13)		
3:30 See It Now	The Hallmark Hall of Fame†* (1/6)	
4:00 CBS Television Workshop†* (1/27)	Meet the Press	
4:30 What in the World?	Juvenile Jury	
5:00 Man of the Week	Zoo Parade	Super Circus
5:30 The Mel Tormé Show† (1/13)	Meet the Masters† (2/24)	Super Circus
6:00 Mr. I Magination (resumed 2/10)	The Roy Rogers Show† (12/30/51)	Space Patrol (resumed 1/27)
6:30 The Sam Levenson Show† (2/10)	Claudia, the Story of a Marriage (Joan McCracken, Hugh Reilly) (1/6)	America's Town Meeting† (1/27)
7:00 The Gene Autry Show	Sound-Off Time	The Paul Whiteman Revue
7:30 This Is Show Business	Young Mr. Bobbin	The Adventures of Ellery Queen (as of 1/27)
8:00 The Toast of the Town	The Colgate Comedy Hour	King's Crossroads† (films) (1/13)
8:30 The Toast of the Town	The Colgate Comedy Hour	King's Crossroads (films)
9:00 The Fred Waring Show	The Philco Television Playhouse alternating with The Goodyear Theatre	The Arthur Murray Party (resumed 1/13)
9:30 The Fred Waring Show	The Philco Television Playhouse alternating with The Goodyear Theatre	films
10:00 Celebrity Time	The Red Skelton Show	Billy Graham Crusade
10:30 What's My Line?	Cameo Theatre* (resumed 1/6)	Youth On the March

Monday

CBS	NBC	ABC
7:00 local	Kukla, Fran and Ollie	John Daly World News/ Sports with Russ Hodges
	7:15: The Goldbergs (resumed 2/4)	7:15: Candid Camera
7:30 News 7:45: The Perry Como Show	Those Two 7:45: News Caravan	Hollywood Screen Test

	CBS	NBC	ABC
8:00	The Lux Video Theatre	The Paul Winchell Show	The Amazing Mr. Malone alternating with Mr. District Attorney
8:30	Arthur Godfrey's Talent Scouts	The Voice of Firestone	Life Begins at 80
9:00	I Love Lucy	Lights Out	You Asked for It† (Art Baker) (1/7)
9:30	It's News to Me	Robert Montgomery Presents (in weekly format as of 12/31/51)	theatrical films
10:00	Studio One	Robert Montgomery Presents	theatrical films
10:30	Studio One	Dangerous Assignment† (Brian Donlevy) (3/10)	theatrical films

7:30-8:55 WOR weeknights The Broadway Television Theatre†* (4/14)

Tuesday

7:00	local	Kukla, Fran and Ollie	John Daly World News/ Sports with Russ Hodges
		7:15: The Stork Club (as of 2/11)	7:15: The Carmel Myers Show
7:30	News	The Dinah Shore Show	Beulah (Louise Beavers) (resumed 4/29)
	7:45: The Stork Club	7:45: Camel News Caravan	
8:00	The Frank Sinatra Show	Texaco Star Theatre	Charlie Wild, Private Detective
8:30	The Frank Sinatra Show	Texaco Star Theatre	How Did They Get That Way?
9:00	Crime Syndicated	Fireside Theatre	United or Not?
9:30	Suspense	The Armstrong Circle Theatre	news reports
10:00	Danger	The Ted Mack Original Amateur Hour	film
10:30	My Friend Irma† (Marie Wilson, Cathy Lewis) (1/8)	The Ted Mack Original Amateur Hour	Actors' Hotel

9-9:30 WABD Battle of the Ages (1/1)
9:30-10:00 WABD Quick on the Draw† (Bob Duncan, host) (1/1)

Wednesday

7:00	local	Kukla, Fran and Ollie	John Daly World News/ Sports with Russ Hodges
		7:15: The Goldbergs	7:15: Candid Camera
7:30	News	Those Two	The Name's the Same† (Robert Q. Lewis) (12/19/51)
	7:45: The Perry Como Show	7:45: Camel News Caravan	
8:00	Arthur Godfrey and His Friends	The Four Star Revue (The Kate Smith Evening Hour)	The Paul Dixon Show (resumed 1/2)

	CBS	NBC	ABC
8:30	Arthur Godfrey and His Friends	The Four Star Revue (The Kate Smith Evening Hour)	The Paul Dixon Show
9:00	Strike It Rich	The Kraft Television Theatre	P. D. Q. Quiz Show
9:30	The Web	The Kraft Television Theatre	Newsstand Theatre† (1/16) followed by Rendezvous† (Ilona Massey, hostess) (2/13)
10:00	The Wednesday Night Fights	Your Prize Story† (repeats) (4/2)	Celanese Theatre alternating with Pulitzer Prize Playhouse
10:30	The Wednesday Night Fights	Pantomine Quiz (resumed 1/2) followed by The Unexpected†* (3/5)	Celanese Theatre alternating with Pulitzer Prize Playhouse

9:00-9:30 WABD Famous Jury Trials (12/5/51)

Thursday

	CBS	NBC	ABC
7:00	local	Kukla, Fran and Ollie	John Daly World News/ Sports with Russ Hodges
		7:15: The Stork Club	7:15: Walter Coveli Solo Drama (1/13)
7:30	News 7:45: The Stork Club	The Dinah Shore Show 7:45: Camel News Caravan	The Lone Ranger
8:00	The George Burns-Gracie Allen Show alternating with The Garry Moore Show	You Bet Your Life	Stop the Music
8:30	Amos 'n' Andy	Treasury Men in Action	Stop the Music
9:00	The Alan Young Show	Dragnet† (Jack Webb, Ben Alexander) (12/16/51) followed by The Gangbusters† (3/20)	The Herb Shriner Show
9:30	Big Town	The James Melton Show	Meet the Champ† (1/13)
10:00	Racket Squad	Martin Kane, Private Eye	Football Highlights
10:30	Crime Photographer	Foreign Intrigue	The At Home Show

9:30-10:00 WABD The Cases of Eddie Drake† (Don Haggerty, Patricia Medina) (3/6)
9-9:30 WABD The Gruen Guild Playhouse* (resumed 3/27) alternating with repeats of The Firestone Theatre (4/4)

Friday

	CBS	NBC	ABC
7:00	local	Kukla, Fran and Cllie	John Daly World News/ Sports with Russ Hodges
		7:15: The Goldbergs	7:15: Candid Camera

	CBS	NBC	ABC
7:30	News 7:45: The Perry Como Show	Those Two 7:45: Camel News Caravan	Life with Linkletter
8:00	I Remember Mama	The RCA Victor Show with Dennis Day† (3/21)	The Mark Saber Mystery Theatre
8:30	Man Against Crime	We, the People	The Trouble with Father
9:00	The Schlitz Playhouse of the Stars	The Big Story	Rebound†* (2/8)
9:30	The Schlitz Playhouse of the Stars	The Aldrich Family	Tales of Tomorrow
10:00	Police Story†* (4/4)	The Friday Night Fights	The Black Spider† (films) (2/8)
10:30	Presidential Timber† (4/4)	The Friday Night Fights	local

Summer Programming, 1952

Saturday
7-7:30 NBC The Schaefer Century Theatre†* (5/24)
8-8:30 NBC Duffy's Tavern† (Ed Gardner) (6/21)
9:30-10:00 NBC The Saturday Night Dance Party† (Jerry Lester) (6/7)
10:30-11:00 NBC Assignment: Manhunt† (J. Pat O'Malley, Ralph Stantley)
(7/5)

Sunday
12:30-1:00 afternoon NBC Through the Enchanted Gate† (5/11)
3:30-4:00 CBS Story for Americans† (7/6)
6-6:30 NBC Are You Positive?† (sports quiz) (7/6)
7:30-8:00 CBS Your Lucky Clue† (Basil Rathbone) (7/13)
10-10:30 ABC Hour of Decision† (Billy Graham) (7/6)
10-10:30 NBC The Hallmark Hall of Fame* (this time as of 6/29)

Monday
8-8:30 NBC The Quiz Kids (resumed 7/7)
8-8:30 NBC Masquerade Party (resumed 7/14)
9-9:30 CBS My Little Margie† (Charles Farrell, Gale Storm) (6/16)
9:30-10:00 CBS Who's There?† (Arlene Francis) (7/14)
10-11:00 ABC The Harlem Talent Show† (Lionel Hampton, Ralph Cooper)(6/9)

Tuesday
7:30-8:00 WABD The Gruen Guild Playhouse* (as of 7/29)
7:45-8:00 CBS Tuesday and Thursday The Patti Page Show† (7/1)
9-9:30 NBC The Boss Lady† (Lynn Bari, Glenn Langan) (8/26)

Wednesday
9:30-10:00 CBS The Hunter† (Barry Nelson) (7/3) [first episode only, Thursday 9:00-9:30 CBS]
10-10:30 NBC Where the People Stand† (Elmer Roper, host) (6/4)

Thursday
8-8:30 ABC Hollywood Off Beat† (Melvyn Douglas, Mary Beth Hughes)(6/12)
8-8:30 CBS The Al Pearce Show† (7/10)
8:30-9:00 CBS The Steve Allen Show† [alternating with Amos 'n' Andy] (7/3)
9:30-10:00 NBC Mr. Peepers† (Wally Cox, Norma Crane, Joseph Foley,
David Tyrell) (7/3)

CBS	NBC	ABC

Friday
8-8:30 NBC Curtain Call†* (6/20)
9-9:30 NBC Doorway to Danger† (Roland Winters) (7/4)
9:30-10:00 CBS Footlights Theatre† [repeats of Bigelow-Sanford Theatre] (7/4)
9:30-10:00 NBC Playhouse† [repeats of Gruen Guild Playhouse and Stars Over Hollywood] (6/6)
10:30-11:00 CBS Candidate Closeups† (6/27)

1952-53 SEASON

Saturday

	CBS	NBC	ABC
7:00	The Stork Club	local	The Paul Whiteman TV Teen Club (9/6)
7:30	Beat the Clock	My Hero† (Robert Cummings) (11/8)	Live Like a Millionaire (9/6)
8:00	The Jackie Gleason Show† (9/20)	The All-Star Revue (9/6)	Comedy Cameos† (films) (9/6)
8:30	The Jackie Gleason Show	The All-Star Revue	theatrical films
9:00	My Little Margie (13/4) followed by Meet Millie (Elena Verdugo, Ross Ford, Florence Halop) (10/25)	Your Show of Shows (9/6)	theatrical films
9:30	Jane Froman's Canteen† (10/18)	Your Show of Shows	theatrical films
10:00	Balance Your Budget† (Bert Parks) (10/18)	Your Show of Shows	theatrical films
10:30	Battle of the Ages† (Morey Amsterdam) (9/6)	Your Hit Parade (8/30)	theatrical films

7-7:30 WABD Wild Bill Hickok [continuing]

Sunday

	CBS	NBC	ABC
3:00		Victory at Sea†* (10/26)	
3:30	local	local	
4:00	The Quiz Kids (9/14)	Kukla, Fran and Ollie (8/24)	
4:30	Omnibus†* (11/9)	The Hallmark Hall of Fame* (8/24)	Papa Cellini† (Carlo de Angelo) (9/28)
5:00	Omnibus	Zoo Parade (8/24)	Super Circus (9/28)
5:30	Omnibus	Meet the Masters (9/24)	Super Circus
6:00	Man of the Week (9/14)	Meet the Press	Captain Midnight† (Sid Melton, Richard Webb) (10/5)
6:30	See It Now	The Roy Rogers Show (8/31)	The Billy Daniels Show† (10/5) 6:45: The Walter Winchell Show† (10/5)
7:00	The Gene Autry Show (9/28)	The Red Skelton Show (9/28)	You Asked for It (Art Baker) (10/5)

	CBS	NBC	ABC
7:30	This Is Show Business (9/28) alternating with The Jack Benny Show (10/5)	Mr. Peepers (9/3; 10/26) alternating with Doc Corkle† (Eddie Mayehoff, Chester Conklin, Arnold Stang, Hope Emerson, Connie Marshall) (10/5)	The Hot Seat† (Stuart Scheftel) (10/5)
8:00	The Toast of the Town	The Colgate Comedy Hour [Eddie Cantor, Bob Hope, Martin & Lewis, et al.]	theatrical films
8:30	The Toast of the Town	The Colgate Comedy Hour	theatrical films
9:00	The Fred Waring Show (9/28)	The Philco Television Playhouse* alternating with The Goodyear Theatre* (9/14)	theatrical films
9:30	Break the Bank (9/28)	The Philco Television Playhouse alternating with The Goodyear Theatre	Enterprise, U.S.A.† (industrial films) (10/19)
10:00	The Web* (9/28)	The Doctor† (Warner Anderson) (8/24)	Billy Graham Crusade
10:30	What's My Line?	The Schaefer Century Theatre* (10/5)	Anywhere, U.S.A.† (on health neglect, Eddie Dowling, Robert Preston) (11/9)

5-6:00 WABD The New York Times Youth Forum† (9/14)
10-10:30 WABD The Arthur Murray Party (10/12)

Monday

7:30	News	Meet Your Match† (Jan Murray) (8/25)	Hollywood Screen Test
	7:45: The Perry Como Show (8/25)		
8:00	The Lux Video Theatre* (8/25)	The Paul Winchell Show (8/25)	Inspector Mark Saber, Homicide Squad (10/6)
8:30	Arthur Godfrey Talent Scouts (8/25)	The Voice of Firestone	Dark Adventure† (films) (8/25)
9:00	I Love Lucy (9/15)	Hollywood Opening Night†* (10/6)	The All Star News Hour† (8/25)
9:30	Life with Luigi† (J. Carrol Naish, Alan Reed) (9/22)	Robert Montgomery Presents* (9/1)	The All Star News Hour
10:00	Studio One* (9/22)	Robert Montgomery Presents	Boxing
10:30	Studio One	Dangerous Assignment (10/6)	Boxing

7:30-8:55 WOR The Broadway Television Theatre* (9/15)
7:30-8:00 WABD Easy Chair Theatre† [repeats of Fireside Theatre] (9/22)

Tuesday

7:15-7:30: Short Short Drama†* (9/30)

CBS	NBC	ABC
7:30 News	The Dinah Shore Show (8/26)	Beulah (Louise Beavers) (9/2) displaced by The Greatest Man on Earth† (12/3)
7:45: Heaven for Betsy† (Jack Lemmon, Cynthia Stone) (9/30)	7:45: News Caravan	
8:00 Leave It to Larry† (Eddie Albert) (10/4)	The Texaco Star Theatre (9/16) displaced monthly by The Circus Hour† (Joe E. Brown, John Raitt) (10/7)	Story Theatre (repeats) (9/2)
8:30 The Red Buttons Show† (10/14)	The Texaco Star Theatre displaced monthly by The Circus Hour†	theatrical films
9:00 Crime Syndicated (10/14)	Fireside Theatre* (9/30)	theatrical films
9:30 Suspense* (10/14)	The Armstrong Circle Theatre* (9/2)	theatrical films
10:00 Danger* (10/14)	Two for the Money† (Herb Shriner) (9/30)	theatrical films
		10:15: Comedy Cameos
10:30 Your Jeweler's Show-case†* (11/11)	Club Time† (10/7)	

7:30-8:00 WABD Death Valley Days† (10/7)
7:30-8:00 WABD Terry and the Pirates† (William Tracy, Gloria Saunders) (11/25)

Wednesday

CBS	NBC	ABC
		7:15: Sports, with Tommy Henrich† (8/27)
7:30 News	Those Two (8/27)	The Name's the Same (8/27)
7:45: The Perry Como Show (8/25)	7:45: News Caravan	
8:00 Arthur Godfrey and His Friends (10/1)	I Married Joan† (Joan Davis, Jim Backus) (10/15)	theatrical films
8:30 Arthur Godfrey and His Friends	The Patti Page Music Hall† (10/8) alternating with Cavalcade of America†* (10/1)	theatrical films
9:00 Strike It Rich (10/1)	The Kraft Television Theatre* (10/1)	The Adventures of Ellery Queen (8/27)
9:30 Man Against Crime (10/1)	The Kraft Television Theatre	films
10:00 The Wednesday Night Fights	This Is Your Life† (Ralph Edwards) (10/1)	Wrestling (from Chicago)
10:30 The Wednesday Night Fights	The Unexpected* (10/1)	Wrestling

	CBS	NBC	ABC

Thursday

	CBS	NBC	ABC
		7:15: Short Short Drama†	7:15: Sports, with Tommy Henrich†
7:30	News	The Dinah Shore Show	The Lone Ranger (9/18)
	7:45: Heaven for Betsy†	7:45: News Caravan	
8:00	The George Burns-Gracie Allen Show (10/2)	You Bet Your Life (9/18)	A Date with Judy† (Mary Linn Beller) (9/18)
8:30	Amos 'n' Andy (9/18) alternating with Four Star Playhouse†* (9/25)	Treasury Men in Action (8/28)	Chance of a Lifetime (Dennis James) (9/18)
9:00	Biff Baker, U.S.A. † (Alan Hale, Randy Stuart) (11/6)	Dragnet (8/28)	Perspective† (films) (9/18)
9:30	Big Town (10/2)	Ford Theatre†* (10/2)	The Maggie McNellis Show† (9/18)
10:00	My Little Margie (10/2)	Martin Kane, Private Eye (9/18)	documentary films
10:30	I've Got a Secret† (10/2)	Foreign Intrigue (9/18)	documentary films

Friday

	CBS	NBC	ABC
			7:15: Sports, with Tommy Henrich†
7:30	News	Meet Your Match† (8/29)	The Trouble With Father (10/17)
	7:45: The Perry Como Show	7:45: News Caravan	
8:00	I Remember Mama (9/5)	The Dennis Day Show (10/3)	Ozzie and Harriet† (10/3)
8:30	My Friend Irma (10/3)	Gulf Playhouse†* (10/3)	local
			8:45: Rudolph Halley Reports† (10/3)
9:00	The Schlitz Playhouse of the Stars* (10/3; half hour format as of 5/23/52)	The Big Story (8/29)	Life Begins at 80 (10/3)
9:30	Our Miss Brooks† (Eve Arden, Gale Gordon, Richard Crenna) (10/3)	The Aldrich Family (9/5)	Tales of Tomorrow* (10/3)
10:00	Mr. and Mrs. North† (Barbara Britton, Richard Denning) (10/3)	The Friday Night Fights	theatrical films
10:30	Teledrama† (10/3) followed by The Abbott and Costello Show† (12/5)	The Friday Night Fights	theatrical films

8-8:30 WABD The Boston Blackie† (Kent Taylor, Lois Collyer) (10/3)
8:30-9:00 WABD Rebound (resumed 11/21)

	CBS	NBC	NBC

1952-53 MIDSEASON

Saturday

	CBS	NBC	NBC
6:30	Rod Brown of the Rocket Rangers† (Cliff Robertson) (4/18)	Hopalong Cassidy (from 5:30)	
7:00	The Stork Club	Star Time Kids† (4/25)	The Paul Whiteman TV Teen Club
7:30	Beat the Clock	Ethel and Albert† (Peg Lynch, Alan Bunce) (4/25)	Live Like a Millionaire
8:00	The Jackie Gleason Show	My Hero (as of 4/25)	Complete Theatre† (theatrical films)
8:30	The Jackie Gleason Show	The Amateur Show (4/25)	Complete Theatre
9:00	Allinone† (1/31)	Your Show of Shows	Complete Theatre
9:30	Meet Millie	Your Show of Shows	Complete Theatre
10:00	The Quiz Kids	Your Show of Shows	films
10:30	Its News to Me	Your Hit Parade	films

Sunday

	CBS	NBC	NBC
3:00		(via New York channel 4): Life in New York† (5/10)	
3:30	local	local	
4:00	The Quiz Kids	Kukla, Fran and Ollie	
4:30	Omnibus	Zoo Parade	The Range Rider (Jock Mahoney) (resumed 2/1)
5:00	Omnibus	The Hallmark Hall of Fame	Super Circus
5:30	Omnibus	Meet the Veep (2/1) 5:45: A Window on Washington† (2/1)	Super Circus
6:00	You Are There† (2/1)	Meet the Press	Captain Midnight
6:30	See It Now	The Roy Rogers Show	The Walter Winchell Show 6:45: The Rosemary Clooney Show† (4/12)
7:00	The Gene Autry Show	The Red Skelton Show	You Asked for It
7:30	This Is Show Business alternating with Private Secretary† (Ann Sothern, Don Porter) (2/1)	Mr. Peepers	The ABC Album†* (a.k.a. The Plymouth Playhouse) (4/12)
8:00	The Toast of the Town	The Colgate Comedy Hour	The All Star News
8:30	The Toast of the Town	The Colgate Comedy Hour	The All Star News
9:00	The Fred Waring Show alternating with The General Electric Theatre†* (2/1)	The Philco Television Playhouse alternating with The Goodyear Theatre	film

	CBS	NBC	ABC
9:30	The Ken Murray Show (as of 2/8) alternating with The Alan Young Show (as of 2/1)	The Philco Television Playhouse alternating with The Goodyear Theatre	This Is the Life (films)
10:00	The Web	The Doctor	The Billy Graham Crusade 10:15: Joe Franklin's Memory Lane (12/21/51)
10:30	What's My Line?	Your Favorite Story†* (1/11)	local 10:45: Screen Shots (12/21/51)

Monday

3:30-4:00 weekdays:
Action in the Afternoon† (western, with
Jack Valentine) (2/2)

7:00		The Cisco Kid (Duncan Renaldo) (began 1/20/51; resumed here 1/19)	
7:30	News 7:45: The Perry Como Show	Those Two 7:45: News Caravan	Hollywood Screen Test
8:00	The Burns and Allen Show (as of 3/30)	The Paul Winchell	films
8:30	Arthur Godfrey's Talent Scouts	The Voice of Firestone	Dark Adventure
9:00	I Love Lucy	Eyewitness†* (3/30)	The Little Theatre (films)
9:30	The Red Buttons Show (as of 1/5)	Robert Montgomery Presents	The Army Talent Patrol† (Steve Allen) (1/19)
10:00	Studio One	Robert Montgomery Presents	comedy films
10:30	Studio One	Dangerous Assignment	mystery films

Tuesday

		7:15-7:30: Our Place† (Jimmy Stearns) (4/14)	
7:30	News 7:45: Jane Froman's U.S.A. Canteen (as of 1/6)	The Dinah Shore Show 7:45: News Caravan	Beulah
8:00	The Ernie Kovacs Show† (1/6)	The Texaco Star Theatre	Short Story Theatre
8:30	The Ernie Kovacs Show	The Texaco Star Theatre	Film Previews
9:00	City Hospital (resumed 1/6)	Fireside Theatre	theatrical films
9:30	Suspense	The Armstrong Circle Theatre	theatrical films

	CBS	NBC	ABC
10:00	Danger	Two for the Money	The Dog Show of Champions
10:30	Your Jeweler's Showcase alternating with Demi Tasse Tales† [repeats of Silver Theatre] (1/6)	Club Time	The Name's the Same

7:15-7:30 WPIX This Is Charles Laughton† (readings) (1/6)

Wednesday

	CBS	NBC	ABC
7:00	local	The March of Time	local
7:30	News	Those Two	A Date With Judy (resumed 1/7)
	7:45: The Perry Como Show	7:45: News Caravan	
8:00	Arthur Godfrey and His Friends	I Married Joan	Twentieth Century Tales† [repeats of Stars Over Hollywood and Hollywood Opening Night] (2/25)
8:30	Arthur Godfrey and His Friends	The Patti Page Music Hall alternating with Cavalcade of America	The Adventures of China Smith† (Dan Duryea) (5/13)
9:00	Strike It Rich	The Kraft Television Theatre	Wrestling
9:30	Man Against Crime	The Kraft Television Theatre	Wrestling
10:00	The Wednesday Night Fights	This Is Your Life	Wrestling
10:30	The Wednesday Night Fights	Douglas Fairbanks Jr. Presents†* (1/7)	Spotlight on Music† (1/7)

Thursday

	CBS	NBC	ABC
		7:15-7:30: Our Place†	
7:30	News	The Dinah Shore Show	The Lone Ranger
	7:45: Jane Froman's U.S.A. Canteen	7:45: News Caravan	
8:00	The George Burns-Gracie Allen Show	You Bet Your Life	The Greatest Man on Earth (as of 3/19)
8:30	Amos 'n' Andy alternating with The Four Star Playhouse	Treasury Men In Action	Chance of a Lifetime
9:00	The Lux Video Theatre (as of 4/2)	Dragnet	The Turning Point† [repeats of Stars Over Hollywood, Hollywood Opening Night and Gruen Guild Playhouse] (2/5) followed by Major City Bouts† (3/19)
9:30	Big Town	Ford Theatre	Major City Bouts†
10:00	My Little Margie	Martin Kane, Private Eye	The Dog Show of Champions† (3/19)

	CBS	NBC	ABC

10:30 I've Got a Secret   Foreign Intrigue   Personality Puzzle†
(Robert Alda) (3/19)

[Note: President Truman's Farewell Address, all stations 10:30-11:00
1/15/53]

Friday

7:15-7:30: The Herman
Hickman Show (1/2)

7:30 News   Those Two   The Trouble with Father
7:45: The Perry   7:45: News Caravan
Como Show

8:00 I Remember Mama   The Dennis Day Show   Ozzie and Harriet
8:30 My Friend Irma   The Life of Riley†   This Is Charles Laugh-
(William Bendix,   ton† (1/9)
Marjorie Reynolds,
Wesley Morgan,
Gloria Blondell,
Tom D'Andrea) (1/2)

8:45: Rudolph Halley
Reports

9:00 The Schlitz Play-   The Big Story   Appointment with Love†
house of the Stars   [repeats of The Gruen
Guild Playhouse] (1/2)

9:30 Our Miss Brooks   The Aldrich Family   Tales of Tomorrow
10:00 Mr. and Mrs. North The Friday Night   Papa Cellini (resumed
Fights   1/2)
10:30 The Abbott and Cos- The Friday Night   Black Spider (films)
tello Show   Fights

Summer Programming, 1953

Saturday
2-2:45 afternoon CBS Camera Three† (6/6)
6-6:30 WPIX Ramar of the Jungle (resumed 8/29)
7-7:30 NBC The Hunter (resumed 7/11)
7:30-8:00 NBC My Son Jeep† (Jeffrey Lynn) (7/11)
8-9:00 CBS The Larry Storch Show† (7/11)
10-10:30 CBS The Chrysler Medallion Theatre†* (7/11)

Sunday
1:30-2:00 afternoon ABC The Better Living Theatre† (6/21)
5:00-5:30 NBC Recital Hall† (7/5)
5:30-6:00 NBC The Nature of Things (resumed 7/5)
5:00-6:00 CBS Adventure† [produced under the auspices of the American
Museum of Natural History; later aired 6:30-7:00 (5/10)]
7:00-7:30 NBC Operation Neptune† (Tod Griffith) (6/28)
7:30-8:00 ABC Straw Hat Theatre† [repeats of Gruen Guild Playhouse] (7/5)
7:45-8:00 ABC The Orchid Award† (Bert Lytell) (6/21)
9:00-9:30 ABC Martin Agronsky Comments† (7/12)
9:30-10:00 CBS The Arthur Murray Party (resumed 6/28)
9:30-10:00 ABC The Fitzgeralds (resumed 7/12)
10:00-10:30 NBC Liberace at the Piano† (7/5)
10:00-10:30 WABD What's the Story?† (Al Capp) (7/12)

CBS	NBC	ABC

Monday
Monday, Wednesday and Friday 7:45-8:00 CBS Top Tunes† (7/13)
8:00-8:30 CBS The Masquerade Party (resumed 6/22)
7-7:30 NBC Wonderful John Acton† (Harry Holcombe, Virginia Dwyer, Ronnie
    Walken, Ian Martin) (7/13)
8-8:30 NBC Name That Tune† (7/6)
9-9:30 NBC The Juvenile Jury (resumed 7/6)
9-9:30 ABC Twilight Theatre† [repeats of Gruen Guild Playhouse] (6/1)
11:00-Midnight ABC The Talk of the Town† (4/27)

Tuesday
7:45-8:00 CBS Summertime U.S.A. † (7/7)
8-8:30 CBS The Gene Autry Show (resumed 7/7)
8-8:30 NBC The Revlon Mirror Theatre†* (6/23)
9-9:30 NBC Follow the Leader† (Vera Vogue) (7/7)
9:30-10:00 NBC Candid Camera (resumed 6/2)
10:30-11:00 CBS Hollywood Off Beat (resumed 6/16)
10:30-11:00 CBS Youth Takes a Stand† (8/18)

Wednesday
8-8:30 NBC Take a Guess† (7/22)
8-9:00 CBS The Red Skelton Revue† (7/22)
8:30-9:00 ABC The China Smith Adventures (resumed 7/8)
10:30-11:00 CBS The Blue Angel† (Orson Bean) (7/22)

Thursday
8-8:30 WABD Drama at Eight† [repeats of Schaefer Century Theatre] (8/6)
8:30-9:00 CBS Ben Hecht's Tales of the City†* (6/25)
8:30-9:00 NBC Place the Face† (Jack Smith) (7/2)

Friday
8-8:30 NBC The Goldbergs (resumed 7/3)
8-8:30 ABC Summer Theatre† [repeats of The Bigelow-Sanford Theatre] (7/3)
8:30-9:00 NBC First Person Playhouse†* (7/10)
9-9:30 NBC Doorway to Danger† (Stacy Harris) (7/3)
9:30-10:00 NBC The Campbell TV Sound Stage†* (7/10)
9:30-10:00 CBS Footlights Theatre [repeats of The Bigelow-Sanford Theatre]
    (resumed 7/3)
9:30-10:00 NBC Double or Nothing† (Bert Parks) (6/5; previous to The Camp-
    bell TV Sound Stage)
9:30-10:00 ABC Double or Nothing† (as of 6/19)
10:30-11:00 WABD Gamble on Love† (7/16)

1953-54 SEASON

[Note: WATV, New York channel 13, initiated 11/14/53]

Saturday
            11-11:30 afternoon:
            Winky Dink and
            You† (Jack Barry)
            (10/9)
            2-2:45: Camera Three
            (9/19)

	CBS	NBC	ABC
7:00	The Stork Club (9/19)	Mr. Wizard† (9/19)	The Paul Whiteman TV Teen Club (10/3)
7:30	Beat the Clock (9/19)	Ethel and Albert (9/19)	Leave It to the Girls (10/3)
8:00	The Jackie Gleason Show (featuring The Honeymooners) (9/19)	Bonino† (Ezio Pinza) (9/12) alternating with The All Star Revue (Martha Raye, et al.) (10/3)	Music from Meadowbrook† (10/3)
8:30	The Jackie Gleason Show	Ted Mack's Amateur Program (9/12) alternating with The All Star Revue	Music from Meadowbrook
9:00	Two for the Money (8/15)	Your Show of Shows (9/12)	Boxing
9:30	My Favorite Husband† (Barry Nelson, Joan Caulfield) (9/12)	Your Show of Shows	Boxing
			9:45: Fight Talk
10:00	The Chrysler Medallion Theatre* (9/12)	Your Show of Shows	Madison Square Garden Sports
10:30	The Revlon Mirror Theatre* (9/19) 11:10: Sports of the Night† (Jim McKay) (9/12)	Your Hit Parade (9/12) 11:15-11:30: Late Date† (Jerry Lester) (10/24)	films

Sunday
4:00		Kukla, Fran and Ollie (9/13)	
4:30		Excursion† (9/13)	
5:00	Omnibus* (10/4)	The Hallmark Hall of Fame* (9/27)	Super Circus (9/13)
5:30	Omnibus	The Hallmark Hall of Fame	Super Circus
6:00	Omnibus	Meet the Press (9/27)	Captain Midnight (9/13)
6:30	You Are There* (8/30)	The Roy Rogers Show (9/13)	The George Jessel Show† (9/13)
7:00	The Quiz Kids (8/30)	The Paul Winchell Show (8/30)	You Asked for It (Art Baker) (9/13)
7:30	The Jack Benny Show (9/13) alternating with Private Secretary (9/20)	Mr. Peepers (9/13)	The Bishop Sheen Program† (9/13)
8:00	The Toast of the Town	The Colgate Comedy Hour (10/4)	Football Films
8:30	The Toast of the Town	The Colgate Comedy Hour	Football Films
9:00	The Fred Waring Show (8/27) alternating with The General Electric Theatre* (9/20)	The Philco Television Playhouse* (9/27) alternating with The Goodyear Theatre*	The Walter Winchell Show (9/6)
			9:15: The Orchid Award (Nanette Fabray) (10/4)

	CBS	NBC	ABC
9:30	The Man Behind the Badge† (Charles Bickford, host and narrator) (10/11)	The Philco Television Playhouse alternating with The Goodyear Theatre	Jukebox Junction† (9/13) alternating with The Plainclothesman
10:00	The Web* (9/20)	A Letter to Loretta (The Loretta Young Show)†* (9/20)	Your Jeweler's Show-case* (8/30)
10:30	What's My Line?	I Led Three Lives† (Rod Cameron, Richard Carlson) (10/4)	films

Monday

	CBS	NBC	ABC
		3-4:00 weekdays: The Kate Smith Hour [continuing]	
7:00	News Parade	Victory at Sea (repeats) (10/5)	Captain Video
			7:15: Marge and Jeff† (8/31)
7:30	News	The Arthur Murray Party (10/5)	Jamie† (Brandon De-Wilde, Ernest Truex, Kathy Nolan, Polly Rowles) (10/5)
	7:45: The Perry Como Show (8/24)	7:45: News Caravan	
8:00	The George Burns-Gracie Allen Show (10/5)	Name That Tune (10/5)	Sky King Theatre (re-sumed 9/28)
8:30	Arthur Godfrey's Talent Scouts (10/5)	The Voice of Fire-stone	The Unexpected† (films) (9/28)
9:00	I Love Lucy (10/5)	The Dennis Day Show (10/5)	The Junior Press Con-ference† (10/5)
9:30	The Red Buttons Show (9/21)	Robert Montgomery Presents* (9/14)	This Is the Life† (9/28)
10:00	Studio One* (9/21)	Robert Montgomery Presents	Boxing
10:30	Studio One	Your Favorite Story* (9/14)	Boxing
			11-11:15: Here's Mor-gan† (9/28)

7:30-8:55 WOR The Broadway Television Theatre* (10/12)

Tuesday

	CBS	NBC	ABC
7:00	News Parade	Henry and Jackie† (9/29)	Captain Video
			7:15: Marge and Jeff†
7:30	News	The Dinah Shore Show	Cavalcade of America* (9/29)
	7:45: Jane Froman's U.S.A. Canteen (8/25)	7:45: News Caravan	

	CBS	NBC	ABC
8:00	The Gene Autry Show (9/8)	The Texaco Star Theatre (9/29) displaced regularly by The Bob Hope Texaco Show† (10/20)	Life Is Worth Living† (The Bishop Sheen Program) (10/13)
8:30	The Red Skelton Show (9/8)	The Texaco Star Theatre displaced regularly by The Bob Hope Texaco Show	The Music Show
9:00	This Is Show Business (Clifton Fadiman) (9/8)	Fireside Theatre* (9/1)	Make Room for Daddy† (Danny Thomas, Jean Hagen, Rusty Hamer, Sherry Jackson) (9/29)
9:30	Suspense* (9/29)	The Armstrong Circle Theatre* (9/1)	The United States Steel Hour†* (10/27) alternating with The Motorola Television Playhouse†* (11/3)
10:00	Danger* (9/29)	Judge for Yourself† (Fred Allen) (8/18)	The United States Steel Hour* alternating with The Motorola Television Playhouse*
10:30	Youth Takes a Stand† (8/18) followed by See It Now (10/7)	The Bob Considine Show† (8/18)	The Name's the Same (Robert Q Lewis) (9/29)

8-8:30 WABD Life Is Worth Living† (The Bishop Sheen Program) (10/13)
10:30-11:00 WABD Death Valley Days (resumed 10/6)

Wednesday

	CBS	NBC	ABC
7:00	News Parade	local	The Gloria DeHaven Show† (10/21) 7:15: Marge and Jeff†
7:30	News	The Eddie Fisher Coke Time† (10/7)	Inspector Mark Saber Mystery Theatre (10/7)
	7:45: The Perry Como Show	7:45: News Caravan	
8:00	Arthur Godfrey and His Friends (10/7)	I Married Joan (9/2)	The Johns Hopkins Science Review (9/30)
8:30	Arthur Godfrey and His Friends	My Little Margie (9/2) following Mr. Mosley, Citizen† (William Demarest) (8/19)	The Adventures of China Smith
9:00	Strike It Rich	The Kraft Television Theatre* (9/2)	Joe Franklin's Memory Lane (9/2)
9:30	I've Got a Secret (9/2)	The Kraft Television Theatre	Dollars a Second (9/2)
10:00	Blue Ribbon Bouts (boxing)	This Is Your Life	Boxing
10:30	Blue Ribbon Bouts	Douglas Fairbanks Jr. Presents* (9/9)	Boxing

9-9:30 WABD Colonel Humphrey J. Flack† (Alan Mowbray, Frank Jenks) (10/7)
10-10:30 WABD I Am the Law (George Raft) [continuing 9/9]

CBS	NBC	ABC

Thursday

	CBS	NBC	ABC
7:00	News Parade/Its Worth Knowing	Lights, Camera, Questions† (9/3)	Captain Video
			7:15: Marge and Jeff†
7:30	News 7:45: Jane Froman's U. S. A. Canteen	The Dinah Shore Show 7:45: News Caravan	The Lone Ranger (10/15)
8:00	Meet Mr. McNutley† (Ray Milland) (9/17)	You Bet Your Life (9/17) alternating with The Dave Garroway Show (10/2)	Quick as a Flash† (Bud Collyer) (9/10)
8:30	The Four Star Playhouse* (9/10)	Treasury Men In Action (8/20)	Where's Raymond?† (Ray Bolger, Betty Lynn) (10/8)
9:00	The Lux Video Theatre* (10/8)	Dragnet (10/1)	Back the Fact† (Joey Adams) (10/22); subsequently The Dotty Mack Show†
9:30	Big Town (9/10)	Ford Theatre* (10/1)	Home Garden† (10/1) subsequently replaced by The Kraft Television Theatre* (twice weekly as of 10/15)
10:00	Playhouse†* (10/1)	Foreign Intrigue (James Daly)(10/8)	Comeback† (George Jessel) (10/1) subsequently replaced by The Kraft Television Theatre
10:30	Place the Face† (9/24)	Martin Kane, Private Eye† (Mark Stevens) (10/22)	The Adventures of China Smith; subsequently House Detective† (10/22)

Friday

	CBS	NBC	ABC
7:00	News Parade	Father McQuade† (Jim Carroll) (9/4)	Captain Video
			7:15: Marge and Jeff†
7:30	News 7:45: The Perry Como Show	The Eddie Fisher Coke Time† 7:45: News Caravan	The Trouble with Father (9/18)
8:00	I Remember Mama (9/4)	The Goldbergs (9/4)	Ozzie and Harriet (9/18)
8:30	Topper† (Robert Sterling, Anne Jeffreys, Leo G. Carroll, Lee Patrick) (10/9)	The Life of Riley (9/18)	The Pepsi Cola Playhouse†* (10/2)
9:00	The Schlitz Playhouse of the Stars* (9/4)	The Big Story (9/4)	The Pride of the Family† (Paul Hartman, Bobby Hyatt, Natalie Wood, Fay Wray) (10/2)
9:30	Our Miss Brooks (10/2)	The Campbell TV Sound Stage* (10/16)	Comeback Story† (9/18)

	CBS	NBC	ABC
10:00	Mr. and Mrs. North (10/2)	The Friday Night Fights	Your Chevrolet Show-room† (9/18)
10:30	Person to Person† (Edward R. Murrow) (10/2)	The Friday Night Fights	Your Chevrolet Show-room

1953-54 MIDSEASON

Saturday

	CBS	NBC	ABC
			6:30-7:00 Success Story† (Dwight Wiest) (4/2)
7:00	The Stork Club	Mr. Wizard	The Paul Whiteman TV Teen Club
7:30	Beat the Clock	Ethel and Albert	Leave It to the Girls
8:00	The Jackie Gleason Show	Bonino; alternating the hour with The	theatrical films
8:30	The Jackie Gleason Show	All Star Revue	theatrical films
9:00	Two for the Money	Your Show of Shows	Boxing
9:30	My Favorite Husband	Your Show of Shows	Boxing 9:45: Fight Talk
10:00	That's My Boy† (Eddie Mayehoff, Gil Stratton Jr.) (4/10)	Your Show of Shows	Madison Square Garden Sports
10:30	Orient Express† (Paul Lukas) (12/19/53)	Your Hit Parade	films

Sunday

	CBS	NBC	ABC
4:00		Kukla, Fran and Ollie	
4:30		Excursion	
5:00	Omnibus	The Hallmark Hall of Fame	Super Circus
5:30	Omnibus	The Hallmark Hall of Fame	Super Circus
6:00	Omnibus	Meet the Press	Captain Midnight
6:30	You Are There	The Roy Rogers Show	The George Jessel Show
7:00	Life with Father† (Leon Ames, Lurene Tuttle, Ralph Reed, Ronald Keith, Freddie Leiston, Harvey Grant) (11/22/53)	The Paul Winchell Show	You Asked for It
7:30	The Jack Benny Show alternating with Private Secretary	Mr. Peepers	The Bishop Sheen Program
8:00	The Toast of the Town	The Colgate Comedy Hour	The Mask†* (1/10)
8:30	The Toast of the Town	The Colgate Comedy Hour	The Mask
9:00	The General Electric Theatre alternating with The Fred Waring Show; regularly	The Philco Television Playhouse alternating with The Goodyear Theatre	The Walter Winchell Show

	CBS	NBC	ABC

			displaced by The Bing Crosby Specials† (1/3)	

	CBS	NBC	ABC
			9:15: The Martha Wright Show† (4/18)
9:30	The Man Behind the Badge	The Philco Television Playhouse alternating with The Goodyear Theatre	The Plainclothesman alternating with Juke-box Jury
10:00	The Web	The Loretta Young Show	local
10:30	What's My Line?	I Led Three Lives	local

Monday

7-9:00 weekdays: The Morning Show† (Walter Cronkite, Charles Collingwood, The Bil Baird Puppets) (3/14)

1:15-1:30 weekdays: Portia Faces Life† [continuing drama] (Frances Reid, Renee Jarrett, Donald Woods) (4/26)

7:00	News Parade	Victory at Sea (repeats)	Captain Video
			7:45: Marge and Jeff
7:30	News	The Arthur Murray Party	Jamie
	7:45: The Perry Como Show	7:45: News Caravan	
8:00	The George Burns-Gracie Allen Show	Name That Tune	Sky King Theatre
8:30	Arthur Godfrey's Talent Scouts	The Voice of Firestone	The Unexpected
9:00	I Love Lucy	The Dennis Day Show	Junior Press Conference
9:30	The Red Buttons Show	Robert Montgomery Presents	This Is the Life
10:00	Studio One	Robert Montgomery Presents	Boxing
10:30	Studio One	Your Favorite Story	Boxing
			11-11:15: Here's Morgan

11-11:30 WOR The Man from Times Square† (1/18)

Tuesday

7:00	News Parade	Henry and Jackie	Captain Video
			7:15: Marge and Jeff
7:30	News	The Dinah Shore Show	Cavalcade of America
	7:45: The Jo Stafford Show† (3/30)	7:45: News Caravan	
8:00	The Gene Autry Show	The Texaco Star Theatre	Life Is Worth Living
8:30	The Red Skelton Show	The Texaco Star Theatre	The Music Show

	CBS	NBC	ABC
9:00	This Is Show Business	Fireside Theatre	Make Room for Daddy
9:30	Suspense	The Armstrong Circle Theatre	The United States Steel Hour alternating with The Motorola Television Hour
10:00	Danger	Judge for Yourself	The United States Steel Hour alternating with The Motorola Television Hour
10:30	See It Now	Mr. and Mrs. North (as of 1/26)	The Name's the Same

8-8:30 WABD The Goldbergs (resumed 4/13)

Wednesday

	CBS	NBC	ABC
7:00	News Parade	local	The Gloria De Haven Show 7:45: Marge and Jeff
7:30	News 7:45: The Perry Como Show	The Eddie Fisher Coke Time 7:45: News Caravan	Inspector Mark Saber Mystery Theatre
8:00	Arthur Godfrey and His Friends	I Married Joan	The Johns Hopkins Science Revue
8:30	Arthur Godfrey and His Friends	My Little Margie	Salute to Racing† (interviews) (3/31)
9:00	Strike It Rich	The Kraft Television Theatre	Joe Franklin's Memory Lane
9:30	I've Got a Secret	The Kraft Television Theatre	Dollars a Second
10:00	Blue Ribbon Bouts	This Is Your Life	local
10:30	Blue Ribbon Bouts	Douglas Fairbanks Jr. Presents	Angel Auditions† (Broadway play previews) (4/21)

Thursday

	CBS	NBC	ABC
7:00	News Parade	Lights, Camera, Questions	Captain Video 7:15: Marge and Jeff
7:30	News 7:45: The Jo Stafford Show†	The Dinah Shore Show 7:45: News Caravan	The Lone Ranger
8:00	Meet Mr. McNulty (title change)	You Bet Your Life	Quick as a Flash
8:30	The Four Star Playhouse	Justice†* (4/15)	Where's Raymond?
9:00	The Lux Video Theatre	Dragnet	Open Hearing† (John Daly) (4/1) [first episode devoted to the Army-McCarthy controversy]
9:30	Big Town	Ford Theatre	The Kraft Television Theatre
10:00	The Public Defender† (Reed Hadley) (3/11)	Foreign Intrigue	The Kraft Television Theatre

	CBS	NBC	ABC
10:30	Place the Face	local	The Adventures of China Smith

Friday

	CBS	NBC	ABC
7:00	News Parade	Father McQuade	Captain Video 7:15: Marge and Jeff
7:30	News 7:45: The Perry Como Show	The Eddie Fisher Coke Time 7:45: News Caravan	The Trouble with Father
8:00	I Remember Mama	The Goldbergs	Its About Time† (Bergan Evans) (3/4)
8:30	Topper	The Life of Riley	The Pepsi Cola Playhouse
9:00	The Schlitz Playhouse of the Stars	The Big Story	The Pride of the Family
9:30	Our Miss Brooks	The Campbell TV Sound Stage	Comeback Story
10:00	local/Mr. and Mrs. North	The Friday Night Fights	Your Chevrolet Showroom
10:30	Person to Person	The Friday Night Fights	Your Chevrolet Showroom

9:30-10:00 WOR Inner Sanctum†* (1/29)

Summer Programming, 1954

Saturday
8-9:00 CBS Stage Show† (7/3)
9-10:00 NBC The Saturday Night Revue† (Eddie Albert, host) (6/12)
10:30-11:00 CBS Two in Love† (quiz, with Bert Parks) (6/12)
10:30-11:00 WABD Colonel Humphrey J. Flack (resumed 5/8)

Sunday
5-6:00 CBS Adventure† (4/4)
5-6:00 NBC Out on the Farm† (7/11)
6-6:30 CBS The American Week† (Eric Sevareid) (4/4)
6-6:30 NBC Dr. Frank Baxter's Now and Then† (8/1)
6:30-7:00 NBC The Man of the Week (resumed, 7/4)
7-7:30 NBC The College of Musical Knowledge (Tennessee Ernie Ford, host) (7/4)
7:30-8:00 ABC The Pepsi Cola Playhouse* (this day as of 7/4)
7:30-8:00 CBS: Your Play Time† [repeats of Mirror Theatre and Pepsi Cola Playhouse] (6/13)
8-9:00 ABC On the Boardwalk† (Paul Whiteman, host) (5/30)
10-10:30 NBC Dollars a Second (resumed 7/4)

Monday
3:45-4:00 NBC weekdays Concerning Miss Marlowe† [continuing drama] (Louise Albritton, Efrem Zimbalist Jr.) (7/5)
7:30-8:00 NBC weeknights The World of Mr. Sweeney† (Charles Ruggles) (6/30)
7:45-8:00 CBS Monday, Wednesday, Friday TV's Top Tunes (resumed, 6/28)
8:30-9:00 ABC The Roberta Peters Show† (6/14)

Tuesday
7:30-8:00 ABC Men of Tomorrow† [Boy Scouts series] (6/29)

CBS	NBC	ABC

8-8:30 NBC Midwestern Hayride† (6/15)
8:30-9:00 CBS Juvenile Jury (resumed, 6/22)
8:30-9:00 NBC The Arthur Murray Party (resumed, 6/15)
8:30-9:00 WABD One Minute Please† (7/6)
9-9:30 NBC Summer Playhouse† [repeats of Ford Theatre; Nelson Case, host] (7/6)
9:30-10:00 ABC Center Stage†* (6/1) alternating with The United States Steel Hour* (as of 6/8)
9:30-10:00 NBC Top Plays of '54 [repeats of Ford Theatre] (6/1)

Wednesday
8-8:30 NBC Bank on the Stars† (5/12)
10-10:30 ABC Foreign Intrigue (James Daly) (resumed, 5/26)
9-9:30 WABD Summer in the Park† (6/23)

Thursday
8-9:30 ABC Melody Tour† (7/8)
8-8:30 CBS What's in a Word?† (Clifton Fadiman) (7/22)
9-9:30 CBS What Do You Have in Common? (resumed 7/1)
9-9:30 NBC Adventure in Java† (Tim Holt) (7/8)
10-10:30 CBS The Telltale Clue† (Anthony Ross, host) (7/8)
10-10:30 NBC The Marriage† (Hume Cronyn, Jessica Tandy, Susan Strasberg, Malcolm Broderick) (7/1)

Friday
8-8:30 NBC The Duke† (Paul Gilbert) (7/2)
8:30-9:00 ABC Who's the Boss?† (Walter Kiernan, host) (7/2)
9-9:30 ABC So You Want to Lead a Band (Sammy Kaye and Orchestra) (resumed, 7/2)
9-9:30 WABD The Stranger† [mystery series] (6/25)
9-9:30 NBC The Best in Mystery† [repeats of Mirror Theatre and The Pepsi Cola Playhouse] (7/16)
10:00-10:30 CBS Award Performance† [repeats of Mirror Theatre and Pepsi Cola Playhouse] (7/9)
10:30-11:00 CBS Its News to Me† [Walter Cronkite, host; John Henry Faulk was the first guest] (7/9)

1954-55 SEASON

Saturday

11-11:30 A. M. Space Patrol (Ed Kemmer) (9/4)

1:30-2:00 afternoon America in the Making† (11/13)
2-2:45 afternoon Camera Three (9/11)
4:45-5:00 Stop the Experts† (sports quiz) (12/18)
5:30-6:00 Amos 'n' Andy (9/25)

	CBS	NBC	ABC
7:00	The Gene Autry Show (9/25)	The Playhouse† (films) (10/2)	local
7:30	Beat the Clock (9/25)	Ethel and Albert (9/4)	Dangerous Assignment (9/8)
8:00	The Jackie Gleason Show (9/25)	Hey, Mulligan† (The Mickey Rooney Show) (8/24)	Let's Dance† (9/18)
8:30	The Jackie Gleason Show	Place the Face (9/4)	Let's Dance
9:00	Two for the Money (8/28)	The Imogene Coca Show† (10/2)	Boxing
9:30	My Favorite Husband (9/11)	The Texaco Star Theatre: The Jimmy Durante Show† (10/2)/ The Donald O'Connor Show† (10/9)	Boxing
10:00	That's My Boy (9/18)	The George Gobel Show† (10/2)	The Stork Club (9/18)
10:30	Willy† (June Havoc) (9/18)	Your Hit Parade (9/11)	Victory at Sea [repeats] (9/25)

Sunday

	CBS	NBC	ABC
	10-10:30 A.M. Lamp unto My Feet (10/13)		
3:30	Adventure (9/26)		
4:00	local		
4:30	The Search (10/17)	The Zoo Parade	
5:00	Omnibus* (10/17)	The Hallmark Hall of Fame* (9/5)	Super Circus (9/5)
5:30	Omnibus	Background† (9/5)	Super Circus
6:00	Omnibus	Meet the Press	Meet Corliss Archer† (Ann Baker, Bobby Ellis) (9/5)
6:30	You Are There* (8/29)	The Roy Rogers Show (9/19)	My Hero (Robert Cummings) (9/5)
7:00	Lassie† (Jeff Miller, Tommy Rettig, Jan Clayton, George Cleveland; subsequently Cloris Leachman, Jon Shepodd; subsequently June Lockhart, Hugh Reilly, Jon Provost) (9/12)	People Are Funny† (Art Linkletter, host) (9/19)	You Asked for It (9/5)
7:30	Private Secretary (9/12) alternating The Jack Benny Show (10/3)	Mr. Peepers (9/19)	The Pepsi Cola Playhouse* (10/3)
8:00	The Toast of the Town (fifth anniversary: 6/20/54)	The Colgate Comedy Hour (9/19)	The Ruggles (The Charles Ruggles Show) (9/5)
8:30	The Toast of the Town	The Colgate Comedy Hour	The Big Picture† (films) (9/5)

	CBS	NBC	ABC
9:00	The General Electric Theatre* (9/26) regularly displaced by The Fred Waring Show (11/7)	The Philco Television Playhouse* (9/19) alternating with The Goodyear Theatre*	The Walter Winchell Show (9/5)
			9:15: Martha Wright (9/12)
9:30	Honestly, Celeste!† (Celeste Holm) (10/10)	The Philco Television Playhouse alternating with The Goodyear Theatre	Life Begins at 80 (9/26) alternating with Dr. I. Q. (James McLain, host) (10/3)
10:00	Father Knows Best† (Robert Young, Jane Wyatt, Elinor Dona-hue, Billy Gray, Lauren Chapin) (10/3)	The Loretta Young Show* (8/29)	Break the Bank (9/5)
10:30	What's My Line?	The Hunter (Barry Nelson) (9/19) [9-10:30 above, Max Liebman Presents The Sunday Spectacu-lar (9/12) monthly displaced program-ming]	Victory at Sea [repeats] (9/5)

6-6:30 WPIX Hans Christian Andersen (10/30)

Monday

	CBS	NBC	ABC
		4:30-4:45 weekdays: The World of Mr. Sweeney (10/4) 4:45-5:00 Modern Romance† (10/4) alternating with True Story†	
7:00	News Parade	The Adventures of Sherlock Holmes† (Ronald Howard, H. Marion Crawford) (10/18)	Kukla, Fran and Ollie (9/6)
			7:15: News Jamie (9/27)
7:30	News	The Tony Martin Show† (10/4) 7:45: News Caravan	
	7:45: The Perry Como Show (8/23)		
8:00	The George Burns-Gracie Allen Show (10/4)	The Sid Caesar Hour† (9/27)	Colonel March of Scot-land Yard† (Boris Karloff) (9/27)
8:30	Arthur Godfrey's Talent Scouts (10/4)	The Sid Caesar Hour	The Voice of Firestone (10/4)
9:00	I Love Lucy (10/4)	Medic†* (9/13)	local
9:30	December Bride† (Frances Rafferty, Dean Miller, Spring Byington, Harry Mor-gan, Verna Felton) (10/4)	Robert Montgomery Presents* (9/20)	Lifeline† (films) (10/4)

	CBS	NBC	ABC
10:00	Studio One* (9/20)	Robert Montgomery Presents	Boxing
10:30	Studio One	Big Town (10/18)	Boxing 10:45: Neutral Corner
		Producer's Showcase†* (10/18) monthly dis-placed programming 8:30-10:00 above. 11:30-1:00 weeknights: The Tonight Show† (Steve Allen, host) (9/27)	

Tuesday

	CBS	NBC	ABC
7:00	News Parade	Janet Dean, Registered Nurse (Ella Raines) (from 3/23; 10/5)	Kukla, Fran and Ollie
			7:15: News
7:30	News	The Dinah Shore Show (10/5)	Cavalcade of America* (9/28)
	7:45: The Jo Staf-ford Show (10/5)	7:45: News Caravan	
8:00	The Red Skelton Show (9/21)	The Buick Show with Milton Berle† (9/21)	A&P Playhouse† [repeats of Ford Theatre] (9/28)
8:30	The Halls of Ivy† (Ronald Colman, Benita Hume, John Lupton) (10/19)	The Buick Show with Milton Berle†	Twenty Questions† (9/28)
9:00	Meet Millie (9/28)	Fireside Theatre* (8/31)	Make Room for Daddy (9/21)
9:30	Danger* (8/31)	The Armstrong Circle Theatre* (8/31)	The Elgin Hour†* (10/5) alternating with The United States Steel Hour* (9/14)
10:00	Life with Father (8/24)	Truth or Consequences (9/7)	The Elgin Hour alter-nating with The United States Steel Hour
10:30	See It Now (8/24)	It's a Great Life† (James Dunn, Wil-liam Bishop, Michael O'Shea) (9/7)	Stop the Music (9/7)
			11-11:30 Tuesday and Thursday: Sealy's TV Playhouse† [repeat dramas] (9/7)

9-9:30 WABD Studio '57†* (9/21)

Wednesday

	CBS	NBC	ABC
7:00	News Parade	It Seems Like Yester-day† (filmed high-lights) (9/29)	Kukla, Fran and Ollie
			7:15: News
7:30	News	Eddie Fisher's Coke Time (10/6)	Disneyland†* (10/27)

	CBS	NBC	ABC
	7:45: The Perry Como Show	7:45: News Caravan	
8:00	Arthur Godfrey and His Friends (9/15)	I Married Joan (9/29)	Disneyland
8:30	Arthur Godfrey and His Friends	My Little Margie (9/29)	The Stu Erwin Show (10/27)
9:00	Strike It Rich (9/15)	The Kraft Television Theatre* (9/29)	Masquerade Party (9/29)
9:30	I've Got a Secret (9/15)	The Kraft Television Theatre	Dollars a Second (10/6)
10:00	Blue Ribbon Bouts (boxing)	This Is Your Life (9/29)	The Wednesday Night Fights
10:30	Blue Ribbon Bouts	Douglas Fairbanks Jr. Presents The Rheingold Theatre* (9/29)	The Wednesday Night Fights
	[The Best of Broadway†* (9/15) monthly displaced Blue Ribbon Bouts and programming 10-11:00 above]		

8:30-9:00 WABD The Royal Playhouse† [repeats of Fireside Theatre] (11/3)
9:30-10:00 WOR Your Favorite Story* (resumed 10/13)

Thursday

	CBS	NBC	ABC
7:00	News Parade	Foreign Intrigue (repeats, 9/16)	Kukla, Fran and Ollie
			7:15: News
	7:25: Rain Or Shine† (Carol Reid) (9/16)		
7:30	News 7:45: Jane Froman's U.S.A. Canteen (10/7)	The Dinah Shore Show 7:45: News Caravan	The Lone Ranger (10/7)
8:00	Meet Mr. McNulty (9/16)	You Bet Your Life (9/16)	The Mail Story† (from the files of The United States Post Office) (10/7)
8:30	Climax!†* (10/7) alternating with Shower of Stars†* (10/28)	Justice* (9/16)	Treasury Men in Action (10/7)
9:00	Climax! alternating with Shower of Stars	Dragnet (8/26)	The Sammy Kaye Show (10/7)
9:30	Four Star Playhouse* (9/30)	Ford Theatre* (10/7)	The Kraft Television Theatre* (10/7)
10:00	The Public Defender (9/30)	The Lux Video Theatre* (expanded to one hour) (8/26)	The Kraft Television Theatre
10:30	Name That Tune (Bill Cullen) (9/2)	The Lux Video Theatre	Racket Squad (10/7)

8-8:30 WABD They Stand Accused† [unrehearsed courtroom drama] (9/9)

	CBS	NBC	ABC

Friday

7:00	News Parade	The Guy Lombardo Show† (9/17)	Kukla, Fran and Ollie
			7:15: News
7:30	News	Eddie Fisher's Coke Time	Rin Tin Tin† (Lee Aaker, Jim Brown, Joe Sawyer) (10/15)
	7:45: The Perry Como Show	7:45: News Caravan	
8:00	I Remember Mama (9/3)	The Red Buttons Show (10/1) alternating with The Jack Carson Show† (10/22)	Ozzie and Harriet (9/24)
8:30	Topper (10/1)	The Life of Riley (9/24)	The Ray Bolger Show (9/17)
9:00	The Schlitz Playhouse of the Stars* (9/10)	The Big Story (9/10)	Dollars a Second (10/1)
9:30	Our Miss Brooks (10/1)	Dear Phoebe† (Marcia Henderson, Peter Lawford) (9/10)	The Vise†* (10/1)
10:00	The Lineup† (Warner Anderson, Tom Tully) (10/1) [syndicated as San Francisco Beat]	The Friday Night Fights	I Led Three Lives (8/27)
10:30	Person to Person (9/10)	The Friday Night Fights	Mr. District Attorney (10/1)

8:30-9:00 WABD Death Valley Days (Stanley Andrews, host) (resumed 11/5)

1954-55 MIDSEASON

Saturday

	6:15: Playhouse 15† [repeats] (2/19)		
6:30	The Man Behind the Badge (resumed 1/8)	So This Is Hollywood† (Mitzi Green) (1/8)	
7:00	The Gene Autry Show	Henry Fonda Presents The Rheingold Theatre†* (1/8)	Tomorrow† (3/26)
7:30	Beat the Clock	Show Wagon† (4/24)	Dangerous Assignment
8:00	The Jackie Gleason Show	Hey, Mulligan	Soldier Parade† (Arlene Francis) (3/26)
8:30	The Jackie Gleason Show	Place the Face	The Dotty Mack Show (resumed 3/26)
9:00	Two for the Money	The Imogene Coca Show	Boxing
9:30	My Favorite Husband	The Texaco Star Theatre: The Jimmy Durante Show alternating with The Donald O'Connor Show	Boxing

	CBS	NBC	ABC
10:00	That's My Boy [or as Professional Father† (1/8)]	The George Gobel Show	The Stork Club
10:30	Damon Runyon Thea- tre†* (4/16)	Your Hit Parade	Foreign Intrigue

Sunday

3:30	Adventure		
4:00	local		
4:30	The Search	The Zoo Parade	
5:00	Omnibus	The Hallmark Hall of Fame	Super Circus
5:30	Omnibus	Captain Gallant of the Foreign Legion† (Buster Crabbe and son Cuffy) (2/13)	Super Circus
6:00	Omnibus	Meet the Press	Meet Corliss Archer
6:30	You Are There	The Roy Rogers Show	My Hero
7:00	Lassie	People Are Funny	You Asked for It
7:30	The Jack Benny Show alternating with Private Sec- retary	Mr. Peepers	The Pepsi Cola Play- house
8:00	The Toast of the Town	The Colgate Comedy Hour	The Ruggles
8:30	The Toast of the Town	The Colgate Comedy Hour	The Big Picture
9:00	The General Electric Theatre regularly displaced by The Fred Waring Show	The Philco Television Playhouse alternating with The Goodyear Theatre	The Walter Winchell Show
			9:15: Horizons† (12/12/54)
9:30	Stage 7†* (1/30)	The Philco Television Playhouse alternating with The Goodyear Theatre	Pantomine Quiz (resumed 1/16)
10:00	Appointment with Adventure†* (4/3)	The Loretta Young Show	Break the Bank
10:30	What's My Line?	The Hunter	Paris Precinct† (Louis Jourdan, Claude Dauphin) (4/3)

Monday

7:00	News Parade	The Adventures of Sherlock Holmes	Kukla, Fran and Ollie
			7:15: News
7:30	News 7:45: The Perry Como Show	The Tony Martin Show 7:45: News Caravan	Jamie
8:00	The George Burns- Gracie Allen Show	The Sid Caesar Hour	TV Reader's Digest†* (1/17)
8:30	Arthur Godfrey's Talent Scouts	The Sid Caesar Hour	The Voice of Firestone
9:00	I Love Lucy	Medic	The Ruggles
9:30	December Bride	Robert Montgomery Presents	Lifeline

	CBS	NBC	ABC
10:00	Studio One	Robert Montgomery Presents	Boxing
10:30	Studio One	Big Town	Boxing 10:45: Neutral Corner

Tuesday

			6-6:30: The Gloria Swanson Theatre† (12/21)
7:00	News Parade	Janet Dean, Regis- tered Nurse	Kukla, Fran and Ollie
			7:15: News
7:30	News 7:45: The Jo Staf- ford Show	The Dinah Shore Show 7:45: News Caravan	Cavalcade of America
8:00	Life with Father (as of 1/4)	The Buick Show with Milton Berle	A&P Playhouse
8:30	The Halls of Ivy	The Buick Show with Milton Berle	Twenty Questions
9:00	Meet Millie	Fireside Theatre	Make Room for Daddy
9:30	The New Red Skelton Show† (1/4)	The Armstrong Circle Theatre	The Elgin Hour alter- nating with The United States Steel Hour
10:00	Danger (as of 1/4)	Truth or Consequences	The Elgin Hour alter- nating with The United States Hour
10:30	See It Now	It's a Great Life	Stop the Music

8:30-9:00 WABD Studio '57* (this time as of 4/5)

Wednesday

7:00	News Parade	Norby† (David Wayne, Joan Lorring) (1/5)	Kukla, Fran and Ollie
			7:15: News
7:30	News	Eddie Fisher's Coke Time	Disneyland
	7:45: The Perry Como Show	7:45: News Caravan	
8:00	Arthur Godfrey and His Friends	Request Performance† [repeats of Fireside Theatre, Pepsi Cola Playhouse, Ford Thea- tre, Schlitz Playhouse of the Stars] (4/13)	Disneyland
8:30	Arthur Godfrey and His Friends	My Little Margie	Mr. Citizen†* (4/20)
9:00	The Millionaire†* (1/19)	The Kraft Television Theatre	Masquerade Party
9:30	I've Got a Secret	The Kraft Television Theatre	Foreign Intrigue (re- sumed 12/26/54)
10:00	Blue Ribbon Bouts	This Is Your Life	The Wednesday Night Fights
10:30	Blue Ribbon Bouts	Douglas Fairbanks Jr. Presents The Rhein- gold Theatre	The Wednesday Night Fights

10-11:00 monthly: The Best of Broadway

	CBS	NBC	ABC

Thursday

7:00	News Parade	local	Kukla, Fran and Ollie 7:15: News
	7:25: Rain Or Shine		
7:30	News	The Dinah Shore Show	The Lone Ranger
	7:45: Jane Froman's U. S. A. Canteen	7:45: News Caravan	
8:00	Meet Mr. McNultey	You Bet Your Life	Soldier Parade (as of 1/13)
8:30	Climax! alternating with Shower of Stars	Justice	Treasury Men in Action
9:00	Climax! alternating with Shower of Stars	Dragnet	Star Tonight†* (2/3)
9:30	The Four Star Play-house	Ford Theatre	Pond's Theatre†* [under the auspices of the producers of Kraft Theatre] (1/13)
10:00	The Public Defender	The Lux Video Theatre	Pond's Theatre
10:30	Willy (as of 4/7)	The Lux Video Theatre	The Racket Squad

10-10:30 WABD The Conrad Nagel Theatre†* (1/27)

Friday

7:00	News Parade	Science Fiction Thea-tre†* (4/15)	Kukla, Fran and Ollie
			7:15: News
7:30	News	Eddie Fisher's Coke Time	Rin Tin Tin
	7:45: The Perry Como Show	7:45: News Caravan	
8:00	I Remember Mama	The Red Buttons Show alternating with The Jack Carson Show	Ozzie and Harriet
8:30	Topper	The Life of Riley	The Ray Bolger Show
9:00	The Schlitz Play-house of the Stars	The Big Story	Dollars a Second
9:30	Our Miss Brooks	Dear Phoebe	The Vise
10:00	The Lineup	The Friday Night Fights	I Led Three Lives
10:30	Person to Person	The Friday Night Fights	Mr. District Attorney

Summer Programming, 1955

Saturday

7-7:30 ABC Step This Way† (7/23)

8-8:30 NBC The Soldiers† (Tom D'Andrea, Hal March) (6/25)

9-9:30 NBC Musical Chairs† (7/30)

9-10:00 ABC The Lawrence Welk Show† (7/2)

10-10:30 NBC And Here's the Show† (7/9)

10:30-11:00 NBC Your Play Time† [repeats of Pepsi Cola Playhouse and Studio '57] (6/18)

10-11:00 A. M. NBC Captain Safari of the Jungle Patrol† (with Randy Graft and Bongo) (6/4)

11:15-11:45 P. M. NBC Mayor of the Town† (Thomas Mitchell, principal play-er and narrator) (6/4)

| CBS | NBC | ABC |

Sunday
5-5:30 NBC TV Recital Hall† (7/3)
5-6:00 CBS Adventure (resumed 4/17)
6-6:30 CBS I Love Lucy [repeats; 4/17]
7:30-8:00 NBC The Do It Yourself Show (resumed 6/26)
8-9:00 CBS America's Greatest Bands† (6/26)
9:30-10:00 ABC Life Begins at 80 (resumed 7/31)
10-10:30 NBC Cameo Theatre* (resumed 7/3)
11-11:30 ABC What's the Joke? (resumed 6/19)

Monday
3-3:30 weekdays ABC The Ted Mack Matinee† (4/4)
7:30-8:00 ABC The Name's the Same (resumed 5/16)
8-9:30 NBC Wide, Wide, World† (Dave Garroway, host) (6/27)
9-9:30 ABC The Pee Wee King Show† (5/23)
9-9:30 CBS Those Whiting Girls† (Margaret and Barbara Whiting) (7/4)
9:30-10:00 CBS Ethel and Albert (resumed 6/20)

Tuesday
8-8:30 CBS Pantomine Quiz (resumed 7/5)
8-8:30 ABC Talent Varieties† (7/19)
8-8:30 CBS Star Time Playhouse† [repeats of The Schlitz Playhouse of the Stars] (8/2)
8:30-9:00 ABC Who Said That?† (5/17)
9-9:30 NBC Summer Theatre† [repeats of The Four Star Playhouse] (7/5)
9:30-10:00 ABC Mr. District Attorney (David Brian) (resumed 6/28)
9:30-10:00 CBS Spotlight Playhouse† [repeats of The Schlitz Playhouse of the Stars] (6/21)
10-10:30 CBS The $64,000 Question† (Hal March, host) (6/7)

Wednesday
8-8:30 CBS The Robert Cummings Show† (7/7)
8:30-9:00 ABC Playhouse† [repeats of The Schlitz Playhouse of the Stars] (7/20)
9:30-10:00 ABC Penny to a Million† (5/11)
10-11:00 CBS Front Row Center†* (6/1) alternating with The United States Steel Hour (as of 7/6)

Thursday
8-9:00 ABC Soldier Parade (resumed 6/16)
8:30-9:00 NBC Make the Connection† (Gene Rayburn, host) (7/7)
10-10:30 CBS The Johnny Carson Show† (live from Television City in Hollywood) (6/30)

Friday
8:30-9:00 ABC Treasury Men in Action (resumed 6/17)
9-9:30 NBC The Best in Mystery [repeats of The Pepsi Cola Playhouse and Studio '57] (resumed 7/15)
10-10:30 NBC Sports Film† (7/1)
10-10:30 CBS Undercurrent† [repeats of The Pepsi Cola Playhouse and Studio '57] (7/1)
10:30-11:00 CBS Windows†* (7/29)
10:30-11:00 NBC So This Is Hollywood (resumed 7/1)

	CBS	NBC	ABC

1955-56 SEASON

Saturday

	CBS	NBC	ABC
		11-11:30 A. M. Fury† (Bobby Diamond, Peter Graves, William Fawcett) (10/15)	
	11:30-Noon: Tales of the Texas Rangers† (Willard Parker, Harry Lauter) (9/3)		
7:00	The Gene Autry Show (9/10)	Henry Fonda Presents The Rheingold Theatre* (10/29)	Step This Way (9/17)
7:30	Beat the Clock (9/10)	The Big Surprise† (10/8)	Ozark Jubilee† (9/17)
8:00	Stage Show (10/1)	The Perry Como Show (9/17)	Grand Old Opry† (9/17)
8:30	The Honeymooners† (Jackie Gleason, Art Carney, Audrey Meadows) (10/1)	The Perry Como Show	Grand Old Opry
9:00	Two for the Money (The Herb Shriner Show) (9/10)	People Are Funny (9/24)	The Lawrence Welk Show (9/17)
9:30	It's Always Jan† (Janis Paige) (9/10)	The Texaco Star Theatre Presents The Jimmy Durante Show (10/8)	The Lawrence Welk Show
10:00	Gunsmoke† (James Arness, Amanda Blake, Dennis Weaver, Milburn Stone) (9/10)	The George Gobel Show (10/8)	Tomorrow's Careers† (9/17)
10:30	The Damon Runyon Theatre* (10/8) [Ford Star Jubilee†* displaced programming 9:30-11:00, monthly]	Your Hit Parade (9/10)	Boris Karloff Mysteries† (9/17)

Sunday

	CBS	NBC	ABC
4:00	Front Row Center* (9/21)	Wide, Wide World (9/18)	
4:30	Front Row Center	Wide, Wide World	
5:00	Omnibus* (10/9)	Wide, Wide World	Super Circus (9/18)
5:30	Omnibus	Captain Gallant of the Foreign Legion (9/18)	Super Circus
6:00	Omnibus	Meet the Press	The Adventures of Kit Carson [repeats, with Bill Williams, Don Diamond] (9/18)
6:30	You Are There* (9/11)	The Roy Rogers Show (9/18)	The Gene Autry Show [repeats] (9/18)

CBS	NBC	ABC
7:00 Lassie (9/11)	It's a Great Life (9/18)	You Asked for It (9/18)
7:30 Private Secretary (9/11) alternating with The Jack Benny Show (9/25)	Frontier†* (9/25)	Film Festival† (9/18)
8:00 The Toast of the Town (hereafter referred to as The Ed Sullivan Show; seventh anniversary 6/26/55)	The Colgate Comedy Hour (9/18)	Film Festival
8:30 The Toast of the Town	The Colgate Comedy Hour	Film Festival
9:00 The General Electric Theatre* (10/2)	The Philco Television Playhouse* (9/4) alternating with The Alcoa Hour†* (10/16) and The Goodyear Theatre	Chance of a Lifetime (9/18)
9:30 Alfred Hitchcock Presents†* (10/2)	The Philco Television Playhouse alternating with The Alcoa Hour and The Goodyear Theatre	The Ted Mack Original Amateur Hour (10/30)
10:00 Appointment with Adventure* (10/2)	The Loretta Young Show* (8/28)	The Ted Mack Original Amateur Hour
10:30 What's My Line?	Justice* (10/2)	local

6:30-7:00 WABD The New York Times Youth Forum† (10/9)
9-9:30 WABD The Adventures of Ellery Queen (Hugh Marlowe) (resumed 10/2)

Monday

CBS	NBC	ABC
	3-4:00 weekdays: Matinee Theatre†* (10/31)	
		5-6:00 weekdays: The Mickey Mouse Club† (10/31)
7:00		Kukla, Fran and Ollie 7:15: News
7:30 The Adventures of Robin Hood† (Richard Greene, Bernadette O'Farrell, Alan Wheatley, Dorothy Blyth, Alexander Gauge, Peter Hammond, Archie Duncan, Brian Worth, Donald Pleasance, Ronald Howard) (9/26)	The Gordon MacRae Show† (9/19) alternating with The Tony Martin Show (9/12)	Topper (10/3)
	7:45: News Caravan	
8:00 The George Burns-Gracie Allen Show (10/3)	The Sid Caesar Hour (9/26)	TV Reader's Digest* (10/17)
8:30 Arthur Godfrey's Talent Scouts (10/3)	The Sid Caesar Hour	The Voice of Firestone

	CBS	NBC	ABC
9:00	I Love Lucy (10/3)	Medic* (9/26)	The Dotty Mack Show (9/19)
9:30	December Bride (10/3)	Robert Montgomery Presents* (9/12)	Medical Horizons† (9/12)
10:00	Studio One* (9/19)	Robert Montgomery Presents	Dangerous Assignment (9/19)
10:30	Studio One	Douglas Fairbanks Jr. Presents The Rheingold Theatre* (as of 11/7) [Producer's Showcase* (9/19) monthly displaced programming 8-9:30 above]	Boris Karloff Mysteries†

Tuesday

	CBS	NBC	ABC
7:00		The Great Gildersleeve† (Willard Waterman, Stephanie Griffith, Ronald Keith) (9/13)	Kukla, Fran and Ollie
			7:15: News
7:30	Name That Tune (George DeWitt, host) (9/27)	The Dinah Shore Show (9/13)	Warner Brothers Presents: Cheyenne†* (9/20), alternating with King's Row†* (9/13) and Casablanca†* (9/27)
		7:45: News Caravan	
8:00	You'll Never Get Rich† (The Phil Silvers Show) (9/20)	The Martha Raye Show† (9/20) alternating with The Milton Berle Show† (9/27)	Warner Brothers Presents: Cheyenne alternating with King's Row and Casablanca
8:30	Navy Log†* (9/20)	The Martha Raye Show alternating with The Milton Berle Show	Wyatt Earp† (Hugh O'Brian, Mason Alan Dinehart III, Paul Brinegar, Morgan Woodward) (9/6)
9:00	Joe and Mabel† (Larry Blyden, Nita Talbot, Luella Gear) (9/20)	Fireside Theatre* (8/30)	Make Room for Daddy (9/13)
9:30	The Red Skelton Show (9/27)	The Armstrong Circle Theatre* (9/27) alternating with Playwrights '56†* (10/4)	Cavalcade Theatre* (9/13)
10:00	The $64,000 Question (9/20)	The Armstrong Circle Theatre alternating with Playwrights '56	Outside, U.S.A. † (9/13)
10:30	My Favorite Husband (Barry Nelson, Vanessa Brown) (10/4)	Big Town (8/15)	The Ken Murray Show (10/11)

9-9:30 WABD Cavalcade of Stars† [repeats of The Schlitz Playhouse of the Stars] (9/20)

CBS	NBC	ABC

Wednesday

7:00 | | | Kukla, Fran and Ollie
7:15: News
Disneyland* (9/14)

7:30 | Brave Eagle† (Keith Larsen, Kim Winona, Bert Wheeler, Keena Nomkeena) (9/28) | Eddie Fisher's Coke Time (9/14) |

| | | 7:15: News Caravan |

8:00 | Arthur Godfrey and His Friends (9/14) | The Screen Directors' Playhouse†* (10/5) | Disneyland

8:30 | Arthur Godfrey and His Friends | Father Knows Best (8/31) | The MGM Parade† (George Murphy, host) (9/14)

9:00 | The Millionaire* (9/28) | The Kraft Television Theatre* (9/28) | Masquerade Party (9/14)

9:30 | I've Got a Secret (9/14) | The Kraft Television Theatre | Penny to a Million (9/14) followed by Break the Bank (10/26)

10:00 | The United States Steel Hour* (7/6) alternating with The Twentieth Century Fox Hour†* (10/5) | This Is Your Life (9/28) | The Wednesday Night Fights

10:30 | The United States Steel Hour alternating with The Twentieth Century Fox Hour | The Patti Page Show† (11/2) | The Wednesday Night Fights

8-8:30 WABD Case Histories of Scotland Yard† (Edgar Lustgarten, British criminologist, host) (9/14)

Thursday

7:00 | | | Kukla, Fran and Ollie
7:15: News
The Lone Ranger (9/8)

7:30 | Sergeant Preston of the Yukon† (Richard Simmons) (10/6) | The Dinah Shore Show |

| | | 7:45: News Caravan |

8:00 | Love That Bob† (The Robert Cummings Show) (also Rosemary DeCamp, Ann B. Davis, Dwayne Hickman) (10/6) | You Bet Your Life (9/29) | Life Is Worth Living (The Bishop Sheen Program) (10/13)

8:30 | Climax!* (9/29) alternating with Shower of Stars* (10/6) | Dragnet (9/1) | Stop the Music (9/1)

9:00 | Climax! alternating with Shower of Stars | The People's Choice† (Jackie Cooper, Patricia Breslin) (10/6) | Star Tonight†* (9/8)

9:30 | The Four Star Playhouse* (10/6) | Ford Theatre* (10/6) | Down You Go (Bergen Evans) (9/15)

CBS	NBC	ABC
10:00 The Johnny Carson Show (10/6)	The Lux Video Theatre* (9/29)	Outside, U.S.A. (Quincy Howe, commentator) (9/1) supplanted by Hollywood Off Beat [repeats] (9/15)
10:30 Wanted† (Walter McGraw, host) (10/20)	The Lux Video Theatre	Racket Squad

7:30-8:00 WABD The Goldbergs (resumed 9/22)

8-8:30 WABD Long John Silver† (Robert Newton, Connie Gilchrist, Kit Taylor) (9/22)

Friday

	CBS	NBC	ABC
7:00	local	Science Fiction Theatre* (9/2)	Kukla, Fran and Ollie
			7:15: News
7:30	My Friend Flicka† (Johnny Washbrook, Gene Evans, Anita Louise) (9/30)	Eddie Fisher's Coke Time	Rin Tin Tin (9/9)
		7:45: News Caravan	
8:00	I Remember Mama (9/2)	Truth or Consequences (9/9)	Ozzie and Harriet (9/23)
8:30	Our Miss Brooks (9/2)	The Life of Riley (9/16)	Crossroads†* (10/7)
9:00	The Crusader† (Brian Keith, Peter Bourne, Hildegarde Christian, Alf Kjellin, Lisa Golm) (10/7)	The Big Story (9/9)	Dollars a Second (9/9)
9:30	The Schlitz Playhouse of the Stars* (9/30)	Star Stage†* (9/9)	The Vise* (9/9)
10:00	The Lineup (9/30)	The Friday Night Fights	Ethel and Albert (10/14)
10:30	Person to Person (9/2)	The Friday Night Fights	The Adventures of the Falcon† (Charles McGraw) (10/7)

8-8:30 WPIX Duffy's Tavern (Ed Gardner, Pattee Chapman, Alan Reed) (resumed 9/23)

1955-56 MIDSEASON

Saturday

	CBS	NBC	ABC
7:00	The Gene Autry Show	The Turning Point† [repeats of the Pepsi Cola Playhouse] (4/28)	Step This Way
7:30	Beat the Clock	The Big Surprise	Ozark Jubilee
8:00	Stage Show	The Perry Como Show	Grand Old Opry
8:30	The Honeymooners	The Perry Como Show	Grand Old Opry
9:00	Two for the Money	People Are Funny	The Lawrence Welk Show
9:30	It's Always Jan	The Jimmy Durante Show	The Lawrence Welk Show

CBS	NBC	ABC
10:00 Gunsmoke	The George Gobel Show	Tomorrow's Careers
10:30 Damon Runyon Theatre	Your Hit Parade	Boris Karloff Mysteries

Sunday

	CBS	NBC	ABC
4:00	Front Row Center	Wide, Wide, World	
4:30	Front Row Center	Wide, Wide, World	
5:00	Face the Nation (as of 4/15)	Wide, Wide, World	Super Circus
5:30	The American Week (Eric Sevareid) (as of 4/15)	Captain Gallant of the Foreign Legion	Super Circus
6:00	Telephone Time†* (4/8)	Meet the Press	The Adventures of Kit Carson [repeats]
6:30	You Are There	The Roy Rogers Show	The Gene Autry Show [repeats]
7:00	Lassie	It's a Great Life	You Asked for It
7:30	Private Secretary alternating with The Jack Benny Show	Frontier	Film Festival
8:00	The Ed Sullivan Show	The Colgate Comedy Hour	Film Festival
8:30	The Ed Sullivan Show	The Colgate Comedy Hour	Film Festival
9:00	The General Electric Theatre	The Goodyear Theatre alternating with The Alcoa Hour	Chance of a Lifetime
9:30	Alfred Hitchcock Presents	The Goodyear Theatre alternating with The Alcoa Hour	The Ted Mack Original Amateur Hour
10:00	Appointment with Adventure	The Loretta Young Show	The Ted Mack Original Amateur Hour
10:30	What's My Line?	National Bowling Champions† (4/8)	local

Monday

	CBS	NBC	ABC
7:00			Kukla, Fran and Ollie 7:15: News
7:30	The Adventures of Robin Hood	The Gordon MacRae Show 7:45: News Caravan	Topper
8:00	The George Burns-Gracie Allen Show	The Sid Caesar Show	TV Reader's Digest
8:30	Arthur Godfrey's Talent Scouts	The Sid Caesar Show	The Voice of Firestone
9:00	I Love Lucy	Medic	The Dotty Mack Show
9:30	December Bride	Robert Montgomery Presents	Medical Horizons
10:00	Studio One	Robert Montgomery Presents	Dangerous Assignment
10:30	Studio One	Douglas Fairbanks Jr. Presents The Rheingold Theatre	Boris Karloff Mysteries

	CBS	NBC	ABC

Tuesday

7:00		The Great Gildersleeve	Kukla, Fran and Ollie 7:15: News
7:30	Name That Tune	The Dinah Shore Show	Warner Brothers Presents: Cheyenne alternating with King's Row and Casablanca
		7:45: News Caravan	
8:00	You'll Never Get Rich	The Martha Raye Show alternating with The Milton Berle Show	Warner Brothers Presents: Cheyenne alternating with King's Row and Casablanca
8:30	Navy Log	The Martha Raye Show alternating with The Milton Berle Show	Wyatt Earp
9:00	Joe and Mabel	Fireside Theatre	Make Room for Daddy
9:30	The Red Skelton Show	The Armstrong Circle Theatre alternating with Playwrights '56	Cavalcade Theatre
10:00	The $64,000 Question	The Armstrong Circle Theatre alternating with Playwrights '56	Outside, U.S.A.
10:30	My Favorite Husband	Big Town	The Ken Murray Show

Wednesday

7:00			Kukla, Fran and Ollie 7:15: News
7:30	Brave Eagle	Eddie Fisher's Coke Time	Disneyland
		7:45: News Caravan	
8:00	Arthur Godfrey and His Friends	The Screen Director's Playhouse	Disneyland
8:30	Arthur Godfrey and His Friends	Father Knows Best	The MGM Parade
9:00	The Millionaire	The Kraft Television Theatre	Masquerade Party
9:30	I've Got a Secret	The Kraft Television Theatre	Break the Bank
10:00	The United States Steel Hour alternating with The Twentieth Century Fox Hour	This Is Your Life	The Wednesday Night Fights
10:30	The United States Steel Hour alternating with The Twentieth Century Fox Hour	Midwest Hayride† (3/28)	The Wednesday Night Fights

Thursday

7:00			Kukla, Fran and Ollie 7:15: News
7:30	Sergeant Preston of the Yukon	The Dinah Shore Show	The Lone Ranger
		7:45: News Caravan	
8:00	Love That Bob	You Bet Your Life	Life Is Worth Living

	CBS	NBC	ABC
8:30	Climax! alternating with Shower of Stars	Dragnet	Stop the Music
9:00	Climax! alternating with Shower of Stars	The People's Choice	Star Tonight
9:30	The Four Star Play-house	Ford Theatre	Down You Go
10:00	The Johnny Carson Show	The Lux Video Theatre	Hollywood Off Beat [repeats]
10:30	Wanted	The Lux Video Theatre	Racket Squad

8-8:30 WABD The Count of Monte Cristo† (George Dolenz, Nick Cravat, Fortunio Bonanova, Faith Domergue) (3/17)

Friday

7:00	Web of Circum-stances† [repeats] (3/4)	Science Fiction Theatre	Kukla, Fran and Ollie
			7:15: News
7:30	My Friend Flicka	Eddie Fisher's Coke Time	Rin Tin Tin
		7:45: News Caravan	
8:00	I Remember Mama	Truth or Consequences	Ozzie and Harriet
8:30	Our Miss Brooks	The Life of Riley	Crossroads
9:00	The Crusader	The Big Story	Dollars a Second
9:30	The Schlitz Play-house of the Stars	Star Stage	The Vise
10:00	The Lineup	The Friday Night Fights	Ethel and Albert
10:30	Person to Person	The Friday Night Fights	The Adventures of the Falcon

Summer Programming, 1956

Saturday
9-9:30 A.M. CBS To Build a Nation† (7/21)
1-1:30 P.M. ABC The Way† (6/2)
7-7:30 NBC The Open Mind† (7/21)
8-9:00 NBC The Julius LaRosa Show† (6/30)
9:30-10:00 NBC Festival of Stars† [repeats of Ford Theatre] (6/30)
9:30-10:00 CBS The Russ Morgan Show† (7/7)
10-10:30 NBC Encore Theatre† [repeats of the Pepsi Cola Playhouse] (6/30)
10:30-11:00 NBC Adventure Theatre† [repeats] (Paul Douglas, host) (6/30)

Sunday
8-9:00 NBC The Steve Allen Show† (6/24)
10-10:30 NBC Man Against Crime (Frank Lovejoy) (resumed 7/1)

Monday
7:30-8:00 ABC Bold Journey† (John Stephenson, host) (7/16)
8-8:30 ABC The Dotty Mack Show (resumed 7/16)
8-8:30 WPIX Stage 7 [repeats] (6/4)
8-9:00 NBC The Ernie Kovacs Show† (7/2)
9-9:30 CBS The Charlie Farrell Show† (7/2)
9:30-10:00 CBS The Vic Damone Show† (7/2)

	CBS	NBC	ABC

Tuesday
7:30-7:45 NBC Tuesday and Thursday The Frankie Carla Show† (8/17)
8-8:30 CBS Dear Phoebe (resumed 6/26)
8:30-9:00 NBC This Is Show Business (resumed 6/19)
9-9:30 NBC Sneak Preview† [feature film segments] (7/3)
9:00-9:30 ABC The General Electric Summer Originals†* (7/3)
9:30-10:00 CBS Spotlight Playhouse† (6/26)
10:30-11:00 CBS Do You Trust Your Wife?† (6/19)
10:30-11:00 ABC Women Want to Know† (Faye Emerson, hostess and moderator) (6/5)

Wednesday
7-7:30 NBC Death Valley Days (resumed 8/8)
7:30-7:45 NBC Wednesday and Friday The Jaye P. Morgan Show† (7/4)
7:30-8:00 CBS Terrytoons Cartoon Theatre† (Dick Van Dyke, host) (6/13)
8-8:30 NBC Press Conference† (7/4)
10:30-11:00 ABC The Ina Ray Hutton Show† (7/11)

Thursday
8-9:00 ABC The Hour Glass† [feature films] (7/5)
10-10:30 CBS The Arthur Murray Party (resumed 6/8)

Friday
5:30-6:45 CBS The Victor Riesel Interview† (6/29)
7:30-8:00 ABC Combat Sergeant†* (6/29)
8-8:30 CBS Hollywood Summer Theatre† [repeats] (8/17)
9-9:30 NBC The Best in Mystery [repeats of The Four Star Playhouse] (resumed 7/13)
10-10:30 CBS Undercurrent [repeats of Studio '57] (resumed 6/29)
10-10:30 ABC It's Polka Time† (7/13)
10:30-11:00 CBS High Finance† (7/6)
10:30-11:00 ABC Pantomime Quiz (resumed 7/6)
8-8:30 WABD The Adventures of Sherlock Holmes (resumed 6/1)

1956-57 SEASON

Saturday

	CBS	NBC	ABC
7:00	Beat the Clock (9/22)	The Rosemary Clooney Show† (9/22) [hereafter 11:15-11:45 P. M.]	local
7:30	The Buccaneers†* (9/22)	People Are Funny (9/15)	Film Festival
8:00	The Honeymooners (The Jackie Gleason Show) (9/29)	The Perry Como Show (9/15)	Film Festival
8:30	Stage Show (9/15)	The Perry Como Show	Film Festival
9:00	Oh, Susanna! (The Gale Storm Show) (9/29)	The Sid Caesar Hour (9/15)	The Lawrence Welk Show (9/15)
9:30	Hey, Jeannie!† (Jeannie Carson, Alan Jenkins, Jane Dulo) (9/8)	The Sid Caesar Hour	The Lawrence Welk Show

	CBS	NBC	ABC
10:00	Gunsmoke (9/8)	The George Gobel Show (10/6)	Masquerade Party (9/29)
10:30	High Finance (9/8) [Ford Star Jubilee* (10/6) monthly displaced programming 9:30-11:00 above]	Your Hit Parade (9/8)	local

10:30-11:00 WABD I Spy (Raymond Masey) [continuing]

Sunday

5:00	Face the Nation		
5:30	The Bandwagon† (9/30) [See It Now (10/7) regularly displaced programming 5-6:00]		
6:00	Telephone Time* (9/16)		
6:30	Air Power†* (11/11)	The Roy Rogers Show (9/16)	Star Time† (9/9)
7:00	Lassie (9/9)	The 77th Bengal Lancers† (Philip Carey, Warren Stevens, Patrick Whyte, Patrick Knowles, Patricia Medina) (10/21)	You Asked for It (9/23)
7:30	Private Secretary (9/9) alternating with The Jack Benny Show (9/30)	Circus Boy† (Mickey Braddock, Noah Beery Jr., Robert Lowery, Guinn Williams) (9/23)	The Ted Mack Original Amateur Hour (9/23)
8:00	The Ed Sullivan Show (9/16; eighth anniversary 6/24/56)	The Steve Allen Show (9/16)	The Ted Mack Original Amateur Hour
8:30	The Ed Sullivan Show	The Steve Allen Show	It's Polka Time (9/23)
9:00	The General Electric Theatre* (9/30)	The Alcoa Hour* (9/16) alternating with The Goodyear Theatre	Omnibus†* (10/7)
9:30	Alfred Hitchcock Presents* (9/30)	The Alcoa Hour alternating with The Goodyear Theatre	Omnibus
10:00	The $64,000 Challenge (9/30)	The Loretta Young Show* (8/26)	Omnibus
10:30	What's My Line?	National Bowling Champions (8/26)	local

9:30-10:00 WPIX Dr. Hudson's Secret Journal† (John Howard) (9/9)

Monday

	CBS	NBC	ABC
		3-4:00 weekdays: Matinee Theatre* (8/28)	
7:00			Kukla, Fran and Ollie (9/3) 7:15: News
7:30	The Adventures of Robin Hood (10/1)	The Nat King Cole Show† (9/17) 7:45: News Caravan	Bold Journey (10/1)

	CBS	NBC	ABC
8:00	The George Burns-Gracie Allen Show (9/10)	The Adventures of Sir Lancelot†* (9/24)	Make Room for Daddy (10/1)
8:30	Arthur Godfrey's Talent Scouts (10/1)	Stanley† (Buddy Hackett, Carol Burnett) (9/24)	The Voice of Firestone
9:00	I Love Lucy (10/1)	Can Do† (11/26)	Life Is Worth Living (10/1)
9:30	December Bride (10/8)	Robert Montgomery Presents* (9/10)	Lawrence Welk's Top Tunes and Talent† (9/24)
10:00	Studio One* (9/24)	Robert Montgomery Presents	Lawrence Welk's Top Tunes and Talent
10:30	Studio One	Douglas Fairbanks Jr. Presents The Rheingold Theatre* (9/17)	Dr. Christian† (Macdonald Carey) (10/1)

7:15-7:30 weekdays WABD Speaking of Animals† (Herb Sheldon, host) (9/10)
8:30-9:00 WABD The Adventures of Judge Roy Bean† (Edgar Buchanan, Russell Hayden, Jack Beutel) (9/10)

Tuesday

	CBS	NBC	ABC
7:00		Celebrity Playhouse† [retitled repeats] (9/25)	Kukla, Fran and Ollie
			7:15: News
7:30	Name That Tune (9/11)	The Jonathan Winters Show† (10/2)	Conflict†* (9/18) alternating with Cheyenne* (9/11)
		7:45: News Caravan	
8:00	The Phil Silvers Show (9/18)	The Big Surprise (9/18)	Conflict alternating with Cheyenne
8:30	The Brothers† (Gale Gordon, Bob Sweeney) (10/1)	Noah's Ark†* (9/18)	Wyatt Earp (9/11)
9:00	The Herb Shriner Show (10/2)	Jane Wyman Presents The Fireside Theatre* (8/28)	Broken Arrow† (John Lupton, Michael Ansara) (9/25)
9:30	The Red Skelton Show (10/2)	The Armstrong Circle Theatre* (10/2) alternating with The Kaiser Aluminum Hour†* (initially 7/3/56; 9/25)	The DuPont Theatre†* [formerly Cavalcade Theatre) (9/18)
10:00	The $64,000 Question (10/2)	The Armstrong Circle Theatre alternating with The Kaiser Aluminum Hour	The All Star Theatre† (9/18)
10:30	Do You Trust Your Wife? (10/9)	Break the $250,000 Bank† (8/27)	The Damon Runyon Theatre* [repeats] (10/2)

10:30-11:00 WABD The Virginia Graham Theatre† (10/2)
10:30-11:00 WABD The Adventures of Sherlock Holmes (resumed 11/13)

CBS	NBC	ABC

Wednesday

	CBS	NBC	ABC
			6:30: The Frankie Laine Show† (9/19)
7:00			Kukla, Fran and Ollie 7:15: News
7:30	Pick the Winner† (9/12) followed by Giant Step† (11/17)	Eddie Fisher's Coke Time (9/12)	Disneyland (9/12)
		7:45: News Caravan	
8:00	The Adventures of Hiram Holliday† (Wally Cox, Angela Greene) (10/3)	The Big Surprise (9/26)	Disneyland
8:30	The Arthur Godfrey Show (9/26)	Father Knows Best (9/12)	Navy Log* (10/17)
9:00	The Millionaire* (9/12)	The Kraft Television Theatre* (9/19)	Ozzie and Harriet (10/3)
9:30	I've Got a Secret (9/12)	The Kraft Television Theatre	Ford Theatre* (10/3)
10:00	The United States Steel Hour* (9/12) alternating with The Twentieth Century-Fox Hour* (10/3)	This Is Your Life (9/26)	The Wednesday Night Fights
10:30	The Unites States Steel Hour alternating with The Twentieth Century-Fox Hour	Twenty-One† (Jack Barry) (9/12)	The Wednesday Night Fights

8:30-9:00 WABD The Ray Milland Show (resumed 9/12)

Thursday

	CBS	NBC	ABC
7:00			Kukla, Fran and Ollie 7:15: News
7:30	Sergeant Preston of Yukon (9/13)	The Dinah Shore Show (9/20)	The Lone Ranger (9/13)
		7:45: News Caravan	
8:00	Love That Bob (10/4)	You Bet Your Life (a.k.a. The Best of Groucho) (9/27)	Circus Time† (10/4)
8:30	Climax!* (9/27) alnating with Shower of Stars* (11/1)	Dragnet (9/27)	Circus Time
9:00	Climax! alternating with Showers of Stars	The People's Choice (9/13)	Wire Service* (10/4)
9:30	Playhouse 90†* (10/4)	The Tennessee Ernie Ford Show† (10/4)	Wire Service†
10:00	Playhouse 90	The Lux Video Theatre* (9/20)	Ozark Jubilee (9/13)
10:30	Playhouse 90	The Lux Video Theatre	local

	CBS	NBC	ABC
Friday			
7:00		Science Fiction Theatre* (9/28)	Kukla, Fran and Ollie
			7:15: News
7:30	My Friend Flicka (10/12)	Eddie Fisher's Coke Time	Rin Tin Tin (9/7)
		7:45: News Caravan	
8:00	West Point Story†* (10/5)	The Life of Riley (9/14)	The Adventures of Jim Bowie† (Scott Forbes) (9/7)
8:30	The Zane Grey Theatre†* (10/5)	The Walter Winchell Show† (10/5)	Crossroads* (10/5)
9:00	The Crusader (10/5)	On Trial†* (9/14)	Treasure Hunt† (Jan Murray, Marian Stafford) (9/7)
9:30	The Schlitz Playhouse of the Stars* (9/28)	The Big Story (9/7)	The Vise* (9/7)
10:00	The Lineup (9/28)	The Friday Night Fights	The Ray Anthony Show† (10/19)
10:30	Person to Person (9/14)	The Friday Night Fights [The Dinah Shore Show† (9/21) specials regularly displaced programming 9-10:00 above]	The Adventures of the Falcon [continuing]

8:30-9:00 WABD The Ethel Barrymore Theatre†* (9/21)
9-9:30 WABD The Lilli Palmer Theatre†* (9/21)

1956-57 MIDSEASON

	CBS	NBC	ABC
Saturday			
		6:30-7:00: Counterpoint† [repeats of Rebound] (2/2)	
7:00	Beat the Clock	The Rosemary Clooney Show	This Is Galen Drake† (1/12)
7:30	The Buccaneers	People Are Funny	Film Festival
8:00	The Honeymooners	The Perry Como Show	Film Festival
8:30	Stage Show	The Perry Como Show	Film Festival
9:00	Oh, Susanna!	The Sid Caesar Hour	The Lawrence Welk Show
9:30	Hey, Jeannie!	The Sid Caesar Hour	The Lawrence Welk Show
10:00	Gunsmoke	The George Gobel Show	Ozark Jubilee (resumed 12/29/56)
10:30	You're On Your Own† (12/29/56)	Your Hit Parade	The Adventures of the Falcon (resumed 12/29/56)

8:30-9:00 WABD The Racket Squad (resumed 1/4)

	CBS	NBC	ABC
Sunday			
4:00	Odyssey† (1/6)		
4:30	Odyssey		
5:00	I Remember Mama (resumed 12/16/56)		
5:30	The Gerald McBoing Show† (12/16/56)		
6:00	Telephone Time		
6:30	Air Power		
7:00	Lassie	The 77th Bengal Lancers	You Asked for It
7:30	The Marge and Gower Champion Show† (3/31) alternating with The Jack Benny Show	Circus Boy	The Ted Mack Original Amateur Hour
8:00	The Ed Sullivan Show	The Steve Allen Show	The Ted Mack Original Amateur Hour
8:30	The Ed Sullivan Show	The Steve Allen Show	It's Polka Time
9:00	The General Electric Theatre	The Alcoa Hour alternating with The Goodyear Theatre	Omnibus
9:30	Alfred Hitchcock Presents	The Alcoa Hour alternating with The Goodyear Theatre	Omnibus
10:00	The $64,000 Challenge	The Loretta Young Show	Omnibus
10:30	What's My Line?	National Bowling Champions	local
Monday			
7:00			Kukla, Fran and Ollie 7:15: News
7:30	The Adventures of Robin Hood	The Nat King Cole Show 7:45: News Caravan	Wire Service (as of 2/11)
8:00	The George Burns- Gracie Allen Show	The Adventures of Sir Lancelot	Wire Service
8:30	Arthur Godfrey's Talent Scouts	Tales of Wells Fargo†* (3/18)	The Voice of Firestone
9:00	I Love Lucy	Can Do	Life Is Worth Living
9:30	December Bride	Robert Montgomery Presents	Lawrence Welk's Top Tunes and Talent
10:00	Studio One	Robert Montgomery Presents	Lawrence Welk's Top Tunes and Talent
10:30	Studio One	Code Three† (Richard Travis) (3/25)	Dr. Christian
Tuesday			
7:00		Celebrity Playhouse† [repeats] (3/5)	Kukla, Fran and Ollie 7:15: News
7:30	Name That Tune	The Jonathan Winters Show 7:45: News Caravan	Conflict alternating with Cheyenne

	CBS	NBC	ABC
8:00	The Phil Silvers Show	The Big Surprise	Conflict alternating with Cheyenne
8:30	The Brothers	Panic !†* (3/5)	Wyatt Earp
9:00	To Tell the Truth† (1/15)	Jane Wyman Presents The Fireside Theatre	Broken Arrow
9:30	The Red Skelton Show	The Armstrong Circle Theatre alternating with The Kaiser Aluminum Hour	The DuPont Theatre
10:00	The $64,000 Question	The Armstrong Circle Theatre alternating with The Kaiser Aluminum Hour	It's Polka Time (resumed 1/1)
10:30	The Spike Jones Show† (4/2)	Break the $250,000 Bank	Damon Runyon Theatre [repeats]

Wednesday

	CBS	NBC	ABC
			6-6:30: Hawkeye and the Last of the Mohicans† (Lon Chaney Jr., John Hart) (4/3)
			6:30: The Frankie Laine Show
7:00			Kukla, Fran and Ollie 7:15: News
7:30	Giant Step	Eddie Fisher's Coke Time 7:45: News Caravan	Disneyland
8:00	The Adventures of Hiram Holliday	The Big Surprise	Disneyland
8:30	The Arthur Godfrey Show	Father Knows Best	Navy Log
9:00	The Millionaire	The Kraft Television Theatre	Ozzie and Harriet
9:30	I've Got a Secret	The Kraft Television Theatre	Ford Theatre
10:00	The United States Steel Hour alternating with The Twentieth Century-Fox Hour	This Is Your Life	The Wednesday Night Fights
10:30	The United States Steel Hour alternating with The Twentieth Century-Fox Hour	Twenty-One	The Wednesday Night Fights

9-9:30 WGR The O. Henry Playhouse†* (1/23)
10-10:30 WABD The Star and the Story† [repeats of The Rheingold Theatre] (2/13)

Thursday

	CBS	NBC	ABC
7:00			Kukla, Fran and Ollie 7:15: News
7:30	Sergeant Preston of the Yukon	The Dinah Shore Show 7:45: News Caravan	The Lone Ranger

	CBS	NBC	ABC
8:00	Love That Bob	You Bet Your Life	Circus Time
8:30	Climax! alternating with Shower of Stars	Dragnet	Circus Time
9:00	Climax! alternating with Shower of Stars	The People's Choice	Make Room for Daddy (as of 2/14)
9:30	Playhouse 90	The Tennessee Ernie Ford Show	Championship Bowling (as of 2/14)
10:00	Playhouse 90	The Lux Video Theatre	Telephone Time (as of 4/11)
10:30	Playhouse 90	The Lux Video Theatre	local

7:30-8:00 WPIX The Whirlybirds (Craig Hill, Nancy Hale, Kenneth Tobey) (resumed 2/14)

Friday

	CBS	NBC	ABC
7:00		The Silent Service† (Rear Admiral Thomas Dyker, host and narrator) (4/5)	Kukla, Fran and Ollie
			7:15: News
7:30	My Friend Flicka	Eddie Fisher's Coke Time	Rin Tin Tin
		7:45: News Caravan	
8:00	West Point Story	Blondie† (Arthur Lake, Pamela Britton) (1/4)	The Adventures of Jim Bowie
8:30	The Zane Grey Theatre	The Life of Riley (as of 1/4)	Crossroads
9:00	Mr. Adams and Eve† (Howard Duff, Ida Lupino) (1/4)	On Trial	Treasure Hunt
9:30	The Schlitz Playhouse of the Stars	The Big Story	The Vise
10:00	The Lineup	The Friday Night Fights	The Ray Anthony Show
10:30	Person to Person	The Friday Night Fights	The Adventures of the Falcon

8-8:30 WABD The Errol Flynn Theatre†* (3/22)
9-9:30 WOR The Crusader (resumed 1/24)

Summer Programming, 1957

Saturday
6:30-7:00 NBC Hy Gardner Calling† (4/20)
8-8:30 CBS The Jimmy Durante Show (resumed 6/29)
8:30-9:00 CBS Two for the Money (Sam Levenson, host) (resumed 6/29)
8-9:00 NBC The Julius LaRosa Show (resumed 5/11)
9-9:30 NBC The George Sanders Mystery Theatre†* (6/22)
9:30-10:00 CBS S. R. O. Playhouse† [repeats of The Schlitz Playhouse of the Stars] (5/11)
9:30-10:00 NBC Dollar a Second (Jan Murray, host) (resumed 6/22)
10-10:30 NBC Encore Theatre† [repeats of Ford Theatre] (7/6)
10:30-11:00 NBC Adventure Theatre [repeats] (Paul Douglas, host; resumed 5/11)

| CBS | NBC | ABC |

Sunday

5-5:30 CBS Face the Nation (resumed 4/7)

5:30-6:00 CBS World News Round Up† (Eric Sevareid, host) (resumed 4/7)

6-6:30 CBS The Last Word† (4/7)

7:30-8:00 CBS My Favorite Husband (resumed 4/7)

8-8:30 ABC Dangerous Assignment (resumed 4/7)

8:30-9:00 ABC Midwestern Hayride (resumed 4/7)

9-10:00 ABC The Kate Smith Hour (resumed 4/28)

10-10:30 ABC Mike Wallace Interviews† (4/28)

10-10:30 NBC The Web†* (7/7)

Monday

4:45-5:00 weekdays NBC Modern Romances alternating with True Story [continuing]

3-4:30 weekdays ABC American Bandstand† [live and with pre-recorded music] (nationally as of 8/5; Dick Clark, host)

7:30-8:00 NBC The Georgia Gibbs Show† (4/8)

8-8:30 NBC The Charlie Farrell Show (resumed 4/8)

8:30-9:00 NBC Action Tonight† [repeats of The Schlitz Playhouse of the Stars and Studio '57] (7/15)

9-9:30 CBS Those Whiting Girls (Margaret and Barbara Whiting) (resumed 7/1)

9:30-10:00 NBC Richard Diamond, Private Detective†* (7/1)

9:30-10:00 NBC The Arthur Murray Party (resumed 7/1)

10-11:00 NBC The Ted Mack Original Amateur Hour (resumed 7/1)

Tuesday

7-7:30 NBC Celebrity Playhouse† [repeats of Ford Theatre] (7/2)

7:30-7:45 NBC The Andy Williams and June Valli Show† (7/2)

8:30-9:00 NBC Festival of Stars [repeats of The Loretta Young Show] (7/2)

9:00-9:30 Meet McGraw†* (Frank Lovejoy) (7/2)

9:30-10:00 CBS Spotlight Playhouse [repeats of The Ford Theatre] (resumed 7/2)

9:30-10:00 NBC Summer Playhouse [repeats of The Pepsi Cola Playhouse] (resumed 7/2)

10-10:30 NBC The Nat King Cole Show (resumed 7/2)

10:30-11:00 ABC Men of Annapolis† (in association with The United States Naval Academy) (5/7)

Wednesday

7:30-7:45 Wednesday and Friday The Helen O'Connell Show† (7/3) NBC

7:30-8:00 CBS My Friend Irma (resumed 7/3)

8-9:00 CBS The Vic Damone Show† (7/3)

9:30-10:00 Moment of Decision† [repeats of The Ford Theatre] (7/3)

10:30-11:00 NBC The Vise (as of 7/3)

Thursday

7:30-7:45 NBC The Andy Williams and June Valli Show† (7/25)

9-9:30 ABC Theatre Time† [repeats of The Loretta Young Show] (7/25)

9:30-10:00 NBC High-Low† (quiz program) (7/4)

Friday

8:30-9:00 CBS Destiny† [repeats of The Fireside Theatre, The General Electric Theatre, Star Stage and Studio '57] (7/5)

9-9:30 ABC The Key Club Playhouse† [repeats of The Ford Theatre] (5/31)

9:30-10:00 NBC The Big Moment† [sports program] (7/5)

9:30-10:00 ABC A Date with the Angels† [Betty White, Bill Williams] (5/10)

| | CBS | NBC | ABC |

10-10:30 CBS Undercurrent [repeats of The Ford Theatre] (7/19)
10-10:30 ABC The Big Beat† (Alan Freed, host of music program) (7/5)
10:30-11:00 CBS Pantomine Quiz (Mike Stokey, host) (resumed 7/5)

1957-58 SEASON

Saturday

	CBS	NBC	ABC
7:30	Perry Mason†* (9/21)	People Are Funny (9/14)	Keep It in the Family† (Bill Nimmo, host) (10/12)
8:00	Perry Mason	The Perry Como Show (9/14)	Country Music Jubilee† (10/5)
8:30	Dick and the Duchess† (Patrick O'Neal, Hazel Court) (9/28)	The Perry Como Show	Country Music Jubilee
9:00	Oh, Susanna! (9/28)	The Polly Bergen Show (9/21)	The Lawrence Welk Show (10/5)
9:30	Have Gun, Will Travel†* (Richard Boone, Kam Tong, Lisa Lu) (9/14)	The Gisele MacKenzie Show† (9/28)	The Lawrence Welk Show
10:00	Gunsmoke (9/14)	What Is It For?† (10/12)	The Mike Wallace Interview (10/5)
10:30	The Jimmy Dean Show† (9/14)	Your Hit Parade (9/7) [Holiday in Las Vegas† (11/16) regularly displaced The Perry Como Show; Club Oasis† (9/28) regularly displaced The Polly Bergen Show; Command Performance† (11/23) and The Dean Martin Show† (10/5) regularly displaced What Is It For? and Your Hit Parade]	local

Sunday

	CBS	NBC	ABC
4:00		Omnibus* (10/20) [alternating with Wide, Wide World (9/15)]	
4:30		Omnibus [alternating with Wide, Wide World]	
5:00	The Seven Lively Arts†*	Omnibus [alternating with Wide, Wide World]	
5:30	The Seven Lively Arts	Breakthrough† (9/15)	
6:00	local	Meet the Press	

	CBS	NBC	ABC
6:30	The Twentieth Century† (Walter Cronkite, host and narrator) (10/20)	The Ted Mack Original Amateur Hour (9/15)	
7:00	Lassie (9/8)	The Ted Mack Original Amateur Hour	You Asked for It (9/15)
7:30	The Jack Benny Show (9/22) alternating with Bachelor Father† (John Forsythe, Noreen Corcoran, Samee Tong) (9/15)	Sally† (Joan Caulfield, Johnny Desmond, Marian Lorne) (9/15)	Maverick†* (9/22)
8:00	The Ed Sullivan Show (10/6; tenth anniversary 6/29/58)	The Steve Allen Show (9/15)	Maverick
8:30	The Ed Sullivan Show	The Steve Allen Show	Bowling Stars† (9/22)
9:00	The General Electric Theatre* (10/6)	The Dinah Shore Chevy Show† (9/15)	local
9:30	Alfred Hitchcock Presents* (10/6)	The Dinah Shore Chevy Show	The Game of the Week† (9/22)
10:00	The $64,000 Challenge (10/27)	The Loretta Young Show* (10/20)	Case Histories of Scotland Yard [repeats of Dumont series of 9/14/55] (11/17)
10:30	What's My Line? (10/27)	local	local
		[The Bob Hope Show† (10/6) and other specials regularly displaced The Dinah Shore Chevy Show]	

Monday

	CBS	NBC	ABC
		3-4:00 weekdays: Matinee Theatre* (10/15)	
7:30	The Adventures of Robin Hood (9/30)	The Price Is Right† (Bill Cullen, host) (9/23)	American Bandstand (as of 9/9)
8:00	The George Burns-Gracie Allen Show (9/30)	The Restless Gun† (John Payne) (9/23)	The Guy Mitchell Show† (10/7)
8:30	Arthur Godfrey's Talent Scouts (9/30)	The Tales of Wells Fargo* (9/9)	Bold Journey (10/7)
9:00	Make Room for Daddy (10/7)	Twenty-One (9/9)	The Voice of Firestone (9/9)
9:30	December Bride (10/7)	A Turn of Fate†* (composite title for The Alcoa and Goodyear Theatre) (9/30)	Lawrence Welk's Top Tunes and Talent (9/9)
10:00	Studio One* (9/9)	Suspicion†* (9/30)	Lawrence Welk's Top Tunes and Talent
10:30	Studio One	Suspicion	Men of Annapolis (9/9)

CBS	NBC	NBC

Tuesday

	CBS	NBC	NBC
7:30	Name That Tune (9/17)	The Nat King Cole Show (9/17)	Cheyenne* (9/24) alternating with Sugarfoot†* (9/17)
8:00	The Phil Silvers Show (9/17)	The George Gobel Show [expanded to full hour] (9/24)	Cheyenne alternating with Sugarfoot
8:30	The Eve Arden Show† (9/17)	The George Gobel Show	Wyatt Earp (9/17)
9:00	To Tell the Truth (9/17)	Meet McGraw* (9/24)	Broken Arrow (10/1)
9:30	The Red Skelton Show (10/1)	The Robert Cummings Show (9/24)	Telephone Time* (9/10)
10:00	The $64,000 Question (9/17)	The Californians† (Richard Coogan, Sean McClory, Adam Kennedy) (9/24)	West Point [repeats] (10/8)
10:30	Assignment--Foreign Legion† (Merle Oberon, hostess and star) (10/1)	The Vise [repeats] (9/24)	local
	[High Adventure with Lowell Thomas† (11/12) regularly displaced programming 8-9:00 above]	[The Eddie Fisher Show† (10/1) regularly displaced The George Gobel Show; The Jerry Lewis Show† (11/5) regularly displaced Meet McGraw and The Robert Cummings Show]	

8:30-9:00 WABD The White Hunter† (Rhodes Reason) (11/12)

Wednesday

	CBS	NBC	NBC
7:30	I Love Lucy [repeats] (9/11)	Wagon Train†* (9/18)	Disneyland* (9/11)
8:00	The Big Record† (Patti Page, hostess) (9/18)	Wagon Train	Disneyland
8:30	The Big Record	Father Knows Best (9/25)	Tombstone Territory† (Pat Conway, Richard Eastham) (10/16)
9:00	The Millionaire* (9/18)	The Kraft Television Theatre* (9/25)	Ozzie and Harriet (10/2)
9:30	I've Got a Secret (9/18)	The Kraft Television Theatre	The Walter Winchell File†* (10/2)
10:00	The Armstrong Circle Theatre* (10/2) alternating with The United States Steel Hour* (9/25)	This Is Your Life (9/25)	The Wednesday Night Fights
10:30	The Armstrong Circle Theatre alternating with The United States Steel Hour	Code Three (9/25)	The Wednesday Night Fights

	CBS	NBC	ABC

Thursday

	CBS	NBC	ABC
7:30	Sergeant Preston of the Yukon (10/3)	Boots and Saddles: The Story of The Fifth Cavalry† (Jack Pickard, Patrick McVey) (10/31) subsequently displaced by Tic Tac Dough† (quiz) (11/1)	Circus Boy (9/19)
8:00	Harbourmaster† (Barry Sullivan, Nina Wilcox) [subsequently retitled The Adventures at Scott Island, q.v.]	You Bet Your Life (9/26)	Zorro†* (Guy Williams, Joan Evans, Gene Sheldon, Don Diamond, Henry Calvin) (10/10)
8:30	Climax! (9/26) alternating with Shower of the Stars (10/31)	Dragnet (9/26)	The Real McCoys† (Walter Brennan, Richard Crenna, Kathy Nolan) (10/3)
9:00	Climax! alternating with Shower of Stars	The People's Choice (10/3)	The Pat Boone Show† (10/3)
9:30	Playhouse 90* (9/12)	The Tennessee Ernie Ford Show (9/12)	O.S.S.† (Ron Randell) (9/26)
10:00	Playhouse 90	The Rosemary Clooney Show† (9/26)	Navy Log* (9/18; at this time as of 11/17)
10:30	Playhouse 90	Jane Wyman Presents The Fireside Theatre* (9/26) [Command Appearance† (9/19) regularly displaced programming 10-11:00 above]	local

7:30-8:00 WPIX The Whirlybirds (resumed 9/19)
8:30-9:00 WPIX Captain David Grief† (Maxwell Reed) (10/3)
9:30-10:00 WPIX The Gray Ghost† (Tod Andrews) (10/10)
10-10:30 WPIX Frontier Doctor (Rex Allen) (resumed 10/3)
10-10:30 WABD Art Ford's Greenwich Village Party† (9/19)

Friday

	CBS	NBC	ABC
7:00		The Silent Service (8/30)	
7:30	Leave It to Beaver (Jerry Mathers, Tony Dow, Hugh Beaumont, Barbara Billingsley) (10/4)	The Saber of London† (Donald Gray) (9/13)	Rin Tin Tin (9/13)
8:00	Trackdown† (Robert Culp) (10/4)	The Court of Last Resort† (Lyle Bettger) (10/4)	The Adventures of Jim Bowie (9/6)
8:30	Zane Grey Theatre* (10/4)	The Life of Riley (9/13)	The Patrice Munsel Show† (9/13)
9:00	Mr. Adams and Eve (9/20)	M Squad†* (Lee Marvin) (9/20)	The Frank Sinatra Show† (9/13)

	CBS	NBC	ABC
9:30	The Schlitz Play-house of the Stars* (9/13)	The Thin Man† (Peter Lawford, Phyllis Kirk) (9/20)	A Date with the Angels (9/13)
10:00	The Lineup (9/27)	The Friday Night Fights	Colt .45† (Wayde Preston) (10/18)
10:30	Person to Person (9/13)	The Friday Night Fights	The Diamond Playhouse† [repeats] (9/13)

1957-58 MIDSEASON

Saturday

	CBS	NBC	ABC
	Noon-1:00 after-noons, regular specials: The New York Phil-harmonic Young People's Con-certs, with Leo-nard Bernstein† (1/18)		
7:30	Perry Mason	People Are Funny	Keep It in the Family
8:00	Perry Mason	The Perry Como Show	Country Music Jubilee
8:30	Dick and the Duchess	The Perry Como Show	Country Music Jubilee
9:00	Oh, Susanna!	The Polly Bergen Show	The Lawrence Welk Show
9:30	Have Gun, Will Travel*	The Gisele MacKenzie Show	The Lawrence Welk Show
10:00	Gunsmoke	End of the Rainbow† (live audience parti-cipation) (2/1)	The Mike Wallace In-terview
10:30	Sea Hunt† (Lloyd Bridges) (2/1)	Your Hit Parade	local

Sunday

	CBS	NBC	ABC
4:00		Omnibus alternating with Wide, Wide, World	
4:30		Omnibus alternating with Wide, Wide, World	
5:00	The Great Challenge† (2/23)	Omnibus alternating with Wide, Wide, World	
5:30	The Great Challenge	The Saber of London (as of 12/22/57)	
6:00	local	Meet the Press	
6:30	The Twentieth Century	The Ted Mack Ori-ginal Amateur Hour	
7:00	Lassie	The Ted Mack Ori-ginal Amateur Hour	
7:30	The Jack Benny Show alternating with Bachelor Father	Sally	Maverick

	CBS	NBC	ABC
8:00	The Ed Sullivan Show	The Steve Allen Show	Maverick
8:30	The Ed Sullivan Show	The Steve Allen Show	Adventures at Scott Island [previously Harbourmaster] (1/5)
9:00	The General Electric Theatre	The Dinah Shore Chevy Show [regularly displaced by The Bob Hope Show]	Sid Caesar Invites You† (Imogene Coca, Carl Reiner) (1/26)
9:30	Alfred Hitchcock Presents	The Dinah Shore Chevy Show [regularly displaced by The Bob Hope Show]	You Asked for It (as of 1/5)
10:00	The $64,000 Challenge	The Loretta Young Show	Case Histories of Scotland Yard
10:30	What's My Line?	local	local

Monday

7:30	The Adventures of Robin Hood	The Price Is Right	O.S.S. (as of 1/13); displaced by Odyssey† (3/24)
8:00	The George Burns-Gracie Allen Show	The Restless Gun	Love That Jill† (Robert Sterling, Anne Jeffreys) (1/20)
8:30	Arthur Godfrey's Talent Scouts	The Tales of Wells Fargo	Bold Journey
9:00	Make Room for Daddy	Twenty-One	The Voice of Firestone
9:30	December Bride	A Turn of Fate	Lawrence Welk's Top Tunes and Talent
10:00	Studio One	Suspicion	Lawrence Welk's Top Tunes and Talent
10:30	Studio One	Suspicion	Men of Annapolis

1-1:30 weekdays WABD Showcase† (Fanny Hearst, first guest hostess) (1/27)
6:30-7:00 WATZ Report from Rutgers† (Rutgers faculty and Dr. Houston Peterson, Professor of Theology, host) (1/27)

Tuesday

7:30	Name That Tune	Treasure Hunt† (Jan Murray, host; Marian Stafford) (1/28)	Cheyenne alternating with Sugarfoot
8:00	Mr. Adams and Eve (as of 2/11)	The George Gobel Show [regularly displaced by The Eddie Fisher Show]	Cheyenne alternating with Sugarfoot
8:30	The Eve Arden Show	The George Gobel Show [regularly displaced by The Eddie Fisher Show]	Wyatt Earp
9:00	To Tell the Truth	Meet McGraw	Broken Arrow
9:30	The Red Skelton Show	The Bob Cummings Show	Telephone Time
10:00	The $64,000 Question	The Californians	West Point [repeats]
10:30	I Led Three Lives (resumed 12/31/57); displaced by Mike Hammer† (Darren McGavin) (1/28)	The Vise [repeats]	The Twenty-Six Men† (Tristram Coffin, Kelo Henderson) (1/28)

CBS	NBC	ABC

8:30-9:00 WABD Put It in Writing† (on graphology; Sandy Becker, host) (2/25)

Wednesday

	CBS	NBC	ABC
7:30	I Love Lucy [repeats]	Wagon Train	Disneyland
8:00	The Big Record	Wagon Train	Disneyland
8:30	The Big Record	Father Knows Best	Tombstone Territory
9:00	The Millionaire	The Kraft Television Theatre	Ozzie and Harriet
9:30	I've Got a Secret	The Kraft Television Theatre	A Date With the Angels† (as of 1/1/58)
10:00	The Armstrong Circle Theatre alternating with The United States Steel Hour	This Is Your Life	The Wednesday Night Fights
10:30	The Armstrong Circle Theatre alternating with The United States Steel Hour	Code Three	The Wednesday Night Fights

Thursday

	CBS	NBC	ABC
	2-2:30 P.M.: The Way† (ecclesiastical series) (2/13)		
7:30	Sergeant Preston of the Yukon	Tic Tac Dough	Circus Boy
8:00	Richard Diamond, Private Detective* (resumed 1/2)	You Bet Your Life	Zorro
8:30	Climax! alternating with Shower of Stars	Dragnet	The Real McCoys
9:00	Climax! alternating with Shower of Stars	The People's Choice	The Pat Boone Show
9:30	Playhouse 90	The Tennessee Ernie Ford Show	O.S.S. displaced by local programming 1/16
10:00	Playhouse 90	The Rosemary Clooney Show	Navy Log
10:30	Playhouse 90	Jane Wyman Presents The Fireside Theatre	local

7:30-8:00 WABD The White Hunter (resumed 1/9)

Friday

	CBS	NBC	ABC
7:00		The Silent Service	
7:30	Leave It to Beaver	Truth Or Consequences (resumed 12/20/57)	Rin Tin Tin
8:00	Trackdown	The Court of Last Resort	The Adventures of Jim Bowie
8:30	Zane Grey Theatre	The Life of Riley	Colt .45 (resumed 1/3)
9:00	The Phil Silvers Show (as of 2/14)	M Squad	The Frank Sinatra Show (as of 1/3)
9:30	The Schlitz Playhouse of the Stars	The Thin Man	The Patrice Munsel Show (as of 1/3)
10:00	The Lineup	The Friday Night Fights	The Walter Winchell File (resumed 1/3)

	CBS	NBC	ABC
10:30	Person to Person	The Friday Night Fights	Harbour Command (resumed 1/3)

Summer Programming, 1958

Saturday
10:30-11:00 NBC The Betty White Show (resumed 7/6)
10:30-11:00 NBC The Joseph Cotten Show [On Trial] (repeats, 6/14)

Sunday
7:30-8:00 NBC No Warning†* (4/6)
10-10:30 NBC The Web [repeats] (7/6)

Monday
7:30-8:00 ABC The Written Word† (Dr. Frank Baxter, host) (5/12)
8-8:30 ABC Campaign Roundup† (5/12)

Tuesday
8-9:00 NBC The Investigator† (Lonny Chapman, Howard St. John) (6/3)
9-9:30 NBC Dotto† (Jack Narz, host) (7/1)
9:30-10:00 Spotlight Theatre [repeats of The Loretta Young Show] (resumed 6/3)

Wednesday
8-9:00 CBS The Vic Damone Show (resumed 7/2)
9:30-10:00 ABC Traffic Court† (6/18)

Thursday
8:30-9:30 CBS The Verdict Is Yours† (Jim McKay, host) (7/3)
9:30-10:00 NBC Buckskin† (Tommy Nolan, Sallie Brophy) (7/3)
10-10:30 ABC Confession† [Jane Wyman, hostess] (6/26)
10:30-11:00 NBC Music Bingo† (5/29)

Friday
7:30-8:00 NBC The Big Game† (Tom Kennedy, host) (6/20)
8-8:30 NBC Jefferson Drum†* (4/25)
8:30-9:00 CBS Destiny [repeats of The General Electric Theatre] (resumed 7/4)
9:30-10:00 ABC Summer Theatre [repeats of The Ford Theatre] (resumed 6/20)
10-10:30 CBS Undercurrent [repeats of The Ford Theatre] (resumed 6/27)

1958-59 SEASON

	CBS	NBC	ABC
Saturday			
7:30	Perry Mason* (9/20)	People Are Funny (9/13)	The Dick Clark Show (9/20)
8:00	Perry Mason	The Perry Como Show (9/13)	The Billy Graham Crusade† [four weeks only; subsequently displaced by Jubilee, U.S.A. (12/27)] (9/27)

	CBS	NBC	ABC
8:30	Wanted: Dead or Alive† (Steve McQueen) (9/6)	The Perry Como Show	The Billy Graham Crusade [displaced by Jubilee, U.S.A.]
9:00	The Gale Storm Show (10/11)	Steve Canyon† (Dean Fredericks) (9/13)	The Lawrence Welk Dancing Party (9/20)
9:30	Have Gun, Will Travel* (9/27)	Cimarron City†* (George Montgomery, Audrey Totter, Dan Blocker) (10/11)	The Lawrence Welk Dancing Party
10:00	Gunsmoke (9/13)	Cimarron City	The Sammy Kaye Show (9/13)
10:30	Sea Hunt (9/13)	The Brains and Brawn† (Jack Lescoulie, Fred Davis, hosts) (10/11) [The Jerry Lewis Show† (10/18) and other specials regularly displaced programming 9-10:30 above]	Shock Theatre† [repeats] (9/13)

Sunday

4:00	Your Audience's† (10/19)		
4:30	Conquest† (Eric Sevareid, host) (11/16)		
5:00	Boots and Saddles (10/19)	Omnibus* (10/26) alternating with Kaleidoscope† (11/2)	Paul Winchell Show (9/21)
5:30	Face the Nation	Omnibus alternating with Kaleidoscope	The Lone Ranger (9/21)
6:00	The Twentieth Century (10/26)	Meet the Press	The Twenty-six Men (10/26)
6:30	Small World† (Edward R. Murrow, host) (10/26)	The Annie Oakley Show (10/5)	The Roy Rogers Show (10/26)
7:00	Lassie (9/21)	The Saber of London (9/14)	You Asked for It (9/21)
7:30	Bachelor Father (9/14) alternating with The Jack Benny Show (9/21)	Northwest Passage†* (Keith Larsen, Buddy Ebsen, Don Burnett) (9/14)	Maverick* (9/21)
8:00	The Ed Sullivan Show (tenth anniversary 6/22/58)	The Steve Allen Show (10/5)	Maverick
8:30	The Ed Sullivan Show	The Steve Allen Show	Lawman†* (10/5)
9:00	The General Electric Theatre* (9/21)	The Dinah Shore Chevy Show (10/5)	Colt .45 (10/5)
9:30	Alfred Hitchcock Presents* (10/5)	The Dinah Shore Chevy Show	Encounter†* (10/5)
10:00	The $64,000 Question (9/14) subsequently displaced by Keep Talking† (11/9)	The Loretta Young Show* (10/5)	Encounter
10:30	What's My Line?	local	local

	CBS	NBC	ABC

Monday

		1-1:30 weekdays: The Liberace Show† (10/13)	
		2-2:30 weekdays: A Chance for Romance† (10/13)	
		3-3:30 weekdays: Beat the Clock (10/13)	
7:30	Name That Tune (9/29)	Tic Tac Dough (10/6)	Jubilee, U. S. A. (9/29)
8:00	The Texan† (Rory Calhoun) (9/29)	The Restless Gun (9/22)	Jubilee, U. S. A.
8:30	Father Knows Best (9/22)	The Tales of Wells Fargo* (9/15)	Bold Journey (9/8)
9:00	The Danny Thomas Show (10/6)	Peter Gunn†* (10/6)	The Voice of Firestone (John Daly, narrator) (9/8)
9:30	The Ann Sothern Show† (also Don Porter, Ann Tyrrell, Ernest Truex) (10/6)	The Alcoa* (10/6)/ Goodyear Theatre* (9/29)	Anybody Can Play† (9/8)
10:00	The Desilu Play-house†* (10/13) [monthly displaced by The Lucy-Desi Comedy Hour* (10/6]	The Arthur Murray Party (9/29)	This Is Music (9/8)
10:30	The Desilu Play-house [monthly displaced by The Lucy-Desi Comedy Hour]	local; in some areas Decoy† (Beverly Garland) (9/29)	News with John Daly (9/8)

8:30-9:00 WPIX Flight† [General George C. Kenney, USAF (Ret.), host] (9/22)

Tuesday

7:00			Union Pacific† (Jeff Morrow) (9/16)
7:30	Stars in Action† [repeats] (9/30)	Dragnet (9/23)	Sugarfoot* (9/16) alternating with Bronco†* (9/23)
8:00	Keep Talking (9/30) subsequently displaced by The Invisible Man† (11/4)	The George Gobel Show (9/23) alternating with The Eddie Fisher Show (9/30)	Sugarfoot alternating with Bronco
8:30	To Tell the Truth (9/23)	The George Gobel Show alternating with The Eddie Fisher Show	Wyatt Earp (9/9)
9:00	The Arthur Godfrey Show (9/23)	The George Burns Show† (also with Bea Benaderet, Larry Keating) (10/14)	The Rifleman†* (9/30)

	CBS	NBC	ABC
9:30	The Red Skelton Show (9/30)	The Robert Cummings Show (9/16)	The Naked City†* (9/30)
10:00	The Garry Moore Show† (9/30)	The Californians (9/30)	local
10:30	The Garry Moore Show	Mike Hammer (9/30)	local

7-7:30 WATZ This Is Alice† (Patty Ann Gerrity, Tommy Farrell, Phyllis Coates) (10/7)

7:30-8:00 WABD The New Adventures of Charlie Chan† (J. Carrol Naish, James Hong) (11/25)

7:30-8:00 WPIX The Man Without a Gun† (Rex Reason) (10/7)

8-8:30 WATZ How To Marry a Millionaire† (Lori Nelson, Merry Anders, Barbara Eden) (10/7)

8:30-9:00 WATZ Leave It to the Girls (Nancy Connors, moderator) (resumed 10/7)

Wednesday

	CBS	NBC	ABC
7:00			Tugboat Annie† (Minerval Urecal, Walter Sande) (10/2)
7:30	MacKenzie's Raiders† (Richard Carlson) (10/15)	Wagon Train* (10/1)	The Lawrence Welk Show (9/24)
8:00	Pursuit†* (10/22)	Wagon Train	The Lawrence Welk Show
8:30	Pursuit	The Price Is Right	Ozzie and Harriet (10/1)
9:00	The Millionaire* (10/1)	The Milton Berle Show† (10/8)	The Donna Reed Show† (also with Carl Betz, Shelley Fabares, Paul Peterson) (9/24)
9:30	I've Got a Secret (10/1)	Bat Masterson†* (10/8)	The Patti Page Show† (10/1)
10:00	The Armstrong Circle Theatre* (10/1) alternating with The United States Steel Hour* (9/24)	This Is Your Life (9/24)	The Wednesday Night Fights
10:30	The Armstrong Circle Theatre alternating with The United States Steel Hour [High Adventure with Lowell Thomas (10/8) regularly displaced programming 8-9:00 above]	State Trooper (Rod Cameron) (resumed 9/24)	The Wednesday Night Fights

Thursday

	CBS	NBC	ABC
			6:30-7:00: The Huckleberry Hound Show† (animation) (10/2)
7:30	I Love Lucy [repeats] (10/2)	Jefferson Drum* (10/16)	Leave It to Beaver (10/2)

	CBS	NBC	ABC
8:00	December Bride (10/2)	The Ed Wynn Show† (10/2)	Zorro* (10/19)
8:30	Yancy Derringer† (Jock Mahoney, X Brands, Kevin Hagen, Frances Bergen) (10/2)	Concentration† (quiz) (10/2)	The Real McCoys (10/2)
9:00	Zane Grey Theatre* (10/2)	Behind Closed Doors†* (Bruce Gordon, host) (10/2)	The Pat Boone Show (10/2)
9:30	Playhouse 90* (9/25)	The Tennessee Ernie Ford Show (10/2)	The Rough Riders† (Kent Taylor, Jan Miner, Peter Whitney) (10/2)
10:00	Playhouse 90	You Bet Your Life (10/2)	Traffic Court (10/2)
10:30	Playhouse 90	Masquerade Party (10/2)	The Ben Hecht Show (10/2) 10:45: News with John Daly

7:30-8:30 WATZ The Michaels in Africa (family; Michael, Marjorie, daughters Carol and Jane) (11/20)

Friday

	CBS	NBC	ABC
7:30	Your Hit Parade (10/10)	Buckskin (10/10)	Rin Tin Tin (10/3)
8:00	Trackdown (9/26)	The Further Adventures of Ellery Queen†* (9/26)	Walt Disney Presents* (10/3)
8:30	The Jackie Gleason Show (with Buddy Hackett) (10/3)	The Further Adventures of Ellery Queen	Walt Disney Presents
9:00	The Phil Silvers Show (10/3)	M Squad* (9/19)	Man with a Camera† (Charles Bronson) (10/10)
9:30	The Lux Video Playhouse* (10/3) alternating with The Schlitz Playhouse of the Stars* (9/26)	The Thin Man (10/24)	77 Sunset Strip†* (10/10)
10:00	The Lineup (9/26)	The Friday Night Fights	77 Sunset Strip
10:30	Person to Person (9/26)	The Friday Night Fights	The Diamond Playhouse [repeats of The Schlitz Playhouse of the Stars] (9/26)

6:30-7:00 WPIX Casey Jones† (Alan Hale Jr.) (10/3)
8-8:30 WPIX Night Court† (10/24)
10-11:00 WPIX Divorce Court† (10/3)

CBS	NBC	ABC

1958-59 MIDSEASON

Saturday

	CBS	NBC	ABC
7:30	Perry Mason	People Are Funny	The Dick Clark Show
8:00	Perry Mason	The Perry Como Show	Jubilee, U. S. A.
8:30	Wanted: Dead Or Alive	The Perry Como Show	Jubilee, U. S. A.
9:00	The Gale Storm Show	Black Saddle† (Peter Breck, Russell Johnson, Anna Lisa) (1/10)	The Lawrence Welk Dancing Party
9:30	Have Gun, Will Travel*	Cimarron City	The Lawrence Welk Dancing Party
10:00	Gunsmoke	Cimarron City	The Sammy Kaye Show
10:30	Sea Hunt	The D. A.'s Man† [adapted from the James B. Horan book; John Compton, star]	local

Sunday

	CBS	NBC	ABC
4:00	Your Audience's		
4:30	Conquest		
5:00	Boots and Saddles	Omnibus alternating with Kaleidoscope	The Paul Winchell Show
5:30	Face the Nation	Omnibus alternating with Kaleidoscope	The Lone Ranger
6:00	The Twentieth Century	Meet the Press	The Twenty-six Men
6:30	Small World	The Annie Oakley Show	The Roy Rogers Show
7:00	Lassie	The Saber of London	You Asked for It
7:30	Bachelor Father alternating with The Jack Benny Show	The Buddy Bregman Music Shop† (1/11)	Maverick
8:00	The Ed Sullivan Show	The Steve Allen Show [displaced by local programming as of 4/5]	Maverick
8:30	The Ed Sullivan Show	The Steve Allen Show [subsequently displaced by Pete Kelly's Blues†* (4/5)]	Lawman
9:00	The General Electric Theatre	The Dinah Shore Chevy Show	Colt .45
9:30	Alfred Hitchcock Presents	The Dinah Shore Chevy Show	local (as of 11/9/58)
10:00	Richard Diamond, Private Detective* (resumed 2/15)	The Loretta Young Show	local
10:30	What's My Line?	local	Meet McGraw [repeats; as of 2/1]

Monday

	CBS	NBC	ABC
7:30	Name That Tune	Buckskin (as of 1/5)	Tales of the Texas Rangers (as of 1/5)

	CBS	NBC	ABC
8:00	The Texan	The Restless Gun	Polka-Go-Round† (1/5)
8:30	Father Knows Best	The Tales of Wells Fargo	Bold Journey
9:00	The Danny Thomas Show	Peter Gunn	The Voice of Firestone
9:30	The Ann Sothern Show	The Alcoa/Goodyear Theatre	Dr. I. Q. (resumed 12/15/58)
10:00	The Desilu Playhouse [monthly displaced by the Lucy-Desi Comedy Hour]	The Arthur Murray Party	This Is Music
10:30	The Desilu Playhouse [monthly displaced by the Lucy-Desi Comedy Hour]	local/Decoy	News with John Daly
		[The Bell Telephone Hour Adventures in Music† (1/18) regularly displaced programming 8:30-9:30 above]	

Tuesday

7:00			Union Pacific
7:30	Stars In Action	Dragnet	Sugarfoot alternating with Bronco
8:00	MacKenzie's Raiders (as of 2/2)	The George Gobel Show alternating with The Eddie Fisher Show [displaced by Steve Canyon (as of 4/7)]	Sugarfoot alternating with Bronco
8:30	To Tell the Truth	The George Gobel Show alternating with The Eddie Fisher Show [subsequently displaced by The Jimmy Rodgers Show† (3/31)]	Wyatt Earp
9:00	The Arthur Godfrey Show	The George Burns Show [displaced by The Californians (as of 4/7)]	The Rifleman
9:30	The Red Skelton Show	The Robert Cummings Show	The Naked City
10:00	The Garry Moore Show	The David Niven Show†* (4/7)	local
10:30	The Garry Moore Show	Mike Hammer	local

Wednesday

7:00			Tugboat Annie
7:30	New York Confidential† (Lee Tracy) (1/28)	Wagon Train	The Lawrence Welk Show

	CBS	NBC	ABC
8:00	local programming (as of 1/28)	Wagon Train	The Lawrence Welk Show
8:30	Trackdown (as of 1/28)	The Price Is Right	Ozzie and Harriet
9:00	The Millionaire	The Milton Berle Show	The Donna Reed Show
9:30	I've Got a Secret	Bat Masterson	The Patti Page Show
10:00	The Armstrong Circle Theatre alternating with The United States Steel Hour	This Is Your Life	The Wednesday Night Fights
10:30	The Armstrong Circle Theatre alternating with The United States Steel Hour	State Trooper [displaced by Theatre '59† (4/1)]	The Wednesday Night Fights

Thursday

	CBS	NBC	ABC
7:30	I Love Lucy [repeats]	Jefferson Drum	Leave It to Beaver
8:00	December Bride	Steve Canyon (as of 2/5); displaced by The Lawless Years† (James Gregory, Robert Karnes) (4/16)	Zorro
8:30	Yancy Derringer	It Could Be You!† (Bill Leyden, host) (12/4/58); displaced by The Oldsmobile Music Theatre†* (3/26)	The Real McCoys
9:00	Zane Grey Theatre	Behind Closed Doors	The Pat Boone Show
9:30	Playhouse 90	The Tennessee Ernie Ford Show	The Rough Riders
10:00	Playhouse 90	You Bet Your Life	Traffic Court
10:30	Playhouse 90	Masquerade Party	The Ben Hecht Show 10:45: News with John Daly

Friday

	CBS	NBC	ABC
7:30	Your Hit Parade	Buckskin [subsequently displaced by Northwest Passage as of 1/9]	Rin Tin Tin
8:00	Rawhide†* (1/9)	The Further Adventures of Ellery Queen	Walt Disney Presents
8:30	Rawhide	The Further Adventures of Ellery Queen	Walt Disney Presents
9:00	The Phil Silvers Show	M Squad	Tombstone Territory (resumed 3/31)
9:30	The Lux Video Playhouse alternating with The Schlitz Playhouse of the Stars	The Thin Man	77 Sunset Strip

	CBS	NBC	ABC
10:00	The Lineup	The Friday Night Fights	77 Sunset Strip
10:30	Person to Person	The Friday Night Fights	local

Summer Programming, 1959

Saturday
1-1:30 afternoon NBC Ten for Survival† (6/13)
3-4:00 afternoon NBC Woman!† (documentary discussion) (5/19)
7-7:30 CBS Bold Venture† (Dane Clark) (4/4)
8-9:00 NBC Perry Presents† (6/13)
9-9:30 CBS Face of Danger† [repeats of The Schlitz Playhouse of the Stars] (4/18)
9-9:30 CBS Brenner†* (Edward Binns, James Broderick) (6/6)
10:30-11:00 CBS Markham† (Ray Milland) (5/2)
10:30-11:00 ABC Sea Hunt (network change, as of 4/25)

Sunday
Noon-12:30 ABC This Is the Answer† (religious program) (6/21)

Tuesday
9-9:30 CBS Peck's Bad Girl† (Patty McCormack, Wendell Corey, Marsha Hunt) (5/5)

Wednesday
10:30-11:00 NBC Theatre '59† (4/1)

Thursday
8:30-9:00 NBC Too Young to Go Steady† (Brigid Bazlen, Donald Cook, Joan Bennett) (5/14)
9-9:30 NBC Laugh Line† (panel quiz; Dick Van Dyke, host) (4/16)
9:30-10:00 NBC 21 Beacon Street† (Dennis Morgan, Brian Kelly, James Maloney, Joanna Barnes) (7/2)

Friday
10:30-11:00 ABC Rescue 8† [the Los Angeles Rescue Squad documentary dramas; Jim Davis, Lang Jeffries, stars] (5/29)

> [programming schedules continued in Gianakos' Television Drama Series Programming: A Comprehensive Chronicle, 1959-1975 (Metuchen, N.J.: Scarecrow Press, 1978), and with regular supplements.]

SECTION III

Television Drama Series Programming:
A Comprehensive Chronicle, 1947-1959

ACTOR'S STUDIO

The Regulars: Marc Connelly, host with the second season.

The Episodes:

1. "Portrait of a Madonna" [by Tennessee Williams; the basis for
    his 1959 Broadway play; directed by Hume Cronyn] (9-26-48)
    Jessica Tandy
2. "Night Club" (10-3-48) Joan McCracken
3. "The Giant's Stair" [adapted from the Wilbur Daniel Steele
    story] (10-10-48)
4. "The Thousand Dollar Bill" (10-17-48) David Wayne, Jocelyn
    Brando
5. The Catbird Seat" [adapted from the James Thurber story]
    (10-24-48) Hiram Sherman, Mary Wickes
6. "The Inexperienced Ghost" (10-31-48) Dennis King, Rex
    O'Malley, Lou Gilbert
7. "Ropes" (11-7-48) Kim Hunter, Tom Ewell
8. "Esther" [adapted from the Jean Racine play] (11-14-48)
    Margaret Phillips, Will Hare, Jocelyn Brando
9. "Goody Bye, Miss Lizzie Borden" (11-21-48) Mary Wickes,
    Muriel Kirkland
10. "Ten Percent" (11-28-48) George Keane, Ruth Matteson
11. "The Night the Ghost Got In" (12-5-48) Nydia Westman
12. "The Widow of Wasdale Head" (12-12-48) John Forsythe, Lois
    Wheeler
13. "The Man Who Lost Christmas" (12-19-48) Russell Collins,
    George Keane, Jane Hoffman
14. "To the Lovely Margaret" (12-26-48) Bambi Lynn, Billy Red-
    field
15. "A Day in Town" [subsequently restaged for the Medallion The-
    atre episode of 12/12/53] (1-2-49) Warren Stevens, Joce-
    lyn Brando
16. "I'm No Hero" (1-9-49) Harry Bellaver, Marlon Brando
17. "The Little Wife" [adapted by David Shaw from the William
    Marik short story; subsequently restaged for the Revlon
    Mirror Theatre episode of 1/23/53] (1-16-49) Kim Hunter,
    Tom Ewell
18. "The Lady on 142" (1-23-49) Hiram Sherman, Jane Hoffman

19. "A Trip to Czardis" (1-30-49) Julie Harris, Steven Hill
20. "Jim Pemberton and His Boy Trigger" (2-6-49) June Walker, Billy Redfield, Russell Collins

21. "Zone of Quiet" [adapted from the Ring Lardner story] (2-13-49) John Sylvester, Eleanor Lynn, Anne Jackson
22. "The Tell-Tale Heart" [adapted from the Edgar Allan Poe story] (2-20-49) Warren Stevens, Russell Collins
23. "Greasy Luck" (2-27-49) Jocelyn Brando, Steven Hill
24. "Joe McSween's Atomic Machine" (3-6-49) Don Hanmer, Billy Redfield
25. "Dead Man" (3-13-49) Julie Harris, John Sylvester
26. "Concerning a Woman of Sin" (3-24-49) Tom Ewell
27. "Three O'Clock" [adapted from the Cornell Woolrich story] (3-31-49) Steven Hill, Frances Reid, Philip Bourneuf
28. "A Reputation" (4-7-49) Tom Ewell, Edith Atwater
29. "I Can't Breathe" [adapted from the Ring Lardner story] (4-14-49) Mary MacArthur, Kevin McCarthy, Ruth Matteson
30. "From Paradise to Butte" (4-21-49) Elliott Sullivan, Joshua Shelley
31. "Here Comes Spring" (4-28-49) Jack Gilford, Cloris Leachman, Edith King, Don Hanmer, Curt Conway, Ray Font, Nick Pursoff
32. "Somebody Has to Be Nobody" (5-5-49) Byron McGrath, Anne Summers, Lou Polan, Russell Collins, Phyllis Love
33. "Salt of the Earth" (5-12-49) Ann Shepherd, Edith King, Herbert Nelson
34. "Spreading the News" (5-19-49) E. G. Marshall, Julie Harris, Elliott Sullivan
35. "You're Breaking My Heart" (5-26-49) Cloris Leachman, John Sylvester, Richard Boone

Second Season

36. "The Canterville Ghost" [adapted from the Oscar Wilde story] (9-28-49) Edward Ashley, John Shay, Ruth Matteson, Wendy Barrie
37. "Terror in the Streets" (10-5-49) Ann Shepherd, Robert Carroll
38. "It's a Free Country" (10-12-49) Jessie Royce Landis, Don Hanmer, Nancy Franklin
39. "We'll Never Have a Nickel" (10-19-49) John Sylvester, Cloris Leachman
40. "Clarissa" (10-26-49) Jean Muir
41. "The Return to Kansas City" (11-1-49) Kim Hunter, Elliott Sullivan
42. "O'Halloran's Luck" (11-8-49) George Reeves, Cloris Leachman
43. "The Frame-Up" (11-15-49) Joshua Shelley, Cloris Leachman
44. "The Three Strangers" (11-22-49) Steven Hill, John Randolph
45. "The Thousand Dollar Bill" [restaged from 10/17/48] (11-29-49) Don Hanmer, Nancy Franklin

46. "The Man with the Heart in the Highlands" [by William Saroyan] (12-6-49) John McQuade, Butch Cavell
47. "The Midway" (12-13-49) Ann Shepherd, George Reeves
48. "A Child Is Born" [adapted from the Stephen Vincent Benet story; subsequently restaged for the Lux Video Theatre episode of 12/25/50] (12-20-49) Jean Muir
49. "Country Full of Sweden" (12-27-49) Dorothy Sands, Elliott Sullivan, E. G. Marshall
50. "Hannah" (1-3-50) Frances Ingalls, Eva Condon
51. "An Ingenue of the Sierras" (1-10-50) Elliott Sullivan, Nancy Franklin
52. "The Little Wife" [adapted by David Shaw from the William Marik story; restaged from 1/16/49] (1-17-50) Mary McLeod, George Keane
53. "The Timid Guy" (1-24-50) Philip Truex, Patricia Kirkland, Henry Jones
54. "Joe McSween's Atomic Machine" [restaged from 3/6/49] (1-31-50) Conrad Janis, Nancy Franklin
55. "Telas, the King" (2-3-50 at 9-10:00) Robert Pastene, Susan Douglas
56. "Mr. Mummery's Suspicion" (2-17-50 at 9-10:00) George Keane, Ann Shaw

THE PHILCO TELEVISION PLAYHOUSE (subsequently displaced by The Goodyear Theatre and The Alcoa Hour)

    under the auspices of The Equity-Philco Co.; Fred Coe, producer.

The Regulars: Bert Lytell, host (first season only)

The Episodes:

1. "Dinner at Eight" [adapted from the Edna Ferber and George S. Kaufman play; directed by Fred Coe] (10-3-48) Peggy Wood, Dennis King, Mary Boland, Vicki Cummings, Matt Briggs, Royal Beal, Joyce Van Patten, Philip Loeb, Jane Seymour, Judson Laire
2. "Rebecca" [adapted from the Daphne du Maurier novel] (10-10-48) Florence Reed, Bramwell Fletcher, Mary Anderson
3. "Counsellor-at-Law" [adapted from the Elmer Rice play] (10-17-48) Paul Muni
4. "Angel in the Wings" [adapted from the Bob Hilliard and Carl Sigman play] (10-24-48) Paul and Grace Hartman, Hank Ladd
5. "Street Scene" [adapted from the Elmer Rice play] (10-31-48) Betty Field, Erin O'Brien-Moore
6. "This Thing Called Love" (11-7-48) Ralph Bellamy, Peggy Conklin
7. "Camille" [adapted from the Alexandre Dumas story] (11-14-48) Judith Evelyn, Florence Eldridge, Rex O'Malley

8. "An Inspector Calls" [adapted from the J. B. Priestley play] (11-21-48) Walter Abel, George Coulouris
9. "I Like It Here" [adapted from the A. B. Shiffrin play] (11-28-48) Bert Lytell, Oscar Karlweis
10. "Suspect" [adapted from the Edward Percy and Reginald Denham play] (12-5-48) Ruth Chatterton, Bramwell Fletcher
11. "Parlor Story" [adapted from the William McCleery play] (12-12-48) Edith Atwater, Dean Jagger
12. "A Christmas Carol" [adapted from the Charles Dickens classic] (12-19-48) Dennis King; Bing Crosby and The Mitchell Boys' Choir in a film rendition of The Silent Night
13. "The Old Lady Shows Her Medals" [adapted from the James M. Barrie play] (12-26-48) Lucile Watson, Cameron Mitchell
14. "Ramshackle Inn" [adapted from the George Batson play] (1-2-49) Zasu Pitts, Joe Downing, Robert Tome
15. "Cyrano de Bergerac" [adapted from the Edmund Rostand play] (1-9-49) Jose Ferrer, Frances Reid, Robert Carroll, Ernest Graves
16. "Papa Is All" [adapted from the Patterson Greene play] (1-16-49) Mady Christians, Carl Benton Reid
17. "Pride and Prejudice" [adapted from the Jane Austen novel] (1-23-49) Madge Evans, John Baragrey
18. "Dark Hammock" [adapted from the Mary Orr and Reginald Denham play] (1-30-49) Peggy Wood, Sidney Blackmer, Mary Orr, Mary Wickes
19. "The Late Christopher Bean" [adapted from the Sidney Howard play] (2-6-49) Bert Lytell, Lillian Gish (her video debut)
20. "The Story of Mary Surratt" [adapted from the John Patrick play[(2-13-49) Dorothy Gish, Kent Smith
21. "Twelfth Night" [adapted from the Shakespeare classic; directed by Fred Coe] (2-20-49) Marsha Hunt (as Viola), John Carradine (as Malvolio), Vaughn Taylor (as Sir Andrew Aguecheek), Richard Goode (as Sir Toby Belch)
22. "St. Helena" [adapted from the R. C. Sherriff play] (2-27-49) Dennis King
23. "The Druid Circle" [adapted from the John Van Druten play] (3-6-49) Leo G. Carroll, Ethel Griffies
24. "Quality Street" [adapted from the James M. Barrie play] (3-13-49) Alfred Drake, Marsha Hunt
25. "Dinner at Antoine's" [adapted from the novel by Frances Parkinson Keyes] (3-20-49) William Eythe, Janet Blair
26. "Becky Sharpe" [adapted from William Makepeace Thackeray's Vanity Fair] (3-27-49) Clare Luce, Francis Bethencourt
27. "And Never Been Kissed" (4-3-49) Patricia Kirkland, William Redfield
28. "What Makes Sammy Run?" [by Budd Schulberg] (4-10-49) Jose Ferrer

[now under the title REPERTORY THEATRE]

29. "Mr. Mergenthwicker's Lobblies" (4-17-49) Vaughn Taylor

30. "Burlesque" [adapted from the George Manker Watters and Arthur Hopkins play] (4-24-49) Bert Lahr, Vicki Cummings
31. [as The Players' Club] "Macbeth" [adapted from the Shakespeare classic] (5-1-49) Walter Hampden (as Macbeth), Joyce Redman, Walter Abel, Leo G. Carroll

[now under the title ARENA THEATRE]

32. "Romeo and Juliet" [adapted from the Shakespeare classic] (5-15-49) Kevin McCarthy, Patricia Breslin
33. "This Time, Next Year" (6-5-49) Dennis King
34. "It Pays to Advertise" (6-12-49) Frank Albertson, Jean Sincere
35. "Summer Formal" [musical expressly composed for television] (6-19-49) George Canely, Kay Coulter, Jordan Bentley
36. "Jenny Kissed Me" [adapted from the Jean Kerr play] (6-26-49) Leo G. Carroll, Elinor Randel
37. "Dark of the Moon" [adapted from the Howard Richardson and William Berney play] (7-3-49) Carol Stone, Richard Hart
38. "For Love or Money" [adapted from the Frederick Hugh Herbert play] (7-10-49) William Post Jr. , Janet Blake

[resumed under the title THE PHILCO TELEVISION PLAYHOUSE]

39. "The Five Lives of Richard Gordon" (7-17-49) Melvyn Douglas
40. "You Touched Me!" [adapted from the play by Tennessee Williams and Donald Windham] (7-24-49) Dennis King, Mary McCord, William Prince
41. "The Fourth Wall" (7-31-49) Frances Reid, Douglas Clarke-Smith, Philip Tonge
42. "Enter Madame" [adapted from the Gilda Varesi and Dolly Byrne play] (8-7-49) Philip Bourneuf, Carol Goodner
43. "A Murder Has Been Arranged" [adapted from the Emlyn Williams play] (8-14-49) Donald Cook, Louisa Horton, Nancy Sheridan, William Terry
44. "Pretty Little Parlor" [adapted from the Claiborne Foster play] (8-21-49) Marta Linden, Paul Parks, Peggy McCay
45. "Three Cornered Moon" [adapted from the Gertrude Tonkonogy play] (8-28-49) Nina Foch, Kurt Richards

Second Season

46. "What Every Woman Knows" [adapted from the James M. Barrie play] (9-4-49) Margaret Phillips, Wesley Addy
47. "Pride's Castle" (9-11-49) Anthony Quinn, Catherine McLeod, Louise Albritton
48. "The Little Sister" (9-18-49) William Eythe, Jean Carson, Lola Montez, Patricia Breslin
49. "The Lonely" (9-25-49) William Prince, Kim Hunter
50. "The Queen Bee" (10-2-49) Clare Luce, Margaret Phillips, Paul McGrath

51. "Something's Got to Give" (10-9-49) John Beal, Haila Stoddard
52. "The Last Tycoon" [adapted from the F. Scott Fitzgerald novel] (10-16-49) John Baragrey, Leueen MacGrath
53. "Because of the Lockwoods" (10-23-49) Bramwell Fletcher, Marjorie Gateson
54. "Damion's Daughter" (10-30-49) Sidney Blackmer, Hildy Parks, John McQuade
55. "The House of the Seven Gables" [adapted from the Nathaniel Hawthorne classic] (11-6-49) Joan Chandler, Peter Cookson
56. "The Promise" (11-13-49) William Eythe, Kim Hunter
57. "Medical Meeting" (11-20-49) Frances Reid, Philip Bourneuf
58. "The Wonderful Mrs. Ingram" (11-27-49) Carol Goodner, Nydia Westman, Bernard Randall, Stephen Courtleigh
59. "Mist on the Waters" (12-4-49) Torin Thatcher, Margaret Phillips, Dan Morgan
60. "The Beautiful Bequest" (12-11-49) Loring Smith, Eli Wallach, Jean Castle
61. "The Strange Christmas Dinner" (12-18-49) Melvyn Douglas, Vaughn Taylor
62. "In Beauty Like the Night" (12-25-49) Alfred Ryder, Marly Alice Moore, Mercer McLeod, Kathleen Cordell
63. "Little Boy Lost" (1-1-50) John Newland, Alfreda Wallace, Maurice Cavell
64. "Bethel Merriday" [adapted from the Sinclair Lewis play] (1-8-50) Grace Kelly, Oliver Thorndike
65. "Murder at the Stork Club" (1-15-50) Haila Stoddard, Franchot Tone, Valerie Cossart, Ruth Matteson, Mary Orr, Sherman Billingsley
66. "The Marriages" [adapted from the Henry James story] (1-22-50] Henry Daniell, Margaret Phillips, Carol Goodner
67. "Uncle Dynamite" (1-29-50) Arthur Treacher
68. "The Sudden Guest" (2-5-50) John Baragrey, Jean Muir, Florence Reed, Tonio Selwart
69. "Ann Rutledge" (2-12-50) Grace Kelly, Stephen Courtleigh (as Abraham Lincoln)
70. "A Letter to Mr. Priest" (2-19-50) Nelson Olmsted, Leora Dana
71. "Home Town" (2-26-50) Faye Emerson, Barry Nelson, Betty Caulfield, Vinton Hayworth
72. "The Life of Vincent Van Gogh" (3-5-50) Everett Sloane, Chester Stratton, Jeff Morrow
73. "The Uncertain Molly Collicutt" (3-12-50) Lili Palmer, Philip Bourneuf, Ben Lackland
74. "The Trial of Steven Kent" (3-19-50) John Newland, Richard Frazier, Alfreda Wallace, Richard Sanders
75. "The Second Oldest Profession" (3-26-50) Felicia Montealegre, William Prince, Victory Jory
76. "Nocturne" (4-2-50) Leora Dana, Cloris Leachman
77. "Dirty Eddie" (4-9-50) Joseph Buloff, John Buckmaster, Judy Parrish, Vinton Hayworth
78. "The End Is Known" (4-16-50) Kent Smith, Cara Williams
79. "The Man in the Black Hat" (4-23-50) Virginia Gilmore, Les Tremayne, John McQuade

80. "The American" [adapted from the Henry James novel] (4-30-50) John Newland, Tonio Selwart, Irene Worth, Alfred Ryder
81. "The Feast" (5-7-50) Mildred Natwick, Margaret Wycherly, Colin Keith-Johnston
82. "Brat Farrar" (5-14-50) John Baragrey, John Newland
83. "The Charmed Circle" (5-21-50) Alfred Ryder, Betsy Blair
84. "Semmelweis" (5-28-50) Everett Sloane (as Semmelweis), Felicia Montealegre (as his wife), Guy Spaul (as Dr. Doanth), E. G. Marshall
85. "Sense and Sensibility" [adapted from the Jane Austen novel] (6-4-50) John Baragrey, Cloris Leachman, Madge Evans
86. "The Bump on Brannigan's Head" (6-11-50) J. Pat O'Malley, Vinton Hayworth, Leona Powers
87. "Anything Can Happen" (6-18-50) Joseph Buloff, Catherine Lynn
88. "Hear My Heart Speak" (6-25-50) Charlton Heston, Olive Deering
89. "The Reluctant Landlord" (7-2-50) Hume Cronyn, Haila Stoddard
90. "The Tentacles" (7-9-50) E. G. Marshall, John Seymour, Warren Stevens, Alfreda Wallace

Third Season

91. "High Tor" [adapted from the Maxwell Anderson play] (9-10-50) Felicia Montealegre, Vinton Hayworth, Alfred Ryder, Edgar Stehli
92. "The Long Run" (9-17-50) Francis Lederer, Vicki Cummings
93. "Dear Guest and Ghost" (9-24-50) Josephine Hull, Barry Nelson
94. "The Touch of a Stranger" (10-1-50) Leslie Nielsen, E. G. Marshall, Olive Deering
95. "The Vine That Grew on Fiftieth Street" (10-8-50) Bethel Leslie, William Farnum, Dorothy Sands, Frank Maxwell, Florida Friebus
96. "A Husband for Mama" (10-15-50) Muriel Kirkland, Vinton Hayworth, Betty Caulfield
97. "Portrait in Smoke" (10-22-50) Shepperd Strudwick, Olive Deering
98. "The Gambler" [adapted from the Fyodor Dostoevsky novel] (10-29-50) Alfred Ryder, Ethel Griffies, Philip Coolidge, Anne Crawford
99. "The Power Devil" (11-5-50) Kevin McCarthy, Augusta Dabney
100. "The Man Who Got Away with It" (11-12-50) Francis L. Sullivan, Donald Woods, Fred Beir, Margaret Hayes, Richard Sanders, Barbara Robbins
101. "I'm Still Alive" (11-19-50) Burgess Meredith, Haila Stoddard, Howard Smith, Walter Brooke
102. "Torch for a Dark Journey" (11-26-50) Bramwell Fletcher, Felicia Montealegre, Loring Smith

103. "Wacky, the Small Boy" (12-3-50) Butch Cavell, Bill Good-win, Aline MacMahon
104. "Bonanza" (12-10-50) Stanley Ridges, Dan Morgan, William Kemp, Alfreda Wallace
105. "Decoy" (12-17-50) John McQuade, Will Lee, Dulcy Jordan
106. "The Pupil" (12-24-50) John Newland
107. "Leaf out of a Book" (12-31-50) Vicki Cummings, Grace Kelly, Claudia Morgan, Lauren Gilbert, Dorothy Elder
108. "The Symbol: Jefferson Davis" (1-7-51) John Baragrey
109. "The Lost Diplomat" (1-14-51) Scott McKay, Frances Reid
110. "Confession" (1-21-51) John Ireland, Neva Patterson
111. "The Great Escape" [adapted from the Paul Brickall novel] (1-28-51) E. G. Marshall, Everett Sloane, Kurt Katch, Horace Braham
112. "A Matter of Life and Death" (2-4-51) Cloris Leachman, J. Pat O'Malley, John Ericson
113. "Kitty Doone" (2-11-51) Valerie Bettis
114. "Let Them Be Sea Captains" (2-18-51) E. G. Marshall, Florida Friebus, Anne Crawford
115. "The Man Who Bought a Town" (2-25-51) Vinton Hayworth, Dorothy Sands, Catherine Balfour, Oscar Homolka
116. "No Medals on Pop" (3-11-51) Brandon de Wilde, Fritz de Wilde, Ellen Cobb-Hill
117. "The Dark Corridor" (3-18-51) Wesley Addy, Stella Andrew, Viola Roache
118. "Bulletin 120" [based on an actual incident drawn from the files of The United States Public Health Service on conquering pellagra, also known as The Red Death] (3-25-51) Stephen Courtleigh, Robert Quarry, John Randolph, Dan Reed, Elinor Randel
119. "Parnassus on Wheels" (4-1-51) Muriel Kirkland, Russell Hardie, William Post Jr., Una O'Connor
120. "Routine Assignment" (4-8-51) Frank Maxwell, Billy M. Greene, James Westerfield, Stephen Elliott
121. "Hour of Destiny" (4-15-51) Anne Burr, Dorothy Peterson, Phyllis Love
122. "The Birth of the Movies" (4-22-51) John Newland, Jean Pearson; narrated by Lillian Gish
123. "Mr. Arcularis" (4-29-51) Nelson Olmstead, Leora Dana, Eddie Andrews, Stuart MacIntosh
124. "A Secret Island" (5-6-51) Mildred Natwick, Edgar Stehli
125. "The Visitors" (5-13-51) Sylvia Field, Don Murray, Romney Brent, Anne Ives
126. "Justice and Mr. Pleznik" (5-20-51) Joseph Buloff, Leo Penn, Naomi Riordan
127. "Rescue" (5-27-51) Sandy Campbell, Elliott Sullivan, John Randolph, James Westerfield
128. "The Adventures of Hiram Holliday" [the basis for the 1956 film series] (6-3-51) E. G. Marshall, Stella Andrew, Adia Kuzcetzoff
129. "The Fast Dollar" (6-10-51) Vaughn Taylor, Judith Parrish, J. Pat O'Malley

130. "Operation: Airlift" (6-17-51) David Swift, Frank Maxwell, Lauren Gilbert, Russell Hardie
131. "Dr. Hudson's Secret Journal" [adapted from the Lloyd C. Douglas novel; the basis for the 1955 filmed series] (6-24-51) Shepperd Strudwick, Colin Keith-Johnston
132. "The Plot" (7-1-51) Edgar Stehli, Dorothy Elder, Donald Buka, Alfreda Wallace
133. "Case History" (7-8-51) Nydia Westman, Jane Seymour, Peggy Allenby, Robert Pastene, Barbara Joyce, John Baruff, Leslie Woods
134. "I Want to March" [by H. R. Hays; subsequently restaged for Matinee Theatre episode of 2/24/56] (7-15-51) John Hoyt, Katherine Meskill, Enid Markey, Reynold Evans, Sandy Campbell, Patricia Pearton
135. "Pretend I Am a Stranger" (7-22-51) William Prince, Olive Deering, Marjorie Maricle, Henry Berkman, Richard Newton
136. "Television Story" (7-29-51) Sidney Blackmer, Walter Brooke, Gaby Rodgers
137. "The Return" (8-5-51) Biff Elliott, Robert Simon, Jill Kraft
138. "Ephraim Tutt's Clean Hands" (8-12-51) Parker Fennelly, Muriel Kirkland
139. "Come Alive" (8-19-51) Valerie Bettis
140. "Night at the Vulcan" (8-26-51) William Prince, Polly Rowles, Jerome Cowan
141. "This Time Next Year" (9-2-51) Edgar Stehli, Barbara Bolton, Nelson Olmstead
142. "Women of Intrigue" (9-9-51) Robin Craven, Madeleine Carrol, Murray Matheson, Philip Friend, Anthony Dawson
143. "The Wayward Season" (9-16-51) Margaret Wycherly, Kent Smith, Carol Goodner
144. "The Spur" (9-23-51) Alfred Ryder, Wesley Addy
145. "By-Line for Murder" (9-30-51) E. G. Marshall, Irene Moore, Vinton Hayworth
146. "Requiem for a Model A" (10-7-51) Edom Ryan, Mike Lewin, Dortha Duckworth

Fourth Season [now alternating with THE GOODYEAR THEATRE]

147. The Goodyear Theatre [its premiere]: "October Story" (10-14-51) Julie Harris, Leslie Nielsen
148. The Philco Television Playhouse: "Marcia Akers" (10-21-51) Olive Deering, James Gregory, Kendall Clark, James Daly
149. The Goodyear Theatre: "The Copper" (10-28-51) Wally Cox, Pat Carroll
150. The Philco Television Playhouse: "The Education of a Fullback" (11-4-51) Joseph Buloff, Vinton Hayworth
151. The Goodyear Theatre: "Flight to Freedom" (11-11-51) Bramwell Fletcher
152. The Philco Television Playhouse: "A Little Night Music" (11-18-51) Neva Patterson, Paul McGrath
153. The Goodyear Theatre: "The Eleventh Ward" (11-25-51) Margaret Phillips, Lydia St. Clair, Addison Richards, Penny Hays

154. The Philco Television Playhouse: "Incident at Golden's Creek" (12-2-51) Valentina Latimore, Michael Gorrin
155. The Goodyear Theatre: "Money to Burn" (12-9-51) Dan Morgan, Leona Powers, Patricia Breslin
156. The Philco Television Playhouse: "Perspective" (12-16-51) Everett Sloane, Augusta Dabney
157. The Goodyear Theatre: "I Was Stalin's Prisoner" (12-23-51) Edmon Ryan, Robert Vogeler
158. The Philco Television Playhouse: "The Sisters" (12-30-51) Leslie Nielsen, Natalie Schaefer, Dorothy Peterson
159. The Goodyear Theatre: "A Softness in the Wind" (1-6-52) Jean-Pierre Aumont
160. The Philco Television Playhouse: "Without Fear or Favor" [by H. R. Hays on the New York Times' help in dissolving a criminal Tweed political regime; subsequently restaged as a segment of Matinee Theatre (2/13/58)] (1-13-52) E. G. Marshall, Murvyn Vye, Brandon Peters
161. The Goodyear Theatre: "Raymond Schindler, Case One" (1-20-52) Rod Steiger, Frank Maxwell, Joseph Sullivan
162. The Philco Television Playhouse: "Segment" (1-27-52) Eileen Heckart, Mercer McLeod
163. The Goodyear Theatre: "Tour of Duty" (2-3-52) Neva Patterson
164. The Philco Television Playhouse: "Rich Boy" (2-10-52) Gene Lyons, Grace Kelly
165. The Goodyear Theatre: "Crown of Shadows" (2-17-52) Felicia Montealegre, Leslie Nielsen
166. The Philco Television Playhouse: "Tender Age" (2-24-52) Anthony Ross, Stella Andrew
167. The Goodyear Theatre: "Treasure Chest" (3-2-52) Cyril Ritchard, Patricia Crowley, Parker Fennelly
168. The Philco Television Playhouse: "Dusty Portrait" (3-9-52) John Newland
169. The Goodyear Theatre: "Three Letters" (3-16-52) Judith Evelyn
170. The Philco Television Playhouse: "The Best Laid Schemes" (3-23-52) Joseph Buloff, Eileen Heckart
171. The Goodyear Theatre: "Tigers Don't Sing" (3-30-52) John Beal, Wally Cox, Haila Stoddard
172. The Philco Television Playhouse: "The Room Next Door" (4-6-52) Arthur Treacher, Gene Lyons, Dorothy Elder
173. The Goodyear Theatre: "The Medea Cup" (4-13-52) Stella Andrew (as Cleopatra Selene), Harry Andrews (as Juba)
174. The Philco Television Playhouse: "The Basket Weaver" (4-20-52) Robert Keith, Walter Matthau
175. The Goodyear Theatre: "The Travelers" (4-27-52) Janet DeGore
176. The Philco Television Playhouse: "We Were Children" (5-4-52) Polly Rowles
177. The Goodyear Theatre: "The Twenty-third Mission" (5-11-52) Russell Hardie, Luis Van Rooten, Hilde Palmer

178. The Philco Television Playhouse: "A Cowboy for Chris" [by Walter Black and William Mandrek; subsequently restaged for the Matinee Theatre episode of 3/12/56] (5-18-52) Buster Crabbe, Brandon de Wilde

179. The Goodyear Theatre: "The Lantern Copy" (5-25-52) Neva Patterson, Paul Langton

180. The Philco Television Playhouse: "A Man's Game" [by David Swift; subsequently musicalized for the Kaiser Aluminum Hour episode of 4/23/57] (6-1-52) Patricia Benoit, Vinton Hayworth

181. The Goodyear Theatre: "Four Meetings" (6-8-52) John Baragrey, Leora Dana

182. The Philco Television Playhouse: "Flight Into Darkness" (6-15-52) Alfred Ryder, Robert Pastene

183. The Goodyear Theatre: "It's a Small World" (6-22-52) Arthur Treacher, Marcel Hillaire, Gaby Rodgers

184. The Philco Television Playhouse: "The Monument" (6-29-52) Vanessa Brown, E. G. Marshall, John Forsythe

185. The Goodyear Theatre: "Leaf Out of a Book" [restaged from episode of 12/31/50] (7-6-52) Claudia Morgan, Lauren Gilbert, Grace Kelly, Dorothy Elder

186. The Philco Television Playhouse: "A Letter to Mr. Priest" [restaged from 4/19/50] (7-13-52) Nelson Olmstead, Audra Lindley

187. The Goodyear Theatre: "The Trial of Steven Kent" (7-20-52) Paul Langton, Frank Albertson, Gordon Mills

188. The Philco Television Playhouse: "Brat Farrar" [restaged from episode of 5/14/50] (7-27-52) Richard Derr, Robert Pastene

189. The Goodyear Theatre: "The Dusty Drawer" (8-3-52) William Prince, Stefan Gierasch, Connie Ford

190. The Philco Television Playhouse: "The Five Fathers of Pepi" [adapted by Ira and Jane Avery; restaged for the United States Steel Hour episode of 8/29/56] (8-10-52) Jose Perez

191. The Goodyear Theatre: "The Witness" (8-17-52) Darren McGavin, Kim Stanley

192. The Philco Television Playhouse: "Three Sundays" (8-24-52) Walter Matthau, Murray Matheson, Malcolm Keen

193. The Goodyear Theatre: "Roman Fever" [adapted from the Edith Wharton novel; subsequently restaged for the Matinee Theatre episode of 11/18/55] (8-31-52) Eva LeGallienne, Edith Meiser, Peter Brandon

194. The Philco Television Playhouse: "The Last Hour" [adapted by Alvin Boretz from a story by Bob and Wanda Duncan; subsequently restaged for the Matinee Theatre episode of 7/18/57] (9-7-52) Maria Riva

Fifth Season

195. The Goodyear Theatre: "Holiday Song" [by Paddy Chayefsky] (9-14-52) Joseph Buloff, Herbert Berghoff, Frances Cheney, David Kerman

196. The Philco Television Playhouse: "The Thin Air" (9-21-52) Joan Lorring, Jo Van Fleet, Scott Forbes
197. The Goodyear Theatre: "The Room" (9-28-52) Haila Stoddard, Carmen Mathews, Edmund Ryan, Penny Hays
198. The Philco Television Playhouse: "The Black Sheep" (10-5-52) Jeffrey Lynn
199. The Goodyear Theatre: "O Romany" (10-12-52) Luis Van Rooten, Olive Deering, Anatole Winogradoff
200. The Philco Television Playhouse: "Uncertain Heritage" (10-19-52) Margalo Gillmore, Peter Brandon
201. The Goodyear Theatre: "Better Than Walking" (10-26-52) Veronica Lake, Darren McGavin
202. The Philco Television Playhouse: "The Winter of the Dog" (11-2-52) John Forsythe
203. The Goodyear Theatre: "The Darkness Below" (11-9-52) Ralph Meeker
204. The Philco Television Playhouse: "Parole Chief" (11-16-52) Sidney Poitier, Harry Townes
205. The Goodyear Theatre: "The Old Beginning" (11-23-52) Carmen Mathews, Frances Helm
206. The Philco Television Playhouse: "The Gift" (11-30-52) Johnny Johnston, Penny Hays
207. The Goodyear Theatre: "The Search" (12-7-52) Everett Chambers, Anthony Ross, Gene Lyons
208. The Philco Television Playhouse: "Tempest of Tick Creek" (12-14-52) Mildred Natwick, Crahan Denton, Edgar Stehli
209. The Goodyear Theatre: "Mr. Quimby's Christmas Hats" (12-21-52) Parker Fennelly, Ernest Truex
210. The Philco Television Playhouse: "Magic Morning" (12-28-52) Edna Best, Paul McGrath
211. The Philco Television Playhouse: "Double Jeopardy" (1-4-53) Vivian Blaine, Kevin McCarthy, Mary Beth Hughes, Howard St. John
212. The Philco Television Playhouse: "Pride's Way" (1-11-53) Shepperd Strudwick
213. The Philco Television Playhouse: "Two for One" (1-18-53) Cyril Ritchard, Valerie Cossart, Frances Ridgers, Murray Hamilton
214. The Philco Television Playhouse: "Elegy" (1-25-53) Charlton Heston, William Prince, Constance Ford
215. The Goodyear Theatre: "A Medal in the Family" (2-1-53) James Dunn
216. The Philco Television Playhouse: "The Reluctant Citizen" (2-8-53) Joseph Buloff, James Daly
217. The Philco Television Playhouse: "Mr. Pettengill Here" (2-15-53) Arthur Treacher
218. The Philco Television Playhouse: "Wings on My Feet" (2-22-53) Valerie Bettis, Tom Helmore
219. The Philco Television Playhouse: "The Trip to Bountiful" [by Horton Foote; the basis for his 1953 Broadway play] (3-1-53) Lillian Gish, John Beal
220. The Goodyear Theatre: "The Rumor" (3-8-53) Patricia Collinge, Joan Lorring, Leslie Nielsen
221. The Philco Television Playhouse: "The Gesture" (3-15-53)

Eva Gabor, Gene Lyons

222. The Philco Television Playhouse: "The Velvet Mitten" (3-22-53) Edward Everett Horton, Ernest Truex

223. The Goodyear Theatre: "Wish on the Moon" [directed by Delbert Mann] (3-29-53) Phyllis Kirk, Eva Marie Saint, Richard Carlyle

224. The Philco Television Playhouse: "A Young Lady of Property" [by Horton Foote; directed by Vincent J. Donehue and produced by Fred Coe] (4-5-53) Kim Stanley, Dorothy Sands, William Hansen, Joanne Woodward, James Gregory, Vivian Nathan, Fredye Marshall, Margaret Barker, Robert Donley

225. The Philco Television Playhouse: "The Recluse" (4-12-53) Dane Clark, Constance Ford

226. The Goodyear Theatre: "The Long Way Home" (4-19-53) Lloyd Bridges, Gaby Rodgers

227. The Philco Television Playhouse: "Printer's Measure" [by Paddy Chayefsky] (4-26-53) J. Pat O'Malley, Martin Newman, Peg Hillias

228. The Goodyear Theatre: "The Accident" (5-3-53) Jeffrey Lynn, Maureen Stapleton

229. The Philco Television Playhouse: "A Little Something In Reserve" (5-10-53) Tony Randall

230. The Goodyear Theatre: "The Oil Well" [an original story] (5-17-53) Dorothy Gish, E. G. Marshall

231. The Philco Television Playhouse: "Marty" [by Paddy Chayefsky; directed by Delbert Mann; the film version of 1955 earned The Academy Award as Best Picture, in addition to Oscars for Chayefsky and Mann] (5-24-53) Rod Steiger, Nancy Marchand, Esther Minciotti, Augusta Ciolli, Joe Mantell, Betsy Palmer, Lee Philips (Misses Minciotti and Ciolli, and Mr. Mantell repeated their television roles in the United Artists film)

232. The Goodyear Theatre: "Before I Wake" (5-31-53) Vicki Cummings, Betty Field

233. The Philco Television Playhouse: "The Way of the Eagle" (6-7-53) Jean-Pierre Aumont, Grace Kelly

234. The Goodyear Theatre: "Her Prince Charming" (6-14-53) Sylvia Field, James Dunn, Ernest Truex, Carol Wheeler

235. The Philco Television Playhouse: "Expectant Relations" [by Horton Foote] (6-21-53) Lily Cahill

236. The Goodyear Theatre: "Catch a Falling Star" (6-28-53) Faye Emerson, Shepperd Strudwick, Susan Strasberg

237. The Philco Television Playhouse: "The House in Athens" (7-5-53) Lydia St. Clair, Ray Rizzo

238. The Goodyear Theatre: "Nothing to Sneeze At" (7-12-53) Walter Matthau, Elaine Stritch, Maxine Stuart

239. The Philco Television Playhouse: "The Big Deal" [by Paddy Chayefsky] (7-19-53) Anne Jackson, David Opatoshu, Joanna Roos

240. The Goodyear Theatre: "The Young and the Fair" [adapted by N. Richard Nash from his own 1948 Broadway play; subsequently restaged for the Matinee Theatre episode of 5/23/58] (7-26-53) Joanne Woodward, Mildred Dunnock, Louisa Horton, Jenny Eagon

241. The Goodyear Theatre: "The Cipher" (8-2-53) Walter Matthau, Edward Binns, Ernest Truex
242. The Goodyear Theatre: "Ernie Barger Is Fifty" (8-9-53) Ed Begley, Carmen Mathews
243. The Philco Television Playhouse: "The Rainmaker" [by N. Richard Nash; the basis for his Broadway play of 1954; filmed by Paramount 1956] (8-16-53) Darren McGavin, Cameron Prud'homme, Joan Potter
244. The Goodyear Theatre: a) "Fadeout" Sidney Blackmer, Jessie Royce Landis; b) "The New Process" Walter Matthau, Ernest Truex, Geoffrey Lumb, Carole Matthews [teleplays by David Shaw; directed by Delbert Mann and produced by David Susskind; Hedda Hopper was hostess] (8-23-53)
245. The Philco Television Playhouse: "Other People's Houses" (8-30-53) Rod Steiger, Eileen Heckart
246. The Philco Television Playhouse: "Othello" [a streamlined version of the Shakespeare classic, produced by Fred Coe] (9-6-53) Torin Thatcher (as Othello), Walter Matthau (as Iago), Olive Deering (as Desdemona), Gene Lyons (as Cassio), Jack Manning (as Roderigo)
247. The Philco Television Playhouse: "The Baby" (9-13-53) Eli Wallach
248. The Goodyear Theatre: "Holiday Song" [a repeat showing of the Paddy Chayefsky teleplay of 9/14/52] (9-20-53) Joseph Buloff, Herbert Berghoff

Sixth Season

249. The Philco Television Playhouse: "0 for 37" (9-27-53) Arthur O'Connell, Eva Marie Saint, James Broderick
250. The Goodyear Theatre: "The Happy Rest" [by N. Richard Nash; subsequently restaged for the Matinee Theatre episode of 1/6/56] (10-4-53) Wallace Ford, Julie Harris, E. G. Marshall, Mildred Natwick
251. The Philco Television Playhouse: "The Bachelor Party" [by Paddy Chayefsky; filmed by United Artists 1957] (10-11-53) Eddie Albert, Kathleen Maguire
252. The Goodyear Theatre: "The Burgundy Touch" (10-18-53) Elliott Reid
253. The Philco Television Playhouse: "The Girl with the Stop Watch" (10-25-53) Lois Wilson, Betty Miller, Philip Abbott
254. The Goodyear Theatre: "The Haven" [directed by Delbert Mann] (11-1-53) Eileen Heckart, Bart Burns, Gloria Kelly, Charles Taylor
255. The Philco Television Playhouse: "Train to Trouble" (11-8-53) Hugh Marlowe, Maria Riva
256. The Goodyear Theatre: "John Turner" (11-15-53) Clifford Tatum Jr., Katherine Squire, Larry Gates
257. The Philco Television Playhouse: "Up Above the World So High" (11-22-53) Enid Markey
258. The Philco Television Playhouse: "The Sixth Year" (11-29-53) Kim Stanley, Warren Stevens, Kathleen Comegys
259. The Goodyear Theatre: "Madame Aphrodite" (12-6-53)

260. The Philco Television Playhouse: "The Midnight Caller" (12-13-53) Katherine Doucet, Betty Miller
261. The Goodyear Theatre: "Wings Over Barriers" [a documentary tribute to the fiftieth anniversary of powered flight; Eddie Albert, narrator] (12-20-53)
262. The Philco Television Playhouse: "The Glorification of Al Toolum" (12-27-53) Walter Matthau, Betsy Palmer, Murray Hamilton, Maxine Stuart
263. The Goodyear Theatre: "Moment of Panic" (1-3-54) Gene Lyons, Felicia Montealegre, Barbara Baxley
264. The Philco Television Playhouse: "The Hangman in the Fog" (1-10-54) Dane Clark
265. The Goodyear Theatre: "Here's Father" (1-17-54) Cyril Ritchard, Elaine Stritch, Van Dyke Parks, Valerie Cossart
266. The Philco Television Playhouse: "Smoke Screen" (1-24-54) Rod Steiger
267. The Goodyear Theatre: "The Brownstone" (1-31-54) Janice Rule, Kim Stanley, Eli Wallach
268. The Goodyear Theatre: "Game of Hide and Seek" (2-7-54) Mildred Dunnock, Betty Field
269. The Goodyear Theatre: "The Huntress" [by David Shaw] (2-14-54) Judy Holliday (her video debut), Tony Randall, Raymond Bramley, Bert Thorn
270. The Philco Television Playhouse: "Statute of Limitations" [by A. J. Russell; subsequently restaged for the Matinee Theatre episode of 3/15/56] (2-21-56) Martin Balsam, Barbara Baxley, Anne Jackson, Larry Gates
271. The Goodyear Theatre: "Buy Me Blue Ribbons" (2-28-54) Roddy McDowall, Enid Markey, Gale Page
272. The Philco Television Playhouse: "The Dancers" (3-7-54) Joanne Woodward, Janey DeGore, Jamie Broderick
273. The Goodyear Theatre: "The Inward Eye" (3-14-54) Phyllis Kirk, Steven Hill
274. The Philco Television Playhouse: "The Broken Fist" (3-21-54) Claude Dauphin
275. The Goodyear Theatre: "Native Dancer" [half hour segment this day only 9:30-10:00] (3-28-54) Gwen Verdon
276. The Philco Television Playhouse: "The Mother" [by Paddy Chayefsky; directed by Delbert Mann; produced by Fred Coe] (4-4-54) Cathleen Nesbitt, David Opatoshu, Maureen Stapleton, George L. Smith, Estelle Hemsley, Perry Wilson, Katherine Hynes, Dora Weissman, Anna Berger, Violeta Diaz
277. The Goodyear Theatre: "Spring Reunion" [by Robert Alan Aurthur; filmed by United Artists 1957] (4-11-54) Kevin McCarthy, Patricia Neal, Kathleen Maguire
278. The Philco Television Playhouse: "The King and Mrs. Candle" [by Sumner Locke Elliott; musicalized for the Producer's Showcase episode of 8/22/55] (4-18-54) Cyril Ritchard, Joan Greenwood
279. The Goodyear Theatre: "Old Tasselfoot" [by J. P. Miller] (4-25-54) E. G. Marshall, James Mullaney, Sada Thompson, Kevin Coughlin

280. The Philco Television Playhouse: The Joker" (5-2-54) Martin Balsam, Eva Marie Saint
281. The Philco Television Playhouse: "Miss Look-Alike" (5-9-54) Geraldine Page, Bibi Osterwald, Norman Fell
282. The Goodyear Theatre: "And Crown Thy Good" (5-16-54) Nehemiah Persoff, Voytek Dolinski, Anna Berger, Alice Mann, Dina Peskin
283. The Goodyear Theatre: "The Lawn Party" (5-23-54) Geraldine Fitzgerald, Patricia Fay, Larry Gates
284. The Philco Television Playhouse: "The Shadow of Willie Greer" (5-30-54) Dorothy Gish, Wright King, William Hanson
285. The Philco Television Playhouse: "Somebody Special" (6-6-54) Kim Stanley, Patty McCormack, Harry Townes
286. The Philco Television Playhouse: "Adapt or Die" [by Harry Muhelm] (6-13-54) Walter Matthau, John Qualen, Hildy Parks, Geoffrey Lumb
287. The Goodyear Theatre: "Write Me Out Forever" (6-20-54) Richard Kiley, Barbara Baxley, Eva Marie Saint
288. The Philco Television Playhouse: "Friday the Thirteenth" [subsequently restaged for the Matinee Theatre episode of 1/13/56] (6-27-54) Mark Roberts, Bartlett Robinson, Philip Abbott
289. The Goodyear Theatre: "Suitable for Framing" (7-4-54) Larry Blyden, Dorothy Hart, Mercer McLeod
290. The Philco Television Playhouse: "Man Drowning" (7-11-54) William Smithers, Barbara Joyce
291. The Goodyear Theatre: "Dear Harriet Heart-Throb" (7-18-54) Leora Dana, Betsy Palmer, Elliott Reid
292. The Philco Television Playhouse: "The Catamaran" [by J. P. Miller; subsequently restaged for the Matinee Theatre episode of 5/10/56] (7-25-54) Patrick O'Neal, Cloris Leachman, Barbara O'Neil
293. The Goodyear Theatre: "The Arena" (8-1-54) Anthony Franciosa, Steven Hill, Janice Rule, Bert Freed
294. The Philco Television Playhouse: "The Man in the Middle of the Ocean" (8-8-54) Kevin Coughlin, David Opatoshu, Larry Gates
295. The Goodyear Theatre: "Recoil" (8-15-54) Betsy Palmer, Philip Abbott
296. The Goodyear Theatre: "Star in the Summer Night" (8-22-54) Lili Darvas, Mark Richman
297. The Goodyear Theatre: "The Power of Suggestion" (8-29-54) Don DeFore, Phyllis Kirk, Murray Hamilton, Neva Patterson
298. The Philco Television Playhouse: "Run Like a Thief" (9-5-54) James Dean, Kurt Kasznar, Barbara O'Neil
299. The Goodyear Theatre: "The Big Man on Campus" (9-12-54) Richard Jaeckel, Stephen McNally, Constance Ford

Seventh Season

300. The Philco Television Playhouse: "Middle of the Night" [by Paddy Chayefsky; filmed by Columbia 1959] (9-19-54)

Steven Hill, Eva Marie Saint, E. G. Marshall, Mark Richman, Peg Hillias, Anna Berger

301. The Goodyear Theatre: "Guilty Is the Stranger" (9-26-54)
Paul Newman, Fay Bainter, Patricia Crowley

302. The Philco Television Playhouse: "Time Bomb" (10-3-54)
John Ireland, Nancy Kelly

303. The Goodyear Theatre: "The Personal Touch" (10-10-54)
Kevin McCarthy, Celia Lipton, Rex Thompson

304. The Philco Television Playhouse: "Man on the Mountaintop"
[by Robert Alan Aurthur; directed by Arthur Penn and produced by Gordon Duff] (10-17-54) Anne Meara, Steven
Hill, Anthony Rose, Loretta Leversee, Sidney Armus, Mark
Richmond, Gordon Clarke

305. The Philco Television Playhouse: "Time of Delivery" (10-31-
54) Helen Averbach, Martin Brooks, James Broderick

306. The Goodyear Theatre: "Flight Report" (11-7-54) E. G.
Marshall, Walter Matthau

307. The Philco Television Playhouse: "Crime Without Motive"
(11-14-54) William Lundmark, Mark Rydell, Burton Brinckerhoff, George Chandler

308. The Goodyear Theatre: "Thunder of Silence" (11-21-54)
Paul Newman

309. The Philco Television Playhouse: "Beg, Borrow or Steal"
[subsequently restaged for the Matinee Theatre episode of
7/17/56] (11-28-54) Anthony Ross

310. The Goodyear Theatre: "Last Boat from Messina" (12-5-54)
Martin Balsam, Doris Dowling

311. The Philco Television Playhouse: "Catch My Boy on Sunday"
[by Paddy Chayefsky] (12-12-54) Sylvia Sidney

312. The Goodyear Theatre: "Class of '58" [by Louis Peterson;
subsequently restaged for the Matinee Theatre episode of
7/9/56] (12-19-54) Jack Mullaney

313. The Philco Television Playhouse: "Run, Girl, Run" [by Sum-
ner Locke Elliott] (12-26-54) Lee Meriwether (at 19, Miss
America of 1955, in her acting debut), Mary Astor, Robert
Simon, Ann Shoemaker, Margot Stevenson, Lin McCarthy

314. The Goodyear Theatre: "A Case of Pure Fiction" [by Jerome
Ross; subsequently restaged for the Matinee Theatre episode
of 2/13/57] (1-2-55) Constance Ford, Laurence Hugo, Ann
Deere

315. The Philco Television Playhouse: "Walk into the Night" [by
Edmund Morris] (1-9-55) Walter Matthau, Neva Patterson

316. The Goodyear Theatre: "Doing Her Bit" (1-16-55) Janet
Blair, James Daly

317. The Philco Television Playhouse: "Anatomy of Fear" (1-23-
55) Geoffrey Horne, Rod Steiger, Perry Wilson

318. The Goodyear Theatre: "The Way Things Happen" [by George
Baxt] (1-30-55) Peter Lind Hayes, Mary Healey

319. The Philco Television Playhouse: "A Sense of Justice" [by
Gore Vidal] (2-6-55) E. G. Marshall, John Hudson

320. The Goodyear Theatre: "The Rabbit Trap" [by J. P. Miller;
directed by Delbert Mann and produced by Fred Coe; filmed
by United Artists in 1959] (2-13-55) Kevin Coughlin, Philip

Abbott, Kathleen Maguire, James Westerfield, Loretta Daye, Frank Bolger, Frank Rowan, Roy Fant

321. The Philco Television Playhouse: "The Assassin" [by Bernard Woolfe on the life of the exiled Bolshevik leader Trotsky and his Mexico City assassination by Jacques Mornard] (2-20-55) Jacob Ben-Ami, Nehemiah Persoff, Jo Van Fleet, Gaby Rodgers

322. The Goodyear Theatre: "Backfire" [by Marc Brandel; subsequently restaged for the Matinee Theatre episode of 7/12/56] (2-27-55) Mark Richman, Larry Gates

323. The Philco Television Playhouse: "Play Me Hearts and Flowers" (3-6-55) Johnny Desmond, Joey Adams

324. The Goodyear Theatre: "My Lost Saints" [by Tad Mosel; directed by Arthur Penn and produced by Gordon Duff and Robert Alan Aurthur] (3-13-55) Lili Darvas, Eileen Heckart, Richard Hendrick, Barbara Robbins, Tirrell Barbery

325. The Philco Television Playhouse: "Shadow of the Champ" [by Robert Alan Aurthur] (3-20-55) Jack Warden, Eli Wallach, Lee Grant, Tony Canzoneri

326. The Goodyear Theatre: "The Chivington Raid" (3-27-55) Albert Dekker, Steve McQueen, Gene Lyons

327. The Philco Television Playhouse: "Watch Me Die" (4-3-55) John Baragrey

328. The Goodyear Theatre: "Beloved Stranger" [by Sumner Locke Elliott] (4-10-55) Constance Ford, Margaret Hamilton, Hugh Reilly, John Alexander, Elaine Stritch, Maureen Hurley

329. The Philco Television Playhouse: "The Bold and the Brave" [by Calder Willingham as adapted from the 1953 play End as a Man which was the basis for the 1957 Columbia film The Strange One] (4-17-55) John Kerr, Mark Richman, Tom Tully

330. The Goodyear Theatre: "Do It Yourself" [by Jay Presson] (4-24-55) Pat Hingle, E. G. Marshall, Patrick O'Neal, Gena Rowlands

331. The Philco Television Playhouse: "Letter of Recommendation" [by Jerome Ross] (5-1-55) Maureen Hurley, Ross Martin, Miko Oscard, Betty Sue Albert, John Scailim, Augusta Dabney, Louise Busley

332. The Goodyear Theatre: "Visit to a Small Planet" [by Gore Vidal; directed by Jack Smight and produced by Gordon Duff; the basis for Vidal's 1957 Broadway play which was filmed by Paramount in 1960] (5-8-55) Cyril Ritchard, Theodore Bikel, Dick York, Sylvia Davis, Jill Kraft, Edward Andrews, Alan Reed, Bruce Kirby, Louis Edmonds, Alfred de la Fuente

333. The Philco Television Playhouse: "The Pardon-Me Boy" [by J. P. Miller] (5-15-55) Jackie Cooper

334. The Goodyear Theatre: "The Catered Affair" [by Paddy Chayefsky; directed by Robert Mulligan; filmed by Metro Goldwyn Mayer in 1956] (5-22-55) Thelma Ritter, J. Pat O'Malley, Pat Henning, Kathleen Maguire

335. The Philco Television Playhouse: "The Ghost Writer" [by Bernard Woolfe] (5-29-55) Betsy Palmer, Philip Abbott, Shepperd Strudwick

336. The Goodyear Theatre: "Mr. Dorothy Allen" [by Roger O.
      Hirson] (6-5-55) Martha Wright, Gene Lyons
337. The Philco Television Playhouse: "Total Recall" [by David
      Shaw] (6-12-55) Arthur Franz, Loretta Leversee, Robert
      Ellenstein, Lois Wheeler
338. The Goodyear Theatre: "End of the Mission" [by Roger O.
      Hirson] (6-19-55) Lili Darvas, Paul Picerni, Gaby Rod-
      gers, Roger De Koven
339. The Philco Television Playhouse: "Black Frost" (6-26-55)
      Pat Hingle, Bert Freed, Logan Ramsey, Lenka Peterson,
      Lonnie Chapman
340. The Goodyear Theatre: "Tangled Web" [by Audrey and William
      Roos] (7-3-55) John Conte, Joe Mantell, Phyllis Love,
      Tom Poston
341. The Philco Television Playhouse: "Incident in July" [by Calder
      Willingham] (7-10-55) Charles Dingle, Maureen Stapleton,
      Dick York, Peggy Maurer
342. The Goodyear Theatre: "Man on Spikes" [adapted from the
      Eliot Asinof novel] (7-17-55) Robert Morse, Warren Stev-
      ens, William Zuckert, Ned Glass, Janet Ward
343. The Philco Television Playhouse: "The Death of Billy the Kid"
      [by Gore Vidal; filmed by Warner Brothers in 1958 as The
      Left Handed Gun] (7-24-55) Paul Newman (who repeated
      this role in the film), Jason Robards Jr., Frank Overton,
      Michael Strong, Michael Conrad
344. The Goodyear Theatre: "The Prizewinner" [by Jerome Ross;
      subsequently restaged for the Matinee Theatre episode of
      3/7/57] (7-31-55) Betsy Palmer, Joan Lorring, Mark
      Daniels, Lamont Johnson
345. The Philco Television Playhouse: "A Room in Paris" [by
      Peggy Mann] (8-7-55) John Cassavetes, Kathleen Maguire,
      Al Markin
346. The Goodyear Theatre: "The Takers" [adapted from the Wil-
      liam Manchester novel City of Anger] (8-14-55) Martin
      Balsam, Ed Begley, Luis Van Rooten
347. The Philco Television Playhouse: "Gretel" [by Vance Bour-
      jaily; subsequently restaged for the Matinee Theatre episode
      of 8/2/56] (8-21-55) Eva Stern, Geoffrey Horne, Edmon
      Ryan
348. The Goodyear Theatre: "Spring Reunion" [by Robert Alan
      Aurthur; restaged from 4/11/54] (8-28-55) Philip Abbott,
      Kathleen Maguire

Eighth Season [premiering THE ALCOA HOUR]

349. The Philco Television Playhouse: "The Miss America Story"
      [by Roger O. Hirson] (9-4-55) Lee Meriwether, Johnny
      Desmond, Charlotte Rae
350. The Goodyear Theatre: "Suit Yourself" [by James Fritzell,
      author of the Mr. Peepers television series] (9-11-55)
      Eddie Bracken, Kenny Delmar
351. The Philco Television Playhouse: "The Outsiders" [by Bernard
      Woolfe] (9-18-55) Arthur O'Connell, Jason Robards Jr.,
      Eli Wallach, Pat Henning, Jo Rabb

352. The Goodyear Theatre: "The Merry-Go-Round" [by Mann Rubin] (9-25-55) Anne Jackson, Lee Philips
353. The Philco Television Playhouse: "A Man Is Ten Feet Tall" [by Robert Alan Aurthur; filmed by Metro Goldwyn Mayer in 1956 as Edge of the City] (10-2-55) Don Murray, Sidney Poitier, Martin Balsam (Mr. Poitier repeated his role in the film)
354. The Goodyear Theatre: "The Expendable House" [by Reginald Rose] (10-9-55) John Cassavetes, Glenda Farrell, Pat Hingle, Jack Klugman, Paul Hartman, Gena Rowlands
355. The Alcoa Hour (its premiere): "The Black Wings" [by Joseph Schull] (10-16-55) Wendell Corey, Robert Flemyng, Ann Todd
356. The Philco Television Playhouse: "A Business Proposition" [by John Vlahos] (10-23-55) Mildred Dunnock, David Opatoshu, Mikhail Rasumny, Jo Van Fleet, Jean Stapleton
357. The Alcoa Hour: "The Small Servant" (10-30-55) Laurence Harvey, Halliwell Hobbes, Diane Cilento, John Laurie
358. The Philco Television Playhouse: "The Mechanical Heart" [by Al Getto] (11-6-55) Ralph Bellamy, Charles Dingle, Jack Klugman, Edward Binns, Jack Warden
359. The Alcoa Hour: "A Girl Can Tell" (11-13-55) Diana Lynn, William Redfield, Dean Harens, Jack Whiting, Paul McGrath, Carleton Carpenter, Natalie Trundy
360. The Philco Television Playhouse: "One Mummy Too Many" [by Alvin Sapinsley; subsequently restaged for the Matinee Theatre episode of 9/25/57] (11-20-57) Tony Randall, Henry Jones, David Opatoshu, Eva Gabor
361. The Alcoa Hour: "Thunder in Washington" [by David Davidson] (11-27-55) Melvyn Douglas, Ed Begley, James Gregory, Russell Collins, Howard St. John
362. The Philco Television Playhouse: "The Trees" [by Jerome Ross] (12-4-55) Lili Darvas, Sal Mineo, Pat Hingle, Frances Starr, Kay Medford, Edward Binns
363. The Alcoa Hour: "Undertow" [by Jack Kelsey] (12-11-55) John Kerr, Teresa Wright, Thomas Mitchell, Cathleen Nesbitt, Robert Preston
364. The Philco Television Playhouse: "Christmas 'til Closing" [by Ernest Kinoy; directed by Herbert Hirschman] (12-18-55) Jessica Tandy, Hume Cronyn, Eileen Heckart, Natalie Trundy, Malcolm Broderick
365. The Alcoa Hour: "Amahl and the Night Visitors" [the Gian-Carlo Menotti Christmas opera, restaged and sponsored by Showcase Productions] (12-25-55) Bill McIver, soprano, et al.
366. The Philco Television Playhouse: "Rise Up and Walk" [by Robert Anderson] (1-1-56) June Lockhart, Eddie Albert, Jack Klugman
367. The Alcoa Hour: "Man on a Tiger" [by Roger O. Hirson] (1-8-56) Melvyn Douglas, Tony Randall, Keenan Wynn, Polly Rowles
368. The Philco Television Playhouse: "This Land Is Mine" [by Richard Wendley] (1-15-56) Ed Begley, Jack Lord, Pat Hingle, Biff McGuire

369. The Goodyear Theatre: "A Patch of Faith" [by John H. Secon-
dari] (1-22-56) Theodore Bikel, Lee J. Cobb
370. The Philco Television Playhouse: "The Starlet" [by John Vla-
hos] (1-29-56) Ralph Bellamy, Betsy Palmer, Jerome Thor
371. The Alcoa Hour: "Long After Summer" [adapted by Dale Wasserman from the novel by Robert Nathan] (2-5-56) Robert
Preston, Susan Kohner, Cameron Prud'homme
372. The Philco Television Playhouse: "Kyria Katina" [by John
Vlahos] (2-12-56) Viveca Lindfors, William Bendix
373. The Alcoa Hour: "Tragedy in a Temporary Town" [by Reginald Rose; directed by Sidney Lumet] (2-19-56) Lloyd
Bridges, Betty Lou Keim, Edward Binns
374. The Goodyear Theatre: "The Terrorists" [by Jerome Cooper-
smith] (2-26-56) E. G. Marshall, Tom Carlin, Michael
Higgins, Peggy Maurer
375. The Alcoa Hour: "Man on Fire" [by Melvin Wald and Jack
Jacobs; filmed by Metro Goldwyn Mayer in 1957] (3-4-56)
Ed Begley, Tom Ewell, Jerome Thor, Neva Patterson
376. The Goodyear Theatre: "Conspiracy of Hearts" [by Dale Ritt]
(3-11-56) Kim Stanley
377. The Alcoa Hour: "Doll Face" [by Jerome Ross] (3-18-56)
Glenda Farrell, Frank McHugh
378. The Goodyear Theatre: "Joey" [by Louis Peterson] (3-25-56)
Anthony Perkins, Kim Stanley
379. The Alcoa Hour: "Finkle's Comet" [by Herman Raucher]
(4-1-56) David Opatoshu, Hans Conried
380. The Goodyear Theatre: "Footlight Frenzy" [by Jack Kelsey]
(4-8-56) William Bendix, Martha Scott
381. The Alcoa Hour: "Even the Weariest River" [by Alvin Sapinsley; the title derives from Swinburne's Garden of Proserpine]
(4-15-56) Lee Grant, Franchot Tone, Boris Karloff, Jason
Robards Jr., Christopher Plummer
382. The Goodyear Theatre: "Career Girl" [by Jerome Ross]
(4-22-56) Jessie Royce Landis, Betsy Palmer, Gene Lyons
383. The Alcoa Hour: "Paris and Mrs. Perlman" (4-29-56)
Gertrude Berg, Claude Dauphin, Joey Walsh, Sanford Meisner
384. The Goodyear Theatre: "The Sentry" [by John Gay] (5-6-56)
George Grizzard, Frank Overton
385. The Alcoa Hour: "President" [by David Davidson] (5-13-56)
Fred Clark, Mildred Dunnock, Everett Sloane, Claude Rains
386. The Goodyear Theatre: "In the Days of Our Youth" [by John
H. Secondari] (5-20-56) Roddy McDowall, Kim Stanley
387. The Alcoa Hour: "The Confidence Man" [by Ernest Kinoy]
(5-27-56) Hume Cronyn, Dorothy Sands, Jessica Tandy
388. The Goodyear Theatre: "The Primary Colors" [by Jack Par-
tiz] (6-3-56) Judith Evelyn, Cathleen Nesbitt, Tom Carlin
389. The Alcoa Hour: "The Magic Horn" [by Herman Raucher, on
a Dixieland Jazz band in 1920's Chicago] (6-10-56) Sal
Mineo, Ralph Meeker
390. The Goodyear Theatre: "Sound the Pipes of Pan" [by John
Vlahos, on Greek immigrant life in America] (6-17-56)
Theodore Bikel
391. The Alcoa Hour: "The Archangel Harrigan" [by Lorenzo
Semple Jr.] (6-24-56) Darren McGavin, Janice Rule

392. The Goodyear Theatre: "The Film Maker" [by Melvin Wald
      and Jack Jacobs] (7-1-56) Ralph Meeker, House Jameson,
      George Macready, Efrem Zimbalist Jr.
393. The Alcoa Hour: "The Piper of St. James" (7-8-56) Patrick
      O'Neal, Brenda Forbes, Barry Jones
394. The Goodyear Theatre: "Country Fair Time" (7-15-56) An-
      thony Franciosa, Patricia Barry
395. The Alcoa Hour: "Sister" [adapted by William Templeton from
      the Sidney Carroll drama] (7-22-56) Gladys Cooper, Cath-
      leen Nesbitt, Vincent Price
396. The Goodyear Theatre: "Pencil Sketch" [by Abby Mann] (7-
      29-56) Elliott Nugent, Margo Hartman
397. The Alcoa Hour: "Kiss and Tell" [adapted from the Frederick
      Hugh Herbert play] (8-5-56) Robin Morgan, Warren Ber-
      linger, Polly Rowles, Jerome Cowan, Howard St. John, Lois
      Bolton, Marion Randall, John Connell
398. The Goodyear Theatre: "Proud Passage" [by Joseph Schull]
      (8-12-56) Jason Robards Jr., Patricia Cutts, John Drainis
399. The Alcoa Hour: "The Big Vote" [by David Karp] (8-19-56)
      Ed Begley, Walter Matthau, Kathleen Maguire
400. The Goodyear Theatre: "Grow Up" [by Peggy Lamson] (8-26-
      56) Carol Lynley, Clay Hall
401. The Alcoa Hour: "The Girl in Chapter One" [by Elihu Winer]
      (9-2-56) Joanne Woodward, James Daly, Madge Evans
402. The Goodyear Theatre: "Ark of Safety" [by Frank Goforth and
      Howard Richardson] (9-9-56) Beulah Bondi, Andrew Duggan

Ninth Season

403. The Alcoa Hour: "Flight into Danger" [by Arthur Hailey] (9-
      16-56) Macdonald Carey, Liam Redmond, Geoffrey Horne,
      Patricia Barry
404. The Goodyear Theatre: "Maestro" [by John Vlahos] (9-23-56)
      Carmen Mathews, Gregory Ratoff, Kenny Delmar
405. The Alcoa Hour: "The Big Wave" (9-30-56) Hume Cronyn,
      Richard Morse, Carol Lynley, Rip Torn, Joseph Anthony
406. The Goodyear Theatre: "Missouri Legend" [adapted by Ernest
      Kinoy from the story by E. B. Ginty] (10-7-56) Robert
      Preston, Thomas Carlin
407. The Alcoa Hour: "Key Largo" [adapted by Alvin Sapinsley
      from the Maxwell Anderson play] (10-14-56) Anne Ban-
      croft, Alfred Drake, Victor Jory, Lorne Greene, J. Carrol
      Naish
408. The Goodyear Theatre: "All Summer Long" [adapted by Robert
      Anderson from his own 1954 Broadway play] (10-28-56)
      Raymond Massey, Malcolm Broderick, William Shatner
409. The Alcoa Hour: "Morning's at Seven" [adapted by Robert
      Wallstens from the Paul Osborn play] (11-4-56) Dorothy
      Gish, Lillian Gish, Evelyn Varden, David Wayne, June
      Lockhart, Dorothy Stickney
410. The Goodyear Theatre: "Stardust II" [by Herman Raucher]
      (11-11-56) John Forsythe, Martin Balsam, Thomas Carlin,
      Clu Gulager, William Traylor

411. The Alcoa Hour: "Merry Christmas, Mr. Baxter" [adapted by William McCleery from the book by Edward Streeter] (12-2-56) John McGiver, Dennis King, Margaret Hamilton, Cornelia Otis Skinner, Patricia Benoit
412. The Alcoa Hour: "Adventure in Diamonds" (12-9-56) Viveca Lindfors, Gary Merrill, Cameron Prud'homme, Robert Flemyng, Geoffrey Toone
413. The Alcoa Hour: "The Stingiest Man in Town" [a musicalized adaptation of the Charles Dickens classic A Christmas Carol] (12-23-56; 9-10:30 this day only) Basil Rathbone, Vic Damone, Johnny Desmond, Patrice Munsel, Robert Weede, Betty Madigan, Marilyn Greene, The Four Lads
414. The Goodyear Theatre: "A Murder Is Announced" [adapted from the Agatha Christie novel] (12-30-56) Gracie Fields, Roger Moore, Jessica Tandy
415. The Alcoa Hour: "A Double Life" [adapted by Maurice Valency from the 1947 film scenario by Ruth Gordon and Garsin Kanin] (1-6-57) Eric Portman, Nina Foch, Shelley Winters
416. The Alcoa Hour: "Ride the Wild Mare" [by Alfred D. Gato] (1-20-57) Lloyd Bridges, Betty Field
417. The Goodyear Theatre: "Nobody's Town" [by Harold Swanton; filmed by Columbia in 1962 as The Hellions] (1-27-57) Jason Robards Jr., Augusta Dabney, George Maharis
418. The Alcoa Hour: "No License to Kill" [by Alvin Boretz; Victor Reisel was narrator] (2-3-57) Eddie Albert, Hume Cronyn, Maureen Stapleton, Eileen Heckart
419. The Alcoa Hour: "The Animal Kingdom" [adapted from the Philip Barry play] (2-17-57) Robert Preston, Meg Mundy, Joanne Linville
420. The Goodyear Theatre: "The Princess Back Home" [by John Van Druten] (2-24-57) John Beal, Celeste Holm, Richard Derr
421. The Alcoa Hour: "The Last Train to Pusan" [adapted by Theodore Apstein from the story by Vern Sneider] (3-3-57) Gary Merrill
422. The Alcoa Hour: "The Original Miss Chase" (3-17-57) Nanette Fabray, Darren McGavin, Hirman Sherman
423. The Goodyear Theatre: "First Love" [adapted by Ellen McCracken from the play by Gertrude Schweitzer; initially presented on the Matinee Theatre episode of 3/13/57] (3-24-57) James Daly, Lili Darvas, Joel Crothers
424. The Alcoa Hour: "The Big Build-Up" (3-31-57) E. G. Marshall, George Peppard, Jason Robards Jr.
425. The Alcoa Hour: "Nothing to Lose" [by Jerome Ross] (4-14-57) Ralph Bellamy, James Whitmore, Robert Emhardt
426. The Goodyear Theatre: "The Gene Austin Story" [by Ernest Kinoy] (4-21-57) George Grizzard, Eddie Andrews, Scott McKay
427. The Alcoa Hour: "Mechanical Manhunt" [by Harold Swanton] (4-28-57) Richard Kiley, Sallie Brophy
428. The Goodyear Theatre: "A Will to Live" [by Jerome Ross] (5-12-57) Betsy Blair, Walter Matthau
429. The Alcoa Hour: "Protégé" [by Philo Higley] (5-19-57) Betsy Palmer, Ed Wynn, Skip Homeier, Evelyn Varden

430. The Goodyear Theatre: "The Treasure Hunters" [adapted by Michael Dyne from the story by Henry James] (5-26-57) Donald Cook, Roddy McDowall, Rex Thompson, Mary Ellis

431. The Alcoa Hour: "Mrs. Gilling and the Skyscraper" [by Sumner Locke Elliott] (6-9-57) Helen Hayes, Halliwell Hobbes, Jack Klugman, Wilfrid Hyde-White, Leueen McGrath

432. The Goodyear Theatre: "Your Every Wish" [adapted by Clifford Goldsmith from the short story by Walter Brooks] (6-16-57) Don Ameche, Neva Patterson, Audrey Chrustie

433. The Alcoa Hour: "Awake with Fear" [by David Driscoll] (6-23-57) Eddie Bracken, Henry James, Emily Horsley, Lois Bolton, Virginia Kaye, Dennis Kohler

434. The Goodyear Theatre: "The Legacy" [by Steven Gethers] (6-30-57) Melvyn Douglas, Walter Matthau, Philip Abbott, June Dayton, Roland Winters, Sally Chamberlain

435. The Alcoa Hour: "Hostages to Fortune" [by John H. Secondari] (7-7-57) Anne Bancroft, Rip Torn, Charles Korvin

436. The Goodyear Theatre: "Backwoods Cinderella" [by Peggy Lamson] (7-14-57) Abigail Kellogg, Martha Scott, Larry Hagman, Enid Markey, Tuesday Weld, William Traylor, Peg Hillias

437. The Alcoa Hour: "He's for Me" [by Michael Dreyfuss and Michael Brown] (7-21-57) Larry Blyden, Roddy McDowall, Jane Keane, Elaine Stritch, Joan Hovis

438. The Goodyear Theatre: "Rumblin' Galleries" [adapted by Therese Lewis from stories by Booth Tarkington] (7-28-57) Betsy Palmer, John Baragrey, William Redfield, Kurt Kasznar

439. The Alcoa Hour: "Weekend in Vermont" [by Ernest Kinoy] (8-4-57) Tony Randall, Dorothy Stickney, Howard Lindsay, Patricia Barry

440. The Alcoa Hour: "The Trouble with Women" [by John Vlahos] (8-11-57) Audrey Christie, Walter Matthau, Hirman Sherman

441. The Goodyear Theatre: "The Dark Side of the Moon" [by Arthur Sainer] (8-18-57) Alexander Scourby, Kathleen Maguire, Biff McGuire

442. The Alcoa Hour: "The Littlest Little Leaguer" [by Blanche Analts] (8-25-57) Jacob Kalish, Peter Lazer, Nehemiah Persoff, Vivian Nathan

443. The Alcoa Hour: "No License to Kill" [by Alvin Boretz; restaged with Governor Abraham A. Ribicoff of Connecticut as narrator] (9-1-57) Eddie Albert, Maureen Stapleton

444. The Goodyear Theatre: "The House" [by Art Wallace] (9-8-57) Jay C. Flippen, Mark Richman, Hope Emerson

445. The Alcoa Hour: "15 October 1864" [by Louis Pelletier] (9-15-57) Alan Nixon, James Pritchett, Paul Tripp

446. The Alcoa Hour: "Night" [adapted by Bill Barrett] (9-22-57) Franchot Tone, Jason Robards Jr., E. G. Marshall

447. The Goodyear Theatre: "The Best Wine" [by John Vlahos, on a Greek immigrant who became a theatre tycoon] (9-29-57) Walter Slezak, Inga Swenson

As of 9/30/57 The Alcoa Theatre and The Goodyear Theatre (now half-hour programs) alternately played under the title A Turn of Fate, a filmed series which is chronicled elsewhere.

STUDIO ONE

Sponsored by Westinghouse; produced by Worthington Miner.

The Episodes:

1. "The Storm" [adapted from a mystery story] (11-7-48) Margaret Sullavan, Dean Jagger
2. "Let Me Do the Talking" (11-28-48) John Conte, Susan Douglas
3. "The Medium" [the Gian-Carlo Menotti 1947 opera] (12-12-48) Marie Powers, Leo Coleman, Beverly Dame
4. "Not So Long Ago" (12-26-48) Katherine Bard, Karl Weber, Jerome Thor
5. "The Outward Room" (1-9-49) Ruth Ford, Bramwell Fletcher, John Forsythe
6. "Blind Alley" [adapted from the John Warwick play] (1-30-49) Jerome Thor, Bramwell Fletcher
7. "Holiday" [adapted from the Philip Barry play] (2-20-49) Valerie Bettis
8. "Julius Caesar" [a modern dress adaptation of the Shakespeare play; directed by Paul Nickell] (3-6-49) William Post Jr. (as Julius Caesar), Robert Keith (as Brutus), Joseph Silver (as Decius), Vaughn Taylor (as Casca), Emmett Rogers (as Metellus), John O'Shaughnessy (as Cassius), Philip Bourneuf (as Marc Antony), Ruth Ford (as Calpurnia)
9. "Berkeley Square" [adapted from the John L. Balderston and J.C. Squire play] (3-20-49) Leueen MacGrath, William Prince, Leslie Woods
10. "Redemption" [adapted from the Leo Tolstoy play] (4-3-49) Richard Hart, Joan Wetmore
11. "Moment of Truth" (4-17-49) Leo G. Carroll
12. "Julius Caesar" [adapted from the Shakespeare play; restaged from 3/6/49] (5-1-49) William Post Jr., Robert Keith, Richard Hart (as Marc Antony)
13. "The Glass Key" [adapted from the Dashiel Hammett mystery] (5-11-49) Don Briggs, Lawrence Fletcher, Jean Carson
14. "Shadow and Substance" [adapted from the Paul Vincent Carroll play] (5-18-49) Leo G. Carroll, Margaret Phillips
15. "Flowers from a Stranger" (5-25-49) John Conte, Felicia Montealegre, Yul Brynner
16. "The Dybbuk" [adapted from the S. Ansky play; directed by Paul Nickell] (6-1-49) Mary Sinclair, James Lamphier, Arnold Moss
17. "Boy Meets Girl" [adapted from the Samuel and Bella Spewack play] (6-8-49) Hume Cronyn, Michael Harvey, Edward Andrews, Frances Compton
18. "Smoke" (6-15-49) Leueen MacGrath, Charlton Heston, Josephine Brown, Mary Sinclair, Ferdi Hoffman, Guy Spaull
19. "June Moon" [adapted from the Ring Lardner and George S. Kaufman play] (6-22-49) Glenda Farrell, Jean Carson, Eva Marie Saint, Jack Lemmon
20. "The Shadowy Third" [adapted from the Ellen Glasgow play] (6-29-49) Helmut Dantine, Frances Fuller, Margaret Phillips, Sandra Ann Wigginton

Second Season

21. "Kyra Zelas" (9-12-49) Felicia Montealegre, Richard Hart
22. "The Rival Dummy" (9-19-49) Paul Lukas, Anne Francis
23. "The Outward Room" [restaged from 1/9/49] (9-26-49) Ruth Ford, Bramwell Fletcher, Charlton Heston
24. "Mrs. Moonlight" [adapted from the Benn W. Levy play] (10-3-49) Katherine Bard, James MacCall, Una O'Connor
25. "The Light That Failed" [adapted from the Rudyard Kipling classic] (10-10-49) Felicia Montealegre, Richard Hart
26. "The Storm" [restaged from 11/7/48] (10-17-49) Marsha Hunt, John Rodney, Dean Harens
27. "Battleship Bismark" [staged in a 65' by 45' studio; directed by Paul Nickell] (10-24-49) Paul Lukas, Vaughn Taylor
28. "Concerning a Woman of Sin" (10-31-49) Iris Mann, E. G. Marshall, Dean Harens, Hildy Parks, James MacCall
29. "The Husband" (11-7-49) Margaret Phillips, Robert Favart
30. "Two Sharp Knives" (11-14-49) Hildy Parks, Stanley Ridges
31. "Of Human Bondage" [adapted from the William Somerset Maugham classic] (11-21-49) Felicia Montealegre, Charlton Heston
32. "At Mrs. Beam's" [adapted from the C. K. Munro play] (11-28-49) Eva Gabor, John Baragrey, Mildred Natwick, Cathleen Cordell
33. "Henry IV" [adapted from the Luigi Pirandello play] (12-5-49) Richard Purdy, Catherine Willard, Berry Kroeger, Virginia McMahon
34. "Jane Eyre" [adapted from the Charlotte Brontë classic] (12-12-49) Mary Sinclair, Charlton Heston, Mary Malone
35. "Mary Poppins" [adapted from the P. L. Travers classic] (12-19-49) Mary Wickes, E. G. Marshall, Valerie Cossart, Iris Mann, Tommy Rettig
36. "The Inner Light" (12-26-49) Margaret Phillips, Richard Purdy
37. "Riviera" (1-2-50) David Opatoshu, Dolly Haas, Tonio Selwart
38. "Beyond Reason" (1-9-50) Mary Sinclair, Haila Stoddard, Stanley Ridges, Richard Derr
39. "Give Us Our Dream" (1-16-50) Josephine Hull, Butterfly McQueen, Charlotte Keane, Marie Powers
40. "The Rockingham Tea Set" (1-23-50) Louise Albritton, Grace Kelly, Judson Laire, Katherine Emmett, Katherine Willard
41. "Father and the Angels" (1-30-50) Stanley Ridges, Dorothy Peterson
42. "The Loud Red Patrick" [adapted from the John Boruff and Ruth McKenney play] (2-6-50) Dick Foran, Peg Hillias, Joy Geffen
43. "Flowers from a Stranger" [restaged from 5/25/49] (2-13-50) Felicia Montealegre, Yul Brynner
44. "The Wisdom Tooth" [adapted from the Marc Connelly play] (2-20-50) Jack Lemmon, Barbara Bolton
45. "The Willow Cabin" (2-27-50) Priscilla Gillette, Charlton Heston
46. "The Dreams of Jasper Hornby" (3-6-50) David Wayne, Doris Rich, Tom Carney, Alan Stevenson

47. "The Dusty Godmother" (3-13-50) Mary Sinclair, Macdonald Carey, Laura Weber
48. "The Survivors" [adapted from the Irwin Shaw and Peter Viertel play] (3-20-50) Donald Curtis, Leslie Nielsen, Stanley Ridges
49. "Passenger to Bali" (3-27-50) Colin Keith-Johnston, Berry Kroeger, Francis Compton, E. G. Marshall
50. "The Scarlet Letter" [adapted from the Nathaniel Hawthorne classic] (4-3-50) Mary Sinclair, John Baragrey, Richard Purdy
51. "Walk the Dark Streets" (4-10-50) Franchot Tone, Sally Gracie, Patricia Ferris
52. "Torrents of Spring" [adapted from the Ivan Turgenev play] (4-17-50) John Baragrey, Louise Albritton
53. "The Horse's Mouth" (4-24-50) Burgess Meredith, Sally Gracie, Peter Martyn, Francis Bethancourt
54. "Miracle in the Rain" (5-1-50) Jeffrey Lynn, Joy Geffen, Eleanor Wilson
55. "A Wreath of Roses" (5-8-50) Margaret Phillips, Conrad Nagel, Charles Korvin
56. "The Ambassadors" [adapted from the Henry James novel] (5-15-50) Robert Sterling, Judson Laire, Ilona Massey, Katherine Willard
57. "The Room Upstairs" (5-22-50) Mary Sinclair, Donald Curtis, Valerie Bettis, Clay Clement
58. "The Man Who Had Influence" (5-29-50) Robert Sterling, Stanley Ridges, King Calder, Ann Marno
59. "The Taming of the Shrew" [adapted from the Shakespeare play] (6-5-50) Charlton Heston, Lisa Kirk
60. "Zone Four" (6-12-50) Leslie Nielsen, Mary Sinclair, Judson Laire, Eileen Heckart
61. "There Was a Crooked Man" [adapted from the book by Guy Pearce Jones and Constance Bridges Jones] (6-19-50) Robert Sterling, Charles Korvin, Virginia Graham, Richard Purdy
62. "My Granny Van" (6-26-50) Sally Chamberlin, E. G. Marshall, Mildred Natwick, Dean Harens

Third Season

63. "Zone Four" [restaged from 6/12/50] (8-28-50) Mary Sinclair, Judson Laire, Leslie Nielsen, Eileen Heckart
64. "Look Homeward, Hayseed" (9-4-50) Tom Avera, Janet Ward, Jane Seymour
65. "Mist with the Tamara Geba" (9-11-50) Stanley Ridges, Sally Chamberlin
66. "Trilby" (9-18-50) Arnold Moss, Priscilla Gillette
67. "Away from It All" (9-25-50) Kevin McCarthy, Haila Stoddard, Worthington Miner, Katherine McLeod, Richard Purdy
68. "The Passionate Pilgrim" [adapted from the Henry James novel] (10-2-50) Richard Hart, Leueen MacGrath
69. "Spectre of Alexander Wolff" (10-9-50) Leslie Nielsen, Joan Chandler, Murvyn Vye

70. "Good for Thirty Days" (10-16-50) Stanley Ridges, Sally Chamberlin, Helen Fortesque
71. "The Road to Jericho" (10-23-50) Richard Carlson, John Newland, Lydia Clarke, Ann Shoemaker
72. "Wuthering Heights" [adapted from the Emily Brontë classic] (10-30-50) Mary Sinclair, Charlton Heston, Richard Waring
73. "The Blonde Comes First" (11-6-50) Lee Bowman, Virginia Fraser
74. "The Last Cruise" (11-13-50) Don Dickinson, Leslie Nielsen, Richard Webb
75. "The Floor of Heaven" (11-20-50) Glen Langan, Mabel Tallaferro
76. "The Shadow of a Man" (11-27-50) Judson Laire, Ilona Massey, John Van Dreelen, Berry Kroeger
77. "Letter from Cairo" (12-4-50) Charlton Heston, Cecil Parker, Anne Marno
78. "Mary Lou" (12-11-50) Mildred Natwick, Laura Weber
79. "Little Women" [Part I; adapted from the Louisa May Alcott classic] (12-18-50) Mary Sinclair, Nancy Marchand, June Dayton, Lois Hall, Una O'Connor, John Baragrey, Berry Kroeger, Richard Purdy
80. "Little Women" [Part II] (12-25-50) as above.
81. "Collector's Item" (1-1-51) Walter Slezak
82. "England Made Me" (1-8-51) Richard Waring, Joan Wetmore
83. "Track of the Cat" [adapted from the Walter V. Clark novel] (1-15-51) Stanley Ridges, Jane Seymour
84. "The Trial of John Peter Zenger" (1-22-51) Henry Stephenson, Alfreda Wallace, Frank Sundstrom, Judson Laire
85. "Public Servant" (1-29-51) Hume Cronyn, Sally Chamberlin
86. "The Target" (2-5-51) Henry Daniell, Beatrice Straight, Sidney Smith
87. "None But My Foe" (2-12-51) John Forsythe, June Dayton, Howard Freeman, Don Dickinson
88. "The Way Things Are" (2-19-51) Barbara Baxley, Peg Hillias, Richard Carlyle
89. "The Ambassadors" [adapted from the Henry James novel; restaged from 5/15/50] (2-26-51) Robert Sterling, Ilona Massey (as Countess De Vionnet), Judson Laire (as Lambert Strether)
90. "One Pair of Hands" (3-5-51) Denholm Elliott, Mildred Dunnock, Katherine McLeod
91. "A Chill on the Wind" (3-12-51) John Conte, Beatrice Straight, Reba Tassell, Richard Purdy, Sally Chamberlin
92. "Hangman's House" (3-19-51) Kevin McCarthy, Jessica Tandy
93. "The Case of Karen Smith" (3-26-51) Felicia Montealegre, Leslie Nielsen
94. "Wintertime" (4-2-51) Patrick Knowles, Ann Marno
95. "Shake the Stars Down" (4-9-51) Beverly Whitney, Richard MacMurray, Joseph Buloff, Marilyn Monk
96. "The Straight and Narrow" (4-16-51) Patrick Knowles, Judith Evelyn, Maria Riva, Don Dickinson
97. "The Happy Housewife" (4-23-51) June Dayton, John Forsythe, Ann Shoemaker, Gloria Stroock

98. "Portrait by Rembrandt" (4-30-51) Berry Kroeger, Maria
    Riva
99. "No Tears for Hilda" (5-7-51) Mary Sinclair, John Forsythe
100. "The Old Foolishness" [adapted from the Paul Vincent Carroll
    play] (5-14-51) Dick Foran, Una O'Connor, Dennis Harrison
101. "A Chance for Happiness" (5-21-51) Maria Riva, Murray
    Matheson, Frances Compton, Mike McAloney
102. "Here Is My Life" (5-28-51) Vivienne Segal, Judson Laire
103. "Shield for Murder" [by William P. McGivern] (6-4-51) Kevin
    McCarthy, Marcia Henderson, James Nolan
104. "Coriolanus" [adapted by Worthington Miner from the Shake-
    speare play; directed by Paul Nickell; abstract setting by
    Richard Rychtarik] (6-11-51) Richard Greene, Judith
    Evelyn, Frederic Worlock, Sally Chamberlin, Richard Purdy,
    Tom Poston

[now as STUDIO ONE SUMMER THEATRE until new season]

105. "Screwball" (6-18-51) Dick Foran (as Russ Adams), Cloris
    Leachman (as his wife), Lefty Gomez
106. "Lonely Boy" (6-25-51) Mary Sinclair, Jerome Cowan,
    Wright King
107. "The Swan" [adapted from the Ferenc Molnar play] (7-2-51)
    Maria Riva, Alfred Ryder, John Newland
108. "Nightfall" [adapted from the David Goodis play] (7-9-51)
    Margaret Hayes, John McQuade, Herbert Rudley
109. "The Apple Tree" [adapted from the John Galsworthy play]
    (7-16-51) Lucy Vines, William Whitman, John Heldabrand
110. "Tremolo" (7-23-51) Haila Stoddard, Dick Foran
111. "At Mrs. Beam's" [adapted from the C. K. Munro play; re-
    staged from 11/28/49] (7-30-51) Eva Gabor, Jean Adair,
    Enid Markey, Claude Dauphin, Una O'Connor
112. "The Pink Hussar" (8-6-51) Ludwig Donath, Scott McKay,
    Howard Freeman
113. "The Rabbit" (8-13-51) Maria Riva, Richard Purdy
114. "Run from the Sun" (8-20-51) Marc Daniels, Gaby Rodgers
115. "Summer Had Better Be Good" (8-27-51) William Eythe,
    Katherine Bard
116. "Mr. Mummery's Suspicion" (9-3-51) Roland Young, Faith
    Brook, Francis Compton
117. "The Guinea Pig" (9-10-51) Ruth Ford, Richard Kiley, Jack
    O'Brien

Fourth Season

118. "The Angelic Avengers" (9-17-51) Richard Purdy, Maria
    Riva, Mary Sinclair, Murray Matheson
119. "The Little Black Bag" (9-24-51) Harry Townes, Eli Mintz,
    Howard St. John
120. "The Idol of San Vittore" (10-1-51) Eduardo Ciannelli, Maria
    Riva
121. "Mighty Like a Rogue" (10-8-51) Tom Ewell, Nita Talbot,
    Joshua Shelley

122. "Colonel Judas" (10-15-51) Iris Jensen, Anthony Dawson
123. "Macbeth" [adapted from the Shakespeare play] (10-22-51) Charlton Heston, Judith Evelyn
124. "They Serve the Muses" (10-29-51) Priscilla Gillette, Frances Farmer, Noel Leslie, Herbert Evers
125. "The Hero" (11-5-51) Patricia Collinge, Paul Hartman
126. "A Bolt of Lightning" (11-12-51) Charlton Heston, Rita Vale, Romney Brent; Thomas M. Paradine, guest speaker
127. "The King in Yellow" (11-19-51) Carol Bruce, Walter (Jack) Palance
128. "The Dangerous Years" (11-26-51) Maria Riva, Frances Farmer, Harry Townes
129. "Mutiny on the Nicolette" (12-3-51) Boris Karloff, James Westerfield
130. "The Legend of Jenny Lind" (12-10-51) Priscilla Gillette, Thomas Mitchell
131. "The Innocence of Pastor Muller" (12-17-51) Maria Riva, Walter Slezak, John Baragrey
132. "Sara Crewe" (12-24-51) Iris Mann, Henry Stephenson
133. "The Paris Feeling" (12-31-51) Wright King, Ann Gillis
134. "The Devil in Velvet" (1-7-52) Whit Bissell, Phyllis Kirk, Joan Wetmore
135. "Waterfront Boss" (1-14-52) Roy Hargrave, Kent Smith
136. "The Other Father" (1-21-52) Judson Laire, Peg Hillias
137. "Burden of Guilt" (1-28-52) Anthony Ross, Ralph Nelson, Robert Stanton
138. "A Candle for St. Jude" (2-4-52) Tanaquil Le Clercq, Marc Platt, Lilli Darvas, Betty Low
139. "Pagoda" (2-11-52) Sono Osato, John Forsythe
140. "Success Story" [adapted from the John Howard Lawson play] (2-18-52) Harry Townes
141. "Letter to an Unknown Woman" (2-25-52) Viveca Lindfors, Melvyn Douglas, Jean-Pierre Aumont
142. "Ten Thousand Horses Singing" (3-3-52) John Forsythe, Catherine McLeod
143. "The Wings of the Dove" [adapted from the Henry James novel] (3-10-52) Charlton Heston, Stella Andrew, Felicia Montealegre
144. "The Vintage Years" (3-17-52) Walter Slezak, Una O'Connor
145. "Mrs. Hargreaves" (3-24-52) Mary Wickes, Tony Randall
146. "The Story of Meg Mallory" (3-31-52) Wendy Drew, Thomas Mitchell, Skip Homeier
147. "Pontius Pilate" [by Michael Dyne; the basis for his Broadway play Most Honourable Gentleman] (4-7-52) Geraldine Fitzgerald, Cyril Ritchard, Francis L. Sullivan
148. "Hold Back the Night" (4-14-52) John Forsythe, Lee Philips
149. "Lilly, the Queen of the Movies" (4-21-52) Glynis Johns, David B. Greene, Richard Ney
150. "The Deep Dark" (4-28-52) Skip Momeier, Lilli Darvas, Victor Thornley
151. "Treasure Island" [adapted by Donald Davis (who also produced) from the Robert Louis Stevenson classic; directed by Franklin Schaffner] (5-5-52) Peter Avrano (as Jim Hawkins), Francis L. Sullivan (as Long John Silver), Albert Dekker

152. "They Came to Baghdad" (5-12-52) Bramwell Fletcher, Richard Kiley, June Dayton
153. "A Connecticut Yankee in King Arthur's Court" [adapted from the Mark Twain classic] (5-19-52) Thomas Mitchell, Boris Karloff
154. "Abraham Lincoln" (5-26-52) Robert Pastene, Judith Evelyn
155. "Captain-General of the Armies" (6-2-52) Richard Carlson, Victor Jory, Lydia Clarke
156. "Lovers and Friends" (6-9-52) Jane Wyatt, Murray Matheson
157. "International Incident" (6-16-52) Lloyd Bridges, Victor Jory, Patricia Wheel
158. "There Was a Crooked Man" (6-13-52) Judith Parrish, Robert Webber, Butch Cavell, Robert Pastene

[now as STUDIO ONE SUMMER THEATRE until new season]

159. "The Blonde Comes First" [restaged from 11/6/50] (6-30-52) Lee Grant, Tom Helmore
160. "The Rockingham Tea Set" [restaged from 1/23/50] (7-14-52) Scott Forbes
161. "The Last Thing I Do" (7-28-52) Shepperd Strudwick, Whit Bissell, Richard McMurray
162. "Jane Eyre" [adapted from the Charlotte Brontë classic; restaged from 12/12/49] (8-4-52) Katherine Bard, Kevin McCarthy, Doris Roberts
163. "The Man They Acquitted" (8-11-52) Robert Coote, Patricia Wheel
164. "One in a Million" (8-18-52) Reinhold Schunzel, Stefan Schnabel, Royal Dano
165. "The Good Companions" (8-25-52) Edith Fellows, Hamish Menzies (Scottish actor and singer)
166. "Stan, the Killer" [by Georges Simenon; restaged from The Trap episode of 5/20/50] (9-1-52) Romney Brent, Eli Wallach
167. "The Happy Housewife" (9-8-52)
168. "The Shadowy Third" [adapted from the Ellen Glasgow play; restaged from 6/29/49] (9-15-52) Carmen Mathews, Robert Pastene, Geraldine Page

Fifth Season

169. "The Kill" (9-22-52) Nina Foch, Dick Foran, Grace Kelly
170. "The Square Peg" (9-29-52) Thomas Mitchell, Orson Bean
171. "The Doctor's Wife" (10-6-52) John Dall, June Lockhart
172. "Little Man, Big World" (10-13-52) Jack Palance, Shepperd Strudwick
173. "The Great Conspiracy" (10-20-52) Priscilla Gillette, Scott Forbes
174. "The Love Letter" (10-27-52) Dennis King, Richard Waring
175. "The Incredible Mr. Glencannon" (11-10-52) Rhys Williams, John McQuade
176. "Plan for Escape" (11-17-52) Peggy Ann Garner, Frank Overton
177. "The Formula" (11-24-52) Patricia Wheel, Gene Lyons

178. "I Am Jonathan Scrivener" [the lead character remains unseen but for his right hand] (12-1-52) John Forsythe, Maria Riva, John McQuade, Felicia Montealegre, Everett Sloane

179. "The Hospital" (12-8-52) Leslie Nielsen, Victor Jory, Nancy Marchand

180. "The Great Lady" (12-15-52) Rosemary Harris, James Daly, Lilli Darvas, Martita Hunt

181. "The Nativity" (12-22-52) Miriam Wolfe, Hurd Hatfield, Paul Tripp, Thomas Chalmers

182. "Young Man Adam" (12-29-52) Mindy Carson, Alex Nicol, Elspeth Eric, Audrey Christie

183. "Black Rain" (1-5-53) Fay Bainter, Harry Townes, Nan Mc-Farland, Susan Halloran

184. "The Trial of John Peter Zenger" [restaged from 1/22/51] (1-12-53) Eddie Albert, Marian Seldes, Murray Matheson, Frederic Worlock

185. "Signal Thirty-Two" (1-19-53) Roy Roberts, Grace Lyons

186. "To a Moment of Triumph" [adapted from the Pamela Frankau novel] (1-26-53) James Daly (as a cartoonist), Maria Riva (as Cecil), Cecil Parker (as a newspaper publisher)

187. "Mark of Cain" (2-2-53) Mildred Dunnock, Everett Sloane, Warren Stevens

188. "The River Garden" (2-9-53) Patricia Collinge, Richard Webb

189. "The Walsh Girls" (2-16-53) Jane Wyatt, Mary Orr

190. "The Show Piece" (2-23-53) Ernest Parmentier, James Dunn, Jean Jordan

191. "My Beloved Husband" (3-2-53) Ruth Warrick, Fletcher Markle, Mary Alice Moore

192. "The Garretson Chronicle" (3-9-53) Frederick Worlock, Murray Matheson, Tom Taylor, Nana Bryant

193. "A Breath of Air" (3-16-53) Margaret O'Brien, Everett Sloane

194. "The Edge of Evil" (3-23-53) James Daly, Sally Forrest

195. "At Midnight on the Thirty-first of March" (3-30-53) June Lockhart, Anthony Ross, Paul Tripp

196. "Shadow of the Devil" (4-6-53) James Dunn, Mercedes McCambridge, Lin McCarthy

197. "The Magic Lantern" (4-13-53) Dorothy Mackaill, James Dunn, Nils Asther, Carmel Myers, Leatrice Joy, Rex O'Malley

198. "The Fathers" (4-20-53) Shepperd Strudwick, Nancy Kelly

199. "Along Came a Spider" (4-27-53) James Daly, Felicia Montealegre

200. "Birthright" (5-4-53) Jackie Cooper, Everett Sloane, Estelle Winwood, Patricia Benoit

201. "King Coffin" (5-11-53) Zachary Scott, Ruth Ford

202. "The Laugh Maker" (5-18-53) Jackie Gleason, Art Carney, Sally Gracie, Rita Morley

203. "Fly with the Hawk" (5-25-53) James Daly, Mercedes McCambridge

204. "Rendezvous" (6-1-53) Jarmila Novotna, Lorne Greene, Jarmila Dauliek

205. "Conflict" (6-8-53) John Forsythe, Nancy Kelly

[now as STUDIO ONE SUMMER THEATRE until new season]

206. "The Paris Feeling" [directed by Matt Harlib] (6-22-53)
     Adette Myrtil, Lilia Skala, Susan Douglas, Mischa Auer,
     Boris Marshalou, Marshall Thompson, Vinton Hayworth
207. "Greed" (6-29-53) Hurd Hatfield, Donald McKee, Diana
     Douglas
208. "Beyond Reason" [restaged from 1/9/50] (7-6-53) Anthony
     Dawson, Elizabeth Ross, Ann Burr, Patricia Wheel
209. "End of the Honeymoon" (7-13-53) John Kerr, Eva Marie
     Saint, Ruth Warrick
210. "The Shadow of a Man" [restaged from 11/27/50] (7-20-53)
     Claude Dauphin, Lydia St. Clair
211. "The King in Yellow" [restaged from 11/19/51] (7-27-53)
     Kevin McCarthy, Constance Ford, Charles Nolte
212. "The Roman Kid" [by Paul Gallico] (8-3-53) Mike Wallace,
     Victor Varconi, Joe Maross, Patricia Wheel, Santos Ortega
213. "Flowers from a Stranger" [restaged from 5/25/49] (8-10-53)
     Richard Kiley, Katharine Balfour, Everett Sloane
214. "Sentence of Death" (8-17-53) Gene Lyons, Ralph Dunn,
     James Dean, Betsy Palmer
215. "The Gathering Night" [adapted from the Rudyard Kipling clas-
     sic The Light That Failed] (8-24-53) Christopher Plummer,
     Gaby Rodgers, Margaret Phillips, Melville Cooper, Martyn
     Green
216. "Letter from Cairo" [restaged from 12/4/50] (8-31-53) Lilyan
     Chauvin, Peter Hobbs, Herbert Berghoff
217. "Look Homeward, Hayseed" [restaged from 9/4/50] (9-7-53)
     Betsy Palmer, Russell Nype, Margaret Hamilton, Charles
     Dingle
218. "The Storm" [restaged from 11/7/48 and 10/17/49] (9-14-53)
     Georgiann Johnson, Laurence Hugo, Martin Brooks

Sixth Season

219. "1984" [adapted by William Templeton from the George Orwell
     classic; directed by Paul Nickell and produced by Felix Jack-
     son; settings by Henry May and Kim Swados] (9-21-53)
     Eddie Albert (as Winston Smith), Norma Crane (in her video
     debut), Lorne Greene
220. "Hound-Dog Man" (9-28-53) Jackie Cooper, E. G. Marshall
221. "Silent the Song" (10-5-53) Michele Morgan
222. "Music and Mrs. Pratt" (10-12-53) Elsa Lanchester, Philip
     Abbott
223. "Letter of Love" (10-19-53) Sally Forrest, Steve Cochran
224. "Another Caesar" (10-26-53) Robert Keith, Frances Miller,
     Arnold Moss
225. "Crime at Blossom's" (11-2-53) Patricia Collinge, Wesley
     Lau
226. "Camille" [a modern dress adaptation of the Alexandre Dumas
     play] (11-9-53) Michele Morgan, Romney Brent, Arthur
     Franz, Frederic Worlock
227. "A Bargain with God" (11-16-53) Hiram Sherman, Estelle
     Winwood

228. "Buffalo Bill Is Dead" [by Rod Serling] (11-23-53) Anthony Ross
229. "Confessions of a Nervous Man" (11-30-53) Art Carney, Betty Furness
230. "Dry Run" [subsequently restaged for Alfred Hitchcock Presents episode of 11/8/59] (12-7-53) Walter Matthau, Arthur Franz
231. "All My Love" (12-14-53) Nina Foch, Philip Bourneuf, Laurence Hugo
232. "Cinderella '53" [a modernized musical verson of the Charles Perrault children's classic] (12-21-53) Ann Crowley, Conrad Janis
233. "Master of the Rose" (12-28-53) Maria Riva, Peter Capell
234. "The Runaway" (1-4-54) Wallace Ford, Charles Ruggles, Mary Wickes, Jack Carter
235. "The Remarkable Incident at Carson Corners" [by Reginald Rose] (1-11-54) Harry Townes, O. Z. Whitehead, Susan Hallaran, Glen Walken, Stanley Martin, Stefan Olsen, Priscilla Gillette
236. "A Criminal Design" (1-18-54) Richard Kiley, Haila Stoddard, Geraldine Brooks, Luther Adler
237. "A Favor for a Friend" (1-24-54) Vaughn Taylor, Lucile Watson, Georgiann Johnson
238. "Herman, Come By Bomber" (2-1-54) Paul Langton, Gwen Anderson
239. "Man of Extinction" (2-8-54) Margaret Hamilton, Patricia Wheel, Patricia Breslin
240. "Dark Possession" [by Gore Vidal; subsequently restaged for the Matinee Theatre episode of 2/2/56] (2-15-54) Geraldine Fitzgerald, Leslie Nielsen, Barbara O'Neil, Bramwell Fletcher
241. "The Role of a Lover" (2-22-54) Skip Homeier, Betsy Palmer, Steve Cochran
242. "Side Street" (3-1-54) Peter Lind Hayes, Mary Healy, David Opatoshu, Biff McGuire, Joanne Linville
243. "Beyond a Reasonable Doubt" (3-8-54) Leslie Nielsen, Katherine Bard, Susan Hallaran
244. "Thunder on Sycamore Street" [by Reginald Rose; directed by Franklin Schaffner and produced by Felix Jackson] (3-15-54) Whitfield Connor, Nell O'Day, Robert Bussard, Dickie Olsen, Lee Bergere, Anna Cameron, Harry Sheppard, Kenneth Utt, Charlotte Pearson, Tirrell Barbery, Judith Lowry, Charles Penman, Mabel Cochran
245. "The Expendables" [a story of Russian emigrants] (3-22-54) George Voskovec, Martin Kosleck, Flora Campbell, Nelson Olmstead
246. "Paul's Apartment" (3-29-54) Richard Kiley, Eva Gabor, David White
247. "Stir Mugs" (4-5-54) Warren Stevens, Joanne Woodward, Frank Albertson
248. "Jack Sperling, Forty-six" (4-12-54) Chester Morris, Mary Astor, Lois Smith
249. "A Handful of Diamonds" (4-19-54) Patricia Neal, Lorne Greene, Gene Peterson
250. "Romney" (4-26-54) Laurence Hugo, Barbara O'Neil, Oliver Andes, Howard St. John

251. "Cardinal Mindszenty" (5-3-54) Claude Dauphin
252. "Fear Is No Stranger" (5-10-54) Patricia Breslin, Madge
Evans, Jerome Cowan, Peggy Allenby
253. "Castle in Spain" (5-17-54) Joan Lorring, Leslie Nielsen,
Biff McGuire
254. "A Man and Two Gods" (5-24-54) John Baragrey, Charles
Korvin, Patricia Wheel, Paul Stevens
255. "The Death and Life of Larry Benson" [by Reginald Rose]
(5-31-54) Chester Morris, Lee Remick, Skip Homeier,
Peg Hillias
256. "The Strike" [by Rod Serling; directed by Franklin Schaffner
and produced by Felix Jackson] (6-7-54) James Daly,
Frank Marth, Bert Freed, Roy Roberts, William Whitman,
Wyatt Cooper, Douglas Taylor, William Leichester, George
Brenlin, Cy Chermak, Bill Townsend, Ken Mileston, Fred
Scollay, Bill Butler, William Andrews, Tony del Gatto, An-
drew Gainey, Bill Flatley, Harlan Wiltsert, Bob Drew, Jim
Merrick, Bob Boucher, Mel Jurdem, Dan Wright, Herbert
King, Howard and Brad Deilman
257. "A Letter to Mr. Gubbins" (6-14-54) Art Carney
258. "Fandango at War Bonnet" (6-21-54) Royal Dano, Darren
McGavin, Wesley Addy, Monica Boyar, Victor Thorley
259. "Screwball" [restaged from 6/18/51] (6-28-54) Jack Warden,
Sally Gracie

[now as STUDIO ONE SUMMER THEATRE until new season]

260. "The Small Door" (7-5-54) Richard Kiley, Hildy Parks, Edgar Stehli, James Gregory
261. "A Guest at the Embassy" (7-12-54) Leslie Nielsen, Nina
Foch, Betsy Palmer
262. "Home Again, Home Again" (7-19-54) Janice Rule, Robert
H. Harris, Mark Roberts
263. "The Hero" [restaged from 11/5/51] (7-26-54) Bethel Leslie,
Ray Walston, Paul Hartman, James Gregory, Joey Walsh
264. "The Magic Monday" (8-2-54) Dick Foran, Madge Evans,
Joan Wetmore, Mary Linn Beller
265. "Sue Ellen" (8-9-54) Barbara O'Neil, Patrick O'Neal, Inger
Stevens, Addison Richards
266. "The House of Gair" (8-16-54) Basil Rathbone, Hurd Hatfield, Cora Witherspoon, Wesley Addy
267. "Experiment Perilous" (8-23-54) Constance Ford, Gene Lyons,
Augusta Dabney
268. "The Secret Self" (8-30-54) Staats Cootsworth, Nancy Kelly,
Everett Sloane, Peter Cookson
269. "U.F.O." (9-6-54) Parker Fennelly, Dorothy Sands, Jack
Warden
270. "The Cliff" (9-13-54) Maria Riva, Lorne Greene, Hildy Parks

Seventh Season

271. "Twelve Angry Men" [by Reginald Rose; directed by Franklin
Schaffner; filmed by United Artists, 1957] (9-26-54) Robert

Cummings, Edward Arnold, John Beal, Walter Abel, Bart Burns, Franchot Tone, Lee Philips, Paul Hartman, Joseph Sweeney, George Voskovec, Norman Fell, Will West Misters Sweeney and Voskovec repeated their roles for the film.

272. "The Education of H*Y*M*A*N K*A*P*L*A*N" [adapted from the Leonard Q. Ross story] (9-27-54) Jacob Kalich, Maria Riva

273. "Prelude to Murder" (10-4-54) James Daly, Phyllis Kirk, Otto Kruger

274. "Melissa" (10-11-54) Faye Emerson, Walter Brooke, Raymond Bramley, Teal Ames

275. "The Boy Who Changed the World" [commemorating the anniversary of the death of Thomas Edison; this drama is Studio One's first colorcast] (10-18-54) John Beal, Ruth Hussey, Michael Allen (as the young Tom Edison); Charles Edison, guest

276. "Fatal in My Fashion" (10-25-54) Polly Rowles, Charles Korvin, Shepperd Strudwick, Meg Mundy

277. "The Man Who Owned the Town" (11-1-54) Robert Barret, Leslie Nielsen, Paul Stevens, Johnny Devlin

278. "An Almanac on Liberty" [by Reginald Rose, as adapted from the collected essays of William O. Douglas; narrated by Charles Collingwood. This episode sponsored by the B'Nai B'rith; subsequently telecast on the afternoon of May 1, 1955 via CBS] (11-8-54) Pat Hingle, Eli Mintz

279. "Let Me Go, Lover" [the title theme became a popular song standard] (11-15-54) Joe Maross, Anthony Ross, Cliff Norton, Connie Sawyer

280. "Joey" (11-22-54) Orson Bean, Geraldine Brooks, Louise Larabee

281. "The Deserter" (11-29-54) James Gregory, June Lockhart, Margaret Wycherly

282. "Short Cut" (12-6-54) Jackie Gleason, Priscilla Gillette, Lin McCarthy

283. "12:30 A.M." (12-13-54) Van Dyke Parks, Katherine Bard

284. "Two Little Minks" [a New England Christmas story] (12-20-54) Frank McHugh, Walter Hampden, Una Merkel

285. "The Cuckoo in Spring" [adapted by Sam Hall from the Elizabeth Cadell novel] (12-27-54) Charles Coburn, Leatrice Joy, Richard Kiley, David White, Louise King, LeRoi Operti, P. J. Kelly

286. "The Missing Men" (1-3-55) George Macready, Gene Nelson

287. "Grandma Rolled Her Own" (1-10-55) Cathleen Nesbitt, Oliver Andes

288. "Sail with the Tide" [adapted from the Honoré de Balzac story] (1-17-55) Claude Dauphin, Mai Zetterling, Grant Williams

289. "It Might Happen Tomorrow" (1-24-55) Barry Sullivan, Anthony Franciosa, Dana Wynter

290. "The Silent Women" (1-31-55) Margaret Hamilton, Everett Sloane, Gaby Rodgers, Peg Hillias

291. "A Stranger May Die" (2-7-55) Jack Warden, Don Gibson, Martin Rudy

292. "The Broken Spur" (2-14-55) Paul Langton, Royal Dano
293. "The Eddie Chapman Story" [adapted from the Frank Owen book] (2-21-55) Roy Deans
294. "Donovan's Brain" [by Curt Siodmak] (2-28-55) Wendell Corey, E. G. Marshall, June Dayton
295. "Millions of Georges" (3-7-55) Scott Brady, Joan Lorring, Hope Emerson, Barry McGuire
296. "The Conviction of Peter Shea" (3-14-55) Skip Homeier, George Montgomery, Inger Stevens
297. "Miss Turner's Decision" (3-21-55) Nina Foch, Glenda Farrell, Edward Andrews, Cliff Hall
298. "Dominique" [by Ernest Kinoy, from a story idea by Daniel Hollywood; directed by Franklin Schaffner] (3-28-55) Ralph Meeker, Marissa Pavan, John McGiver, Phyllis Hill
299. "Cross My Heart" (4-4-55) Hugh Marlowe, Neva Patterson, Roni Dengal, Jane Seymour
300. "Passage at Arms" (4-11-55) Robert Sterling, Theodore Bikel, Louis Jourdan, Maria Riva, Ralmonda Orselli
301. "Affairs of State" [adapted from the Louis Verneull Broadway play] (4-18-55) Betty Furness, Jeff Morrow
302. "Mrs. Brimmer Did It!" [a mystery drama by Kathleen and Robert Howard Lindsay] (4-25-54) Dennis Price, Margaret Phillips, Brenda Forbes, John McGiver, Frank Compton, Cavada Humphrey
303. "Summer Pavilion" [by Gore Vidal; subsequently restaged for the Matinee Theatre episode of 7/18/56] (5-2-55) Charles Drake, Miriam Hopkins, Elizabeth Montgomery, Joseph Sweeney, Ruth White, Wyatt Cooper
304. "A Picture in the Paper" [by Mann Rubin] (5-9-55) James Dunn, Jason Robards Jr., Doreen Lang, Maxine Stuart
305. "Strange Companion" [adapted by Don Ettlinger from the story by John Van Druten and Christopher Isherwood] (5-16-55) Peggy Ann Garner, Cathleen Nesbitt, Laurence Hugo
306. "Pigeons and People" [adapted from the George M. Cohan Broadway play] (5-23-55) Edward Andrews, George Keane
307. "Operation Home" [by William M. Altman] (5-30-55) John Forsythe, Alan Bunce, Nita Talbot
308. "The Spongers" [by James Yaffe] (6-6-55) Cyril Ritchard, Ernest Truex, Murray Hamilton, Judith Parrish, Alice Pearce
309. "The Incredible World of Horace Ford" [by Reginald Rose; directed by Franklin Schaffner and produced by Felix Jackson] (6-13-55) Art Carney, Jason Robards Jr., House Jameson, Jane Seymour, Leora Dana

[now as STUDIO ONE SUMMER THEATRE until new season]

310. "Heart Song" [by Charles S. Gardner] (6-20-55) Everett Sloane, Phyllis Kirk, Edmon Ryan, Margaret Barker
311. "For the Defense" [by George Bellak] (6-27-55) Mike Wallace, Hildy Parks, Leo Penn, Russell Hicks, Bruce Gordon
312. "The Day Before the Wedding" [by Anthony Spinner] (7-4-55) Inger Stevens, Bigg McGuire, Barbara O'Neil, Russell Collins, Michael Strong

313. "Sane as a Hatter" [by Michael Dyne] (7-11-55) Romney Brent, Rosalind Ivan, Bruce Marshall, Nydia Westman, Frederic Worlock, Margarita Warwick

314. "A Terrible Day" [a western drama by Carey Wilbur] (7-18-55) Jack Klugman, Arthur O'Connell, Mark Lawrence, Bruce Gordon

315. "The Tall Dark Stranger" [by Peter Barry] (7-25-55) Constance Ford, Martin Rudy, Nelson Olmstead, Tom Gorman

316. "Julius Caesar" [a modern dress adaptation by Leo Penn of the Shakespeare play; directed by Don Petrie and produced by Worthington Miner; restaged] (8-1-55) Shepperd Strudwick, Theodore Bikel, Michael Tolan, Maria Brit-Neva, Alfred Ryder, Philip Bourneuf

317. "The Prince and the Puppet" [by Shirley Peterson] (8-8-55) Van Dyke Parks, Phyllis Hill, John Shay, Joseph Sweeney, Bill and Cora Baird and puppets

318. "The Secret" (8-15-55) Hildy Parks, John Baragrey, Catherine McLeod

319. "The Voysey Inheritance" [adapted by Michael Dyne from the Harley Granville-Barker story] (8-22-55) Bramwell Fletcher, Frederic Worlock, Douglas Watson, Gloria Stroock, Dorothy Sands

320. "A Chance at Love" [by Shirley Peterson] (8-29-55) Richard Kiley, Gena Rowlands, Georgiann Johnson

321. "Mama's Boy" [by Mel Goldberg] (9-5-55) Alfred Ryder, Martin Brooks, Ruth White, Morton Rudy, Zorah Alton

322. "The Pit" [a suspense drama by Charles S. Gardner] (9-12-55) Olive Deering, Robert F. Simon, William Smithers

Eighth Season

323. "Like Father, Like Son" [by Kathleen and Robert Howard Lindsay] (9-19-55) Ralph Bellamy, Geoffrey Horne, Keenan Wynn, Vaughn Taylor, Charles Drake, Geraldine Fitzgerald, Charles Dingle

324. "Three Empty Rooms" [by Reginald Rose] (9-26-55) Steve Brodie, Barbara Baxley, Eli Mintz, Joseph Sweeney, Ginger MacManus

325. "A Likely Story" [by Frank Gilroy] (10-3-55) Eddie Bracken, Hope Emerson, Jack Whiting, Patricia Barry

326. "Uncle Ed and Circumstances" [adapted by Frank Gilroy from a short story by Jackie Gleason; the teleplay features Gleason as a contestant on The $64,000 Question] (10-10-55) Jackie Gleason, John Baragrey, Mildred Natwick, Cliff Hall, J. Pat O'Malley, Edward Binns

327. "A Most Contagious Game" [adapted from the Samuel Grafton novel] (10-17-55) Steve Cochran, Kenny Delmar, Edward Andrews, Bert Freed

328. "Private History" [by Jerome Ross] (10-24-55) Cecil Kellaway, Howard St. John, Raymond Bramley, Lee Philips, Louise King

329. "Split Level" [by Joel Hammil] (10-31-55) Cathleen Nesbitt, Dino Di Luca, Alfreda Wallace, Mario Alcalde, Douglas Gordon

330. "Shakedown Cruise" [by Loring D. Mandel] (11-7-55) Richard Kiley, Lee Marvin, George Mathews, Martin Brooks, Don Hastings, Don Gardner, Clint Young

331. "The Judge and the Hangman" [adapted from the Friedrick Durrenmath novel] (11-14-55) Charles Korvin, Herbert Berghoff

332. "Julie" [by David Davidson] (11-21-55) Roni Dengel, Jan Miner, Terry O'Sullivan, Jimmy Sommer

333. "The Man Who Caught the Ball at Coogan's Bluff" [by Rod Serling] (11-28-55) Alan Young, Gisele MacKenzie, Horace MacMahon, Henry Jones

334. "Blow Up at Cortland" [by Paul Monash] (12-5-55) Chester Morris, Neville Brand, Philip Coolidge

335. "The Strongbox" [adapted from the Howard Swiggert novel] (12-12-55) James Daly, Katherine Bard, Meg Mundy

336. "Miracle at Potter's Farm" [by Kathleen and Robert Howard Lindsay] (12-19-55) Frank McHugh, Natalie Wood, Luke Halpin

337. "Fair Play" [adapted from a novelette by John and Ward Hawkins] (12-26-55) Dewey Martin, James Gregory, Joe Mantell, Paul Gibson, Cameron Prud'homme

338. "Dino" [by Reginald Rose; filmed by United Artists, 1957] (1-2-56) Sal Mineo (who repeated his title role for the film), Ralph Meeker

339. "The Talented Mr. Ripley" [adapted by Marc Brandel from the Patricia Highsmith novel] (1-9-56) Keefe Brasselle, Vaughn Taylor, Patricia Smith, William Redfield

340. "Johnny August" [by Carey Wilbur] (1-16-56) Cameron Mitchell, Phyllis Kirk, Charles Korvin, Tina Louise

341. "A Public Figure" [by Harry W. Junkin; filmed by Metro Goldwyn Mayer in 1957 as Slander] (1-23-56) James Daly, Mercedes McCambridge, Shepperd Strudwick

342. "My Son Johnny" [adapted by Kathleen and Robert Howard Lindsay from the John McNulty book] (1-30-56) Neva Patterson, Wendell Corey, Larry Gates, Luke Halpin, Cliff Norton

343. "The Silent Gun" [by Carson A. Wiley] (2-6-56) Lloyd Bridges, Frank McHugh, Anthony Perkins

344. "Manhattan Duet" [by Helen Cotton] (2-13-56) Nina Foch, Geraldine Brooks, Edward Andrews, Dennis O'Keefe

345. "Circle of Guilt" [by Mel Goldberg] (2-20-56) Keenan Wynn, Fred Clark, Julie Adams, Peter Graves, Vaughn Taylor

346. "Always Welcome" [adapted from the Jeanette Kamins play] (2-27-56) Henry Jones, Pat de Simone, Mildred Dunnock, John Lupton

347. "A Favor for Sam" [by John and Ward Hawkins] (3-5-56) James Whitmore, Priscilla Gillette

348. "Flower of Pride" [by Michael Dyne] (3-12-56) Geraldine Fitzgerald, Felicia Montealegre, Trevor Howard, Halliwell Hobbes

349. "The Laughter of Giants" [by Paul Crabtree] (3-19-56) Brian Donlevy, Biff McGuire, Rita Gam, Patrick McVey

350. "The Tale of St. Emergency" (3-26-56) Red Buttons, Cecil Kellaway, Henry Jones, Russell Collins, James Barton, Paul Ford

351. "This Will Do Nicely" [by Thomas Flanagan] (4-2-56) Alan
     Young, Larry Blyden, Felicia Montealegre, Bert Freed
352. "The Arena" [by Rod Serling] (4-9-56) Wendell Corey, Leora
     Dana, Chester Morris, John Cromwell
353. "Regarding File Number 4356" [by Hannah Smith] (4-16-56)
     Dolly Haas, Priscilla Gillette, Lin McCarthy
354. "I Do" [by Ernest Kinoy] (4-30-56) Bobby Driscoll, Gigi
     Perreau
355. "The Drop of a Hat" [by Dick Berg] (5-7-56) Valerie Bettis,
     Nina Foch, Elizabeth Montgomery, Jayne Meadows, George
     Voskovec
356. "The Genie of Sutton Place" [by Kenneth Heuer and George
     Seldon] (5-14-56) Henry Jones, Polly Rowles
357. "The Star-Spangled Soldier" [by David Swift] (5-21-56) Ray
     Collins, Kenny Delmar, Eddie Mayehoff, Vaughn Taylor
358. "Family Protection" [by Palmer Thompson] (5-28-56) Everett
     Sloane, Joanne Woodward, Corey Allen
359. "The Power" [adapted by William A. Altman from the Frank
     Robinson novel] (6-4-56) James Daly, Shepperd Strudwick,
     David White, Paul Stevens

[now as STUDIO ONE SUMMER THEATRE until new season]

360. "Flight" [adapted by Robert Herridge from the John Steinbeck
     story] (6-11-56) Gerald Sarracino, Vivian Nathan, Miriam
     Colon, Jose Perez, Marita Reid
361. "Snap Your Fingers" [by Richard DeRoy] (6-18-56) Nancy
     Sheridan, Philip Abbott, Renee Gadd, Janine Manatis, La-
     raine Grover, John McCay
362. "Mr. Arcularis" [adapted by Robert Herridge from the Con-
     rad Aiken psychological suspense story] (6-25-56) Bram-
     well Fletcher, Jonathan Harris, Nancy Wickwire, John
     Drainie
363. "The Luck of Luke McTigger" [by Leo Brady] (7-2-56) Pat
     Henning, Peg Hillias, Staats Cotsworth
364. "Song for a Summer Night" [by Charles Garment] (7-9-56)
     Herbert Nelson, Joan Chandler, Martin Rudy, Kenneth Ott
365. "Emmaline" (7-19-56) Deirdre Owen, Alexander Scourby,
     Ian Ferrand
366. "An Incident of Love" [by William T. Bode] (7-23-56) Jack
     Lord, Lois Nettleton, Katherine Squire, Michael Strong
367. "The Ballad of Yermo Red" [by Marcel Klauber and William
     T. Grady Jr.] (7-30-56) Biff McGuire, Arch Johnson
368. "Something Ventured" [by Jan Glanzrock] (8-6-56) Larry
     Gates, Joe Maross, Wesley Addy, Jack Sterling, Bryarly
     Lee
369. "Giulio" [by Herbert Abbott Spiro; music from Verdi's La
     Traviata] (8-27-56) Morris Miller, Eleni Klamos
370. "A Day Before Battle" [by Sherman Yellen and Peter Stone]
     (9-3-56) Jack Lord, Gerald Sarracini, Susan Oliver
371. "Cauliflower Heart" [adapted by S. Lee Pogostin from the Ar-
     thur Mayse story] (9-10-56) Clarice Blackburn, Luther
     Adler, Herbert Nelson, Pat De Simone

372. "Dark Morning" [by Arden Casey] (9-17-56) Larry Gates, Joan Potter, Howard Wierum

Ninth Season

373. "A Special Announcement" [by David Aldrich and Peter Van Slingerland] (9-24-56) Robert Cummings; narrated by Alexander Scourby
374. "A Man's World" [adapted by Howard Rodman from the Douglas Farlurn novel] (10-1-56) Rocky Graziano, Lili Darvas, Joanne Woodward, Dick York
375. "The Open Door" [by Loring Mandel] (10-15-56) Albert Salmi, Marian Brach, Robert Simon
376. "The Crimes of Peter Page" (10-22-56) Barry Jones
377. "American Primitive" (10-29-56) Lloyd Bridges, Cameron Prud'homme
378. "The Pilot" [by Paul Crabtree; based on the life of Sister Mary Aquinas] (11-12-56) Nancy Kelly, Barbara O'Neil
379. "The Landlady's Daughter" [adapted by Paul Crabtree from the John Prescott magazine story] (11-26-56) Lee Remick, Richard Kiley, Fred Gwynne, George Mathews, Malcolm Broderick
380. "Portrait of a Citizen" [by Norman Katkov] (12-3-56) Lili Darvas, Walter Slezak
381. "Rachel" [by Kathleen and Robert Howard Lindsay] (12-10-56) Maureen Stapleton, Edward Andrews, Edmond Glover, Everett Sloane
382. "Career" [by Mel Goldberg] (12-17-56) Shepperd Strudwick, Norma Crane, Barry Sullivan
383. "A Christmas Surprise" [by Paul Crabtree] (12-24-56) Orson Bean, Kevin Coughlin, Luke Halpin, Kathleen Maguire, Robert Q. Lewis, Luis Van Rooten
384. "Goodbye Piccadilly" [adapted by Marc Brandel from the John P. Marquand story] (12-31-56) James Daly, Betsy Palmer, Parker McCormick, Donald Marze
385. "Love at Forth Sight" [by Sumner Locke Elliott] (1-7-57) Gisele MacKenzie, William Redfield, Evelyn Varden
386. "The Dark Corner" [by Arthur Wallace] (1-14-57) Fay Bainter, Conrad Nagel, Robert Pastene, Phyllis Thaxter
387. "The Five Dollar Bill" [by Tad Mosel] (1-21-57) Hume Cronyn, Burt Brinckerhoff, Jessica Tandy, Abigail Kellogg
388. "Dead of Noon" [by Carson A. Wiley] (1-28-57) Richard Boone, Cameron Prud'homme
389. "Tale of the Comet" [by Robert Alan Aurthur] (2-4-57) Hal Maria
390. "A Walk in the Forest" [by Howard Rodman] (2-11-57) George Peppard, Alexander Scourby
391. "The Hollywood Complex" [by John Vlahos] (2-18-57) Tony Randall, David Opatoshu, William Redfield, Michael Tolan
392. "The Defender" [Part I; by Reginald Rose; directed by Robert Mulligan and produced by Herbert Brodkin; the basis for the 1961 filmed series] (2-25-57) Ralph Bellamy (as the defense attorney), William Shatner, Martin Balsam (as the prosecutor), Steve McQueen, Dolores Sutton, Ian Wolfe

393. "The Defender" [Part II] (3-4-57) as above.
394. "A Child Is Waiting" [by Abby Mann; filmed by Stanley Kramer for United Artists, 1962] (3-11-57) Pat Hingle, Mary Fickett, Marian Seldes
395. "Walk Down the Hill" [by Ernest Kinoy] (3-18-57) Don Gordon, William Smithers, David Lewis
396. "A Member of the Family" [by Horton Foote; directed by Norman Felton] (3-25-57) Hume Cronyn
397. "The Years in Between" [by Will Schneider and Herman Goldberg] (4-1-57) John Kerr, Phyllis Love
398. "The Playwright and the Stars" [by Sidney Carroll] (4-8-57) Cathleen Nesbitt, Fritz Weaver, Sam Levene
399. "The Rice Sprout Song" [adapted by Loring D. Mandel from the Eileen Chang novel] (4-15-57) David Opatoshu, Olive Deering, Dolores Sutton, Vivian Nathan
400. "The Traveling Lady" [adapted by Horton Foote from his 1954 Broadway play; the basis for the 1965 film, Baby, the Rain Must Fall] (4-22-57) Kim Stanley, Robert Loggia, Mildred Dunnock, Wendy Hiller, Steven Hill
401. "Eight Feet to Midnight" [a drama of the outlawed Irish Republican Army] (4-29-57) Edward Mulhare, Constance Ford, Pat Henning
402. "The Out-of-Towners" [by Tad Mosel] (5-6-57) Eileen Heckart, E. G. Marshall
403. "Babe in the Woods" [by Sumner Locke Elliott] (5-13-57) Betty Furness, Tammy Grimes, Jody McCrea
404. "The Man Who Wasn't Himself" [by Howard Rodman] (5-20-57) Eli Wallach, Patricia Smith
405. "The Weston Strain" (5-27-57) Judson Laire, Aline MacMahon, Conrad Nagel, Dick York, John Drainie
406. "The Furlough" [by Robert Fielder] (6-3-57) James Daly, Mildred Dunnock, Cathleen McGuire, William Smithers

[now as STUDIO ONE SUMMER THEATRE until new season]

407. "The Mother Bit" [by Adrian Spies] (6-10-57) Peter Falk, June Havoc, Harry Guardino, Sam Levene
408. "The Staring Match" (6-17-57) James Daly, Margaret Hamilton, James Gregory
409. "The Goodwill Ambassadors" [by Jerome Ross] (6-24-57) Juano Hernandez, William Redfield, Lenka Peterson
410. "Death and Taxes" [by Laurence Marks] (7-1-57) Theodore Bikel, Vivian Nathan
411. "A Matter of Guilt" [by Alfred Harris] (7-8-57) June Lockhart, Lin McCarthy
412. "Love Me to Pieces" [by Romeo Miller; the theme sung by Jill Corey] (7-15-57) William Hickey, Bennye Gatteys, Cliff Norton, Ned Glass, Parker McCormick, Jerome Cowan, Ralph Hanley
413. "In Love with a Stranger" [by Arthur Rodney Coneybeare] (7-22-57) Jim Backus, Hiram Sherman, Phyllis Love, Audrey Christie, Joanna Roos
414. "The Human Barrier" [by Richard De Roy] (7-29-57) John Beal, Skip Homeier, Patricia Smith, Pat Hingle

415. "My Mother and How She Undid Me" [by Theodore Apstein]
     (8-5-57) Eddie Bracken
416. "The Unmentionable Blues" [by Helen Cotton] (8-12-57) Car-
     men Mathews, Elliott Nugent, Sarah Marshall, Roland Winters
417. "Rudy" (8-19-57) Jacob Ben Ami, Burt Brinckerhoff, Nancy
     Marchand, Madeleine Sherwood, Peter Falk
418. "Guitar" [by Harvey Miller; Ray de La Toire and Charles
     Montoya provided the background music] (8-26-57) Frank
     Silvera
419. "The Dark Intruder" [by Alfred Brenner] (9-2-57) Roland
     Winters, Charles Korvin, House Jameson, David Lewis,
     Joanne Linville

Tenth Season

420. "The Night America Trembled" [by Nelson Bond; a re-enact-
     ment of the Howard Koch and Orson Welles radio play of
     1938 The War of the Worlds broadcast] (9-9-57) Warren
     Beatty, Warren Oates, Alexander Scourby; narrated by Ed-
     ward R. Murrow
421. "First Prize for Murder" [adapted by Phil Reisman Jr.] (9-
     16-57) Darren McGavin, Barbara O'Neil
422. "Mutiny on the Shark" [Part I; by Max Ehrlich] (9-23-57)
     Richard Basehart, Betsy Palmer
423. "Mutiny on the Shark" [Part II] (9-30-57) as above.
424. "The Morning After" [by Tad Mosel] (10-7-57) Barbara Bel
     Geddes, Arthur Hill, Rex Thompson
425. "Act of Mercy" [by Jerome Ross] (10-14-57) Richard Kiley,
     Beatrice Straight
426. "The Deaf Heart" [by Mayo Simon] (10-21-57) Piper Laurie,
     William Shatner
427. "Bend in the Road" [by John Vlahos] (11-4-57) Franchot
     Tone, Cathleen Nesbitt
428. "Twenty-Four Hours 'Til Dawn" [by Patrick Alexander] (11-
     11-57) Lorne Greene, Jason Robards Jr.
429. "Please Report Any Odd Characters" [by Jerome Ross] (11-
     18-57) John Carradine, Henry Jones, Phyllis Love
430. "Escape Route" [by William Mourne] (12-2-57) Robert Flem-
     yng, Leueen McGrath, Juano Hernandez, Murray Matheson,
     Joseph Yadin
431. "No Deadly Medicine" [Part I; by Arthur Hailey; produced by
     Herbert Brodkin] (12-9-57) Lee J. Cobb, William Shatner,
     Gloria Vanderbilt, James Broderick
432. "No Deadly Medicine" [Part II] (12-16-57) as above.

[hereafter titled STUDIO ONE IN HOLLYWOOD]

433. "The Brotherhood of the Bell" [adapted by Dale Wasserman
     from the David Karp novel] (1-6-58) Cameron Mitchell,
     Tom Drake, John Baragrey, Joanne Dru, Pat O'Brien
434. "The Other Place" [adapted by Theodore Apstein from the J.
     B. Priestley play] (1-13-58) Sir Cedric Hardwicke, Rich-
     ard Carlson, Phyllis Avery, Glenda Farrell, Marilyn Ers-
     kine

435. "Trial by Slander" [by Roger O. Hirson] (1-20-58) Franchot Tone, Jackie Cooper, Dennis Hopper, Margaret O'Brien, Rosemary De Camp

436. "Balance of Terror" [adapted by Max Ehrlich from the Peter Shaffer play] (1-27-58) Corrine Calvet, Louis Hayward, Hugh Marlowe, Herbert Marshall, June Lockhart

437. "The Laughing Willow" (2-3-58) Lee Bowman, Nina Foch, Richard Denning, Jane Wyatt

438. "Presence of the Enemy" [by Tad Mosel] (2-10-58) James Gregory, E. G. Marshall, Tom Rettig, Anne Francis, Bethel Leslie

439. "Tide of Corruption" [by Marc Brandel] (2-17-58) Barry Sullivan, Patricia Neal, Murvyn Vye, Ray Danton, Amanda Blake

440. "The Lonely Stage" [by Robert Dozier] (2-24-58) Mary Astor, Macdonald Carey, Jack Klugman, Darryl Hickman, Irene Hervey

441. "The Fair-Haired Boy" [by Herman Raucher] (3-3-58) Darren McGavin, Jackie Cooper, Bonita Granville, Robert H. Harris, Patricia Smith

442. "A Dead Ringer" [by Henry and Madeline Misrock] (3-10-58) Elizabeth Montgomery, Jane Darwell, Gig Young, Marguerite Chapman

443. "The Tongues of Angels" [by John Vlahos] (3-17-58) James MacArthur, Margaret O'Brien, Leon Ames, Frances Farmer

444. "The Award Winner" [by Jerry Davis and Tom August] (3-24-58) Eddie Bracken, Joanna Moore, Gale Gordon, Jack Cakie

445. "The Shadow of a Genius" [by Jerome Ross] (3-31-58) Boris Karloff, Eva LeGallienne, Vivian Nathan, Patricia Barry, Skip Homeier

446. "Mrs. 'Arris Goes to Paris" [adapted by Michael Dyne from the Paul Gallico story] (4-14-58) Gracie Fields, Janet Swanson, Jacques Bergerac

447. "The Desperate Age" [by Abby Mann] (4-21-58) Martin Balsam, Barbara Bel Geddes, Aline MacMahon, Wendell Corey

448. "The Edge of Truth" [by Adrian Spies; directed by David Greene and produced by Norman Felton] (4-28-58) Paul Douglas, Glenda Farrell, John Lupton, Scott Forbes, Robert Bogart

449. "The McTaggert Succession" [by John McGreevey] (5-5-58) Jim Backus, Dennis Day, Hope Emerson, William Gargan

450. "Kurishika Incident" [by Roger O. Hirson] (5-12-58) Sessue Hayakawa, John Cassavetes, Michi Kobi

451. "A Funny-Looking Kid" [by Ben Starr] (5-19-58) Frank McHugh, Joan Blondell, Jack Carson

452. "The Enemy Within" [by Richard DeRoy] (5-26-58) Dane Clark, Dick York, George Tobias, Noah Berry Jr. , Don DeFore

453. "Ticket to Tahiti" [by Robert Bassing] (6-2-58) James MacArthur, Franchot Tone, Kim Hunter, Olive Sturgess

454. "The Strong Man" [by Harold Jack Bloom] (6-9-58) Eric Fleming, Barbara Baxley, James Franciscus, Everett Sloane

455. "The Left-Handed Welcome" [adapted by Robert Presnell from the John D. Weaver story] (6-16-58) Tommy Sands, Elaine Stritch, Judi Meredith
456. "The Man Who Asked for a Funeral" [by Jerome Ross] (6-23-58) Jack Klugman, Terry Moore, Mary Anderson, Corey Allen
457. "The Undiscovered" [by Joseph Landon] (6-30-58) John Lupton, Marilyn Erskine, Edward Andrews, Nancy Hadley
458. "Man Under Glass" [by Dick Berg] (7-14-58) Albert Salmi, Jason Robards Jr., Michael Landon, Peggy Ann Garner
459. "A Delicate Affair" [by Jerome Gruskin] (7-28-58) Robert Horton, Francis Lederer, Charles Ruggles, Joanne Gilbert
460. "The Last Summer" [by Frank Gilroy] (8-4-58) Dennis Hopper, Vivian Nathan, Malcolm Atterbury, Claire Griswold
461. "Tag-Along" (8-11-58) James Gregory, Burt Brinckerhoff, Joel Crothers, Mario Alcalde
462. "Birthday Present" [by Jack Roche] (8-18-58) Cecil Kellaway, Cesar Romero, Mary Beth Hughes, Edgar Buchanan
463. "Bellingham" [adapted by A. J. Carothers and Elliot West from the latter's story] (8-25-58) Leo G. Carroll, Kenneth Haigh, John Abbott, Bill Pottin
464. "The Lady Died at Midnight" [by Charles Lanson; directed by Paul Nickell; as restaged from the Pursuit pilot episode of 2/23/58] (9-1-58) Paul Douglas, Gary Merrill, Earl Holliman
465. "No Place to Run" [by James P. Cavanagh] (9-15-58) Rosemary De Camp, Tommy Rettig, Roberta Haynes
466. "Image of Fear" (9-29-58) Nina Foch, Lili Darvas, Eugenie Leontovich, Rod Taylor

THE FORD THEATRE HOUR

Sponsored by The Ford Motor Company.

The Episodes:

1. "Joy to the World" [on Hollywood habits; by Alan Scott and George Haight] (11-21-48) Eddie Albert, Janet Blair, Philip Coolidge, Myron McCormick, Florida Friebus, Arthur Henderson, Jack Hartley
2. "Night Must Fall" [adapted from the Emlyn Williams play] (12-19-48) Fay Bainter, Oliver Thorndike, Howard St. John, Mildred Dunnock, Cloris Leachman
3. "The Man Who Came to Dinner" [adapted from the George S. Kaufman and Moss Hart play] (1-16-49) Edward Everett Horton, Vicki Cummings, Judy Parrish, Kevin McCarthy, Mary Wickes, Zero Mostel, Rex O'Malley
4. "The Silver Cord" [adapted from the Sidney Howard play] (2-13-49) Mady Christians, Meg Mundy
5. "Outward Bound" [adapted from the Sutton Vane play] (3-13-49) Lillian Gish, Freddie Bartholomew, Mary Boland, Richard Hart

6. "Arsenic and Old Lace" [adapted from the Joseph Kesselring play] (4-11-49) Boris Karloff, Josephine Hull, Anthony Ross

7. "One Sunday Afternoon" [adapted from the James Hagan play] (5-16-49) Burgess Meredith, Hume Cronyn, Francesca Brunning

Second Season

8. "The Twentieth Century" [adapted from the Ben Hecht and Charles MacArthur play] (10-7-49) Fredric March, Lilli Palmer

9. "Kind Lady" [adapted from the Edward Chodorov play] (12-2-49) Fay Bainter, Joseph Schildkraut

10. "Little Women" [adapted from the Louisa May Alcott novel] (12-16-49) Kim Hunter, June Lockhart, Patricia Kirkland, Meg Mundy, Karl Malden

11. "The Farmer Takes a Wife" [adapted from the Marc Connelly and Frank Ball Elser play] (12-30-49) Dane Clark, Geraldine Brooks

12. "The Barker" [adapted from the Kenyon Nicholson play] (1-13-50) Lloyd Nolan, Eileen Heckart, William Redfield, Jean Carson

13. "Laburnum Grove" [adapted from the J. B. Priestley play] (1-29-50) Raymond Massey, Valerie and Ernest Cossart

14. "The Royal Family" [by George S. Kaufman and Edna Ferber, play] (2-10-50) Margaret Wycherly, Carol Goodner, Richard Waring

15. "Uncle Harry" [adapted from the Thomas Job play] (2-24-50) Joseph Schildkraut, Eva LeGallienne

16. "Room Service" [adapted from the John Murray and Allen Boretz play] (3-10-50) Jack Carson, Hume Cronyn

17. "Dear Brutus" [adapted from the James M. Barrie play] (3-24-50) Brian Aherne, Mary Malone, Valerie Cossart, Ralph Riggs

18. "The Little Minister" [adapted from the James M. Barrie play] (4-7-50) Tom Drake, Frances Reid, Ian Keith, Roderick Walker

19. "The School for Scandal" [adapted from the Richard Brinsley Sheridan play] (4-21-50) Leueen McGrath, Margalo Gillmore, Ian Keith, Philip Bourneuf

20. "Father Malachy's Miracle" [adapted from the 1937 play] (5-5-50) Ernest Truex

21. "Subway Express" [adapted from the Eva May Flint and Martha Madison play] (5-19-50) Ian Keith, Mary Mason, Richard Newton, in a cast of fifty.

22. "The Shining Hour" [adapted from the Keith Winter play] (6-2-50) Lois Wheeler, Margaret Lindsay, Richard Derr

23. "On Borrowed Time" [adapted from the Paul Osborn play] (6-30-50) Henry Hull

Third Season [now variously called THE MAGNAVOX THEATRE]

24. "The Traitor" [the Herman Wouk play; directed by Franklin Schaffner] (9-8-50) Lee Tracy, Barbara Ames, Walter Hampden

25. "The Tale of the Wolf" [adapted from the Ferenc Molnar play] (9-15-50) Ilona Massey, John Wengraf, Steven Hill
26. "The Married Look" (9-22-50) Paul Kelly, Lois Wilson, Betsy Blair
27. "The Fog" [adapted from the John Willard play] (9-29-50) Francis L. Sullivan, Jack Manning, Peter Hobbs
28. "The Marble Faun" [adapted from the Nathaniel Hawthorne novel] (10-6-50) Anna Lee, Alan Shayne, Sally Chamberlin
29. "Strange Harbor" (10-13-50) Dane Clark, Geraldine Brooks
30. "Angel Street" [adapted from the Patrick Hamilton play] (10-20-50) Judith Evelyn
31. "Lightnin'" [adapted from the Winchell Smith, Victor Mapes, and Frank Bacon play] (10-27-50) Victor Moore, Jean Gillespie, Leslie Nielsen
32. "Heart of Darkness" [adapted from the Joseph Conrad classic] (11-3-50) Richard Carlson
33. "Father, Dear Father" (11-10-50) Edward Everett Horton, Kim Stanley, Leora Thatcher
34. "The White-Headed Boy" [adapted from the Lennox Robinson play] (11-17-50) Barry Fitzgerald, Biff McGuire, Mildred Natwick, Elinor Randel
35. "The Three Musketeers" [adapted from the Alexandre Dumas classic; the first full hour film made for television] (11-24-50) Charles Lang, Robert Clarke, John Hubbard, Lyn Thomas, Mel Archer, Kristine Miller
36. "Another Darling" (12-1-50) Patricia Crowley, Jack Ewing
37. "The Hurricane at Pilgrim Hill" (12-8-50) Cecil Kellaway, Clem Bevans, Virginia Grey, Leslye Banning
38. "Alice in Wonderland" [adapted from the Lewis Carroll classic] (12-15-50) Iris Mann (as Alice), Richard Waring (as the March Hare), Tiny Schrimp (as the Dormouse), Lervi Operti (as the Mad Hatter), Dorothy Jarnac
39. "Cause for Suspicion" [subsequently restaged for the Matinee Theatre episode of 6/6/56] (12-29-50) Glen Langan, Dean Harens, Louisa Horton
40. "The Presentation of the Look Magazine TV Awards" (1-12-51)
41. "Final Copy" (1-26-51) Robert Sterling, Anna Minot
42. "Spring Again" [adapted from the Isobel Leighton and Bertram Bloch play] (2-9-51) Dorothy Gish, Walter Hampden
43. "The Golden Mouth" (2-23-51) Henry Hull, John Forsythe, Anne Marno, Gerald Mohr, Virginia Gilmore
44. "The Ghost Patrol" (3-9-51) Ernest Truex, Jane Seymour, Dennis Harrison
45. "Heart of Darkness" [adapted from the Joseph Conrad classic; restaged from 11/3/50] (3-23-51) Richard Carlson
46. "Ticket to Oblivion" (4-6-51) Anthony Quinn, Signe Hasso
47. "The Touchstone" (4-20-51) Margaret Sullavan, Paul McGarth, Jerome Cowan
48. "Dead on the Vine" (5-4-51) Margaret Phillips, William Prince, John Alexander, Faith Brook
49. "Peter Ibbetson" [adapted from the George du Maurier novel] (5-18-51) Richard Greene, Stella Andrew, Anna Lee, Iris Mann, Ivan Simpson

50. "Three in a Room" (6-1-51) Judith Evelyn, Louisa Horton, Patricia Kirkland
51. "Night Over London" (6-15-51) Stella Andrew, Hugh Reilly
52. "The Ghost Patrol" [restaged from 3/9/51] (6-29-51) Ernest Truex

THE CHEVROLET TELE-THEATRE

Up to and including the episode of November 8, 1948, this was referred to as THE BROADWAY PLAYHOUSE.

The Episodes:

1. "Home Life of a Buffalo" (9-27-48) John McQuade, Virginia Smith
2. "Mirage in Manhattan" (10-4-48) Jessie Royce Landis, Will Geer
3. "Thinking Aloud" [by Emlyn Williams] (10-11-48) Judith Evelyn, Dean Jagger
4. "Whistle, Daughter, Whistle" (10-18-48) Minerva Pious, Gertrude Berg
5. "His Master's Affairs" (10-25-48) Arthur Treacher, Judy Parrish, Mischa Auer
6. "The Purple Doorknob" (11-1-48) Ethel Griffies, Faye Emerson
7. "A Study in Triangles" (11-8-48) Erni Arneson
8. "No Shoes" (11-15-48) James Dunn, Vinton Hayworth
9. "The Flattering Word" (11-22-48) Zasu Pitts, John Carradine
10. "The Valiant" (11-29-48) Paul Muni
11. "Close Quarters" (12-6-48) Barry Nelson, Louisa Horton
12. "Sham" (12-13-48) Edward Everett Horton, Natalie Schaefer
13. "A Little Matter of Faith" (12-20-48) Frank Conroy, Iris Mann
14. "Who's Your Judge?" (12-27-48) Eddie Albert, Frank M. Thomas
15. "The Mirror and the Manicure" (1-3-49) Guy Kibbee, Glenda Farrell
16. "Good-bye to Larry K" (1-10-49) Buddy Ebsen
17. "Jinxed" (1-17-49) Jackie Cooper, Mary Anderson, Vaughn Taylor
18. "Trapeze" (1-24-49) Louise Rainer, Tod Andrews, Charles Korvin, Clay Clements
19. "All's Fair" (1-31-49) Mary Boland, Roland Young, Patricia Kirkland
20. "Expert Opinion" (2-7-49) Boris Karloff, Dennis King, Vicki Cummings
21. "Miracle in the Rain" (2-14-49) John Dall, Mary Anderson
22. "Suppressed Desires" (2-21-49) Ernest Truex, Ilka Chase, Valerie Cossart
23. "Heat Lightning" (2-28-49) Elizabeth Bergner, Dean Jagger
24. "Mr. Bell's Creation" (3-7-49) Janet Blair, Romney Brent, Ann Thomas, Robert White

25. "Londonderry Air" (3-14-49) Nanette Fabray, John Conte
26. "Smart Guy" (3-21-49) Nancy Coleman, Alan Baxter
27. "The Managers" (3-28-49) Victor Moore, Guy Kibbee
28. "Good Night, Please" (4-4-49) Edward Everett Horton, Natalie Schaefer
29. "The Twelve Pound Look" [adapted from the James M. Barrie play] (4-11-49) Margaret Sullavan, Ralph Forbes
30. "Everybody Loves My Baby" (4-18-49) Jane Withers, Richard Noyes, Calvin Thomas
31. "Tommy Malone Comes Home" (4-25-49) James Dunn
32. "The Suicide Club" [adapted from the Robert Louis Stevenson story] (5-2-49) Francis L. Sullivan, Bramwell Fletcher, Oliver Thorndike
33. "A Passenger to Bali" (5-9-49) Boris Karloff, Stanley Ridges, Vicki Cummings
34. "Manhattan Mary" (5-16-49) Mitzi Green, Bob Scheerer
35. "The Uncertain Hour" (5-23-49) Fay Bainter, Hume Cronyn
36. "Long Lost Brother" (5-30-49) John Carradine, Richard Leone, Donald Hastings
37. "Johnny Cartwright's Camera" (6-6-49) Lee Tracy, Betty George
38. "Weather Ahead" (6-13-49) Brian Donlevy
39. "Heritage of Wimpole Street" (6-20-49) Leo G. Carroll, Valerie Cossart, Emily Lawrence
40. "Half an Hour" (6-27-49) Nina Foch, John Conte
41. "Lesson for Eddy" (7-4-49) Charles Ruggles, Frank Tweddell, Zalia Talma, Betty Ann Nyman

Second Season

42. "Leo and Sagittarius" (9-19-49) Vicki Cummings
43. "Her Majesty, the King" (9-26-49) Ethel Griffies, Barry McCollum, Elaine Williams
44. "The Unguarded Moment" (10-3-49) Paul Lukas, Valerie Bettis, Louis Beachner, Dora Clement, Charles G. Martin, Barbara Townsend
45. "Leave It to Mother" (10-10-49) Irene Rich, Ralph Locke, Mary Malone, Jim Stevens
46. "The Boat Ride" (10-17-49) Dane Clark, John O'Hara
47. "The Birthday Party" (10-24-49) Henry Hull, John Beal, Blanche Yurka
48. "Witness for the Prosecution" [adapted from the Agatha Christie play] (10-31-49) Walter Abel, Nicholas Saunders, Felicia Montealegre, Hilda Vaughn, Anne Ives
49. "His Name Is Jason" (11-7-49) Margo, Jonathan Harris, Norma Jane Marlowe
50. "Temporarily Purple" (11-14-49) Nina Foch, John Conte
51. "Hart to Heart" (11-21-49) Miriam Hopkins, Donald Curtis, Charles Martin, George DeKover
52. "The Door" (11-28-49) Don Ameche, Dennis Harrison, Pamela Rivers, Tom Pedi, Grace Valentine
53. "At Night All Cats Are Grey" (12-5-49) Basil Rathbone, Pamela Conroy, John Moore

54. "Desert Incident" (12-12-49) Guy Kibbee, Joshua Shelley, Iggie Wolfington
55. "The Priceless Gift" (12-19-49) Lee Tracy, Mary Patton, Maurice Fraklin
56. "I Cover Times Square" [the pilot for the 1950 series] (12-26-49) Harold Huber
57. "Hart to Heart" [restaged from 11/21/49] (1-2-50) Dick Foran, Louise Albritton, Roscoe Karns
58. "Midnight Flight" (1-9-50) Barry Nelson, Ferdi Hoffmann
59. "The Chirp of the Cricket" (1-16-50) Noel Leslie, Dennis Harrison, Mercedes McCambridge (her eastern television debut)
60. "The Final Bell" (1-23-50) Canada Lee, Harry Bellaver
61. "The Million Dollar Question" (1-30-50) Faye Emerson, Frank Albertson
62. "Oropalo" (2-6-50) Clarence Derivent, Victor Jory, Jack Arthur, Helen Choate
63. "The Hoosier School-Master" (2-13-50) Wesley Addy, Emily Barnes, Forrest Tucker
64. "Once to Every Boy" (2-20-50) Billy James, Peggy Ann Garner, Carmen Mathews, Howard Smith
65. "Three Smart Girls" (2-20-50) Patricia Crowley, Isobel Elsom, Sally Moffett, Charles Winninger
66. "Queen of Spades" (3-6-50) Margaret Wycherly, Felicia Montealegre, Basil Rathbone
67. "The Man Who Ordered Apple Pie" (3-13-50) Guy Kibbee
68. "The Walking Stick" (3-20-50) Rex Harrison, Dennis King, Una O'Connor, Elizabeth Patterson, Eyleen Peel
69. "The Great Emptiness" (3-27-50) Dick Foran, Peggy Badey
70. "The Voice in the Night" (4-3-50) Dort Clark, Arlene Whelan, Don Hanmer
71. "Once a Gentleman" (4-10-50) Milton Frome, Victor Varconi
72. "The Bone for the Shadow" (4-17-50) John Loder, Flora Campbell, Roberta Jonay
73. "The Californian's Tale" (4-24-50) E. G. Marshall, Edgar Stehli, Dean Harens, Daniel Reed
74. "Introduction" (5-1-50) Philip Bourneuf, Frances Reid, Ben Lackland, William Prince
75. "Welcome Jeremiah" (5-8-50) John McQuade, Mercer McLeod
76. "The Sun" (5-15-50) John Buckmaster, Torin Thatcher, Cara Williams
77. "Highly Recommended" (5-22-50) Mary Wickes, Dara Clement, Philip Tones, Francis Compton
78. "Letter to Edith" (5-29-50) Alfreda Wallace, Nelson Olmstead
79. "The Brave Man with a Cord" (6-5-50) Don Newland, William Post Jr., Marcy Patton
80. "The Way I Feel" (6-12-50) Ellen Cab Hill, Biff McGuire, Edith King
81. "The Fisherman" (6-19-50) Daniel Reed, Betty Caulfield, Dort Clark
82. "The Veranda" (6-26-50) Nydia Westman, Hiram Sherman

THE KRAFT TELEVISION THEATRE

Chronicled from the second season; the series began May 7, 1947, with "Double Door" featuring John Baragrey; Kraft Television Theatre was initially produced by Stanley Quinn and Maury Holland.

Second Season

1. "Her Husband's Wife" (9-22-48) Valerie Cossart, Charles Campbell, Romola Robb
2. "Great Day" (9-29-48) Katherine Meskill, Anna Minot, Maury Hill, Phillipa Bevans
3. "Twin Diamonds" (10-6-48)
4. "The Truth Game" [adapted from the 1930 play] (10-13-48) Joyce Hayward
5. "Criminal at Large" [adapted from the Edgar Wallace play] (10-20-48) Olive Reeves-Smith, Tom Palmer
6. "Biography" [adapted from the Nathaniel Behrman play] (10-27-48) Virginia Gilmore, John Forsythe
7. "Old Lady Robbins" (11-3-48) Ethel Owen, Grace Kelly
8. "The Detour" [adapted from the Owen Davis play] (11-10-48) Curtis Cooksey, Isabel Price, Joan Stanley, James Cootes, Isabelle Robbins
9. "The Ivory Door" [adapted from the A. A. Milne play] (11-17-48) Jackie Cooper, Edith Heyman
10. "Wuthering Heights" [adapted from the Emily Brontë classic] (11-24-48) Louisa Horton, John Forsythe, Ethel Griffies
11. "The Dover Road" [adapted from the A. A. Milne play] (12-1-48) Geoffrey Lumb
12. "The Flashing Stream" [adapted from the Charles Morgan play; subsequently restaged for the Matinee Theatre episode of 4/12/57] (12-8-48) Richard Kirkland, Gwen Anderson, Lorna Kent
13. "The Old Soak" [adapted from the Harry Beresford play] (12-15-48) Guy Kibbee
14. "Hansel and Gretel" [the Humperdinck operetta, staged for television] (12-22-48)
15. "Meet the Prince" [adapted from the A. A. Milne play] (12-29-48)
16. "To Catch the Wind" (1-5-49) Audrey Ridgewell, Mark Roberts, John Conway
17. "Miranda" (1-12-49) Beverly Roberts, Richard Kendrick, Betty Ann Nyman
18. "Duet for Two Hands" [adapted from the Mary Hayley Bell play] (1-19-49) Guy Spaull, Roderick Walker, Valerie Cossart, Louisa Horton
19. "There's Always Juliet" [adapted from the John Van Druten play] (1-26-49) Gwen Anderson, Lex Richards, Margery Maude, Huntington Watts
20. "Her Master's Voice" [adapted from the Clare Kummer play] (2-2-49) Philip Truex, Augusta Dabney, Ethel Owen, Valerie Cossart

21. "Gramercy Ghost" [adapted from the John Cecil Holm play] (2-9-49)

22. "Room Service" [adapted from the John Murray and Allen Boretz play] (2-16-49) Warren Parker, Dudley Sadler, Gage Clark

23. "The Flying Gerardos" [adapted from the Kenyon Nicholson and Charles Robinson play] (2-23-49) Lucille Fenton, Barbara Meyer, Hugh Reilly, Susan Thorne, William Thunkhurst, Winfield Hoeny

24. "A Bill of Divorcement" [adapted from the Clemence Dane play] (3-2-49)

25. "The Arrival of Kitty" (3-9-49) Patricia Kirkland, Gage Clark, Malcolm Beggs, Dort Clark

26. "Consider Lily" (3-16-49) Margaret Phillips, Ann Donaldson, Ron Randell

27. "Village Green" [adapted from the Carl Allensworth play] (3-23-49) Carl Benton Reid, Mark Roberts, Jean Gillespie

28. "Wicked Is the Vine" (3-30-49) Margaret Phillips, Ann Donaldson, Ron Randell

29. "As Husbands Go" [adapted from the Rachel Crothers play] (4-6-49) Ruth Matteson, Betty Ann Nyman, Tonio Selwart, Lawrence Fletcher

30. "The Miracle of Chickerston" (4-13-49) Gage Clark, William Lee, Natalie Schaefer

31. "The Whole Town's Talking" (4-20-49) Lawrence Fletcher, Valerie Cossart, Timothy Lynn Kearse, Andrea Wallace

32. "Green Stockings" (4-27-49) Ruth Matteson, Joseph Allen Jr.

33. "Adam and Eva" [adapted from the Guy Bolton play] (5-4-49) Carl Benton Reid, Mark Roberts, Patricia White

34. "The Oath of Hippocrates" (5-11-49) Guy Spaull, Dean Edwards, Felicia Montealegre

35. "Big Hearted Herbert" [adapted from the Sophia Kerr and A. S. Richardson play; subsequently restaged by Kay Arthur for the Matinee Theatre episode of 11/11/55] (5-18-49) Valerie Cossart, Kirk Brown

36. "Autumn Fire" [adapted from the Thomas C. Murray play] (5-25-49) Martin Lewis, Andrea Wallace, Frank Baxter, Helen Stenborg

37. "The Elephant Shepherd" (6-1-49) Neil Hamilton, Vernon Smith, Madelaine Smith

38. "Payment Deferred" [adapted from the Jeffrey Dell play; restaged from 10/1/47] (6-8-49) Mercer McLeod, Cloris Leachman, Richard Deane, Vilma Kuretz, Grace Carney

39. "Little Brown Jug" [adapted from the Marie Baumer play] (6-15-49) Vaughn Taylor, Katherine Anderson, Malcolm Lee Beggs, John Stephen, Gwen Anderson, John Harvey

40. "Pink Strings and Sealing Wax" (6-22-49) Leslie Barrie, Peter Fernandez, Cloris Leachman, Viola Frayne, Jean Gillespie

41. "Baby Mine" (6-29-49) Kyle MacDonnell, Warren Parker, Margo Mayo

42. "Within the Law" [adapted from the Bayard Veiller play] (7-6-49) Patricia Jenkins, Malcolm Lee Beggs, Polly Coe, Jack Orrison, John Stephen

43. "A Young Man's Fancy" [adapted from the Harry Thurschwell and Alfred Golden play] (7-13-49) Walter Butterworth, Richard Leone, Lee Carney, Joan Shepard
44. "The Curtain Rises" (7-20-49) Nancy Coleman, Lex Richards, Guy Spaull, Peggy French
45. "Time for Elizabeth" [adapted from the Norman Krasna and Groucho Marx play] (7-27-49) John D. Seymour, Nancy Sheridan, Maurice Manson
46. "Heaven and Charing Cross" (8-3-49) Una O'Connor, Elizabeth Ross, Rex O'Malley, Treva Frazee, Louis Beachner
47. "The Misleading Lady" (8-10-49) Patricia Jenkins, Mark Roberts, Vaughn Taylor
48. "Mr. Pim Passes By" [adapted from the A. A. Milne play] (8-17-49) Rex O'Malley, Valerie Cossart, Geoffrey Lumb
49. "Where the Dear Antelope Play" (8-24-49) Mary Young, Joyce Van Patten, Helen Hatch, Edith Meiser, Ruth Hammond
50. "Bedelia" (8-31-49) Julie Haydon, Jim Davidson
51. "Respectfully Yours" (9-7-49) Flora Campbell, Chester Stratton
52. "Little Darling" [adapted from the Eric Hatch play] (9-14-49) Tom Bickley, Marilyn Monk, Nancy Ross, Patricia Pope

Third Season

53. "The Man in Half Moon Street" [adapted from the Barre Lyndon story; subsequently restaged for the Matinee Theatre episode of 1/9/57] (9-21-49) John Newland, Mercer McCleod, Anne Jackson
54. "Climax" (9-28-49) John Arthur, Felicia Montealegre, Oliver Thorndike
55. "Apple of His Eye" [adapted from the Kenyon Nicholson and Charles Robinson play] (10-5-49) Kenyon Nicholson, Charles Robinson (adapted and starred); Larry Fletcher, Vaughn Taylor, Pamela Rivers
56. "Your Friendly Nabors" (10-12-49) Valerie Cossart, Warren Parker, Enid Markey, Lawrence Fletcher
57. "Accidentally Yours" (10-19-49) Valerie Cossart, Mercer MacLeod, Cloris Leachman
58. "To Dream Again" (10-26-49) Lauren Gilbert, Janet DeGore, Leon Shaw, Robert Craven, Velma Royton
59. "Whistling in the Dark" [adapted from the Lawrence Gross and E. C. Carpenter play] (11-2-49) Jack Lemmon, Rosemary Rice, Donald Briggs
60. "Happy Ending" (11-9-49) Jim Davidson, June Dayton, Isabel Price, Florence Robinson
61. "The Happiest Years" [adapted from the Thomas Coby and William Roerick play] (11-16-49) James Daly, Ethel Owen, Lewis Martin, Hildy Parks, Alan Bunce
62. "In Love with Love" (11-23-49) Anne Francis, Maury Hill
63. "Seen But Not Heard" [adapted from the Martin Berkeley play] (11-30-49) George Reeves, Warren Parker, Tommy Rettig, Toni Halloran, Kathleen Maguire, Larry Fletcher, Jackie Collins
64. "The Comedy of Errors" [adapted from the Shakespeare classic] (12-7-49) Stewart Bradley, James Daly, Harry Townes, Kurt Richards

65. "The Nantucket Legend" (12-14-49) Vaughn Taylor, Phil Faversham, Myrtle Ferguson, Edith Gresnam
66. "The Glove" (12-21-49) Margaret Phillips, Dennis Harrison
67. "New Brooms" [adapted from the Frank Craven play] (12-28-49) William Lee, Will Hare, Frances Waller, June Dayton
68. "That Naborly Feeling" [sequel to episode of 10/12/49] (1-4-50) Valerie Cossart, Warren Parker, Enid Markey
69. "As Husbands Go" [adapted from the Rachel Crothers play; restaged from 4/6/49] (1-11-50) Mary Alice Moore, Donald Briggs
70. "The Vinegar Tree" [adapted from the Paul Osborn play] (1-18-50) Raymond Bramley, Bess Winburn, Edmon Ryan
71. "Kelly" (1-25-50) Anne Francis, E. G. Marshall, Mark Roberts, George Reeves
72. "The Old Ladies" [adapted from the Rodney Ackland play] (2-1-50) Katherine Meskill, Mildred Natwick, Doris Rich
73. "The Dark Tower" [adapted from the George S. Kaufman and Alexander Woollcott play] (2-8-50) E. G. Marshall, Flora Campbell, John Newland
74. "The Silent Room" (2-15-50) Neva Patterson, Thomas Nello
75. "Valley Forge" [adapted from the Maxwell Anderson play] (2-22-50) E. G. Marshall, Judson Laire, Vaughn Taylor
76. "Mrs. Moonlight" [adapted from the Benn W. Levy play] (3-1-50) Mary Sinclair, E. G. Marshall, Ethel Ramy
77. "The Nineteenth Hole" [adapted from the Frank Craven play] (3-8-50) Alan Stevenson, Enid Markey, Hildy Parks
78. "Ladies in Retirement" [adapted from the Edward Percy and Reginald Denham play] (3-15-50) Mildred Natwick, Richard Newton, Jean Cameron, Marge Ann Deighton
79. "The Queen's Husband" [adapted from the Robert Emmett Sherwood play] (3-22-50) Mercer McLeod, Katherine Meskill, Richard Purdy
80. "The Copperhead" [adapted from the Augustus Thomas play] (3-29-50) John Shellie, Doris Rich, Flora Campbell
81. "A Doll's House" [adapted from the Henrik Ibsen classic] (4-5-50) Felicia Montealegre, Joan Wetmore, John Newland, Theodore Newton
82. "The Lucky Finger" [adapted from the 1948 play] (4-12-50) Lois Holmes, Eleanor Wilson, Dan Morgan, Claude Horton
83. "Make Way for Lucia" [adapted from the John Van Druten and E. F. Benson play] (4-19-50) Doris Dalton, Fellippa Revana, Geoffrey Lumb
84. "Black Sheep" [adapted from the 1932 play] (4-26-50) Anne Francis, Richard McMurray, Eileen Heckart
85. "The Fourth Step" (5-3-50) Augusta Dabney, Leslie Nielsen
86. "Macbeth" [adapted from the Shakespeare classic] (5-10-50) E. G. Marshall, Uta Hagen
87. "Storm in a Teacup" [adapted from the Bruno Frank London play] (5-17-50) Doris Rich, George Reeves, Ivan Simpson, Andrea Wallace
88. "The House Beautiful" [adapted from the 1931 play] (5-24-50) Valerie Cossart, Warren Parker, Dudley Sadler
89. "The Luck of Guldeford" (5-31-50) Leslie Nielsen

90. "The Doctor in Spite of Himself" [adapted from the Moliere classic] (6-7-50) George Englund, Ulrich Haupt, Robert Chisholm, Flora Campbell

91. "Good Housekeeping" [adapted by William McCleery from his own 1949 play; subsequently restaged for the Matinee Theatre episode of 5/8/58] (6-14-50) Anne Francis, Nelson Olmstead, Arthur Walch

92. "Noah" [adapted from the Andre Obey play] (6-21-50) Vaughn Taylor, Doris Rich, Stewart Bradley

93. "The Wind Is Ninety" [adapted from the Ralph Nelson play] (6-28-50) George Reeves, Nancy Coleman

94. "Jeannie" [adapted from the 1940 play] (7-5-50) Elizabeth Ross, Mercer McLeod, Warren Burmeister

95. "Murder on the Nile" [adapted from the 1946 play] (7-12-50) Guy Spaull, Patricia Wheel

96. "Accent on Youth" [adapted from the Samson Raphaelson play] (7-19-50) Melville Ruick, Marilyn Erskine

97. "Mr. Barry's Etchings" [by Walter Bullock and Daniel Archer] (7-26-50) John Shellie

98. "January Thaw" [adapted from the William Ross and Bellamy Partridge play] (8-2-50) Vaughn Taylor

99. "Feathers in a Gale" [adapted from the Pauline Jamerson and Reginald Lawrence play] (8-9-50) E. G. Marshall, George Reeves, Kyle MacDonnell

100. "September Tide" [adapted from the Daphne du Maurier story; subsequently restaged from the Matinee Theatre episode of 8/31/56] (8-16-50) Ruth Matteson, Robert Pastene

101. "The First Mrs. Fraser" [adapted from the John G. St. Ervine play] (8-23-50) Dorothy Peterson, E. G. Marshall, Lex Richards

102. "The Detour" [adapted from the Owen Davis play] (8-30-50) Ethel Remy, James Coates, Blair Davies

103. "The Last Trump" [adapted from the 1938 play] (9-6-50) Mercer McLeod, Richard Purdy

104. "The Great Big Doorstep" [adapted from the Frances Goodrich, Albert Hackett and E. P. O'Donnell play] (9-13-50) Robert Chisholm, Philip Tonge, Florida Friebus

105. "The Last Stop" [adapted from the Irving Kaye Davis play] (9-20-50) Mildred Dunnock, Isabel Price

Fourth Season

106. "The Green Pack" (9-27-50) James Daly, Mercer McLeod

107. "I Like It Here" [adapted from the A. B. Shiffrin play] (10-4-50) Donald Buka, Anne Francis, Stefan Schnabel, Carmen Mathews

108. "The Great Broxopp" [adapted from the A. A. Milne play] (10-11-50) Chester Stratton, Faith Brook, Philip Tonge, Rex O'Malley

109. "Old Lady Robbins" [restaged from 11/3/48] (10-18-50) Enid Markey, Augusta Dabney, Herbert Nelson

110. "Truant in Park Lane" (10-25-50) Blanche Yurka, Dan Morgan

111. "Dolphin's Reach" (11-1-50) Mercer McLeod, Carmen Mathews, Enid Pulver, Stefan Schnabel
112. "Sixteen" (11-8-50) Anna Lee, Patricia Crowley, Donald Curtis
113. "The Romantic Age" [adapted from the A. A. Milne play] (11-15-50) Bethel Leslie, Dean Harens
114. "The Romantic Young Lady" [adapted from the Gregorio Martinez Sierra play] (11-22-50) Betty Caulfield, Ethel Griffies, E. G. Marshall
115. "Windows" [adapted from the John Galsworthy play] (11-29-50) Valerie Cossart, Lex Richards, Mercer McLeod, Joyce Sullivan
116. "Short Story" [adapted from the Robert Morley play] (12-6-50) Bramwell Fletcher, Viola Keats, Jane Sutherland
117. "Michael and Mary" [adapted from the A. A. Milne play] (12-13-50) Felicia Montealegre, John Newland, Peter Fernandez
118. "The Village Green" [adapted from the Carl Allensworth play] (12-20-50) Glen Denning, Raymond Van Sickle, Wendy Drew
119. "Rip Van Winkle" [adapted from the Washington Irving classic] (12-27-50) E. G. Marshall
120. "Paper Moon" (1-3-51) Frances Robinson, Richard Kiley
121. "Kelly" [restaged from 1/25/50] (1-10-51) Olive Deering, Mark Roberts, E. G. Marshall
122. "The Best Years" [adapted from the 1932 play] (1-17-51) Augusta Dabney, Dorothy Sands, Leslie Nielsen, Bonnie Baken
123. "The Spring Green" (1-24-51) Conrad Janis, Helene Seamon, Herbert Nelson, Flora Campbell
124. "The Sound of Hunting" [adapted from the Harry Brown play] (1-31-51) Ralph Meeker, Joseph Di Reda, Biff Elliott
125. "The Glass Mountain" (2-7-51) Blanche Yurka, Robert Pastene, Patricia Wheel
126. "Engaged" (2-14-51) Louis Edmonds, Lloyd Bochner, Jean Gillespie, Pat Englund, Elizabeth Ross, Dan Morgan
127. "The Fortune Hunter" (2-21-51) Jack Lemmon, Margot Moser
128. "Jane Eyre" [adapted from the Charlotte Brontë classic] (2-28-51) Kathleen Crowley, John Baragrey
129. "Delicate Story" [adapted from the Ferenc Molnar play] (3-7-51) Felicia Montealegre, John Ericson, Nelson Olmstead
130. "On Stage" (3-14-51) E. G. Marshall, Vaughn Taylor, Barbara Joyce, Pat Englund
131. "Of Famous Memory" (3-21-51) Nancy Marchand, Leslie Nielsen, Mercer McLeod
132. "The Silent Room" (3-28-51) Meg Mundy, Dan Morgan
133. "Yours Truly" [adapted from the 1927 play] (4-4-51) Lisa Kirk, Judith Parrish, John Randolph, Richard Derr
134. "Mrs. Dane's Defense" [adapted from the Henry Arthur Jones play] (4-11-51) Cyril Ritchard, Madge Elliott, Faith Brook
135. "Mr. Mergenthwirker's Lobblie" (4-18-51) Vaughn Taylor, Vinton Hayworth
136. "Brief Music" [by Emmet Lavery; subsequently restaged for the Matinee Theatre episode of 5/23/56] (4-25-51) Pat Conway, Patricia Kirkland, Joyce Van Patten

137. "Brief Candle" [by Robert Powell; subsequently restaged for the Matinee Theatre episode of 6/28/57] (5-2-51) Douglas Watson, Isobel Elsom, Mary Howard
138. "Till Death Do Us Part" (5-9-51) John Newland, Gwen Anderson, Charles Summers
139. "The Intimate Strangers" [adapted from the Booth Tarkington play] (5-16-51) Peggy Conklin, Nelson Olmstead
140. "A Play for Mary" (5-23-51) Cloris Leachman, Bramwell Fletcher, James Daly
141. "Ben Franklin" (5-30-51) Robert Emhardt, Jocelyn Brando
142. "A Seacoast in Bohemia" [by Ben Radin] (6-6-51) Raymond Rizzo, Joyce Van Patten, Philip Coolidge, Lili Darvas, Biff Elliott, Dan Morgan, Stuart MacIntosh
143. "Stranglehold" (6-13-51) Gene Lyons, Marilyn Monk, Enid Markey
144. "Only the Heart" [adapted by Horton Foote from his 1944 play] (6-20-51) Jack Ewing, Isobel Price, Isobel Robins, Dorothy Sands
145. "Merry Madness" (6-27-51) Cameron Prud'homme, Regina Wallace
146. "The Adventures of Tom Sawyer" [adapted from the Mark Twain classic] (7-4-51) Charles Taylor, Susan Harris, Joey Walsh
147. "Vienna Dateline" (7-11-51) Robert Dale Martin, John Stephen, Mary Jones, Natalie Core
148. "Zone Four" (7-18-51) Richard Kiley, Louisa Horton
149. "Bright Shadow" (7-25-51) Frederick Worlock, Raynold Evans, Richard Aherne, Valerie Cardew
150. "Hilda McKay" [a modernized version of Henrik Ibsen's Hedda Gabler] (8-1-51) Polly Rowles, John Baragrey, Robert Pastene, Wendy Drew
151. "Old Doc" (8-8-51) Vaughn Taylor, John Stephen, Dorothy Sands, Judy Parrish
152. "John Wilkes Booth" (8-15-51) John Baragrey, Oliver Thorndike, Raymond Bramley
153. "With Rosemary Rice" (8-22-51) William Daniels, Vaughn Taylor, Enid Markey
154. "Ashes in the Wind" (8-29-51) Emily Lawrence, Herbert Rudley
155. "The Easy Mark" [adapted from the 1924 play] (9-5-51) Jack Lemmon, Frances Waller

Fifth Season

156. "The Tale of the Wolf" [adapted from the Ferenc Molnar play] (9-12-51) Katherine Bard, Donald Curtis
157. "The Wren" [adapted from the Booth Tarkington play] (9-19-51) Pat Browning, Janet DeGore, Alan Shayne, Howard Wierum
158. "The Climax" [adapted from the 1909 play; restaged from 9/28/49] (9-26-51) Jack Arthur, Oliver Thorndike, Olive Deering
159. "Irish Eyes" (10-3-51) Dick Foran, Andrea Wallace, Paul Langton

160. "Seen But Not Heard" [adapted from the Martin Berkeley play; restaged from 11/30/49] (10-17-51) Jean Gillespie, Eleanor Wilson, Lawrence Fletcher

161. "Moon Over Mulberry Street" [adapted from the 1935 play] (10-19-51) Tiger Andrews, Dolores Sutton, William Edmunds

162. "Intolerance" (10-24-51) Margaret Phillips, Alfreda Wallace, John Stephen, Bramwell Fletcher

163. "Hour of Crisis" (10-31-51) Hazel Dawn Jr., Billy Lynn, Cliff Hall

164. "Justice" [adapted from the John Galsworthy play] (11-7-51) Malcolm Keen, Fred Stewart, Eileen Martin, Alan Shayne

165. "Never Be the Same" (11-14-51) Jean Adair, Howard Freeman, Dan Morgan, Christine Miller

166. "Dear Brutus" [adapted from the James M. Barrie play] (11-21-51) Tom McElhaney, Faith Brook, Joseph Anthony, Joan Wetmore

167. "The Fair Haired Boy" (11-28-51) Frances Helm, Dick Foran, Nelson Olmstead, Richard Carlyle

168. "Loyalties" [adapted from the John Galsworthy play] (12-5-51) Philip Friend, Lloyd Bochner, Toby Robins

169. "The Golden Slate" (12-12-51) Dorothy Malone, Jane Rose, J. Pat O'Malley, Edgar Stehli, Logan Ramsey

170. "Incident on Fifth Avenue" (12-19-51) Joseph Sweeney, Gene Lee, Hildy Parks

171. "The Nantucket Legend" [restaged from 12/14/49] (12-26-51) Vaughn Taylor, Brook Byron

172. "The New Gossoon" [adapted from the G. Shiels play] (1-2-52) E. G. Marshall, Carmen Mathews

173. "Philip Goes Forth" [adapted from the George Kelly play] (1-9-52) Roddy McDowall, Blanche Yurka

174. "The Round Table" (1-16-52) Katherine Bard, Gene Lyons, Chris White, John Cameron

175. "The Peaceful Warrior" (1-23-52) Dick Foran, Nancy Marchand, Nita Talbot, Melville Cooper

176. "Mrs. O'Brien Entertains" (1-30-52) Peg Hillias, John McGiver, Patrick O'Neal

177. "Follow the Dream" (2-6-52) Vivian Ferrar

178. "The Skin Game" [adapted from the John Galsworthy play] (2-13-52) Tom Helmore

179. "The Mollusc" [adapted from the Hubert Henry Davies play] (2-20-52) John Newland, Ernest Truex, Dortha Duckworth

180. "September Tide" [adapted from the Daphne du Maurier story; restaged from 8/16/50] (2-27-52) Esther Ralston, Robert Pastene

181. "What Anne Brought Home" (3-5-52) William Redfield, Beverly Dennis, Tom Shirley, Michael Dreyfuss

182. "The Thief" [adapted from the Henry Bernstein play] (3-12-52) Carol Weber, Robert Shakleton, Vaughn Taylor, Beverly Whitney, Laurence Gilbert

183. "The Bride the Sun Shines On" [adapted from the 1931 play] (3-19-52) John Newland, Cloris Leachman

184. "The Rugged Path" [adapted from the Robert E. Sherwood play] (3-26-52) E. G. Marshall, Carmen Mathews, Dan Morgan, Philip Kenneally

185. "That Ryan Girl" (4-2-52) Audrey Christie, Una O'Connor, Edmond Ryan
186. "The Last Mile" [adapted from the John Wexley play] (4-9-52) John Newland, Ben Gazzara, Robert Keith Jr.
187. "Green Cars Go East" (4-16-52) William Harrigan, James Dayton
188. "The Summit" (4-23-52) E. G. Marshall, Carmen Mathews
189. "The Man In Half Moon Street" [adapted from the Barre Lyndon story; restaged from 9/21/49] (4-30-52) John Newland, Anne Jackson
190. "She Stoops to Conquer" [adapted from the Oliver Goldsmith classic] (5-7-52) John Baragrey, Kate Hardcastle, Stella Andrew
191. "The Inn" (5-14-52) Rod Steiger, Margaret Hayes, Warner Anderson
192. "Prologue to Glory" [adapted from the E. P. Conkle play] (5-21-52) Thomas Coley, Patricia Breslin, Una O'Connor
193. "The Third Visitor" (5-28-52) Glenn Anders, Berry Kroeger, Carol Wheeler
194. "At Mrs. Beam's" [adapted from the C. K. Munro play] (6-4-52) David Greene, Lisa Ferrady, Phoebe MacKay
195. "The Cricket on the Hearth" [adapted from the Charles Dickens classic] (6-11-52) Grace Kelly, Russell Hardie
196. "The Death of Kid Slawson" (6-18-52) Jaime Smith, Duncan Baldwin, Walter Matthau
197. "Thorn in the Flesh" (6-25-52) Beatrice Straight, Peter Cookson
198. "A Time for Turning" (7-2-52) Emily Lawrence, Gaby Rodgers, David McKay
199. "The Great Big Doorstep" [adapted from the Frances Goodrich, Albert Hackett, and E. P. O'Donnell play; restaged from 9/13/50] (7-16-52) E. G. Marshall, Florida Friebus
200. "The Music Master" [adapted from the Charles Klein play] (7-30-52) Don Murray, Stefan Schnabel, Roland Winters, Jacqueline Holt
201. "Six by Six" (8-6-52)
202. "Lace on Her Petticoat" [adapted from the Aimee Stuart play] (8-13-52) Valerie Cossart, Herbert Rudley, Una O'Connor, Denise Alexander
203. "Indian Summer" [adapted from the 1913 play] (8-20-52) Anna Lee, Edmond Ryan, Russell Hardie, Jayne Meadows
204. "The Small Hours" [adapted from the George S. Kaufman and Leueen MacGrath play] (8-29-52) Lauren Gilbert, Grace Kelly, Katherine Meskill
205. "Mr. Barry's Etchings" [adapted by Walter Bullock and Daniel Archer from their own Kraft Theatre play; restaged from 7/26/50] (9-3-52) Geoffrey Lumb
206. "Letters to Lucerne" [adapted from the Fritz Hotter and Allen Vincent play] (9-10-52) Bethel Leslie
207. "The Grass Harp" [by Truman Capote and Virgil Thomson; as adapted from their own 1952 Broadway play] (9-17-52) Mildred Natwick, Russell Collins
208. "Background" (9-24-52) Katharine Bard, Joseph Anthony, Don Briggs, Patsy Bruder

Sixth Season

209. "Michael and Mary" [adapted from the A. A. Milne play; re-staged from 12/13/50] (10-1-52) Maria Riva, Scott Ford
210. "The New Tenant" (10-8-52) Alan Bunce, Blanche Yurka, Katherine Meskill
211. "A Kiss for Cinderella" [adapted from the James M. Barrie play] (10-15-52) Leslie Nielsen, Melville Cooper, Mary Stearns
212. "A Long Night in Forty Miles" (10-22-52) John Baragrey, Hildy Parks, Fred Stewart
213. "The Divine Drudge" [adapted from the 1933 play] (10-29-52) Felicia Montealegre, Harry Townes, Robert Pastene
214. "Melody Jones" (11-5-52) Janet Lally, Patsy Bruder
215. "Hilda McKay" [the modernized version of Henrik Ibsen's Hedda Gabler as restaged from 8/1/51] (11-12-52) Haila Stoddard, Shepperd Strudwick
216. "The Quiet Wedding" [adapted from the 1938 play] (11-19-52) Alan Haines, Patricia Lothian
217. "Mr. Lazarus" [adapted from the 1916 play] (11-26-52) Don Murray, E. G. Marshall, Dortha Duckworth
218. "The Iron Gate" (otherwise known as "The Empty House") [an original drama by John T. Chapman] (12-3-52) Henry Daniell, Margaret Phillips, Beatrice Straight, Patricia Breslin
219. "The Intimate Strangers" [adapted from the Booth Tarkington play] (12-10-52) Nelson Olmstead, Peggy Conklin, Isabel Price
220. "The Guest" (12-17-52) Ethel Ramey, Judith Parish, Gene Lyons
221. "A Christmas Carol" [adapted from the Charles Dickens classic] (12-24-52) Malcolm Keene, Harry Townes
222. "The Paper Moon" (12-31-52) Richard Kiley, Ilka Chase, Ruth Matteson
223. "The Fire Below and the Devil Above" (1-7-53) Richard Newton, Bethel Leslie
224. "Zone Four" [restaged from 7/18/51] (1-14-53) John Newland, Richard Kiley, Mary Fickett, Lawrence Gilbert
225. "A Square Peg" [adapted from the 1923 play] (1-21-53) Evelyn Varden, Frank M. Thomas, Irene Vernon, Lois Bolton
226. "Duet" (1-28-53) Jack Lemmon, Ray Rizzo, Sally Brook, Anatole Winodograff
227. "The Chess Game" [by Robert Howard Lindsay; produced and directed by Maurice Holland] (2-4-53) Russell Collins, Robert Carroll
228. "Right You Are! (If You Think So)" [adapted from the Luigi Pirandello play] (2-11-53) Olive Blakely, Tom Helmore
229. "Snooksie" [adapted from the Thomas A. Johnstone play] (2-18-53) Jack Lemmon, J. Pat O'Malley, Andrea Wallace, Vinton Hayworth
230. "Star Bright" (2-25-53) William Roerick, Jay Varney, Georgianna Johnson
231. "My Brother's Keeper" (3-4-53) Rod Steiger (in his first starring role), James Gregory, John Connell, Captain Ray Hall

232. "So Very Young" (3-11-53) Henry Jones, Patty O'Neill
233. "Autumn Story" (3-18-53) Alan Bunce, Perry Wilson
234. "Miss Mabel" [adapted from the 1948 play] (3-25-53) Estelle Winwood, Malcolm Keen, Frederic Worlock
235. "The Summer Place" (4-1-53) Blanche Yurka, John Newland
236. "Next of Kin" (4-8-53) Frederic Tozere, James Daly, Pat Ferris, Jack Arthur
237. "Rain No More" (4-15-53) Edward Binns
238. "The New Servant" (4-22-53) Helen Averbach, Katherine Meskill, John D. Seymour, Wright King
239. "Hoodlum with a Halo" (4-29-53) Frank Albertson, Joe Maross, Constance Ford
240. The Sixth Anniversary Show [offering scenes from previous dramas televised on The Kraft Theatre] a) "Queen Elizabeth I" Nancy Marchand; b) "January Thaw" (initially staged 8/2/50) Vaughn Taylor; c) "Wuthering Heights" (initially staged 11/24/48) John Baragrey; d) "My Brother's Keeper" (initially staged 3/4/53) Rod Steiger (5-6-53)
241. "Final Edition" (5-13-53) Chester Morris
242. "One Left Over" [by Robert Howard Lindsay; subsequently restaged for the Matinee Theatre episode of 1/10/56] (5-20-53) Isobel Price, Harry Townes, Patricia Wheel
243. "The Twilight Rounds" (5-27-53) Barbara Baxley, J. Pat O'Malley, Tony Canzoneri
244. "The Ascent of P. J. O'Hara" (6-10-53) Cliff Hall
245. "Boy of Mine" (6-17-53) Grace Kelly, Martin Newman, Henry Jones
246. "The Rainy Day" [adapted from the 1923 play] (6-24-53) Ernest Truex, Joey Walsh, Sylvia Field, Joe Maross
247. "The Diehard" (7-1-53) Jackie Cooper
248. "The House Beautiful" [adapted from the 1931 play; restaged from 5/24/50] (7-8-53) Perry Wilson, Harry Townes, Beverly Whitney
249. "The Blind Spot" (7-15-53) John Baragrey, Ruth Matteson, Richard Waring
250. "The Adventures of the Kind Mr. Smith" (7-22-53) Marcel Hillaire, Martin Green, Rene Paul
251. "The Intruder" [adapted from the 1928 play] (7-29-53) John Beal, Valerie Cossart, Patsy Bruder, Kathleen Comegys
252. "Old Macdonald Had a Curve" (8-5-53) Cameron Prud'homme. Olin Howlin
253. "Day of the Vision" (8-12-53) Harry Townes, Ilka Chase, John McGovern
254. "In Albert's Room" (8-19-53) Tony Randall, Dorothy Donohue, Joe Maross
255. "The Blues for Joey Menotti" [by Rod Serling] (8-26-53) Dan Morgan, Constance Ford

Seventh Season

256. "Quite a Guy" (9-2-53) Allen Nourse, Barry McGuire, Patty McCormack, Richard Carlyle, Nancy Devlin
257. "Double in Ivory" (9-9-53) Lee Remick, Robert Pastene, Beverly Whitney

258. "Her Father's Butler" (9-16-53) Chester Stratton, Cameron Prud'homme, Constance Ford, Richard Kiley
259. "Corinth House" (9-23-53) Kathleen Comegys, Edgar Stehli
260. "Lobblies Never Lie" [sequel to episode of 4/18/51] (9-30-53) Vaughn Taylor, Leora Dana
261. "Cap'n Jonas" (10-7-53) Fred Stewart, Paul Flannagan, Mark Roberts
262. "Keep Our Honor Bright" (10-14-53) James Dean, Addison Richards, Michael Higgins

[now twice weekly]

263. "Johnny Came Home" (10-15-53) Sylvia Sidney, Frank McHugh
264. "The Picket Fence" (10-21-53) Lois Bolton, Lee Remick
265. "Alias Jimmy Balentine" [adapted from the O. Henry short story] (10-22-53) Murray Hamilton, Patricia Smith, James Gregory
266. "The Threshold" (10-28-53) Edward Binns, Joey Walsh, Marian Seldes
267. "The Barretts of Wimpole Street" [adapted from the Rudolph Besier play] (10-29-53) Valerie Cossart, Alexander Scourby, Frederic Tozere
268. "Dream House" [by Arthur Cavanaugh; subsequently restaged for the Matinee Theatre episode of 2/20/56] (11-4-53) Rod Steiger, Doris Rich, Kenny Delmar
269. "Next Year" [by Robert Howard Lindsay] (11-5-53) Robert Pastene, Colin Keith-Johnston, E. G. Marshall, Susan Shaw
270. "A Long Time Till Dawn" (11-11-53) James Dean, Naomi Riordan, Ted Osborn
271. "The Bitter Wind" (11-12-53) Mary Pickett, Lawrence Weber
272. "The Gate" [by Kathleen Lindsay; subsequently restaged for the Matinee Theatre episode of 1/9/56] (11-18-53) Audra Lindley, Addison Richards
273. "The Apple Tree" [adapted from the John Galsworthy story] (11-19-53) Johnny Stewart, Lois Smith
274. "Gavin" (11-25-53) Richard Kendrick, Beatrice Straight
275. "The White Carnation" [by R. C. Sheriff] (11-26-53) Ian Keith, Valerie Cossart, Francis Compton
276. "The Rose Garden" (12-2-53) Enid Markey
277. "The Patsy" (12-3-53) Lois Bolton, Cloris Leachman, Chandler Cowles
278. "A Room and a Half" (12-9-53) Joe Maross, Patricia Smith
279. "The Amazing Mr. Gladstone" (12-10-53) Eli Mintz, Benjamin Fishbein, David Medoff
280. "To Live in Peace" (12-16-53) Arnold Moss, Anne Bancroft, Doro Merande, Florenz Ames
281. "Smilin' Through" (12-17-53) Bethel Leslie, Richard Ney, Jack Sweeney
282. "Rip Van Winkle" [adapted from the Washington Irving classic; restaged from 12/27/50] (12-23-53) E. G. Marshall, Raymond Bramley
283. "A Christmas Carol" [adapted from the Charles Dickens classic] (12-24-53) Melville Cooper, Noel Leslie, Denis Greene, Harry Townes, Geoffrey Lumb, Valerie Cossart

284. "A Cup of Kindness" (12-30-53) Constance Ford, Lilia Skala, Mark Roberts, Elaine Stritch
285. "Candlelight" [adapted from the P. G. Wodehouse version of the Siegfried Geyer story] (12-31-53) Mary Sinclair, Bramwell Fletcher, Siegfried Geyer (adapted and co-starred), Leueen MacGrath
286. "The Thankful Heart" (1-6-54) Florenz Ames, John Stephen, Grace Kelly
287. "Babylon Revisited" [adapted from the F. Scott Fitzgerald story] (1-7-54) Kevin McCarthy, Theodore Newton
288. "The Atherton Boy" (1-13-54) Louisa Albritton, Grant Sullivan
289. "Burlesque" [adapted from the George Manker Waters and Arthur Hopkins play] (1-14-54) Art Carney, Constance Ford
290. "One Man in a Million" (1-20-54) James Barton, Ed Begley
291. "Wednesday's Child" [adapted from the Leopold Atlas story; subsequently restaged for the Matinee Theatre episode of 3/3/58] (1-21-54) Edward Binns, Gaby Rodgers, Carole Mathews, Ken Walkes
292. "The Antique Touch" (1-27-54) Tony Randall, Dorothy Donahue
293. "The Shining Palace" [by Peggy Phillips; subsequently restaged for the Matinee Theatre episode of 3/8/56] (1-28-54) Arthur Franz, Mary Fickett, Gene Lyons
294. "The Missing Years" (2-3-54) Ted Brenner, Mary Astor, Anthony Perkins
295. "Elisha and the Long Knives" [by Dale Wasserman and Jack Balch; subsequently restaged for the Matinee Theatre episode of 12/27/55] (2-4-54) Van Dyke Parks, Jared Reed, Dan Morgan, Royal Beal
296. "The Barn" (2-10-54) Felicia Montealegre (in a three-character role), Edward Binns
297. "The Thinking Heart--A Lincoln Biography" (2-11-54) Andrew Duggan, Nancy Marchand; narrated by Anthony Ross
298. "The Cuckoo Clock" (2-17-54) Hans Schumm, Gaby Rodgers, Edgar Stehli
299. "Icewater, Please" (2-18-54) Carmen Mathews, Peter Capell
300. "Gallin--All American" (2-24-54) Don Dubbins, Judson Pratt, Joanna Roos
301. "Night Must Fall" [adapted from the Emlyn Williams play] (2-25-54) Terence Kilburn, Evelyn Varden, Una O'Connor
302. "Two Weeks in the Country" [by Kathleen and Robert Howard Lindsay] (3-3-54) Frances Reid, Paul Langton, Charles Saari
303. "Delicate Story" [adapted from the Ferenc Molnar play; restaged from 3/7/51] (3-4-54) Eli Wallach, Gaby Rodgers
304. "The Picture Window" (3-10-54) Arthur Franz, Kathleen Maguire, Leora Thatcher, Raymond Bramley
305. "Dark Victory" [adapted from the George Emerson Brewer and Bertram Bloch play] (3-11-54) Leora Dana, Duane McKinney
306. "You Touched Me!" [adapted from the Tennessee Williams and Donald Windham play] (3-17-54) Terence Kilburn, Martyn Green, Catherine Willard
307. "Home at Seven" [by R. C. Sheriff; subsequently restaged for the Matinee Theatre episode of 7/27/56] (3-18-54) Tom Helmore, Valerie Cossart

308. "Pardon My Prisoner" (3-24-54) Cliff Hall, Helen Gallagher, Dennis James
309. "Angel Street" [adapted from the Patrick Hamilton play] (3-25-54) Leueen MacGrath, Sally Chamberlin, Howard St. John, Elizabeth Patterson, Jerome Kilty
310. "A Hat for Winter" (3-31-54) Bart Burns, Mary Fickett, Bert Thorn
311. "Glorious Morning" (4-1-54) Colin Keith-Johnston, Elizabeth Ross
312. "Mr. Candido" (4-7-54) Jose Perez, Patrick McVey, Jose Ferrer, Carlos Montalban, Muriel Berkson, Kimetha Over-backer
313. "The Old Maid" [adapted from the Zoe Akins play] (4-8-54) Nancy Marchand, Jayne Meadows, Eva Marie Saint, Bill Lundmark
314. "The People Next Door" (4-14-54) Louisa Horton, Charles Drake, Audrey Christie, Anne Mary Tallon
315. "A Marriage Made in Heaven" (4-15-54) Jennie Goldstein, Michael Strong, E. A. Krumschmidt
316. "The Little Gods Sell Tamales" (4-21-54) Henry Lascoe
317. "Spring 1600" [adapted from the Emlyn Williams play] (4-22-54) John Baragrey, Janet DeGore, Valerie Cossart
318. "Dr. Rainwater Goes A-Courtin'" [adapted from the William Brandon short story] (4-28-54) Heywood Hale Brown, Jack Warden, Peter Kelly, Pat Smith
319. "Unequal Contest" [an eighteenth-century tale] (4-29-54) Darren McGavin, Joanne Woodward, Joan Hopkins
320. "Alice in Wonderland" [adapted from the Lewis Carroll classic] (5-5-54) Art Carney, Arthur Treacher, Ernest Truex, Blanche Yurka, Joey Walsh, Bobby Clark, James Barton, Edgar Bergen and Charlie McCarthy
321. "Arrowsmith" [adapted from the Sinclair Lewis classic] (5-6-54) Richard Kiley, Biff McGuire, Joseph Wiseman, June Dayton
322. "The Stake" (5-12-54) John Baragrey, Louisa Horton, Joe Maross, Leon Belasco
323. "The Worried Songbirds" (5-13-54) Mildred Dunnock, Carmen Mathews
324. "A Touch of Summer" (5-19-54) Cora Witherspoon, Jerome Cowan, Ruth Matteson
325. "All Our Yesterdays" (5-20-54) Arthur O'Connell, Nancy Marchand, Joan Potter
326. "The Scarlet Letter" [adapted from the Nathaniel Hawthorne classic] (5-26-54) Kim Stanley, Leslie Nielsen, Margaret Wycherly, Bramwell Fletcher
327. "Dodsworth" [adapted from the Sinclair Lewis classic] (5-27-54) Anthony Ross, Irene Manning, Flora Campbell, Nils Asther
328. "Citizen Miller" (6-2-54) Vaughn Taylor, Enid Markey, Edgar Stehli, Marie Carroll, Bruno Wick
329. "The House on Woldwood Lane" [by George Lowther; restaged for the Matinee Theatre episode of 11/17/55] (6-3-54) Joseph Anthony, Kathleen Bard, Dickie Allen

330. "Romeo and Juliet" [adapted from the Shakespeare classic] (6-9-54) Liam Sullivan, Susan Strasberg (aged sixteen), Carroll McComas, Noel Leslie, Felix Deebank

331. "Blind Alley" [adapted from the James Warwick play] (6-10-54) Darren McGavin, Herbert Berghoff, Frances Heflin

332. "The Man Who Took to His Bed" (6-16-54) Pat Smith, Roy Bromley, Perry Fiske, Jack Hartley

333. "Deliver Me from Evil" (6-17-54) Anthony Ross, Claudia Morgan, Grant Williams

334. "The Long Road Home" (6-23-54) Peggy Conklin, Sara Haden, James Gregory

335. "See You on Sunday" (6-24-54) Patricia Breslin, Joe Maross, Kathleen Meskill, Allen Nourse

336. "The Man Most Likely" (6-30-54) Eli Mintz, Rod Steiger, Wright King

337. "Mr. Simmons" (7-1-54) Mildred Natwick, Arthur O'Connell, Richard Newton

338. "Wish Tonight" (7-7-54) Patrick McVey, Beverly Roberts, Susan Halloran

339. "A Connecticut Yankee in King Arthur's Court" [adapted from the Mark Twain classic] (7-8-54) Jack Livesey (as King Arthur), Carl Reiner (as Sir Kay), Joey Walsh (as Clarence, the page), Edgar Bergen (as Yankee), Victor Jory (as Merlin), Eva Leonard-Boyne (as Queen Guinevere)

340. "An American Lyric" (7-14-54) Joe Verdi, Carlo DiAngela, Gloria Marlowe

341. "Petticoat Fever" [adapted from the Mark Reed play] (7-15-54) Douglas Watson, Frances Robinson, Dodie Baurer, Anthony Kemble-Cooper

342. "Knight in a Business Suit" (7-21-54) Arthur O'Connell, Valerie Cossart

343. "Forty Weeks of Uncle Tom" (7-22-54) Robin Morgan, Polly Rowles, Carl Reiner, Nydia Westman, Joel Grey

344. "Edie and the Princess" (7-28-54) William Smith, Susan Hallaran, Pat Smith

345. "The Dashing White Sergeant" (7-29-54) Conrad Janis, Christopher Plummer, Jill Kraft

346. "The Happy Touch" (8-4-54) Margaret Hamilton, ZaSu Pitts, Chester Stratton, Doro Merande

347. "Nothing Personal" (otherwise known as "Flowers in a Book") (8-5-54) Nancy Kelly, Walter Matthau

348. "Charm Bracelet" (8-11-54) Una O'Connor, Joanna Roos, Frank Overton

349. "The Bishop Misbehaves" [adapted from the Frederick Jackson play] (8-12-54) Bramwell Fletcher, Nydia Westman

350. "The Worried Man's Blues" (8-18-54) Joe Maross, William Dillard, John Shellie, Edgar Stehli

351. "The Shining Hour" [adapted by Richard McCracken from the story by Keith Winters; subsequently restaged for the Matinee Theatre episode of 11/9/56] (8-19-54) Valerie Bettis, Richard Waring

352. "Short Story" [adapted from the Robert Morley play; restaged from 2/6/50] (8-25-54) Murray Matheson, Carmen Mathews

353. "Uncle Harry" [adapted from the Thomas Job play] (8-26-54)
Art Carney, Mildred Dunnock, Sally Gracie, Zamah Cunning-
ham
354. "Kidnapped" [adapted from the Robert Louis Stevenson classic]
(9-1-54) Frederic Worlock, Jack Livesey, Jerome Kilty,
Raymond Worlock, John Stewart
355. "Philip Goes Forth" [adapted from the George Kelly play; restaged from 1/9/52] (9-2-54) Roddy McDowall, Blanche
Yurka, Frank M. Thomas
356. "Party for Jonathan" (9-8-54) Carl Betz, Betty Sinclair
357. "Albert" [a German prisoner-of-war camp drama with an all
male cast] (9-9-54) Tom Helmore, Jack Livesey, Stefan
Schnabel
358. "The Witch Child" (9-15-54) Adele Newton, Stevie Briggs
359. "Guest in the House" [adapted from the Hagar Wilde, Dale
Eunson and Katherine Albert play] (9-16-54) Dorothy Sands,
Karl Swenson, Lenka Peterson, Joan Tompkins
360. "The Light Is Cold" (9-22-54) Elizabeth Montgomery, Lilia
Skala, Don Dubbins
361. "Professor Jones and the Missing Link" (9-23-54) Roger
Price, Estelle Winwood, Murray Matheson, Isobel Elsom

Eighth Season

362. "A Simple Matter" (9-29-54) Joey Walsh, Harry Townes
363. "The Oath of Hippocrates" [restaged from 5/11/49] (9-30-54)
Lloyd Bochner, Sally Chamberlin, John Stephen
364. "The Office Dance" (10-6-54) Nancy Marchand, Phyllis Love,
Doris Rich, Sammy Kaye
365. "The Man Who Made the Kaiser Laugh" (10-7-54) Hurd Hatfield, Woodrow Parfrey, E. A. Krumschmidt
366. "Papa Was a Sport" (10-13-54) Lilia Skala, Barnard Hughes,
Richard Jaeckel
367. "The Passionate Bystander" (10-14-54) Ernest Truex, Katherine Haymes, Gene Lyons, Josephine Brown
368. "The Luck of Roaring Camp" [adapted from the Bret Harte
story] (10-20-54) Cliff Hall, J. Pat O'Malley, Jared Reed,
William Harrigan
369. "The Shop at Sly Corner" (10-21-54) Roddy McDowall, Dino
Di Luca, Margaret Wycherly, Una O'Connor
370. "Split Level" (10-27-54) Biff McGuire, Pat Smith, Nydia
Westman
371. "The Happy Journey" [adapted from the Thornton Wilder one-
act play] (10-28-54) Mildred Dunnock, Frank McHugh
372. "Full of the Old Harry" (11-3-54) Fritz Lieber, Douglass
Montgomery, Leora Dana
373. "The Day the Diner Closed" (11-4-54) Conrad Janis, Carmen
Mathews, Bibi Osterwald, Nancy Andrews
374. "The World and the Werners" (11-10-54) Mikhail Rasumny,
Dorothy Raimon
375. "One Sunday Afternoon" [adapted from the James Hagen play]
(11-11-54) Claudia Morgan, Kenneth Nelson, Valerie Cossart, John Shellie, Frank Albertson

376. "The Independent" (11-17-54) Jeffrey Lynn, Joe Fallon,
Frances Robinson
377. "My Son, the Doctor" (11-18-54) Martin Newman, Woodrow
Parfrey, Patricia Wheel, Olga Fabian
378. "Emma" [adapted from the Jane Austen classic] (11-24-54)
Felicia Montealegre, Roddy McDowall, Peter Cookson
379. "Run for the Money" [by Frank D. Gilroy; subsequently restaged for the Matinee Theatre episode of 10/22/57] (11-25-
54) Phyllis Love, Joseph Sweeney
380. "Camille" [adapted from the Alexandre Dumas classic] (12-1-
54) Signe Hasso, Jacques Bergerac, Lilia Skala
381. "Kitty Foyle" [adapted from the Christopher Morley story and
scenario] (12-2-54) Hazel Dawn, Cloris Leachman, Judson
Laire
382. "Career" [an Iron Curtain drama] (12-8-54) Nancy Marchand,
Bryon Sanders, J. Pat O'Malley, E. A. Krumschmidt
383. "The Consul" [adapted from the Richard Harding Davis short
story] (12-9-54) Noel Leslie
384. "Account Rendered" [adapted from the John Turner play] (12-
15-54) Jessie Royce Landis, Craig Kelly, Richard Kendrick
385. "Time of the Drought" (12-16-54) Ed Begley, Joe Maross,
Vaughn Taylor, June Dayton, Valerie Cossart
386. "The Little Stone of God" (12-22-54) Felicia Montealegre,
Tom Helmore, Mary Howard
387. "A Child Is Born" [adapted from the Stephen Vincent Benét
story; previously dramatized for the Lux Video Theatre
(q. v.)] (12-23-54) Mildred Dunnock, Harry Townes, Nancy
Marchand; the St. Thomas Boys' Choir and Chamber Orchestra
388. "Strangers in Hiding" [by Robert Thomson] (12-29-54) Bradford Dillman, Inger Stevens, Harold Lang
389. "Death Takes a Holiday" [adapted by Walter Ferris from the
Alberto Casella play] (12-30-54) Joseph Wiseman, Malcolm Lee Beggs, Stiana Braggiotti
390. "One Hill, One River" (1-5-55) Conrad Janis, Wright King,
Lee Remick, Crahan Denton
391. "A Bit of Love" (1-6-55) Harry Townes, Margaret Phillips,
Katherine Hynes
392. "Patterns" [by Rod Serling; Fielder Cook directed; filmed by
United Artists in 1956] (1-12-55) Ed Begley, Richard
Kiley, Everett Sloane, Joanna Roos, Elizabeth Wilson
(Misters Begley and Sloane; Miss Roos and Miss Wilson
repeated their roles for the film adaptation)

[hereafter weekly] [Note: The Television Theatre's second weekly
drama actually continued under the management of Pond's as
POND'S THEATRE (q. v.)]

393. "The Written Word" (1-19-55) David Cole, Edward Binns,
J. Pat O'Malley
394. "Boys Will Be Boys" [adapted from the Irving S. Cobb story]
(1-26-55) Ed Begley, James Barton, Heywood Hale Brown
395. "The Skin Game" [adapted from the John Galsworthy play; re-

staged from 2/13/52] (2-2-55) Jack Livesey, Frederic Tozere, Richard Newton, J. Pat O'Malley

396. "Patterns" [by Rod Serling and directed by Fielder Cook; restaged from 2/9/55 and sponsored by the J. Walter Thompson Agency] (2-9-55) Ed Begley, Richard Kiley, Everett Sloane, Joanna Roos, Elizabeth Wilson

397. "Departure" (2-16-55) Neva Patterson, Mikhail Rasumny, Anne Appel

398. "The Emperor Jones" [adapted from the Eugene O'Neill play; sponsored by the J. Walter Thompson Agency] (2-23-54) Ossie Davis (in the title role), Rex Ingram, Everett Sloane

399. "Half the World's a Bride" (3-2-55) Carmen Mathews, Loretta Leversee, George Voskovec

400. "The Night Watcher" (3-9-55) Constance Ford, Mark Roberts, Edward Binns

401. "Jeannie" [adapted from the 1940 play; restaged from 7/5/50] (3-16-55) Elizabeth Ross, James Daly, Dan Morgan, Stuart MacIntosh

402. "The Story of Mary Surratt" [adapted from the John Patrick play] (3-23-55) Doreen Lang, Alexander Scourby, Anne Pearson, Bruce Gordon

403. "The Southwest Corner" [a condensed version of the John Cecil Holm Broadway play with the original cast] (3-30-55) Eva LeGallienne, Enid Markey, Parker Fennelly

404. "Whim of Iron" [a drama of Byzantine Emperor Justinian and Empress Theodora] (4-6-55) Anthony Franciosa, Claudia Morgan

405. "Now, Where Was I?" (4-13-55) Gisele MacKenzie, Robert Webber, June Dayton; an appearance by Vincent Sardi Jr. of Sardi's

406. "Gramercy Ghost" [adapted from the John Cecil Holm play; restaged from 2/2/49] (4-20-55) Pat Carroll, Conrad Janis, James Broderick

407. "A Seacoast in Bohemia" [by Ben Radin; restaged from 6/6/51] (4-27-55) Ray Rhodes, George Macready, Theodore Bikel, Jeff Harris

408. "Flowers for 2-B" [by Edward DeBlasco] (5-4-55) Virginia Vincent, Benny Baker

409. "Judge Contain's Hotel" [by William Mourne] (5-11-55) John Cassavetes, Charles Dingle, Elizabeth Fraser

410. "The Braveness of Christy Fellon" [by Arthur Cavanaugh] (5-18-55) Frances Starr, Cliff Hall, Arthur Shields

411. "Million Dollar Rookie" [by Mel Goldberg] (5-25-55) Buster Crabbe, Richard York

412. "A Woman for Tony" [by Richard Wendley] (6-1-55) James Daly, Zolya Talma, Marian Seldes, Catherine McLeod

413. "Someone to Hang" [by Robert Garris] (6-8-55) George Mitchell, Kathleen Maguire, Russell Hardie, Philip Abbott

414. "My Aunt Daisy" [by Albert Halper and Joseph Schrank] (6-15-55) June Lockhart, Jamie Smith, Richard Davalos, Doretta Duckworth, Bill Thunkhurst

415. "Drop on the Devil" [adapted by Dale Wasserman from the Terence Kilpatrick story] (6-22-55) Everett Chambers, Ford Rainey, Joan Chambers

416. "The Mob" [adapted from the John Galsworthy play] (6-29-55) Claudia Morgan, Frederic Worlock, J. Pat O'Malley, Michael Clarke Laurence

417. "Impasse" [by Julian Maxwell Snyder] (7-6-55) Georgiann Johnson, Larry Weber, Joseph Foley, Royal Bear, Josephine Brown, William Gideon

418. "The Straw" [adapted from the Eugene O'Neill play] (7-13-55) Kathleen Maguire, Lin McCarthy, Cliff Hall, Murray Hamilton

419. "In the La Banza" [by Sam Elkin] (7-20-55) Joe Maross, Andy Sanders, Hildy Parks, Dennis Patrick, Larry Gates

420. "Meet a Body" [adapted from the Frank Launder and Sidney Gilliat murder mystery farce] (7-27-55) James Broderick, Joyce Smight, Raymond Bramley, Lee Goodman, Guy Raymond

421. "Spur of the Moment" [by Oliver Crawford] (8-3-55) Arthur Franz, Michael Tolan, Jane Seymour, Marian Randall, Robert F. Simon

422. "Two Times Two" (8-10-55) Jack Klugman, June Dayton, Joe Maross, Larry Gates, Marcel Hillaire

423. "The Failure" [by George Lowther] (8-17-55) Henry Jones, Judith Evelyn, David White, Mary Lee Deering, Warren Berlinger

424. "The Haunted" [adapted by Cyril Hume from the story by Richard Carlson] (8-24-55) Felicia Montealegre, John Baragrey, James Gregory

425. "The Chess Game" [by Robert Howard Lindsay; restaged from 2/4/53] (8-31-55) Melvyn Douglas, Lin McCarthy, Richard Morse, Constance Wilson

426. "Woman of Principle" [by Will Lorin] (9-7-55) Mary Pickett, Helen Shields, Larry Weber, Richard Kendrick

427. "It's Only Money" [by Judith Parrish] (9-14-55) Henry Jones, Peter Turgeon, Lois Bolton, John McGiver

428. "The King's Bounty" [by Michael Dyne] (9-21-55) Christopher Plummer, Hurd Hatfield, Everett Sloane, Lilia Skala, Romney Brent, Carol Goodner, Betsy Von Furstenberg

Ninth Season

429. "The Diamond as Big as the Ritz" [adapted from the F. Scott Fitzgerald fantasy; this episode, if chronicled from May 7, 1947, marks the five hundredth teleplay in the Kraft Theatre series] (9-28-55) Lee Remick, Signe Hasso, Elizabeth Montgomery, George Macready, Richard Franchot, Mario Alcalde

430. "The Beautiful Time" [adapted from the magazine short story by Czensi Ormonde] (10-5-55) Lili Darvas, Claudia Morgan, Edward Andrews, Kimetha Laurie, George Voskovec

431. "Trucks Welcome" [adapted from the Albert Halper story] (10-12-55) Rita Gam, James Gregory, Una Merkel, Joe Maross, Johnny Studer

432. "I, Mrs. Bibb" [by Paul Crabtree] (10-19-55) Lillian Gish, Richard Ney

433. "One" [by David Karp] (10-26-55) Barry Jones, Harry Townes, Laurence Hugo, Helen Shields
434. "Number Four with Flowers" [by Louis Pelletier] (11-2-55) Jack Klugman, Parker McCormick, Lois Bolton
435. "The Ticket and the Tempest" [by Frank Kulla] (11-9-55) Arthur Shields, Cameron Prud'homme, J. Pat O'Malley, Alice Pearce
436. "Summer's End" (11-16-55) James Barton, Ian Turner
437. "Day of Judgment" [by Harry Julian Fink] (11-23-55) Dino Di Luca, Lydia St. Clair, Lorne Greene
438. "Once a Genius" [by Dick Berg] (11-30-55) Herbert Berghoff, Eva Gabor, Lilia Skala, Lawrence Hugo, Martin Rudy
439. "Lady Ruth" [by Jack Partiz] (12-7-55) Jo Van Fleet, Barbara Barrie, Ruth Attaway
440. "A Nugget from the Sunrise" [by Jess Gregg] (12-14-55) Henry Jones, Elizabeth Ross, Harry Townes, John McGiver, Jane Rose
441. "A Christmas Dinner" [by Harold Flander] (12-21-55) Ian Turner, James Barton
442. "Eleven O'Clock Flight" [by Jerry DeBono] (12-28-55) Joanne Woodward, Richard Shepard, Al (David) Hedison
443. "The Thieving Magpie" (1-4-56) James Gregory, Jo Van Fleet
444. "The Sears Girl" [by Victor Woolfson] (1-11-56) Fay Bainter, Leora Dana
445. "The Devil as a Roaring Lion" [by John Gay] (1-18-56) James Whitmore, E. G. Marshall, Dennis Patrick, Van Dyke Parks, Loretta Leversee
446. "Home Is the Hero" [by Walter Maken] (1-25-56) Anthony Perkins, Brian Donlevy, J. Pat O'Malley, Anne Thomas, Glenda Farrell
447. "Five Minutes to Live" [by Palmer Thompson] (2-1-56) Basil Rathbone, Felicia Montealegre, Neil Hamilton, Dennis O'Keefe, Richard Shepard
448. "Good Old Charlie Faye" [by David Karp] (2-8-56) Paul Hartman, Lee Tracy
449. "Man on Roller Skates" [by Louis Pelletier] (2-15-56) Steven Allen, Henry Jones
450. "Snapfinger Creek" [by William Noble] (2-22-56) Jo Van Fleet, John Shellis, Hope Lange, Richard Shepard
451. "Bobbie" [by Narda Stokes] (2-29-56) Nancy Malone, Neil Harrison, Joe Maross, Pat Englund
452. "The Fool Killer" [adapted by Dale Wasserman from the Helen Eustle novel] (3-7-56) Audra Lindley, Jane Rose, Lee Marvin, Larry Gates, Malcolm Broderick
453. "The Lost Weekend" [adapted from the Charles Jackson novel and film scenario] (3-21-56) Joe Maross, Mary Fickett
454. "A Night to Remember" [adapted from the Walter Lord account of The Titanic incident; directed by George Roy Hill] (3-28-56) Claude Rains (who also narrated) and a cast of 107.
455. "Paper Foxhole" [by James Edwards] (4-4-56) Kenny Delmar, Hal March, Joe Mantell, Felix Munro
456. "The Last Showdown" (4-11-56) Elizabeth Montgomery, Edward Arnold, Glenda Farrell, Victor Jory

457. "No Riders" [by Wendell Mayes; restaged from his Pond's Theatre episode of 4/14/55] (4-18-56) James Daly, Audra Lindley

458. "The Gentle Grafters" [adapted by Dale Wasserman from the 1926 play] (4-25-56) Kenny Delmar, Kay Ballard, Charles Coburn

459. "A Night to Remember" [a repeat showing of the episode of 3/28/56 on the Walter Lord account of the Titanic incident] (5-2-56)

460. "Death Is a Spanish Dancer" [by Wendell Mayes; restaged from his Pond's Theatre episode of 6/30/55] (5-9-56) James Daly, Kim Stanley, Bert Freed, David Stewart

461. "A Profile In Courage" [adapted from the John Fitzgerald Kennedy book focussing on the Edmund G. Ross chapter, which was again enacted for the series Profiles in Courage 3/21/65; Senator Kennedy, aged thirty-eight, introduces this program] (5-16-56) James Whitmore, Victor Jory, Robert H. Harris

462. "Bedroom Twelve on the Appalachian Waterfall" [by Harry Muheim] (5-23-56) Elliott Nugent, June Dayton

463. "Box 704" [by James Herlihy] (5-30-56) Paul Carr

464. "The Night of May Third" [adapted by Robert Shaw from the Anna Mary Wells book] (6-6-56) Phyllis Thaxter, Laurence Hugo, Kenny Delmar

465. "Boy in a Cage" [by Paul Monash] (6-13-56) Burt Brincker-hoff, James Gregory

466. "Flying Object at Three O'Clock High" [by DeWitt S. Copp] (6-20-56) Everett Sloane, George Peppard, Biff McGuire, Robert Simon

467. "Starfish" [by William Noble] (6-27-56) Joanne Woodward, Farley Granger

468. "Tear Open the Skies" [this episode, and all hereafter, are colorcast] (7-4-56) Richard Carlson, Geoffrey Lumb, Bruce Gordon, Nancy Marchand

469. "Long Arm" [by Marjorie and George Faulkner] (7-11-56) John Ericson, Phyllis Love, Elizabeth Montgomery

470. "Babies for Sale" (7-18-56) Leora Dana, Paul Langton

471. "Prairie Night" [by John Gay] (7-25-56) Victor Jory, Robert Simon, Martha Scott, Charles Mendick

472. "One Way West" [by Louis Pelletier] (8-1-56) Leora Dana, Kurt Kasznar, Peter Turgeon, Patrick Macnee

473. "Anna Santonello" [by Robert Crean] (8-8-56) Eileen Heckart, Will Kuluva, Joseph Campanella, Nehemiah Persoff, Simon Oakland, James Gregory

474. The Magic Box [the 1952 J. Arthur Rank film] (8-15-56) Robert Donat, Maria Schell, Margaret Johnston, Richard Attenborough are among the principals.

475. "The Girls Who Saw Too Much" [adapted by Robert J. Shaw] (8-29-56) Betsy Palmer, Robert Middleton, Russell Hurd, Joe Maross

476. "Mock Trial" [by Edith and Samuel Grafton] (9-5-56) Ed Begley, Henry Jones, Richard York; Attorney Joseph N. Welch, guest host.

477. "Shadow of Evil" [adapted by Calvin Tomkins from the James Cawell story] (9-12-56) Richard Carlson, Conrad Nagel

Tenth Season

478. "Out to Kill" [by William Mourne] (9-19-56) James Whitmore
479. "The Plunge" [by Grace Garnett] (9-26-56) Norman Lloyd, Robert Emhardt, Lois Wheeler, Menasha Skulnik
480. "The Life of Mickey Mantle" [by Nicholas E. Baehr] (10-3-56) James Olson
481. "The Murder of a Sand Flea" [by James Lee Barrett] (10-10-56) Eric Torn, Lynwood McCarthy, Joe Maross
482. "I Am Fifteen and Don't Want to Die" [adapted from the Christine Anthony story] (10-17-56) Bennye Gatteys, Grant Williams, Nehemiah Persoff
483. "Ten Grapefruit to Lisbon" [by Frank D. Gilroy] (10-24-56) Eva Gabor, Michael Ingram, Russell Hardie
484. "Hit and Run" [adapted from the Gertrude Schweitzer magazine story] (10-31-56) Conrad Nagel, Louise Platt, Paul Brinckerhoff
485. "Shadow of Suspicion" [by Arthur Hailey] (11-7-56) Robert Lansing, Russell Collins, Audra Lindley, Philip Abbott
486. "Before It's Too Late" [adapted from the Gertrude Schweitzer story] (11-14-56) Wallace Rooney, Phyllis Newman, Judy Sanford, Biff McGuire, Charles Aidman
487. "The Day of the Hunter" [adapted from the John and Ward Hawkins story] (11-21-56) Joe Mantell, Clay Hall
488. "Time Lock" [by Arthur Hailey; filmed by Distributors Corporation of America in 1959] (11-28-56) Chester Morris, Peter Lazer
489. "The Ninth Hour" [adapted by Will Loren from the Ben Benson novel] (12-5-56) Jack Klugman
490. "Teddy Bear" [by James Lee Barrett] (12-12-56) Michael Tolan, Tom Carlin, Brett Somers, Marion Brash
491. "The Wonderful Gift" [by Robert Crean] (12-19-56) Conrad Nagel, Mildred Dunnock, Valerie Cossart, Ruth McDevitt
492. "The Just and the Unjust" [adapted by Don and Katrina Ettlinger from the James Gould Cozzens novel] (12-26-56) Richard Kiley, June Dayton
493. "Hang Up My Guns" [by Wendell Mayes; restaged from his Pond's Theatre episode of 4/28/55] (1-2-57) Harry Townes, Bruce Gordon, Pamela Simpson
494. "Six Hours of Terror" [adapted by John Whedon from the Francis Didelot novel] (1-9-57) Theodore Bikel
495. "No Warning" [by Junius Eddy] (1-16-57) Pat Hingle, Mike Kellin, James Broderick, Joseph Campanella
496. "Most Blessed Woman" [by Wendell Mayes] (1-23-57) Albert Salmi, Paul Hartman, John McGiver, Betsy Von Furstenberg, Jane Rose
497. "The Singin' Idol" [by Paul Monash; filmed by Twentieth Century-Fox in 1958 as Sing, Boy, Sing] (1-30-57) Tommy Sands (who repeated his role for the film), Fred Clark
498. "The Discoverers" [by Max Rosenfeld and George Talver-

son] (2-6-57) Richard Kiley, Joe Maross, William Shatner

499. "The Man Who Couldn't Say No" [by Don Witty] (2-13-57) Barbara Cook, Robert Culp

500. "Give Me the Courage" [by Frances O'Neil] (2-20-57) Louisa Horton, Gene Lyons

501. "A Travel from Brussels" [adapted by Joel Ross from a story by Philip Freuner] (2-27-57) Orson Bean, Hiram Sherman

502. "The Duel" [by Leslie Stevens] (3-6-57) Roland Winters, Dan O'Herlihy, E. G. Marshall, Doreen Lang, Conrad Nagel, Elizabeth Montgomery

503. "Collision" [by Norman Vane] (3-13-57)

504. "Night of the Plague" [by Lester Powell] (3-20-57) Maggie Smith, Edward Mulhare

505. "Sheriff's Man" [by Robert Van Scoyk] (3-27-57) Mark Richman, Paul Hartman

506. "The Medallion" [adapted by Dale Wasserman from the Gritta Sereny story] (4-3-57) Christopher Snell, Lorne Greene, Kevin McCarthy, Leora Dana

507. "A Matter of Life" [by Oliver Crawford] (4-17-57) Raymond Massey, Robert Pastene

508. "A Night of Rain" [adapted by Robert Lindsay from the Jacques Deval play] (4-24-57) Harry Townes, Roddy McDowall, Nina Foch

509. "Drummer Man" [by Mel Goldberg] (5-1-57) Sal Mineo (aged eighteen)

510. "Flesh and Blood" [by Anthony Spinner] (5-8-57) Tommy Sands, Victor Jory

511. "The Glass Wall" [by Roger Hirson] (5-15-57) Kim Stanley, Richard Kiley, Jack Klugman, Mary Fickett

512. "Man of Prey" [by Leonard Heideman] (5-22-57) Chester Morris, Bruce Gordon, Georgiann Johnson

513. "All Those Beautiful Girls" [by Richard DeRoy] (5-29-57) Betsy Palmer, Neva Patterson, Robert Webber

514. "The Roaring Twentieth" [by Calvin Tomkins] (6-5-57) Roland Winters, Wally Cox, Dennis Patrick, Robert Emhardt, Patrick Smith, Minnie Jo Curtis

515. "Fire and Ice" [by Richard Fielder] (6-12-57) Dan O'Herlihy, Geraldine Page, Henry Jones, Frank McHugh

516. "Nothing Personal" (6-19-57) Robert Preston, Nina Foch

517. "The Curly Headed Kid" [by David Davidson] (6-29-57) Warren Beatty, Raymond Massey, Dan Morgan, Nancy Malone, Leslie Barrett, Wallace Rooney, Bill Zuckert

518. "The Long Flight" [by DeWitt S. Copp; a drama of Strategic Air Command] (7-3-57) George Peppard, James Gregory, Patricia Bosworth, Loren Tindall

519. "The First and the Last" [adapted from the John Galsworthy play] (7-10-57) Edward Mulhare, Frank Conroy, Geoffrey Tonnie

520. "The Big Break" [by Jack Klugman] (7-17-57) Cliff Robertson, Kathleen Maguire, James Barton, Alexander Scourby, Patsy Kelly, Joe Sweeney, Frank McHugh

521. "Welcome to a Stranger" [by Burton and James Benjamin]
     (7-24-57) Jane White, Jose Perez, David J. Stewart, Mar-
     tin Newman, Jimmy Gavin, Marita Reid
522. "Success!" [by Virginia Ratcliffe and William Hurt] (7-3-57)
     Kent Smith, Everett Sloane, Ann Rutherford, Eileen Heckart
523. "Sextuplets" [by Johnny Morin] (8-7-57) Tammy Grimes,
     Fred Gwynne, William Redfield, Ferlin Husky
524. "Circle of Fear" (8-14-57) Lee Remick, Farley Granger,
     Sylvia Sidney, Don Dubbins
525. "Ride into Danger" [by Fred Edge] (8-21-57) Dick York,
     Victor Jory, Richard Emhardt
526. "Sing a Song" [by Don Ettlinger] (8-28-57) Patty McCormack,
     Jean-Pierre Aumont, Jules Munshin
527. "Triumph" [by Theodore and Mathilde Ferro] (9-4-57) Henry
     Jones, Ralph Bellamy, Betty Field, Murray Matheson, Robert
     Pastene, David White
528. "The Old Ticker" [by John Whedon] (9-11-57) Sam Levene,
     Glenda Farrell, Paul Hartman, Eddie Bracken, Larry Blyden
529. "The Killer Instinct" [by Cy Chermak] (9-18-57) Rip Torn,
     Peggy Ann Garner, Ruth White

Eleventh Season

530. "Vengeance" [by Joseph Cochran] (9-25-57) Cliff Robertson,
     Ward Costello, Richard Shepard
531. "Barefoot Soldier" [by Bruce Bassett] (10-2-57) Sal Mineo,
     Nancy Marchand, Collin Wilcox
532. "Smart Boy" [by Harry Junken] (10-9-57) Ed Begley, Skip
     Homeier, Loretta Leversee
533. "A Cook for Mr. General" [by Steven Gethers; the basis for
     his 1961 Broadway play] (10-16-57) Bill Travers (who re-
     peated his role for the stage), Roland Winters, William
     Redfield
534. "Man in a Trance" [by Will Loren] (10-23-57) Farley Grang-
     er, Nehemiah Persoff
535. "Gun at a Fair One" [by Bruce Bassett] (10-30-57) Ben
     Piazza, Nancy Malone, Burt Brinckerhoff
536. "The Category Is Murder" [by George Harmon Coxe] (11-6-
     57) Betsy Palmer, Gene Lyons
537. "The Big Heist" [by Newton Melzer] (11-13-57) Mildred Nat-
     wick, Patty Duke, Bert Lahr, Fred Gwynne
538. "The Sound of Trouble" [by Jack Partiz] (11-20-57) Mildred
     Dunnock, Jill Corey, James Westerfield
539. "Come to Me" [by Peter Lind Hayes and Robert J. Crean;
     Hayes, with Robert Allen, also authored the title song and
     Lilac Chiffon] (12-4-57) Margaret O'Brien, Farley Granger,
     Julie Wilson, J. Pat O'Malley, Steve Dunne
540. "Heroes Walk on Sand" [by George E. Dyslin] (12-11-57)
     Basil Rathbone, Elliott Nugent, Walter Abel, Ann Harding
541. "Polka" [by Robert J. Crean] (12-18-57) Shelley Winters,
     Glenda Farrell, James Gregory, Torin Thatcher, Clay Hall,
     Kimetha Laurie
542. "The Other Wise Man" [adapted by Robert J. Crean from the

Henry Van Dyke story] (12-25-57) Richard Kiley, Dolores Vitina, Alexander Scourby, Robert Pastene

543. "The Battle for Wednesday Night" [by Robert Van Scoyk] (1-1-58) Rudy Vallee, Virginia Gibson, Earl Holliman, Jack Oakie

544. "The Velvet Trap" [by David Davidson] (1-8-58) Thomas Mitchell, William Shatner, Russell Collins, Peggy Ann Garner

545. "Code of the Corner" [by Jack Klugman] (1-15-58) Walter Matthau, Howard Morris, Nancy Walker, Barton MacLane, Nancy Gates [the first dramatic roles for Mr. Morris and Miss Walker]

546. "Eddie" [by Sam Dann] (1-22-58) Fay Wray, Pat O'Brien, Rip Torn, Ruth White

547. "Run, Joe, Run" [by James Lee Barrett] (1-29-58) Jan Sterling, Alex Nicol, Neville Brand, Harry Guardino, Paul Hartman

548. "The Spell of the Tigress" [adapted by Michael Dyne from the Lady Cynthia Asquith story] (2-5-58) Ilka Chase, Viveca Lindfors, Patty McCormack, Henry Daniell

549. "Material Witness" [by Henry Denker] (2-18-58) Nancy Marchand, Richard Kiley, Tim Hovey, Milton Berle

550. "The Women at High Hollow" [adapted by Edward Mabley from the Margaret Manners story] (2-26-58) Skip Homeier, Estelle Winwood, Gene Nelson, Susan Oliver

551. "Dog in a Bus Tunnel" (3-5-58) Cameron Mitchell, Gloria Vanderbilt, Martin Balsam, Frank McHugh

552. "The Sea Is Boiling Hot" [by Shimon Wincelberg] (3-12-58) Sessue Hayakawa, Earl Holliman

553. "Look What's Going On" [by Dale Wasserman and Rufus Henry] (3-19-58) Ed Begley, Lee Grant, Neville Brand, Harry Townes

554. "Angry Angel" [by Alfred Brenner] (3-26-58) Lynn Loring, Audra Lindley, Laurence Weber

555. "The Man in Authority" (4-2-58) Henry Jones, Rosemary Harris, Max Adrian, William Redfield, Florence Reed

556. "Three Plays by Tennessee Williams" [Williams composed and introduces] a) "Moony's Kid Don't Cry," Ben Gazzara, Lee Grant; b) "The Last of My Solid Gold Watches," Thomas Chalmers, Gene Saks, Alonzo Bozan; c) "This Property Is Condemned," Zina Bethune, Martin Huston (4-16-58)

557. "Angry Harvest" [adapted by David Davidson from the Stanislau Mierzenski and Herman Field novel] (4-23-58) Ina Balin, Theodore Bikel

558. "Fifty Grand" [adapted by A. E. Hotcher from the Ernest Hemingway story] (4-30-58) Ralph Meeker

559. "The Outcasts of Poker Flat" [adapted by Phil Reisman Jr. from the Bret Harte story] (5-7-58) Larry Hagman, George C. Scott, Burton Mallory, Ruth White, Barbara Lord

560. "All the King's Men" [Part I; adapted by Don Mankiewicz from the Robert Penn Warren Pulitzer Prize novel] (5-14-58) Neville Brand (as Willie Stark), Maureen Stapleton (as Sadie Burke), William Prince, Robert Emhardt, Frank Conroy, Fred J. Scollay

561. "All the King's Men" [Part II] (5-21-58) as above.
562. "A Boy Called Ciske" [adapted by J. P. Miller from the Piet Bakker novel] (5-28-58) Peter Cookson, Peter Lazer
563. "The Last of the Belles" [adapted by James P. Cavanagh from the F. Scott Fitzgerald story] (6-4-58) Jody McCrea, Roddy McDowall, Janice Rule, Ann Williams

[now as KRAFT MYSTERY THEATRE]

564. "Killer's Choice" [adapted by Alvin Boretz from the Ed McBain (Evan Hunter) story] (6-11-58) Michael Higgins, Staats Cotsworth, Joanne Linville, Martin Rudy, Joan Copeland
565. "Now Will You Try for Murder?" [adapted by Harry Olesker from his own novel] (6-18-58) Fred J. Scollay, Carl Frank, Lois Nettleton, Al Morgenstern
566. "The Eighty Seventh Precinct" [adapted by Larry Cohen from the Ed McBain story; the basis for the 1961 television series] (6-25-58) Robert Bray, Martin Rudy
567. "Next Door to Death" [adapted by Michael Dyne from the Charlotte Armstrong novel] (7-2-58) Abigail Kellogg, Patrick MacNee
568. "Cop Killer" [adapted by Art Wallace from the George Bagby novel] (7-9-58) Fred J. Scollay, Paul Hartman, Edward Binns
569. "The Man Who Didn't Fly" [adapted by Jerome Coopersmith from the Margot Bennett story] (7-16-58) William Shatner, Patricia Bosworth, Walter Brooke, Jonathan Harris
570. "Focus on Murder" [adapted by Mel Goldberg from the George Harmon Coxe story] (7-23-58) Simon Oakland, Phyllis Hill, Olive Deering
571. "Death Wears Many Faces" (7-30-58) Mark Richman, Warren Berlinger, Robert Emhardt
572. "Death for Sale" [adapted by Vance Bourjaily from the Henry Kane book] (8-6-58) Shepperd Strudwick, Joanna Moore
573. "Night Cry" [by Larry Cohen] (8-13-58) Jack Klugman, John McQuade
574. "We Haven't Seen Her Lately" [adapted by Sumner Locke Elliott from the E. X. Ferrars novel] (8-20-58) George C. Scott, Angela Thorton
575. "Web of Guilt" [by Mel Goldberg] (8-27-58) Michael Higgins, Fred J. Scollay, Simon Oakland, Lois Wheeler, Ann Hillary
576. "Back Track" [by Samuel Elkin] (9-3-58) John Baragrey, Phyllis Hill, Lawrence Weber
577. "Trick or Treat" [adapted by Doris Miles Disney from the Vance Bourjaily story] (9-10-58)
578. "A Cup of Kindness" [adapted by Alvin Boretz from the William Iverson story] (9-17-58) Norma Crane, Leo Penn, Philip Bourneuf
579. "Riddle of a Lady" [adapted by Jerome Coopersmith from the Anthony Gilbert novel] (9-24-58) David Hurst, David White, Nancy Marchand, Lisa Daniels, Lee Richardson

NBC PRESENTS

The Episodes:

1. "Fancy Meeting You Here" (1-3-49) Mary Wickes, Eva Condon
2. "The Haunting Years" (1-10-49) Alexander Kirkland, Peggy Conklin, Edward Forbes, Lawrence Tibbett Jr.
3. "Murder by Choice" (1-17-54) Myrtle Tannahill, Audrey Dobney, William H. Neil
4. "Ring Once for Central" (1-24-49) Eva Condon, Andy (Andrew) Duggan, Howard Wendell
5. "A Husband's Rights" (1-31-49) Ian Keith, John Harvey, Melba Rae
6. "Tough Kid" (2-7-49) Ivan McDonald, Ralph Theodore, Richard Astor, Andy Duggan, Jeanne Shepherd
7. "Anything But Love" (2-14-49) Joy Geffen, Herbert Evers, Dorothy Beattie, Si Vario
8. "The Girl" (2-21-49) Guy Spaull, Jean Carson, Tod Andrews
9. "Security" (2-28-49) Augusta Dabney, Paul Park, John Froelick, John Glendenning
10. "The Florist Shop" (3-7-49) Ruth Gilbert, David Orrick
11. "Alison's Lad" (3-14-49) William Whitman, Lois Hector, Neil Fitzgerald
12. "Right of Way" (3-21-49) Jeanne Shepherd, Andy Duggan, Bill Storey
13. "Sundae Punch" (3-28-49) Phil Arthur, Philip Huston, Patricia Kirkland
14. "Sugar and Spice" (4-4-49) Bonnie Baker, Bill Storey, Francesca Bruning, Roy Beal, Jane Compton
15. "Fairly Won" (4-11-49) Margaret Wycherly
16. "Just for Tonight" (4-18-49) Neva Patterson, Patricia Shay, John Forsythe
17. "Mistress Sims Inherits" (4-25-49) Mabel Tallaferro, Nancy Sheridan, Dean Harens, Gloria Strook, Eva Condon
18. "Tin Can Skipper" (5-2-49) Sidney Blackmer, Steve Cochran, Jess White, James Lamphier
19. "Lady, Look Out!" (5-9-49) Cloris Leachman, Philip Truex, Natalie Schaefer, David Orrick
20. "Lady in the Lobby" (5-16-49) Louisa Horton, Hugh Reilly, Jess White
21. "First Dance" (5-23-49) Sally Moffatt, Michael Steele, Joan Wetmore
22. "Entrapment" (5-30-49) John Howard, Karen Stevens, Doug Rutherford, Peggy Carnegie
23. "Concerning a Lady's Honor" (6-6-49) Edith Atwater, Byron McGrath
24. "Applause of Thousands" (6-13-49) Valerie Cossart, Mel Ceane
25. "Assignment--Main Street" (6-20-49) Louise Albritton
26. "All Things Come Home" (6-27-49) Neil Hamilton, Jeanne Shepherd, Philip Arthur, Merle Maddern
27. "Mr. and Mrs. North" [pilot for the 1952 series] (7-4-49) Joseph Allen Jr., Mary Lou Taylor

Second Season

28. "Expert Opinion" (8-8-49) Richard Hart
29. "The Key in the Lock" (8-15-49) Nancy Coleman, Rory Mallinson
30. "What Price Story?" (8-22-49) Mary K. Wells, Dort Clark
31. "Old Flames" (8-29-49) Donald Buka, Sally Moffatt, John Boruff
32. "My Wife Is a Liar" (9-5-49) Erin O'Brien-Moore, William Post Jr. , Walter Von Wagen
33. "Perkins Finds $3,400,000" (9-12-49) Romney Brent, Lester Carr, Eddie Hymans, Philip Huston
34. "The Loan" (9-19-49) Tom Ewell
35. "The Contest" (9-26-49) Tom Ewell
36. "Picture of the Bride" (10-3-49) Nancy Coleman, A. J. Herbert, Roberta Bollenger, Dean Harens
37. "Grandma, Barn Alice" (10-10-49) Kathleen Comegys, Stuart Nedd, Anna Minot

SUSPENSE [after the radio series]

The Episodes:

1. "Revenge" [directed by Robert Stevens] (3-1-49) Eddie Albert, Margo
2. "Suspicion" (3-15-49) Ernest Truex, Sylvia Field, Viola Roche
3. "Cabin B-13" [by John Dickson Carr] (3-29-49) Charles Korvin, Eleanor Lynn
4. "The Man Upstairs" (4-5-49) Anthony Ross, Mildred Natwick
5. "After Dinner Story" (4-12-49) Otto Kruger
6. "The Creeper" (4-19-49) Nina Foch, Anthony Ross
7. "A Night at an Inn" (4-26-49) Boris Karloff
8. "Dead Ernest" (5-3-49) Margaret Phillips, Tod Andrews, Will Hare, Joshua Shelley
9. "Post Mortem" (5-10-49) Peggy Conklin, Sidney Blackmer
10. "The Monkey's Paw" [adapted from the W. W. Jacobs classic] (5-17-49) Boris Karloff, Mildred Natwick
11. "Murder Through the Looking Glass" (5-24-49) William Prince, Ruth Madison, Peter von Zernich
12. "The Door's on the Thirteenth Floor" (5-31-49) Louisa Horton, Robert Sterling, Anthony Ross
13. "The Yellow Scarf" (6-7-49) Boris Karloff
14. "Help Wanted" (6-14-49) Otto Kruger
15. "Stolen Empire" (6-21-49) Kenneth Lynch, Audrey Christie
16. "The Hands of Mr. Ottermole" [adapted from the Thomas Burke story] (6-28-49) Ralph Bell

Second Season

17. "Lunch Box" (9-6-49) Lon McAllister, Abe Vigoda
18. "Collector's Item" (9-13-49) Lon McAllister

19. "Dr. Jekyll and Mr. Hyde" [adapted from the Robert Louis Stevenson classic] (9-20-49) Ralph Bell
20. "The Comic Strip Murder" (9-29-49) Lilli Palmer
21. "Doctor Violet" (10-4-49) Hume Cronyn, Evelyn Varden
22. "The Cask of Amontillado" [adapted from the Edgar Allan Poe classic] (10-11-49) Bela Lugosi
23. "The Serpent Ring" (10-18-49) Donald Buka
24. "The Murderer" (10-25-49) Jeffrey Lynn
25. "Black Passage" (11-1-49) William Prince, Stella Adler
26. "Suspicion" [restaged from 3/15/49] (11-8-49) Meg Mundy, Edgar Stehli, Russell Collins, Charlton Heston
27. "The Thin Edge of Violence" (11-15-49) George Reeves, Leonore Aubert, Emily Lawrence
28. "The Third One" (11-22-49) Iris Mann, Margaret Phillips, Theodore Newton
29. "The Man in the House" (11-29-49) Alan Baxter, Boyd Crawford
30. "The Scar" (12-6-49) Edgar Stehli
31. "The Gray Helmet" (12-13-49) Jack Lemmon, Mort Stevens, Bernard Kates
32. "The Seeker and the Sought" (12-20-49) Philip Loeb, Grace Valentine, Eileen Heckart, Joseph Holland
33. "The Case of Lady Sannox" (12-27-49) Stella Adler, Berry Kroeger, Henry Brandon
34. "Morning Boat to Africa" (1-3-50) Nina Foch
35. "The Bomber Command" (1-10-50) Susan Douglas, George Reeves
36. "Summer Storm" (1-17-50) E. G. Marshall, Jackie Diamond
37. "The Horizontal Man" (1-24-50) Mildred Natwick
38. "The Distant Island" (1-31-50) Patricia Kirkland
39. "Escape This Night" (2-7-50) Donald Buka, Peter Capell, Robert Harris
40. "The Suicide Club" [adapted from the Robert Louis Stevenson story] (2-14-50) Donald Buka, Ralph Clanton
41. "Roman Holiday" (2-21-50) Leslie Nielsen, Jack Simond
42. "The Man Who Talked in His Sleep" (2-28-50) Don Briggs, Edith Atwater
43. "The Ledge" (3-7-50) Dick Foran, E. G. Marshall
44. "The Parcel" (3-14-50) Conrad Janis, Ann Thomas
45. "The Old Man's Badge" (3-21-50) Barry Nelson, Steven Hill
46. "The Second Class Passenger" (3-28-50) Leslie Nielsen, Monica Boyer, Alfreda Wallace
47. "One Thousand Dollars to One for Your Money" (4-4-50) Tom Drake, Carol Williams, Betty Garde, Paul Stewart
48. "Steely, Steely Eyes" (4-11-50) Betty Garde
49. "Murder at the Mardi Gras" (4-18-50) Hume Cronyn, Tom Drake
50. "The Gentleman from America" (4-25-50) Barry Nelson
51. "Death of a Dummy" (5-2-50) Conrad Janis
52. "Red Wine" (5-9-50) Tom Drake, Hume Cronyn
53. "One and One's a Lonesome" (5-16-50) Nina Foch, Scott McKay, Meg Mundy, Robert Emhardt
54. "Photo Finish" (5-23-50) Ralph Clanton, Eileen Heckart

55. "Listen, Listen" (5-30-50) Mildred Natwick
56. "Black Bronze" (6-6-50) Franchot Tone, Joan Diener
57. "I'm No Hero" (6-20-50) Hume Cronyn, Mark Roberts
58. "Wisteria" (6-27-50) Conrad Janis, Marjorie Gateson

Third Season

59. "Poison" [by Roald Dahl] (8-29-50) Arnold Moss
60. "A Pocketful of Murder" (9-5-50) Steven Hill, Barry Nelson
61. "Edge of Panic" (9-12-50) Patrick McVey, Louisa Horton, Haila Stoddard
62. "Dark Shadows" (9-19-50) William Redfield, Robert Harris
63. "Six to One" (9-26-50) Edith Atwell
64. "The Monkey's Paw" [adapted from the W. W. Jacobs classic; restaged from 5/17/49] (10-3-50) Mildred Natwick, Stanley Ridges
65. "Criminal's Mark" (10-10-50) Catherine McLeod, Richard Kiley, Joseph Wiseman
66. "The Man Who Would Be King" [adapted from the Rudyard Kipling classic] (10-17-50) Francis L. Sullivan
67. "Breakdown" [by Francis Cockrell and Louis Polloch] (10-24-50) Ellen Violett, Don Briggs
68. "Halloween Hold-Up" (10-31-50) Conrad Janis
69. "Nightmare" (11-7-50) Richard Kiley, Berry Kroeger
70. "The Brush-Off" (11-14-50) Leslie Nielsen, Mary Sinclair
71. "The Death Cards" (11-21-50) Francis L. Sullivan
72. "The Hands of Mr. Ottermole" [adapted from the Thomas Burke story; restaged from 6/28/49] (11-28-50) Lawrence Fletcher, Robert Emhardt
73. "The Guy from Nowhere" (12-5-50) Barry Nelson, Catherine McLeod, Lawrence Fletcher
74. "The Mallet" (12-12-50) Walter Slezak, Pamela Gordon, Claire Williams, Victor Beecroft
75. "Dancing Dan's Christmas" [subsequently restaged for the Damon Runyon Theatre episode of 4/23/55] (12-19-50) Wally Cox
76. "The Tip" (12-26-50) Stanley Ridges, Felicia Montealegre
77. "Death in the River" (1-2-51)
78. "Tough Cop" (1-9-51) Barry Nelson, Katherine Bard
79. "The Fool's Heart" (1-16-51) Henry Hull
80. "Dead Fall" (1-23-51) Barry Nelson
81. "The Rose Garden" (1-30-51) Mildred Natwick, Estelle Winwood
82. "Night Break" (2-6-51) E. G. Marshall, Jane Seymour, Anne Marno
83. "Double Entry" (2-13-51) Robert Emhardt, Virginia Gilmore
84. "The Victims" (2-20-51) Stanley Ridges, Eileen Heckart
85. "Margin for Safety" (2-27-51) Denholm Elliott, Francis Bethencourt
86. "Dr. Jekyll and Mr. Hyde" [adapted from the Robert Louis Stevenson classic; restaged from 9/20/49] (3-6-51) Basil Rathbone
87. "On a Country Road" (3-13-51) Mildred Natwick, John Forsythe, Mary Sinclair

88. "Telephone Call" (3-20-51) Russell Collins, Eileen Heckart, Robert Emhardt
89. "The Three of Silence" (3-27-51) Walter Slezak, Betty Garde
90. "Go Home Dead Man" (4-3-51) Jackie Cooper
91. "The Foggy Night Visitor" (4-10-51) Leslie Nielsen, Cloris Leachman
92. "The Juice Man" (4-17-51) Cloris Leachman
93. "The Meeting" (4-24-51) Jackie Cooper, Mildred Natwick, Wally Cox
94. "No Friend Like an Old Friend" (5-1-51) Judith Evelyn, Ruth Ford, Tom Helmore
95. "Murder in the Ring" (5-8-51) Don Briggs, Hiram Sherman, Audrey Christie
96. "Too Hot to Live" (5-15-51) Billie Redfield, Olive Deering
97. "Escape This Night" [restaged from 2/7/50] (5-22-51) Judith Evelyn, Theo Goetz
98. "Vamp Till Dead" (5-29-51) Mary Sinclair
99. "The Call" (6-5-51) Cloris Leachman, Billy Redfield, Lawrence Fletcher, Paul Langton
100. "De Mortuis" [adapted from the John Collier story] (6-12-51) Walter Slezak, Olive Deering
101. "A Killing in Abilene" (6-19-51) William Prince
102. "The Greatest Crime" [a documentary drama] (6-26-51) Walter Slezak
103. "Blood on the Trumpet" (7-3-51) John Forsythe, Cloris Leachman, Virginia Gibson
104. "Tent on the Beach" (7-10-51) Eileen Heckart, Paul Langton
105. "Wisteria Cottage" (7-17-51) Billy Redfield, Marjorie Gateson
106. "The Incident at Story Point" (7-24-51) Donald Buka, Russell Hardie, Rusty Lane
107. "A Vision of Death " (7-31-51) Henry Hull, Jerome Cowan
108. "Killers of the City" (8-7-51) Conrad Janis
109. "Death Sabre" (8-14-51) Felicia Montealegre, Leslie Nielsen
110. "This Is Your Confession" [Part I] (8-21-51) William Bishop, Eva Gabor, Sidney Blackmer
111. "This Is Your Confession" [Part II] (8-28-51) as above.
112. "This Way Out" (9-4-51) Jean Parker, Richard Coogan
113. "Strange for a Killer" (9-11-51) John Forsythe, Anthony Ross

Fourth Season

114. "Merryman's Murder" (9-18-51) Red Buttons
115. "Doctor Anonymous" (9-25-51) Walter Slezak, Josephine Brown
116. "Santa Fe Flight" (10-2-51) Charlton Heston, Margaret Phillips
117. "High Street" (10-9-51) Mary Sinclair, Mildred Natwick
118. "The Fifth Dummy" (10-16-51) Francis L. Sullivan
119. "The Train from Czechoslovakia" (10-23-51) Maria Riva, Richard Kiley; General Lucius Clay, Royce G. Martin, guests.
120. "Court Day" (10-30-51) Richard Coogan, Parker Fennally, Steve Holland

121. "Moonfleet" [Part I] (11-6-51) Jack Diamond, John Baragrey, Edgar Stehli
122. "Moonfleet" [Part II] (11-13-51) as above.
123. "Frisco Payoff" (11-20-51) Anthony Ross, Paul Langton
124. "Mikki" (11-27-51) Joan Chandler, Brandon Peters
125. "The Man Without a Face" (12-4-51) Judith Evelyn, Douglas Watson, Henry Jones
126. "Meditation in Mexico" (12-11-51)
127. "Pier 17" (12-18-51)
128. "The Lonely Place" (12-25-51) Robin Morgan, Boris Karloff, Judith Evelyn; the Westminster Choir
129. "Routine Patrol" (1-1-52)
130. "Flare Week" (1-8-52) Eileen Heckart, Conrad Janis, Edmon Ryan
131. "The Spider" (1-15-52) Olive Deering, Arnold Moss
132. "The Red Signal" (1-22-52) Thomas Helmore, Beatrice Straight
133. "Death Drum" (1-29-52) Maria Riva
134. "Betrayal in Vienna" (2-5-52) Claude Dauphin, Irja Jensen
135. "North of Shanghai" (2-12-52) Thomas Mitchell, Dorothy Peterson
136. "Summer Night" (2-19-52) Carmen Mathews, Parker Fennelly
137. "Night Drive" (2-26-52) Neva Patterson, Robert H. Harris
138. "Day of Infamy" (3-4-52) Signe Hasso
139. "Four Days to Kill" (3-11-52) Robert Keith Jr., Joseph Buloff
140. "The Mystery of Edwin Drood" [Part I; adapted from the Charles Dickens novel] (3-18-52) John Baragrey
141. "The Mystery of Edwin Drood" [Part II] (3-25-52) as above.
142. "Black Panther" (4-8-52) Chester Morris
143. "Night of Evil" (4-15-52) Henry Hull, Patricia Crowley, Skip Homeier
144. "Alibi Me" (4-22-52) Don Hanmer
145. "The Letter" [adapted from the Somerset Maugham story] (4-29-52) Mary Sinclair, Arnold Moss
146. "The Mandarin Murders" (5-6-52) Cloris Leachman, William Redfield
147. "Fingers of Fear" (5-13-52) Robert Keith Jr., Lawrence Fletcher
148. "Hunted Down" (5-20-52) John Baragrey
149. "The Debt" (5-27-52) Conrad Janis, Robert Keith Jr.
150. "Murder of Necessity" (6-3-52) John Forsythe
151. "House of Masks" (6-10-52) Geraldine Fitzgerald, William Redfield
152. "Phantom of the Riviera" (6-17-52) Olive Deering, John Baragrey
153. "Night of Reckoning" (6-24-52) John Baragrey, Gusti Huber
154. "Fifty Beautiful Girls" [by Halstead Welles; subsequently restaged for the Schlitz Playhouse of the Stars episode of 6/21/57] (7-1-52) Grace Kelly, Robert Keith Jr., Joseph Anthony, Rusty Lane
155. "For the Love of Randi" (7-15-52) Rita Lynn, Darren McGavin, Jack Banning

156. "The Crooked Frame" (7-29-52) Richard Kiley, Neva Patterson
157. "Death Cargo" (8-5-52) Anthony Ross, Robert Keith Jr.
158. "Remember Me" (8-12-52) Cloris Leachman, Martin Brooks
159. "Her Last Adventure" (8-19-52) Arlene Francis, Lloyd
Bridges
160. "Woman in Love" (8-26-52) Gaby Rodgers, Arnold Moss
161. "The Cld Lady of Bayeux" (9-2-52) Nicole Stephan
162. "Call from a Killer" (9-9-52) Anne Jackson
163. "The Return of Dr. Bourdette" (9-16-52) William Prince,
John Baragrey
164. "Set-Up for Death" (9-23-52) Robert Keith Jr., Mary Sinclair
165. "The Beach of Falesa" (9-30-52) John Forsythe
166. "The Man in the Mirror" (10-7-52) Constance Ford, Gerald
S. O'Loughlin

Fifth Season

167. "Blue Panther" (10-14-52) Phyllis Brooks
168. "The Man Who Had Seven Hours" (10-21-52) Robert Sterling
169. "All Hallow's Eve" (10-28-52) Franchot Tone
170. "The Moving Target" (11-11-52) Jamie Smith, Irja Jensen,
Joseph Anthony
171. "Monsieur Vidocq" (11-18-52) Luis Van Rooten, Jacques Aubuchon, Nigel Greene
172. "The Whispering Killer" (11-25-52) Richard Webb, Nita Talbot, George Mathews, Bert Conway
173. "A Time of Innocence" (12-2-52) Thomas Mitchell, Patricia
Hitchcock (in her video debut), Louise Larrabee
174. "The Girl Who Saw Tomorrow" (12-9-52) Lois Wheeler,
Thomas Coley, Eugene Ruyman
175. "The Tortured Hand" (12-16-52) Peter Lorre
176. "The Deadly Lamb" (12-23-52) Dick Haymes, Patricia Breslin; the Choir of Westminster College
177. "The Invisible Killer" (12-30-52) John Dall, Jackie Cooper,
Anne Sargent
178. "Little Camorra" (1-6-53) Mary Sinclair, William Prince
179. "Mr. Matches" (1-13-53) Warren Stevens, Henry Jones,
Eleanor Wilson
180. "Vacancy for Death" (1-20-53) Joan Blondell, Steven Elliott
181. "Career" (1-27-53) Fay Bainter
182. "Mutiny Below" (2-3-53) Eddie Albert, Murray Hamilton
183. "A Study in Stone" (2-10-53) Roger Dann, Wesley Addy, Joan
Wetmore, Jay Barney
184. "The Quarry" (2-17-53) James Daly, Jeffrey Lynn, Robert
Middleton
185. "They Haven't Killed Me Yet" (2-24-53) Harry Lowe, Shizu
Moriya
186. "The Kiss-Off" (3-3-53) Jack Palance, Virginia Baker
187. "The Legend of Lizzie (Borden)" (3-10-53)
188. "The Black Prophet" (3-17-53) Boris Karloff
189. "Portrait of Constance" (3-24-53) Ann Rutherford, Hugh Reilly
190. "Death in the Cave" (3-31-53) Zachary Scott

191. "Kiss Me Again, Stranger" [adapted from the Daphne du Maurier story] (4-14-53) Maria Riva, Richard Waring
192. "The Duel" (4-21-53) Eva Gabor, Roger Dann
193. "F. O. B. Vienna" (4-28-53) Walter Matthau
194. "The Suitor" (5-5-53) Mildred Natwick
195. "Death of an Editor" (5-12-53) Anthony Ross, Mario Gallo, Wolfe Barzell, Frank Marth
196. "Come into My Parlor" (5-19-53) John Carradine, John Kerr, Martin Newman
197. "The Adventure of the Black Baronet" [adapted by Michael Dyne from the story by Adrian Conan Doyle and John Dickson Carr; an extension of the Sherlock Holmes tales] (5-26-53) Basil Rathbone, Martyn Green
198. "The Queen's Ring" (6-2-53) Mildred Dunnock, Scott Forbes, Jack Livesey
199. "The Man Who Cried Wolf" (6-9-53) Martin Brooks, Marion Winters, David Stewart, Logan Ramsey
200. "See No Evil" (6-16-53) Betty Jane Watson, John Conte
201. "The Signal Man" [adapted from the Charles Dickens story] (6-23-53) Boris Karloff, Alan Webb
202. "The Fury of Señorita Gomez" (6-30-53) Nina Foch, Harold Gordon
203. "The Mascot" (7-7-53) Mike Wallace, Margaret Hayes
204. "The Dutch Schultz Story" (7-14-53) Rod Steiger, Harry Bellaver
205. "Pigeon in the Cage" (7-21-53) John Howard, Jacqueline Susann
206. "The Dance" [adapted from the F. Scott Fitzgerald story] (7-28-53) Katherine Bard, John Baragrey
207. "Vial of Death" (8-4-53) Claude Dauphin
208. "Point Blank" (8-11-53) Chester Morris, Janis Carter
209. "Nightmare at Ground Zero" (8-18-53) O. Z. Whitehead, Louise Larabee
210. "Death in the Passing" (8-25-53) Sir Cedric Hardwicke
211. "Paradise Junction" (9-1-53) Dorothy Donahue, Tod Andrews
212. "Reign of Terror" (9-8-53) Miroslava, Peter Capell, Leonard Barry, Rosa Stradner
213. "The Darkest Night" [with an all-female cast] (9-15-53) Sally Forrest
214. "The Riddle of Mayerling" (9-22-53) Christopher Plummer, Viveca Lindfors

Sixth Season

215. "The Sister" (9-29-53) Judith Evelyn, Martha Scott
216. "Death at Skirkerud Pond" [a documentary on the Norwegian Underground Movement; narrated by Quentin Reynolds] (10-6-53)
217. "The Accounting" [a biographical drama of Emile Zola] (10-13-53) Everett Sloane
218. "The Valley of the Kings" (10-20-53) Herbert Berghoff, Jack Livesey
219. "The Others" (10-27-53) Geraldine Fitzgerald, Hugh Reilly

220. "The Interruption" (11-3-53) Sir Cedric Hardwicke, Evelyn Varden
221. "Needle in a Haystack" (11-10-53) Lee Marvin, Edwin Cooper
222. "The Newcomer" (11-17-53) Zachary Scott
223. "My Short Walk to Freedom" (11-24-53) Joseph Anthony, John Baragrey
224. "Laugh It Off" (12-1-53) Dick Haymes
225. "The Dance" [adapted from the F. Scott Fitzgerald story; re-staged from 7/28/53] (12-8-53) John Baragrey
226. "Cagliostro and the Chess Player" (12-15-53) Jack Palance
227. "The Gift of Fear" (12-22-53) Bud Flannagan, Paul Hartman
228. "Mr. Nobody" (12-29-53) Art Carney, Constance Bennett
229. "Diamonds in the Sky" (1-5-54) Annabella, Eddie Garr, Jackson Young
230. "The Scrap Iron Curtain" (1-12-54) Bart Burns
231. "The Haunted" (1-19-54) John Archer, Augusta Dabney, Helmut Dantine
232. "An Affair with a Ghost" (1-26-54) Felicia Montealegre, Darren McGavin
233. "The Man Who Wouldn't Talk" (2-2-54) Harry Townes, Peter Capell; narrated by Quentin Reynolds
234. "The Moonstone" [adapted from the Wilkie Collins novel] (2-9-54) Phyllis Kirk, Noel Leslie
235. "The Execution" (2-16-54) Katherine Bard, Joseph Anthony
236. "Death of the Screen" (2-23-54) Paul Langton, Don Hanmer
237. "I Do Solemnly Swear" (3-2-54) Nancy Kelly, Royal Dano
238. "Before the Act" (3-9-54) Jeffrey Lynn, Jo Van Fleet
239. "The Fourth Degree" (3-16-54) Joseph Wiseman
240. "The Tenth Reunion" (3-23-54) John Dall, Margaret Hayes, Patricia Barry
241. "Torment" (3-30-54) Luise Rainer, Martin Kosleck
242. "Operation: Barracuda" (4-13-54) Otto Preminger, Frank Marth, Dana Wynter
243. "The Return Journey" (4-20-54) Art Carney, Roxanne, Kay Medford
244. "The Terror Begins" [on the Stalin Party purge] (4-27-54) Everett Sloane, Stefan Schnabel
245. "Smoke" [adapted from the William Faulkner story] (5-4-54) E. G. Marshall, George Mitchell
246. "Operation: Nightmare" [a biographical drama of Lieutenant Ann Bernatitus] (5-11-54) Anne Burr, Douglas Rodgers
247. "Breakout" (5-18-54) Anthony Ross
248. "Fingerprints" (5-25-54) John Emery
249. "Race Against Murder" [a documentary on solo research flight] (6-1-54)
250. "North Side" (6-8-54) Edward Binns
251. "The Pistol Shot" (6-15-54) Hurd Hatfield, Dana Wynter
252. "String" (6-22-54) Harry Townes, Richard Merrill, Jack Lord
253. "The Hunted" (6-29-54) Ward Bond, John Kerr
254. "The Girl in Car Thirty-two" (7-6-54) Edith Adams, Gene Barry
255. "Conversation at an Inn" (7-13-54) Maria Riva, Mildred Natwick, Jacques Aubuchon

256. "Once a Killer" (7-20-54) Lenka Peterson, Michael Strong, Martin Brooks
257. "Main Feature: Death" (7-27-54) Nina Foch
258. "The Last Stand" (8-3-54) Joan Lorring, Pat Hingle
259. "The Iron Cop" (8-10-54) J. Pat O'Malley, Ray Walston, Dara Seegar
260. "Barn Burning" [adapted from the William Faulkner short story] (8-17-54) E. G. Marshall, Charles Taylor

BELIEVE IT OR NOT [after the radio series]

The Regulars: Robert L. Ripley, cartoonist and creator, who also adapted the series for television, host

The Episodes (initially began 3/1/49, untitled):

1. "Murder in Duplicate" (1-4-50)
2. "The Voice of Obsession" (1-11-50) Hildy Parks, John Hudson, Grace Kelly
3. "Voyage of Destiny" (1-25-50) Pat Jenkins
4. "Wheels of Chance" (2-1-50) Henry Hart, Ann Sorg, Maurice Manson
5. "The Man Without a Country" [adapted from the Edward Everett Hale classic] (2-8-50) John Stephen, Anne Francis
6. "The Case of the Missing Model" (2-15-50) Charles Summers, Barbara Joyce
7. "The Diamond Eye" (2-22-50) William Keane, Hi Enzel
8. "Journey Through the Darkness" (3-1-50) Anna Minot, George Reeves
9. "Murder to Come" (3-8-50) Vicki Marsden
10. "Cross of Valor" (3-15-50) Leonard Ceeley, Frederick Bradlee
11. "The Secret of Nefertiti" (3-22-50) Rita Gam, Ralph Bunker, Stewart Bradley, Romola Robb
12. "The Frightened City" (3-29-50) Patricia Benoit, Barbara Bolton, Wesley Addy, Robert Carricart
13. "The Bandit of Ballingry Ridge" (4-5-50)
14. "Casket of Doom" (4-19-50)
15. "The Pointing Finger" (4-26-50)
16. "Murder Makes the Headlines" (5-3-50) Mark Roberts, Gaye Jordon
17. "The Mystery of the Missing Guests" (5-10-50)
18. "The Bodark Tree" (5-18-50) Virginia McMahon, Jim Davidson
19. "Passport to Zermatt" (6-1-50) Gordon Mills, Marguerite Lewis
20. "Death Calls the Time" (6-8-50) Catherine Maskell, Warren Burmeister
21. "Rose of Vengeance" (6-15-50)
22. "Murder by Moonlight" (6-22-50) Louis Hector, Faith Brooke
23. "The Bleeding Heart" (6-29-50) Dayton Lummis, Jean Gillespie
24. "The Million Dollar Corpse" (7-6-50) Constance Moorehead, Dean Harens

25. "Double Jeopardy" (7-13-50)
26. "The Well of Despair" (7-20-50)
27. "Murder with a Payoff" (7-27-50) King Calder
28. "Loser Take All" (8-3-50)
29. "The Ghostly Will" (8-10-50) Justine Johnson, Elizabeth Ross
30. "Corpus Delicti" (8-17-50) John Stephen, Geoffrey Lumb, Dan Morgan
31. "The Emerald Tattoo" (8-24-50) Marcel Rousseau, Dan Morgan
32. "The Blood Call" (8-31-50) Gene Barry, Theodore Newton, Jean Gillespie
33. "Murder in Diamonds" (9-7-50) Herbert Evers, Wolf Barzell
34. "The Dead Will Speak" (9-21-50) Adia Kuznetzoff, Miriam Goldina
35. "Homicide" (9-28-50) John Marley

FIRESIDE THEATRE

Segments from the third season produced and directed by Frank Wisbar in Hollywood.

The Episodes:

1. "Friend of the Family" (4-5-49) Virginia Gilmore, Yul Brynner, Peter Barry
2. "Ghost Story" (4-12-49) Eda Heinemann, Dorothea Jackson, Ethel Remey, Michael Sivy
3. "Leonard Sillman's New Faces" [adapted from the Broadway revue] (4-19-49) Wally Cox, June Carroll
4. "Meet My Sister" (5-3-49) Betty and Jane Kean
5. "Time Bomb" (5-10-49) Jack Mitchum, Robert Bice, Robert Stevenson
6. "Brainy Bobby" (5-17-49)
7. "Make a Wish" (5-24-49)
8. "Feature Story" (6-7-49)
9. "Dance Discoveries" (6-14-49) Paul Draper, Igor Youskevitch
10. a) "The Stronger"; b) "A Terribly Strange Bed" [adapted from the Wilkie Collins classic] (6-21-49)
11. "Father" (6-28-49) Harry Bannister, Jane Walker, Curt Conway

Second Season

12. a) "Smooth Fingers"; b) "Germelshausen" (9-6-49)
13. a) "Vain Glory"; b) "Out of the River" (9-20-49)
14. a) "The Spy"; b) "The Postmistress of Laurel Rim" (9-27-49)
15. a) "Like Money in the Bank"; b) "Magic Skin" (10-4-49)
16. a) "Scream in the Night"; b) "Troubled Harbor" (10-11-49)
17. a) "Bandit, Banker and Blonde"; b) "The Wall" (10-18-49)
18. a) "Heartbeat"; b) "Mardi Gras" (10-25-49)
19. a) "Checkmate"; b) "Solange" (11-1-49)
20. a) "Night Owl"; b) "Another Road" (11-8-49)
21. a) "Stagecoach Driver McLean"; b) "Cowboy's Lament" (11-15-49)

22. a) "The Room"; b) "Epilogue" (11-29-49)
23. a) "Sealed Orders"; b) "Battle Scene" (12-6-49)
24. "The Pardoner's Tale" [adapted from Geoffrey Chaucer's Can-terbury Tales] (12-13-49)
25. a) "The Doll"; b) "The Bet" (12-20-49)
26. a) "The Gambler"; b) "Threshold" (12-27-49)
27. a) "Dinner for Three" Fay Baker, John Archer; b) "The Vam-pire" Muriel Mansell, Jodi Lawrence (1-3-50)
28. a) "The Devil's Due" Douglas Dumbrille; b) "Rendezvous" Irene Vernon, Jim Anderson (1-10-50)
29. a) "The Golden Ball"; b) "Just Three Words" (1-17-50)
30. a) "Confession" John Warburton; b) "Reprieve" (1-24-50)
31. a) "Of Thee I Love"; b) "Double Jeopardy" (1-31-50)
32. a) "The Imp in the Bottle" Clark Howatt; b) "The Stronger" [restaged from 6/21/49] Geraldine Fitzgerald (2-7-50)
33. a) "The Shot"; b) "The Red by the Window" (2-14-50)
34. a) "Anniversary" Michail Blake; b) "Jungle Terror" Mack Wil-liams (2-21-50)
35. a) "A Terribly Strange Bed" [adapted from the Wilkie Collins classic; restaged from 6/21/49]; b) "The Stronger" [restaged from 6/21/49 and 2/7/50] (2-28-50)
36. a) "Germelshausen" [restaged from 9/6/49]; b) "Sealed Orders" [restaged from 12/6/49] (3-7-50)
37. a) "The General's Coat"; b) "Vain Glory" [restaged from 9/20/49] (3-14-50)
38. "Leather Heart" (3-21-50) Irene Vernon
39. "The Bunker" (3-28-50) Dick Wessel, Jack Mitchum
40. "The Tangled Web" (4-11-50) Alan Wells, Byron Foulger, Basil Talon
41. "No Strings Attached" (4-18-50) Gertrude Michael, Reginald Sheffield, John Warburton, Wilton Graff
42. "Boys Will Be Men" (4-25-50) Stephen Salina, Ken Harvey
43. "Operation Mona Lisa" (5-2-50) Ralph Byrd, Marian Martin
44. "The Parasol" (5-9-50) Frances Ford, Jack Mitchum
45. "The Hired Girl" (5-16-50) Shirley Jones, James Anderson
46. "Big Ben" (5-23-50)
47. "The Man Without a Country" [adapted from the Edward Everett Hale classic] (5-30-50) Ralph Byrd, John Warburton, Regi-nald Sheffield, June Lang, Lester Matthews
48. a) "The Human Touch" Albert Dekker; b) "The Assassin" (6-6-50)
49. a) "Dinner for Three" [restaged from 1/3/50] Fay Baker, John Archer; b) "The Devil's Due" [restaged from 1/10/50] (6-13-50)
50. a) "The Courting of Bell" Jack Mitchum, Art Millan; b) "Ren-dezvous" [restaged from 1/10/50] (6-20-50)
51. "The Ear" (6-27-50) Whit Bissell

Third Season

52. "Polly" (8-29-50) Ann Savage, Kenneth Harvey
53. "Stopover" (9-5-50) Gertrude Michael
54. "Leather Heart" [restaged from 3/21/50] (9-12-50) Irene Ver-non, Wilton Graff, Art Millan, John Baer

55. "Incident in the Rain" (9-19-50) Irene Vernon, Warren Douglas, Frances Williams
56. "Andy's Old Man" (9-26-50) Trude Marshall, Cynthis Corby,
   Kathleen Freeman
57. "International Incident" (10-3-50) Wilton Graff, John Baer
58. "Lucy and the Stranger" (10-10-50) Margaret Lambert
59. "Hope Chest" (10-17-50) Frieda Inescourt, Mary Sinclair
60. "The Amber Gods" (10-24-50) Mary Sinclair
61. "Mother's Mutiny" (10-31-50) Virginia Mullen
62. "Judas" (11-7-50) Gertrude Michael, Ann Savage
63. "Party Line" (11-14-50) Ginny Jackson, Gertrude Michael,
   Walter McGrail, Don Beddoe
64. "The Love of Mike" (11-21-50) Irene Vernon, Anthony Caruso
65. "Three Strangers" (11-28-50) John Call, Myron Healey, George
   Calhoun, Kay Lee, George Clancy
66. "The Green Convertible" (12-5-50) Frances Dee, Gertrude
   Michael, John Warburton, Joan Miller, Dabbs Greer
67. "The Case of Marina Goodwin" (12-12-50) Mary Sinclair, Edgar Barrier, Wilton Graff
68. "Miggles" (12-19-50) Mary Sinclair, Hugh O'Brian, Grant
   Calhoun
69. "No Children, No Dogs" (12-26-50) Irene Vernon, Warren
   Douglas
70. "Flight Thirteen" (1-2-51) Walter Coy, Patricia Dane, Dorothy
   Bruce
71. "Neutral Corner" (1-9-51) George Wallace, Anthony Caruso,
   Peter Brocco
72. "Looking Through" (1-16-51) Irene Vernon, Edgar Barrier
73. "Drums in the Night" (1-23-51) Malcolm Keane, Lester Matthews
74. "A Child in the House" (1-30-51) Frances Dee
75. "Hottest Day of the Year" (2-6-51) James Anderson, Carol
   Matthews, Sheilah Watson
76. "Substance of His House" (2-13-51) Jimmy Hickman, Lillian
   Albertson, Jack Daly
77. "Going Home" (2-20-51) Hugh O'Brian, Dabbs Greer, Noreen
   Nash
78. "Copy Boy" (2-27-51) Bob Ellis, Hunter Gardner, David Bruce,
   John Warburton
79. "Malachi's Cove" (3-6-51) Tony McMillon, Sally Owen, Wilfred Walters
80. "Shifting Sands" (3-13-51) Gertrude Michael, Hugh O'Brian
81. "Eleventh Hour" (3-20-51) Hugh O'Brian, Lynne Roberts,
   John Dunbar
82. "Unwritten Column" (3-27-51) Virginia Farmer, Edward Earl,
   Frieda Inescourt, Marjorie Steele
83. "The Gentleman from La Porte" (4-3-51) Eve Miller, Warren
   Douglas
84. "Hot Spot" (4-10-51) Eve Miller, Clark Howatt
85. "Close Shave" (4-17-51) James Anderson, Ginni Jackson
86. "The Celebrated Mrs. Rowland" (4-24-51) Gertrude Michael,
   John Warburton
87. "The Moment of Truth" (5-1-51) Edward Norris, Richard
   Avonde

88.　"The Tunnel"　(5-8-51)　Dickie Le Roy, R. B. Norman

Fourth Season

89.　"Back to Zero"　(6-26-51)　Bernard Miles, June Rodney
90.　"Moment of Glory"　(7-3-51)　Vaughn Taylor
91.　"The Vigil"　(7-10-51)
92.　"A Little Light Music"　(7-17-51)
93.　"A Jury of Her Peers" [adapted from the Susan Glaspell story]　(7-24-51)
94.　"Deliver Us from Evil"　(7-31-51)　Robert Crozler, Franklin Fox
95.　"Agnew Jones and the Giants"　(8-7-51)
96.　"Make Believe"　(8-14-51)　Don Wigginton
97.　"The Lottery" [adapted from the Shirley Jackson story]　(8-21-51)　Margaret Hayes
98.　"Comes the Day"　(8-28-51)　Tom Powers, Sheila Bromley
99.　"Second Chance"　(9-4-51)　Anthony Caruso, Robert Einer
100.　"Homer Takes a Bride"　(9-11-51)　Robert North, Evelynn Eaton
101.　"Solitaire"　(9-18-51)　Gertrude Michael, Margaret Field
102.　"White Violet"　(9-25-51)　Eve Miller, Jim Davis
103.　"The Birds Are Walking"　(10-2-51)　Edward Norris, Jimmy Smith
104.　"Doctor Mac"　(10-9-51)　Tom Powers, Emory Parnell
105.　"Treasure of the Heart"　(10-16-51)　William Fawcett, Douglas Dick, Garry Lee Jackson
106.　"Torture"　(10-23-51)　Ken Harvey, Dabbs Greer, Garry Lee Jackson
107.　"Party Dress"　(10-30-51)　Robert North
108.　"Big Night in Boonetown"　(11-6-51)　John Mitchum
109.　"The Seven Graces"　(11-13-51)　Jim Davis, Jessie Cavitt
110.　"Handcuffed"　(11-20-51)　Dorothy Comingore
111.　"Not a Bit Like Jason"　(11-27-51)　Lynne Roberts, John Sutton, Tom Cook, Gloria Marshall
112.　"The Squeeze"　(12-4-51)　Clancy Cooper, William Lester
113.　"A Question of Wills"　(12-11-51)　Maura Murphy, Tom Powers
114.　"Black Savannah"　(12-18-51)　Joan Leslie, Lester Mathews
115.　"A Christmas Carol" [adapted from the Charles Dickens classic]　(12-25-51)　Sir Ralph Richardson, Arthur Treacher
116.　"The Saint and Senorita"　(1-1-52)　Rita Moreno, William Henry
117.　"Hunt for Death"　(1-8-52)　Lynne Roberts, George Wallace, William Lester
118.　"Land of Destiny"　(1-15-52)　Charlita, William Bishop
119.　"Flame of Faith"　(1-22-52)　Maura Murphy
120.　"Twilight Song"　(1-29-52)　Jay M. Karrigan, Moina McGill
121.　"The Exile"　(2-5-52)　Clancy Cooper, Ann Savage, Dabbs Greer
122.　"The Old Talbot"　(2-12-52)　Alf Kjellin, Anna Q. Nilsson
123.　"The Broken Chord"　(2-19-52)
124.　"The Co-Signer"　(2-26-52)　Jay Novello
125.　"M'liss"　(3-4-52)　Rita Moreno, William Bishop

126. "The Secret" (3-11-52) Marguerite Churchill, Gary Gray
127. "Washington Rendezvous" (3-18-52) Lisa Ferraday
128. "Hurray, Hurray" (3-25-52) George Reeves, Mary Castle
129. "Sound in the Night" (4-1-52) Lee Marvin
130. "The Living Thing" (4-8-52) Scott Forbes
131. "Brown of Calaveras" (4-15-52) William Bishop, Marjorie Lord
132. "Deadline" (4-22-52) Douglas Kennedy, William Lester
133. "The Last Stop" (4-29-52) John Warburton, Carol Mathews
134. "The Haunted Wedding" (5-6-52) Gar Moore, Margaret Field
135. "The Rivals" (5-13-52) Claudia Dell, Robert Paige
136. "To Stand Alone" (5-20-52) William Fawcett
137. "The Imposter" (5-27-52) Joan Leslie, Craig Stevens
138. "Another Harvest" (6-3-52) Ruth Warrick
139. "Mirage" (6-10-52) Marjorie Lord, Bill Henry, John Picard, Robert Foulk
140. "The Serpent's Tongue" (6-17-52) Robert Paige, Louise Currie, Alix Talton
141. "The Boxer and the Stranger" (6-24-52) Isabel Jewell, George Wallace

Fifth Season

142. "The Next to Crash" [an airforce drama] (9-30-52) John Agar, Milburn Stone
143. "A Grand for Grandma" (10-7-52) Mabel Paige
144. "The People's Choice" (10-14-52) Kristine Miller, Barbara Brown, Tom Powers
145. "The Sheriff" (10-21-52) Jim Davis, Andrea King
146. "Visit from a Stranger" (10-28-52) Marjorie Lord, Marshall Thompson
147. "I Send Your Son into Battle" (11-11-52) Bob Ellas, Jim Davis, Peter Adams
148. "The Roof" (11-18-52) Kenneth Tobey, Ed Tierney, Leslie Banning
149. "That's How It Is" (11-25-52) Hannelore Axmann, Ed Tierney
150. "Feet of Clay" (12-2-52) Grandon Rhodes, Bill Phipps, Angela Green
151. "Honor" (12-9-52) Larry Carr, John Hoyt
152. "Love Without Wings" (12-16-52) Jane Wyatt
153. "Ward of the Golden Gate" (12-23-52) Marshall Thompson, Susan Morrow
154. "A Kiss for Aunt Sophie" (12-30-52) Robert Hutton, Peggy Castle
155. "Let the Cards Decide" (1-6-53) Paula Raymond, Craig Stevens
156. "Many Happy Returns" (1-13-53) Eve Miller, Phil Terry
157. "The Critic" (1-20-53) Helen Parrish, John Warburton, Jody Lawrence
158. "The Lady Wears a Star" (1-27-53) Shirley O'Hara, George Nader, Russ Conway
159. "I Cover Korea" (2-3-53) Marguerite Chapman, Donald Woods
160. "Return" (2-10-53) Garry Moore, Marjorie Lord

161. "Boundary Line" (2-17-53) George Nader, Joy Page, Adam Williams
162. "The Juror" (2-24-53) Anita Louise, John Warburton
163. "Grey Gardens" (3-3-53) Arthur Franz, Frances Gifford, Fay Roope
164. "Money Under the Tree" (3-10-53) Madge Meredith, Walter Reed
165. "A Grand Cop" (3-17-53) John Bromfield, Shirley O'Hara
166. "Unexpected Wife" (3-24-53) William Bishop, Maria Palmer, Ruth Clifford
167. "A Man of Peace" (3-31-53) Ralph Faulkner, Robert Arthur
168. "Cocoon" (4-7-53) Barbara Brown
169. "Top Kick" (4-14-53) Clancy Cooper
170. "Mission to Algiers" (4-21-53) William Bishop, Joe Kerr, Kristine Miller
171. "The Pemberton Boy" (4-28-53)
172. "The Hitchhiker" (5-5-53) Marjorie Lord
173. "The Gift Horse" (5-12-53) Robert Paige, Ruth Warrick
174. "Safety Island" (5-19-53) Grandon Rhodes, Maura Murphy, James Hickman
175. "The Day the Greek's Was Closed" (5-26-53)
176. "One Plus One" (6-2-53) Laura Mason, Lisa Clark, Bill Lester, Walter Reed
177. "The Deauville Bracelet" (6-9-53) Reginald Denny, Phyllis Stanley
178. "In the Carquinez Woods" (6-16-53) Andrea King, Jim Davis
179. "Night in the Warehouse" (6-23-53) Clancy Cooper, Robert Blake
180. "The Snake" (6-30-53) Madge Meredith, Leslie Bradley

Sixth Season

The Regulars: Gene Raymond, host

181. "The Traitor" [drama of an American prisoner-of-war in North Korea] (9-1-53) Hugh Beaumont, Don Keefer, Jerry Paris
182. "Bless the Man" (9-8-53) William Bishop, Joyce Holden, Jonathan Hale
183. "Man Enough for Millie" (9-15-53) Eve Miller, Jim Davis, Barton MacLane
184. "His Name Is Jason" (9-22-53) Gertrude Michael, John Warburton
185. "Domestic Tranquility" (9-29-53) George Givot, Ric Vallin
186. "Refuge" (10-6-53) George Nader, Amanda Blake
187. "The Favorable Signs" (10-13-53) Barton MacLane, Jacqueline DeWitt
188. "Phantom of the Bridge" (10-20-53)
189. "Full Portrait" (10-27-53) Gene Raymond
190. "Man of the Comstock" (11-3-53) Bruce Bennett, Morris Ankrum, Andrea King
191. "The Shattered Dream" (11-10-53) Douglas Kennedy, Aurelio Galfi, Madge Meredith

192. "Appointment with Death" (11-17-53) George Nader, Eve Miller
193. "We'll Never Have a Nickel" (11-24-53) Hayden Rorke, Ann Doran, Gloria Talbott, Taylor Holmes
194. "Alien" (12-1-53)
195. "The Boy Down the Road" (12-8-53) Lee Aaker
196. "The Suitors" (12-15-53) Peter Graves, Peggie Castle
197. "Practically Christmas" (12-22-53) Anthony Caruso, Renata Vanni
198. "The Wild Earth" (12-29-53) Jim Davis, Pamela Duncan
199. "Moses and Mr. Aiken" (1-5-54) Porter Hall, Lillian Culver
200. "The First Prize" (1-12-54) Billy Gray, Grandon Rhodes
201. "The Insufferable Woman" (1-19-54) Robert Hutton, Eve Mc-Veach, William Bakewell
202. "The Uncrossed River" (1-26-54) Bruce Bennett, Andrea King
203. "The Old Order Changeth" (2-2-54) Frieda Inescourt, Ann Doran, Hayden Rorke
204. "Joe Giordano and Mr. Lincoln" (2-9-54) Mario Siletti, Peter Price
205. "The Grass Is Greener" (2-16-54) Gene Raymond, Frances Robinson
206. "Touch the Earth" (2-23-54) Irene Hervey, George Wallace
207. "The Desert Answer" (3-2-54) Frances Robinson, James Millican
208. "The Farnsworth Case" (3-9-54) John Agar, Ruth Clifford
209. "Ringo's Last Assignment" (3-16-54) Tom Powers, Mary Orr
210. "Retribution" (3-23-54) Faith Domergue, Ken Tobey
211. "The Relentless Weavers" (3-30-54) John Lupton, Alan Wells
212. "Invitation to Marriage" (4-6-54) Lola Albright, Gene Raymond
213. "Beyond the Cross" (4-13-54) Peter Graves, Suzanne Dalbert, John Hudson
214. "Nine Quarts of Water" (4-20-54) Amanda Blake, Jane Darwell, Jeff York
215. "A Case of Independence" (4-27-54) George Givot, Ric Vallin, with the Four Greeks
216. "Trial Period" (5-4-54) Marjorie Lord, Hugh Sanders
217. "Fight Night" (5-11-54) Hugh Beaumont, Mary Beth Hughes
218. "Harvest of Wrath" (5-18-54) Charles Drake, Faith Domergue
219. "Juror on Trial" (5-25-54) Julie Bishop, John Shelton, Wally Cassell, Jonathan Hale
220. "The Whole Truth" (6-1-54) Barbara Billingsley, Hayden Rorke, Peter Price
221. "Bread upon the Waters" (6-8-54) Peter Graves, John Banner, Brigit Nielsen
222. "The Kiss" (6-15-54) Andrea King, Jim Davis
223. "Valley of Shadows" (6-22-54)
224. "Acts of God Notwithstanding" (6-29-54) Bill Henry, Kim Spalding

Seventh Season [Gene Raymond remains host]

225. "Second Elopement" (8-31-54) Gene Raymond
226. "Crusade Without Conscience" (9-7-54) Walter Coy, Frances Rafferty

227. "Smoke and Fire" (9-14-54) Randy Stuart, Dan Barton
228. "The Sporting Doctor" (9-21-54) Gene Raymond
229. "Afraid to Live" (9-28-54) Thomas Mitchell, Charles Drake, Dorothy Malone
230. "Member of the Jury" (10-5-54) Karen Verne
231. "The Reign of Amelika Jo" (10-12-54) Keye Luke, James Edwards
232. "The Man Who Sold Himself" (10-19-54) Dan Barton, Betty Lynn
233. "The Wife Who Lived Twice" (10-26-54) Marisa Pavan, John Hudson
234. "Thank You Dr. Russell" (11-2-54) Rhys Williams, Tom Cook
235. "Lost Perspectives" (11-9-54) Gertrude Michael, Regis Toomey, Rhys Williams
236. "Girl Not Wanted" (11-16-54) Kathleen Crowley, Philip Terry
237. "The Last Hat" (11-23-54) John Warburton, Betty Lynn, Jim Davis
238. "Three Missions West" (11-30-54) Virginia Field, Virginia Grey, Paula Raymond, Robert Hutton
239. "His Father's Keeper" (12-7-54) Bobby Driscoll, Paul Kelly
240. "The Mural" (12-14-54) John Warburton
241. "Our Son" (12-21-54) Dorothy Malone, Wilton Graff
242. "A Mother's Duty" (12-28-54) June Havoc, Willard Parker, Tom Cook, Karen Sharpe
243. "The Indiscreet Mrs. Jarvis" (1-4-55) George Brent, Angela Lansbury, Martha Vickers, William Lundigan
244. "Sergeant Sullivan Speaking" (1-11-55) William Bendix, Joan Blondell
245. "The Double Life of Barney Peters" (1-18-55) Bobby Driscoll, Gene Raymond
246. "Not Captain Material" (1-25-55) Arthur Franz, Virginia Grey, Dennis Morgan
247. "Brian" (2-1-55) Maureen O'Sullivan
248. "Mr. Onion" (2-8-55) William Bendix, Irene Hervey, Dorothy Malone
249. "No Place to Live" (2-15-55) Tom Drake, Martha Vickers
250. "Marked for Death" (2-22-55) Paul Kelly, Beverly Washburn
251. "Return in Triumph" (3-1-55) George Brent, Gertrude Michael, Kathleen Crowley
252. "The Poachers" (3-8-55) Ernest Borgnine, Dan Barton, Barbara Whiting
253. "No Time for Susan" (3-15-55) Virginia Field, Melinda Markey
254. "The Failure" (3-22-55) Alan Wells, Nana Bryant
255. "It's Easy to Get Ahead" (3-29-55) George Brent, Gene Raymond, Marilyn Erskine, Irene Hervey
256. "Not the Marrying Kind" (4-5-55) Dan Barton, Kathleen Crowley
257. "The Blessing of the Pets" [of a Mexican ritual] (4-12-55) Jay Novello, David Colmans, Alma Belram
258. "Luxurious Ladies" (4-19-55) Hillary Brooke
259. "Bitter Grapes" (4-26-55) Peter Graves, John Banner, Jody Lawrence, Kurt Katch, Rod Williams

260. "The Innocent and the Guilty" (5-3-55) Alan Wells, Grandon Rhodes, Frank Wilcox, Lisa Golm, Jean Howell
261. "Cheese Champion" (5-10-55) John Mitchum, Constance Dowling, Edward Foster, Sydney Melton, Don Haggerty, Alan Wells
262. "Night of Terror" (5-17-55) Donald Murphy, George Wallace, Betty Lynn
263. "A Dream for Jimmy" (5-24-55) Robert Crosson, Fern Bennett, Hugh Sanders, Paul Brinegar
264. "The Ninety-ninth Day" (5-31-55) Lauren Chapin, Arthur Franz, Virginia Grey, Claude Akins
265. "Murderer's Wife" (6-7-55) Audrey Totter, John Howard, June Kenny
266. "The Man Who Likes to Kill" [by Herbert Little Jr. and David Victor] (6-14-55) John Hudson, Ian MacDonald, Barbara Logan, John Close
267. "A Ring for Nell" (6-21-55) Dorothy Green, Alan Hale Jr.
268. "An Argument with Death" (6-28-55) Kenneth Tobey, Sallie Brophy, Rudy Lee

Eighth Season [hereafter as JANE WYMAN PRESENTS THE FIRESIDE THEATRE]

269. "Technical Charge of Homicide" (8-30-55) John Harmon, Argentina Brunetti, Nan Boardman, William Ching
270. "Gusher City" (9-6-55) Rod Cameron
271. "The Director" [by Rod Serling] (9-13-55) Jack Carson, James Barton, Nancy Gates
272. "Holiday in Autumn" (9-20-55) Jane Wyman, Fay Wray
273. "The Little Guy" [an Emmy nominee for film editing, 1955] (9-27-55) Dane Clark, Lee Marvin
274. "The Sport" (10-4-55) Keenan Wynn, Jayne Meadows, Reginald Denny, Paul Harvey
275. "Stephen and Publius Cyrus" (10-11-55) Marguerite Chapman, Peter Lawford
276. "One Last September" (10-18-55) Jane Wyman, Don Murray
277. "The Smuggler" (10-25-55) Gilbert Roland, Henry Daniell, Lita Milan, Vince Edwards
278. "Nailed Down" (11-1-55) Dan Duryea, Gene Barry
279. "Ride with the Executioner" (11-8-55) Jane Wyman, Neville Brand
280. "The Key" (11-15-55) Carolyn Jones, Jane Wyman
281. "His Maiden Voyage" (11-22-55) James Barton, Charles Winninger
282. "Women at Sea" (11-29-55) Ruth Hussey, John Baragrey, Katherine Bard
283. "Bamboo Cross" (12-6-55) Jane Wyman, Betty Lynn, Sichi Sao, James Hong
284. "As Long as I Live" (12-13-55) Brian Keith, Dan O'Herlihy, Sallie Brophy
285. "Along Came a Bachelor" (12-20-55) Jane Wyman, Patric Knowles, Harvey Grant

286. "Big Joe's Comin' Home" (12-27-55) Victor McLaglen, Wallace Ford, Richard Jaeckel, Douglass Dumbrille
287. "Once Upon a Nightmare" (1-3-56) Jane Wyman
288. "The Liberator" (1-10-56) Dane Clark, Sebastian Cabot
289. "The House on Elm Street" (1-17-56) Jane Wyman
290. "Excuse Me for Living" (1-24-56) Jane Wyman, Arthur Franz, Edith Evanson
291. "The Velvet Trap" (1-31-56) James Whitman, Phyllis Thaxter
292. "Not What She Pretended" (2-7-56) Tom Tryon
293. "Kristi" (2-14-56) Jane Wyman, Jack Kelly, Charles Coburn
294. "The Thread" (2-21-56) Jane Wyman, Chuck Connors, Penny Santon
295. "The Mirror" (2-28-56) Joanne Dru, Tom Tryon
296. "Echo Out of the Past" (3-6-56)
297. "Scent of Roses" (3-13-56) Nancy Gates, Jack Kelly
298. "Shoot the Moon" (3-20-56) Ozzie Nelson
299. "Sound of Thunder" (3-27-56) Charles Drake, Jane Wyman, Carl Esmond
300. "In a Different Life" (4-3-56) Jane Wyman, Scott Forbes
301. "This Land Is Mine" (4-10-56) John Ireland, Joy Page
302. "The Past Is Always Present" (4-17-56) Lawrence Dobkin, John Baragrey
303. "The Hidden People" (4-24-56) Jane Wyman

Ninth Season

304. "Ten Percent" (8-28-56) William Hopper, George Montgomery
305. "Dirty Face" (9-4-56) Jane Wyman
306. "Approved by Censor" (9-11-56) Jane Wyman, Mark Richman, Tom Brown
307. "The Way to Heaven" (9-18-56) Gene Lockhart
308. "Let Yesterday Die" (9-25-56) Jane Wyman, Jimmy Baird
309. "Assignment Champ" (10-2-56) Donald Curtis, Leo Gordon
310. "No More Tears" (10-16-56) Jane Wyman
311. "Between Jobs" [an Emmy nominee for film editing, 1956] (10-30-56) Neville Brand, Ralph Meeker
312. "Father Forgets" (11-13-56) Jane Wyman, Bruce Gordon
313. "The Marked Bullet" (11-20-56) Jane Wyman, Joseph Wiseman
314. "A Time to Live" (11-27-56) Jane Wyman
315. "Helpmate" (12-4-56) Imogene Coca, Dabbs Greer
316. "While There's Life" (12-11-56) Henry Jones, Vivi Janiss, Gordon Jones
317. "A Point of Law" (12-18-56) Virginia Grey
318. "A Place on the Bay" (12-25-56) Gene Barry, Connie Gilchrist, Kurt Kasznar, Gloria Talbott
319. "The Little Black Lie" (1-1-57) Dane Clark, Carolyn Jones
320. "Twenty Dollar Bride" (1-8-57) Jane Wyman, Jeff Morrow, Gordon Jones, Jim Haywood, Claude Akins, Paul Wexler
321. "Portrait in Fear" (1-15-57) Jane Wyman
322. "The Golden Door" (1-22-57) Jane Wyman, Benny Rubin
323. "Killer's Pride" (1-29-57) John Kerr, Mae Clarke, Fay Wray
324. "Birthright" (2-5-57) Gail Kobe, Tom Tryon, Jane Wyman, Jeanette Nolan

325. "Small Talk" (2-12-57) Jane Wyman
326. "Farmer's Wife" (2-19-57) John Dehner, Beverly Washburn
327. "A Dangerous Thing" (2-26-57) Jeannie Carson
328. "Married to a Stranger" (3-5-57) Jane Wyman, Simon Scott
329. "The Pendulum" (3-12-57) Gene Barry
330. "The Wildcatter" (3-19-57) Claude Akins, Virginia Grey
331. "Mama Bufano's" (4-9-57) Jane Wyman
332. "Not for Publication" (4-16-57) Jane Wyman, Tom Conway
333. "Harbor Patrol" (4-23-57) Neville Brand, Cara Williams
334. "The Man in the Car" (4-30-57) Craig Stevens
335. "There Comes One Moment" (5-7-57) Jane Wyman
336. "Night of Terror" (5-14-57) Jane Wyman
337. "Two Sides to Everything" (6-11-57) Jane Wyman, Simon Scott

Tenth Season

338. "The Way Home" (9-26-57) Robert Bray, Steve Dunne, Jane Wyman
339. "Contact" (10-3-57) Joseph Cotten
340. "The Man on the Thirty-fifth Floor" (10-10-57) Macdonald Carey
341. "The Animal Instinct" (10-31-57) Jane Wyman
342. "Roadblock Number Seven" (11-7-57) Margaret O'Brien, Mark Richman
343. "A Reasonable Doubt" (11-28-57) Hugh Marlowe, Mark Stevens, Jimmy Gavin
344. "Death Rides the 12:15" (12-5-57) Jane Wyman, Edward Platt
345. "The Perfect Alibi" (12-12-57) Vincent Price
346. "The Night After Christmas" (12-26-57) Jane Wyman
347. "The Elevator" [adapted by Michael Fessier from the story by James and Pamela Mason] (1-2-58) Linda Darnell, John Baragrey
348. "A Widow's Kiss" (1-9-58) Jane Wyman
349. "Day of Glory" (1-16-58) Paul Douglas
350. "A Guilty Woman" (1-30-58) Virginia Grey, Jan Sterling
351. "My Sister Susan" (2-6-58) Jane Wyman (as twin sisters)
352. "He Came for the Money" (2-13-58) Ruth Roman
353. "Tunnel Eight" [a post-Civil War drama] (2-20-58) Preston Foster, Grant Williams
354. "Prime Suspect" (2-27-58) William Bendix, Nita Talbot
355. "The Doctor Was a Lady" [otherwise known as "My Darling Doctor"] (3-27-58) Jane Wyman, Keith Andes, Frances Bergen
356. "Swindler's Inn" (4-10-58) Jane Wyman
357. "The Bravado Touch" (4-17-58) Fernando Lamas
358. "Man of Taste" (4-24-58) Paul Henreid
359. "On the Brink" (5-1-58) Richard Beymer, Mercedes McCambridge
360. "The Last Test" (5-8-58) Gary Merrill
361. "Hide and Seek" (5-22-58) Everett Sloane, Jane Wyman

YOUR SHOW TIME

Sponsored by the American Tobacco Company for the Lucky Strike Cigarette.

The Regulars: Arthur Shields, host and storyteller

The Episodes:

1. "The Necklace" [adapted from the Guy de Maupassant story] (1-21-49) John Beal
2. "The Sire de Maletroit's Door" [adapted from the Robert Louis Stevenson story] (1-28-49) Dan O'Herlihy, Morris Carnovsky, Allene Roberts
3. "Mademoiselle Fifi" [adapted from the Guy de Maupassant story] (2-4-59) Hurd Hatfield, Roman Bohnen, Jeanne Page, Frank Reicher, Jay Adler, Tannis Chandler
4. "The Mummy's Foot" [adapted from the Theophile Gautier story] (2-11-49) Phyllis Coates, Peggy Dow, J. Edward Bromberg, Herbert Anderson, Hand Henry
5. "The Substitute" (2-18-49) Robert Alda, Suzanne Dalbert
6. "The Invisible Wound" (2-25-49) Reginald Denny, Maria Palmer
7. "A Capture" [adapted from the Henry C. Bunner story] (3-4-49) Jeanne Cagney, Sterling Holloway, Housely Stevenson, Richard Travis
8. "The Real Thing" [adapted from the Henry James story] (3-11-49) John Archer, Marjorie Lord
9. "The Treasure of Franchard" (3-18-49) Alan Reed, Selena Royle, Dan Seymour
10. "The Adventure of the Speckled Bird" [adapted from the Arthur Conan Doyle story] (3-25-49) Alan Napier, Melville Cooper, Evelyn Ankers
11. "The Tenor" [adapted from the Henry C. Bunner story] (4-1-49) Hugo Haas, Carol Brennan, Lee Patrick, Betty Adams
12. "The Manchester Marriage" (4-8-49) Jan Clayton, Richard Travis
13. "The Lady or the Tiger" [adapted from the Frank Stockton story] (4-15-49) Leif Erickson, Eve Miller, William Frawley, Peggy Knudsen
14. "A Confession on New Year's Eve" (4-22-49) John Archer, Stanley Waxman
15. "The Mysterious Picture" (4-29-49) Marc Daniels, Hugo Haas, Mark Stevens
16. "An Old, Old Story" (5-6-49) Eric Blore, Selena Royle
17. "The Marquise" (5-13-49) Elizabeth Fraser, Leif Erickson
18. "The Million Pound Bank Note" (5-20-49) Ross Ford, Paula Raymond
19. "Birthday of the Infants" [otherwise known as "The Infants of Spain"] (5-27-49) Gene Reynolds, Frank Wilcox, Gloria Holden
20. "Why Thomas Was Discharged" (6-3-49) Marc Daniels, Marcia Jones, Gil Stratton Jr., Tom Stevenson
21. "The Bishop's Experiment" (6-10-49) Leif Erickson, Ludwig Donath

22. "The Celebrated Jumping Frog of Calaveras County" [adapted from the Mark Twain story] (6-17-49) Kristine Miller, Kirby Grant
23. "An Only Son" (6-24-49) Richard Crane, Judy Sochor
24. "Colonel Starbottle for the Plaintiff" [adapted from the Bret Harte story] (7-1-49) Robert Warwick
25. "Cricket on the Hearth" [adapted from the Charles Dickens story] (7-8-49) Heather Wilde, Thomas P. Dillon
26. "A Lodging for the Night" [adapted from the Robert Louis Stevenson story] (7-15-49) Stanley Waxman, Eva Gabor

LIGHTS OUT

Under the sponsorship of Admiral.

The Regulars: Jack La Rue, host and narrator; subsequently displaced by Frank Gallup (with episode of 4/24/50)

The Episodes:

1. "Episode One" (7-19-49) Frances Reid, Phil Arthur, Anita Anton, Gladys Clark
2. "Episode Two" (7-26-49) William Post Jr., Mary Patton, Eva Marie Saint
3. "Long Distance" (8-2-49) Jan Miner
4. "Conquerer's Isle" (11-7-49) Richard Derr, Mercer McLeod, Vinton Hayworth, Sarah Benham
5. "The Fall of the House of Usher" [adapted from the Edgar Allan Poe classic] (11-21-49) Helmut Dantine, Pamela Conroy, Stephen Courtleigh
6. "I Dreamt I Died" (11-28-49) Alfreda Wallace, Philip Truex, Karen Stevens, Ross Martin
7. "Something in the Wind" (12-5-49) John Graham, Douglas Chandler, Inga Adams
8. "Justice Lies Waiting" (12-12-49) Larry Fletcher, Ray Rand, Mercer McLeod, Pat Jones, John Boruff
9. "The Elevator" (12-19-49) Jack Hartley, Helene Dumas, James Van Dyke, Dolores Badioni
10. "The Man Who Couldn't Lose" (12-26-49) Dean Harens, Alfreda Wallace
11. "The Riverman" (1-2-50) Athena Lorde, Elizabeth Moore, Henry Brandon
12. "Judgment Reversed" (1-9-50) King Calder, Nancy Coleman, Ralph Riggs, Bernard Nedell
13. "The Green Dress" (1-16-50) Lynn Salisbury, Robert Pastene, Mercedes Gilbert, Candy Montgomery
14. "The Devil to Pay" (1-23-50) Alfreda Wallace, Arnold Moss
15. "Reservation--For Four" (1-30-50) Mercer McLeod, Dean Harens
16. "Dead Pigeon" (2-6-50) Phil Coolidge, Joel Ashley, John Boruff, Florida Friebus

17. "The Invisible Staircase" (2-13-50) Clairence and Elfreda Derwent
18. "Graven Image" (2-20-50) Pat Jenkins, Dean Harens, John Glendinning
19. "Portrait of a Dead Man" (2-27-50) Horace Braham, Dick Fraser
20. "The Strange Case of John Kingman" (3-6-50) John Newland, Richard Purdy
21. "The Emerald Lavalier" (3-13-50) Felicia Montealegre, Theodore Newton
22. "The Scarab" (3-20-50) Vinton Hayworth, Richard Derr, Melba Rae
23. "Mary" (3-27-50) Carol Ohmart, George Englund, Gage Jordan, John McQuade
24. "The Queen Is Dead" (4-3-50) Mildred Natwick, Una O'Connor
25. "The Faithful Heart" (4-10-50) Anne Francis, Liam Sullivan, Dorothy Francis, James O'Neil
26. "A Toast to Sergeant Farnsworth" (4-17-50) Ross Martin, Dan Morgan
27. "The Man Who Couldn't Remember" (4-24-50) Jack Palance, Tom Walsh, Roger De Koven
28. "The Gloves of Gino" (5-1-50) Ross Martin, Bernard Nedell, Sarah Anderson, Leslie Barrett
29. "The Silent Voice" (5-8-50) Douglas Parkhirst
30. "The House That Time Forgot" (5-15-50) Dulcey Jordan
31. "Rendezvous" (5-22-50) Richard MacMurray, Inge Adams
32. "How Love Came to Professor Guildea" (5-29-50) Arnold Moss
33. "The Heart of Jonathan O'Rourke" (6-5-50) Alfreda Wallace, Peter Capell, William Windom
34. "The Determined Lady" (6-12-50) Ethel Griffies
35. "A Child Is Crying" (6-19-50) David Cole, Frank Thomas Jr., Leslie Nielsen
36. "Encore" (6-26-50) Don Hanmer
37. "I Dreamt I Died" [restaged from 11/28/49] (7-3-50)
38. "The Devil to Pay" [restaged from 1/23/50] (7-17-50) Theodore Marcuse, Grace Kelly, Jonathan Harris
39. "The Strange Case of John Kingman" [restaged from 3/6/50] (7-31-50) Philip Coolidge, Oliver Cliff, John Baragrey
40. "The Queen Is Dead" [restaged from 4/3/50] (8-14-50)

Second Season

41. "The Ides of April" (8-28-50) Ella Raines, George Reeves, Horace MacMahon
42. "Benuili Chant" (9-4-50) Tom Drake, Ed Begley, Jean Sheppard
43. "The Dark Corner" (9-11-50) John Newland, Mary Sinclair, Alan Marshall
44. "The Leopard Lady" (9-18-50) Boris Karloff
45. "Sisters of Shadow" (9-25-50) William Eythe, Elinor Randel
46. "The Posthumous Dead" (10-2-50) Ed Begley
47. "Just What Happened" (10-9-50) John Howard, Richard Purdy, Rita Lynn

48. "The Thing Upstairs" (10-16-50) Florence Reed, Freddy Bartholomew, Peggy Nelson
49. "The Skeptics" (10-23-50) E. G. Marshall
50. "The Martian Eyes" (10-30-50) Burgess Meredith, David Lewis, J. Pat O'Malley, Gavin Gordon
51. "The Half-Pint Flask" (11-6-50) John Carradine, Kent Smith
52. "The Waxwork" (11-13-50) John Beal, Nelson Olmstead
53. "Dr. Heidegger's Experiment" [adapted from the Nathaniel Hawthorne classic] (11-20-50) Billie Burke, Gene Lockhart, Halliwell Hobbes, Thomas Poston
54. "The Mule Man" (11-27-50) Charles Korvin, Melba Rae, James O'Neil
55. "Beware This Woman" (12-4-50) Veronica Lake, Glenn Denning
56. "Masque" (12-11-50) Estelle Winwood, Mary Stewart, Lynn Salisbury
57. "The Men on the Mountain" (12-18-50) Lee Tracy, William Free, Vern Collett
58. "Jaspar" (12-25-50) Janis Carter, Johnny Johnston, Meg Mundy
59. "The Haunted Skyscraper" (1-1-51) Felicia Montealegre, Don Dickinson, Virginia Gilmore
60. "Bird of Time" (1-8-51) Jessica Tandy, David Lewis, Julie Bennett, Irving Ulinter
61. "The Bottle Imp" (1-15-51) Donald Buka, Glenn Langan
62. "For Release Today" (1-22-51) K. T. Stevens, Herbert Rudley, Vinton Hayworth
63. "The Masque of the Red Death" [adapted from the Edgar Allan Poe classic] (1-29-51) Hurd Hatfield
64. "The House of Dust" [advertised as "the most daring and unusual drama ever presented on Lights Out"] (2-5-51) Nina Foch, Anthony Quinn
65. "Curtain Call" (2-12-51) Otto Kruger, Alan Bunce, Elinor Randel
66. "Strange Legacy" (2-19-51) Robert Stack, Margaret Hayes, Henry Hart, Joseph Sweeney
67. "The Dispossessed" (2-26-51) Jeffrey Lynn, June Dayton, Stefan Schnabel
68. "The Man With the Astrakhan Hat" (3-5-51) Paul Stewart, Ross Martin, Jim Bender, Peter Capell
69. "Leda's Portrait" (3-12-51) Felicia Montealegre, George Reeves, John Emery
70. "Western Night" (3-19-51) Richard Derr, Biff Elliott, William Free
71. "The Power of the Brute" (3-26-51) Tom Drake, Richard Carlyle, Reba Tassell
72. "The Mad Dullaghen" (4-2-51) Glen Langan, Stella Andrew, Berry Kroeger
73. "The Crushed Rose" (4-9-51) John Beal, Barbara Britton, Richard Purdy
74. "The Witness" (4-16-51) Dane Clark, Howard Smith, Florence Standley
75. "The Fonceville Curse" (4-23-51) Patrick Knowles, Rosalind Ivan, Alma Lawton, Donald Morrison
76. "Grey Reminder" (4-30-51) Beatrice Straight, John Newland

77. "The Lost Will of Dr. Kant" (5-7-51) Leslie Nielsen, Pat Englund, Russell Collins
78. "Dead Man's Coat" (5-14-51) Basil Rathbone, Norman Ross, William Post
79. "The Cat's Cradle" (5-21-51) Martha Scott, Murvyn Vye, Larry Kerr
80. "The Pattern" (5-28-51) John Forsythe, June Dayton, David Lewis
81. "The Martian Eyes" [restaged from 10/30/50] (6-4-51) Burgess Meredith, J. Pat O'Malley, David Lewis, John Baragrey
82. "Pit of the Dead" (6-11-51) Joseph Buloff, John Dall, Beatrice Kraft, Bill Darriet
83. "Dead Freight" (6-18-51) Charles Dingle, Louisa Horton
84. "The Passage Beyond" (6-25-51) John Buckmaster, Stella Andrew
85. "And Adam Begot" (7-2-51) Kent Smith
86. "The Meddlers" (7-9-51) John Carradine, E. G. Marshall, Dan Morgan
87. "The Devil in Glencairn" (7-16-51) Richard Carlson
88. "Zero Hour" (7-23-51) Denise Alexander, John O'Hare, Richard Wigginton
89. "The Fingers" (7-30-51)
90. "The Faceless Man" (8-6-51) Robert Sterling, Ted Hecht, Gregory Morton
91. "The Man with the Watch" (8-13-51) Francis L. Sullivan, Gordon Clarke, Peggy French, Peter Capell
92. "Follow Me" (8-20-51) Peter Cookson, Doris Rich

Third Season

93. "Mrs. Manifold" (8-27-51) Leslie Nielsen, Adelaide Klein, J. Pat O'Malley
94. "Blackwood Halt" (9-3-51) Stella Andrew, Frederick Tozere
95. "Prophet of Darkness" (9-10-51) Sidney Blackmer, Ronola Robb
96. "To See Ourselves" (9-17-51) Cathy O'Donnell, Henry Barnard, Mercer McLeod
97. "Rappaccini's Daughter" [adapted from the Nathaniel Hawthorne classic] (9-24-51) Eli Wallach, Hope Miller
98. "Will-o'-the-Wisp" (10-1-51) Robert Stack, Louanna Gardner, Pat Browning
99. "Dark Image" (10-8-51) Donald Woods, Ann Shepherd, Leni Stengel, Beatrice Kraft
100. "I Spy" (10-15-51) Henry Hull, Dorothy Stickney, Dale Engel, Alfreda Wallace
101. "The Deal" (10-22-51) Tom Ewell, Joseph Wiseman, Anne Marno, Martin Gabel
102. "The Veil" (10-29-51) Lee J. Cobb, Arlene Francis
103. "The Chamber of Gloom" (11-5-51) Geraldine Brooks, Arnold Moss
104. "The Beast in the Garden" (11-12-51) Margaret Phillips, Jack Marivale
105. "Friday the Nineteenth" (11-19-51) Eddie Albert

106. "Far-Cff Island" (11-26-51) Richard Greene, Gregory Morton, Lenka Peterson
107. "The Silent Supper" (12-3-51) Vanessa Brown
108. "The Angry Birds" (12-10-51) John Forsythe, Constance Dowling
109. "Perchance to Dream" (12-17-51) William Eythe, Louanna Gardner
110. "This Way to Heaven" (12-24-51) Burgess Meredith
111. "Of Time and Third Avenue" (12-31-51) Henry Daniell, Bethel Leslie, Edward Gargan
112. "School for the Unspeakable" (1-7-52) Donald Buka, Don Hanmer
113. "Blood Relation" (1-14-52) Nina Foch, Franchot Tone
114. "The Intruder" (1-21-52) Chester Morris, Jane Wyatt
115. "The Third Door" (1-28-52) Vincent Price
116. "The Chain" (2-4-52) Raymond Massey
117. "Cries the String" (2-11-52) Signe Hasso, Gregory Morton
118. "The Eyes from San Francisco" (2-18-52) Thomas Mitchell, Mary Heath, Stephen Hill
119. "The Perfect Servant" (2-25-52) Henry Daniell, Albert Dekker, Joe Allen Jr.
120. "Private--Keep Out" (3-3-52) Melvyn Douglas
121. "The Upstairs Floor" (3-10-52) John Forsythe, Josephine Hull
122. "The Borgia Lamp" (3-17-52) Grace Kelly, Robert Sterling, Hugh Griffith
123. "Another Country" (3-24-52) Yvonne De Carlo
124. "The Pit" (4-7-52) Murvyn Vye
125. "The Men on the Mountain" [restaged from 12/18/50] (4-14-52)
126. "A Lucky Piece" (4-21-52) Adelaide Klein, Henry Jones
127. "For Rent" (4-28-52)
128. "Journey into the Shadows" (5-5-52) Robert Pastene, Katherine Bard
129. "The Green Thumb" (5-12-52) George Mitchell, Victor Thorley
130. "Little Girl" (5-19-52) Patsy Bruder, Frieda Altman
131. "The Death's Head" (5-26-52) Steven Hill, Edgar Stehli
132. "Night Walk" (6-2-52) Don Hanmer, Susan Douglas
133. "Blind Man's Bluff" (6-9-52) Mercer McLeod, Mary Farrell
134. "Nightmare" (6-16-52) Joe Mantell, Perry Wilson, Mary Alice Moore
135. "Coins of Death" (6-23-52) Joseph Anthony, Berry Kroeger
136. "The Lonely Albatross" (6-30-52) John Carradine, William Redfield, Hildy Parks, Charles Egglestom
137. "The Corpse in Room Thirteen" (7-7-52) Everett Sloane, Eleanor Lynn, Harold Gary, Charles Jordan
138. "The Bog-Oak Necklace" (7-14-52) Jane Seymour, Carol Wheeler
139. "Death Trap" (7-28-52) Clare Luce, Leslie Nielsen, John McQuade, J. Pat O'Malley
140. "Man in the Dark" (8-4-52) Joseph Wiseman, Margaret Draper, Romney Brent, Joe De Santis

141. "The Killer's Moon" (8-11-52) June Lockhart, Alfred Ryder, Michael Garrett, Neil Fisher
142. "Twist of Fate" (8-18-52) E. G. Marshall, Constance Ford, Howard Smith
143. "Death Is a Small Monkey" (8-25-52) Kevin McCarthy, Francis L. Sullivan, Constance Dowling
144. "The Verdict" (9-1-52) Everett Sloane
145. "The Red Rose" [by Milton Lewis] (9-8-52) John Newland, Mary Phillips
146. "The Darker Night" (9-15-52) Louisa Horton, Richard Derr
147. "Flight Thirteen" (9-22-52) Josephine Hull, Alan Bunce
148. "The Hollow Man" (9-29-52) William Bendix, Doris Dowling, Art Smith, Harry Bellows

ACADEMY THEATRE [experimental plays]

The Episodes:

1. "The Stolen Prince" [by Dan Totheroh] (8-1-49) Shirley Dale, Ivan MacDonald, Collins Bain
2. "Drums of Oude" (8-8-49) Richard Newton, Emily Lawrence, Peter Pagan
3. "In the Shadow of the Glen" (8-15-49) Anne Jackson, Barry McCullen, Paul Anderson, Peter Wynn
4. "Two Plays by Thornton Wilder": a) "Love and How to Cure It"; b) "Such Things Only Happen in Books" (8-22-49)
5. "Summer Comes to the Diamond O" (8-29-49) Mark Roberts, Jack Davis, Bob Bolger
6. "Aria da Capo" [adapted from the Edna St. Vincent Millay 1923 play] (9-5-49) Robert Gairinger, Michael Higgins

1949-1950 SEASON

VIDEO THEATRE

The Episodes:

1. "Retaliation" (10-16-49)
2. "Young Stacey" (10-23-49) Norma Jane Marlowe
3. "The Old Lady Shows Her Medals" [adapted from the James M. Barrie play] (10-30-49) Florence Reed
4. "Remember the Day" (11-6-49) Donald Ross, Hershel Bentley
5. "O'Brien" (11-13-49) Phil Arthur, Joan Pugsley
6. "News Item" (11-20-49) James Engler, Mary Alice Moore
7. "Daughters Are Different" (11-27-49) Marta Linden, Dean Harens, Wendy Drew, Mary K. Wells
8. "Company for Dinner" (12-4-49) Dorothy Kelton, Mary K. Wells, John Baragrey, Harry Bannister
9. "A Trip to Czardia" (12-11-49) Butch Cavell, Norma Jane Marlowe
10. "The Pearls" (12-18-49) Renold Evans, Donald Buka
11. "Blessed Are They" (12-25-49) Ian Keith, Norma Jane Marlowe
12. "I'll Marry You Later" (1-1-50) Walter Klavan, Robert Gonay
13. "Second Generation" (1-8-50) Carroll Ashburn, Neva Patterson
14. "Bert's Wedding" (1-15-50) Parker Fennally, Wendy Drew, Frank Thomas Jr.
15. "Two for a Penny" (1-22-50) Neva Patterson, William Post Jr.
16. "Abby, Her Farm" (1-29-50) Jimsey Somers, Joan Castle, Jack Diamond, John Newland
17. "The Trap" (2-5-50) Oliver Thorndyke, Mary K. Wells
18. "The Brave and Early Fallen" (2-12-50) Royal Dano
19. "The Karpoldi Letter" (2-19-50) William Neil
20. "The Long Young Dreams" (2-26-50) Richard McMurray, Alfreda Wallace, Dean Harens
21. "Neither a Borrower" (3-5-50) Leona Maricle, Perry Wilson
22. "Always a Knife in the Back" (3-12-50) Vicki Cummings
23. "Blackmail" (3-19-50) William Post Jr., Virginia Gilmore
24. "The Green Bomb" (3-26-50) Robert Feyti, Eleanor Lynn, Jonathan Marlowe
25. "Burden of Guilt" (4-2-50) Clay Clement
26. "Motive for Murder" (4-9-50) John Baragrey, Pam Duncan
27. "Double Entry" (4-16-50) Florence Reed, Robert Feyti
28. "The Witness to the Crime" (4-23-50) Joe Glendinning, June Dayton
29. "The Lawbeaters" (4-30-50) Lee Tracy

30. "The Suitable Present" (5-7-50) Kathleen Comegys
31. "Revenge by Proxy" (5-14-50) Nancy Coleman, Phil Arthur,
    Bernard Kates, Victor Sutherland
32. "Change of Murder" (5-21-50) Bernard Nedell, Charles Jor-
    dan, Alfred Hosson
33. "South Wind" (5-28-50) William Post Jr., Peggy French
34. "I Got What It Takes" (6-4-50)
35. "The Hotel of the Three Kings" (6-11-50) Elwyn Harvey, Sara
    Anderson, William Beach
36. "Hands of the Enemy" (6-18-50) Alfreda Wallace, Kem Dibbs,
    Richard McMurray
37. "Satan's Waitin'" (6-25-50) Jeanne Cagney, Pierre Watkins

SILVER THEATRE

The Regulars: Conrad Nagel, host.

The Episodes:

1. "L'Amour the Merrier" (10-3-49) Eva Gabor, Burgess Meredith
2. "'Til Death Do Us Part" (10-10-49) Faye Emerson, John Loder
3. "Rhapsody in Discord" (10-17-49) Paul Lukas, Kim Hunter
4. "School for Love" (10-24-49) John Payne
5. "The Farewell Supper" (10-31-49) Charles Korvin, Lenore
   Aubert, Myron McCormick
6. "Patient Unknown" (11-7-49) Felicia Montealegre, John Baragrey
7. "Don't Give Up the Ship" (11-14-49) Louise Albritton, Henry
   Morgan
8. "Silent as the Grave" (11-21-49) Marsha Hunt, George Reeves
9. "Much to Do About Something" (11-28-49) Jean Pugsley, Larry
   Hugo
10. "Star over Bridgeport" (12-5-49) Richard Hart
11. "Strange Rebound" (12-12-49) Vicki Cummings
12. "The Guilding Star" (12-19-49) Clem Bevans
13. "Four Callers" (12-26-49) Donald Buka
14. "The First Snow of 1950" (1-2-50) Conrad Nagel, George
    Reeves, Joyce Mathews
15. "Papa Romani" (1-9-50) Chico Marx, William Frawley, Mar-
    garet Hamilton
16. "Happy Marriage" (1-16-50) Carol Bruce
17. "The Great Nikoli" (1-23-50) Mikhail Rasumny, Peter Capell
18. "Never Hit a Pigeon" (1-30-50) Gene Anton Jr., Joanne Dolan
19. "The Late Mr. Beasley" (2-6-50) Donald Curtis
20. "Gaudy Lady" (2-13-50) Glenda Farrell
21. "My Brother's Keeper" [the first attempt at putting on film this
    normally "live" drama; thereby overcoming deficiencies in
    kinescope recording] (2-20-50) Ward Bond, Glenn Corbett,
    Beverly Tyler
22. "For Richer, for Poorer" (2-27-50) Geraldine Brooks, Rich-
    ard Derr

23. "Lucky Pierre" (3-6-50) George Ripka, Skippy Housier; radio-television editor Ben Gross, guest
24. "Quiet Neighborhood" (3-13-50) Nancy Coleman
25. "Concerning the Soul of Felicity" (3-20-50) Ilka Chase
26. "The Howland Fling" (3-27-50) Carol Goodner, Vinton Hayworth
27. "Coals of Fire" (4-3-50) Carol Thurston, William Erwin, Vinton Hayworth
28. "Minor Incident" (4-10-50) Nancy Kelly, Donald Woods, Sue England, Dorothy Tree, Rita LeRoy
29. "Double Feature" (4-17-50) Don DeFore, Diana Lynn
30. "Bad Guy" (4-24-50) Lee Bowman, Barbara Lawrence, John Archer
31. "The First Hundred Years" (5-1-50) Barbara Whiting, William Frawley, Jimmy Lydon, Allene Roberts
32. "Lady with Ideas" (5-8-50) Pamela Britton, Gig Young, Mikhail Rasumny
33. "Papa Romani" [repeat of episode of 1/9/50] (5-15-50)
34. "Wedding Anniversary" (5-22-50) Virginia Bruce, Rita LeRoy, Louis Jean Heydt
35. "Close-Up" (5-29-50) Ann Dvorak, Donald Woods
36. "Walt and Lavinia" (6-5-50) Don DeFore, Diana Lynn
37. "Double Feature" [repeat of episode of 4/17/50] (6-12-50)
38. "Bad Guy" [repeat of episode of 4/24/50] (6-19-50)
39. "My Heart's in the Highlands" [adapted from the 1939 William Saroyan play] (6-26-50) Howard Da Silva, Byron Folgar, Tommy Pihl, Adelaide DeWalt Reynolds, Art Smith

THE CLOCK

The Episodes [chronicled from the eleventh telecast]:

1. "The Web" (11-16-49) Oliver Thorndike, Alfreda Wallace, Moaltrie Patton
2. "Reverse" (11-23-49) Bramwell Fletcher
3. "Cousin Maria" (11-30-49) Wilma Kuver, Ann Summers, John Shay
4. "Maniac at Large" (12-7-49) Dort Clark
5. "Lease of Death" (12-14-49) Oliver Thorndike, Adelaide Klein, Ed Latimer, Ruth White
6. "Romance" (12-21-49) Pamela Rivers, Philip Faversham
7. "Mark Wade, D.A." (12-28-49) William Post, Bob Morgan, Treva Frazee, James Little
8. "The Firebug" (1-4-50) Helen Marcy, Philip Arthur, Priscilla Towers
9. "The Book Seller" (1-11-50) Phillippe Bevans, Jason Johnson, Theodore Marcuse, Iggie Wolfington
10. "Who Is This Man?" (1-18-50) Dora Clement, Elizabeth Ross, Dean Harens
11. "Dig Your Own Grave" (1-25-50) David Kerman, Parker Mc-Cormick
12. "The Cat" (2-1-50) Beverly Roberts, Richard Purdy
13. "William and Mary" (2-8-50) Byron Russell, Helen Kingstead

14. "Bury Her Deep" (2-15-50) Arnold Moss, Alan Bunce, Carol Mathews
15. "The Take" (2-22-50) Gene Barry, Dulcie Jordan, Peter Capell
16. "Woman in the Road" (3-1-50) Mildred Natwick, Joy Reese, Bob Smith
17. "The Graveyard Shift" (3-8-50) Tom Drake
18. "What Makes a Murderer?" (3-15-50) Dennis Harrison, Arthur McCormick
19. "The Hypnotist" (3-22-50) Charlton Heston, Cara Williams, Charlie Jordan, Mitchell Arguss
20. "Open the Door for Murder" (3-29-50) Paul McGrath
21. [unknown title] (4-7-50)
22. "Rain in the Night" (4-21-50) John Newland
23. "Voyage West" (5-5-50) Berry Kroeger, Walter Brooke
24. "Just a Minute" (5-19-50) Helmut Dantine, Heywood Brown, Sid Paul, Sandy Bickart
25. "I Keep Forgetting" (6-2-50) Donald Curtis, Philip Coolidge, Augusta Dabney
26. "The Caller" (6-16-50) Dan Morgan, Kurt Hatch, Mary Mace
27. "Someone Must Die" (6-30-50) Vinton Hayworth
28. "A Grave Plot" (7-14-50) John Boruff, Sarah Anderson
29. "Jump, Elbert, Jump" (7-28-50) Oliver Thorndyke
30. "The Checked Suit" (8-11-50) Leon Tokatyan, Anna Lee
31. "Rumble in Manhattan" (8-25-50) Dennis Harrison, Muriel Landers, Vito Christie

Second Season

32. "Prescription for Death" (9-8-50) Leslie Nielsen, Philip Sterling, Julie Bennett, Helen Donaldson, Maggi M. Thomas
33. "The Morning After" (9-22-50) Raymond Massey, Mady Christians
34. "The Joke" (10-6-50) Ian Keith, James Daly
35. "Vengeance" (10-20-50) Torin Thatcher
36. "The Brief Case" (11-3-50) Dennis Harrison
37. "Ninth Life" (11-17-50) Ian Keith, John Newland
38. "The Old Woman" (12-1-50) Ethel Griffies, Olive Deering
39. "The Last Tomorrow" (12-15-50) Cloris Leachman, Richard Kiley
40. "The New Year Caper" (12-29-50) John Van Dreelen
41. "A Dream for Susan" (1-12-51) Arlene Francis, Laura Weber
42. "Whenever I'm Alone" (1-26-51) Charles Korvin, Louisa Horton, Henry Hart
43. "Runaway" (2-9-51) Peter Capell, Adelaide Klein, Martin Newman, Louis Sorin
44. "Accident on Canigou" (2-23-51) Richard Carlyle, Richard Kiley, Leni Stengel, Monty Banks Jr.

Third Season

45. "Journey Across the River" (7-6-51) Martha Scott
46. "The Hidden Thing" (7-13-51) Robert Sterling
47. "The Lily Pond" (7-20-51) Kent Smith

48. "Last Adventure" (7-27-51) Alan Marshall, Susan Shaw, William Crane
49. "Dream Beach" (8-3-51) Jackie Cooper, Silby Parks
50. "The Traveler" (8-10-51) Charles Dingle
51. "Love Is Contraband" (8-17-51) Julie Haydon, Donald Buka
52. "The Affliction" (8-24-51) Jeffrey Lynn
53. "A Right Smart Trick" (8-31-51) John Dahl

Fourth Season

54. [unknown title] (10-17-51) Maurice Holbert, Adia Kutznetzoff, Charles Cooper
55. "The Silver Frame" (10-24-51)
56. "The Devil's Wine" (10-31-51) Greg Juarez, Frank Milan
57. "The Silent Hand" (11-7-51)
58. "Death Trap" (11-14-51)
59. "Balzac Murder" (11-21-51)
60. "Just for the Record" (11-28-51)
61. "Weather Station" (12-5-51)
62. "Somebody" (12-12-51)
63. "Assignment" (12-19-51)
64. "No Witnesses" (12-26-51)
65. "Incident at Cotdumer" (1-2-52)
66. "Sight Unseen" (1-9-52)

THE BORIS KARLOFF MYSTERY PLAYHOUSE

The Regulars: Boris Karloff, host

The Episodes:

1. "Five Golden Guineas" (9-22-49) Boris Karloff, Mildred Natwick
2. "The Mask" (9-29-49)
3. "Mungahara" (10-6-49)
4. "Mad Illusion" (10-13-49)
5. "Perchance to Dream" (10-20-49)
6. "The Devil Takes a Bride" (10-27-49)
7. "The Moving Finger" (11-3-49)
8. "The Twisted Path" (11-10-49)
9. "Fake Face" (11-17-49) Jean Muir
10. "Cranky Bill" (11-24-49)
11. "Three O'Clock" (12-1-49)
12. "The Shop at Sly Corner" (12-8-49) Oliver Thorndike, Mary Malone
13. "The Night Reveals" (12-15-49)

THEATRE OF ROMANCE

The Episodes:

1. "Camille" [adapted from the Alexandre Dumas classic] (11-3-49) Ruth Ford, Richard Hylton, Malcolm Keane
2. "Sometime, Every Summertime" (11-17-49) Dean Harens, Mary Sinclair
3. "The M. P. and the Mouse" (12-1-49) Susan Douglas, Steven Hill
4. "Michael and Mary" [adapted from the A. A. Milne play] (12-15-49) Jean Gillespie, Jack Manning
5. "The Afternoon of a Faun" (12-29-49) Steven Hill, Cara Williams, Bethel Leslie

STARLIGHT THEATRE

The Episodes:

1. "Second Concerto" (4-2-50) Meg Mundy, Barry Nelson, Larry Fletcher
2. "Night Before Sailing" (4-9-50) Valerie Cossart, Larry Fletcher, Mildred Natwick
3. "The M. P. and the Mouse" [restaged from the Theatre of Romance episode of 12/1/49] (4-16-50) William Prince, Susan Douglas
4. "White Mail" (4-23-50) George Reeves, Margaret Phillips
5. "The Sire de Maletroit's Door" [adapted from the Robert Louis Stevenson story] (4-30-50) Douglas Watson, Mary Sinclair
6. "The Song the Soldiers Sang" (5-7-50) Scott McKay
7. "The Roman Kid" [adapted from the Paul Gallico story] (5-14-50) Barry Nelson, Joan Chandler
8. "Her Son" (5-21-50) Oliver Thorndike, Mildred Natwick, Neil Hamilton
9. "The Juggler" (5-28-50) Barry Nelson, Betty Garde, Judy Parrish
10. "The Winner and Champion" (6-4-50) Mark Roberts, Virginia Gilmore
11. "Verna" (6-11-50) Don Matthews, Bernie Kates, Dulcie Jordan
12. "The Witch of Woonsapucket" (6-18-50) Mary Malone, Conrad Janis
13. "The Afternoon of a Faun" [restaged from the Theatre of Romance episode of 12/29/49] (6-25-50) Donald Buka
14. "Much Ado About Spring" (7-3-50) Ernest Truex, Sylvia Field
15. "The Last Kiss" (7-10-50) Mary Sinclair, John McQuade
16. "The Great Nonentity" (7-20-50) Arnold Stang, George Reeves, Cliff Hall, Cara Williams
17. "Three Hours Between Planes" [adapted from the F. Scott Fitzgerald story] (7-27-50) Virginia Gilmore, Alfred Ryder
18. "Passing Fancy" (8-3-50) Warren Stevens, Olive Deering, James Little

19. "The Poet Takes a Wife" (8-10-50) Hiram Sherman, Jane Hoffman
20. "Forgotten Melody" (8-17-50) Felicia Montealegre
21. "Fumble" (8-24-50) Conrad Janis, Gloria Stroock, Joshua Shelley
22. "The Philanderer" (8-31-50) Ernest Truex, Sylvia Field
23. "The Face Is Familiar--But" (9-7-50) Barbara Whiting, Joshua Shelley

Second Season

24. "Welcome Home" (11-16-50) Nancy Kelly, Robert Webber, Dorothy Rohr
25. "Before You Came Along" (11-30-50) Wendy Barrie, Frank Albertson
26. [unknown title] (12-14-50)
27. [unknown title] (12-28-50) Lee Bowman, Mary Sinclair, Ralph Riggs
28. "Relatively Speaking" (1-11-51) Melvyn Douglas
29. "Be Nice to Mr. Campbell" (1-25-51) Augusta Dabney, Frank McHugh, Jean Parker
30. "Julie" (2-8-51) Eve Arden
31. "The Magic Wire" (2-22-51) Leslie Nielsen, Geraldine Brooks, Frank Sylvern
32. "Miss Buell" (3-8-51) Judith Evelyn, Patricia Peardon, Lonny Chapman
33. "Flaxen-Haired Mannequin" (3-22-51) Margaret Hayes, Gil Lamb, Fred Stewart, Julie Bennett
34. "Season for Marriage" (4-5-51) Coleen Gray, Charles Korvin, William Prince
35. "The Magnificent Faker" (4-17-51) Dorothy Gish
36. "I Guess There Are Other Girls" (5-3-51) Wally Cox
37. "Bernice Bobs Her Hair" [adapted from the F. Scott Fitzgerald story] (5-17-51) Julie Harris, Anita Loos, Mary Sinclair
38. "The Come-Back" (5-31-51) Glenda Farrell, Nils Asther, Melville Cooper
39. "The Fascinating Mr. Hogan" (6-14-51) Jackie Cooper
40. "Three Hours Between Planes" [restaged from 7/27/50] (6-28-51) Virginia Gilmore, John Forsythe
41. "The Big Head" (7-12-51) Dulcie Moore
42. "In a Military Manner" (7-26-51) John Forsythe, Alfred Ryder
43. "With Baited Breath" (8-9-51) Henry Hull
44. "Lunch at Disalvo's" (8-23-51) Franchot Tone, Donald Curtis
45. "Act of God Notwithstanding" (9-6-51) Chester Morris
46. "The Gravy Train" (9-20-51) Dane Clark, Elinor Lynn, Loring Smith

ROBERT MONTGOMERY PRESENTS YOUR LUCKY STRIKE THEATRE

The Regulars: Robert Montgomery, host

The Episodes:

1. "The Letter" [adapted from the William Somerset Maugham story] (1-30-50) Madeleine Carroll, Theodore Newton, William Post Jr. , Howard Wierum
2. "Kitty Foyle" [adapted from the Christopher Darlington Morley story] (2-13-50) Jane Wyatt, Richard Derr, Farrell Pelly, Peter Cookson
3. "The Male Animal" [adapted from the James Thurber and Elliott Nugent play] (2-27-50) Elliott Nugent, Martha Scott
4. "The Egg and I" [adapted from the Betty MacDonald novel] (3-13-50) June Havoc, Barry Nelson, Vaughn Taylor, Ann Shoemaker
5. "Ride the Pink Horse" (3-27-50) Robert Montgomery, Thomas Gomez, Susan Douglas, Vaughn Taylor; Burgess Meredith, host for the episode.
6. "Our Town" [adapted from the Thornton Wilder play] (4-17-50) Burgess Meredith, Jean Gillespie
7. "The Phantom Lady" [adapted from the Cornell Woolrich story] (4-24-50) Ella Raines, Hugh Reilly, Gordon Mills
8. "Pitfall" (5-8-50) Lee Bowman, Nancy Coleman, Jean Carson
9. "Rebecca" [adapted from the Daphne du Maurier novel] (5-22-50) Barbara Bel Geddes, Peter Cookson
10. "The Champion" [adapted from the Ring Lardner story] (6-5-50) Richard Kiley, Louise Albritton, Vicki Cummings
11. "The Citadel" [adapted from the Archibald Joseph Cronin novel] (6-19-50) Robert Montgomery, Angela Lansbury

Second Season

12. "The Awful Truth" [adapted from the Arthur Richman story] (9-11-50) Lee Bowman, Jane Wyatt, Donald Curtis, Edna Heinemann
13. "The Big Sleep" [adapted from the Raymond Chandler novel] (9-25-50) Zachary Scott, Patricia Gaye
14. "Arrowsmith" [adapted from the Sinclair Lewis novel] (10-9-50) Van Heflin, June Dayton, Bruno Wick
15. "The Petrified Forest" [adapted from the Robert Emmett Sherwood play] (10-23-50) Robert Montgomery, John McQuade, Glenn Denning, Ralph Briggs, Morton Stevens
16. "The Seventh Veil" [adapted from the play] (11-6-50) Brian Aherne, Leueen McGrath, Dennis Hoey
17. "The Canterville Ghost" [adapted from the Oscar Wilde play] (11-20-50) Margaret O'Brien, Cecil Parker
18. "The Philadelphia Story" [adapted from the Philip Barry play] (12-4-50) Barbara Bel Geddes, Richard Derr, Leslie Nielsen
19. "Mrs. Mike" [adapted from the Benedict and Nancy Freedman novel] (12-18-50) Barbara Britton, Glenn Langan, Bill Martel, Margarita Warwick
20. "Kiss and Tell" [adapted from the Frederick Hugh Herbert play] (1-1-51) Betty Caulfield, Walter Abel, William Windom
21. "Victoria Regina" [adapted by Thomas W. Phipps from the Laurence Housman play] (1-15-51) Helen Hayes (as Queen

Victoria), Kent Smith (as Prince Albert), Robert Harris (as Lord Braconsfield), Alexander Clark, Olga Fabian

22. "Quicksand" (1-29-51) Skip Homeier, Claire Kirby, Martin Newman, Cara Williams

23. "A Star Is Born" [adapted from the William A. Wellman and Robert Carson film scenario] (2-12-51) Conrad Nagel, Kathleen Crowley

24. "The Last Tycoon" [adapted from the F. Scott Fitzgerald novel] (2-26-51) Robert Montgomery, June Duprez, Judy Parrish, Louis Hector

25. "The Young in Heart" [adapted from the Ida Alexa Ross Wylie story] (3-12-51) Alan Mowbray, Adrienne Allen

26. "Dark Victory" [adapted from the George Emerson Brewer play] (3-26-51) John Forsythe, Dorothy McGuire

27. "Stairway to Heaven" [adapted from the Michael Powell and Emerie Pressburger story] (4-9-51) Richard Greene, Jean Gillespie, Bramwell Fletcher, Francis Compton; Lee Bowman, guest host.

28. "The Bishop's Wife" [adapted from the 1947 film scenario which was adapted from the 1938 Robert Nathan novel In Barley's Fields] (4-23-51) Martha Scott, Janet Alexander, Philip Bourneuf, Richard Derr

29. "Ladies in Retirement" [adapted from the Edward Percy and Reginald Denham story] (5-7-51) Lillian Gish, Una O'Connor, Betty Sinclair, Michael McAloney

30. "The House of the Seven Gables" [adapted from the Nathaniel Hawthorne classic] (5-21-51) Leslie Nielsen, Gene Lockhart, June Lockhart, Richard Purdy

31. "For Love or Money" [adapted from the Daniel Taradash, Bernard Feiss, and Julian Blaustein play] (6-4-51) John Loder, Vicki Cummings, June Lockhart

32. "Three O'Clock" (6-18-51) Robert Montgomery, Olive Deering, Vaughn Taylor

33. "When We Are Married" [adapted from the J. B. Priestley play] (7-2-51) Bramwell Fletcher, Roddy McDowall

Third Season

34. "Bubbles" (9-10-51) Richard Derr, Denise Alexander, J. Pat O'Malley

35. "I Am Still Alive" (9-24-51) Donald Woods, Judy Parrish, Audra Lindley

36. "To Walk the Night" (10-8-51) John Baragrey, Geraldine Fitzgerald

37. "I Wouldn't Want to Be in Your Shoes" (10-22-51) Vaughn Taylor, Katherine Squire

38. "An Inspector Calls" [adapted from the J. B. Priestley play] (11-5-51) Herbert Marshall, Faith Brook

39. "The Kimballs" (11-19-51) Vanessa Brown, Boris Karloff

40. "Top Secret" (12-3-51) Robert Montgomery, Elizabeth Montgomery (her video debut), Margaret Phillips, Anthony Dawson

41. "A Christmas Gift" (12-17-51) Jean-Pierre Aumont, Margaret Draper, Donald Briggs

[hereafter weekly]

42. "Class of '67" [a documentary drama telecast live from a New York hospital] (12-31-51)
43. "The Farmer's Hotel" (1-7-52) Thomas Mitchell
44. "Cashel Byron's Profession" [adapted from the George Bernard Shaw play] (1-14-52) Charlton Heston, June Lockhart, Melville Cooper
45. "The Tender Men" (1-21-52) Skip Homeier, Anthony Ross, Jean Gillespie
46. "Eva? Caroline?" (1-28-52) Jayne Meadows, Viola Roache, Richard Carlson
47. "Rise Up and Walk" (2-4-52) Lloyd Bridges, Kim Hunter
48. "The Moonstone" [adapted from the Wilkie Collins novel] (2-11-52) Richard Greene, Stella Andrew
49. "Sheppey" (2-18-52) Geraldine Fitzgerald, Melville Cooper
50. "Those in Favor" (2-25-52) Raymond Massey, Herbert Berghoff
51. "Happy Birthday, George" (3-3-52) Jeffrey Lynn, Anna Jackson, Gaby Rodgers
52. "Guardian of the Clock" (3-10-52) Jack Hartley, Helen Shields, Marcia Van Dyke
53. "The Wall" (3-17-52) Douglass Montgomery, Jane Wyatt, Lydia Westman
54. "Claire Ambler" [adapted from the Booth Tarkington novel] (3-24-52) Peggy Ann Garner, Margalo Gillmore
55. "See No Evil" (3-31-52) Tom Ewell, Betty Field
56. "O Evening Star" (4-7-52) Fay Bainter, Robert H. Harris
57. "Operation Hitch-Hike" (4-14-52) June Lockhart
58. "And Never Come Back" (4-21-52) Teresa Wright, Audra Lindley, Mike Kellin
59. "The Truth About Blayds" [adapted from the A. A. Milne play] (4-28-52) Anna Lee, Leslie Barry, Romney Brent; Robert Cummings, guest host.
60. "The Lonely" (5-5-52) Leueen McGrath, Robert Sterling, Dorothy Peterson
61. "Lita, My Love" (5-12-52) Robert Cummings, Gaby Rodgers
62. "The Longest Night" (5-19-52) Joan Caulfield, John Newland, Alice Frost, Eva Condon
63. "The Ringmaster" (5-26-52) Paul Lukas, Vincent Price, Anna Lee
64. "Candles for Theresa" (6-2-52) Robert Sterling, Grace Kelly
65. "Penny" (6-9-52) Joanne Woodward, Walter Abel, Ann Seymour
66. "Of Lena Geyer" [adapted by Mathilde and Theodore Ferro from the Marcia Davenport novel] (6-16-52) Cameron Prud'homme, Mimi Benzell (the lyric soprano in her video debut), Anthony Dawson
67. "Till Next We Meet" (6-23-52) James Daly, Barbara Britton, Roland Winters
68. "King of the Castle" (6-30-52) Melville Cooper, Robert Coote, Frederic Worlock, J. Pat O'Malley

[now as SUMMER STOCK THEATRE until new season]

69. "The Catbird Seat" [adapted by Robert J. Shaw from the James Thurber story; subsequently restaged for the Matinee Theatre episode of 2/16/56] (7-14-52) John Newland, Margaret Hayes, Vaughn Taylor (the three forming the repertory company for the duration of the summer)
70. "Advice to the Lovelorn" [adapted from the Christopher Morley story] (7-28-52) Hayes, Taylor, Newland
71. "Mr. Dobie Takes a Powder" (8-4-52) Taylor, Hayes, Newland
72. "Summer Story" (8-11-52) Hayes, Taylor, Newland
73. "Stand-In Bride" (8-18-52) Hayes, Taylor, Newland
74. "Nostradamus Beery" (8-25-52) Taylor, Hayes, Newland

Fourth Season

75. "Unclouded Summer" (9-1-52) Signe Hasso
76. "The Law Abiding" (9-8-52) Chester Morris
77. "The Fairfield Lady" (9-15-52) June Havoc, Hugh Reilly, Donald Buka, Tom Coley
78. "There Once Was a Diamond Ring" (9-22-52) Robert Pastene, Joan Wetmore
79. "Precinct" (9-29-52) Cliff Robertson, Paul Kelly, Miriam Goldina
80. "Señora Isobel" (10-6-52) Constance Bennett, Edmon Ryan
81. "The Fall Guy" (10-13-52) Jackie Cooper, Geraldine Page
82. "Keane Versus Keane" (10-20-52) James Daly, Barbara Baxley, Wanda Hendrix
83. "The Sheffield Story" (10-27-52) David Niven, Martin Koslick, Frederic Worlock
84. "The Beach in the Park" (11-3-52) Walter Hampden, Margaret Hayes
85. "The Biarritz Scandal" (11-10-52) Gene Lockhart, June Lockhart
86. "The Davidian Report" (11-17-52) Robert Sterling Maria Riva
87. "The Valari Special" (11-24-52) Ezio Pinza, Bruno Wick
88. "The Post Road" (12-1-52) Vaughn Taylor, Dorothy Gish
89. "The Inward Eye" [by Peggy Bacon] (12-8-52) Jane Wyatt, Richard Purdy
90. "Victory" (12-15-52) Sidney Blackmer, Margaret Phillips, E. A. Krumschmidt, Anthony Kimble-Cooper
91. "The Christmas Cards" (12-22-52) Lydia Reed, John Newland, Henry Jones
92. "The Closed Door" (12-29-52) Charlton Heston, Jan Miner, James Gregory, Boris Aplon
93. "Keep Your Head Up, Mr. Putnam" (1-5-53) Robert Sterling, Donald Symington, Olive Blakeney
94. "Ricochet" (1-12-53) Edmond O'Brien, Patricia Benoit
95. "Maggie, Pack Your Bags" (1-19-53) Margaret Hayes, Robert Preston, Roland Winters
96. "The Outer Limit" (1-26-53) Jackie Cooper, Robert H. Harris, Howard St. John, Hugh Reilly
97. "Element of Risk" (2-2-53) Brian Aherne, Diana Douglas, Isobel Elsom
98. "The Shadow Line" (2-9-53) Skippy Homeier

99. "The Burtons" (2-16-53) Gene Lockhart, Kathleen Lockhart (Mrs. Gene Lockhart), June Lockhart
100. "Dinah, Kip, and Mrs. Barlowe" (2-23-53) Jack Lemmon, Diana Lynn, Vaughn Taylor
101. "Betrayed" (3-2-53) Joanne Dru, Richard McMurray, Jane Wyatt
102. "The Centrifuge" (3-9-53) Patric Knowles, Lisa Ferraday, James Hanley
103. "Tomorrow We'll Sing" (3-16-53) Robert Alda, Theresa Celli
104. "The Big Night" (3-23-53) Chester Morris, Joan Lorring
105. "The Burden of Proof" (3-30-53) Boris Karloff
106. "Second-Hand Sofa" (4-6-53) Leslie Nielsen, Ann Rutherford, Beverly Roberts, Nelson Olmstead
107. "The Glass Cage" (4-13-53) Lee Bowman, Marilyn Erskine
108. "World By the Tail" (4-20-53) Diana Lynn, Hildy Parks
109. "Summer Tempest" (4-27-53) Geraldine Fitzgerald
110. "Linda" (5-4-53) Maria Riva, John Newland
111. "Appointment in Samarra" [adapted by Irving Gaynor Neiman from the John O'Hara novel; directed by Herbert Swope Jr.] (5-11-53) Robert Montgomery, Margaret Hayes
112. "The Wind Cannot Read" (5-18-53) Donald Woods, Roger Moore, Geoffrey Lumb
113. "All Things Grand and Beautiful" (5-25-53) Fay Bainter
114. "Storm" [by George R. Stewart] (6-1-53) Frank Thomas Sr.
115. "No Head for Moonlight" (6-8-53) Dennis O'Keefe, Mary Sinclair
116. "The Woman Who Hated Children" (6-22-53) Leora Dana, Jeffrey Lynn, Kent Smith
117. "Half a Kingdom" (6-29-53) Wendell Corey, Abby Lewis, Lynn Loring

[now as SUMMER STOCK THEATRE until new season (segments variously directed by Norman Felton and Herbert Swope)]

118. "The Half-Millionaire" (7-6-53) John Newland, Margaret Hayes, Vaughn Taylor, Elizabeth Montgomery (the four forming the repertory company for the summer)
119. "Two of a Kind" (7-13-53) Newland, Taylor, Hayes, E. Montgomery
120. "A Summer Love" (7-20-53) Newland, E. Montgomery, Taylor, Hayes
121. "Anne's Story" (7-27-53) Judy Parrish, Hayes, E. Montgomery, Newland, Taylor
122. "Duet for Two Hands" (8-3-53) Newland, Taylor, Hayes, E. Montgomery
123. "Red Robin Rides Again" (8-10-53) Newland, Taylor, Marshall Thompson, Hayes, E. Montgomery
124. "Pierce, 3098" (8-17-53) Newland, Taylor, Hayes, E. Montgomery
125. "Grass Roots" (8-24-53) Newland, Taylor, Hayes, E. Montgomery

Fifth Season

126. "The First Vice President" [adapted by S. N. Savage from the novel by Joan Transue; directed by Gerald Savory (his first directorial assignment for this series)] (8-31-53) Addison Richards, Chester Stratton, Olive Blakeney
127. "Private Purkey's Private Peace" (9-7-53) Jackie Cooper
128. "The Lost and Found" (9-14-53) Kent Smith
129. "September Time" (9-21-53) Ruth Warrick
130. "The Big Money" (9-28-53) Wendell Corey, Jeanne Shepherd
131. "Breakdown" (10-5-53) Brian Aherne, Margaret Phillips, Scott Forbes, Frederic Worlock
132. "A Criminal Assignment" (10-12-53) Sir Cedric Hardwicke, Harold Vermilyea, Halliwell Hobbes, Richard Ahern
133. "The Sunday Punch" (10-19-53) Gig Young, Frank Wilson, Barbara Joyce
134. "Cakes and Ale" [adapted from the William Somerset Maugham story] (10-26-53) Angela Lansbury, Bramwell Fletcher
135. "No Picnic at Mt. Kenya" (11-2-53) Gary Merrill, George Chandler, Bruce Gordon
136. "Week-End Pass" (11-9-53) Brian Keith
137. "The Deep Six" (11-16-53) John Payne, Scott Forbes
138. "Harvest" [a Thanksgiving story] (11-23-53) Dorothy Gish, Ed Begley, James Dean, Vaughn Taylor
139. "The Soprano and the Piccolo Player" (11-30-53) Francis L. Sullivan, Dana Wynter
140. "Really the Blues" [adapted from the Mezz Mezzrow autobiography] (12-7-53) Jackie Cooper
141. "No Visible Means" (12-14-53) Robert Montgomery, Claudia Morgan, Patricia Breslin
142. "What About Christmas?" [vignettes] (12-21-53) John Newland, Rex Thompson, Hugh Reilly
143. "The Greatest Man in the World" [adapted from the James Thurber story] (12-28-53) Chester Morris
144. "The Steady Man" (1-4-54) Arthur Franz, Leatrice Joy, June Lockhart
145. "A Case of Identity" (1-11-54) Robert Ellenstein, Florence Anglin
146. "Machinal" (1-18-54) Joan Lorring, Robert Webber, Malcolm Lee Boggs
147. "Richard Said No" (1-25-54) John Newland, Phyllis Kirk, Phyllis Thaxter
148. "The Seventeenth of June" [a documentary of an uprising in the anti-Communist Russian zone of Germany] (2-1-54) Wendell Corey
149. "Mr. Whittle and the Morning Star" (2-8-54) Elliott Nugent
150. "Our Hearts Were Young and Gay" [episodes adapted from the Cornelia Otis Skinner and Emily Kimbrough novel] (2-15-54) Sally Kemp, Elizabeth Montgomery, Marjorie Gateson, Elliott Reid
151. "Land of Happiness" (2-22-54) Osa Massen, John Newland
152. "Such a Busy Day Tomorrow" (3-1-54) Walter Hampden
153. "Paradise Cafe" (3-8-54) Barbara Baxley, James Dunn

154. "The Quality of Mercy" (3-15-54) Lillian Gish
155. "The Pink Hippopotamus" (3-22-54) Oscar Homolka, Mary Laslo, Herman Schwedt
156. "The Little Girl" (3-29-54) James Dunn, William Lundmark
157. "For These Services" (4-5-54) Arthur Franz, Raymond Massey, Gale Page
158. "The Pale Blonde of Sands Street" (4-12-54) Joan Lorring, Billy Halop
159. "Big Boy" (4-19-54) Ed Begley, Katherine Squire, John Connell
160. "No Need of Favor" (4-26-54) Geraldine Fitzgerald, John Newland, Frederic Worlock
161. "The Wages of Fear" (5-3-54) Louis Jourdan, Hope Miller
162. "Pilgrim's Pride" (5-10-54) Elliott Nugent, Cliff Robertson, Audrey Christie
163. "Sky Block" (5-17-54) Zachary Scott, Vaughn Taylor
164. "The Power and the Prize" [adapted from the Howard Swaggert novel] (5-24-54) Gusti Huber, Robert Montgomery
165. "Once Upon a Time" (5-31-54) Peggy Ann Garner, Elizabeth Montgomery
166. "The Patriot from Antibes" (6-7-54) Francis Lederer, Joan Wetmore
167. "Great Expectations: The Promise" [Part I; an excerpt from the Charles Dickens classic] (6-14-54) Rex Thompson, Estelle Winwood, Roddy McDowall, Scott Forbes, Malcolm Lee Beggs, Jacques Aubuchon
168. "Great Expectations: The Reality" [Part II] (6-21-54) as above.

[now as SUMMER STOCK THEATRE until new season]

169. "In His Hands" (6-28-54) Cliff Robertson, Elizabeth Montgomery, John Newland, Vaughn Taylor, Jan Miner [the five, together with Anne Seymour (who later appears), forming the repertory for the summer]
170. "The Expert" (7-5-54) Robertson, Newland, Miner, E. Montgomery
171. "Story on Eleventh Street" (7-12-54) Newland, Kevin Coughlin, E. Montgomery
172. "It Happened in Paris" (7-19-54) Orson Bean, E. Montgomery
173. "Patricia" (7-26-54) E. Montgomery, Newland, Katherine Anderson
174. "Home Town" [by Cleveland Amory] (8-2-54) Robertson, E. Montgomery, Frank Albertson
175. "About Sara Caine" (8-9-54) Miner, E. Montgomery
176. "Invitation to Murder" [by James Parrish] (8-16-54) Claudia Morgan, Newland, Taylor
177. "Personal Story" [directed by Norman Felton] (8-23-54) Newland, Anne Seymour, Miner, E. Montgomery, Taylor
178. "A Matter of Luck" (8-30-54) Newland, E. Montgomery
179. "The People You Meet" (9-6-54) Seymour, Newland, Taylor, Miner

180. "Ten Minute Alibi" (9-13-54) Robertson, E. Montgomery, Taylor, Seymour

Sixth Season

181. "Diary" [by Robert Emmett Sherwood, expressly composed for television] (9-20-54) Janice Rule, John Cassavetes
182. "A Dream of Summer" (9-27-54) Jackie Cooper
183. "Two Wise Women" (10-4-54) Carl Betz, Signe Hasso, Paul McGrath
184. "Autumn Crocus" [adapted from the C. L. Anthony play] (10-11-54) Julie Haydon, George Voskovec, Betty Sinclair
185. "A Foreign Affair" (10-18-54) Signe Hasso, Katherine Bard, Steve Cochran
186. "Remote" [on the role of television coverage in the public interest] (10-25-54) George Forrest, E. G. Marshall, Frank Schofield, Ellen Cobb Hill
187. "The Gentleman" (11-1-54) Donald Woods, Joan Wetmore, J. Pat O'Malley, Lauren Gilbert
188. "The Hunchback of Notre Dame" [Part I; adapted from the Victor Hugo novel] (11-8-54) Hurd Hatfield, Frederic Worlock, Mary Sinclair, Bramwell Fletcher, Celia Lipton, Robert Ellenstein
189. "The Hunchback of Notre Dame" [Part II] (11-15-54) as above.
190. "Homecoming" (11-22-54) John Lupton, Don Taylor, Joanne Woodward, June Dayton, Patricia Breslin
191. "Judith" (11-29-54) Margaret Phillips
192. "Dr. Ed" (12-6-54) Walter Matthau, Lucy Lancaster
193. "End of a Mission" (12-13-54) Leslie Nielsen, Joan Elan
194. "David Copperfield" [Part I; adapted by Doria Folliott from the Charles Dickens classic] (12-20-54) David Cole, Earl Montgomery, Rex Thompson, Cavada Humphrey, Ralph Bunker, Frederic Worlock, J. Pat O'Malley, Sarah Marshall, Ethel Owen, Carolyn Lee
195. "David Copperfield: The Reward" [Part II] (12-27-54) as above.
196. "Death and the Sky Above" [adapted from the novel] (1-3-55) Gale Page, Staats Cotsworth, Jeffrey Lynn, Nancy Guild
197. "A Night for Dreaming" (1-10-55) Midge Ware, Inger Stevens, Carol Gustafson
198. "The Cypress Tree" [by Robert J. Shaw; subsequently restaged for the Matinee Theatre episode of 7/30/56] (1-17-55) Katherine Squire, Dorothy Stickney, June Walker
199. "Joe's Boy" (1-24-55) James Dunn, Jo Van Fleet, Loretta Leversee, Lee Bergere
200. "Deadline" (1-31-55) Peggy Ann Garner
201. "The Lost Weekend" [adapted from the Charles Reginald Jackson novel] (2-7-55) Robert Montgomery (as Don Birnam), Leora Dana (as his girl friend), Walter Matthau (as the bartender), Edward Andrews (as his friend)
202. "The Breaking Point" (2-14-55) Barry Jones, Geoffrey Horne

203.   "Coming of Age" [by Harold and Joanna Brodkey; subsequently restaged for the Matinee Theatre episode of 12/19/55] (2-21-55) Lee Bowman, Robin Morgan, Jan Miner

204.   "A Very Special World" (2-28-55) Jackie Cooper, Bramwell Fletcher, Lee Remick

205.   "A Matter of Dignity" (3-7-55) John Newland, Elizabeth York, Barbara Towsend, Anne Seymour

206.   "A Stone for His Son" (3-14-55) Walter Matthau, Gale Page, Lin McCarthy, Jo Ralib

207.   "N. Y. to L. A." (3-21-55) Charles Drake, Pamela Rivers, Edward Binns

208.   "The Iron Cobweb" (3-28-55) Geraldine Fitzgerald, Polly Rowles, Hugh Reilly

209.   "The Tender Leaves of Hope" [by Robert J. Shaw; subsequently restaged for the Matinee Theatre episode of 12/20/57] (4-4-55) Raymond Massey, Anne Seymour

210.   "P. J. Martin and Son" [by Robert J. Shaw] (4-18-55) Lynn McCarthy, Jack Mullaney, Edna Best

211.   "The Tall, Dark Man" [adapted from the Anne Chamberlain novel] (4-25-55) Ben Yaffee, Robin Morgan, Mary Jackson, Rosemary Murphy, Anita Bayless, Margarita Warwick

212.   "Belle Fleace Gave a Party" [adapted by Doria Folliott (using an Irish setting) from the Evelyn Waugh short story] (5-2-55) Fay Bainter, Frederic Worlock, J. Pat O'Malley, Chester Stratton, Ralph Bunker, John McLiam, Ronald Long

213.   "The Great Gatsby" [adapted by Alvin Sapinsley from the F. Scott Fitzgerald novel] (5-9-55) Robert Montgomery (as Gatsby), Phyllis Kirk (as Daisy), Lee Bowman, Gena Rowlands, Frederic Worlock, Scott Tennyson, John Newland

214.   "The Cage" [by Joseph Graham and Paul Manning] (5-16-55) Colin Keith-Johnston, Christopher Hewitt, Samuel Gray

215.   "The Drifter" [by John Vlahos] (5-23-55) Zachary Scott, William Windom, Sally Gracie, Jack Manning, Coe Norton

216.   "Now or Never" [by Martha Wilkerson; subsequently restaged for the Matinee Theatre episode of 8/23/57] (5-30-55) Barbara Britton, Charles Drake, Dorothy Blackburn, James Millhallin

217.   "The Killer" [by Milton Gelman] (6-6-55) Luther Adler, Katherine Squire, Jack Mullaney, Luis Van Rooten, Harry Bellaver, Jenny Egan

218.   "Second Chance" [by Theodore and Mathilde Ferro] (6-13-55) Henry Garrard, Ruth Saville, Ken Konopka, George Gilbreath, Dana Gentner

219.   "There's No Need to Shout" [adapted by Doria Folliott from the novel by Frances Warfield] (6-20-55) Nancy Malone, Mark Roberts, Eric Sinclair, Chris White, William A. Lee

220.   "Towhead" [by John McLiam] (6-27-55) Charles Drake, Glen Walken, Audra Lindley, Dierdre Owens, Thomas Coley

[now as SUMMER STOCK THEATRE until new season (some segments variously directed by John Newland)]

221.   "The Fourth of July" [by S. S. Schweitzer] (7-4-55) Charles

Drake, House Jameson, Gale Page, Eric Sinclair, Carlos Montalban, Coe Norton, Swea Grunfeld, Luis Van Rooten [Drake, Jameson, Page, Sinclair, Montalban together with Augusta Dabney and Dorothy Blackburn (who later appear) form the summer repertory]

222. "The Paper Hero" [by Dagny Delph] (7-18-55) John Gibson, Elizabeth Eustis, Jameson, Dorothy Blackburn

223. "The Diamond Curtain" [by Thomas Phipps] (7-18-55) Augusta Dabney, Blackburn, Jameson, Drake

224. "Decision by Morning" [adapted from the Sylvia Cooper novel] (7-25-55) Drake, Dabney, Jameson, Blackburn, Sinclair

225. "A Slightly Important Man" [by Noel B. Gerson] (8-1-55) Jameson, Dabney, Sinclair

226. "Uncle Snowball" [by Doria Folliott] (8-8-55) Drake, Dabney, Jameson, Blackburn

227. "Late Love" [adapted by Gail Ingram from the Rosemary Casey play; subsequently restaged for the Matinee Theatre episode of 12/20/56] (8-15-55) Drake, Dabney, Jameson, Sinclair

228. "Rosie" [by Milton Gelman] (8-22-56) Bibi Osterwald, Sinclair, Montalban

229. "The Return of Johnny Burro" (8-29-56) Drake, Dabney, Sinclair

230. "My Dear Emily" [by Elaine Corrington] (9-5-55) Drake, Dabney, Jameson, Sinclair, Blackburn

Seventh Season

231. "Woman in the Window" [adapted by Nunnally Johnson from his own film scenario of 1944 which was adapted from J. H. Wallis' Once Off Guard] (9-12-55) Maria Riva, Robert Preston

232. "Mr. and Mrs. Monroe" [adapted from the James Thurber story] (9-19-55) Edward Andrews, Augusta Dabney

233. "Along Came Jones" [adapted by Doria Folliott from the 1945 western film scenario which was adapted from Alan Lemay's The Useless Cowboy] (9-26-55) Charlton Heston, Louis Lytton, Pat Roe, Lonny Chapman

234. "The Stranger" [by Doria Folliott] (10-3-55) John Baragrey, Barbara Britton, Parker Fennelly, Luis Van Rooten, Jack Livesy

235. "Paper Town" [by Robert J. Shaw; directed by John Newland] (10-10-55) Sidney Blackmer, Pat Sales, Jan Miner, Jack Mullaney, Brandon Peters

236. "Tomorrow Is Forever" [by Roy Bailey] (10-17-55) Gale Storm, William Windom, Robert Ellenstein

237. "Man Lost" (10-24-55) Franchot Tone, Lee Remick, Philip Bourneuf

238. "In a Foreign City" [adapted from a story by Robert M. Coates] (10-31-55) John Hudson, Joseph Campanella

239. "The World to Nothing" [by Abby Mann] (11-7-55) Eddie Albert, Dolores Sutton, Brett Somers, Patricia Bosworth, Burt Brinckerhoff, Tommy Holleran

240. "Cry Silence" (11-14-55) Edward Andrews, George Mathews

241. "Isabel" [by Doria Folliott] (11-21-55) Geraldine Fitzgerald, Anne Meacham, Robert Carrol, Viola Roach, Alfred Ryder
242. "End of the Rainbow" [adapted from a story by Vern Sneider] (11-28-55) George Voskovec
243. "Lucifer" [by J. Harvey Howells] (12-5-55) John Newland, Audra Lindley, House Jameson, Charles Dingle
244. "See the Man" [by Theodore and Mathilde Ferro] (12-12-55) Skip Homeier, Milette Alexander, Jan Miner
245. "Quality Town" [adapted from the story by Margaret Cousins] (12-19-55) Lee Bowman, Piper Laurie
246. "The Second Day of Christmas" [by Sandra Michael, on the romance between Hans Christian Anderson and Jenny Lind] (12-26-55) Charles Taylor, Frank Scoffield, Lois Smith
247. "Three Men from Tomorrow" [by Robert J. Shaw] (1-2-56) Jack Mullaney, William Daniels, Lee Remick
248. "End of the Tether" [adapted by Abby Mann from the Joseph Conrad novel] (1-9-56) Barry Jones
249. "The Tyrant" [by Franklin Barton] (1-16-56) Roy Bramley, June Havoc, Gale Page
250. "Aftermath" [by Mervin Gerard] (1-23-56) Charles Drake, Martin Ritt, Olive Deering
251. "Mr. Tutt Baits a Hook" [adapted by Murray Burnett from the Arthur Train story] (1-30-56) Parker Fennelly
252. "Good Friday, 1865" [adapted by John Lewellen from the William J. Ferguson autobiography] (2-6-56) Michael Allan
253. "The Man Who Vanished" [by Robert Coates] (2-13-56) Gene Rayburn, Augusta Dabney, Frederic Worlock
254. "An Excuse for Sharks" [by Gilbert S. Faust] (2-20-56) William Redfield
255. "End of Morning" [by William Kendall Clarke] (2-27-56) Jackie Cooper, Joan Lorring
256. "Adam's Son" [by Theodore and Matthilde Ferro] (3-5-56) Raymond Massey
257. "The Briefcase" [by J. Harvey Howells] (3-12-56) Gloria DeHaven, John Hudson, Edmon Ryan
258. "The Secret" [by Milton Gelman] (3-19-56) Don Gordon, Nita Talbot, Edward Holmes
259. "The Long Way Home" [by Robert Wallace] (3-26-56) John Beal
260. "Death Insurance" [by Martha Wilkerson] (4-2-56) Henry Jones
261. "Pistolero" [by John Vlahos] (4-9-56) Farley Granger, Suellen Blake
262. "Portrait of a Man" [by William Kendall Clarke] (4-16-56) Robert Ellenstein, Nina Hansen, Beverly Lunsford, Peter von Aernick, Ray Boyle
263. "The Baobab Tree" [by Doria Folliott] (4-23-56) Charles Drake, Martha Scott, Elizabeth Montgomery
264. "Don't Do Me Any Favors" [by Robert J. Shaw] (4-30-56) Katherine Meskill, Betsy Von Furstenberg, Johnny Desmond, Joe De Santis
265. "Jack Be Nimble" [by Doria Folliott] (5-7-56) John Newland, June Lockhart, Augusta Dabney

266. "The Right Thing" [by Elliott Baker] (5-14-56) Forrest Tucker
267. "All Expenses Paid" [by Robert J. Shaw] (5-21-56) Lee
    Bowman, Gale Page, Lee Remick
268. "Who?" [by Robert Wallace] (5-28-56) Tom Poston
269. "Honored Guest" [by William Kendall Clarke] (6-4-56) Henry
    Gerrard, Walter Slezak, Lilia Skala, Raymond Bramley,
    William A. Lee
270. "Storm over Swan Lake" [by Kevin McKay] (6-11-56) John
    Shellie, Haila Stoddard, Jan Miner, Frederic Tozere
271. "The Soldier Room" [adapted by Milton Gelman from the novel
    by Anne Chamberlain] (6-18-56) John Newland, Dierdre
    Owens
272. "An Elephant for Peanuts" [by Stanley Brown] (6-25-56) Lin
    McCarthy, Lesley Woods, Glenn Walken

[now as SUMMER STOCK THEATRE until new season]

273. "Dream No More" (7-2-56) Charles Drake, Jan Miner, Tom
    Middleton, Elizabeth Montgomery, John Gibson, Mary K.
    Wells (all forming the repertory company for the summer)
274. "A Matter of Conscience" [by Theodore and Mathilde Ferro]
    (7-9-56) Drake, Miner, Wells
275. "Day of Grace" (7-16-56) Drake, Miner, Wells
276. "Catch a Falling Star" [by David Levy] (7-23-56) E. Mont-
    gomery, Drake, Miner, Wells
277. "Southern Exposure" [adapted by Doria Folliott from the Owen
    Criemps Broadway comedy] (7-30-56) Drake, Miner, E.
    Montgomery, Gibson, Wells
278. "Maybe Tomorrow" [by William Hamilton] (8-6-56) Drake,
    Wells, Gibson, Miner
279. "The Company Wife" [by Martha Wilkerson] (8-27-56) E.
    Montgomery, Drake, Wells, Miner, Gibson, Raymond Bramley
280. "Mr. Parker's Rhubarb" (9-3-56) Drake, E. Montgomery,
    Gibson, Middleton, Miner

Eighth Season

281. "Soldier from the Wars Returning" [by Robert Wallace] (9-10-
    56) James Cagney
282. "Onions in the Stew" [adapted by Doria Folliott from the novel
    by Betty McDonald] (9-17-56) Constance Bennett
283. "After All These Years" [by Robert J. Shaw] (9-24-56)
    Claudette Colbert, Staats Cotsworth, David DeHaven, Leona
    Powers
284. "The Last Trip of the Hindenburg" [a documentary drama by
    Burton and James Benjamin; narrated by Robert Montgomery]
    (10-1-56) Gale Page
285. "September Affair" [by Theodore and Mathilde Ferro] (10-8-
    56) John Newland, Alexis Smith
286. "Pilgrimmage" [by Theodore and Mathilde Ferro] (10-15-56)
    John Hudson, Joyce Holden, John Griggs, Theo Goetz, Betty
    Lou Keim
287. "Goodbye, Grey Flannel" [by J. Harvey Howells] (10-22-56)

Lee Bowman, Diana Douglas
288. "One Bright Day" [adapted by Doria Folliott from the play by Sigmund Miller] (10-29-56) Sidney Blackmer, House Jameson
289. "Mr. Tutt Goes West" [adapted by Murray Burnett from the story by Arthur Train] (11-5-56) Parker Fennelly, Lenka Peterson
290. "Harvest" [repeat showing of the Thanksgiving story of 11/23/53] (11-12-56)
291. "The Misfortunes of Mr. Minihan" [a fantasy by Martha Wilkerson] (11-19-56) William Bendix, Horace MacMahon
292. "Plainfield Teachers College" [by James Beach] (11-26-56) Jerry Lester
293. "Sunset Boulevard" [adapted by Doria Folliott from the 1950 film scenario by Billy Wilder, Charles Brackett and D. M. Marshman Jr.] (12-3-56) Mary Astor, Darren McGavin
294. "The Young and the Beautiful" [by Sally Benson] (12-10-56) Geoffrey Horne, Lee Remick, Terry O'Sullivan, Leslie Woods, Barry McGuire, Douglas Watson, Fran Carlon
295. "Miracle at Lensham" [adapted from the British short story] (12-17-56) Elsa Lanchester, Barry Jones
296. "Amahl and the Night Visitors" [the Gian-Carlo Menotti Christmas opera, restaged] (12-24-56) Kirk Jordan, Rosemary Kuhlmann, Andrew McKinley, David Acken, Leon Lishner, Francis Monachino
297. "Music for Your New Year's Eve" [a revue special] (12-31-56) Dorothy Olsen, Eddie Heywood, Teddi Kunig, Henry Levine, Eddie Dano, Ann Gilbert, The Night Cops; all performing musicians
298. "The Liar" [by J. Harvey Howells] (1-7-57) Norma Moore, Jan Miner
299. "Give and Take" [adapted by Gail Ingram from the story by Phyllis Bentley] (1-14-57) Martha Scott, Kent Smith
300. "Crisis at Sand Cave" [adapted by Burton Benjamin from the story of the effort to save the life of Floyd Collins] (1-21-57) Ray Boyle
301. "The Clay Pigeon" [by Dick Berg] (1-28-57) Farley Granger, Phyllis Kirk, Frank Maxwell, Paul McGrath
302. "The Week the World Stood Still" [by Burton Benjamin] (2-4-57) John Beal
303. "The Grand Prize" [adapted by Doria Folliott from the play by Ronald Alexander] (2-11-57) Judith Braun, June Lockhart, John Newland
304. "Wait for Me" [by William Kendall Clarke] (2-18-57) Jim Backus, Scott Brady, Barbara Barrie
305. "Reclining Figure" [adapted by Doria Folliott from the Harry Kurnitz Broadway play] (2-25-57) Scott McKay, Sally Kemp, Eddie Andrews
306. "The Enemy" [by Pearl Buck] (3-4-57) Shirley Yamaguchi, Kate Deei, Aki Aleong, Naol Kondo, Shigu Moriya, Sho Onodera
307. "The Last Train to Kildevil" [by Milton Gelman] (3-11-57) Charles Korvin, Martha Scott, David White
308. "His Name Was Death" (3-18-57) Henry Jones

309. "One Minute to Ditch" [adapted by James Benjamin from an article by Cornelius Ryan] (3-25-57) Gale Page, Charles Cooper, Frank Maxwell

310. "A Slice of Life" [by J. Harvey Howells] (4-1-57) J. Pat O'Malley, Ruth McDevitt, Peggy McKay

311. "Victoria Regina" [adapted from the Laurence Housman play] (4-8-57) Claire Bloom, Paul Stevens

312. "Fear Street" [by William Kendall Clarke] (4-15-57) Robert Alda, Joseph Campanella

313. "The Trial of Pontius Pilate" [an original teleplay by Robert E. Sherwood] (4-22-57) Bruce Gordon, Maria Palmer, Max Adrian, House Jameson

314. "The New World" [adapted by Sebastian Simms from the book by Dr. Arthur H. Compton] (4-29-55) Melville Ruick, Philip Bourneuf

315. "Longing for to Go" [by Martha Wilkerson] (5-6-57) Robert Culp, Lenka Peterson, Joan Hotchkiss, Belle Flower, James Kincaid

316. "Return Visit" [by Milton Gelman] (5-13-57) Joe Maross, Joanne Linville

317. "Sturdevant's Daughter" [by Kevin McKay] (5-27-57) Joan Wetmore, Nancy Malone

318. "One Smart Apple" [by J. Harvey Howells] (6-3-57) Mary Alice Canfield, George Abandor

319. "The Last Trip of the Hindenburg" [a repeat showing of the documentary drama of 10/1/56] (6-10-57)

320. "The Weather Cover" [by Milton Gelman] (6-17-56) Joseph Campanella, Edward Andrews, Norman Rose

321. "Faust '57" [by Robert Wallace] (6-24-57) Bruce Gordon, Alfred Ryder, Louis Edmonds, House Jameson

THE PLAY'S THE THING

The Episodes:

1. "The Apple Tree" [adapted from the John Galsworthy play] (3-3-50) John Merivale, Patricia Kirkland, Grace Kelly

2. "The Pink Hussar" (3-17-50) Joseph Buloff, George Keane, Leonore Aubert

3. "The Salt of the Earth" (3-31-50) Ann Shepherd, Robert Pastene

4. "Sanctuary in Paris" (4-14-50) Elliott Sullivan, Joan Chandler

5. "Screwball" (4-28-50) Jack Gilford, Lee Grant, Edith King

6. "Alison's House" [adapted from the Susan Glaspell Pulitzer Prize play] (5-21-50) Flora Campbell, John Merivale, Reginald Mason

7. "The Token" (5-26-50) Mark Roberts, Grace Kelly

8. "The Swan" [adapted from the Ferenc Molnar play] (6-9-50) George Keane, Grace Kelly, Alfred Ryder

9. "The Good Companions" [adapted from the John Boynton Priestley book and 1933 film scenario] (6-23-50) Edith Atwater, Nancy Franklin, James Noble

THE TRAP

The Regulars: Joseph De Santis, host and narrator.

The Episodes:

1. "Puzzle for Friends" (4-29-50) George Keane, Jean Carson, Vera Allen
2. "Lonely Boy" (5-6-50) Wright King, Howard Wierum, Dorothy Sands
3. "The Last Thing I Do" (5-13-50) Richard Purdy, John D. Seymour, Robert Pastene
4. "Stan, the Killer" (5-20-50) E. G. Marshall, Herbert Berghoff, Michael Ozep
5. "Sentence of Death" (5-27-50) George Reeves, Leslie Nielsen, Joseph Boland, Kim Stanley
6. "Chocolate Cobweb" (6-3-50) Nancy Franklin, Peter Brandon, Luella Gear
7. "The Man They Acquitted" (6-10-50) Torin Thatcher
8. "Three Blind Mice" (6-17-50) Augusta Dabney, John Newland, Bertha Belmore
9. "The Dark Corner" (6-24-50) Frieda Altman, Warren Stevens, Mary MacLeod, Elliott Sullivan

MASTERPIECE PLAYHOUSE

1. "Hedda Gabler" [adapted from the Henrik Ibsen classic] (7-23-50) Jessica Tandy (as Hedda), Margaret Phillips (as Thea Elvsted), Walter Abel (as George Tesman), Kent Smith (as Judge Brack), Richard Hart (as Eilert Lovborg)
2. "Richard III" [adapted from the Shakespeare classic] (7-30-50) William Windom (as King Richard III), Douglas Watson, Rita Colton, William Post Jr. , Blanche Yurka, Hugh Williams
3. "The Rivals" [adapted from the Richard Brinsley Sheridan play] (8-6-50) Hurd Hatfield, Constance Ford, Ralph Forbes, Mary Boland, Diana Douglas
4. "Six Characters in Search of an Author" [adapted from the Luigi Pirandello play] (8-13-50) Joseph Schildkraut, Betty Field
5. "The Importance of Being Earnest" [adapted from the Oscar Wilde play] (8-20-50) Brooke Byron, Hurd Hatfield, Margaret Lindsay, Margaret Phillips
6. "Othello" [adapted from the Shakespeare classic] (8-27-50) Torin Thatcher, Alfred Ryder, Olive Deering
7. "Uncle Vanya" [adapted from the Anton Chekhov play] (9-3-50) Tod Andrews, Boris Karloff, Walter Abel, Isobel Elsom, Eva Gabor, Leora Dana, Eda Heinemann

THE WEB

The Web was to have become a filmed series, so becoming the first non-live project of Mark Goodman-Bill Toddman productions, but this was never achieved.

The Regulars: Jonathan Blake, host.

The Episodes:

1. "The Twelfth Juror" (7-4-50) Robert Pastene, John Shay
2. "The Orderly Mr. Appleby" (7-11-50) Jonathan Harris, Selena Royle, Howard Wierum
3. "The Memory of Murder" (7-18-50) Warren Stevens
4. "Solo to Singapore" (7-25-50) Guy Spauli, Robert Chisholm, Berry Kroeger
5. "Help Wanted" (8-1-50) Howard Wierum, Peggy French, Robert Downing
6. "Heaven Ran Last" (8-8-50) John McQuade
7. "Home for Christmas" (8-15-50) Leslie Nielsen, George Reeves, Millicent Brower
8. "Man in the Velvet Hat" (8-22-50) Vinton Hayworth, Morton Stevens, Rudolph Justice Watson
9. "Key Witness" (8-30-50) Diana Douglas, Richard MacMurray, Charles Mendrick
10. "Dark Cross Roads" (9-6-50) Colin Keith-Johnston, Richard Frazer, Eva Thomas
11. "Talk of the Town" (9-13-50) Don Hanmer, George Reeves
12. "Murder's Challenge" (9-20-50) Ralph Bell, E. G. Marshall
13. "The Witness" (9-27-50) Richard Kollmar
14. "Blessed Are the Meek" (10-4-50) Jonathan Harris, Robert Harris, Morton Stevens, Peter Capell, Adelaide Klein
15. "The Dark Curtain" (10-11-50) Haila Stoddard, John Newland
16. "Never Say Die" (10-18-50) Richard Carlyle
17. "Journey by Night" (10-25-50) Richard Webb, Richard Kiley, Marilyn Monk
18. "Mirror of Delusion" (11-1-50) Grace Kelly, Anna Lee, Mary Stuart, Hugh Franklin
19. "Fit to Kill" (11-8-50) Conrad Janis
20. "The Boy" (11-15-50) Jane Seymour, Joey Walsh
21. "The Amateur" (11-22-50) Murvyn Vye
22. "The Creeper" (11-29-50) Mary K. Wells, Robert Nelson, Gene Lyons, Natalie Priest
23. "The Deadly Friend" (12-6-50) Richard Purdy, E. G. Marshall, Raymond Bramley, Jimmy Sommer
24. "Fifty Dollars Reward" (12-13-50) Dennis Harrison, Jean Gillespie
25. "The Friendly Hearts" (12-20-50) Mildred Dunnock
26. "Stone Cold Dead" (12-27-50) John Carradine, John Marrioth, Richard Webb, Catherine McLeod; the Duke of Iron, calypso singer, guest.
27. "Dark Legacy" (1-3-51) Charles Korvin, Kathleen Comegys, James McDonald, Audra Lindley

28. "The Man Who Had No Friends" (1-10-51) Steve Elliot, Haila Stoddard
29. "Essence of Strawberry" (1-17-51) Michael O'Halloran, Leslie Pave, Sally Gracie
30. "You Killed Elizabeth" (1-24-51) Jerome Thor, Leslie Nielsen
31. "The Crisis of Dirk Diamond" (1-31-51) Alfred Ryder, Robert Emhardt
32. "The Wallet" (2-7-51) Joey Walsh, Joseph Derrida (De Rida), John Marley
33. "Thread of Life" (2-14-51) Meg Mundy, Herbert Rudley
34. "For Laura" (2-21-51) Will Hare, Barbara Joyce, Don Briggs
35. "Star Witness" (2-28-51) Katherine Bard, Clark Gordon, Charles Mendrick
36. "The Shadowy Men" (3-7-51) E. G. Marshall, Audra Lindley, Viola Roche
37. "Finders Keepers" (3-14-51) Russell Hardy
38. "Incident in a Blizzard" (3-21-51) Alfreda Wallace, Robert Pastene, Lynn Loring
39. "The Great Diamond Discovery" (3-28-51) Robert Allen, Guy Sorel
40. "Guardian Angel" (4-4-51) John Stephens, Jerome Thor, Edith King
41. "Mr. Fish" (4-11-51) Roland Winters, Bert Conway, Preston Hanson
42. "The Dream" (4-18-51) Wesley Addy, Judith Parrish, Lawrence Fletcher
43. "The Kid's Last Fight" (4-25-51) Russell Hardie, Cliff Hall, Howard Smith
44. "Solid Gold" (5-2-51) Clay Clement, Polly Rowles
45. "Trojan Horse" (5-9-51) Jerome Thor, Joseph Anthony
46. "The Judas Bullet" (5-16-51) Mary Sinclair, Mark Daniels, Lawrence Fletcher
47. "A Switch in Time" (5-23-51) Henry Jones, Audrey Christie, Herbert Rudley
48. "Cops Must Be Tough" (5-30-51) Jack Lemmon
49. "All the Way Home" (6-6-51) Alfreda Wallace, Jane Seymour, John Randolph
50. "Checkmate" (6-13-51) Jerome Cowan, John Newland, Neva Patterson
51. "Wanted, Someone Innocent" (6-20-51) Anna Lee, Diana Olsen, Peter Pagan
52. "No Escape" (6-27-51) Judith Parrish, Richard Kiley
53. "Old Jim's Second Woman" (7-4-51)
54. "The Man in the Goldfish Bowl" (7-11-51)
55. "Breakup" (7-18-51) Dan Briggs, Jim Nolan, Billy Green
56. "Wolf Cry" (7-25-51)
57. "According to Regulations" (8-1-51)
58. "Murder for a Friend" (8-8-51)
59. "The Edge of Error" (8-15-51) Paul Langton, Robert Emhardt, Beverly Whitney
60. "The Dishonorable Thief" (8-22-51) Henry Jones, Irene (Eileen) Heckart
61. "Too Late to Run" (8-29-51) Judith Parrish, Russell Hardie

62. "The Practical Joke" (9-5-51) Maria Riva, Anthony Ross
63. "Hand in Glove" (9-12-51) Donald Buka, Bertha Belmore
64. "The Contradictory Case" (9-19-51) Jack Grimes, Rita Lynn, Marc Kramer, Donald Curtis

Second Season

65. "The Customs of the Country" (9-26-51) Peter Cookson, Ann Marno, Joseph Anthony, Gene Gross
66. "All the Way to the Moon" (10-3-51) Henry Jones, Eleanor Wilson, James Gregory
67. "Volcano" (10-10-51) Alfred Ryder, Oliver Thorndyke, Lois Wheeler, Russell Hardie
68. "The House Guests" (10-17-51) Marc Cramer, Lenka Peterson
69. "Beyond the Sea of Death" (10-24-51) Richard Purdy, Katherine Bard, Ann Shoemaker
70. "A Man Dies" (10-31-51) Jerome Cowan, Reba Tassell
71. "He Was Asking for You" (11-7-51) Patricia Wheel
72. "Golden Secret" (11-14-51) John Carradine, Tamara Geva
73. "Danger in the Shadows" (11-21-51)
74. "Shine, Mister?" (11-28-51)
75. "St. Petersburg Dilemma" (12-5-51) Jerome Cowan
76. "The Package" (12-12-51)
77. "The Man Who Was Always Right" (12-19-51) Joseph Anthony, Jackie Diamond
78. "Model Murder" (12-26-51) Whit Bissell, John Baragrey
79. "Sentence of Death" (1-2-52)
80. "After the Fact" (1-9-52) Leslie Nielsen
81. "Indian Sign" (1-16-52) Alfred de Leo, Lawrence Fletcher, Flora Campbell
82. "Second Chance" (1-23-52) Ray Boyle, Christine White
83. "Honeymoon at the Grand" (1-30-52) Billy Redfield, Haila Stoddard, Rusty Lane
84. "Witness to Murder" (2-6-52) Don Hanmer, Lois Wheeler
85. "The Brass Ring" (2-13-52) Judy Parrish, Perry Wilson, Peter Hobbs, Edgar Stehli
86. "Sleeping Dogs" (2-20-52) Ann Jackson, E. G. Marshall, James Dean
87. "Friends of the Devil" (2-27-52) Frances Helm
88. "Hear Footsteps" (3-5-52) Beatrice Straight, Peter Cookson
89. "The Phantom of the Bridge" (3-12-52) Bobby Santon
90. "Death Mask" (3-19-52) Tom Helmore, Luella Gear, Betty Field
91. "Nemesis" (3-26-52) Edmon Ryan
92. "The Terrible Truth" (4-2-52) Patricia Crowley
93. "Rehearsal for Death" (4-9-52) Leon Tokatvan, Andy Ackers
94. "Rx Death" (4-16-52) Peter Hobbs, Edward Binns
95. "Prelude to Murder" (4-23-52) Paul Langton
96. "Broken Date" (4-30-52) William Redfield, Ian Martin
97. "The Handcuff" (5-7-52) Mildred Dunnock, Joseph Anthony
98. "Kill with Kindness" (5-14-52) Charles Dingle, Sidney Blackmer
99. "The Perfect Out" (5-21-52) Whit Bissell, Richard Webb, Virginia Vincent

100. "The Vanished Hours" (5-28-52) James Daly, Anne Jackson, Anne Seymour
101. "Serpent's Tooth" (6-4-52) Neva Patterson, Vincent Price
102. "The Giant Killer" (6-11-52) Gene Reynolds
103. "The Quiet Room" (6-18-52) Anthony Ross
104. "The Dark Shore" (6-25-52) John Raitt, Carmen Mathews, Stella Andrew
105. "The Poison Tree" (7-2-52) Blanche Yurka, Vaughn Taylor, Luella Gear, Martin Newman

Third Season

106. "Deadlock" (9-28-52) Eli Wallach
107. "The Homecoming" (10-5-52) Robert Sterling, Richard Webb
108. "Tiger in the Closet" (10-12-52) Hurd Hatfield
109. "Shadow in the Sun" (10-19-52) J. P. Anthony
110. "The Keyhole" (10-26-52) Audra Lindley
111. "K for Killer" (11-2-52)
112. "Turn Back" (11-9-52) Darren McGavin, Joan Copeland
113. "The Switch" (11-16-52) Jerome Cowan
114. "The Unafraid" (11-23-52)
115. "The Best of Everything" (11-30-52) Dean Harens
116. "Backfire" (12-7-52)
117. "Night Alarm" (12-14-52)
118. "Fatal Alibi" (12-21-52) Robert Sterling
119. "The Tower" (12-28-52) Sidney Blackmer
120. "Stranger in the Park" (1-4-53) John Connell
121. "The Beast" (1-11-53) Richard Webb
122. "Midnight Guest" (1-18-53) Patricia Collinge, Alexander Scourby
123. "Dark Meeting" (1-25-53) Alan Bunce
124. "Long Shot" (2-1-53)
125. "Time for the Piper" (2-8-53) Michael Higgins
126. "The Patsy" (2-15-53)
127. "The Last Chance" (2-22-53) Jack Palance, Eva Marie Saint
128. "The Real Thing" [adapted from the Henry Jones story] (3-1-53) Brandon de Wilde
129. "A Time for Dying" (3-8-53) Joseph Schildkraut
130. "The Joke" (3-15-53) Mary Sinclair
131. "The Curve" (3-22-53)
132. "Passport" (3-29-53)
133. "Cry of Trumpets" (4-5-53)
134. "The Boy in the Front Row" (4-12-53) Mildred Dunnock, James Lipton
135. "Fair Warning" (4-19-53) Virginia Gibson
136. "A Time for Hate" (4-26-53) Jessie Royce Landis
137. "Somewhere in Korea" (5-3-53)
138. "The Thirty-second Floor" (5-10-53)
139. "A Fair Exchange" (5-17-53) John Newland, Eva Marie Saint
140. "The Trouble at San Rivera" (5-24-53) Harold Huber
141. "A Matter of Vengeance" (5-31-53) Alan Webb
142. "Dear Sister" (6-7-53) Martha Scott
143. "A Perfect Imitation" (6-14-53)

144. "Unseen" (6-21-53)
145. "Encore" (6-28-53) Felicia Montealegre
146. "A Case of Escape" (7-5-53) Ben Gazzara, Leora Dana
147. "The Line of Duty" (7-12-53) Richard Kiley
148. "The Bells of Damon" (7-19-53) James Costigan, Paul Newman
149. "The Badger Game" (7-26-53) John Raitt, Harry Townes
150. "Like Father" (8-2-53) Mildred Dunnock, George Mathews, David Winters
151. "Death Sentence" (8-9-53) Beverly Whitney, Eric Dressler
152. "End of the Line" (8-16-53) Jayne Meadows
153. "Rainy Day" (8-23-53) Susan Hallaran
154. "Speak No Evil" (8-30-53) Mildred Dunnock
155. "The Lake" (9-6-53) Henry Jones
156. "You've Got to Stop Sometime" (9-13-53) Jennie Goldstein, Terry Becker

Fourth Season

157. "One for the Road" (9-20-53) Paul Newman, Grace Raynor, Wally Brown
158. "Combination for Murder" (9-27-53) Evelyn Varden
159. "A Design for Execution" (10-4-53) Gene Lyons, Marjorie Gateson, J. Pat O'Malley
160. "Kind Stranger" (10-11-53) Richard Kiley, Joan Copeland
161. "Cave of Chambery" (10-18-53) Hildy Parks
162. "Strange Sanctuary" (10-25-53) E. G. Marshall
163. "The Winner" (11-1-53) Frank McHugh
164. "The Perfect Wife" (11-8-53) June Dayton, Joe Maross
165. "The Leech" (11-15-53) Wesley Addy
166. "The World My Cage" (11-22-53) James Costigan, Mildred Natwick, Maureen Hurley
167. "The Scrap" (11-29-53) Dino Di Luca
168. [unknown title] (12-6-53)
169. "Figurine" (12-13-53) Dorothy Donahue, Eric Dressler
170. "The Closing Net" (12-20-53) Phyllis Kirk
171. "The Blue Bottle" (12-27-53) Catherine McLeod
172. "Enough Rope" (1-3-54) Louise Albritton
173. "The Well" (1-10-54) Henry Hull
174. "The Hunted" (1-17-54) Howard St. John, Mary Alice Moore, Ross Martin, Guy Raymond
175. "The Barrier" (1-24-54) Royal Dano, Bill Zuckert
176. "The Visit" (1-31-54)
177. "A Handful of Stars" (2-7-54) Arthur Franz, Cloris Leachman, Patty McCormack
178. "Rock-Bound" (2-14-54) Howard St. John, Mike Wallace, Chester Morris
179. "Paper Doll" (2-21-54) Wynne Gibson
180. "The Circle Closes" (2-28-54)
181. "Sheep's Clothing" (3-7-54) Christopher Plummer
182. "A Piece of Gray Cloth" (3-14-54) James Dunn
183. "Night Fare" (3-21-54)
184. "The Favorite" (3-28-54)
185. "Stopover" (4-4-54) Kay Medford

186. "Scapegoat" (4-11-54)
187. "The Lonely Heart" (4-18-54)
188. "Snow" (4-25-54)
189. "Grand Finale" (5-2-54) Henry Lascoe, Lisa Ferraday
190. "Blind Man's Bluff" (5-9-54) O. Z. Whitehead, James Nolan
191. "Brush-Off" (5-16-54) Paul Langton
192. "The Primitive Touch" (5-23-54)
193. "Death Has Nine Lives" (5-30-54) Haila Stoddard
194. "Top Gun" (6-6-54) Dickie Moore, Carl Albertson, Alfred Hopson
195. "Hurricane Coming" (6-13-54) Maria Riva, Kurt Kasznar
196. "Look at the Clown" (6-20-54)
197. "Missing Person" (6-27-54) James Daly
198. "My Sister's Keeper" (7-4-54)
199. "The Treadmill" (7-11-54) Mark Roberts, Phyllis Love, Carroll Baker
200. "The Trouble with Diamonds" (7-18-54) Harry Townes, Joseph Buloff
201. "A Name for Death" (7-25-54) Leora Dana, Frederic Worlock
202. "I'll Buy a Dream" (8-1-54) Biff McGuire, Patricia Breslin, Cameron Prud'homme
203. "Matter of Degree" (8-8-54) Joe Maross
204. "The Pinball" (8-15-54)
205. "The Bait" (8-22-54) Patrick O'Neal, Alan Bunce, Betsy Palmer
206. "The House" (8-29-54) Joanna Roos, Marian Russell, Charles Dingle
207. "The Crackpot" (9-5-54) Phyllis Kirk, Charles Aidman
208. "A Sense of Honor" (9-12-54)
209. "The Face on the Shadow" (9-19-54) Fay Bainter
210. "Welcome Home" (9-26-54) Biff McGuire, Jim Backus

CAMEO THEATRE

Produced by Albert McCleery.

The Episodes:

1. "It Takes a Thief" (5-16-50) Marjorie Gateson, Jack Hartley
2. "The Great Merlini" (5-23-50) Chester Morris, Mary K. Wells
3. "The Long Walk" (5-30-50) Richard Carlyle, Patricia Breslin, Robert Bolger
4. "Manhattan Footstep" (6-7-50) Sam Wanamaker, Tod Andrews
5. "The Lottery" [adapted from the Shirley Jackson story] (6-14-50)
6. "Weep for the Heart" (6-21-50) Ernest Truex
7. "A Daughter to Think About" (6-28-50) Tod Andrews, Ruth Ford
8. "The Canon's Curtain" (7-19-50) Ernest Truex, Eva Conden, Grace O'Malley

9. "Line of Duty" (7-26-50) Ed Begley
10. "Googan" (8-2-50) Billy M. Green, John Harvey, Judy Parrish
11. "The Triumph of Justice" [by Irwin Shaw] (8-9-50)
12. "A Point of View" (8-16-50) William Post Jr.
13. "Sarah Lee's Children" (8-23-50) Mildred Natwick
14. "The Westland Case" (9-13-50) Preston Foster, Frank Jenks, Carol Hughes
15. "The Paper Sack" (9-20-50) Dennis Harrison, Gavin Gordon, James Little
16. "Murder Is a Matter of Opinion" [adapted from the Jules Archer story] (9-27-50) Fred Bartholomew

Second Season

17. "Special Delivery" (6-18-51) June Havoc, Rusty Lane
18. "Blackout" (6-25-51) Jeffrey Lynn, Barbara Britton
19. "Betrayal" (7-2-51) Nina Foch, Philip Reed
20. "Avalanche" (7-9-51) Richard Carlson, Constance Bennett
21. "Deception" (7-16-51) Madge Evans
22. "Of Unsound Mind" (7-23-51) Clare Luce, Philip Reed, Donald Briggs
23. "The Third Time" (7-30-51) Ilona Massey
24. "Strange Identity" (8-6-51) Jan Miner, Donald Briggs

Third Season

25. "Dark of the Moon" [adapted from the Howard Richardson and William Berney play] (1-6-52) Alfred Drake, Rita Gam
26. "The Gathering Twilight" (1-13-52) Sylvia Sidney
27. "The Visit" [adapted from the Frederick Durrenmatt play] (1-20-52) John Newland
28. "The Paper Sack" [restaged from 9/20/50] (1-27-52) Dennis Harrison, Judy Parrish
29. "Problem Child" (2-3-52) Butch Cavell
30. "The Man Who Played Lincoln" (2-10-52)
31. "The Thompsons" (2-17-52)
32. "Peer Gynt" [adapted from the Henrik Ibsen play; Part I] (2-24-52) Clare Luce, Douglass Montgomery, Rita Gam
33. "Peer Gynt" [Part II] (3-2-52) as above.
34. "Peer Gynt" [Part III] (3-9-52) as above.
35. "The Canon's Curtain" [restaged from 7/19/50] (3-16-52) Ernest Truex
36. "The Heart Is Young" (3-23-52)
37. "Debut" (3-30-52)
38. "The Legend of Liz" (4-6-52)

Fourth Season

39. "The Inca of Perusalem" [a Graustarkian story of George Bernard Shaw] (7-3-55) Sir Cedric Hardwicke, Mary Scott
40. "Bending of the Bough" (7-17-55) Guy Williams, Barbara Jean Wong
41. "The Grown Ones" [by Arthur Rodney Coneybeare] (7-24-55) Karen Sharpe, James Drury, Dorothy Granger

42. "Hutch" (7-31-55)
43. "Company" (8-7-55)
44. "The Man from the South" [by Roald Dahl; subsequently restaged for the Alfred Hitchcock Presents episode of 3/13/60] (8-14-55)
45. "A Little Night Music" (8-21-55)

THE ARMSTRONG CIRCLE THEATRE

From the fifth season William Corrigan directed the series; Ralph Nelson produced.

The Regulars: Nelson Case, host.

The Episodes:

1. "The Magnificent Gesture" (6-6-50) Brian Aherne
2. "Jackpot" (6-13-50) Stuart Erwin
3. "Only This Night" (6-20-50) Nina Foch
4. "The Chair" (6-27-50) Vaughn Taylor, Lucile Watson
5. "The Sky Rocket" (7-4-50) Ed Begley, Jane Seymour
6. "Local Stop" (7-11-50) Vaughn Taylor, Jimmy Sonner, David Burke
7. "The Bald Spot" (7-18-50) Bob Duncan
8. "The Rocking Horse" (7-25-50)
9. "The Big Day" (8-1-50) Neil Hamilton, Louise Larabee
10. "Man of Action" (8-8-50) Dan Reed
11. "Ring Around My Finger" (8-15-50)
12. "Remember, Remember?" (8-22-50) Don McClelland, Valerie Cossart, Barbara Townsend
13. "Blaze of Glory" (8-29-50) Judson Pratt, Mary Patton, Reed Brown Jr., Dort Clark
14. "The First Formal" (9-5-50) Jane Sutherland, Ruth Matteson, Edwin Bruce
15. "The Oldest Son" (9-12-50)
16. "The Other Woman" (9-19-50) Louise Albritton, Glenn Langan
17. "The Elopement" (9-26-50) Betty Caulfield, Robert Allen
18. "Round-Up" (10-3-50) Zachary Scott, Klock Ryder, Jeanne Sheppard
19. "Give and Take" (10-10-50) Frank Albertson
20. "It's Only a Game" (10-17-50) Donald Woods
21. "Time of Their Lives" (10-24-50) Frank Thomas
22. "Man and Wife" (10-31-50) Paul McGrath
23. "Person to Person" (11-7-50) Lawrence Hugo, Gloria Stroock
24. "Best Trip Ever" (11-14-50) Enid Markey, Elizabeth Patterson, Alexander Campbell
25. "The Perfect Type" (11-21-50) Richard Derr, Romney Brent, Augusta Dabney, Ruth Ford
26. "Anything But Love" (11-28-50) Julie Haydon, Karl Malden, Charles Mendick, Jean Casto
27. "The Happy Ending" (12-5-50) Otto Kruger, Helen Gillett, Cathleen Cordell

28. "Green Eyes" (12-12-50) Judith Evelyn, Lili Valenty, Tom Helmore, Joyce Mathews
29. "The Diet" (12-19-50) Lawrence Fletcher, Lois Wilson
30. "Christopher Beach" (12-26-50) Barbara Britton, Tyler Carpenter
31. "That Man Is Mine" (1-2-51) Margaret Lindsay, Philip Reed
32. "Rooftop" (1-9-51) Jean Pearson, Biff McGuire
33. "The Younger Generation" (1-16-51) Loring Smith
34. "Silver Service" (1-23-51) Geraldine Brooks, John Archer
35. "Those Wonderful People" (1-30-51) James Van Dyke, Peter Fernandez, Bess Johnson
36. "Super Highway" (2-6-51) Ed Begley, John Hamilton
37. "A Different World" (2-13-51) Joan Chandler, Tom Avera
38. "That's Simon's Girl" (2-20-51) Bonita Granville, Robert Pastene
39. "Twenty-One Days" (2-27-51) Skip Homeier, Lola Albright, Joan Morgan
40. "The Partnership" (3-6-51) John Newland, Lucille Watson, Harry Sheppard
41. "The Patcher-Upper" (3-13-51) Vinton Hayworth, Judy Parrish, Neva Patterson
42. "The Hero" (3-20-51) William Tabbert, Kathleen Crowley
43. "Double Exposure" (3-27-51) Edmond Ryan, Ruth Matteson
44. "The Moment of Decision" (4-3-51) Bruce Cabot, Will Hare
45. "Ghost Town" (4-10-51) Henry Hull
46. "Honor Student" (4-17-51) Donald Buka, Walter Starken, Jean Gillespie
47. "Backstage" (4-24-51) William Prince, Patricia Wheel
48. "The Big Rainbow" (5-1-51) Lawrence Fletcher, June Walker
49. "The Open Heart" (5-8-51) Ivan Simpson, Gaby Rodgers
50. "Jury Duty" (5-15-51) Howard Smith
51. "The Vote Getter" (5-22-51) Arthur Vinton, Muriel Kirkland
52. "Over the Fence" (5-29-51) Dick Foran, Barbara Britton
53. "Lover's Leap" (6-5-51) Leslie Nielsen, Grace Kelly, Don Murphy, Michael Keith, Charles Mendick, Larry Buchanan, Alan Abel
54. "The Rookie" (6-12-51) Douglas Watson, Naomi Riordan, Ellen Mahar
55. "Close Harmony" (6-19-51) Lawrence Tibbett, Madeleine Clive, Romney Brent
56. "Buckaroo" (6-26-51) Cloris Leachman
57. "Leave It to Mother" (7-3-51) Enid Markey
58. "Table for Two" (7-10-51) Henry Daniell, Ruth Matteson, Hazel Dawn
59. "Last Chance" (7-17-51) Isobel Elsom, Sidney Blackmer, Jack Lemmon
60. "A Beautiful Friendship" (7-24-51) Jerome Cowan, Sheila Bromley
61. "Mountain Song" (7-31-51) James Lipton, Marcia Henderson
62. "The Mistake" (8-7-51) Felicia Montealegre, Frances Reid
63. "The Man in the Bookshop" (8-14-51) William Prince
64. "Bone of Contention" (8-21-51) Coleen Gray, Richard Derr
65. "Johnny Pickup" (8-28-51) Art Keegan, Anne Jackson

66. "By the Book" (9-4-51) Beverly Whitney, Ernest Graves
67. "Sleight of Hand" (9-11-51) Richard Kollnar, Hildy Parks

Second Season

68. "Flame-Out" (9-18-51) Leslie Nielsen, Ann Marno
69. "Danny's Tune" (9-25-51) George Hall, Mary Kay Stearn
70. "The Runaway Heart" (10-2-51) Judith Evelyn, John Newland, Mary Orr, Sunny Lewbel
71. "The Commandant's Clock" (10-9-51) Ben Cooper, Richard Cleary, Melville Ruick, Woody Morgan
72. "The Lost and Found" (10-16-51) Cara Williams, Chester Stratton
73. "The Long View" (10-23-51) Thomas Mitchell
74. "Night Song" (10-30-51) Geraldine Fitzgerald, Donald Woods
75. "Fog Station" (11-6-51) William Eythe, Constance Ford
76. "Day Dreams" (11-13-51) Beatrice Pearson
77. "The Oldster" (11-20-51) Henry Hull, Butch Cavell
78. "Brand from the Burning" (11-27-51) Thomas Coley
79. "Key Witness" (12-4-51) Kent Smith
80. "Marionettes" (12-11-51) Beatrice Pearson, Henry Jones; the Bill Baird marionettes
81. "Disaster" (12-18-51) Gene Reynolds, Jack Lambert
82. "Enter Rosalind" (12-25-51) Enid Markey
83. "The Snow Deer" (1-1-52) Beverly Whitney, Charles Cooper
84. "Pandora's Box" (1-8-52) Dorothy Stickney, John Boyd
85. "It Takes All Kinds" (1-15-52) Hildy Parks, William Redfield
86. "Price Tag" (1-22-52) Anne Jackson, Jack Grimes
87. "Yesterday's Magic" (1-29-52) Jerome Cowan, Frances Robinson
88. "Image" (2-5-52) Beatrice Straight, Edmon Ryan
89. "The Yards of Poetry" (2-12-52) Michael Gorrin
90. "The Hat from Hangtown" (2-19-52) Mabel Tallafero
91. "Mrs. Bemmis Takes a Trip" (2-26-52) E. G. Marshall, Diana Douglas
92. "Domenico" (3-4-52) Henry Hull, Luis Van Rooten
93. "The Man in 308" (3-11-52) Leslie Nielsen, Frances Helm
94. "The Shoes That Laughed" (3-18-52) Paul Valentine, Patricia Crowley
95. "High Ground" (3-25-52) Noel Leslie
96. "Way of Courage" (4-1-52) Douglass Montgomery, Martha Scott, Brandon Peters
97. "Troubled Sands" (4-8-52) Hildy Parks
98. "The Darkroom" (4-15-52) Louise Albritton, John Newland, Walter Matthau, Glenda Farrell
99. "Wedding Day" (4-22-52) Mari Kennedy, Edgar Stehli
100. "The Sergeant" (4-29-52) Don Hanmer
101. "The Lucky Suit" (5-6-52) Stuart Erwin
102. "Dismal Swamp" (5-13-52) Oliver Thorndyke, Lloyd Knight
103. "Breakaway" (5-27-52) Joy Hodges, Richard Kendrick
104. "Fairy Tale" (6-3-52) Patricia Crowley
105. "Situation Normal" (6-17-52) Philip Huston

106. "Cappie's Candles" (6-24-52) Katherine Bard, Wesley Addy, John Hamilton
107. "City Editor" (7-1-52) Shepperd Strudwick, Louise Albritton, Grace Kelly
108. "For Worse" (7-15-52) Leslie Nielsen, Nancy Malone, Andy Milligan
109. "Changing Dream" (7-29-52) Anne Seymour, Ben Cooper
110. "The Vase" (8-5-52) E. G. Marshall, Dennis Hoey, Muriel Kirkland
111. "Return the Favor" (8-12-52) James Daly, Doris Dowling
112. "A Man and His Conscience" (8-19-52) William Prince, Michael Stanley
113. "Round Robin" (8-26-52) Marc Cramer, Susan Shaw
114. "Recapture" (9-2-52) Grace Kelly, Barbara Baxley, Darren McGavin
115. "Caprice" (9-9-52) Paul Lukas
116. "The Thirteenth" (9-16-52) Evelyn Varden, Frederick Tozere, Doris Dalton

Third Season

117. "Red Tape" (9-30-52) Peggy Conklin
118. "Remembrance Island" (10-7-52) Raimonda Orselli, Jaimie Smith
119. "Betrayal" (10-14-52) Maria Riva, Judith Evelyn
120. "The Gentle Rain" (10-28-52) Edith Fellows, Frederic Tozere, Whit Bissell
121. "A Godmother for Amy" (11-11-52) Bunny Lewbel, Stefan Olsen
122. "A Volcano Is Dancing Here" (11-18-52) Barbara Baxley, William Prince, Edgar Stehli
123. "Fable of Honest Harry" (11-25-52) Robert Armstrong
124. "The Lights Are Bright" (12-9-52) Andy Milligan, Walter Burke, James Little
125. "The Nothing Kid" (12-16-52) Jack Whiting, Bill Hayes
126. "The Visitor" (12-23-52) Shepperd Strudwick, Haila Stoddard
127. "Billy Adams, American" (12-30-52) E. A. Krumschmidt, Richard Wigginton
128. "The Thirty-eighth President" (1-6-53) Alan Bunce, Audrey Christie
129. "Ski Story" (1-13-53) Nina Foch, Robert Shackleton
130. "Before Breakfast" (1-20-53) Scotty Beckett, Ed Begley. Chris White
131. "Black Wedding" (1-27-53) Patricia Breslin, Lili Darvas, Florence Reed, Eric Sinclair
132. "Pilgrimage" (2-3-53) Fay Bainter, Jessie Royce Landis
133. "The Marmalade Scandal" (2-10-53) Melville Cooper, Mildred Natwick, J. Pat O'Malley
134. "Recording Date" (2-17-53) Melville Ruick, Fritzi Scheff, Reinhold Schunzel
135. "The Anchorage" (2-24-53) Ernest Truex, Una O'Connor, Addison Richards

136. "The Twenty-ninth Theme" (3-3-53) Perry Fiske, Gene Lyons
137. "House of Tears" (3-10-53) Ruth Ford
138. "The Checkerboard Heart" (3-17-53) Jack Lemmon, Betsy Von Furstenberg
139. "The Parrot" [an opera program] (3-24-53) Josephine Schillig, soprano
140. "Transfusion" (3-31-53) Murray Hamilton, James Gregory, Kathleen McLean
141. "A Slight Case of April" (4-7-53) Hildy Parks
142. "The Straight and Narrow" (4-14-53) Walter Matthau, Glenda Farrell, Staats Cotsworth
143. "Judy and the Brain" (4-21-53) Lee Remick, Richard Franchot, Lorna Lynn
144. "On the Beat" (4-28-53) Ann Hillary, Donald Richards, Dennis Harrison
145. "Sunday Storm" (5-5-53) Mary Fickett, Edward Bryce, Russell Hicks
146. "Candle in a Bottle" (5-12-53) Phyllis Kirk, Leslie Nielsen
147. "A Matter of Opinion" (5-19-53) Philip Bevins, Bibi Osterwald, Jimmy Jamail
148. "The Middle Son" (5-26-53) Jackie Cooper
149. "The Right Approach" (6-2-53) Elizabeth Montgomery, Ona Munson

Fourth Season

150. "Judgment" [by Nicholas E. Baehr; directed by James Sheldon and produced by Judson Fausett] (9-1-53) Madge Evans, Robert Keith, Larry Robinson
151. "Two Prisoners" (9-8-53) William Prince, Louisa Horton, Dick Ewell
152. "A Story to Whisper" (9-15-53) Betsy Palmer, Leslie Nielsen, Ethel Owen
153. "The Last Tour" (9-22-53) Jo Van Fleet, Jessie Royce Landis, Melville Ruick, Vaughn Taylor
154. "A Time to Live" (9-29-53) Leora Dana, Hugh Reilly
155. "Tour of Duty" (10-6-53) Ed Begley, Jackie Cooper, Joseph Wiseman, Thomas Cole
156. "The Free Choice" [by Hamilton Benz] (10-13-53) Kent Smith, Douglas Dick, Mary Johnson
157. "Herman" (10-20-53) Larry Blyden, Sally Gracie
158. "Julie's Castle" (10-27-53) Lili Darvas, Sally Forrest, Joe Maross
159. "The Honor of Littorno" (11-3-53) Martin Brooks, Robert H. Harris, Geraldine Brooks
160. "The Right Approach" [restaged from 6/2/53] (11-10-53) Ona Munson, Claudia Morgan
161. "The Bells of Cockaigne" (11-17-53) James Dean, Gene Lockhart
162. "The Beard" (11-24-53) Leslie Nielsen, Sir Cedric Hardwicke
163. "A Little Moaning to Sell" (12-1-53) Hugh Reilly
164. "The Marshal of Misery Gulch" (12-8-53) Peter Lind Hayes, Mary Healy, Wallace Ford

165. "The Debt" (12-15-53) William Prince, Louisa Horton
166. "The Tree in the Empty Room" (12-22-53) Margaret Hayes, Arthur Cassell
167. "Return to Ballygally" (12-29-53) Melville Cooper, Scott Forbes, Maureen Hurley
168. "For Ever and Ever" (1-5-54) Kevin Coughlin, Richard Kendrick, Marcia Van Dyke
169. "The Piano Tuner" (1-12-54) Fay Bainter, Otto Kruger
170. "The Millstone" (1-19-54) Elizabeth Montgomery, Walter Brooke, Rebecca Sand
171. "The Old Man's Gold" (1-26-54) Katherine McLeod, James Gregory
172. "Pride of Jonathan Craig" (2-2-54) Jack Whiting, Valerie Cossart
173. "The Fight" (2-9-54) Joey Walsh, Jean Carson, Tod Andrews
174. "Run to the Magic" (2-16-54) Anna Lee, John Archer
175. "Evening Star" (2-23-54) Arthur Franz, Jarmila Novotna, Sarah Marshall
176. "Tam O'Shanter" (3-9-54) Arthur Treacher, Mildred Natwick
177. "The Fugitive" (3-16-54) Anthony Perkins, Dolly Haas
178. "So Close the Stars" (3-23-54) Biff McGuire, Leora Dana
179. "The Military Heart" (3-30-54) Sidney Blackmer
180. "My Client MacDuff" (4-6-54) Roddy McDowall, Patricia Breslin
181. "The Three Tasks" [an Easter story] (4-13-54) Arthur Treacher, Francis L. Sullivan
182. "Treasure Trove" (4-20-54) Gene Lockhart, Mildred Dunnock, June Lockhart, Wallace Ford
183. "Gang-Up" (4-27-54) Ed Begley, Carmen Mathews
184. "The Hand of the Hunter" (5-4-54) Joseph Schildkraut, E. A. Krumschmidt
185. "Man Talk" (5-11-54) Enid Markey, Gage Clark
186. "Breakdown" (5-18-54) Carmen Mathews, William Redfield, Patricia Smith
187. "The Use of Dignity" (5-25-54) Ed Begley, Cliff Robertson, Joe Downing

Fifth Season

188. "The Beautiful Wife" [by David Shaw] (8-31-54) Janet Blair, Tony Randall, Bert Thorn, Maxine Stuart
189. "The First Born" (9-7-54) Mary Boland, E. G. Marshall, Carmen Mathews
190. "Judy and Me" (9-14-54) James Dunn, Patty McCormack
191. "Explosion" (9-21-54) Joe Maross, Frank Overton
192. "The Judged" (9-28-54) Walter Abel
193. "The Runaway" (10-5-54) Fay Bainter, Philip Abbott
194. "Half a Hero" (10-12-54) Larry Blyden
195. "Lie Detector" (10-19-54) Skip Homeier
196. "The Scandal That Rocked Paris" (10-26-54) Marcel Le Bon
197. "Fred Allen's Sketchbook" [a revue; Allen narrates three "droll stories"] (11-9-54) Fred Allen, Barbara Nichols
198. "Flare-Up" (11-16-54) Leora Dana, Philip Abbott
199. "Brink of Disaster" (11-23-54) Ed Begley, Joanne Woodward

200. "The Contender" (11-30-54) Paul Newman, Frank McHugh
201. "H Is for Hurricane" (12-7-54) Kim Stanley
202. "Hit a Blue Note" (12-14-54) Walter Matthau, Carol Bruce
203. "Ring Twice for Christmas" (12-21-54) Joey Faye, Nat Frey
204. "Run Away Fast" (12-28-54)
205. "Save Me from Treason" (1-4-55) Ed Begley, Mildred Dunnock
206. "The Fatal Trap" (1-11-55) Jessie Royce Landis, Nita Talbot
207. "The Invisible Handcuffs" [a study of juvenile delinquincy] (1-18-55)
208. "Thunder in the House" (1-25-55) E. G. Marshall, Philip Abbott, Patricia Collinge, Joey Walsh
209. "Ladders of Lies" (2-1-55) Georgiann Johnson, John Cassavetes
210. "No Room to Breathe" (2-8-55) Dane Clark
211. "I Found Sixty Million Dollars" [based on the story of Charles A. Steen] (2-15-55) Jackie Cooper
212. "Sudden Disaster" (2-22-55) Leora Dana
213. "Stay Away, Stranger" (3-1-55)
214. "Crack-Up" (3-8-55) Ernest Truex
215. "Trapped" (3-15-55) Judith Evelyn, Jo Van Fleet, Philip Abbott
216. "TV or Not TV" [by Jerome Ross] (3-22-55) William Redfield
217. "Buckskin" (4-5-55) Jack Lord, John Cassavetes
218. "Leap for Freedom" (4-12-55) Martin Brooks
219. "The Secret of Emily du Vane" (4-19-55) Geraldine Fitzgerald
220. "Fight for Tomorrow" [by Irving Elman] (4-26-55) Margaret Hayes, William Prince
221. "Crisis" (otherwise known as "Jet Pilot") [by Douglas Stone] (5-3-55) William Smithers, Lori March
222. "Here at Home" [by Mann Rubin] (5-10-55)
223. "East of Nowhere" [a drama of Chinese communism] (5-17-55) Oscar Homolka, Joan Tetzel
224. "The Narrow Man" [by Anne Howard Bailey] (5-24-55) Harry Townes, Catherine McLeod
225. "The Hallelujah Corner" [by Greer Johnson] (5-31-55) Fay Bainter
226. "The Honorable Mrs. Jones" [by Jerome Coopersmith] (6-14-55) Edith Atwater, Peter Cookson
227. "Time for Love" [by Don Taylor] (6-21-55) John Cassavetes, Gena Rowlands, Joseph Sweeney
228. "Moment of Truth" [by Newton Meltzer] (6-28-55) Joe Maross, Kathleen Maguire

Episodes continued with Television Drama Series Programming: A Comprehensive Chronicle 1959-1975.

STAGE 13

The Episodes:

1. "Midsummer's Eve" (5-3-50) Richard MacMurray, J. Pat O'Malley, Emily Barnes
2. "Never Murder Your Grandfather" (5-10-50) Robert Gallagher, Leslie Nielsen, Barbara Bolton
3. "Permission to Kill" (5-17-50) Alice Reinheart, Daniel Morgan
4. "The Last Man" (5-24-50) Vinton Hayworth, Kathleen Cordell
5. "Now You See Him" (5-31-50) Dennis Harrison
6. "You Have Been Warned" (6-21-50) James Monks, Jane White
7. "No More Wishes" (6-28-50) Donald Briggs, Lucille Patton, Philip Sterling

1950-1951 SEASON

THE LUX VIDEO THEATRE [after the radio series]

The Episodes:

1. "Saturday's Children" [adapted from the Maxwell Anderson play]
   (10-2-50) Joan Caulfield, Dean Harens, John Ericson
2. "Rosalind" (10-9-50) Luise Rainer
3. "Shadow on the Heart" (10-16-50) Veronica Lake
4. "The Valiant" (10-23-50) Nina Foch, Zachary Scott
5. "Mine To Have" (10-30-50) Nina Foch, Andrew Duggan
6. "The Wonderful Night" (11-6-50) Angela Lansbury, Glenn
   Langen, Cliff Hall
7. "Gallant Lady" (11-13-50) Ruth Hussey, Herbert Rudley, John
   Stephen
8. "Goodnight, Please" (11-20-50) Franchot Tone
9. "The Token" (11-27-50) Wanda Hendrix, Dean Harens, June
   Dayton
10. "To Thine Own Self" (12-4-50) Melvyn Douglas
11. "The Lovely Menace" (12-11-50) Walter Abel, Mercedes Mc-
    Cambridge
12. "Down Bayou DuBac" (12-18-50) Lon McAllister, Diana Lynn
13. "A Child Is Born" [adapted from the Stephen Vincent Benét
    Christmas story] (12-25-50) Gene Lockhart (as the inn-
    keeper), Fay Bainter (as his wife)
14. "A Well-Remembered Voice" (1-1-51) Brian Aherne
15. "The Purple Doorknob" (1-8-51) Josephine Hull
16. "Purple and Fine Linen" (1-15-51) Ilona Massey, Basil Rath-
    bone
17. "Manhattan Pastorale" (1-22-51) Teresa Wright
18. "The Shiny People" (1-29-51) Robert Cummings
19. "The Choir Rehearsal" (2-5-51) Martha Scott, Robert Sterling
20. "Abe Lincoln in Illinois" [adapted from the Robert E. Sherwood
    play] (2-12-51) Raymond Massey, Muriel Kirkland, Frank
    Tweddell
21. "To the Lovely Margaret" (2-19-51) Margaret O'Brien, Skip
    Homeier
22. "The Irish Drifter" (2-26-51) Pat O'Brien, Jonathan Marlowe
23. "Not Guilty--Of Much" (3-5-51) Dane Clark, Bonita Granville
24. "Long Distance" (3-12-51) Miriam Hopkins, Lila Lee
25. "No Shoes" (3-19-51) Jack Carson
26. "The Treasure Trove" (3-26-51) Barbara Britton, Bruce Cabot,
    Dick Foran
27. "The Old Lady Shows Her Medals" [adapted from the James M.
    Barrie play] (4-2-51) Robert Preston, Margaret Wycherly

28. "Column Item" (4-9-51) Laraine Day
29. "Heritage of Wimpole Street" (4-16-51) Walter Hampden, Patricia Wheel, Judson Ross
30. "Hit and Run" (4-23-51) Edmond O'Brien
31. "The Speech" (4-30-51) Fredric March, Florence Eldridge
32. "The Sire de Maletroit's Door" [adapted from the Robert Louis Stevenson story] (5-7-51) Richard Greene, Coleen Gray
33. "Local Storm" (5-14-51) Betty Field
34. "Wild Geese" (5-21-51) Evelyn Keyes
35. "Sweet Sorrow" (5-28-51) Sarah Churchill, Jeffrey Lynn
36. "Consider the Lillies" (6-4-51) Kay Francis
37. "Weather for Today" (6-11-51) Lynn Bari, Lee Bowman
38. "Inside Story" (6-18-51) Lola Albright, Robert Sterling
39. "The Promise" (6-25-51) Vincent Price

Second Season

40. "The Pacing Goose" (8-27-51) Celeste Holm
41. "Forever Walking Free" (9-3-51) Wendell Corey
42. "It's a Promise" (9-10-51) Laraine Day
43. "A Family Affair" (9-17-51) Roland Young, Lorna Lynn
44. "A Matter of Life" (9-24-51) Edmond O'Brien
45. "Grandma Was an Actress" (10-1-51) Josephine Hull
46. "Route Nineteen" (10-8-51) Dennis O'Keefe, Robert Stack, Vanessa Brown, Charlton Heston
47. "Cafe Ami" (10-15-51) Robert Preston, Maria Riva
48. "The Twinkle in Her Eye" (10-22-51) Diana Lynn, Dick Foran
49. "The Doctor's Wife" (10-29-51) June Lockhart
50. "Confession" (11-5-51) Thomas Mitchell
51. "No Will of His Own" (11-12-51) Gene Lockhart, Binnie Barnes
52. "Stolen Years" (11-19-51) Lola Albright, Richard Greene, Robert Sterling, Francis L. Sullivan
53. "Dames Are Poison" (11-26-51) Nina Foch, William Eythe
54. "Tin Badge" (12-3-51) Pat O'Brien
55. "Second Sight" (12-10-51) Celeste Holm
56. "The Blues Street" (12-17-51) Veronica Lake, Roddy McDowall
57. "A Child Is Born" [the Stephen Vincent Benét Christmas story; restaged] (12-24-51) Thomas Mitchell, Fay Bainter
58. "The Jest of Hahalaba" (12-31-51) Boris Karloff
59. "Mr. Finchley Versus the Bomb" [by Rod Serling; Fielder Cook directed] (1-7-52) Henry Hull, Arlene Francis, Roland Winters
60. "Ceylon Treasure" (1-14-52) Edmond O'Brien, Maria Riva
61. "The Sound of Breaking Waves" (1-21-52) Teresa Wright, Kent Smith
62. "For Heaven's Sake" (1-28-52) Jack Carson, June Lockhart
63. "Kelly" (2-4-52) Robert Preston, Geraldine Brooks
64. "The Game of Chess" [by Robert Howard Lindsay; subsequently restaged for the Kraft Theatre episode of 2/4/53] (2-11-52) Vincent Price
65. "Life, Liberty and Orrin Dooley" [subsequently restaged for the Ford Television Theatre episode of 10/2/52] (2-18-52) Jackie Cooper

66. "The Bargain" (2-25-52) Celeste Holm
67. "Night Be Quiet" (3-3-52) Sylvia Sidney
68. "The Promotion" (3-10-52) Thomas Mitchell, Anne Jackson
69. "The Foggy, Foggy Dew" (3-17-52) James Barton
70. "Julie" (3-24-52) Miriam Hopkins
71. "Taste" (3-31-52) Peter Lorre
72. "Hunt the Man Down" (4-7-52) Broderick Crawford, Carmen Mathews
73. "Decision" (4-14-52) Burgess Meredith
74. "Operation Week-End" (4-21-52) Angela Lansbury
75. "Salad Days" (4-28-52) Peggy Ann Garner, Roddy McDowall
76. "Masquerade" (5-5-52) Basil Rathbone
77. "Marriage Is the Beginning" (5-12-52) Diana Lynn
78. "Ferry Crisis at Friday Point" (5-19-52) Fredric March, Florence Eldridge, Henry Jones
79. "Pattern for Glory" (5-26-52) Robert Cummings, Sylvia Sidney
80. "Garneau '83" (6-2-52) Janet Beecher
81. "The Lesson" (6-9-52) Gene Raymond, Nancy Coleman, Geraldine Page
82. "Gilia" (6-16-52) Leueen MacGrath
83. "Welcome Home Lefty" (6-23-52) Chester Morris
84. "I Can't Remember" (6-30-52) Robert Alda
85. "Lady from Washington" (7-7-52) Constance Cummings
86. "Son Wanted" (7-14-52) Aina Niemela
87. "Brigadier" (7-21-52) Henry Hull
88. "Two Pale Horsemen" (7-28-52) Anthony Ross, Marian Winters
89. "Two Makes Four" (8-4-52) Lewis Scholle, Johnny Coleman
90. "The Orchard" (8-11-52) Geraldine Brooks, Peggy Ann Garner, Skip Homeier, Henry Jones
91. "You Be the Bad Guy" (8-18-52) Macdonald Carey

Third Season

92. "The Magnolia Touch" (8-25-52) Nina Foch, Donald Cook, John Newland
93. "The Return of Ulysses" (9-1-52) Sir Cedric Hardwicke
94. "Ile" [adapted from the Eugene O'Neill play] (9-8-52) Fay Bainter, Gene Lockhart
95. "Stone's Throw" (9-15-52) Angela Lansbury, Jeffrey Lynn
96. "Happily, But Not Forever" (9-22-52) June Lockhart, Robert Preston
97. "A Message for Janice" (9-29-52) Jackie Cooper, Grace Kelly
98. "Legacy of Love" (10-6-52) Corinne Calvet, Steven Hill
99. "The Country Lawyer" (10-20-52) Thomas Mitchell
100. "Three Hours Between Planes" (10-27-52) Lilli Palmer, Joseph Anthony
101. "The Face of Autumn" (11-3-52) Pat O'Brien, Tony Canzoneri
102. "Something to Celebrate" (11-10-52) Edward Arnold, Signe Hasso, Paul Lukas
103. "The Man Who Struck It Rich" (11-17-52) Barry Fitzgerald
104. "The Hill" (11-24-52) Mercedes McCambridge

105. "Amo, Amas, Amat" (12-1-52) Lizabeth Scott, Ralph Meeker
106. "Fear" (12-8-52) Boris Karloff, Gene Lockhart, Bramwell Fletcher
107. "Song for a Banjo" (12-15-52) Dick Haymes
108. "A Child Is Born" [the Stephen Vincent Benét Christmas story; restaged] (12-22-52) Gene Lockhart, Fay Bainter
109. "The Key" (12-29-52) Nina Foch
110. "Two for Tea" (1-5-53) Brian Aherne, Robert Helpmann, Glynis Johns
111. "Thanks for a Lovely Evening" (1-12-53) Art Carney, Veronica Lake, Jeffrey Lynn
112. "To Babette" (1-19-53) Corinne Calvet
113. "The Inn of the Eagles" (1-26-53) Macdonald Carey, Brian Keith
114. "The White Gown" (2-2-53) Margaret O'Brien, John Kerr
115. "Bouquet for Caroline" (2-9-53) Luise Rainer
116. "Miss Marlowe at Play" (2-16-53) Binnie Barnes, Basil Rathbone
117. "Autumn Nocturne" [by Ann Howard Bailey] (2-23-53) Viveca Lindfors, Robert Sterling
118. "A Time for Heroes" (3-2-53) Dennis O'Keefe
119. "One of Those Things" (3-9-53) Donald Cook, Nancy Guild
120. "The Wednesday Wish" (3-16-53) Josephine Hull
121. "One for the Road" (3-23-53) Pat O'Brien
122. "The Brooch" [adapted by William Faulkner from his own story] (4-2-53) Dan Duryea, Sally Forrest, Mildred Natwick
123. "With Glory and Honor" (4-9-53) Wendell Corey
124. "Measure of Greatness" (4-16-53) Arlene Francis
125. "Long Distance" (4-23-53) Miriam Hopkins
126. "The Ascent of Alfred Fisilkettle" (4-30-53) Robert Newton
127. "Listen, He's Proposing!" (5-7-53) Phyllis Kirk
128. "The Betrayer" (5-14-53) Robert Preston, Grace Kelly
129. "Tunnel Job" (5-21-53) Brian Donlevy
130. "Lost Sunday" (5-28-53) Celeste Holm
131. "Ten Days to Forever" (6-4-53) Barry Sullivan
132. "Make Believe Bride" (6-11-53) Lizabeth Scott, Don DeFore
133. "Wind on the Way" (6-18-53) Phyllis Thaxter
134. "This Is Jimmy Merrill" (6-25-53) Millard Mitchell, Madge Evans
135. "Force of Circumstance" [adapted from the William Somerset Maugham story] (7-2-53) Robert Alda, Lisa Ferraday
136. "Tango" (7-9-53) Joan Blondell, James Dunn
137. "The Corporal and the Lady" (7-16-53) Eddie Bracken, Gloria Marlowe
138. "A Man in the Kitchen" (7-23-53) William Lundigan
139. "The Odyssey of Jeffrey Sewell" (7-30-53) Dennis O'Keefe, Patrice Wymore
140. "Something to Live For" (8-6-53) Virginia Bruce, Otto Kruger
141. "The Lovely Day" (8-13-53) Robert Paige, Ann Sheridan, Tom Powers
142. "Women Who Wait" (8-20-53) Laraine Day, William Ching, Randy Stuart
143. "Some Call It Love" (8-27-53) Gene Raymond, Carole Mathews

144. "Message in a Bottle" (9-3-53) Ronald Reagan, Maureen O'Sullivan
145. "The Second Meeting" (9-10-53) Frank Lovejoy, Arlene Whelan
146. "Witness for the Prosecution" [adapted from the Agatha Christie mystery] (9-17-53) Edward G. Robinson
147. "Return to Alsace" (9-24-53) Scott Brady, Suzanne Dalbert
148. "Anniversary" (10-1-53) Phyllis Thaxter

Fourth Season

149. "The Moon for Linda" (10-8-53) Ruth Hussey, Barbara Lawrence
150. "Guilty Knowledge" (10-15-53) Stephen McNally, Frances Dee
151. "The Cruel Time" (10-22-53) Jean-Pierre Aumont, George Pascal, Nancy Gates
152. "The Return of Socko Renard" (10-29-53) Broderick Crawford
153. "Will Power" (11-5-53) Charles Coburn
154. "Lady of Suspicion" (11-12-53) Edmond O'Brien, Faith Domergue
155. "The Moment of the Rose" (11-19-53) Claude Dauphin, Patricia Morison
156. "Three Just Men" (12-10-53) Steve Cochran
157. "A Bouquet for Millie" (12-17-53) Marge and Gower Champion
158. "Call Off the Wedding" (1-7-54) Joanne Dru
159. "All Dressed in White" (1-14-54) Richard Carlson, Phyllis Kirk
160. "The Bachelor of Granby Oaks" (1-21-54) Macdonald Carey, Nancy Kelly
161. "A Place in the Sun" [adapted from the film scenario of Theodore Dreiser's An American Tragedy] (1-28-54) John Derek, Ann Blyth, Marilyn Erskine, Ronald Reagan
162. "The Small Glass Bottle" (2-4-54) Miriam Hopkins
163. "Shall Not Perish" [adapted by William Faulkner from his own short story; updated from the World War II setting to the Korean conflict] (2-11-54) Fay Bainter, Raymond Burr
164. "Final Round" (2-18-54) Wendell Corey, Martha Hyer
165. "Borrowed Wife" (2-25-54) Diana Lynn, Lee Bowman
166. "Miracle at the Waldorf" (3-4-54) Paul Lukas, Joan Weldon
167. "Call Me Mrs." (3-11-54) Laraine Day, Hugh Beaumont
168. "The Exposure of Michael O'Reilly" (3-18-54) Victor McLaglen, Vera Miles
169. "Spent in Silence" (3-25-54) Nancy Olsen
170. "The Way I Feel" (4-1-54) Margaret O'Brien, Michael Chafin
171. "Pick of the Litter" (4-8-54) William Talman, Joan Leslie, Bethel Leslie
172. "The Girl Who Couldn't Cry" (4-15-54) Gigi Perreau, Phyllis Thaxter
173. "Gavin's Darling" (4-22-54) Barbara Rush, Herbert Marshall
174. "Chair for a Lady" (4-29-54) Angela Lansbury, Paul Richards
175. "Two Dozen Roses" (5-6-54) Janet Gaynor, Frank Wilcox
176. "The Queen's English" (5-13-54) Ann Harding, Gene Lockhart
177. "Blind Fury" (5-20-54) Dean Jagger

178. "I'll Never Love Again" (5-27-54) Suzan Ball, Richard Long
179. "The Outside Witness" (6-3-54) William Bendix
180. "Waiting for Onorio" (6-10-54) J. Carrol Naish, Argentina Brunetti
181. "The Pretext" (6-17-54) Patricia Crowley, Wilton Graff
182. "Perished Leaves" (6-24-54) Faith Domergue, Anne Francis

Fifth Season [as hour series]

The Regulars: James Mason, host.

183. "To Each His Own" [adapted from the Charles Brackett film scenario] (8-26-54) Dorothy McGuire, James Mason
184. "Welcome Stranger" [adapted from the Frank Butler film scenario] (9-2-54) Bill Goodwin, J. M. Kerrigan, Martha Hyer
185. "Christmas in July" [adapted from the Preston Sturgess film scenario] (9-9-54) Nancy Gates, Alex Nicol, Raymond Walburn
186. "Hold Back the Dawn" [adapted from the Charles Brackett and Billy Wilder film scenario of the Ketti Frings novel] (9-16-54) Fernando Lamas, Toni Gerry, Robert Emmett Keane
187. "The Heiress" [adapted from the Ruth and Augustus Geotz film scenario which was adapted from their play] (9-23-54) Marilyn Erskine, Vincent Price
188. "Meet Jo Cathcart" (9-30-54) Virginia Bruce, Bruce Bennett
189. "The Mansion" (10-7-54) Zachary Scott
190. "A Visit from Evelyn" (10-14-54) Ann Harding, Lynn Bari, Jon Sheppod
191. "An Angel Went AWOL" (10-21-54) Joanne Dru, George Nader
192. "September Tide" [adapted from the Daphne du Maurier story] (10-28-54) Maureen O'Sullivan, John Sutton
193. "Imperfect Lady" [adapted from the Ladislas Fodor film scenario] (11-4-54) Patricia Medina
194. "Five Star Final" [adapted from the film scenario of the Louis Weitzenkorn play] (11-11-54) Edmond O'Brien, Joanne Woodward, Mae Clarke
195. "Captive City" [adapted from the Alvin M. Josephy Jr. film scenario] (11-18-54) Gig Young, Betsy Palmer
196. "A Medal for Benny" [adapted from the John Steinbeck and Jack Wagner film scenario] (11-25-54) J. Carol Naish, James Mason, Anne Brancroft
197. "Craig's Wife" [adapted from the film scenario of the George Kelly play] (12-2-54) Ruth Hussey
198. "Ladies in Retirement" [adapted from the film scenario of the Edward Percy and Reginald Denham play] (12-9-54) Claire Trevor, Elsa Lanchester, Isobel Elsom, Sean McClory
199. "Double Indemnity" [adapted from the Billy Wilder and Raymond Chandler film scenario of the James M. Cain novel] (12-16-54) Laraine Day, Frank Lovejoy
200. "September Affair" [adapted from the 1950 film scenario] (12-23-54) Arlene Dahl, John Howard
201. "The Chase" [adapted from the film scenario of Cornell Wool-

rich's The Black Path of Fear] (12-30-54) James Arness, Pat O'Brien, Ruth Roman

202. "Sunset Boulevard" [adapted from the Billy Wilder, Charles Brackett and D. M. Marshman Jr. film scenario] (1-6-55) Miriam Hopkins, James Daly, Nancy Gates

203. "Penny Serenade" [adapted from the film scenario of the Martha Cheavens short story] (1-13-55) Don Taylor, Phyllis Thaxter

204. "Love Letters" [adapted from Ayn Rand film scenario of the Chris Massie novel] (1-20-55) Diana Lynn, Dan O'Herlihy, Judith Evelyn

205. "So Evil My Love" [adapted from the film scenario of Joseph Shearing's For Her to See; after the drama, a film award is presented by Wade H. Nichols] (1-27-55) Marilyn Erskine, Louis Hayward

206. "One Foot in Heaven" [adapted from the film scenario of the Hartzell Spence novel] (2-3-55) Patsy Kelly, Ellen Drew, Hugh Marlowe

207. "A Bell for Adano" [adapted from the film scenario of the Paul Osborn play of John Hersey's novel] (2-10-55) Edmond O'Brien

208. "The Copperhead" (2-17-55) John Ireland, Betty Field

209. "So Dark the Night" [adapted from the Aubrey Wisberg film scenario] (2-24-55) Joseph Schildkraut

210. "Casablanca" [adapted from the Julius J. Epstein, Philip G. Epstein and Howard Koch film scenario] (3-3-55) Paul Douglas, Arlene Dahl, Hoagy Carmichael

211. "The Life of Emile Zola" [adapted from the Heinz Herald, Geza Herczeg, and Norman Reilly Raine film scenario] (3-10-55) Lee J. Cobb

212. "It Grows on Trees" [adapted from the film scenario of the Leonard Praskins and Barney Slater story] (3-17-55) Ruth Hussey, Robert Preston

213. "Shadow of a Doubt" [adapted from the Gordon McDonnell film scenario] (3-24-55) Frank Lovejoy, Barbara Rush

214. "My Name Is Julia Ross" [adapted from the film scenario of the Anthony Gilbert novel The Woman in Red] (3-31-55) Fay Bainter, Beverly Garland, Paul Richards

215. "The Browning Version" [adapted from the film scenario of the Terrence Rattigan play] (4-7-55) Herbert Marshall, Rod Taylor, Judith Evelyn, Robert Douglas

216. "No Sad Songs for Me" [adapted from the film scenario of the Ruth Southard novel] (4-14-55) Claire Trevor, William Hopper, Katharine Bard

217. "An Act of Murder" [adapted from the film scenario of the Ernest Lothar novel The Mills of God] (4-21-55) Ann Harding, Thomas Mitchell

218. "The Great McGinty" [adapted from the Preston Sturges film scenario] (4-28-55) Brian Donlevy, Thomas Gomez, Jessie White

219. "Remember the Night" [adapted from the Preston Sturges film scenario] (5-5-55) Jan Sterling, Dennis O'Keefe

220. "Eight Iron Men" [adapted from the film scenario of the Harry
        Brown novel A Sound of Hunting] (5-12-55) Alex Nicol,
        Paul Gilbert, Gene Reynolds
221. "Make Way for Tomorrow" [adapted from the film scenario
        of the Josephine Laurence novel The Years Are So Long]
        (5-19-55) Ernest Truex, Sylvia Field
222. "Thunder on the Hill" [adapted from the film scenario of the
        Charlotte Hastings novel Bonadventure] (5-26-55) Rex
        Reason, Phyllis Thaxter, Beverly Garland
223. "The Suspect" [adapted from the film scenario of the James
        Ronald novel This Way Out] (6-2-55) Robert Newton, Erin
        O'Brien-Moore
224. "Lightning Strikes Twice" [adapted from the film scenario of
        the Margaret Echard novel A Man Without Friends] (6-9-55)
        Tab Hunter, Dan O'Herlihy, Janet Blair
225. "Inside Story" [adapted from the Ernest Lehman and Geza
        Herczeg scenario] (6-16-55) James Barton, Vera Miles;
        Thomas Mitchell, program host.
226. "Forever Female" [adapted from the film scenario of the James
        M. Barrie play Rosalind] (6-23-55) Anita Louise, Anne
        Bancroft, Fred Clark

[now as SUMMER VIDEO THEATRE until new season]

227. "Last Year's Snow" [adapted from the Don Tracy novel] (6-
        30-55) Steve Brodie, Constance Ford, Paul Langton
228. "The Creaking Gate" [adapted from the mystery melodrama]
        (7-7-55) Philip Abbott, Beverly Garland
229. "Dark Tribute" (7-14-55) Rod Taylor, Robert Coote, Gage
        Clark
230. "Desperate Glory" [by Joseph Cochran] (7-21-55) Joe De
        Santis, Reba Waters
231. "The Bride Came C. O. D. " [adapted from the film scenario of
        the story by Kenneth Earl and M. M. Musselman] (7-28-55)
        Ron Randell, Joyce Holden
232. "The Nine-Penny Dream" [by Don M. Mankiewicz] (8-4-55)
        Lloyd Corrigan, Betty Sinclair, Lisa Daniels
233. "Perilous Deception" [by Catherine Turney] (8-11-55) Karen
        Katler, David Janssen, April Kent
234. "Nor All Your Tears" [by Frank Partos and Frank Waldman]
        (8-18-55) Arlene Whelan, Richard Shannon
235. "June Bride" [adapted from the film scenario of the Graeme
        Lorimer and Eileen Tighe play] (8-25-55) Marguerite
        Chapman, Jerome Thor
236. "The Last Confession" [adapted from an article by Rene Bel-
        benoit, on French priest Father Pierre's twenty-three year
        stay on Devil's Island] (9-1-55) Eduard Franz, Steve Colt
237. "The Happy Man" [by Rafael Hayes] (9-8-55) Kurt Kasznar,
        Judith Evelyn, Marilyn Erskine, Robert Emhardt; Otto Kru-
        ger, program host.
238. "The Lucky Finger" [by Lennox Robinson] (9-15-55) Edith
        Barrett, Alan Napier, J. Pat O'Malley

239. "The Eyes of Father Tomasino" [by Edwin Blum] (9-22-55) Keefe Brasselle, Gloria Talbot, Joe De Santis

Sixth Season

240. "The Enchanted Cottage" [adapted from the film scenario of the Arthur Wing Pinero play] (9-29-55) Dan O'Herlihy, Teresa Wright
241. "The Amazing Mrs. Halliday" [adapted from the Sonya Levien film scenario] (10-6-55) Barbara Rush, Grant Williams
242. "The Two Dollar Bettor" (10-13-55) Gene Lockhart, Karen Sharpe, Peter Hansen, King Donovan, Diane Jergens, Barney Phillips
243. "The Human Jungle" [adapted from the William Sackheim film scenario] (10-20-55) Dennis O'Keefe, Joan Vohs
244. "The Lady Gambles" [adapted from the Louis Meltzer and Oscar Saul film scenario] (10-27-55) Martha Hyer, Lyle Bettger
245. "Appointment for Love" [adapted from the Ladislaus Bus Fekete film scenario] (11-3-55) Julie Adams, Cesar Romero
246. "Bedtime Story" [adapted from the Horace Jackson and Grant Garrett film scenario] (11-10-55) Gene Raymond, Marguerite Chapman
247. "The Hunted" [by Sandy Barnett] (11-17-55) Richard Boone, Helen Westcott
248. "Miss Susie Slagle's" [adapted from the film scenario of the Augusta Tucker novel] (11-24-55) Dorothy Gish, Virginia Gibson, Craig Hill, Gerald Charlesboise
249. "The Web" [adapted from the Harry Kurnitz film scenario] (12-1-55) Raymond Burr, Arlene Whelan, Ray Danton
250. "Suspicion" [adapted from the Samson Raphealson scenario of the Francis Iles novel Before the Fact] (12-8-55) Kim Hunter, Louis Hayward, Melville Cooper
251. "Branded" [adapted from the Sydney Boehm and Cyril Hume film scenario of the Evan Evans novel Montana Rides Again] (12-15-55) Brian Keith, Jay C. Flippen, Josephine Hutchinson
252. "Holiday Affair" [adapted from the film scenario of the John D. Weaver novel Christmas Gift] (12-22-55) Phyllis Thaxter, Scott Brady, Robert Hutton, Chris Olsen
253. "Cover Up" [adapted from the 1948 film scenario] (12-29-55) William Bendix (repeating his film role), Jane Howard
254. "Hands Across the Table" [adapted from the film scenario of the Vina Delmar novel Bracelets] (1-5-56) Anne Jeffreys, Robert Sterling
255. "The Unfaithful" [adapted from the 1947 film scenario which was inspired by William Somerset Maugham's The Letter] (1-12-56) Jan Sterling
256. "Ivy" [adapted from the film scenario of the Marie Adelaide Loundes novel Story of Ivy] (1-19-56) Martha Hyer
257. "Witness to Murder" [adapted from the Chester Erskine film scenario] (1-26-56) Paul Langton, Audrey Totter, Onslow Stevens
258. "The Green Promise" [adapted from the Monty F. Collins film scenario] (2-2-56) James Barton, Jean Howell

259. "The Star" [adapted from the Katherine Albert and Dale Eunson film scenario] (2-9-56) William Hopper, Mary Astor
260. "Night Song" [adapted from the Dick Irving Hyland film scenario] (2-16-56) Barbara Rush, Richard Contino
261. "Hired Way" [adapted from the Alma Sioux Scarberry film scenario] (2-23-56) Anne Bancroft, Lex Barker
262. "Here Comes the Groom" [adapted from the Virginia Van Upp, Liam O'Brien and Myles Connolly film scenario of the Robert Riskin and Liam O'Brien story] (3-1-56) Robert Sterling, Patricia Crowley, Steve Dunne
263. "Criminal Code" [adapted from the film scenario of the Martin Flavin Broadway play] (3-8-56) Dewey Martin
264. "Little Boy Lost" [adapted from the film scenario of the Marghanita Laski novel] (3-15-56) Dennis O'Keefe, Carl Esmond
265. "The Steel Trap" [adapted by S. H. Barnett from the Andrew Stone film scenario] (3-22-56) Howard Duff
266. "It Started with Eve" [adapted from the Hans Kraly film scenario] (3-29-56) David Janssen, Joan Weldon, Thomas Mitchell
267. "Tabloid" (4-5-56) Scott Brady, Karen Sharpe, Anthony Caruso
268. "Temptation" [adapted from the film scenario of the Robert Smythe Hichens novel Bella Donna] (4-12-56) Sarah Churchill
269. "I Married a Stranger" [adapted from the film scenario of the Thorne Smith novel] (4-19-56) Patrick O'Neal, Marilyn Erskine, Robert Horton
270. "Impact" [adapted from the 1949 film scenario] (4-26-56) Brian Donlevy (repeating his film role)
271. "Has Anybody Seen My Gal?" [adapted from the Eleanor H. Porter film scenario] (5-3-56) Gene Lockhart
272. "The Night of January Sixteenth" [adapted from the film scenario of the Ayn Rand play] (5-10-56) Phyllis Thaxter
273. "Princess O'Rourke" [adapted from the Norman Krasna film scenario] (5-17-56) Diana Lynn
274. "Millie's Daughter" [adapted from the film scenario of the Donald Henderson Clarke novel] (5-24-56) June Havoc
275. "Indiscreet" [adapted from the film scenario of the Norman Krasna play Kind Sir] (5-31-56) Margaret Lindsay
276. "She Married Her Boss" [adapted from the Thyra Samter Winslow film scenario] (6-7-56) Jan Sterling, Patric Knowles

[now as SUMMER VIDEO THEATRE until new season]

277. "A House of His Own" (6-14-56) Richard Boone
278. "The Corrigan Case" [adapted from the Laurence Riley stage play] (6-21-56) Anne Bancroft, Steve Brodie, Frances Bavier
279. "A Yankee Cousin" (6-28-56) Kurt Kasznar
280. "A Marriage Day" [by Merle Miller] (7-5-56) Marilyn Erskine, Ray Collins, Cloris Leachman, Andrew Duggan
281. "Sting in the Tail" (7-12-56) Vincent Price, Mabel Albertson, Ellen Corby
282. "No One To Cry With" (7-19-56) Marguerite Chapman, Constance Ford, John Betley

283. "Miss Mabel" [adapted by Harry Kronman from the R. C. Sheriff play] (7-26-56) Elsa Lanchester, Irene Anders, Frederic Worlock; Ken Carpenter, program host
284. "The Quick and the Dead" (8-2-56) James Whitmore, Ray Danton
285. "Rebuke Me Not" [by Herbert Abbott Spiro] (8-9-56) Jan Sterling, Forrest Tucker
286. "The Wayward Saint" [adapted from the Paul Vincent Carroll play] (8-30-56) Roland Winters, Liam Redmond, Ann B. Davis, Sallie Brophy
287. "Road of Fear" [by Thomas Patrick Cullinan] (9-6-56) Scott Brady, Catherine McLeod, Johnny Crawford, Jimmy Baird
288. "The Top Rung" [by Reuben Bercovitch] (9-13-56) Lee Bowman, Irene Hervey, William Hopper

Seventh Season

289. "Mildred Pierce" [adapted from the Ranald MacDougall and Catherine Turney film scenario of the James M. Cain novel] (9-20-56) Virginia Bruce, Zachary Scott (repeating his film role), Patric Knowles
290. "Only Yesterday" [adapted from the film scenario of the Frederick Lewis Allen novel] (9-27-56) Joan Caulfield, Richard Eyer, Don Taylor
291. "Now, Voyager" [adapted from the Casey Robinson film scenario of the Olive Higgins Prouty novel] (10-4-56) Laraine Day, Herbert Marshall, Richard Carlson
292. "The Guilty" [adapted from the film scenario of the Cornell Woolrich novel Two Men in a Furnished Room] (10-11-56) Ralph Meeker, Skip Homeier, Carol Ohmart
293. "Flamingo Road" [adapted from the film scenario of the Robert and Sally Wilder novel] (10-18-56) Raymond Burr, Joanne Dru, Robert Middleton
294. "Because of You" [adapted from the Thelma Robinson film scenario] (10-25-56) Vera Miles, John Benteley, Irene Hervey, Sandy Descher
295. "You Can't Escape Forever" [adapted from the film scenario of Roy Chanslor's Hi Nellie] (11-1-56) Don DeFore, Virginia Gregg
296. "Jezebel" [adapted by Catherine Turney from the Clements Ripley, Aben Finkel and John Huston film scenario of the Owen Davis play] (11-8-56) Martha Hyer
297. "The Glass Web" [adapted from the film scenario of Max Simon Ehrlich's Spin the Glass Web] (11-15-56) George Nader
298. "The Gay Sisters" [adapted from the film scenario of the Stephen Longstreet novel] (11-22-56) Alexis Smith, Helen Westcott, Tim Hovey, Karen Steele
299. "Old Acquaintance" [adapted from the film scenario of the John Van Druten play] (11-29-56) Ruth Hussey, Lynn Bari, Joan Evans
300. "Christmas in Connecticut" [adapted from the Lionel Houser and Adele Commandini film scenario of the Aileen Hamilton story] (12-13-56) Mona Freeman

301. "Hollywood's Musical Holiday Revue" (12-20-56) Gordon Mac-Rae, Shirley Jones, Nelson Eddy, Jeanette MacDonald
302. "Michael and Mary" [adapted from the film scenario of the A. A. Milne play] (12-27-56) Maureen O'Sullivan
303. "It Happened on Fifth Avenue" [adapted from the Herbert Clyde Lewis and Frederick Stephani film scenario] (1-3-57) Gene Lockhart, Ernest Truex, Leon Ames, Diane Jergens, William Campbell
304. "Just Across the Street" [adapted from the Roswell Rogers and Joe Malone film scenario] (1-10-57) Julie Adams, Jack Kelly, Cecil Kellaway; Gordon MacRae, host
305. "To Have and Have Not" [adapted by Sanford Barnett from the Jules Furthman and William Faulkner film scenario of the Ernest Hemingway novel] (1-17-57) Edmond O'Brien
306. "Vice Squad" [adapted from the film scenario of the Leslie T. White novel] (1-24-57) Pat O'Brien
307. "One Sunday Afternoon" [adapted from the film scenario of the James Hagan play] (1-31-57) Peter Lind Hayes, Mary Healy, Gordon MacRae, Sheila MacRae
308. "The Undesirable" (2-7-57) Vivian Blaine, Richard Denning
309. "Dark Victory" [adapted from the Casey Robinson film scenario of the George Emerson Brewer and Bertram Bloch play] (2-14-57) Shirley Jones, Jack Cassidy
310. "One Way Street" [adapted from the Lawrence Kimble film scenario] (2-21-57) George Nader, Nancy Gates
311. "Possessed" [adapted from the film scenario of the Edgar Selwyn play] (2-28-57) Laraine Day, Brian Keith
312. "One Way Passage" [adapted from the Wilson Mizer and Joseph Jackson film scenario of the Robert Lord story] (3-7-57) Barry Sullivan, Bonita Granville, Barton MacLane
313. "Eileen" [adapted from the Victor Herbert musical comedy] (3-14-57) Gordon MacRae, Wendy Martin, Patricia Morison
314. "The Great Lie" [adapted from the film scenario of the Polan Banks novel Far Horizon] (3-21-57) Jan Sterling, Catherine McLeod, Glenn Langan
315. "The Black Angel" [adapted from the film scenario of the Cornell Woolrich story] (3-28-57) Marilyn Erskine, John Ireland, Anne Bancroft
316. "Adam Had Four Sons" [adapted from the film scenario of the Charles Bonner novel Legacy] (4-4-57) Leon Ames, Valentina Cortesa
317. "The Taggart Light" (4-18-57) John McIntire, Vera Miles, Roger Moore
318. "The Man Who Played God" [adapted from the film scenario of the Jules E. Goodman play which was based upon the Governeur Morris short story] (4-25-57) Boris Karloff, Mary Astor, June Lockhart
319. "The Hard Way" [adapted from the Daniel Fuchs and Peter Viertel film scenario of the Jerry Wald story] (5-2-57) Ann Sheridan, Nancy Gates

[now as SUMMER VIDEO THEATRE until new season]

The Regulars: Ken Carpenter, host.

320. "Stand-In for Murder" (5-9-57) Dewey Martin
321. "Death Do Us Part" (5-16-57) Alexis Smith, Kent Smith
322. "The Armed Venus" [by Richard McDonagh and William Stuart] (5-23-57) Steve Forrest, Peter Graves, Esther Williams
323. "Paris Calling" [adapted from the John S. Toldy and Benjamin Glazer film scenario] (5-30-57) Joanne Dru, Grant Williams
324. "Payment in Kind" (6-6-57) Ruth Hussey
325. "Design for November" (6-13-57) Julie Adams
326. "Edge of Doubt" (6-20-57) Philip Carey, Kathleen Crowley
327. "The Latch Key" [adapted by Paul Franklin from the Ronald Mitchell story] (6-27-57) Janis Paige, Michael Connors
328. "Who Is Picasso?" [by Louis Pelletier] (7-4-57) Marilyn Erskine, Hugh Marlowe, Steve Dunne, K. T. Stevens
329. "The Softest Music" [by Robert Presnell Jr.] (7-11-57) Forrest Tucker, Peggy McKay
330. "Summer Return" [by Anne Howard Bailey] (7-18-57) Kent Smith, Joan Evans
331. "High Tension" [adapted from the J. Robert Bren and Norman Houston film scenario] (7-25-57) John Howard
332. "Dark Hammock" (8-1-57) Barton MacLane, Frances Reid, Jack Carson, Mary Wickes
333. "Barren Harvest" (8-8-57)
334. "Judge Not" (8-15-57) Alan Mowbray, Lloyd Corrigan, Audrey Dalton, Rex Evans
335. "Diagnosis--Homicide" (8-22-57) Craig Stevens
336. "Old Witch, Old Witch" (9-5-57) Margalo Gillmore, Maury Hill
337. "The Last Act" (9-12-57) Jack Cassidy, Lilia Skala, Liam Sullivan, Veola Vienn

Eighth Season [as half hour series LUX PLAYHOUSE and alternating with the SCHLITZ PLAYHOUSE OF THE STARS]

338. "The Best House in the Valley" (10-3-58) Polly Bergen, Rod Taylor
339. "The Four" (10-17-58) Anne Baxter
340. "The Connoisseur" (10-31-58) Michael Rennie, Barbara Rush, John Maxwell
341. "A Game of Hate" (11-14-58) Kathryn Grayson, Tom Laughlin
342. "Coney Island Winter" (11-28-58) Edmond O'Brien, Kathleen Crowley
343. "Drive a Desert Road" (12-12-58) Barry Nelson, Audrey Totter
344. "A Deadly Guest" (1-9-59) Philip Carey, Jane Wyman
345. "Deathtrap" (2-6-59) Virginia Mayo, James Gregory
346. "Various Temptations" (2-20-59) Hurd Hatfield, Ida Lupino
347. "Stand-In for Murder" (3-6-59) Jan Sterling
348. "Frederick" (3-20-59) Regis Toomey, Phyllis Thaxter
349. "The Dreamer" (4-3-59) John Cassavetes
350. "This Will Do Nicely" (4-17-59) Zsa Zsa Gabor, Richard Haydn

351. "The Case of the Two Sisters" (5-1-59) Michael Wilding, Fred Clark, Phyllis Coates
352. "Boy on a Fence" (5-15-59) Richard Eyer, Diana Lynn
353. "Mirror, Mirror" (5-29-59) Anne Jeffreys
354. "The Miss and Missiles" (6-12-59) Gisele MacKenzie, John Forsythe

MUSICAL COMEDY TIME

The Episodes:

1. "Anything Goes" [adapted from the 1934 Broadway musical; book by Guy Bolton, P. G. Wodehouse, Howard Lindsay and Russel Crouse; music and lyrics by Cole Porter] (10-2-50) Martha Raye, John Conte, Billy Lynn
2. "Whoopee" [adapted from the 1928 Broadway musical; book by William A. McGuire from a play by Owen Davis; lyrics by Gus Kahn and music by Walter Donaldson] (10-16-50) Johnny Morgan, Nancy Walker, Beverly Tyler
3. "The Chocolate Soldier" [adapted from the 1909 Broadway musical; book and lyrics by Rudolph Bernauer and Leopold Jacobson from George Bernard Shaw's Arms and the Man; music by Oscar Straus] (10-30-50) Mimi Benzell, Wilbur Evans, Billy Gilbert
4. "Rio Rita" [adapted from the 1927 Broadway musical; book by Guy Bolton and Fred Thompson; lyrics by Joseph McCarthy and music by Harry Tierney] (11-13-50) Patricia Morison (as Rio Rita), Bert Wheeler (repeating his Chuck Bean role), John Tyers (as ranger Jim), Hal LeRoy, Donald Buka
5. "The Merry Widow" [adapted from the 1907 Broadway musical; book by Victor Leon and Leo Stein; music by Franz Lehar and lyrics by Adrian Ross] (11-27-50) Irra Retina, Wilbur Evans, Melville Cooper
6. "Hit the Deck" [adapted from the 1927 Broadway musical; book by Herbert Fields as based on the Hubert Osborne play; lyrics by Leo Rolun and Clifford Grey; music by Vincent Youmans] (12-11-50) John Beal, Iva Withers, Jack Gilford
7. "Babes in Toyland" [adapted from the 1903 Broadway musical; music by Victor Herbert; book and lyrics by Glen MacDonough] (12-25-50) Robert Weade (as Santa Claus and The Toymaker), Dennis King (as Dr. Electron), Edith Fellows (as Jane), Dorothy Jarnac, Robert Dixon, Gil Lamb
8. "Miss Liberty" [adapted from the 1949 Broadway musical; book by Moss Hart and Robert Emmett Sherwood; music and lyrics by Irving Berlin] (1-8-51) Kenny Baker, Carol Bruce, Doretta Morrow, Gloria De Haven
9. "Louisiana Purchase" [adapted from the 1940 Broadway musical; book by Morrie Ryskind; music and lyrics by Irving Berlin] (1-22-51) Victor Moore (repeating his role as Oliver P. Loganberry), Irene Bordoni (repeating her role as Madame Bordelaise)

10. "Mademoiselle Modiste" [adapted from the 1905 Broadway musical; book and lyrics by Henry Blossom; music by Victor Herbert] (2-5-51) Fritzi Scheff (whose initial role was Fifi), Marguerite Piazza, Brian Sullivan, Frank McHugh
11. "Revenge with Music" [adapted from the 1934 Broadway musical; book and lyrics by Howard Dietz; music by Arthur Schwartz] (2-19-51) Anne Jeffreys, Billy Gilbert, John Raitt, Audrey Christie
12. "No! No! Nanette!" [adapted from the 1925 Broadway musical; book by Otto Harbach and Frank Mandel; music by Vincent Youmans; lyrics by Irving Caesar and Otto Harbach] (3-5-51) Ann Crowley, Danny Schall, Jackie Gleason, Ruth Matteson
13. "Flying High" [adapted from the 1930 Broadway musical; book by Lew Brown; music by Ray Henderson and lyrics by B. G. DeSylva] (3-19-51) Bert Lahr (repeating his role as "Rusty" Krause)

SURE AS FATE

The Regulars: Francis L. Sullivan, host.

The Episodes:

1. "Nightfall" (9-5-50) John McQuade
2. "Child's Play" (9-12-50) Victor Jory, Robert Lantin
3. "Run from the Sun" (9-19-50) Robert Cummings, Jean Gillespie
4. "Mary Had a Little Lad" (9-26-50) Felicia Montealegre, Douglas Watson
5. "Beyond Reason" (10-3-50) Haila Stoddard, Joseph Boland, Peggy French
6. "The Vanishing Lady" (10-17-50) Kim Stanley, Jeff Morrow
7. "Three Blind Mice" (10-31-50) John McQuade
8. "Ten Days to Spring" (11-14-50) Sara Anderson, Theodore Newton
9. "The Dancing Doll" (11-28-50) Arlene Francis, John Newland, Haila Stoddard, James Nolan
10. "Nightfall" (12-12-50) Chester Stratton, E. G. Marshall, Augusta Dabney
11. "Tremolo" (12-26-50) John McQuade, Luella Gear, Mary Patton
12. "Macbeth" [a modern dress adaptation of the Shakespeare classic] (1-9-51) John Carradine, Judith Evelyn
13. "Distinguished Gathering" (1-23-51)
14. "The Devil Takes a Bride" (2-6-51) Leslie Nielsen, Lawrence Fletcher
15. "The Rabbit" (2-28-51) Martin Brooks, Maria Riva
16. "One in a Million" (3-6-51) Joseph Schildkraut
17. "Errand for Noonan" (3-20-51) Jerome Thor, Dickie Moore, Teddy Wilson

18. "The Guinea Pigs" (4-3-51) Marsha Hunt, Dane Clark; Mrs. Alben W. Barkley and Douglas Fairbanks Jr., guests.

DANGER

Episodes under the supervision of Yul Brynner and Sidney Lumet; Sheldon Reynolds directed some segments.

The Episodes:

1. "August Heat" [adapted from the W. F. Harvey story] (9-26-50) Alfred Ryder
2. "The Fearful One" [adapted from the Saki story] (10-3-50) Iris Mann, Nan McFarland, John Shellie
3. "Dressing Up" (10-10-50) Lee Grant
4. "The Green and Gold String" (10-17-50) Lee Tracy
5. "See No Evil" (10-24-50) Leo Penn, Nancy Franklin
6. "The Liquor Glass" (10-31-50) Fay Bainter
7. "Witness for the Prosecution" [adapted from the Agatha Christie mystery] (11-7-50) Sarah Churchill
8. "The Man in the Cage" (11-14-50) Joseph Anthony
9. "Borderline Affair" (11-21-50) Iris Mann
10. "Taste of Ashes" (11-28-50) Rod Steiger, Mary Patton, Joseph Anthony, Sydna Scott
11. "Another Man's Poison" (12-5-50) John Newland
12. "The Hungry Woman" (12-12-50) Marsha Hunt
13. "The Sergeant and the Doll" (12-19-50) Laura Weber, James Westerfield
14. "Surprise for the Boys" (12-26-50) Henry Burke Jones, John McGovern, Joseph Julian
15. "Charles Markham, Antique Dealer" (1-2-51) Jerome Thor
16. "Footfalls" (1-9-51) Walter Slezak, Henry Jones
17. "Appointment with Death" (1-16-51) Dean Harens, Jerome Thor
18. "The Ghost Is Your Heart" (1-23-51) Frank Albertson
19. "The Anniversary" (1-30-51) Kim Stanley
20. "Ask Me Another" (2-6-51) Wally Cox, Philip Leeds
21. "The Net Draws Tight" (2-13-51) E. G. Marshall, Wright King
22. "The Corpse and Tighe O'Kane" (2-20-51) J. Pat O'Malley, Don Hanmer
23. "Will You Walk into My Parlor?" (2-27-51) Geraldine Brooke, Joseph Anthony, Lawrence Hugo
24. "The Night of March Fifteenth" (3-6-51) Tom Ewell
25. "Mr. John Nobody" (3-13-51) David Opatoshu
26. "Nightmare" (3-20-51) Dane Clark, Tony Mottola
27. "Head Print" (3-27-51) Leo G. Carroll
28. "The Undefeated" (4-3-51) Walter Slezak
29. "The Undertaker Calls" (4-10-51) Chester Morris
30. "The Great Gilson Bequest" (4-17-51) Franchot Tone
31. "Blue" (4-24-51) Anthony Quinn, Coleen Gray
32. "The Killer Scarf" (5-1-51) Anne Marno, Greg Morton

33. "The Eye Witness Who Couldn't See" (5-8-51) June Dayton, John Sylvester
34. "The Mirror" (5-15-51) Judith Evelyn
35. "A Clear Case of Suicide" (5-22-51) John Forsythe, Joan Bennett
36. "The Trumpet of Doom" (5-29-51) Bobby Sherwood, Maria Riva, Teddy Wilson
37. "The Fatal Step" (6-5-51) Ann Shephard, Paul Mann, Anne Jackson, Mickey Knox, Sylvia Davis
38. "Operation Murder" (6-12-51) Maria Riva, Jerome Thor
39. "The Knave of Diamonds" (6-19-51) Walter Slezak, Roger De Koven
40. "Marley's Ghost" (6-26-51) Joseph Anthony, Rita Gam
41. "The Paper Box Kid" [by Mark Hellinger] (7-3-51) Martin Ritt
42. "Criminal at Large" [adapted from the Edgar Wallace mystery] (7-10-51) Bobby Santon, George Matthews
43. "Mr. Lupescu" (7-17-51)
44. "Sparrow Cup" (7-24-51) Jack Lemmon, Robin Morse
45. "Death Gambles" (7-31-51) Henry Jones, Frieda Altman
46. "Goodbye, Hannah" (8-7-51) Paul Langton, John Randolph
47. "Murderer's Face" (8-14-51) Robert Pastene, Ann Marno
48. "Motive for Murder" (8-21-51) Richard Kiley, Judy Parrish
49. "Mad Man of Midville" (8-28-51) Walter Slezak, Everett Sloane
50. "Death Among the Relics" (9-4-51) Joey Walsh, Edward Binns
51. "In the La Banza" (9-11-51) Jack Warden

Second Season

52. "The Fourth Confession" (9-18-51) Harold Vermilyea, Stephen Elliott
53. "Love Comes to Miss Lucy" (9-25-51) Maria Riva
54. "Free Zoo" (10-2-51) Gene Lyons, Judy Parrish
55. "Sleep and Tell" (10-9-51) Maria Riva, Marc Kramer, Paul Langton
56. "Inherit Murder" (10-16-51) Anthony Ross, Paul Langton, Rita Gam
57. "Final Rejection" (10-23-51) Ernest Truex
58. "Deadline" (10-30-51) Richard Kiley, Joseph Anthony
59. "High Wire, High Steel" (11-6-51) James Westerfield, Steven Hill
60. "Death Beat" (11-13-51)
61. "The Killer Instinct" (11-20-51) Martin Ritt
62. "The Friend Who Killed" (11-27-51)
63. "The Captain Has Bad Dreams" (12-4-51) Joseph Anthony
64. "The Face of Fear" (12-11-51)
65. "The Lady on the Rock" (12-18-51) Don Hanmer, Olive Deering
66. "Passage for Christmas" (12-25-51) Mary Sinclair, Joseph Anthony
67. "Love Trap" (1-1-52) Jayne Meadows
68. "Fresh as a Daisy" (1-8-52) Ben Gazzara
69. "The Intruders" (1-15-52) Eileen Heckart, Edmond Ryan
70. "The Business Affairs of Gentlemen" (1-22-52) Alan Webb, Chester Stratton, Betty Sinclair

71. "Windfall" (1-29-52) Joshua Shelley, Lou Gilbert
72. "Prelude to Death" (2-5-52) Grace Kelly, Carmen Mathews
73. "The Hands of the Enemy" (2-12-52) Richard Kiley
74. "Primary Decision" (2-19-52) Robert Pastene
75. "You're Wanted on the Phone, Al" (2-26-52) Don Dammer
76. "Benefit Performance" (3-4-52) Monty Ritt, Joshua Shelley
77. "Tattoo of Terror" (3-11-52)
78. "The Way of Freedom" (3-18-52) Polly Rowles, E. G. Marshall
79. "The Hero" (3-25-52) Steven Hill
80. "The Escape Artist" (4-1-52) Cloris Leachman, John Conte
81. "The Black Tie" (4-8-52) Leo Penn
82. "Cornbelt Kid" (4-15-52) Joshua Shelley, Eddie Binns
83. "Hello, Mr. Lutz" (4-22-52) Maria Riva, Martin Ritt
84. "Border Incident" (4-29-52) Paul Langton
85. "Dark As Night" (5-6-52) Lee Grant
86. "The Strong Finish" (5-13-52) Gene Reynolds, Philip Pine
87. "A Buck Is a Buck" (5-20-52) Walter Matthau
88. "The Gold Watch" (5-27-52) Sylvia Davis, Terry Becker
89. "The Paper Box Kid" [repeat of episode of 7/3/51] (6-3-52) Martin Ritt
90. "The System" (6-10-52) Kim Stanley
91. "Death Amond the Relics" [repeat of episode of 9/4/51] (6-17-52) Joey Walsh, Edward Binns
92. "Death for the Lonely" (6-24-52) Lee Grant, Richard Kiley, Howard Wierum
93. "The Double Deal" (7-1-52) James Daly, Neva Patterson
94. "The Net Draws Tight" [restaged from 2/13/51] (7-15-52) Whit Bissell
95. "A Date at Midnight" (7-29-52) Joshua Shelley, Cloris Leachman
96. "Murder Takes the 'A' Train" (8-5-52)
97. "Flowers of Death" (8-12-52) Don Murray, Stella Andrew
98. "Pickup" (8-19-52)
99. "The Face of Fear" [restaged from 12/11/51] (8-26-52) Lee Grant, Sidney Lumet
100. "Backfire" (9-2-52)
101. [unknown title] (9-9-52)
102. "Death Signs an Autograph" (9-16-52) Richard Kiley, Robin Morgan
103. "Change Up" (9-30-52) Edward Binns
104. "The Thread of Scarlett" (10-7-52) Darren McGavin, Bramwell Fletcher, Carmen Mathews, Philip Bourneuf

Third Season

105. "Buttons" (10-14-52) Mildred Natwick
106. "The Pay-Off Girl" (10-21-52)
107. "Club Date" (10-23-52) Hildy Parks
108. "The Fix" (11-11-52) John Forsythe
109. "The Hanging Judge" (11-18-52) Walter Slezak, Thomas Chalmers
110. "Boomerang" (11-25-52) Leslie Nielsen

111. "King of the Cons" (12-2-52)
112. "The Gunman" (12-9-52) John Baragrey
113. "The Next Stop Death" (12-16-52) Richard Kiley
114. "The Man Who Tried to Kill Christmas" (12-23-52)
115. "Death Pulls the Strings" (12-30-52) Chester Morris, Bill Baird
116. "Death in a Penthouse" (1-6-53)
117. "A Shawl for Sylvia" (1-13-53)
118. "Honestly, It's the Best Policy" (1-20-53)
119. "Stand-In for Danger" (1-27-53)
120. "Footfalls" [restaged from 1/9/51] (2-3-53) Walter Slezak
121. "The Second Cup" (2-10-53) James Westerfield, Irene Vernon
122. "Said the Spider to the Fly" (2-17-53) Jack Palance
123. "Cage a Killer" (2-24-53)
124. "Mortal Enemy" (3-3-53)
125. "Diego" (3-10-53) Joey Walsh
126. "Words Fail Me" (3-17-53)
127. "Car Pool" (3-24-53) William Prince, Hildy Parks, Richard MacMurray
128. "Inside Straight" (3-31-53) Veronica Lake
129. "Family Jewels" (4-7-53) Gary Merrill
130. "No Room" (4-14-53) James Dean, Kate Smith, Irene Vernon, Martin Kingsley
131. "Hand Me Down" (4-21-53) Nina Foch, Walter Matthau
132. "Sing for Your Life" (4-28-53) Johnny Desmond
133. "Last Stop Before Albany" (5-5-53) Constance Ford, James Gregory, James Broderick
134. "Squeeze Play" (5-12-53) John Baragrey, Shepperd Strudwick, Georgiann Johnson
135. "Jam Session" (5-19-53) John Connell, Constance Ford, Frank Albertson
136. "Subpoena" [by Jeremy Daniel] (5-26-53) Eddie Albert, Hildy Parks
137. "Return Flight" (6-2-53) Edward Binns, Augusta Dabney, Karen Preiss
138. "Borrowed Furs" (6-9-53) Broderick Crawford, Hildy Parks
139. "Circus Story" (6-16-53) Reba Tassell, Joseph Wiseman
140. "Operation Nightmare" (6-23-53) John Kerr, Beverly Dannis, Russell Collins
141. "Surface Tension" (6-30-53) Constance Ford, James Gregory
142. "Windy" (7-7-53) Rod Steiger
143. "Prodigal Returns" (7-14-53) Polly Rowles, Leo Penn, Alan Morgan
144. "Trial By Jungle" (7-21-53) Richard Kiley, William Prince, Henry Hull
145. "Missing Night" (7-28-53) Leslie Nielsen, Norma Connolly
146. "I'll Be Waiting" (8-4-53) Art Carney, Dorothy Hart
147. "Cokkle's Tour" (8-11-53) Jackie Miles, Jim Nolan, Leonard Bell, Ziska Coles
148. "Letter of Thanks" (8-18-53) Kevin McCarthy, Ed Begley, Henriette Moore
149. "Death Is My Neighborhood" (8-25-53) James Dean, Walter Hampden, Betsy Palmer

150. "The Innocent and the Guilty" (9-1-53) Jerome Thor, Lili Darvas
151. "The Boys on the Corner" (9-8-53) Robert Preston, John Cornell, Madeleine Sherwood
152. "Five Minutes to Die" (9-15-53) Steve Allen, Jayne Meadows

Fourth Season

153. "Once Over Lightly" (9-29-53) Joe Maross, Christie White, Charles Mendrick
154. "Help Wanted" (10-6-53) Arthur Franz, Georgiann Johnson
155. "But the Patient Died" (10-13-53) Gene Lockhart
156. "Father of the Man" (10-20-53) Dan Morgan, Perry Wilson
157. "Blackmail" (10-27-53) Warren Stevens
158. "Face of a Stranger" (11-3-53) Don Dubbins, Dick Robbins
159. "Flamingo" [by Steve Allen] (11-10-53) Steve Allen, Jayne Meadows
160. "The Educated Heart" (11-17-53) Basil Rathbone, Margaret Phillips
161. "Towerman" (11-24-53) Jackie Cooper, Chester Morris
162. "The Man with the Gun" [Part I] (12-1-53)
163. "The Man with the Gun" [Part II] (12-8-53)
164. "The Christmas Present" (12-15-53) Joseph Walsh, Andrew Duggan
165. "Prelude to Death" (12-22-53) Frances Reid, Lonnie Chapman
166. "The Psychological Error" (12-29-53) Leslie Nielsen, Carole Mathews
167. "Night of Reckoning" (1-5-54) Edward Binns, Constance Ford, Walter Matthau
168. "Sudden Shock" (1-12-54) Georgiann Johnson
169. "Riviera Revisited" (1-19-54) Carmen Mathews
170. "Sredni Vashtar" [adapted from the Saki (Hector Hugh Munroe) classic] (1-26-54) Rex Thompson
171. "Freedom to Get Lost" (2-2-54) Charlton Heston, Hildy Parks
172. "In Line of Duty" (2-9-54) Joanne Woodward, Paul Langton
173. "Fall Guy" (2-16-54) James Gregory, E. G. Marshall, Larry Robinson
174. "Shorty" (2-23-54) Norman Shelby, Joe Maross, Harry Bellaver
175. "A Dip in the Pool" [adapted from the Roald Dahl short story] (3-2-54) Harry Townes
176. "The First Hold Up" (3-9-54) Ben Gazzara, Bethel Leslie
177. "The Actor" (3-16-54) Dane Clark, Catherine McLeod
178. "The Bet" (3-23-54) Kim Stanley, Edward Binns
179. "The Little Woman" (3-30-54) James Dean
180. "The Runaways" (4-6-54) Jeanne Eagen, Ray Boyle
181. "Road Happy" (4-13-54) Conrad Janis
182. "Live and Let Live" (4-20-54) David Opatoshu, Mario Alcaide, Maurice Tarplin
183. "Escape Route" (4-27-54)
184. "The Ring of Death" [otherwise known as "Title Fight"] (5-4-54)
185. "Outlaw's Boots" (5-11-54) James Gregory, William Smithers

186. "De Castries of Dienbienphu" (5-18-54)
187. "Deadly Counter" (5-25-54) Ian Tucker
188. "The Bouncer" (6-1-54)
189. "Lonesome Road" (6-8-54) John Cassavetes, Raymond Bramley
190. "The Big Man" (6-15-54) Joan Lorring, Philip Abbott
191. "One Can't Help Feeling Sorry" (6-22-54)
192. "An Affair of Delicacy" (6-29-54) Philip Bourneuf, Joan Wetmore
193. "The Gunman" (7-6-54) Ben Gazzara
194. "The Lion's Mouth" (7-13-54)
195. "Never Come Home" (7-20-54) Barbara Britton, Leslie Nielsen
196. "The Trophy" (7-27-54) George Kilroy
197. "The Key" (8-3-54) Michael Strong, Abby Lewis, Bob Lieb
198. "Handful of Salt" (8-10-54) Eva Gabor, Berry Kroeger, David J. Stewart
199. "An Angel of Clay" (8-17-54) Hildy Parks, Frank Marth, William Gargan
200. "One Day's Pay" (8-24-54) James Daly, Jacqueline Susann, Elspeth Eric

Fifth Season

201. "The Shadow on the Sun" (8-31-54) Sylvia Dawell
202. "Knee-High to a Corpse" (9-7-54) Walter Burke, Frank Campanella, Carole Mathews, Doug Rodgers
203. "One for the Angels" (9-14-54)
204. "See No Evil" (9-21-54) Nina Foch
205. "Cornered" (9-28-54) Everett Sloane
206. "Obsession" (10-5-54) Barbara Baxley, Ruth White
207. "Death Is My Neighbor" (10-12-54) Harry Townes, Jo Van Fleet
208. "Stranglehold" (10-19-54) Barry Jones, Scott Forbes
209. "The Pattern of Truth" (10-26-54) Russell Hardie
210. "Padlocks" (11-9-54) James Dean, Mildred Dunnock
211. "Experiment with Death" (11-16-54) Lorne Greene, George Voskovec
212. "Circle of Doom" (11-23-54) Mary Astor
213. "Silent Witness" (11-30-54)
214. "Knife in the Dark" (12-7-54) Paul Newman, James Gregory
215. "A Taste for Murder" (12-14-54) Jeffrey Lynn, George Macready
216. "Treasure of Argo" (12-21-54)
217. "Menace from the East" [a documentary on America's radar defenses] (12-28-54)
218. "Precinct Girl" (1-4-55) Peggy Ann Garner
219. "Sign of the Vulture" (1-11-55)
220. "No Passport for Death" [dramatizing the 1907 New York smallpox scare] (1-18-55) John Cassavetes
221. "Death Trap" (1-25-55) Joey Walsh, Russell Hardie
222. "The Dark Curtain" (2-1-55) Beatrice Straight, Wesley Addy
223. "Murder on Tenth Street" (2-8-55) John Baragrey, Katherine Bard

224. "Rampage" (2-15-55)
225. "The Blue Hotel" [adapted from the Stephen Crane story] (2-22-55) Henry Hull
226. "Journey with a Lady" (3-1-55) Jo Van Fleet
227. "Silent Mutiny" [based upon Captain Jan Civillinski's story of the reason for his flight from the Polish liner Batory] (3-8-55) George Voskovec
228. "Wire Tap" (3-15-55) Grant Richards, John Cassavetes, Neva Patterson, David Lewis
229. "The Belled Buzzard" [adapted from the Irving S. Cobb story] (3-22-55) Sidney Blackmer
230. "Season for Murder" (3-29-55) Carroll Baker
231. "The Last Duel in Virginia City" (4-5-55) Todd Karns
232. "Sandy River Blues" (4-12-55) Conrad Janis, Barbara Nichols
233. "Telegram" (4-19-55) Harry Townes, Gene Perrson, David White
234. "The Piano" [adapted from the Ben Ames Williams short story] (4-26-55) Jack Warden, Ford Rainey, Leora Thatcher
235. "Nightmare" (5-3-55)
236. "The Decision" (5-10-55)
237. "The Soldiers" [a composite of four Ambrose Bierce Civil War short stories as adapted by George Bellak] (5-17-55)
238. "The Operator" [adapted by Halstead Welles] (5-24-55) Lee Philips, Roni Dengal
239. "The Birds" [adapted from the Daphne du Maurier story; the same source was the basis for the 1963 Alfred Hitchcock feature] (5-31-55)

BILLY ROSE'S PLAYBILL

Sponsored by the Hudson Motor Car Company.

The Episodes:

1. "The Night They Made a Bum Out of Helen Hayes" (10-3-50) Murvyn Vye, Jackie Miles
2. "The Night Billy Rose Should'a Stood in Bed" (10-10-50) Burgess Meredith (as Billy Rose), Ruth McDevitt, Guy Kibbee
3. "George III Once Drooled in This Plate" (10-17-50) Burgess Meredith (as Billy Rose), Faye Emerson, Ludwig Donath, Leonard Elliott
4. [unknown title] (10-24-50) Frank Albertson (as Billy Rose), Linda Watkins
5. "The Murder Club" [an original story by Ben Hecht] (10-31-50) Walter Hampden, Richard Derr
6. "Ibsen Comes to Second Avenue" (11-7-50) Ludwig Donath, Jennie Goldstein
7. "Drink to Me Only with Thine Ice" (11-14-50) Harry Mc-Naughton, Cara Williams
8. "If You're an Actor--Act!" (11-21-50) Lee Tracy, Alfred Drake, Meg Mundy

9. "The Benefit of the Doubt" (11-28-50) Walter Hampden, Leo G. Carroll, Romney Brent
10. [unknown title] (12-5-50) Mary Sinclair
11. "One More Night to Go" (12-12-50) John Loder
12. "Kind Hearts and Gentle People" (12-19-50) Lionel Stander, Murvyn Vye
13. "Moon Over Miami" (12-26-50) John Loder, Frank Albertson, Cloris Leachman
14. "Pick Up" (1-2-51) Donald Cook, Dolly Haas
15. "The Galoshes of Fortune" (1-9-51) Frank Albertson, Wally Cox
16. "The Old Flame" (1-16-51) Brian Aherne
17. "Whirligig of Life" [adapted from the O. Henry story] (1-23-51) Tom Ewell, Otto Preminger, Mary Sinclair, Murray Hamilton
18. "Sugar O'Hara" (1-30-51) Lee Tracy
19. "Flowers for Millie" (2-6-51) Pamela Rivers, Ludwig Donath, Murray Hamilton
20. "My Aunt Frieda's Love Affair" (2-13-51) Ludwig Donath, Jenny Goldstein
21. "Duet for Two Actors" (2-20-51) Cyril Ritchard, Frank Albertson
22. "Julie the Jinx" (2-27-51) Jack Gilford
23. "Farewell Appearance" (3-6-51) Judith Anderson
24. "The Old Magician" (3-13-51) Walter Hampden
25. "Bright Golden Girl" (3-27-51)

STARS OVER HOLLYWOOD

The Episodes:

1. "Not a Bad Guy" (9-27-50) Edmon Ryan, Bruce Cabot
2. "Some Small Nobility" (10-4-50) Joan Banks
3. "Rock Against the Sea" (10-11-50) Mary Stuart
4. "Texas Parson" (10-18-50) Ross Ford, Lynne Roberts
5. "Showdown" (10-25-50) Lurene Tuttle
6. "A Model Young Lady" (11-1-50) Sally Parr
7. "Midnight" (11-8-50) Gloria Saunders, Herb Patterson
8. "This Little Pig Cried" (11-15-50) Frances Rafferty, Robert Rockwell
9. "Winter Love" (11-22-50) Ellen Corby, Art Smith
10. "Landing at Daybreak" (11-29-50) Anita Louise, Marsha Van Dyke, Ray Montgomery
11. "Small Town Story" (12-6-50) Ross Ford, Alan Mowbray
12. "My Rival Is a Fiddle" (12-13-50) Hans Conried, Maria Palmer
13. "Merry Christmas for Sweeney" (12-20-50) Bruce Cabot
14. "Never Trust a Redhead" (12-27-50) Herb Patterson, Sandra Dorn
15. "My Nephew Norwell" (1-3-51) Harold Peary
16. "The Ace of Spades" (1-10-51) Leon Ames
17. "Yang Yin and Mrs. Wiswell" (1-17-51) Adele Jergens, Helen Parrish

18. "Moon on Wires" (1-24-51) Dorothy Patrick
19. "Cutie Pie" (1-31-51) Carole Matthews
20. "The Return of Van Sickle" (2-7-51) Cliff Arquette
21. "Hand on My Shoulder" (2-14-51) Frank Jenks
22. "Son of the Rock" (2-21-51) Ellen Corby, Stanley Andrews, John Qualen
23. "Autumn Flames" (2-28-51) Maria Palmer, Onslow Stevens
24. "When the Devil Is Sick" (3-7-51) Larry Blake, Dorothy Adams
25. "Prison Doctor" (3-14-51) Cameron Mitchell, Raymond Burr
26. "Conqueror's Isle" (3-21-51)
27. "Old Mother Hubbard" (3-28-51) Ellen Corby
28. "Pearls from Paris" (4-4-51) Raymond Burr, Suzanne Dalbert, Gerald Mohr
29. "Tails for Jeb Mulcahy" (4-11-51) Bruce Cabot
30. "The Kirbys" (4-18-51) Ann Rutherford, Cameron Mitchell
31. "Pretty Boy" (4-25-51) Robert Clarice, Lynne Roberts, Richard Benedict
32. "Girl or Ghost" (5-2-51) Herbert Patterson, Gloria Saunders
33. "The Devil You Say" (5-9-51) Fred Sherman
34. "Nor Gloom of Night" (5-16-51) Buddy Ebsen

THE NASH AIRFLYTE THEATRE

The Regulars: William Gaxton, host.

The Episodes:

1. "A Double-Dyed Deceiver" (9-21-50) Van Heflin, John Payne, Ralph Riggs, Ian Keith
2. "Borrowed Memory" (9-28-50) Ruth Hussey, Torin Thatcher, Chester Stratton
3. "Portrait of Lydia" (10-5-50) David Niven, Mary Beth Hughes
4. "The Boor" (10-12-50) Fredric March
5. "The Box Supper" (10-19-50) Marguerite Piazza, Dorothy Peterson
6. "Municipal Report" (10-26-50) Herbert Marshall
7. "The Cut Glass Bowl" (11-12-50) Martha Scott
8. "I Won't Take a Minute" (11-9-50) Dane Clark
9. "Suppressed Desires" (11-16-50) Lee Bowman, Meg Mundy
10. "The Doll in the Pink Silk Dress" (11-23-50) Ann Rutherford, Otto Kruger
11. "Trial by Jury" [adapted from the Gilbert and Sullivan play; conducted by Alexander Semmler] (11-30-50) Patricia Morison, Ralph Riggs, Donald Clark, Stanley Carlson
12. "The Case of the Missing Lady" (12-7-50) Ronald Reagan
13. "The Windfall" (12-14-50) Peggy Conklin, Gene Lockhart
14. "Molly Morgan" (12-21-50) Barbara Bel Geddes, James Broderick, Jane Seymour
15. "The Kind Mr. Smith" (12-28-50) Basil Rathbone, Bethel Leslie, Vinton Hayworth
16. "Waltz Dream" (1-4-51) Kitty Carlisle, Jimmy Carroll, Marcia Van Dyke

17. "The Lipstick" (1-11-51) Robert Pastene, Kitty Carlisle, Jane Wyatt, Donald Curtis, Jimmy Carroll
18. "Pot o' Gold" (1-18-51) Joan Blondell, Richard Arlen
19. "The Case of the Calico Dog" (1-25-51) Nina Foch, Barbara Rollins, Lucile Watson
20. "The Crisis" (2-1-51) Laraine Day
21. "Peggy" (2-8-51) Joan Bennett, Katherine Alexander
22. "Pearls Are a Nuisance" (2-15-51) Dane Clark, Lionel Stander, Constance Dowling
23. "A Kiss for Mr. Lincoln" (2-22-51) Richard Greene
24. "Scandalous Conduct" (3-1-51)
25. "The Fiddling Fool" (3-8-51) Parker Fennelly, Nathan Milstein
26. "The Professor's Punch" (3-15-51) John Beal

THE PRUDENTIAL FAMILY PLAYHOUSE

The Episodes:

1. "Biography" [adapted from the Samuel Nathaniel Behrman play] (10-10-50) Gertrude Lawrence, Kevin McCarthy, Hiram Sherman
2. "Dodsworth" [adapted from the Sinclair Lewis novel] (10-24-50) Ruth Chatterton, Walter Abel
3. "Call It a Day" [adapted from the Dodie Smith play] (11-7-50) Peggy Ann Garner, Kay Francis, John Loder, John McQuade
4. "Three Men on a Horse" [adapted from the John Cecil Holm and George Abbott play] (11-21-50) Hiram Sherman
5. "The Barretts of Wimpole Street" [adapted from the Rudolph Besier play] (12-5-50) Helen Hayes, Bethel Leslie, Gene Lockhart, Robert Pastene
6. "Over Twenty-One" [adapted from the Ruth Gordon play] (12-19-50) Ruth Gordon, Paul Stewart
7. "Burlesque" [adapted from the George Manker Watters and Arthur Hopkins play] (1-2-51) Donald Curtis, Haila Stoddard, Bert Lahr, Carol Stone
8. "Skylark" [adapted from the Samson Raphealson play] (1-16-51) Donald Curtis, John McQuade, Haila Stoddard, Donald Cook, Gertrude Lawrence
9. "Icebound" [adapted from the Owen Davis Pulitzer Prize play] (1-30-51) Jessica Tandy, Kevin McCarthy
10. "Berkeley Square" [adapted from the John L. Balderston play] (2-13-51) Richard Greene, Grace Kelly, Rosalind Ivan, Mary Scott
11. "The Ruggles of Red Gap" [adapted from the Harry Leon Wilson play] (2-27-51) Cyril Ritchard, Glenda Farrell, Walter Abel
12. "One Sunday Afternoon" [adapted from the James Hagen play] (3-13-51) Richard Carlson, June Lockhart, Virginia Gilmore
13. "The Bishop Misbehaves" [adapted from the Frederick Jackson play] (3-27-51) Walter Hampden, Dorothy Gish

SOMERSET MAUGHAM THEATRE (a. k. a. TELLER OF TALES)

The Regulars: Somerset Maugham, host.

The Episodes:

1. "The Creative Impulse" (10-18-50) Mildred Natwick, Alan Bunce, Sylvia Field, Chester Stratton
2. "McKintosh" (10-25-50) Torin Thatcher, Francis L. Sullivan, Richard Malek
3. "Winter Cruise" (11-1-50) Adrienne Allen
4. "The Unconquered" (11-8-50) Rex Williams, Olive Deering
5. "Episode" (11-15-50) Leo Penn, Grace Kelly
6. "Lord Mountdrago" (11-22-50) Luis Van Rooten, Arnold Moss
7. "The String of Beads" (11-29-50) Anna Lee, John Van Dreelen
8. "Force of Circumstance" (12-6-50) Dennis Harrison, Virginia Gilmore
9. "The Round Dozen" (12-13-50) Mildred Dunnock, J. Pat O'Malley
10. "Footprints in the Jungle" (12-20-50) Dennis Hoey, Ronald Alexander, Patricia Wheel
11. "Virtue" (12-27-50) Ruth Madison, John Merivale
12. "The Treasure" (1-3-51) Tom Helmore, Beatrice Straight
13. "The Man from Glasgow" (1-10-51) Jessica Tandy, Robert Harris
14. "The Vessel of Wrath" (1-17-51) Martha Scott, Bramwell Fletcher
15. "Honolulu" (1-24-51) Luther Adler, Roberta Haines
16. "Partners" (1-31-51) Dane Clark, Anthony Quinn, Perry Bruskin
17. "The Romantic Young Lady" (2-7-51) Joan Chandler, Art Smith
18. "The Dream" (2-14-51) Joan Bennett, Francis Lederer
19. "The People You Meet" (2-21-51) John Conte, Howard Freeman, Laura Pierpont
20. "The Outstation" (2-28-51) Otto Kruger, Edith Atwater, Stefan Schnabel; Joyce Mathews, hostess
21. "The Back of Beyond" (3-7-51) Meg Mundy
22. "Halfway to Broadway" (3-14-51) William Prince, Katherine Bard
23. "The Luncheon" (3-21-51) Robert Cummings
24. "End of Flight" (3-28-51) Signe Hasso, Alfred Ryder

Second Season

25. "Of Human Bondage" (4-2-51) Tom Helmore, Cloris Leachman, John Baragrey, Betty Sinclair
26. "Theatre" (4-16-51) Judith Anderson, Robert H. Harris, Vicki Cummings, John Baragrey
27. "The Moon and Sixpence" (4-30-51) Lee J. Cobb, Romney Brent, Bramwell Fletcher
28. "The Facts of Life" (5-14-51) Veronica Lake
29. "Cakes and Ale" (5-28-51) June Havoc

30. "The Narrow Corner" (6-11-51) Dennis King, Susan Douglas, Harry Landers, Farrell Relly, Treva Standards, Harry Mc-haffey
31. "The Letter" (6-25-51) Judith Evelyn
32. "The French Governor" (7-9-51) Alfred Ryder, Peggy McCay
33. "The Promise" (7-16-51) Haila Stoddard
34. "In Hiding" (7-23-51) Nina Foch, John Baragrey
35. "The Ardent Bigamist" (7-30-51) Romney Brent
36. "Bewitched" (8-1-51) Martha Scott
37. "The Great Man" (8-13-51) Murray Matheson
38. "The Yellow Streak" (8-20-51) Elliott Sullivan
39. "A Woman of Fifty" (8-27-51) Sylvia Field
40. "Appearances and Reality" (9-3-51) Joseph Schildkraut

Third Season [now as hour series]

41. "The Mother" (9-17-51) Mildred Natwick, William Redfield
42. "Grace" (10-1-51) Betty Field
43. "Masquerade" (10-15-51) Bonita Granville
44. "The Fall of Edward Bernard" (10-29-51) Richard Greene
45. "Before the Party" (11-12-51) Geraldine Fitzgerald
46. "Home and Beauty" (11-26-51) Constance Bennett
47. "Smith Serves" (12-10-51) Eddie Albert, Joan Bennett

THE PULITZER PRIZE PLAYHOUSE

Under the sponsorship of Frigidaire and Schlitz Beer; awarded the best dramatic series by the Academy of Television Arts and Sciences for the year 1950.

The Regulars: Elmer Davis, narrator.

The Episodes:

1. "You Can't Take It with You" [adapted from the George S. Kaufman and Moss Hart play] (10-6-50) Charles Coburn, Ella Raines
2. "The Canton Story" (10-13-50) Richard Carlson
3. "Abe Lincoln in Illinois" [adapted from the Robert Emmett Sherwood play] (10-20-50) Raymond Massey, Betty Field
4. "The Late Christopher Bean" [adapted from the Sidney Howard play] (10-27-50) Charles Dingle, Helen Hayes (her video debut)
5. "The Magnificent Ambersons" [adapted from the Booth Tarkington novel] (11-3-50) Ruth Hussey, Florence Eldridge, Richard Hylton
6. "The Raven" [adapted from the Marquis James biography of Texan Sam Houston] (11-10-50) Zachary Scott
7. "Knickerbocker Holiday" [adapted from the Maxwell Anderson play, which had music by Kurt Weill] (11-17-50) Dennis King, John Raitt, Doretta Morrow

8. "The End Game" (11-24-50) Barry Nelson, Richard Derr, Kent Smith
9. "Our Town" [adapted from the Thornton Wilder play] (12-1-50) Edward Arnold, Elizabeth Patterson, Charles Dingle, Dorothy Peterson
10. "The Ponzi Story" (12-8-50) Hume Cronyn, Colleen Gray, Blanche Yurka, Quentin Reynolds
11. "Bethel Merriday" [adapted from the Sinclair Lewis play] (12-15-50) Barbara Bel Geddes, Philip Reed, Betty Garde
12. "The Pharmacist's Mate" (12-22-50) Gene Raymond, Brian Donlevy
13. "Mrs. January and Mr. Ex" [adapted from the Zoe Akins play] (12-29-50) Penny Singleton, Melvyn Douglas
14. "Portrait of a President" (1-5-51) Walter Hampden, Fay Bainter
15. "Ned McCobb's Daughter" [adapted from the Sidney Howard play] (1-12-51) Miriam Hopkins, Gig Young, Charles Dingle, Anthony Quinn
16. "Light Up the Sky" [adapted from the Moss Hart play] (1-19-51) Lee Tracy, Patricia Morison
17. "The Silver Cord" [adapted from the Sidney Howard play] (1-26-51) Dame Judith Anderson, Joanne Dru, Joan Chandler
18. "Alison's House" [adapted from the Susan Glaspell play] (2-2-51) Otto Kruger, Madge Evans, Patricia O'Quinn O'Hara
19. "Broken Dishes" [adapted from the Martin Flavin play] (2-9-51) James Dunn, Marcia Henderson, Robert Stack
20. "Mary of Scotland" [adapted from the Maxwell Anderson play] (2-16-51) Helen Hayes, Mildred Natwick, John Emery
21. "Valley Forge" [adapted from the Maxwell Anderson play] (2-23-51) Albert Dekker, Victor Sutherland, Wright King, Guy Aubrey
22. "The Wisdom Tooth" [adapted from the Marc Connelly play] (3-2-51) Jean Parker, John Beal, Helen Donaldson
23. "The Haunted House" [adapted from the Owen Davis play] (3-9-51) Barbara Britton, Howard St. John, Constance Dowling
24. "The Royal Family" [adapted from the George S. Kaufman and Edna Ferber play] (3-16-51) Florence Reed
25. "Blockade" (3-23-51) Robert Pastene, Vanessa Brown
26. "The Just and the Unjust" (3-20-51) Charles Dingle, Jan Sterling, June Lockhart, Richard Kiley
27. "Night Over Taos" [adapted from the 1932 play] (4-6-51) Riza Royce, Joseph Gallela, Murvyn Vye
28. "Icebound" [adapted from the Owen Davis play] (4-13-51) Edmond O'Brien, Charles Dingle, Nina Foch
29. "Rebellion in Jackson County" (4-20-51) James Dunn, Valerie Bettis, Everett Sloane, Muriel Kirkland
30. "Second Threshold" [adapted from the Philip Barry play] (4-27-51) Clive Brook, Betsy Von Furstenberg, Hugh Reilly
31. "The Happy Journey" (5-4-51) Spring Byington, Jack Lemmon, Wanda Hendrix
32. "The Thousand Yard Look" [narrated by Hal Boyle] (5-11-51)
33. "The Queen's Husband" [adapted from the Robert Emmett Sherwood play] (5-18-51) Roland Young

34. "The Stolen City" (5-25-51) Charles Dingle
35. "Detour" [adapted from the Owen Davis play] (6-1-51) Dorothy Gish, William Harrigan
36. "Hostage" (6-8-51) Paul Porter, Donald Devion
37. "The Buccaneer" [adapted from the Maxwell Anderson play] (6-15-51) Brian Aherne, Nina Foch
38. a) "The Pen" b) "You're Not the Type" c) "The Weak Spot" [three one-act plays] (6-22-51) Sidney Blackmer, Edna Best
39. "The Big Break" (6-29-51) James Dunn, Lynn Bari

Second Season

40. "The Skin of Our Teeth" [adapted from the Thornton Wilder play] (12-19-51) Thomas Mitchell, Mildred Natwick, Nina Foch, Peggy Wood
41. "Alison's House" [restaged from 2/2/51; adapted from the Susan Glaspell play] (1-2-51) Ruth Chatterton, Otto Kruger
42. "The Town" [adapted from the Conrad Richter novel] (1-16-52) Aline MacMahon, John Forsythe, Joseph Hardy
43. "Years of Grace" [adapted from the Margaret Ayer Barnes novel] (1-30-52) Ann Harding, Lucille Watson
44. "Hill 346--A Report on Korea" [adapted by Norman Lessing from the Marguerite Higgins documentary drama; directed by Lawrence Carra; Miss Higgins narrated] (2-13-52) Philip Bourneuf, Philip Coolidge, Vaughn Taylor
45. "Melville Goodwin, U.S.A." [adapted from the John P. Marquand story] (2-27-52) Paul Kelly, Margalo Gillmore, Jayne Meadows
46. "Monsieur Beaucaire" [adapted from the Booth Tarkington novel] (3-12-52) Vincent Price, Anna Lee, Audrey Meadows
47. "Robert E. Lee" [adapted from the Douglas Southall Freeman biography] (3-26-52) Robert Keith, Ilka Chase
48. "The Jungle" [adapted from the James Michener novel] (4-9-52) Nina Foch, Robert Preston, Kent Smith
49. "The Fascinating Stranger" [adapted from the Booth Tarkington novel] (4-23-52) Thomas Mitchell, Polly Rowles
50. "The Return of Mr. Motto" [adapted from the John P. Marquand character series] (5-7-52) James Daly, Eva Gabor, Harold Vermilyea
51. "The American Leonardo: The Life of Samuel F. B. Morse" [adapted from the Carleton Mabee biography] (5-21-52) John Forsythe, Gene Raymond, Wanda Hendrix
52. "Daisy Mayme" [adapted from the George Kelly play] (6-4-52) June Havoc, Shepperd Strudwick

THE FAITH BALDWIN PLAYHOUSE [FAITH BALDWIN'S THEATRE OF ROMANCE]

The Regulars: Faith Baldwin, author, hostess and narrator.

The Episodes:

1. "To My Beloved Wife" (1-20-51) Walter Abel, Sylvia Field
2. "Shot in the Dark" (1-27-51) Robert Warrick, Charles Starrett
3. "Bride from Broadway" (2-3-51) Nina Foch
4. "Follow Fat Flora" (2-17-51) William Eythe, Betsy Von Furs-
    tenberg
5. "Fountain of Youth" (3-3-51) Glenda Farrell
6. "A Doctor's Dream" (3-17-51) Jeffrey Lynn
7. "Portrait of Niki" (3-31-51) Neva Patterson, Luther Adler
8. "I'm Not for You" (4-14-51) Russell Nype
9. "When a Wife's Away" (4-28-51) Nancy Carroll
10. "Waiting for Love" (5-5-51) Joseph Schildkraut
11. "Woman Overboard" (5-19-51) Luise Rainer
12. "Black Sheep" (6-2-51) Russell Nype
13. "Success Story" (6-16-51) Susan Douglas, Paul Stewart
14. "Barry and the Beautiful Doll" (6-30-51) John Carradine
15. "Love Letters" (7-14-51) Constance Bennett
16. "Careless Love" (7-28-51) Robert Sterling
17. "Inspiration" (8-11-51) Robert Alda, Millicent Browar
18. "A Job for Jenny" (8-25-51) Coleen Gray
19. "We Have These Hours" (9-8-51) Sarah Churchill
20. "Henry's Harem" (9-22-51) Paul Hartman
21. "The Sleeping Beauty" (10-6-51) Ilona Massey
22. "What's Yours Is Mine" (10-20-51) Nancy Kelly

COSMOPOLITAN THEATRE

The Episodes:

1. "The Secret Front" (10-2-51) Lee Tracy, Marsha Hunt
2. "Be Just and Fear Not" (10-9-51) Joseph Schildkraut, Jane Walker
3. "Incident in the Blizzard" (10-16-51) Betty Field, E. G. Marshall
4. "Reward, One Million" (10-23-51) Dennis Hoey, Beatrice Straight
5. "Mr. Pratt and the Triple Horror Bill" (10-30-51) Tom Ewell, Constance Dowling
6. "Last Concerto" (11-6-51) Lon Chaney Jr., Susan Douglas
7. "I'll Be Right Home, Ma" (11-13-51) Charles Nolte
8. "The Tourist" (11-20-51) John Hoyt, John Boruff, Peggy Allenby
9. "Time to Kill" (11-27-51) John Forsythe, Torin Thatcher, Phyllis Love
10. "The Beautiful Time" (12-4-51) Joseph Buloff, Lili Darvas
11. "Mr. Whittle and the Morning Star" (12-11-51) Bramwell Fletcher, Peggy Conklin
12. "The Sighing Sounds" (12-18-51) Bethel Leslie, Gordon Mills
13. "One Red Rose for Christmas" (12-25-51) Jo Van Fleet

CELANESE THEATRE

Sponsored by the Celanese Corporation of America; winner of a Peabody Award.

The Episodes:

1. "Ah, Wilderness!" [adapted from the Eugene O'Neill play] (10-3-51) Thomas Mitchell, Howard St. John, Roddy McDowall, Dorothy Peterson
2. "Susan and God" [adapted from the Rachel Crothers play] (10-17-51) Pamela Brown, Wendell Corey, Albert Dekker, Helen Craig
3. "Winterset" [adapted from the Maxwell Anderson play] (10-31-51) Eduardo Ciannelli, Richard Carlyle, Joan Chandler, Ralph Morgan

4. "Old Acquaintance" [adapted from the John Van Druten play] (11-14-51) Edna Best, Ruth Chatterton
5. "Counsellor-at-Law" [adapted from the Elmer Rice play] (11-28-51) Alfred Drake, Ruth Hussey
6. "No Time for Comedy" [adapted from the Samuel Nathaniel Behrman play] (12-12-51) Sarah Churchill, Jean-Pierre Aumont, Ronald Howard
7. "The Joyous Season" [adapted from the Philip Barry play] (12-26-51) Lillian Gish, Wesley Addy
8. "Reunion in Vienna" [adapted from the Robert Emmett Sherwood play] (1-9-52) Signe Hasso, Melvyn Douglas, Ernest Truex
9. "Anna Christie" [adapted from the Eugene O'Neill play] (1-23-52) June Havoc, Richard Burton, John Qualen
10. "Brief Moment" [adapted from the Samuel Nathaniel Behrman play; directed by Alex Segal] (2-6-52) Veronica Lake, Robert Sterling, Burgess Meredith, Anthony Ross
11. "The Petrified Forest" [adapted from the Robert Emmett Sherwood play] (2-20-52) David Niven, Kim Hunter
12. "The Animal Kingdom" [adapted from the Philip Barry play] (3-5-52) Wendell Corey, Meg Mundy
13. "Saturday's Children" [adapted from the Maxwell Anderson play] (3-19-52) Mickey Rooney
14. "Street Scene" [adapted from the Elmer Rice play] (4-2-52) Ann Dvorak, Paul Kelly, Coleen Gray, Michael Wager
15. "Morning's at Seven" [adapted from the Paul Osborn play] (4-16-52) Aline MacMahon, Patricia Collinge
16. "They Knew What They Wanted" [adapted from the Sidney Howard play] (4-30-52) Betty Field, Frank Puglia, Robert Stack
17. "The Distaff Side" [adapted from the John Van Druten play] (5-14-52) Celia Johnson, Eileen Peel, John Merivale
18. "Yellow Jacket" [adapted from the Sidney Howard and Paul de Kruif play] (5-28-52) Richard Kiley, Macdonald Carey, Walter Abel
19. "When Ladies Meet" [adapted from the Rachel Crothers play] (6-11-52) Claudia Morgan, Patricia Morison, Richard Carlson
20. "On Borrowed Time" [adapted from the Paul Osborn and Lawrence Edward Watkin play] (6-25-52) Ralph Morgan, Mildred Dunnock, Billy Chapin, Melville Cooper

THE GRUEN GUILD PLAYHOUSE

Originating in Hollywood.

The Episodes:

1. "Unfinished Business" (9-27-51) Dane Clark, Alan Mowbray, Ann Rutherford
2. "The Driven Snow" (10-4-51) Kristine Miller, Bruce Cabot
3. "Hit and Run" (10-11-51) Robert Hutton, Bonita Granville
4. "Angel" (10-18-51) Steve Brodie
5. "Return to Vienna" (10-25-51) Ruth Warrick, Cameron Mitchell

6. "Peril in the House" (11-1-51) Marjorie Reynolds
7. "That Time in Boston" (11-8-51) Jorja Curtwright
8. "One Strange Day" (11-15-51) Bonita Granville, Steve Brodie
9. "Ballerina" (11-22-51) Ann Dvorak
10. "The Case of the Cavorting Statue" (11-29-51) Cesar Romero, Ann Rutherford
11. "The Luckiest Guy in the World" (12-6-51) Gordon Oliver, Marjorie Reynolds
12. "Swami" (12-13-51) Morris Ankrum, Bernadine Hayes
13. "Joe Santa Claus" (12-20-51) Sigrid Gurie, Maria Palmer

Second Season

14. "The Bachelor's Week-End" (3-27-52) Robert Paige, Ann Doran
15. "Dream Man" (4-10-52) Vincent Price, Andrea King, Harry Carey Jr.
16. "The Tiger" (4-24-52) Raymond Burr, Ludwig Donath, Randy Stuart
17. "Al Haddon's Lamp" (5-8-52) Buddy Ebsen, Robert Hutton
18. "A Boy Wears a Gun" (5-22-52) Francis Ford, Billy Gray
19. "Counterplot" (6-5-52) John Hudson, Marj Alden
20. "Bird of Prey" (6-19-52) Elizabeth Frazer, Patrick O'Neal
21. "For Life" (7-3-52) Shirley Jones, Bill Lester
22. "The Corner Shop" (7-29-52) Craig Stevens, Ruth Warrick
23. "Emergency" (8-12-52) Robert Hutton, Dorothy Patrick, John Hoyt
24. "Out of the Dark" (8-26-52) Ludwig Donath
25. "The Leather Coat" (9-9-52) Raymond Burr, Randy Stuart
26. "Face Value" (9-23-52) Raymond Burr

THE SCHLITZ PLAYHOUSE OF THE STARS

Segments were syndicated under a variety of titles HERALD PLAYHOUSE and THE PLAYHOUSE among them.

The Episodes [initially as hour series]:

1. "Not a Chance" (10-5-51) Helen Hayes, David Niven
2. "The Name Is Bellingham" (10-12-51) John Payne, Romney Brent
3. "Never Wave at a WAC" (10-19-51) Rosalind Russell
4. "Still Life" (10-26-51) Margaret Sullavan, Wendell Corey
5. "The Lucky Touch" (11-2-51) Helen Hayes
6. "Decision and Daniel Webster" (11-9-51) Charles Dingle, Walter Hampden, Matt Briggs
7. "The Memoirs of Aimee Durant" (11-16-51) Diana Lynn
8. "One Is a Lonesome Number" (11-23-51) Charlton Heston, June Lockhart
9. "Two Living and One Dead" (11-30-51) Fay Bainter, Walter Hampden
10. "The Nymph and the Lamp" (12-7-51) Robert Preston, Margaret Sullavan

11. "Exit" (12-14-51) John Payne, Coleen Gray
12. "Dark Fleece" (12-21-51) Helen Hayes, Anthony Quinn, Carmen Mathews
13. "Girl in a Million" (12-28-51) Joan Caulfield, John Forsythe
14. "Clean Sweep for Lavinia" (1-4-52) Josephine Hull
15. "Billy Budd" [adapted from the Herman Melville classic] (1-11-52) Walter Hampden, Peter Hobbs, Charles Nolte, Chester Morris
16. "The Man That I Marry" (1-18-52) John Ireland, Diana Lynn, Jeffrey Lynn, Steven Hill, John Baragrey
17. "P. G. " (1-25-52) Dan Duryea, John Forsythe, Henry Jones, Billy Redfield, Teresa Celli
18. "Lady with a Will" (2-1-52) Ann Sothern, Edmond Ryan
19. "The Daughter" (2-8-52) Geraldine Fitzgerald (as Mary Todd Lincoln), Juanita Hall (as Mammy Salby)
20. "Fifty Grand" (2-15-52) Dane Clark
21. "World So Wide" (2-22-52) Nina Foch, John Forsythe, John Baragrey
22. "Apple of His Eye" (2-29-52) Ward Bond, June Lockhart, Henry Jones
23. "The Haunted Heart" (3-7-52) Polly Bergen, William Eythe
24. "Make Way for Teddy" (3-14-52) Walter Hampden, Irene Manning, Philip Abbott, Anne Crowley
25. "The Human Touch" (3-21-52) Diana Lynn, Vincent Price
26. "The Autobiography of Grandma Moses" (3-28-52) Lillian Gish, Jonathan Marlowe
27. "Experiment" (4-4-52) Sylvia Sidney
28. "Four's a Family" (4-11-52) Celeste Holm
29. "Now's the Time" (4-18-52) Walter Hampden
30. "Fear" (4-25-52) Geraldine Fitzgerald
31. "Doctors Should Never Marry" (5-2-52) Diana Lynn, Jamie Smith
32. "Appointment with the Past" (5-9-52) Mark Stevens
33. "Autumn in New York" (5-16-52) Polly Rowles, Skip Homeier, Donald Briggs

[now as half hour series; Irene Dunne, hostess for the summer]

34. "Love Came Late" (5-23-52) Luise Rainer, Joseph Anthony
35. "A Quarter for Your Troubles" (5-30-52) Richard Haydn, Ned Young, Ned Glass
36. "Souvenir from Singapore" (6-6-52) Dan Duryea
37. "Dress in the Window" (6-13-52) Teresa Wright
38. "Say Hello to Pamela" (6-20-52) Barbara Britton, Leif Erickson
39. "The Von Linden File" (6-27-52) Joan Leslie, Steve Brodie
40. "The House of Death" [otherwise known as "Death House"] (7-4-52) Boris Karloff
41. "A Southern Lady" (7-11-52) Jane Wyatt
42. "Early Space Conquerors" (7-18-52) Bobby Driscoll
43. "A Man's World" (7-25-52) Pat O'Brien
44. "Crossroads" (8-1-52) Sir Cedric Hardwicke, Amanda Blake, Charmienne Harker
45. "So Help Me" (8-8-52) Jean Wallace
46. "Double Exposure" (8-15-52) John Beal, Amanda Blake, Jack Daly

47. "Mr. and Mrs. Trubble" (8-22-52) Virginia Field, Willard Parker
48. "Port of Call" (8-29-52) Victor McLaglen, Gertrude Michael
49. "Homecoming" (9-5-52) Leif Erickson
50. "The Marriage of Lit-Lit" [adapted from the Jack London story] (9-12-52) Don DeFore, Rita Moreno
51. "I Want To Be a Star" (9-19-52) James Dunn, Elinor Donahue
52. "The Trial" (9-26-52) Lon Chaney Jr.

Second Season [Irene Dunne remains hostess]

53. "Come What May" (10-3-52) Wallace Ford
54. "Trouble in Pier Twelve" (10-10-52) Akim Tamiroff, Rochelle Hudson
55. "This Plane for Hire" (10-17-52) Lloyd Bridges
56. "Drawing Room A" (10-24-52) William Bishop
57. "Enchanted Evening" (10-31-52) Eddie Albert, Margo
58. "Tango" (11-7-52) Cesar Romero, Ann Savage
59. "The House of Pride" (11-14-52) Robert Hutton, Coleen Gray
60. "The Pussyfootin' Rocks" (11-21-52) Joan Blondell, Buddy Ebsen
61. "Barrow Street" [a series pilot] (11-28-52) Sally Forrest, Jim Young
62. "Mr. Thayer" (12-5-52) Peggy Ann Garner, Francis L. Sullivan,
63. "The White Cream Pitcher" (12-12-52) Frances Rafferty, Walter Slezak
64. "The Playwright" (12-19-52) Richard Carlson
65. "A String of Beads" [adapted from the William Somerset Maugham story] (12-26-52) Joan Caulfield, Tom Drake
66. "Jenny" (1-2-53) Fay Bainter
67. "The Unopened Letter" (1-9-53) John Newland, Geraldine Wall, Phyllis Avery
68. "Guardian of the Clock" (1-23-53) Edmund Gwenn, Una Merkel
69. "Point of Honor" (1-30-53) Joseph Schildkraut
70. "Manhattan Robin Hood" (2-6-53) Preston Foster
71. "Mr. Greentree and Friend" (2-13-53) Hans Conried
72. "The Devil's Other Name" (2-20-53) Arthur Franz, Marjorie Lord
73. "Girl of My Dreams" (2-27-53) Marguerite Chapman, Donald Woods, Jeff Donnell
74. "Big Jim's Boy" (3-6-53) Jackie Cooper, Phyllis Avery
75. "Nineteen Rue Marie" (3-13-53) David Brian, Maria Palmer
76. "Parents' Week-End" (3-20-53) Maureen O'Sullivan, Jerome Cowan, Skip Homeier
77. "Happy Ending" (3-27-53) Helmut Dantine
78. "The Governess" (4-3-53) Ellen Drew, Onslow Stevens, Lillian Bronson
79. "The Mirror" (4-10-53) Victor Jory, Ian MacDonald
80. "Papa Goes to the Ball" (4-17-53) Harold Peary
81. "Allen of Harper" (4-24-53) John Newland, Anne Seymour, Robert Warwick
82. "Medicine Woman" (5-1-53) George Brent, Andrea King
83. "The Copper Ring" (5-8-53) Charles Bickford

84. "Vacation for Ginny" (5-15-53) Barbara Hale
85. "Pursuit" (5-22-53) Richard Carlson
86. "The Girl That I Married" (5-29-53) Gene Raymond, Suzanne Dalbert, Beverly Tyler
87. "Twenty-two Sycamore Road" (6-5-53) Nancy Davis, Willard Parker
88. "The Widow Makes Three" (6-12-53) Betty Lou Gerson, Broderick Crawford
89. "Operation Riviera" (6-19-53) Lon McAllister, Randy Stuart
90. "The Ledge" (6-26-53) Regis Toomey, Skip Homeier, Allene Roberts
91. "Richard and the Lion" (7-3-53) Joanne Dru, Jackie III
92. "Storm Warnings" (7-10-53) Arthur Franz, Robert Stack
93. "The Journey" (7-17-53) Merle Oberon, Patrick O'Neal, Grandon Rhodes
94. "Knave of Hearts" (7-24-53) Mark Stevens
95. "The Doctor Comes Home" (7-31-53) Ronald Reagan, Barbara Billingsley
96. "Simplon Express" (8-7-53) Eddie Bracken, Aline Towne, Laura Mason
97. "Miracle in the Night" (8-14-53) Ann Harding
98. "Sheila" (8-21-53) Elisabeth Risdon, Vincent Price, Griff Barnett
99. "Two Lives Have I" (8-28-53) Patricia Medina, Philip Carey, Janine Perreau

Third Season

100. "The Perfect Secretary" (9-4-53) Margaret Hayes, John Newland
101. "Lost and Found" (9-11-53) Edward Arnold, Percy Helton
102. "Boomerang" (9-18-53) John Barrymore Jr., William Wright, Tommy Cook
103. "Desert Tragedy" (9-25-53) Broderick Crawford, Eddy Waller, Edward Clark
104. "The Prize" (10-2-53) Ann Sothern, Walter Coy
105. "The Long Shot" (10-9-53) Edmond O'Brien, Dave Willock, Patrick O'Neal
106. "In the Pincers" (10-16-53) Sir Cedric Hardwicke, Judith Evelyn
107. "Second Sight" (10-23-53) Pat O'Brien, Lurene Tuttle
108. "The Sail" (10-30-53) Vera Miles, Skip Homeier
109. "Lineman's Luck" (11-6-53) Edmond O'Brien, William Bishop, Margaret Fields
110. "Lucky Thirteen" (11-13-53) Walter Brennan, Ruth Brennan
111. "Fresh Start" (11-20-53) William Campbell, Wanda Hendrix
112. "The Closed Door" [a psychological drama] (11-27-53) Gene Lockhart, Beverly Washburn
113. "Storm Swept" (12-4-53) Angela Lansbury
114. "No Compromise" (12-11-53) Stephen McNally, Robert Strauss
115. "Part of the Game" (12-18-53) Peter Graves, Gig Young
116. "The Baker of Barnbury" (12-25-53) Elsa Lanchester, Robert Newton

117. "Go Away a Winner" (1-1-54) Ellen Drew, Richard Egan, Richard Travis
118. "Rim of Violence" (1-8-54) Scott Brady, Martin Milner, Marcia Patrick
119. "Pearl-Handled Guns" (1-15-54) Zachary Scott, Harey Stephens, Lee Aaker
120. "At the Natchez Inn" (1-22-54) Peter Lawford, Marian Carr
121. "Give the Guy a Break" (1-29-54) William Lundigan, Frances Rafferty
122. "Four Things He'd Do" (2-5-54) Michael O'Shea, Lee Van Cleef, Maxine Cooper
123. "Man from Outside" (2-12-54) Broderick Crawford, Alexander Campbell, Ted de Corsia
124. "The Jungle Trap" (2-19-54) Ronald Reagan, Barbara Billingsley
125. "Night Ride to Butte" (2-26-54) William Bishop, Arlene Whelan, James Millican, Scott Elliott
126. "The Great Lady" (3-5-54) Ann Harding, Douglas Kennedy, Vera Miles
127. "Groundloop" (3-12-54) Alex Nicol, Randy Stuart, Robert Ellis
128. "Her Kind of Honor" (3-19-54) Marjorie Lord, Hugh Marlowe, Pamela Mason
129. "The Edge of Battle" (3-26-54) Ronald Reagan, Neville Brand
130. "Tapu" (4-2-54) Richard Denning, Jane Wooster, Hilo Hattie
131. "The Plugged Nickel" (4-9-54) Macdonald Carey
132. "Something Wonderful" (4-16-54) Claude Dauphin, Marcia Patrick, John Bryant
133. "Dawn at Damascus" (4-23-54) Gene Raymond, Paula Corday, Donald Murphy
134. "Decision at Sea" [a documentary drama on the late Admiral Marc A. Mitscher] (4-30-54) Don Taylor, Peter Lawford, William Phillips, Carl Benton Reid, Floyd Carl
135. "Prisoner in the Town" (5-7-54) John Ireland, Carolyn Jones
136. "The Pearl Street Incident" (5-14-54) Nancy Davis, Horace MacMahon, Jacqueline de Witt
137. "Blizzard Bound" (5-21-54) Forrest Tucker, William Phillips, Donna Martell
138. "Little War at San Dede" (5-28-54) John Agar, Willard Parker, Ross Elliott, Pilar del Ray, Rodolfo Hoyos
139. "The Whale on the Beach" (6-4-54) John Qualen, Charles Winninger, Hope Emerson
140. "The Treasure of Santo Domingo" (6-11-54) James Dunn, Murvyn Vye
141. "The Black Mate" [adapted from the Joseph Conrad story] (6-18-54) Paul Kelly, Lee Van Cleef, Robert Cornthwaite, William Phillips
142. "The Man Who Escaped from Devil's Island" (6-25-54) Victor Jory, Romney Brent
143. "How the Brigadier Won His Medals" [adapted from the Sir Arthur Conan Doyle story] (7-2-54) Claude Dauphin, Pat O'Moore, Eugenia Paul
144. "Rabbit Foot" (7-9-54) Stephen McNally, Paul Langton
145. "Showdown at Sunset" (7-16-54) Tom Tully, Daryl Hickman, Jan Shepard

146. "The General's Boots" (7-23-54) Basil Rathbone, John Dehner, Melville Cooper
147. "By-Line" (7-30-54) Marilyn Erskine, Arthur Franz
148. "The Roman and the Renegade" [on the life of Hannibal; the episode received an Emmy nomination for film editing, 1954] (8-6-54) Scott Forbes, Faith Domergue
149. "Gift of the Devil" (8-13-54) Will Rogers Jr., Joan Campden, Sally Fraser
150. "Captain in Command" (8-20-54) James Whitmore, Jeff Donnell, Donald Murphy
151. "Hemmed In" (8-27-54) Richard Carlson, Jean Byron
152. "Some Delay at Fort Bess" (9-3-54) Barbara Billingsley, Sterling Hayden

Fourth Season

153. "The Secret" (9-10-54) Tom Drake, Francis X. Bushman, Tom Moore, Madge Kennedy, Doris Kenyon
154. "Reunion at Steepler's Hill" (9-17-54) John Ireland, John Larch
155. "The Pipe" [adapted from the L. J. Baeston story] (9-24-54) Peter Lorre, Michael Pate, Lowell Gilmore
156. "The Viking" (10-1-54) Charles Bickford, Lamont Johnson, Margaret Field
157. "The Net Draws Tight" (10-8-54) Edmond O'Brien, Skip Homeier
158. "Square Shootin'" (10-15-54) John Newland, Marcia Patrick, Walter Sande
159. "The Best of Everything" (10-22-54) Don Taylor, Sally Frazer, Ann Tyrrell, Gar Moore
160. "The Sensation Club" (10-29-54) Francis L. Sullivan
161. "No Rescue" (11-5-54) Francis Lederer, Nancy Evans, Rodolfo Hoyos Jr.
162. "Midnight Haul" (11-12-54) Kevin McCarthy, K. T. Stevens
163. "The Long Trail" (11-19-54) Anthony Quinn, John Bryant
164. "Mystery of Murder" (11-26-54) Bruce Bennett, Frances Rafferty
165. "Volturio Investigates" [sequel to episode of 7/23/54] (12-3-54) Basil Rathbone, Melville Cooper, John Dehner
166. "Spangal Island" (12-10-54) Arthur Franz
167. "Woman Expert" (12-17-54) Howard Duff, Nancy Gates, Gertrude Michael
168. "Day of Good News" (12-24-54) Cecil Kellaway
169. "The Dumbest Man in the Army" (12-31-54) Neville Brand, Donald Murphy, William Boyett, Russ Conway
170. "The Cool One" (1-7-55) Stephen McNally, Hildy Parks, Paul Langton
171. "Man Out of the Rain" (1-14-55) Phyllis Thaxter, Skip Homeier
172. "Underground" (1-21-55) Paul Kelly, John Lupton, Dennis Weaver, Peggy O'Connor
173. "Murder in Paradise" (1-28-55) John Ireland, Lynn Allen, Steven Geray
174. "The Last Pilot Schooner" (2-4-55) Marshall Thompson, John Hoyt, King Donovan

175. "The Schoolmarm" (2-11-55) Will Rogers Jr., Martin Milner
176. "The Way to Freedom" (2-18-55) Patric Knowles, Robert Warwick, Rhys Williams
177. "Fast Break" (2-25-55) Jackie Cooper
178. "Fedar" (3-4-55) Scott Forbes, Ian Keith, Toni Gerry
179. "Visitor in the Night" (3-11-55) Ellen Drew, Willard Parker, Dorothy Green
180. "Ride to the West" (3-18-55) John Ireland
181. "Log the Man Innocent" (3-25-55) Dan O'Herlihy
182. "Tourists--Overnight" (4-1-55) Barbara Hale, Norma Varden
183. "Mr. Ears" (4-8-55) Walter Brennan, Tommy Rettig
184. "O'Brien" (4-15-55) Dan Duryea, Margaret Field, Virginia Lee, Lillian Bronson
185. "Who's the Blonde?" (4-22-55) Don Taylor
186. "The Brute Next Door" [adapted from the William Fay story] (4-29-55) Hans Conried, Hal Baylor
187. "The Unlighted Road" [by Walter C. Brown] (5-6-55) James Dean, Murvyn Vye, Edgar Stehli, Pat Hardy, Charles Wagenheim
188. "Too Many Nelsons" [by Richard Wormser] (5-13-55) Eddie Albert
189. "Sentence of Death" [adapted by George Bruce from the Thomas Walsh story] (5-20-55) Cecil Kellaway, Bonita Granville, Paul Langton
190. "The Argonauts" (5-27-55) Robert Newton, Jeanette Nolan, John Alderson, Barbara Self
191. "Visa for X" [adapted from the Barry Perouin story] (6-3-55) Cecil Kellaway, Joan Elan, Anthony Eustrel, Bruce Lester
192. "O'Connor and the Blue-Eyed Felon" [by Nord Riley] (6-10-55) Chuck Connors, Diana Lynn
193. "A Mule for Santa Fe" (6-17-55) Will Rogers Jr., Karin Booth, Stephen Wootton
194. "Splendid with Swords" (6-24-55) Farley Granger, Lili Fontaine, Eduard Franz
195. "The Ordeal of Dr. Sutton" [adapted from a story by Benjamin Siegel] (7-1-55) Raymond Burr, Marilyn Erskine
196. "Ambitious Cop" (7-8-55) Gene Evans
197. "Meet Mr. Justice" [adapted from the Jerry McGill story] (7-15-55) Joe E. Brown, Kathleen Crowley, John Baer, Jonathan Hale, Nancy Kulp
198. "Visibility Zero" [adapted by George Broadst from the Richard Thornton story] (7-22-55) Dean Jagger, Barry Kelley
199. "The Direct Approach" [adapted from the Richard Stern story] (7-29-55) Mona Freeman, John Archer
200. "Too Late to Run" (8-5-55) Bobby Driscoll, Beverly Garland, Arthur Franz
201. "On Leave" (8-12-55) Claude Dauphin, Robert Easton, Michael Pate, Maurice Marsac
202. "Jury of One" (8-19-55) Paul Kelly, Bill Henry, Ken Tobey, Eleanor Tanin, Addison Richards
203. "The Case for the State" (8-26-55) Marshall Thompson, Mark Herron, Hayden Rorke, Nancy Howard
204. "Three Months to Remember" (9-2-55) Don Taylor, Sallie Brophy, Diane Jergens

205. "The Uninhibited Female" (9-9-55) Marilyn Erskine, Barry
     Nelson
206. "Wild Call" (9-16-55) J. Carrol Naish, Herb Vigran, Ross
     Elliott, Bill Leicester
207. "The Quitter" (9-23-55) Raymond Hatton, Frances Rafferty,
     Noah Beery Jr., Craig Stevens

Fifth Season

208. "The Last Out" (9-30-55) Thomas Mitchell, Regis Toomey,
     Touch (Michael) Connors, Richard Erdman, Edward Binns
209. "Bandit's Hide-Out" (10-7-55) Anthony Quinn, Gloria Saunders,
     Eduard Franz, Joseph Waring
210. "Two-Bit Gangster" (10-14-55) Keenan Wynn, Addison Rich-
     ards, Robert J. Wilke, Barton MacLane
211. "The Girl Who Scared Men Off" (10-21-55) Phyllis Avery,
     Hans Conried
212. "Nothing to Do Till Next Fall" (10-28-55) James Dunn, Willis
     Bouchey
213. "A Gift of Life" (11-4-55) Barbara Billingsley, Don DeFore
214. "No Trial by Jury" (11-11-55) Alex Nicol, May Wynn, Touch
     (Michael) Connors
215. "Night of the Big Swamp" (11-18-55) Scott Brady, Myron
     Healey, Joan Vohs
216. "The Careless Cadet" (11-25-55) Don Taylor, Regis Toomey
217. "Moment of Triumph" (12-2-55) Kevin McCarthy, Eduard
     Franz
218. "On the Nose" (12-9-55) Neville Brand, Richard Deacon, Ben
     Cooper
219. "The Baited Hook" [by Sam Thomas] (12-16-55) Dane Clark,
     Morris Ankrum
220. "Christmas Guest" (12-23-55) Dan O'Herlihy, Phyllis Avery,
     Hayden Rorke
221. "Well of Anger" [adapted from the Morgan Lewis story] (12-
     30-55) Bill Williams, Nancy Gates
222. "Fool Proof" [by Charles Smith and Ralph Rose] (1-6-56)
     Claire Trevor
223. "Dealer's Choice" (1-13-56) Philip Ahn, John Ireland
224. "The Big Payday" [adapted by William Foy] (1-20-56) James
     Whitmore, Richard Crane
225. "The Day I Died" [by Jerome Gruskin] (1-27-56) David Brian
226. "The Gentle Stranger" (2-3-56) Joanne Dru, John Miljan,
     John Hudson
227. "Top Man" (2-10-56) John Lupton, James Ramsey Ullman,
     Scott Forbes
228. "On a Dark Night" (2-17-56) Will Rogers Jr., Tina Carver
229. "Ordeal" [by Miles Tolner] (2-24-56) John Ireland
230. "Showdown at Painted Rock" (3-2-56) Lyle Bettger
231. "Web of Circumstance" (3-9-56) Hugh Beaumont, Thomas
     Mitchell
232. "The Young and the Brave" [by Jackland Marmur] (3-16-56)
     John Ericson
233. "The Waiting House" [by Betty Ullius] (3-23-56) Phyllis
     Kirk, Paul Langton

234. "The Finger of God" (3-30-56) Jeff Morrow
235. "Angels in the Sky" (4-6-56) Marcia Henderson, Bill Williams
236. "The Bitter Land" (4-13-56) John Newland, Jack Diamond
237. "The Mysterious Cargo" (4-20-56) J. Carrol Naish
238. "Step Right Up and Die" (4-27-56) Lyle Bettger
239. "Formosa Patrol" (5-4-56) Eddie Bracken
240. "Plague Ship" (5-11-56) Ward Bond, Jon Shepodd
241. "Officer Needs Help" (5-18-56) Stephen McNally
242. "Date for Tomorrow" (5-25-56) John Ericson, Susan Kohner
243. "The Roustabout" (6-8-56) Scott Brady, Jeanne Moody, Harry Antrim
244. "Pattern for Pursuit" (6-15-56) Arthur Franz, Maggie Mahoney
245. "Witness to Condemn" (6-22-56) Warren Stevens, Teresa Wright
246. "Weapon of Courage" (6-29-56) Kevin McCarthy, Victor Jory, Maxine Cooper, John Dennis, Michael Winkleman, Frank Gerstle, Baynes Barron
247. "The Mechanical Cook" (7-6-56) William Bendix, Audrey Totter, Harry Tyler
248. "The Happy Sun" (7-13-56) Walter Brennan, George Brent, Kenneth Tobey, Nancy Hadley
249. "The Bankmouse" (7-20-56) Joan Caulfield, Betty Caulfield, Jon Shepodd
250. "Dara" (7-27-56) Phyllis Thaxter, Donald Curtis, Gerald Mohr
251. "Flowers for Jenny" [adapted from the Louis L'Amour story] (8-3-56) Claudia Barrett, Dale Robertson
252. "Repercussion" (8-10-56) Dan Duryea, Marcia Henderson
253. "Strange Defense" (8-24-56) David Brian, Constance Ford
254. "I'll Wait for You" (8-31-56) Ben Cooper, Joan Evans
255. "The Press Agent" (9-7-56) Jack Carson, John Lupton, Nancy Gates
256. "Midnight Kill" (9-14-56) Phyllis Avery, James Whitmore, Carl Benton Reid
257. "Top Secret" (9-21-56) Lee Bowman, Patricia Hardy

Sixth Season

258. "Moment of Vengeance" (9-28-56) Ward Bond, Gene Nelson
259. "The House That Jackson Built" (10-5-56) Arthur Franz, Diana Lynn
260. "The Trophy" (10-12-56) Jack Carson, Patricia Morison
261. "Always the Best Man" (10-26-56) Don Taylor, Angie Dickinson, Greta Thyssen
262. "The Night They Won the Oscar" (11-9-56) Richard Carlson, June Lockhart
263. "The Letter" [adapted from the William Somerset Maugham story] (11-23-56) John Ericson, Vera Miles
264. "Once Upon a Time" (11-30-56) Peter Lawford, Rudy Lee, Ray Ferrell
265. "Washington Incident" (12-7-56) Mark Stevens, Dean Stockwell
266. "A Tale of Wells Fargo" [adapted from the Zane Grey story; the basis for Tales of Wells Fargo, the 1957 series] (12-14-56)

Dale Robertson (initiating his role as Jim Hardie), Helen Westcott

267. "A Light in the Desert" (12-21-56) Lew Ayres, Virginia Field
268. "The Big Payoff" (12-28-56) Ralph Bellamy, Nat Pendleton
269. "The Lady Was a Flop" (1-4-57) Mickey Rooney
270. "Tower Room 14-A" (1-11-57) Richard Jaeckel, Edmond O'Brien, Ruta Lee
271. "Terror in the Streets" (1-18-57) Richard Long, Linda Darnell, K. T. Stevens
272. "The Enchanted" (1-25-57) Anna Maria Alberghetti, John Ericson, Kurt Kasznar
273. "One Left Over" (2-1-57) Robert Cummings, Beverly Washburn, Steve Brodie
274. "Sometimes You Break Even" (2-8-57) Mona Freeman, Barry Atwater
275. "Night Drive" (2-15-57) Constance Cummings, Everett Sloane
276. "The Wedding Present" (2-22-57) Celeste Holm, Gary Merrill
277. "The Life You Save" (3-1-57) Gene Kelly (in his video debut), Janice Rule, Agnes Moorehead
278. "Carriage from Britain" (3-8-57) Eduardo Ciannelli, Janet Leigh
279. "The Girl in the Grass" (3-15-57) Carolyn Jones, Ray Milland, Fay Baker
280. "For Better, for Worse" (3-22-57) Bette Davis, Anne Baxter
281. "The Restless Gun" [the pilot film for the 1957 filmed western series] (3-29-57) John Payne (initiating his role as Vint Bonner), William Hopper, Michael Landon
282. "Clothes Make the Man" (4-5-57) Hume Cronyn, Jessica Tandy
283. "The Blue Hotel" [adapted from the Stephen Crane story] (4-12-57) Vincent Price, Lee Van Cleef
284. "Girl with a Glow" (4-19-57) Patricia Crowley, John Forsythe
285. "Hey, Mac" (4-26-57) Gary Merrill, Sue George, Marion Marsh, Gordon Gebert
286. "The Traveling Corpse" (5-3-57) John Baragrey, Dennis O'Keefe, Gertrude Michael, Leora Dana
287. "Sister Louise Goes To Town" (5-24-57) Teresa Wright, Josephine Hutchinson
288. "The Sword" (5-31-57) Jacques Sernas, Nicola Michaels
289. "Old Spanish Custom" (6-7-57) Dolores Del Rio, Cesar Romero
290. "Fifty Beautiful Girls" [by Halstead Welles; restaged from his Suspense episode of 7/1/52] (6-21-57) Barbara Bel Geddes
291. "The Dead Are Silent" (7-19-57) Glynis Johns
292. "Easy Going Man" (8-2-57) Lee Marvin, Virginia Grey
293. "Hands of the Enemy" (8-9-57) Kevin McCarthy
294. "Sporting Chance" (8-16-57) Mark Stevens, John Baragrey

Seventh Season

295. "Three Dollar Bill" (9-13-57) Steve Forrest, Patricia Crowley
296. "One Way Out" (9-20-57) Stephen McNally, Vanessa Brown, Harry Guardino
297. "Storm Over Rapallo" (9-27-57) Ricardo Montalban, Yvonne De Carlo

298. "Switch Station" (10-4-57) Charlton Heston, John Carradine
299. "Smarty" (10-11-57) Shelley Winters
300. "High Barrier" (10-18-57) Carolyn Jones, Jeff Richards, Vincent Price
301. "Bitter Parting" (10-25-57) Laraine Day, Paul Henreid
302. "Dual Control" (11-1-57) Robert Cummings, Susan Kohner
303. "The Hole Card" (11-8-57) Tallulah Bankhead
304. "The Lonely Wizard" [a documentary drama on Charles Proteus Steinmetz; the episode received an Emmy nomination for its film editing, 1957] (11-15-57) Rod Steiger (in the title role), Diane Brewster
305. "No Second Helping" (11-22-57) Myrna Loy, Jill St. John, Tom Helmore
306. "Outlaw's Boots" (11-29-57) Steve Cochran, Roland Winters, Keenan Wynn
307. "Neighbors" (12-6-57) Joseph Cotten
308. "French Provincial" (12-13-57) Barbara Bel Geddes
309. "Rich Man, Poor Man" (12-20-57) Gilbert Roland
310. "Pattern for Death" (12-27-57) Eddie Albert, Noreen Nash
311. "Guys Like O'Malley" (1-10-58) Neville Brand, John Ericson, James Best
312. "Home Again" (1-17-58) Janis Paige, Mark Richman, Don Taylor
313. "No Boat for Four Months" (1-31-58) James Mason, Faith Domergue
314. "Heroes Never Grow Up" (2-7-58) Dane Clark, Alex Nicol, Barbara Turner
315. "East of the Moon" (2-14-58) Sterling Hayden, Lisa Lu, Warren Hoieh
316. "Man on a Rack" (2-21-58) Tony Curtis, Everett Sloane, Dolores Hart
317. "Two Lives Have I" [restaged from 8/28/53] (2-28-58) Ernest Borgnine, Judith Evelyn
318. "Night of the Stranger" (3-7-58) Valentina Cortesa, George Saunders
319. "The Honor System" (3-14-58) Paul Douglas
320. "Bluebeard's Seventh Wife" (3-21-58) Phyllis Avery, Hugh Marlowe, Ralph Meeker
321. "I Shot a Prowler" (3-28-58) Craig Stevens, Alexis Smith, Helmut Dantine, Morey Amsterdam
322. "Papa Said No" (4-4-58) Scott Brady
323. "A Contest of Ladies" (4-18-58) Louis Hayward, Alan Mowbray
324. "The Kind Mr. Smith" (4-25-58) Vincent Price, Valerie French
325. "Penny Wise" (5-2-58) Vera Miles
326. "The Town That Slept with the Lights On" (5-16-58) Edmond O'Brien, Shepperd Strudwick
327. "Lottery for Revenge" (5-30-58) Kevin McCarthy, Thomas Gomez
328. "Way of the West" (6-6-58) John Forsythe, Abby Dalton, Michael Landon
329. "You'll Have To Die Now" (6-20-58) Steve Forrest, James Gregory, Paula Raymond

330. "Curfew at Midnight" (6-27-58) Rory Calhoun, Robert Alda

Eighth Season

331. "A Thing to Fight For" [by Paul Monash] (9-26-58) Rod
Steiger, Rod Taylor, Marianne Stewart, Kim Charney
332. "The Hasty Hanging" (10-10-58) Fess Parker
333. "The Trouble with Ruth" (10-24-58) Jeanne Craine
334. "False Impression" (11-7-58) Macdonald Carey, Patricia
Breslin
335. "Last Edition" (11-21-58) Eddie Albert
336. "Third Son" (12-5-58) Steve Forrest
337. "No Answer" (12-19-58) Donald Cook, Keenan Wynn
338. "A Fistful of Love" (1-2-59) Lee Marvin
339. "You Can't Win 'Em All" (1-16-59) Guy Madison, Karen
Steele, Burt Reynolds
340. "And Practically Strangers" (1-30-59) Richard Carlson, Paula
Raymond, John Dall
341. "The Man Who Had No Friends" (2-13-59) Ralph Meeker
342. "On the Brink" (2-27-59) Mercedes McCambridge, Richard
Beymer, Barry Kelley
343. "Ivy League" (3-13-59) William Bendix, Tim Hovey
344. "The Salted Mine" (3-27-59) Scott Brady, Ernie Kovacs,
Marie Windsor
345. "The Rumor" (6-5-59) Hal March, Patricia Crowley
346. "Hostage" (6-19-59) Jim Brown

THE HALLMARK HALL OF FAME [after the radio series]

The Regulars: Sarah Churchill (daughter of Sir Winston), hostess as
of 1/6/52 through the fourth season.

The Episodes:

1. "Amahl and the Night Visitors" [the premiere performance of
the Gian-Carlo Menotti Christmas opera of the Magi on their
way to Jerusalem; an NBC Opera presentation produced by
Samuel Chotzinoff] (12-24-51 Monday 9:30-10:30 NBC)

[now as Sunday afternoon series]

2. "Dr. Serocold" (1-6-52) Sarah Churchill
3. "Love Story" (1-13-52) Beatrice Straight
4. "The Big Build-Up" (1-20-52) Grace Kelly, Richard Derr
5. "The Story of Roger Williams" (1-27-52) John Beal, Barbara
Bolton
6. "Florence Nightingale" (2-3-52) Sarah Churchill
7. "Woman with a Sword" (2-10-52) Jayne Meadows
8. "The Plot to Kidnap General Washington" (2-17-52) Joshua
Shelley
9. "Mistress of the White House" (2-24-52) June Lockhart
10. "Prelude" (3-2-52) Sarah Churchill

11. "Juliette Low and the Girl Scouts" (3-9-52) Lucille Watson
12. "Constitution Island" (3-16-52) Frances Starr
13. "Harriet Quimby" (3-23-52) Sarah Churchill
14. "The Vision of Father Flanagan" (3-30-52) Dennis Harrison
15. "Ordeal by White House" (4-6-52) E. G. Marshall, Alfreda Wallace
16. "Amahl and the Night Visitors" [the Gian-Carlo Menotti opera; restaged from 12/24/51] (4-13-52 4-5:00 NBC) Rosemary Kuhlmann, Andrew McKinley, David Allen, Leon Lishner, Francis Monachino
17. "Anne Bradstreet, Puritan Poetess" (4-20-52) Sarah Churchill
18. "Miracle in May" (4-27-52) Richard Waring
19. "The Face of Spain" (5-4-52) Berry Kroeger (as Francesco Goya), Ruth Ford
20. "A Woman for the Ages" (5-11-52) Sylvia Field
21. "Reign of Terror" (5-18-52) Sarah Churchill, Wesley Addy
22. "The Magnificent Failure" (5-25-52) Val Dufour, Beatrice Straight
23. "The King's Author" (6-1-52) James Westerfield
24. "Nefretiti" (6-8-52) Sarah Churchill
25. "Mr. and Mrs. Freedom" (6-15-52) William Darrid, Alfreda Wallace
26. "Forgotten Children" (6-2-52) Cloris Leachman, Don McHenry
27. "Our Sister Emily" (6-29-52) Sarah Churchill
28. "The Legend of Josiah Blow" (7-6-52) Biff McGuire, Christine White
29. "The Real Glory" (7-13-52) Alan Bunce
30. "Salvage" (7-20-52) Ian Keith
31. "Twenty-One Plus" (7-27-52) Neil Harrison, Isobel Elsom, Natalie Core, John O'Hare
32. "The Carlson Legend" (8-3-52) Tod Andrews
33. "The Last Command" (8-10-52) Curtis Cooksey
34. "I Lift My Lamp" (8-17-52) Maria Riva

Second Season

35. "Crabapple Saint" (8-24-52)
36. "The Refresher Course" (8-31-52) Marjorie Gateson
37. [unknown title] (9-7-52)
38. "Horns of the Dilemma" (9-14-52) Frances Reid
39. "The Bride's Tea Pot" (9-21-52) Peggy McCay
40. "Sometimes She's Sunday" (9-28-52) Bruno Wick
41. "The Bachelor and the Ballot" (10-12-52) Marc Cramer, Beverly Whitney
42. "Faith Is a Nine Letter Word" (10-19-52)
43. "The Secret Vote" (10-26-52)
44. "Line of Duty" (11-2-52) William Post Jr.
45. "Bread of Freedom" (11-9-52)
46. "Blue and White Lamp" (11-16-52)
47. "Mrs. Thanksgiving" (11-23-52) Madge Evans
48. "Ten Thousand Words" (11-30-52) Cliff Robertson
49. "Joan of Arc" (12-7-52) Sarah Churchill, E. G. Marshall
50. "The Hills Are Green" (12-14-52) Sarah Churchill, narrator.

51. "The Small One" (12-21-52) Kate Smith
52. [unknown title] (12-28-52)
53. "Fanny Stevenson" (1-4-53) Sarah Churchill
54. "Span of Time" (1-11-53)
55. "The General's Bible" (1-18-53)
56. "Socrates' Wife" (1-25-53) Katina Paxinou
57. "To My Valentine" (2-1-53) Sarah Churchill
58. "Lincoln's Little Correspondent" (2-8-53)
59. "Crown of Audubon" (2-15-53)
60. "Dinner for the General" (2-22-53)
61. "The Accused" (3-1-53) Sarah Marshall
62. "Horace Mann's Miracle" (3-8-53)
63. "The Harp of Erin" (3-15-53)
64. "Photograph by Brady" (3-22-53)
65. "A Queen Is Born" (3-29-53) Sarah Churchill
66. "The Other Wise Man" (4-5-53) Wesley Addy
67. "Skipper of the Skies" (4-12-53)
68. "The World on a Wire" (4-19-53)
69. "Hamlet" [the first video presentation of the Shakespeare classic; directed by George Schaefer and produced by Albert McCleery; sponsored by J. C. Hall, President of Hallmark Cards] (4-26-53 Sunday 3:30-5:30 NBC) Maurice Evans (in the title role; his video debut), Barry Jones (as Polonius), Sarah Churchill (as Ophelia), Ruth Chatterton (as Queen Gertrude), Joseph Schildkraut (as King Claudius)
70. "No Man Is an Island" (5-3-53)
71. "The Lady of Liberty" (5-10-53)
72. "Soldier of Peace" (5-17-53)
73. "Proudly I Love" (5-24-53)
74. "Spark of Genius" [Marconi] (5-31-53)
75. "The Clay of Kings" (6-7-53)
76. "Scott's Castle" (6-14-53)
77. "Man Against Pain" (6-21-53)
78. "The Mercer Girls" (6-28-53) Sarah Churchill, Bibi Osterwald

Third Season [episodes produced and directed by Albert McCleery]

79. "A Smile for Danger" [Christina Granville] (9-27-53) Sarah Churchill
80. "Of Time and the River" [a drama of the composition of the Thomas Wolfe novel] (10-4-53) Lamont Johnson (as the son), Thomas Mitchell (as William Oliver Gant), Sara Haden (as his wife), Sarah Churchill
81. "A Queen's Way" [Catherine Parr, wife to Henry VIII] (10-1-53) Sarah Churchill
82. "McCoy of Abilene" (10-18-53) George Nader
83. "Never Kick a Man Upstairs" [Theodore Roosevelt, previous to his ascension to the Presidency] (10-25-53) Sidney Blackmer
84. "The Imaginary Invalid" [adapted from the Molière play] (11-1-53) Barry Jones, Sarah Churchill
85. "The Lonely Path" [John Fremont, American explorer of the Far West] (11-8-53) Gene Barry, Sarah Churchill
86. "Of Time and the River" [a drama of the composition of the

Thomas Wolfe novel; restaged from 10/4/53] (11-15-53)
Thomas Mitchell, Lamont Johnson, Sara Haden, Sarah
Churchill

87. "The Courtship of Miles Standish" [adapted from the Henry
Wadsworth Longfellow classic] (11-22-53) Kenneth Tobey,
Roger Pace, Jeff Donnell

88. "The Last Voyage" [Benjamin Franklin in Paris] (11-29-53)
Maurice Manson, Richard Garland

89. [unknown title] (12-6-53)

90. "Aesop and Rhodope" [adapted from the Greek legend of the
love between two slaves] (12-13-53) Lamont Johnson, Sarah
Churchill

91. "Amahl and the Night Visitors" [the Gian-Carlo Menotti Christmas opera; restaged from 12/24/51 and 4/13/52] (12-20-53
Sunday 5-6:00 NBC) Rosemary Kuhlmann, William McIver

92. "Blaze of Darkness" [the blind poet John Milton] (12-27-53)
John Sutton

93. "John Marshall and the Burr Case" [Aaron Burr, the United
States Vice-President charged with treason in 1807] (1-3-
54) Robert Emmett Keane, Dan Riss, Richard Garland

94. "Crusade to Liberty" [James Edward Oglethorpe] (1-10-54)
Douglass Montgomery

95. "The St. Cloud Storm" [Jane Grey Swisshelm, pioneer reporter]
(1-17-54) Dorothy Green, Jan Lowry

96. "King Richard II" [the first video presentation of the Shakes-
peare classic; directed by George Schaefer and produced by
Albert McCleery] (1-24-54 Sunday 4-6:00 NBC) Maurice
Evans (in the title role), Sarah Churchill (as the Queen),
Frederic Worlock (as John of Gaunt), Kent Smith (as Boll-
ingbroke), Bruce Gordon (as Thomas Mowbray), Richard
Purdy (as the Duke of Aumerle)

97. "Lone Star" [Sam Houston's efforts to liberate Texas from
Mexico] (1-31-54)

98. "The Hands of Clara Schumann" [a story of the love between
composer Robert Schumann and pianist Clara Weick] (2-7-
54) Sarah Churchill, Patrick O'Neal

99. "Crusader Against Cruelty" [Henry Bergh] (2-14-54) Kent
Smith, Gertrude Michael

100. "Miss Tracy of Mount Vernon" [a young woman's efforts to
preserve the Washington home as a national shrine during
the Civil War] (2-21-54) Sarah Churchill

101. "The Turbulent Air" [the eighteenth-century French scientist
Lavoisier] (2-28-54) John Hudson

102. "The Good Samaritan" [on the evolution of the Red Cross Move-
ment] (3-7-54) Douglass Montgomery

103. "The Road to Tara" [St. Patrick's conversion of Ireland to
Christianity] (3-14-54) Patrick O'Neal

104. "Out of Jules Verne" (3-21-54) George Nader

105. "The Ordeal of Thomas Jefferson" [concerning the French Rev-
olution] (3-28-54) Warner Anderson

106. "Young William Penn" [on the reformation of the seventeenth-
century English courts] (4-4-54)

107. "The Liberator" [Simon Bolivar] (4-11-54) Joseph Jefferson

108. "The Story of Ruth" [adapted from the Bible] (4-18-54) Maria
 Riva, Fay Bainter, Margaret Hayes
109. "Lafayette for Freedom" (4-25-54)
110. "Petticoat Revolution" [on the first successful American femin-
 ist movement] (5-2-54)
111. "Portrait by Whistler" (5-9-54) Keith Larsen, Doris Lloyd
112. "Moby Dick" [adapted from the Herman Melville allegorical
 novel; produced and directed by Albert McCleery] (5-16-54
 Sunday 5-6:00 NBC) Victor Jory (as Ahab), Lamont Johnson
 (as Ishmael), Harvey Stephens (as Stubb), Hugh O'Brian (as
 Starbuck)

[now as half hour series]

113. "The Story of Father Juniper Serra" [on the establishment of
 the first mission in San Francisco, 1775] (5-23-54) Robert
 Warrick
114. "The Armour-Bearer" [on the founding of Temple University,
 Philadelphia] (5-30-54)
115. "A Reckless Youth" [story of the love between Samuel Clemens
 and Olivia Langdon] (6-6-54)
116. "Come to the Window" [Jenny Lind] (6-13-54) Jan Clayton
117. "Flight from Cathay" [the friendship between Marco Polo and
 a Chinese princess] (6-20-54) Sarah Churchill
118. "Wife Unto Caesar" [Calpurnia] (6-27-54) Sarah Churchill
119. "John Paul Jones" (7-4-54) Lamont Johnson, Gloria Jean

Fourth Season [variously as half-hour or hour dramas]

120. "Dynamite" [story of Alfred Nobel] (9-5-54) Wesley Addy,
 Osa Massen
121. "Don't Cry for Me" [Stephen Foster] (9-12-54) John Sheppard
122. "John Wanamaker" (9-19-54) Peter Graves
123. "The Story of Moses" (9-26-54) John Barrymore Jr.
124. "The Story of Johann Sebastian Bach" (10-3-54)
125. "Immortal Oath" [Hippocrates] (10-10-54) John Baer, Vera
 Miles
126. "The Story of John Paulding" (10-17-54)
127. "Lady in the Wings" [Mrs. Edward MacDowell, wife of the
 American composer] (10-24-54) Rosemary DeCamp, Peter
 Hansen, Ludwig Stossel, Michael Whelan
128. "Path of Peace" [the Horace Greeley defense of the defeated
 Jefferson Davis] (10-31-54)
129. "The Story of Daniel Boone" (11-7-54)
130. "A Matter of Principle" [the John Adams defense of British officers after a riot] (11-14-54)
131. "President for a Day" [David Rice Atchison] (11-21-54)
132. "Macbeth" [adapted from the Shakespeare classic; directed by
 George Schaefer and produced by Albert McCleery] (11-28-
 54 Sunday 4-6:00 NBC) Maurice Evans (in the title role),
 Staats Cotsworth (as Banquo), Dame Judith Anderson (as
 Lady Macbeth), House Jameson (as King Duncan), Richard
 Waring (as Macduff)

133. "With One Heart and One Mind" [Alexander Hamilton] (12-5-54)
134. "The Province of Man" [William Harvey] (12-12-54)
135. "Amahl and the Night Visitors" [the Gian-Carlo Menotti Christmas opera; restaged from 12/24/51, 4/13/52 and 12/20/53] (12-19-54 Sunday 5-6:00 NBC) Rosemary Kuhlmann, William McIver, William Aiken
136. "The Joyful Tydings" [Pastor William Tyndale versus Henry VIII and Cardinal Wolsey on the English translation of the Bible] (12-26-54)
137. "William Tell" (1-2-55)
138. "First Mintmaster" [John Hull of the Commonwealth of Massachusetts] (1-9-55)
139. "Crusade for Freedom" [Benjamin Franklin's efforts on behalf of freedom of the press] (1-16-55)
140. "Dr. Harvey Wiley" [his fight for a pure food and drug act] (1-23-55)
141. "A Tribute to Henry Ford" (1-30-55)
142. "Patrick Henry" (2-6-55)
143. "A Tribute to Alcuin" [who initiated the first European schools] (2-13-55)
144. "The Courtship of George Washington and Martha Custiss" (2-20-55)
145. "A Tribute to Alexander Graham Bell" [how the telephone evolved out of his aid to a deaf child] (2-27-55)
146. "A Tribute to Lieutenant Marcus Contee" [a member of the Captain Matthew C. Perry 1853 expedition to Japan to negotiate the first treaty with the United States] (3-6-55) John Barrymore Jr.
147. "A Tribute to Edward Livingston" [the aide-de-camp to General Andrew Jackson in the War of 1812] (3-13-55)
148. "Soldier's Bride" [story of the love between Knox Taylor (daughter of Colonel Zachary Taylor) and Jefferson Davis] (3-20-55) Sarah Churchill, John Baragrey, Olive Blakeney, Robert Brubaker, Richard Gaines
149. "The Finest Gift" [Lord Byron's efforts to liberate Greece] (3-27-55) Tod Andrews
150. "Ethan Allen" (4-3-55) William Bishop
151. "Lydia" [a pagan Greek lady living in ancient Rome saves the Apostle Paul] (4-10-55)
152. "The Story of Dr. James Ewing" (4-17-55)
153. "The Story of Aimee Rivery" [a French girl who brought reforms to Turkey] (4-24-55)
154. [unknown title] (5-1-55)
155. "Cradle Song" [Mme. Ernestine Schumann-Heink, whose five sons served in the Second World War; one on the side of the enemy] (5-8-55) Osa Massen
156. "The Story of Damon and Pythias" (5-15-55)
157. "The Man with a Camera" [George Eastman] (5-22-55) Gene Reynolds, Lyle Talbott, Olive Blakeney
158. "The Story of Paul P. Harris" [founder of Rotary International] (5-29-55)
159. "The Hammer and the Sword" [Baron Von Steuben, the German soldier who trained troops in the American Revolution] (6-5-55) Joseph Schildkraut

160. "Edgar Allan Poe at West Point" [by Will Price and Marcia Dealy] (6-12-55)
161. "The Story of Milton S. Hershey" (6-19-55)
162. "The Farmer of Monticello" [Thomas Jefferson] (6-26-55)

Fifth Season [hereafter as a series of specials]

The Regulars: Maurice Evans, host and narrator.

163. "Alice in Wonderland" [adapted from the Lewis Carroll classic; directed by George Schaefer; costumes by Noel Taylor] (10-23-55 Sunday 4-5:30 NBC) Gillian Barber (as Alice), Martyn Green (as the White Rabbit), Bobby Clark (as The Duchess), J. Pat O'Malley (as the Gryphon), Reginald Gardiner (as the White Knight), Hiram Sherman (as the King of Hearts), Burr Tillstrom (as the Mock Turtle and Puppeteer), Elsa Lanchester (as the Red Queen), Eva LeGallienne (as the White Queen), John Payne; narrated by Maurice Evans
164. "The Devil's Disciple" [adapted from the George Bernard Shaw play; directed by George Schaefer] (11-20-55 Sunday 4-5:30 NBC) Maurice Evans, Ralph Bellamy, Teresa Wright, Dennis King
165. "Dream Girl" [adapted from the Elmer Rice play; directed by George Schaefer] (12-11-55 Sunday 4-5:50 NBC) Vivian Blaine (as Georgiana Allerton), Hal March, Evelyn Varden, Donald Symington, Edmon Ryan

Episodes continued with Television Drama Series Programming: A Comprehensive Chronicle, 1959-1975 and with regular supplements.

THE GALLERY OF MME. LIU-TSONG

Having chosen the beauteous legendary screen star Anna May Wong, the Dumont network inaugurated this short-lived adventure-- a proper blend of Oriental intrigue and mysticism.

The Regulars: Anna May Wong, hostess and performer.

The Episodes:

1. [unknown title] (8-27-51)
2. "The Golden Women" (9-3-51)
3. "The Spreading Oak" (9-10-51)
4. "The Man with a Thousand Eyes" (9-17-51)
5. "Burning Sands" (9-24-51)
6. "Shadow of the Sun God" (10-1-51)
7. "The Tinder Box" (10-31-51)
8. "The House of Quiet Dignity" (11-7-51)
9. "Boomerang" (11-14-51)
10. "The Face of Evil" (11-21-51)

TALES OF TOMORROW

The Episodes:

1. "Verdict from Space" (8-3-51) Lon McCallister, Martin Brandt
2. "A Child Is Crying" (8-17-51) Walter Abel, Robin Morgan
3. "The Last Man on Earth" (8-31-51) John McQuade, Cloris Leachman
4. "Errand Boy" (9-7-51) Joey Walsh
5. "The Monsters" (9-14-51) Paul Langton, Bert Kalmar Jr., Barbara Boulton
6. "The Dark Angel" (9-28-51) Meg Mundy, Sidney Blackmer
7. "The Crystal Egg" (10-12-51) Thomas Mitchell
8. "Test Flight" (10-26-51) Lee J. Cobb
9. "The Search for the Flying Saucer" (11-9-51) Jack Carter, Olive Deering, Vaughn Taylor
10. "Enemy Unknown" (11-23-51) Lon McCallister, Walter Abel, Edith Fellows, Vince Otis
11. "Sneak Attack" (12-7-51) Zachary Scott
12. "The Invaders" (12-12-51) Eva Gabor, William Eythe
13. "The Dune Roller" (1-4-52) Bruce Cabot, Virginia Gilmore
14. "Frankenstein" [adapted from the Mary Shelley classic] (1-18-52) John Newland, Lon Chaney Jr.
15. "Twenty Thousand Leagues Under the Sea: The Chase" [Part I; adapted from the Jules Verne classic] (1-25-52) Thomas Mitchell, Leslie Nielsen, Bethel Leslie
16. "Twenty Thousand Leagues Under the Sea: The Escape" [Part II] (2-1-52) as above.
17. "What You Need" (2-8-52) Billy Redfield, Edgar Stehli
18. "Age of Peril" Phyllis Kirk, Dennis Harris
19. "Memento" (2-22-52) Boris Karloff, Barbara Joyce
20. "The Children's Room" (2-29-52) Clare Luce, Terry Greene, Una O'Connor
21. "Bound Together" (3-7-52) Nina Foch
22. "The Diamond Lens" (3-14-52) Franchot Tone
23. "Fountain of Youth" (3-21-52) Tom Drake
24. "Flight Overdue" (3-28-52) Veronica Lake
25. "And a Little Child" (4-4-52) Frank McHugh, Iris Mann
26. "Sleep No More" (4-11-52) Jeffrey Lynn
27. "Time to Go" (4-18-52) Sylvia Sidney
28. "Plague from Space" (4-25-52) Gene Raymond
29. "Red Dust" (5-2-52)
30. "The Golden Ingot" (5-9-52) Gene Lockhart
31. "Black Planet" (5-16-52) Leslie Nielsen, Frank Albertson
32. "World of Water" (5-23-52) Victor Jory
33. "Little Black Bag" (5-30-52) Joan Blondell
34. "The Exile" (6-6-52) Chester Morris
35. "All the Time in the World" (6-13-52) Esther Ralston
36. "The Miraculous Serum" (6-20-52) Lola Albright, Richard Derr
37. "Appointment to Mars" (6-27-52) Leslie Nielsen, William Redfield
38. "The Duplicates" (7-4-52) Darren McGavin

39. "Ahead of His Time" (7-18-52) Paul Tripp
40. "Sudden Darkness" (8-1-52) Olive Deering
41. "Ice from Space" (8-8-52)
42. "A Child Is Crying" (8-15-52) Bert Lytell, Robin Morgan
43. "A Bird In Hand" (8-22-52) Gina Niemilla, Peter Munsen
44. "Thanks" (8-29-52)
45. "The Seeing-Eye Surgeon" (9-5-52) Bruce Cabot
46. "The Cocoon" (9-12-52) Jackie Cooper, Edith Fellows
47. "The Chase" (9-19-52) Walter Abel
48. "Youth on Tap" [otherwise known as "Young Blood"] (9-26-52)
    Robert Alda

Second Season

49. "Substance 'X'" (10-3-52) Vicki Cummings
50. "The Horn" (10-10-52) Franchot Tone
51. "Double Trouble" (10-17-52) Paul Tripp, Ruth Enders
52. "Many Happy Returns" (10-24-52) Gene Raymond
53. "The Tomb of King Tarus" (10-31-52) Walter Abel
54. "The Window" (11-7-52)
55. "The Camera" (11-14-52) Olive Deering, Donald Buka
56. "The Quiet Lady" (11-21-52) Una O'Connor, John Conte
57. "The Invigorating Air" (11-28-52) Joseph Buloff
58. "The Glacier Giant" (12-5-52) Edith Fellows, Chester Morris,
    Murray Tannenbaum
59. "The Fatal Flower" (12-12-52) Victory Jory, John Hammer
60. "The Machine" (12-19-52) Gene Lockhart, Georgianne Johnson
61. "The Bitter Storm" (12-26-52) Arnold Moss
62. "The Mask of Medua" (1-2-53) Raymond Burr
63. "Conquerer's Isle" (1-9-53) Ray Montgomery
64. "Discovered Heart" (1-16-53) Susan Hallaran
65. "The Picture of Dorian Gray" [adapted from the Oscar Wilde
    classic] (1-23-53) John Newland, Peter Fernandez
66. "Two-Faced" (1-30-53) Richard Kiley
67. "The Build-Box" (2-6-53) Glenda Farrell
68. "Another Chance" (2-13-53) Leslie Nielsen
69. "The Great Silence" (2-20-53) Burgess Meredith
70. "Lonesome Village" (2-27-53) Constance Clausen
71. "The End of the Cocoon" (3-6-53) Nancy Coleman, Peter Capell
72. "The Squeeze Play" (3-13-53) John McQuade, Elizabeth Yorke
73. "Read to Me, Herr Doktor" (3-20-53) Everett Sloane, Mer-
    cedes McCambridge; Paul Lukas, program host
74. "Ghost Writer" (3-27-53) Leslie Nielsen, Gaby Rodgers
75. "Past Tense" (4-3-53) Boris Karloff, Robert F. Simon
76. "Homecoming" (4-10-53) Edith Fellows
77. "The Rival" (4-17-53) Mary Sinclair, Anthony Ross
78. "Please Omit Flowers" (4-24-53) Ann Burr
79. "The Evil Within" (5-1-53) Margaret Phillips
80. "The Vault" (5-8-53) Dorothy Peterson, Cameron Prud'homme
81. "Ink" (5-15-53) Mildred Natwick, Joseph Anthony
82. "The Spider Web" (5-22-53) Nancy Coleman
83. "Lazarus Walks" (5-29-53) William Prince, Olive Deering
84. "What Dreams May Come" (6-12-53) Arnold Moss

CBS TELEVISION WORKSHOP

The Episodes:

1. "Don Quixote" [adapted from the Cervantes classic] (1-13-52) Boris Karloff, Jimmy Salvo
2. "Careless Love" (1-20-52) Conrad Janis
3. "Into the Valley" (1-27-52)
4. "The Angel Was a Yankee" (2-3-52) John McQuade
5. "Tom Sawyer, the Gloria Whitewasher" [adapted from the Mark Twain classic] (2-10-52) Ken Walking
6. "The Sound Machine" (2-17-52) Richard Purdy, Tom Chalmers
7. "The Rose and the Ring" (2-24-52) Philip Bourneuf
8. "The Beggar's Opera" [adapted from the John Gay classic] (3-2-52) Dorothea Morrow
9. "The Talking Cure" (3-9-52) John Baragrey
10. "Rocket" (3-16-52) Katharine Squire, Martin Ritt
11. "The Gallows Tree" (3-23-52) Geraldine Fitzgerald, Frederic Worlock
12. "Riders to the Sea" (3-30-52) Cathleen Nesbitt
13. "My Eyes Have a Cold Nose" (4-6-52) Albert Dekker
14. "Rainy Day in Paradise Junction" (4-13-52) Audrey Hepburn

THE BROADWAY TELEVISION THEATRE

The Episodes:

1. "The Trial of Mary Dugan" [adapted from the Bayard Veiller play] (4-14-52) Ann Dvorak, Thomas Heaphy, Richard Derr, Vinton Hayworth
2. "Three Men on a Horse" [adapted from the George Abbott and John Cecil Holm play] (4-21-52) Orson Bean, Ann Thomas, Murvyn Vye
3. "The Jazz Singer" [adapted from the Samson Raphaelson play and 1927 film scenario] (4-28-52) Celia Adler, Lionel Ames
4. "Angel in the Pawnshop" [adapted from the A. B. Shiffrin play] (5-5-52) Ernest Truex, Sylvia Field
5. "Angel Street" [adapted from the Patrick Hamilton play] (5-12-52) Victor Jory, Lola Montez, Melville Cooper
6. "The Night-Cap" [adapted from the play] (5-19-52) Edward Everett Horton, Lola Montez, Melville Cooper
7. "The Fortune Hunter" [adapted from the 1909 play] (5-26-52) Peter Cookson, William Post Jr.
8. "Within the Law" [adapted from the Bayard Veiller play] (6-2-52) Lola Montez, Cara Williams
9. "Nothing But the Truth" [adapted from the James Montgomery play] (6-9-52) Orson Bean, Ernest Truex, Sylvia Field
10. "The Barker" [adapted from the Kenyon Nicholson play] (6-16-52) Sidney Blackmer, Virginia Gilmore, Gloria McGhee, Jack Diamond
11. "The Patsy" [adapted from the Barry Conners play] (6-23-52)

Luella Gear, Curtis Cooksey, Douglas Watson, Christine White

12. "Burlesque" [adapted from the George Manker Waters and Arthur Hopkins play] (6-30-52) Buddy Ebsen, Gloria McGhee, Jean Bartell

13. "The Velvet Glove" [adapted from the Rosemary Casey play] (7-7-52) Bramwell Fletcher, Lola Montez, Richard Derr

14. "The Night of January Sixteenth" [adapted from the Ayn Rand play] (7-14-52) Neil Hamilton, Virginia Gilmore, Stella Andrew

15. "For Love or Money" [adapted from the Frederick Hugh Herbert play] (7-28-52) Tom Helmore, Vicki Cummings, Buddy Ebsen, Diana Herbert

16. "Three Cornered Moon" [adapted from the Gertrude Tonkonogy play] (8-4-52) Bethel Leslie, William Post Jr.

17. "It's a Boy!" [adapted from the Austin Melford play] (8-11-52) Frederic Tozere, Hope Miller, Michael Higgins, James Kirkwood Jr.

18. "Night Must Fall" [adapted from the Emlyn Williams play] (8-18-52) Bethel Leslie, Ruth Gates, Anthony Kemble-Cooper, Wright King

19. "Jenny Kissed Me" [adapted from the Jean Kerr play] (8-25-52) Christine White, Melville Cooper, Warren Wade

20. "Rebecca" [adapted from the Daphne du Maurier novel] (9-1-52) Patricia Breslin, Scott Forbes

21. "Mrs. Moonlight" [adapted from the Benn W. Levy play] (9-8-52) Beverly Whitney, Una O'Connor, Stephen Courtleigh

Second Season

22. "Blind Alley" [adapted from the James Warwick play] (9-15-52) Roy Hargrave, Ernest Groves, Beverly Roberts

23. "The Bishop Misbehaves" [adapted from the Frederick Jackson play] (9-22-52) Gene Lockhart, Alice Pearce

24. "Theatre" [adapted from the William Somerset Maugham and Guy Bolton play] (9-29-52) Sylvia Sidney

25. "Suspect" [adapted from the Edward Percy and Reginald Denham play] (10-6-52) Florence Reed

26. "It Pays to Advertise" [adapted from the Roi Cooper Megrue and Walter Hackett play] (10-13-52) Roddy McDowall, Barbara Baxley

27. "The Two Mrs. Carrolls" [adapted from the Martin Vale (Mauguerite Veiller) play] (10-20-52) Signe Hasso

28. "The Nervous Wreck" [adapted from the Owen Davis play] (10-27-52) Buddy Ebsen

29. "The Letter" [adapted from the William Somerset Maugham story] (11-3-52) Sylvia Sidney, Gene Raymond

30. "Seven Keys to Baldpate" [adapted from the George M. Cohan and Earl Derr Biggers play] (11-17-52) Buddy Ebsen

31. "Craig's Wife" [adapted from the George Kelly play] (11-17-52) Osa Munson, Mildred Dunnock

32. "Outward Bound" [adapted from the Sutton Vane play] (11-24-52) John Dall, Jean Adair, Ernest Truex, Estelle Winwood

33. "This Thing Called Love" [adapted from the Edwin Burke play] (12-1-52) Gene Raymond, Ruth Warrick
34. "One Sunday Afternoon" [adapted from the James Hagan play] (12-8-52) Gloria McGhee, Mimi Kelly
35. "I Like It Here" [adapted from the A. B. Shiffrin play] (12-15-52) Bert Lytell, Oscar Karlweiss
36. "The Enchanted Cottage" [adapted from the Arthur Wing Pinero play] (12-22-52) Judith Evelyn
37. "The Gold Diggers" [adapted from the Avery Hopwood play] (12-29-52) Gloria McGhee, John Newland
38. "Death Takes a Holiday" [adapted from the Alberto Casella play] (1-5-53) Nigel Green, Wendy Drew
39. "Adam and Eva" [adapted from the Guy Bolton and George Middleton play] (1-12-53) Hugh Reilly, Katherine Bard
40. "Smilin' Thru" [adapted from the Jane Cowl and Jane Murfin play] (1-19-53) William Prince, Beverly Whitney, Wesley Addy
41. "The Acquittal" [adapted from the 1920 play] (1-26-53) John Baragrey, Judith Evelyn
42. "Criminal at Large" [adapted from the Edgar Wallace play] (2-2-53) Basil Rathbone, Estelle Winwood, Anthony Kimble-Cooper
43. "R. U. R." ("Rossum's Universal Robots") [adapted from the Karel Capek and Joseph Capek play] (2-9-53) Hugh Reilly, Dorothy Hart
44. "Candlelight" [adapted from the Siegfried Geyer play] (2-16-53) Clare Luce, Ian Keith, Rex O'Malley
45. "Guest in the House" [adapted from the Hagar Wilde and Dale Eunson play] (2-23-53) Richard Webb, Bonita Granville, Meg Mundy
46. "The Firebrand" [adapted from the Edwin Justin Mayer play; Barbara Brigham applied the make-up] (3-2-53) Basil Rathbone (as Benevenuto Cellini), Claudia Morgan, Esmond Knight
47. "Whistling in the Dark" [adapted from the Lawrence Gross and Edward Childs Caroenter play] (3-9-53) Edward Everett Horton, Marjorie Gateson
48. "The Kick-In" [adapted from the Willard Mack play] (3-16-53) Meg Mundy, Richard Webb
49. "In Any Language" [adapted from the Edmund Beloin and Henry Garson play] (3-23-53) Micha Auer, Audrey Christie
50. "George and Margaret" [adapted from the Gerald Savory play] (3-30-53) Ernest Truex, Sylvia Field
51. "Wuthering Heights" [adapted from the Emily Brontë classic] (4-6-53) William Prince, Meg Mundy
52. "Meet the Wife" [adapted from the Lynn Starling play] (4-13-53) Edith Meiser, Loring Smith, Murray Matheson
53. "The Noose" [adapted from the Willard Mack play] (4-20-53) Richard Hylton, Jay Jostyn, Lee Grant, Esther Ralston
54. "Her Master's Voice" [adapted from the Clare Kummer play] (4-27-53) Cliff Norton, Nydia Westman, June Walker
55. "Interference" [adapted from the Harold Dearden play] (5-4-53) Conrad Nagel, Clare Luce

56. "The Village Green" [adapted from the Carl Allensworth play] (5-11-53) Marc Connelly
57. "Climax" [adapted from the Edward Locke play] (5-18-53) Sylvia Sidney, Russell Hardie
58. "The Witching Hour" [adapted from the Augustus Thomas play] (5-25-53) Ian Keith, Sarah Burton, Warren Wade

Third Season

59. "The Twentieth Century" [adapted from the Ben Hecht and Charles MacArthur play] (10-12-53) Fred Clark, Constance Bennett
60. "The Front Page" [adapted from the Ben Hecht and Charles MacArthur play] (10-19-53) Edward Everett Horton
61. "Seventh Heaven" [adapted from the Austin Strong play] (10-26-53) Hurd Hatfield, Geraldine Brooks, Ian Keith
62. "The Hasty Heart" [adapted from the John Patrick play] (11-2-53) Hurd Hatfield, John Dall
63. "Janie" [adapted from the Josephine Bentham and Herschel V. Williams play] (11-9-53) Bert Lytell, Marjorie Gateson, Jay Jostyn
64. "Dark Victory" [adapted from the George Emerson Brewer Jr. and Bertram Block play] (11-16-53) Sylvia Sidney, Christopher Plummer, Ian Keith
65. "The Bat" [adapted from the Mary Roberts Rinehart and Avery Hopwood play] (11-23-53) Estelle Winwood, Jay Jostyn, Alice Pearce
66. "Kind Lady" [adapted from the Edward Chodorov play] (11-30-53) Sylvia Sidney
67. "Your Uncle Dudley" [adapted from the Howard Lindsay and Bertrand Robinson play] (12-7-53) Edward Everett Horton
68. "The Last of Mrs. Cheyney" [adapted from the Frederick Lonsdale play] (12-14-53) Vicki Cummings, Patricia Jenkins, John Baragrey
69. "Angel Street" [adapted from the Patrick Hamilton play; restaged from 5/12/52] (12-21-53) Sylvia Sidney, Victor Jory, Melville Cooper
70. "The Thirteenth Chair" [adapted from the Bayard Veiller play] (12-28-53) Clare Luce
71. "The Gramercy Ghost" [adapted from the John Cecil Holm play] (1-4-54) Veronica Lake, Richard Hylton
72. "Room Service" [adapted from the John Murray and Allen Boretz play] (1-11-54) Lew Parker
73. "Reflected Glory" [adapted from the George Kelly play] (1-18-54) Clare Luce
74. "The Patsy" [adapted from the Barry Conners play; restaged from 6/22/53] (1-25-54) Charles and Roxanne Pursell, Mary Johnson

THE UNEXPECTED

The Regulars: Herbert Marshall, host and narrator

The Episodes:

1. "Calculated Risk" (3-5-52) Rochelle Hudson
2. "The Hitchhiker Was a Lady" (3-12-52) Jane Nigh
3. "The Man from Yesterday" (3-19-52) Jane Nigh, John Archer
4. "Fury and Sound" (3-26-52) Lois Hall
5. "The Slide Rule Blonde" (4-2-52) Marjorie Reynolds
6. "Born Again" (4-9-52) Dolores Mann, Billy Halop
7. "Split Second" (4-16-52) Veda Ann Borg
8. "Mardi Gras" (4-23-52) Mary Anderson
9. "Legal Tender" (4-30-52) Jeanne Cagney
10. "House of Shadows" (5-7-52) Phyllis Avery
11. "Eclipse" (5-14-52) Margo
12. "The Professional Touch" (5-21-52) Virginia Grey
13. "The Witch of the Eight Islands" (5-28-52) Paula Drew, John Kellogg
14. "The Eyeglasses" (6-4-52) Philip Terry
15. "Lifeline" (6-11-52) Ann Tyrell, Robert Paige
16. "False Colors" (6-18-52) Sheila Ryan, Robert Shayne
17. "Merry-Go-Round" (6-25-52)
18. "The Magnificent Lie" (7-2-52) Raymond Burr
19. "The Perfectionists" (7-16-52) Veda Ann Borg, Anthony Caruso, Kenneth Tobey
20. "Slightly Dead" (7-30-52) J. M. Kerrigan
21. "Leopard's Enlightening" (8-6-52)
22. "The Emperor of Nothing" (8-13-52) Todd Karns
23. "The Perfect Mrs. Chesney" (8-20-52) Martha Vickers
24. "One for the Money" (8-27-52) Katherine Locke, Isabel Jewell
25. "The Mask" (9-3-52) John Hudson
26. [unknown title] (9-10-52)
27. "The Puppeteers" (9-17-52) Gale Storm, Robert Hutton
28. "The Woman Who Left Herself" (9-24-52) Bonita Granville

Second Season

29. "Blackmail" (10-1-52) Marie Windsor
30. "Mr. O" (10-8-52) Ludwig Donath
31. "High Adventure" (10-15-52) Paula Raymond
32. "Bright Boy" (10-22-52) Tom Drake
33. "Confidentially Yours" (10-29-52) Alan Mowbray
34. "Landscape in Black" (11-5-52) Coleen Gray
35. "Desert Honeymoon" (11-12-52) John Agar
36. "The Numbers Game" (11-19-52) Marshall Thompson
37. "Beyond Belief" (11-26-52) John Hoyt, Lois Collier
38. "Escape to Nowhere" (12-3-52) Lowell Gilmore
39. "Some Day They'll Give Us Guns" (12-10-52) Bobby Driscoll, Kyle James
40. "Lifeline" (12-17-52)

REBOUND

The Episodes:

1. "The Cheat" (2-8-52) Onslow Stevens
2. "The Treasure" (2-15-52) Martin Garralaga
3. "The Boarder" (2-22-52) Janet Stewart, John Doucette, Dorothy Adams, Robert Foulk
4. "The Mine" (2-29-52) Robert Osterloch, Ned Glass, Lee Marvin
5. "The Prize" (3-7-52) George Macready, Roberta Haynes
6. "The Match" (3-14-52) Gloria Saunders, Mario Siletti, Miner-
   val Urecal
7. "Joker's Wild" (3-21-52) Raymond Burr, Onslow Stevens
8. "The Losers" (3-28-52) Mervin Williams, Dorothy Comingore
9. "One Night Stand" (4-4-52)
10. "The Wreck" (4-11-52)
11. "The Money" (4-18-52)
12. "The Wedding" (4-25-52)
13. "A Matter of Honor" (5-2-52) Jeff York, Elizabeth Fraser
14. "The Thief" (5-9-52)
15. "The Witness" (5-16-52)
16. "The Henchmen" (5-23-52) Robert Osterloh, James Hayward
17. "The Honeymoon" (5-30-52) Damian O'Flynn

Second Season [alternating with the series DARK OF NIGHT]

18. "The Good Turn" (11-21-52) George Macready, Rita Johnson,
    Hayden Rorke
19. "I'm You" (12-5-52) Dave Willock, John Doucette
20. "Simple" (1-2-53)
21. "Quiet Sunday" (1-16-53) Fay Baker

POLICE STORY

Drawn from actual police files.

The Episodes:

1. "Detective Sergeant, Martin Stephens" (4-4-52) James Gregory, Leni Stengel, Al Remsen
2. "The San Francisco Story" (4-11-52) Jay Barney
3. [unknown title] (4-18-52) Peg Hillias
4. "The New Orleans Story" (4-25-52) Ralph Stanley
5. "The Detroit Story" (5-2-52) Victory Thorley
6. "The Richmond Story" (5-9-52) Edmon Ryan
7. "The Springfield, Massachusetts Story" (5-16-52) E. G.
   Marshall
8. "The Portland, Oregon Case" (5-23-52)
9. "The Cleveland, Ohio Case" (5-30-52)
10. "The Philadelphia Story" (6-6-52) Joshua Shelley

11. "The Dallas, Texas Story" (6-13-52)
12. "The Alleghany County Story" (6-20-52) Russell Hardie
13. "The Miami, Florida Story" (6-27-52)
14. "The Indianapolis Case" (7-4-52)
15. "The Boston Case" (7-18-52) Edward Binns
16. "The California Case" (8-1-52) Robert Keith Jr., Hope Miller

CURTAIN CALL

The Episodes:

1. "The Promise" (6-20-52) Carol Bruce, Robert Preston
2. "The Soul of the Great Bell" (6-27-52) Boris Karloff
3. "Azaya" (7-4-52) Victoria Ward, Jack Palance, Richard Kiley
4. "The Season of Divorce" (7-11-52) John Forsythe, Shepperd Strudwick, Richard Kiley, Leora Dana
5. "The Party" (7-18-52) Miriam Hopkins
6. "Summer Evening" (7-25-52) Raimonda Orselli, Lee Bowman
7. "Swell Girl" (8-1-52) Victoria Ward, Wendell Corey, Charles Cooper, Reginald Mason
8. "The Vexations of A. J. Wentworth B.A." (8-15-52) Harry Townes, Melville Cooper
9. "The Liar" [adapted from the Henry James story] (8-27-52) Ilona Massey, Charlton Heston, Frederic Tozere, Susan Harris
10. "The Summer People" (8-29-52) James Dunn, Frances Fuller, Paul Ford
11. "The Model Millionaire" (9-5-52)
12. "Mutiny in the Zoo" (9-12-52) Louise Larrabe, Howard Smith
13. "Carrie Marr" (9-19-52) Maureen Stapleton, Frederic Tozere, Val Dufour
14. "Concert in Brooklyn" (9-26-52) Worthington Miner, Priscilla Gillette

THE SCHAEFER CENTURY THEATRE

The Episodes:

1. "Portrait of Toby" (5-24-52) Lynne Roberts, John Qualen
2. "Annual Honeymoon" (5-31-52) Bonita Granville, Garry Moore, Alan Mowbray
3. "Mr. and Mrs. Spring" (6-7-52) Ruth Warrick, Onslow Stevens
4. "Shooting Star" (6-14-52) Lynne Roberts, Whitfield Connor
5. "From Such a Seed" (6-21-52) Frieda Inescourt
6. "Yesterday's World" (7-9-52) Robert Rockwell, Bonita Granville
7. "The Red Balloon" (7-30-52) Randy Stuart, John Sutton
8. "A Mansion for Jimmy" (8-6-52) Robert Paige
9. "Playmates" (8-20-52) Natalie Wood

10. "Cafe Berlin" (8-27-52) Robert Hutton
11. "The Other Woman" (9-9-52) Lynn Bari

Second Season

12. "Portfolio Twelve" (10-5-52) Robert Hutton
13. "Lesson in Hot Lead" (10-12-52) Billy Gray
14. "The Juvenile Genius" (11-2-52) Robert Paige

VICTORY AT SEA

A reverent, brilliantly detailed study of the World War II Naval Theatre became the first major video documentary undertaking. As produced by Henry Salomon Jr. and put to the music of Richard Rodgers (whose score was arranged by Robert Russell Bennett) "Victory at Sea," still popular in syndication, yet splashes home the emblematical Nike achieved by the combatants.

The Regulars: Leonard Graves, narrator.

The Episodes:

1. "Design for War" (10-26-52)
2. "The Pacific Boils Over" (11-2-52)
3. "Sealing the Breach" (11-9-52)
4. "Midway Is East" (11-23-52)
5. "The Mediterranean Mosaic" (11-30-52)
6. "The Pacific Bolls Over" (12-7-52)
7. "Guadalcanal" (12-14-52)
8. "Rings Around Rabout" (12-21-52)
9. "Mare Nostrum" (12-28-52)
10. "Sea and Sound" (1-4-53)
11. "Beneath the Southern Cross" (1-11-53)
12. "Magnetic North" (1-18-53)
13. "Conquest of Micronesia" (1-25-53)
14. "Malanesian Nightmare" (2-1-53)
15. "Roman Renaissance" (2-8-53)
16. "D-Day" (2-15-53)
17. "The Killers and the Killed" (2-22-53)
18. "The Turkey Shoot" (3-1-53)
19. "Two If By Sea" (3-8-53)
20. "The Battle for Leyte Gulf" (3-15-53)
21. "The Return of the Allies" (3-22-53)
22. "Full Fathom Five" (3-29-53)
23. "The Fate of Europe" (4-5-53)
24. "Target Suribachi" (4-12-53)
25. "The Road to Mandalay" (4-19-53)
26. "Suicide for Glory" (4-26-53)

OMNIBUS

Produced under the auspices of The Ford Foundation Television-Radio Workshop; William Spier, producer.

The Regulars: Alistair Cooke, host.

The Episodes:

1. a) scenes from The Mikado [adapted from the Gilbert and Sullivan musical play; Lehman Engel conducted] Martyn Green; b) "The Trial of Anne Boleyn" [adapted by Maxwell Anderson from his own Anne of the Thousand Days; directed by Alex Segal] Rex Harrison, Lili Palmer; c) "The Bad Men" [an original teleplay by William Saroyan]; d) "The Witch Doctor" [a short film on the Haitian voodoo dance]; e) "Camera Miracles" [a documentary on the X-ray] (11-9-52)
2. a) "Mr. Lincoln: 'The Birth and Death of Abraham Lincoln'" [Part I; "The Early Years," beginning a series of teleplays expressly composed for television, by James Agee] Royal Dano, Jerome Courtland, Joanne Woodward; b) "The Telephone" [by Gian-Carlo Menotti]; c) "Leonardo da Vinci: The Renaissance Man" [a documentary]; d) "The Lonely Hearts Club" [with The Paris Ballet]; e) "The Dog Club" (11-16-52)
3. a) "The Twelve Pound Look" [adapted from the James M. Barrie play] Helen Hayes; b) Julio de Diego, painting to music; c) "The Stranger Left No Card" [a British film thriller featuring Alan Badel]; d) Philippe Halsman photographs Eva Gabor and Linda Christian (11-23-52)
4. a) "The Christmas Tie" [an original teleplay by William Saroyan] Helen Hayes, Burgess Meredith; b) "Nancy Hanks"; c) "Mr. Lincoln: 'The Birth and Death of Abraham Lincoln'" [Part II] Royal Dano, et al. (11-30-52)
5. a) "The Trial of Ben Jonson" [an original teleplay by Maxwell Anderson] June Lockhart, Alexander Scourby; b) feature films (12-7-52)
6. a) "A Mother Goose Suite" Helen Hayes; b) "Mr. Lincoln: 'The Birth and Death of Abraham Lincoln'" [Part III, "Lincoln's Boyhood"]; c) feature films (12-14-52)
7. "The Trial of Mr. Pickwick" [as adapted from the Charles Dickens novel] Sir Cedric Hardwicke (12-21-52)
8. a) "My Brother Henry" [adapted from the James M. Barrie play] Michael Redgrave; b) scenes from Walt Disney's Peter Pan (1952) (12-28-52)
9. "The Bear" [adapted from the Anton Chekhov play] Michael Redgrave, June Havoc (1-4-53)
10. a) "Henry V" [adapted from the Shakespeare classic] Brian Aherne; b) "New Salem" Joanne Woodward; c) "Mr. Lincoln: 'The Birth and Death of Abraham Lincoln'" [Part IV] Royal Dano, et al. (1-11-53)
11. a) a report on the film work of Raymond Loeury; b) "Servant with the Two Masters" [with The Paris Ballet]; c) "Vive" [an original teleplay by William Saroyan] Bert Lahr, Bobby Driscoll (1-18-53)

12. a) The Benny Goodman Trio; b) "Thomas Hart Benton at Home";
    c) an episode from Roberto Rossellini's feature film The
    Flowers of St. Francis (1953) (1-25-53)
13. Die Fledermaus [the Johann Strauss opera sung in English; the
    Metropolitan Opera Company's first production from a tele-
    vision studio; Eugene Ormandy, conducting] (2-1-53) Jar-
    mila Novotna, soprano, et al.
14. a) "Napoleon's Letters" James and Pamela Mason; b) "The Pel-
    ican" [a film short subject]; c) "Mr. Lincoln: 'The Birth
    and Death of Abraham Lincoln'" [Part V] Royal Dano, et al.;
    d) The Paris Ballet (2-8-53)
15. a) "The Oyster and the Pearl" [an original teleplay by William
    Saroyan] Paul Douglas; b) "Wheat Field"; c) The Cellini-
    Cup Exhibition; d) The Paris Ballet (2-15-53)
16. La Boheme [the Puccini opera, originating from the Metropolitan
    Opera House; Alberto Eredi conducting the Metropolitan or-
    chestra] (2-22-53) Nadine Conner, soprano; Brian Sullivan,
    bass; Brenda Lewis, Frank Guarrera, Alessio de Paolis
17. a) "The Happy Journey" Helen Hayes; b) "Five Gifts" [a ballet];
    c) a feature on the Coronation Ceremony of Queen Elizabeth
    II; d) "The History of the Income Tax" [a documentary]
    (3-1-53)
18. a) "A Lodging for the Night" [adapted from the Robert Louis
    Stevenson story] Yul Brynner (as François Villon); b) so-
    prano guitarist Olga Coelho; c) a Pimpinella fairy tale
    (3-8-53)
19. a) "The Last Night of Don Juan" [adapted from the Edmond
    Rostand play] Fredric March, Joseph Schildkraut; b) William
    Capell, at the piano; c) "Country Editor" [a documentary];
    d) "Genesis" [an experimental film] (3-15-53)
20. a) "Three Maidens and a Devil" [the premiere of an American
    ballet choreographed by Agnes de Mille] Yurek Lazowski (as
    "The Devil"), Agnes de Mille (as "The Priggish Maiden"),
    Lucia Chase (as "The Greedy Maiden"), Janet Reed (as "The
    Lustfull Maiden"); b) "Happy Birthday, Aunt Sarah" June
    Havoc (3-22-53)
21. a) "Lord Byron's Love Letter" [an original play by Tennessee
    Williams] Ethel Barrymore, Patricia Collinge, Nydia West-
    man; b) "135th Street" [the George Gershwin operetta (a
    variation on the Frankie and Johnnie theme), lyrics by Buddy
    de Sylva; orchestrated by George Bassman] Betta Warren,
    Baun Spearman, Jimmy Rushing, principals in the all-black
    cast (3-29-53)
22. a) "Everyman" [adapted from the fifteenth century morality play]
    Burgess Meredith; b) "Grandma Moses at Home" [a docu-
    mentary]; c) "A Trip to the Moon" [the Melies classic]
    (4-5-53)
23. a) "Toy Symphony" [by Haydn; Leopold Stokowski conducting];
    b) "A Young Person's Guide to the Orchestra" [by Benjamin
    Britten] (4-12-53)
24. a) "The Abracadabra Kid" [an original teleplay by William Sa-
    royan] Maria Riva; b) "Trial by Jury" [adapted from the
    Gilbert and Sullivan play]; c) "Paul Revere's Ride" Raymond
    Massey (4-19-53)

25. a) Emlyn Williams reads from Charles Dickens' A Tale of Two
    Cities; b) "Gaieté Parisienne" [a ballet]; c) "The Figgerin'
    of Aunt Wilma" [an original play by James Thurber] (4-26-53)
26. "Arms and the Man" [adapted from the George Bernard Shaw
    play; directed by John Burrell, director of the London Old
    Vic Theatre; costumes by Leslie Renfield (CBS designer)
    and Julia Sze (head of CBS costumes)] (5-3-53) Walter
    Slezak (as Major Paul Petkoff), Jean-Pierre Aumont (as
    Captain Bruntschi), Nanette Fabray (as Raina), Kent Smith
    (as Major Sergius), Gwen Anderson (as the servant girl),
    Martita Hunt

Second Season

27. a) "Glory in the Flower" [an original teleplay by William Inge]
    Jessica Tandy, Hume Cronyn, James Dean; b) excerpts from
    Oklahoma! with the current Broadway cast; c) "This Little
    Kitty Stayed Cool" [an original teleplay by James Thurber]
    Carol Channing, Elliott Reid; d) "The Big Dome" (10-4-53)
28. a) "The Battler" [adapted from the Ernest Hemingway short
    story] Jack Palance, Chester Morris; b) "Games" [a ballet];
    c) "Operation: Hurricane" [a documentary]; d) preview of
    the forthcoming Omnibus adaptation of "King Lear" (10-11-53)
29. "King Lear" [a 73-minute condensation of the Shakespeare clas-
    sic; directed by Peter Brook] (10-18-53) Orson Welles (as
    King Lear), Beatrice Straight (as Goneril), Margaret Phil-
    lips (as Regan), Scott Forbes (as the Duke of Cornwall),
    Bramwell Fletcher (as the Earl of Kent), Alan Badel (as the
    Fool), Wesley Addy (as the King of France), Frederic Wor-
    lock, Larry Blyden
30. a) an interview with Frank Lloyd Wright; b) "The Gold Dress"
    [adapted from the Stephen Vincent Benet story]; c) "Stock-
    holm, Sweden" [a documentary]; d) a recording session with
    Les Paul and Mary Ford (10-25-53)
31. a) "The Man of Destiny" [adapted from the George Bernard
    Shaw play] Alan Badel; b) "The Life of Melies" [a documen-
    tary on the pioneer filmmaker]; c) The Columbia University
    Football Team (11-1-53)
32. a) "The X-Ray Machine" [a documentary, and an interview with
    Dr. Raymond Gramiak of the University of Rochester Medi-
    cal School]; b) "Billy the Kid" [the Agnes de Mille ballet,
    choreographed to the Aaron Copland score] John Kriza, Ruth
    Ann Koesun, Fernand Nault, Scott Douglas; c) "Romance of
    Transportation" [a documentary travelogue]; d) "A Jury of
    Her Peers" [adapted from the Susan Glaspell mystery drama]
    Louisa Horton, Carmen Mathews, Arthur O'Connell, John
    Shellie (11-8-53)
33. a) "The Raspberry Queen" [the story of a press agent's effort
    to make a drum majorette of sixteen the Queen of Wynndotte
    Valley]; b) "The Moor Pavane" [a modern dress ballet of
    Othello; Jose Limon and Company]; c) "The Sea Horse" [a
    documentary study of the life cycle] (11-15-53)
34. a) "Toine" [adapted from the Guy de Maupassant short story]
    Elsa Lanchester, Walter Slezak; b) an interview with Paul

Frischen, an arctic explorer; c) the St. Paul's Cathedral
Choir of London; d) "A Demonstration of the X-Ray Motion
Picture Technique" [a documentary, with Dr. Raymond Gra-
miak of the University of Rochester] (11-22-53)

35. "The Horn Blows at Midnight" [adapted from the Aubrey Wisberg
scenario, on an angel's errand to destroy a wicked world]
(11-29-53) Jack Benny

36. a) "The Capital of the World" [the Ballet Theatre rendition of
the Ernest Hemingway story; b) "The Capital of the World"
[a dramatization of the Hemingway story]; c) "Laughing Gas"
[Italian feature film; narrated by Alistair Cooke]; d) "On the
Christmas Windows of Lord and Taylor" (12-6-53)

37. a) "The Birth of a Modern Twenty Piece Dance Band"; b) "The
Nature of the Beast" [adapted from the uncompleted Moss
Hart play] Mel Ferrer; c) a documentary on the reaction of
laboratory animals during a thirty-seven mile high rocket
flight over the New Mexico desert (12-13-53)

38. a) "Irish Linen" Helen Hayes; b) "Mom and Leo" Helen Hayes;
c) "The 51st Dragon" [an animated feature adapted from the
Heywood Broun satire on private schools]; d) "The Young
Fighter" [a documentary utilizing a newly-developed camera
technique] (12-20-53)

39. a) "The Sojourner" [adapted by Carson McCullers from her own
short story on American Bohemians] Neva Patterson, David
Wayne, Frances Starr; b) "Chicken Little" [the premiere
performance of an Alec Wilder operetta based on the children's story]; c) "Melies the Great: Magician of the Movies"
[documentary on the film pioneer] (12-27-53)

40. a) "Nobody's Fool" [adapted from the John Steinbeck story "Pas-
tures of Heaven"] Thomas Mitchell; b) "Palle Alone in the
World" [on the reactions of a Danish boy who believes he
solely occupies the earth] Lars Henning Jenson; c) "Village
Incident in India" [a documentary]; d) Alistair Cooke reads
Benediction (1-3-54)

41. a) "The Remarkable Case of Mr. Bruhl" [adapted from the
James Thurber short story; narrated by Edward Everett
Horton] Elliott Nugent; b) a demonstration of the detection
of art forgeries by art expert M. M. Van Dantzig; c) "Latest
Advances in Laboratory Chemistry" [a documentary]; d) Alistair Cooke interviews the Casadesus family of classical
pianists (1-10-54)

42. a) "Undersea Archaelogy" [Part I; a documentary by Jacques
Yves Cousteau on the recovery of art treasures from a
Greek ship sunk twenty-two years ago]; b) "The Duchess
and the Smugs" [by Pamela Frankau] Susan Strasberg, John
Beal, Lili Darvas (1-17-54)

43. a) "Nothing So Monstrous" [an original teleplay by John Stein-
beck] Lew Ayres, Randy Stuart, Thomas Rettig, Arthur
Shields; b) a demonstration of atom smashing by Dr. Dunning
at a Columbia University laboratory; c) "The Hunter" [a
documentary with music]; d) an interview with Broadway sign
builder Douglas Leigh (1-24-54)

44. a) The Sleeping Beauty [the premiere performance of Ottorino
Respighi's opera] Jim Hawthorne (as the prince), Jo Sullivan

(as the princess); b) an interview with Sir Edmund Hillary, conqueror of Mount Everest   (1-31-54)

45.   a) "Undersea Archaelogy" [Part II, with Jacques Yves Cousteau];
b) "Mr. Lincoln: The End and the Beginning" [excerpts from the James Agee drama on the early and last days of Abraham Lincoln]; c) John Jay discusses experiences in photographing skiers in action; d) Victor Borge is interviewed   (2-7-54)

46.   a) The Azuma Kabuki dancers of Japan; b) "Pazo Doble" [by Budd Schulberg, on a young bullfighter forced into the sport by his father]; c) "The Confidential Clerk" [scenes from the T. S. Eliot play] Claude Rains, Douglas Watson; d) "The Whale Who Wanted to Be a Submarine" [a tale]   (2-14-54)

47.   a) "The Merry Wives of Windsor" [a Yale University production of the Shakespeare classic]; b) "Time Out of War" [an original feature film produced under the auspices of the U. C. L. A. School of Cinematography, on the friendship between a Northerner and a Confederate]; c) Southern African songs by Marais and Miranda   (2-21-54)

48.   a) Captain Jacques Yves Cousteau discusses his most recent underwater exploration off the Persian gulf; b) "A Marriage Has Been Arranged" [between a woman in her twenties and a man in his forties] Joan Greenwood; c) "Hilde and the Turnpike" [a surrealist drama] Peggy McCay   (2-28-54)

49.   a) "Treason 1780" [an historical drama on Benedict Arnold] Martin Brooks; b) "The House" [adapted from the John Steinbeck story] Buddy Ebsen, Mabel Paige   (3-7-54)

50.   a) "The Gambler, The Nun and The Radio" [adapted from the Ernest Hemingway short story] Geraldine Fitzgerald, Harry Townes; b) "Shoot the Nets" [a documentary on the Dutch herring fleet]; c) three original skits by Hermione Gingold: "Hate," "Holiday," "Conquest"   (3-14-54)

51.   a) The John Destine Dancers; b) "Arteriosclerosis" [a documentary]; c) a British satire on a trip to the dentist; d) [at 5:45] live coverage and remote broadcast from the New York Times on how the Monday front page is put together; Alistair Cooke interviews Arthur Hays Sulzberger; managing editor Turner Catledge, and editor Charles Mertz   (3-21-54)

52.   a) "The Apollo of Bellac" [a comedy play by Jean Giraudoux] Claude Dauphin, Gaby Rodgers, Francis Compton; b) a cavalcade of highlights from previous episodes of the season   (3-28-54)

Third Season

53.   a) Fred Allen previews his forthcoming book Treadmill to Oblivion; b) "Percussion" with Saul Goodman, chief, and members of the percussion section of the New York Philharmonic; c) "Dance to Freedom" [a documentary on two Hungarian dancers' escape through the Iron Curtain]; d) "Around the World in Fifteen Minutes" [on traveling a non-stop flight]   (10-17-54)

54.   a) "The Man with the Diamond" [a contemporary folk tale of the mid-west; the premiere program for the Omnibus repertory company]; b) "The Man Who Married a Dumb Wife"

[adapted from the Anatole France story] Zachary Scott, Nita Talbot; c) "A Child's View of the United Nations" [interviews]; d) "Farewell to Native Dancer" [from Sagamore Farm, Maryland] (10-24-54)

55. a) "A Clean Fresh Breeze" E. G. Marshall, Richard Kiley; b) "Toby and the Tall Corn" [a touring tent show with the Touring Players] (10-31-54)

56. a) a review of Pearl Buck's My Several Worlds; b) "Brewsie and Willie" [adapted from the Gertrude Stein story, with the Touring Players, Inc.]; c) wrestling match: U. S. Naval Academy versus Penn State College; d) a demonstration of professional wrestling with Bert Schurtleff (11-7-54)

57. a) "An Analysis of the First Movement of Beethoven's Fifth Symphony" with Leonard Bernstein; b) the story of a sixty-one-year-old beginner; c) "Small College Football" [the effect of the game on a midwestern town] (11-14-54)

58. a) "Antigone" [adapted from the Sophocles tragedy] Beatrice Straight, Shepperd Strudwick, Kevin McCarthy, Marian Seldes, Philip Bourneuf, Barry Jones; b) Dick Button demonstrates figure skating (11-21-54)

59. a) "The Virtuous Island" [adapted from the Jean Giraudoux play]; b) a musical lesson on the brass section of a symphony orchestra; c) "The Capture of the Musk-Ox" [a documentary]; d) Orson Bean in profile (11-28-54)

60. a) a visit with a Maine lobsterman; b) "Toys"; c) French puppeteers; d) a visit to the New York Lexington's school for the deaf (12-5-54)

61. a) "The Contrast" [adapted from the Royall Tyler play, one of the first produced in America] (12-12-54) Nita Talbot

62. a) a drama staged in The Cloisters; b) The Vienna Boys' Choir; c) Christmas readings by Hume Cronyn and Jessica Tandy (12-19-54)

63. The Merry Widow [the Franz Lehar opera; directed by Cyril Ritchard, with the Symphony of the Air conducted by Eugene Ormandy] (12-26-54) Patrice Munsel, Theodore Uppman, Martyn Green, Dorothy Coulter, Jim Hawthorne, Jerome Kilty

64. a) "The Trial of St. Joan" [adapted from the George Bernard Shaw play] Kim Hunter, Larry Blyden, Everett Sloane; b) "Architecture" [a documentary on its history; Eliot Noyes, narrator] (1-2-55)

65. a) "The Adams Family: John Adams" [Part I, the first in a series of drama documentaries depicting four generations of the Adams Family, as interpreted by historian Allan Nevins] Robert Preston, Carmen Mathews; b) skin divers battling a shark; c) a profile of New York's Grand Central Station (1-9-55)

66. a) Gilbert and Sullivan interpretations by Martyn Green; b) the story of Nobel Prize laureate Hideki Yukawa, a Japanese physicist (the 1949 recipient for "theoretical deductions of the existence of mesons") (1-16-55)

67. a) a violin lesson by Yehudi Menuhin; b) "The Adams Family: John Quincy Adams" [Part II, as interpreted by Allan Nevins]

Hume Cronyn, Jessica Tandy; c) an interview with Professor Nevins   (1-23-55)

68.   a) scenes from Shakespeare's Hamlet, with the Canadian Players Ltd., Walter Kerr, host; b) a fencing demonstration by the United States Olympic team; c) a story of high-altitude flight (1-30-55)

69.   "Mr. Lincoln" [a condensation of the five-part documentary drama by James Agee]   (2-6-55)   Royal Dano, Joanne Woodward, Marian Seldes, Blanche Chalet, Joanna Roos

70.   a) "The Turn of the Screw" [adapted by Gore Vidal from the Henry James story] Geraldine Page, Rex Thompson, Cathleen Nesbitt, Nina Reader; b) "The Romance of Playing Cards" [a dance interpretation]; c) the story of France's first oil well   (2-13-55)

71.   a) "The New World" [adapted from the James M. Barrie play] Barry Jones; b) sessions in remedial reading with instructors from the Teachers' College of Columbia University; c) maritime paintings by Winslow Homer are used to tell the story of the sea   (2-20-55)

72.   a) "The Adams Family: Charles Francis Adams" [Part III, as interpreted by Allan Nevins] Shepperd Strudwick; b) "Command post" [on the use of radar installations for defensive purposes]; c) "Parts of the Human Body: The Brain" [Part I, first in a documentary series]   (2-27-55)

73.   a) The Mighty Casey [a new American opera adapted from the Ernest L. Thayer baseball poem; Samuel Krachmalnuk, conductor] E. G. Marshall, Danny Scholl; b) a close-up of rare jewels and what goes into their final show casing   (3-6-55)

74.   a) "A Different Drummer" [an original play created for the Drama Department of Baylor University, on a youth's attempt to establish his own identity] Clu and Miriam Gulager, Jack Dempsey; b) "The Human Body: The Heart" [Part II in the documentary series]; c) "American Boyhoods" [Part I, with recollections by Attorney Joseph Welch on his growing up in Iowa]   (3-13-55)

75.   a) "The Adams Family: The Education of Henry Adams" [Part IV, as interpreted by Allan Nevins] James Daly, William Windom, Lori March, Brooks Adams; b) "A Tribute to Spring"; c) "The Story of Wheat" [a documentary]   (3-20-55)

76.   a) the story of the confederate states prior to the outbreak of hostilities; b) a baseball player's minor league training; c) a profile of an Australian Royal mail carrier; d) "The Independent Man" [a report]   (3-27-55)

77.   "The Iliad" [adapted by Andrew K. Lewis in free dramatic form from the Homer classic, focussing on Achilles]   (4-3-55) Paul Sparer, Alexander Scourby, Dorothy Hart, Michael Higgins, Frederic Tozere, Michael Kane

78.   a) "Uncle Tom's Cabin" [adapted from the Harriet Beecher Stowe classic; an excerpt] James Daly; b) the debut of classical dancer Shanta Rao and instrumentalist Ali Akbar Khan of India, with interpretations by Yehudi Menuhin; c) the medieval tradition of bell-changing   (4-10-55)

Fourth Season

79. "The Birth of Modern Times" [an original teleplay by Robert
Coughlean; an examination of the Renaissance period of the
fifteenth century] (10-9-55) Charlton Heston, Everett Sloane,
Betsy Von Furstenberg, Peter Donat, James Daly, Nancy
Marchand

80. a) "The Jazz World: From Blues to Rock 'n' Roll" [as seen and
interpreted by Leonard Bernstein]; b) "American Boyhoods:
The Boyhood of William Saroyan" [Part II in the series]
Sal Mineo, Pat DeSimone (10-16-55)

81. a) "Television Magic" [a dramatization of new techniques]; b)
"A Cockney's View of London"; c) "The Adams House" [the
concluding segment on The Adams Family series, where five
generations of the family lived]; d) "Survival in the Bush"
[a documentary on man's survival in the Canadian wilds]
(10-23-55)

82. a) "Advice to Bathers" [with Esther Williams, Walter Kiphuth
and the Walter Reed Women's Swimming team in a telecast
from Yale University]; b) "Favorite Theatrical Courtship
Scenes" with Jessica Tandy and Hume Cronyn (10-30-55)

83. a) "Toby and the Tall Corn" [the story of America's oldest traveling
tent show; repeat of episode of 10/31/54]; b) Antonio and his
Spanish Ballet Company; c) "Excursion House" [a report on the
house boom in America] (11-6-55)

84. a) a comedy monologue with Art Carney; b) scenes from the Gilbert
and Sullivan operetta The Pirates of Penzance with the D'Oyly
Carte Opera Company; c) "American Boyhoods" [Part III;
filmed interviews with Navy Captain John M. Elliott, who
served under Admiral Dewey at Manila] (11-13-55)

85. "She Stoops to Conquer" [adapted from the Oliver Goldsmith
classic; telecast live from New York] (11-20-55) Barbara
Jefford, Hermione Gingold, Michael Redgrave, Walter Fitzgerald, Rex Everhart

86. a) "The Art of Conducting an Orchestra: From Beethoven to
Jazz" with Leonard Bernstein; b) "American Boyhoods" [Part
IV; an interview with the Reverend Dr. Harry Emerson Fos-
dick]; c) the Harlem Globetrotters display basketball tricks,
with narration by Bud Palmer (12-4-55)

87. a) "The Royal Game" [adapted by David Shaw from the Stefan
Zweig play] Joseph Anthony, Carmen Mathews; b) "Jack Me
Normal" [a story of the dispute of the constitution of the
"normal" child, by Arnold Sundgard] Darren McGavin, Dickie
Olsen, Edward Binns (12-11-55)

88. a) "Salome" [adapted from the Oscar Wilde play] Eartha Kitt
(as Salome; her television debut), Leo Genn (as King Herod),
Patricia Neal (as Herodias), Elsa Lanchester; b) an interview
with English concert comedienne Anna Russell (12-18-55)

89. The Messiah [the Handel masterpiece; Leonard Bernstein conducting the Symphony of the Air; The Schola Cantorum directed by Hugh Ross] (12-25-55)

90. "The Best Year in the History of the Whole World" (1-1-56)
Paul Hartman, Orson Bean

91. "Dear Brutus" [adapted from the James M. Barrie play] (1-8-56) Helen Hayes, Dorothy Sands, Susan Strasberg, Franchot Tone, Neva Patterson

92. a) "The Great Forgery" Hal March, Harry Townes, Elliott Reid; b) "The Great Adventure" [Part I; the first feature-length production of Swedish documentary filmmaker Arne Sucksdorff] (1-15-56)

93. a) "The Great Adventure" [1953 documentary; Part II]; b) the debut of the Yugoslavian National Folk Ballet in America; c) a profile of ski champion Dick Durrance (1-22-56)

94. a) "Minds Over Manners" [a study of United States etiquette since 1858] Jessica Tandy, Hume Cronyn, Dorothy Sands; b) a report on boxing with "Sugar" Ray Robinson (1-29-56)

95. "One Nation" [Part I; a documentary drama study of the United States Constitution; Attorney Joseph N. Welch, host] (2-5-56) Bramwell Fletcher, Jacques Aubuchon, Larry Gates, Alan Hewitt, Jerome Kilty, Victor Jory, Jack Lord, Harry Townes, Lilia Skala

96. "Mr. Lincoln" [a condensation of the five-part documentary drama by James Agee; a repeat of episode of 2/6/55] (2-12-56) Royal Dano, et al.

97. "One Nation Indivisible" [Part II of the documentary drama on the United States Constitution; Attorney Joseph Welch, host] (2-19-56) Bramwell Fletcher, et al.

98. a) "The Evolution of the Ballet" with Agnes de Mille; b) "The Exploration of the Function and Tradition of the Organ" with E. Power Biggs; c) "Assault on the Eiffel Tower" [by four French Alpinists] (2-26-56)

99. a) "With Liberty and Justice for All" [Part III of the documentary drama on the United States Constitution; Attorney Joseph Welch, host] Bramwell Fletcher, et al.; b) an interview with James Thurber (3-4-56)

100. a) "Something About the Sky" [an "essay" on clouds]; b) "The Museum That Jack Built" [a tour of the Boston museum]; c) "The Better Half" [adapted by Maurice Valency from the Eric Knight story] Hume Cronyn, Jessica Tandy (3-11-56)

101. "The Role of the University in American Life" with Harvard President Nathan W. Pusey (3-25-56)

102. "Trial by General Court-Martial: William Mitchell, Air Service" [adapted by E. J. Kahn from the Milton Sperling and Emmett Lavery story] (4-1-56) James Daly, Richard Carlson, Neva Patterson, Marjorie Lord

103. The American Musical Comedy [Leonard Bernstein, host, illustrates its history by way of scenes from musicals of the past century; Black Crook (1866), Floradora (1900), Revue of 1914 (which had music by Irving Berlin), Oh, Kay! (1926), Of Thee I Sing (1931), others] (10-7-56)

104. a) "Androcles and the Lion" [adapted from the George Bernard Shaw play] Bert Lahr; b) scenes from the 1956 documentary film "The Silent World," with Jacques Yves Cousteau; c) "Presidents--The Ones Who Made It, The Ones Who Didn't" [a retrospective] (10-14-56)

105. a) "The Last Days of Manolete" [narrated by Barnaby Conrad];

        b) "The Silent World" [excerpts from the Jacques Cousteau film: Part II]; c) a folk ballet choreographed by Agnes de Mille (10-21-56)

106.   a) "All About Horses" [adapted from the sports story "Horsemanship"]; b) "My Heart's in the Highlands" [adapted by William Saroyan from his own 1939 play] James Daly, Everett Sloane; c) "The Silent World" [excerpts from the Jacques Cousteau film; Part III] (10-28-56)

107.   a) Eartha Kitt sings international folk songs; b) "Let There Be Farce" [by Raymond Walsh] Judith Evelyn, Jonathan Harris, Enid Markey; c) "Fads of the Roaring Twenties" (11-4-56)

108.   a) "The School for Wives" [adapted by Walter Kerr from the Molière classic comedy] Bert Lahr, William Shatner; b) a post-game session with the Princeton football team, with Coach Charles Caldwell (11-11-56)

109.   a) "The Plough and the Stars, " "Juno and the Paycock, " "The White-Headed Boy, " "Is Life Worth Living?" [adaptations of the Sean O'Casey plays by Lennox Robinson] Siobhan McKenna (the featured performer for all four segments); b) "On the Bowery" [a "Skid Row" film documentary]; c) "Era of a Wonderful Nonsense" [on the 1920's] 11-18-56)

110.   "The Blue Hotel" [adapted from the Stephen Crane short story] (11-25-56) Rip Torn, Arthur O'Connell

111.   a) "Amicable Parting" [by Mr. and Mrs. George S. Kaufman]; b) "The Man Without a Country" [a modern dress adaptation of the Edward Everett Hale classic]; c) a jam session with an Indian drummer and American jazz musicians (12-2-56)

112.   a) "The Art of Murder" [by Sidney Carroll; inspired by the works of Rex Stout, Poe and Doyle] James Daly; b) "Adventure" [a Swedish nature study]; c) an interview with comedienne Alice Pearce (12-9-56)

113.   a) "The Christmas Tie" [by William Saroyan; a repeat of episode of 11/30/52] Helen Hayes, Burgess Meredith; b) "Drugstore Sunday Noon" [by Horton Foote] Helen Hayes; c) an interview with Mr. and Mrs. Sandor Szabor; d) an interview with musical comedy star Kato Barczy and two sons (12-16-56)

114.   a) "Star of Bethlehem" [at the Hayden Planetarium]; b) The Columbus Boys' Choir; c) a parody of the Omnibus program with a Bill Baird puppet as Alistair Cooke (12-23-56)

115.   a) "The Evolution of the Dance" with Agnes de Mille; b) "Gunmanship" [a satire by comedians Bob and Ray] (12-30-56)

116.   "Oedipus the King" [adapted from the Sophocles classic] (1-6-57) Christopher Plummer, Carol Goodmer, William Shatner, Donald Davis, Robert Goodier

117.   a) "After Wagner--What?" [Leonard Bernstein discusses serious modern music]; b) "The Flight of Hungarian Refugees" [a documentary] (1-13-57)

118.   "Lee at Gettysburg" [by Alvin Sapinsley] (1-20-57) James Daly, Bruce Gordon, Dick Moore

119.   a) "The Big Wheel" [an original teleplay by S. J. Perelman] Bert Lahr; b) "The Burlesque Entertainment of Yesterday"; c) "The Message" [on the futility of war] (1-27-57)

120. "The Louisiana Story" [by Robert Flaherty] (2-3-57)
121. a) "The Ballad of Baby Doe" [a musical drama by John La-
     Touche and Douglas Moore] Martha Lipton, Virginia Cope-
     land, William Johnson; b) "The Last Days of Maonlete" [nar-
     rated by Barnaby Conrad; a repeat of episode of 10/21/56]
     (2-10-57)
122. a) "Call It Courage" [on physical stress tests]; b) an interview
     with Senator John Fitzgerald Kennedy; c) "White Mane" [a
     nature study] (2-17-57)
123. a) "The Boyhood of William Shakespeare" [a chronicle by Wal-
     ter Kerr]; b) "America's High Society of Former Years";
     c) "Baptiste" with French pantominist Jean Louis Barrault
     (2-24-57)
124. a) scenes from ancient Greek, Elizabethan and contemporary
     theatre showing the development of stage techniques; b) "And
     Joy Is My Witness" [a ballet choreographed and performed
     by Pearl Lang and Company, to the music of Bach] (3-3-57)
125. "The Trial of Captain Kidd" (3-10-57) Victor Jory, Nancy
     Marchand
126. a) "The Story of Amelia Earhart" [a documentary drama nar-
     rated by Burgess Meredith] Meg Mundy; b) the current ex-
     hibit at the Museum of Modern Art (3-17-57)
127. a) Attorney Joseph Welch comments on the Lizzie Borden case;
     b) Agnes de Mille dances to "Fall River Legend, " a ballet
     fashioned after the Lizzie Borden story; c) "The Trial of
     Lizzie Borden" [a dramatization] Richard Kiley, Margaret
     Hamilton, Christopher Plummer (3-24-57)
128. "The Music and Techniques of Bach" with a commentary, by
     Leonard Bernstein (3-31-57)

Sixth Season

129. "Stover at Yale" [adapted from the magazine serial by Owen
     Johnson] (10-20-57) Bradford Dillman, Peter Benzoni
130. a) "American Trial by Jury" [narrated by Attorney Joseph N.
     Welch]; b) "Staff of Life" [how picture magazines are pro-
     duced] (11-3-57)
131. "American Trial by Jury" [Part II; Attorney Joseph Welch,
     host] (11-17-57)
132. a) scenes from "Mary Stuart" [the current off-Broadway pro-
     duction of the Friedrich Schiller 1932 play] Irene Worth (as
     Stuart), Eva LeGallienne (as Queen Elizabeth I), Max Adrian;
     b) Leonard Bernstein and Felicia Montealegre narrate a
     filmed record of their trip to Israel (12-1-57)
133. "The Life of Samuel Johnson" [a dramatization of the James
     Boswell classic] (12-15-57) Kenneth Haigh (as Boswell),
     Peter Ustinov (as Johnson), Eithne Dunn
134. "Suburban Revue" [a variety program] (1-14-58) Bert Lahr,
     Pat Stanley, Mike Nichols and Elaine May
135. "La Perichole" [the Maurice Valency English adaptation of the
     Jacques Offenbach comic opera] (1-26-58) Cyril Ritchard,
     Laura Hurley (soprano), Theodor Uppman (baritone), Oslo
     Hankins (bass), Paul Franke (tenor), Alissio de Paole (tenor)

136. "I Found the Bones of The Bounty" [a filmed record on the discovery of the remains of The Bounty, sunk in 1790] (2-9-58)
137. "Moment of Truth" [adapted by Peter Ustinov from his own 1952 play] (2-23-58) Peter Ustinov, Jason Robards Jr., Rosemary Harris, Fritz Weaver
138. "Mrs. McThing" [adapted from the Mary Chase play] (3-9-58) Helen Hayes, Sam Levene, Eddie Hodges
139. "What Music Means to an Opera Libretto," with Leonard Bernstein [telecast live from the Metropolitan Opera House] (3-23-58)
140. "The Lady's Not for Burning" [adapted by Walter Kerr from the Christopher Fry play] (4-6-58) Christopher Plummer, Mary Ure, John McGiver, Noel Leslie, Geoffrey Lumb
141. "Nine Lives" (1957); "The Reindeer Men" (1957) [foreign films on the Second World War; the former derived from David Howarth's We Die Alone] (4-20-58)

Seventh Season

142. "Capital Punishment--Its Pros and Cons" [by James Lee, who also directed; Attorney Joseph Welch, host] (10-26-58) Edward Asner, Val Avery, Joseph Sullivan, Ed Holmes, Bill Zuckert, Ruth Manning
143. "The Submariners" [their training and life under water, with Esther Williams in interview] (11-9-58)
144. "The So-Called Human Race" [a satire on psychiatry by George Panetta] (11-23-58) Menasha Skulnick
145. "The Empty Chair" [by Peter Ustinov] (12-7-58) George C. Scott (as Robespiere), Peter Ustinov (as George Danton), Joseph Ruskin (as Jacques Hebert)
146. "Dancing Is a Man's Game" [Gene Kelly, host and principal participant] (12-21-58)
147. "Prince Orestes" [adapted from the Aeschylus trilogy by Leo Brady; staged by E. Martin Browne] (1-4-59) Christopher Plummer, Irene Worth, Mary Grant, Neil Burnside
148. "Malice in Wonderland: Three Hollywood Cameos" [by S. J. Perelman, as adapted from his own stories "And Thou Beside Me, Yacketing in the Wilderness," "Rent Me, And I'll Come to You," "Physician, Steel Thyself"; directed by James Lee] (1-18-59) Keenan Wynn, Julie Newmar, Pat Englund, Norma Crane
149. "Abraham Lincoln: The Early Years" [by James Agee; a repeat of episode of 11/16/52] (2-1-59) Royal Dano, et al.
150. The Medium [the Gian-Carlo Menotti opera; restaged] (2-15-59) Claramae Turner (contralto; as the medium), Lee Venora (soprano), Jose Perez, Donald P. Morgan, Belva Kibler, Beverly Dame
151. "Ah, Sweet Mystery of Mrs. Murphy" [an original teleplay by William Saroyan] (3-1-59) Hugh Griffith, Kate Wilkinson, George Grizzard, Daniela Bori
152. "Forty-five Minutes from Broadway" [adapted from the George M. Cohan 1906 musical] (3-15-59) Tammy Grimes, Robert

Morse, Larry Blyden, Diana Millay, David Burns, Russell Nype
153. "Power Among Men" [a 1959 motion picture on "man's capacity to create and destroy"; directed by Gian Luigi Polidoro under the supervision of Alexander Hammid; a sixty-minute condensation of the ninety-minute film] (3-29-59) Laurence Harvey, featured performer
154. "The Strange Ordeal of the Normanflier" [the story of the English tramp steamer disaster at sea as recounted by one of two survivors; adapted from the published book] (4-12-59) Rex Thompson, principal player
155. "Professor Tim" [a 1959 motion picture adapted from the Irish dramatist George Shiel's comedy Professor Tim and Paul Twyning] (4-26-59) The Abbey Players of Dublin: Seamus Kavanagh (as Professor Tim), Ray McAnally, Maire O'Donnell, Marie Kean, Philip O'Flynn, John Hoey, Geoffrey Golden, Michael O'Brien, Eileen Furlong, Brid Lynch, Bill Foley, Robert Mooney, Mike Malone, Jack Howarth
156. "H. M. S. Pinafore" [adapted from the Gilbert and Sullivan operetta; directed by Norman Campbell; choreography by Dina Krupska] (5-10-59) Cyril Ritchard (as Sir James Porter), Jacquelyn McKeever, Susan Johnson, Nathaniel Frey, William Chapman, Loren Driscoll

Eighth Season [now as a special series; telecast via NBC Sundays 5-6:00]

157. "He Shall Have Power" [a documentary examination of the office of the American Presidency] (11-13-60) Larry Blyden, Philip Abbott, Michael Tolan, Larry Gates, Harry Townes, Roland Winters; Dean McGeorge Bundy of Harvard University, narrator
158. "Abraham Lincoln: The Early Years" [by James Agee; a repeat of episode of 11/16/52] (2-5-61) Royal Dano, et al.
159. "The New Drama As Viewed by William Saroyan" [Saroyan examines the avant garde with excerpts from four theatre works] (3-5-61) a) "The Time of Your Life" (William Saroyan) Mike Kellin, Nancy Wickwire; b) "Krapp's Last Tape" (Samuel Beckett) Myron McCormick; c) "The Killer" (Eugene Ionesco); d) "The Sand Box" (Edward Albee)
160. "The Western Hemisphere--1971" [a discussion on government, education, sociology, economics and culture] (4-16-61) Professor Samuel H. Beer, Harvard University; Dr. Clodimir Vianna Moog of Brazil; Dr. Raul Prebisch of Argentina; Dr. Claude Bissell, President of the University of Toronto; Dr. German Arciniegas of Columbia are panel participants.

HOLLYWOOD OPENING NIGHT

The Episodes:

1. "Terrible Tempered Tolliver" (10-6-52) William Bendix, Peggy Ann Garner
2. "Let Georgie Do It" (10-13-52) Ann Sothern, Richard Egan
3. "Delaying Action" (10-20-52) John Hodiak, John Agar
4. "Somebody I Know" (10-27-52) Peggy Ann Garner, James Dunn, Ann Harding
5. "Welcome Home, Stranger" (11-3-52) Teresa Wright, Mark Stevens
6. "Thirty Days" (11-10-52) Robert Stack, Edward Arnold
7. "Hope Chest" (11-17-52) Macdonald Carey, Joan Caulfield
8. "The Singing Years" (11-24-52) Dorothy Lamour
9. "The Lucky Coin" (12-1-52) Maureen O'Sullivan, Wendell Corey
10. "Mysterious Ways" (12-8-52) Ethel Barrymore
11. "Sword Play" (12-15-52) David Niven
12. "Josie" (12-22-52) Jane Darwell, Ann Whitfield, James Dunn
13. "The Priceless Gift" (12-29-52) Ronald Reagan
14. "Legal Affair" (1-5-53) Franchot Tone, Nina Foch
15. "The Living Image" (1-12-53) Paul Douglas
16. "Interlude" (1-19-53) Ezio Pinza
17. "Mrs. Genius" (1-26-53) Celeste Holm
18. "The Shepherd's Touch" (2-2-53) Diana Lynn, Henry Brandon
19. "False Witness" (2-9-53) Virginia Field
20. "The Pattern" (2-16-53) Gloria Swanson
21. "The Romantic Type" (2-23-53) June Havoc, Don DeFore
22. "The Invited Seven" (3-2-53) Boris Karloff
23. "Uncle Fred Flits By" [adapted from the P. G. Wodehouse story; subsequently restaged for the Four Star Playhouse episode of 5/3/55] (3-9-53) Roland Young, David Niven
24. "Mr. Barber's Love Affair" (3-16-53) Robert Newton
25. "My Boss and I" (3-23-53) Richard Carlson, Marguerite Chapman

SHORT, SHORT DRAMA

The Regulars: Ruth Warrick, hostess

The Episodes:

1. [unknown title] (9-30-52)
2. "The Boat Ride" (10-2-52)
3. "The Man with Black Hair" (10-7-52)
4. "Act of Divorce" (10-9-52) Neva Patterson, Robert Pastene
5. "The Witness" (10-14-52)
6. "The Diary" (10-16-52) Leslie Nielsen, Olive Blakeney
7. "The Man Who Remembered" (10-21-52) Peter Hobbes, Lois Wheeler
8. "Flat Feet" (10-23-52) Gene Lyons, Paul Ford
9. "That Certain Flavor" (10-28-52) Mark Roberts
10. "Double Negative" (10-30-52) Shepperd Strudwick
11. "The Cloud" (11-4-52) Peggy Allenby, Loretta Day
12. "City Slicker" (11-6-52) Jed Proudy

13. "The Return" (11-11-52) Julie Lawrence, Frank Albertson, Ruth Woods
14. "Meet Me at the Liberty" (11-13-52) Henry Jones
15. "The Fix" (11-18-52) Jay Barney
16. "Hat Trick" (11-20-52) June Dayton, Ann Thomas, Dean Harens
17. "A Portrait of General Garrity" (11-25-52) Cliff Robertson, E. G. Marshall
18. "The Unknown Factor" (11-27-52) Richard Kiley, Eileen Heckart
19. "The Gift" (12-2-52) Olive Deering, John Boruff
20. "Woman in His Life" (12-4-52) Harriet MacGibbon
21. "I Am Not Alone" (12-9-52) Jay Giffen, John Rodney, Somer Alberg
22. "The Light Touch" (12-11-52) Leo Penn
23. "Night School" (12-16-52) Henry Jones
24. "The Escape" (12-18-52) Guy Tomajan
25. "Missing Heir" (12-23-52)
26. "Success Story" (12-25-52) Richard Derr
27. "The Matchmaker" (12-30-52) Joe Maross
28. "Thin Ice" (1-1-53) Cynthia Stone
29. "The Countess" (1-6-53) Lisa Ferraday, Vaughn Taylor
30. "The Present" (1-8-53) June Dayton
31. "The Dowry" (1-13-53) Theo Goetz
32. "The New Book" (1-15-53) Richard Bishop
33. "Lapse of Memory" (1-20-53) James Gregory
34. "Buried Treasure" (1-22-53) Una O'Connor, Ruth McDevitt, Joe Graham
35. "Paper Profits" (1-27-53) William Mills
36. [unknown title] (1-29-53)
37. "Operation Sunshine" (2-3-53) George Petrie
38. "Reasonable Facsimile" (2-5-53) Loretta Day
39. "The Interruption" [Part I] (2-10-53) Wesley Addy
40. "The Interruption" [Part II] (2-12-53) Wesley Addy
41. "The Wrestler" (2-17-53) Murvyn Vye, Alan Lee
42. "The Doctor's Deceit" (2-19-53) Russell Collins
43. "To Whom It May Concern" (2-24-53) Tony Randall, Bethel Leslie
44. "The Real Thing" [adapted from the Henry James story] (2-26-53)
45. "The Calculated Risk" (3-3-53) Lisa Howard
46. "Act of Bravery" (3-5-53) Richard Kiley
47. "Public Relations" (3-10-53) E. G. Marshall, Frank Thomas
48. "The Gambler" (3-12-53) Vaughn Taylor
49. "The Double Cross" (3-17-53) Darren McGavin, Margaret Hayes
50. "Appointment with Love" (3-19-53) Terry Becker
51. "The Will" (3-24-53) Jay Hodges
52. "The Unheard Song" (3-26-53)
53. "Follow-Up" (3-31-53) Frank Albertson
54. "The Winning Ticket" (4-2-53) June Dayton
55. "Partners in Law" [Part I] (4-7-53)
56. "Partners in Law" [Part II] (4-9-53)

YOUR JEWELER'S SHOWCASE

The Episodes:

1. "Like the Rich People" (11-11-52) Barbara Whiting, Ruth Warrick, Robert Sweeney
2. "Operation, E. S. P. " (11-18-52) Barbara Whiting
3. "Study in Charcoal" (11-25-52) Ellen Corby, James Griffith, Robert Foulk, Mary Powell
4. "Teacher of the Year" (12-2-52) Martha Hyer, Lee Aaker
5. "Tenampa" (12-9-52) Sheldon Leonard, Virginia Grey
6. "Marked X" (12-16-52) Barry Kelley
7. "Tiger Bait" (12-23-52) Sheldon Leonard, Lisa Howard
8. "Something for Ginger" (12-30-52) Elizabeth Frazer, Whitfield Connor
9. "The Rocking Horse" (1-13-53)
10. "Three and One Half Musketeers" (1-27-53) Jan Clayton, Dave Willock
11. "Roman Interlude" (2-10-53) Gladys George, Ray Teal
12. "The Woman of Bally Runion" (2-24-53) Arthur Shields
13. "Bridal Suite" (3-10-53) Myron Healey, Marian Carr
14. "The Bean Farm" (3-24-53) Phyllis Coates, Robert Hutton
15. "The Monkey's Paw" [adapted from the W. W. Jacobs classic] (4-7-53) Una Merkel
16. "A Very Old Murder" (4-21-53) Barton MacLane, Edith Evans
17. "Week-End with Wal'tuh" (5-5-53) Barbara Whiting, Robert Sweeney
18. "Heart's Desire" (5-19-53) Celeste Holm, George Nader
19. "Never Trust a Lady" (6-9-53) June Vinson

CAVALCADE OF AMERICA [after the radio series]

Note: biographical subjects are enclosed in brackets or a character role in parentheses.

The Episodes:

1. "Poor Richard" [Benjamin Franklin] (10-1-52) Cecil Kellaway, Dabbs Greer
2. "All's Well with Lydia" (10-15-52) Ruth Warrick, Reginald Denny, John Dodsworth, Esther Dale
3. "The Man Who Took a Chance" [Eli Whitney] (10-29-52) Richard Denning, Rhys Williams
4. "A Romance to Remember" [Nathaniel Hawthorne] (11-12-52) Dan O'Herlihy, Fay Baker
5. "What God Had Wrought" [Samuel Morse] (11-26-52) Eduard Franz, Tom Henry
6. "No Greater Love" [Nurse Clara Maass, who fought against yellow fever] (12-10-52) Mary Anderson, Arthur Franz
7. "In This Crisis" [an espionage drama] (12-24-52) Tom Tully, Ann Doran, John Hoyt, Richard Gaines
8. "The Arrow and the Bow" [Andrew Jackson] (1-7-53) Sean McClory, Eleana Verdugo, Booth Coleman, O. Z. Whitehead

9. "What Might Have Been" (1-21-53) Dayton Lumis (as Joseph Davis), Ross Ford (as Jefferson Davis), Nancy Hale (as Sarah Knox)
10. "New Salem Story" (2-4-53) James Griffith (as Abraham Lincoln), Jeff Donnell (as Ann Rutledge)
11. "A Matter of Honor" [Sam Houston] (2-18-53) Onslow Stevens, Randy Stuart
12. "Experiment at Monticello" [Thomas Jefferson] (3-4-53) Raymond Greenleaf, Brandon Rhodes, Barbara Woodele
13. "Mightier Than the Sword" [the John Peter Zenger case] (3-18-53) Douglas Kennedy, Adele Longmire
14. "Indomitable Blacksmith" [documentary drama on the Vermont blacksmith who invented the first electric motor] (4-1-53) Whitfield Connor, Peggy Webber
15. "The Gingerbread Man" [historical drama of the Baker-General of the Continental Army] (4-15-53) Otto Waldis, Edith Angold, John Hamilton
16. "Night Strike" (4-29-53) Glenn Langen, Richard Garrick, Russell Simpson
17. "Slater's Dream" (5-13-53) Terence Kilburn, Mary Ellen Kay, Howard Wendall
18. "The Pirate's Choice" [Jean Lafitte] (5-27-53) William Bishop, Rhys Williams, Morris Ankrum, Donna Martel
19. "John Yankee" [John Adams] (6-10-53) Whitfield Connor, Helen Parrish, Raymond Greenleaf
20. "The Tenderfoot" [Theodore Roosevelt] (6-24-53)

Second Season

21. "Sam and the Whale" (9-29-53) Cecil Kellaway, Evelyn Ankers
22. "Stolen General" (10-6-53) Reginald Denny, Barbara Billingsley, Dorothea Meadows
23. "Breakfast at Nancy's" (10-13-53) Amanda Blake, Charles McGraw
24. "Sunset at Appomattox" (10-20-53) William Johnston, Henry Morgan
25. "And to Fame Unknown" [a documentary on the life of a high school teacher] (10-27-53) Rolland Gladieux
26. "Time to Grow" (11-3-53) Booth Coleman
27. "The Tiger's Tail" [Thomas Nast and the Boss Tweed Ring] (11-17-53) Robert Cornthwaite
28. "The Last Will of Daniel Webster" (11-24-53) Ray Collins, Ann Doran
29. "Major Pauline" (12-1-53) Gertrude Michael
30. "The Betrayal" [Benedict Arnold] (12-8-53) Dan O'Herlihy
31. "Riders of the Pony Express" (12-15-53) Robert Warrick
32. "One Nation Indivisible" [the Horace Greeley crusade to release Jefferson Davis] (12-22-53) Edgar Buchanan, Fay Wray
33. "Mr. Pearce's Dinosaur" (12-29-53) Lowell Gilmore, Lurene Tuttle
34. "G Is for Goldberger" [Dr. Joseph Goldberger's fight to conquer pellagra] (1-12-54) Walter Coy, William Forrest, Emlen Davies

35. "Smyrna Incident" [adapted from the Robert Louis Stevenson story] (1-19-54) Carl Benton Reid, John Wengraf
36. "Man of Glass--The Story of a Glassmaker" (1-26-54) Robert Strauss, Carl Benton Reid, Jane Whitley
37. "Plume of Honor" (2-9-54) Maurice Marsal
38. "Margin for Victory" [on the American Revolution] (2-16-54) Francis L. Sullivan, Edward Ashley
39. "The Absent Host" (3-2-54) Don Kennedy
40. "Duel at the O. K. Corral" (3-9-54) Kenneth Tobey, Henry Morgan, Morgan Jones, Jim Bannon
41. "The Splendid Dream" [William Penn] (3-16-54) Richard Stapley, Leo G. Carroll
42. "Young Andy Jackson" (3-23-54) Billy Gray, Douglass Dumbrille
43. "Escape--The Story of Carl Schurz" (3-30-54) David Albert, Dabbs Greer
44. "Riddle of the Seas" (4-6-54) Lamont Johnson, Laura Elliott
45. "Crazy Judah" (4-13-54) Ross Elliott, Frances Rafferty
46. "The Paper Sword" (4-27-54) Patrick O'Neal, Margaret Field
47. "Gentle Conquerer" (5-4-54) Wilton Graff
48. "Spindletop--Texas' First Oil Gushers" (5-11-54) William Bishop, Nancy Hale
49. "Moonlight School" (5-18-54) Lon Chaney Jr., George Nader, Emlen Davies
50. "A Strange Journey" (6-1-54) Robert Easton
51. "The Skipper's Lady" (6-8-54) Paul Langton, Sally Brophy, Harvey Stephens
52. "Courage in Connecticut" [pre-Revolutionary America] (6-22-54) Booth Coleman, Sean McClory, Anne Kimbell

Third Season

53. "Mountain Man" [a Kentuckian in the early days of California] (9-28-54) Gregory Walcott
54. "The Great Gamble" [the Cyrus Field attempt to lay the first Atlantic cable] (10-5-54) Whitfield Connor, Marjorie Lord
55. "The Forge" [Eliphalet Remington] (10-26-54) Kathleen Crowley, George Nader
56. "Moonlight Witness" [Abraham Lincoln's defense of a boy charged with murder] (11-2-54) Bruce Bennett, Rhys Williams, Claire De Brey
57. "Saturday Story" [Illinois high school football coach Mark Wilson] (11-9-54) Ralph Moody, Otto Graham, Dabbs Greer, Charles Meredith, Joyce MacKenzie; Mark Wilson, Frank Leahy
58. "The American Thanksgiving--Its History and Meaning" (11-23-54) Helen Van Tuyle, Walter Coy, Dick Rich, Richard Gaines, Larry Johns
59. "Ordeal in Burma" (11-30-54) Toni Gerry, Donald Murphy
60. "A Man's Home" (12-28-54) Hillary Brooke, Ross Elliott
61. "The Marine Who Was Two Hundred Years Old" [on a veteran leatherneck] (1-4-55) Ward Bond
62. "Message from Garcia" [a Spanish-American War drama] (1-18-55) Donald Murphy, Salvador Baguez

63. "Petticoat Doctor" [Dr. Elizabeth Blackwell's fight against prejudice] (1-25-55) Paula Raymond
64. "Take Off Zero" (2-1-55) Lamont Johnson
65. "Decision for Justice" (2-15-55) Jeff Morrow, Marjorie Lord, Marilyn Erskine, Dayton Lummis
66. "The Hostage" (2-22-55) Glenn Langan
67. "That They Might Live" (3-8-55) Booth Coleman (as Dr. Abraham Jacobi), Emlen Davies (as Dr. Mary Putnam Jacobi)
68. "Man on the Beat" [a drama of a police officer] (3-15-54) William Campbell, Constance Ford
69. "The Ship That Shook the World" [the invention of the Monitor by John Ericson and its battle with the Merrimac] (3-29-55) Alex Gerry, Richard Hale
70. "The Gift of Dr. Minot" [Dr. George R. Minot, 1934 Nobel Laureate in Medicine for his liver treatment of anemia] (4-12-55) Walter Coy, Phyllis Coates
71. "How to Raise a Boy" [by Edith Sonmer and Robert Soderberg] (4-26-55) Paul Kelly, Gordon Gilbert, Erin O'Brien-Moore
72. "Stay On, Stranger" [the story of Mrs. Alice Lloyd who founded a school in the Kentucky mountains] (5-3-55) Peggy Converse, Lon Chaney Jr., Edgar Buchanan
73. "Sunrise on a Dirty Face" [James E. West's efforts to help juvenile delinquents] (5-10-55) Jack Kelly, Peter Reynolds, Lois Collier
74. "Six Hours to Deadline" (5-24-55) John McIntire, Sara Haden, Will Wright, King Donovan
75. "The Palmetto Conspiracy" [Allan Pinkerton's thwarting of the plot to assassinate Abraham Lincoln] (6-7-55)
76. "The Rescue of Dr. Beanes" [a dramatization of the events leading to Francis Scott Key's composition of the national anthem, the "Star-Spangled Banner"] (6-21-55) Donald Murphy, Paula Raymond, Christopher Dark, Griff Barnett

Fourth Season [now as DUPONT PRESENTS THE CAVALCADE THEATRE]

77. "A Time for Courage" [Olympic swimming champion Nancy Merlus' battle to overcome polio] (9-13-55) Gloria Talbott, Hugh Beaumont
78. "The Texas Rangers" (9-27-55) William Talman, Jim Davis
79. "Toward Tomorrow" [Dr. Ralph Bunche] (10-4-55) James Edwards, McHenry Norman, Ruby Goodwin, Maidie Norman
80. "Disaster Patrol" (10-18-55) Steve Brodie, Joan Ruth
81. "The Swamp Fox" (10-25-55) Hans Conried (as General Francis Marion), Nancy Hadley, Paul Brinegar, Ron Randell
82. "A Chain of Hearts" [by Frederic Brady] (11-1-55) Joyce McCluskey, Charles Bronson
83. "One Day at a Time" (11-15-55) James Daly, John Litel, Eve March, James Best, James Bell
84. "Crisis in Paris" (11-29-55) Howard St. John, Leslie Gray, Liam Sullivan, Noel Drayton
85. "Doctor on Wheels" (12-13-55) Lamont Johnson, Betty Lynn
86. "Barbed Wire Christmas" [a documentary drama of American Prisoners-of-War in Germany, 1944] (12-20-55) Chuck Connors,

Strother Martin, John Bryant
87. "Postmark: Danger" (12-27-55) Barry Atwater, Scott Forbes
88. "The Boy Who Walked to America" (1-3-56) Hugh Beaumont, John Dennis, Dennis Chang
89. "Prison Within" [adapted by John Meredyth Lucas from a story by David Dresser] (1-17-56) Gloria Talbott, Claire Carleton
90. "Star and Shield" (1-24-56) Walter Sande, Joi Lansing, Mark Damon, Elizabeth Patterson
91. "The Secret Life of Joe Swedie" (2-7-56) Chick Chandler, Linda Sterling
92. "Call Home the Heart" (2-21-56) Teru Shimada, Kristine Miller
93. "The Listening Hand" (3-6-56) John Craven, Barbara Ellar
94. "Life to Live By" [by Laszlo Gorog] (3-20-56) John Ericson, Sally Frazer
95. "The Doll Who Found a Mother" (4-3-56) Cheryl Callaway, Peggy Weber, Mort Mills
96. "The Jackie Jenson Story" [an autobiographical drama] (4-17-56) Jackie Jenson
97. "Diplomatic Outpost" (5-1-56) Richard Loo, John Hudson, Cynthia See
98. "Danger at Clover Ridge" (5-8-56) Robert Horton
99. "Who Is Byington?" (5-22-56)
100. "The Mayor of St. Lou" (6-5-56) Peter Graves, Nick Dennis, Frank Gerstle, Morris Ankrum, Robert Cossen, Ed Kemmer

Fifth Season [now as DUPONT THEATRE]

101. "Monument to a Young Man" (9-18-56) John Beradino, Michael Fox, Miguel Landa, Perry Lopez
102. "Bed of Roses" (9-25-56) Susan Kohner, Kathryn Card
103. "The Boy Nobody Wanted" (10-2-56) Johnny Crawford, Ron Haggerthy
104. "The People and General Glancy" (10-9-56) Minor Watson
105. "Wild April" (10-16-56) John McIntire
106. "The Hobo Kid" (10-23-56) Reba Waters, Robert Foulk, Caroline Craig
107. "Date with a Stranger" (10-30-56) Judith Braun, Arthur Franz, Madge Blake
108. "Innocent Bystander" (11-13-56) Don Taylor
109. "Women's Work" [by John Weaver] (11-20-56) Walter Brennan, James Best, Jane Darwell, Mary Murphy
110. "Return of a Bombardier" (11-27-56) Skip Homeier
111. "Pursuit of a Princess" (12-4-56) Fred Clark, Brian Aherne
112. "Once a Hero" (12-11-56) Ward Bond, Richard Eyer, Ben Johnson
113. "The Blessed Midnight" (12-18-56) Maureen O'Sullivan, Danny Richards Jr.
114. "Three Young Kings" [a Christmas story] (12-25-56) Tony Terry, Robert Hernandes, Carlos Vera
115. "The Two Worlds of Nicols" (1-1-57) Peter Reynolds
116. "The House of Empty Rooms" (1-8-57) Ann Harding, Helen Westcott, Ross Ford

117. "Leap to Heaven" [documentary drama on Olympic pole vault champion The Reverend Robert Richards and his mentor The Reverend Merlin Garber] (1-15-57)
118. "Dowry for Ilona" [adapted by Laszlo Gorog from the Al Martin story] (1-22-57) Oscar Homolka
119. "The Man from St. Paul" (1-29-57) Harry Townes, Michael Landon
120. "Are Trees People?" (2-5-57) Ruth Donnelly
121. "Decision for a Hero" (2-12-57) John Ericson, Joan Evans
122. "Frightened Witness" (2-19-57) Dan Duryea, Barbara Billingsley, Herbert Rudley
123. "The Man Who Asked No Favors" (3-5-57) Lew Ayres
124. "Dan Marshall's Brat" (3-19-57) Patty McCormack, Russell Johnson, Paul Fix, Barbara Eiles
125. "The Widow Was Willing" (3-26-57) Anne Jeffreys, Robert Sterling
126. "The Last Signer" (4-2-57) Kevin McCarthy, Lisa Montell, Vladimir Sokoloff
127. "The Jackie Jensen Story" [a documentary drama] (4-16-57)
128. "Shark of the Mountain" (4-23-57) Richard Eyer, James Gleason
129. "Chicago 2-1-2" (4-30-57) Frank Lovejoy, Roy Thinnes

THE FORD TELEVISION THEATRE [after the radio series]

The Episodes:

1. "Life, Liberty and Orrin Dooley" (10-2-52) Will Rogers Jr., Marguerite Chapman
2. "Junior" (10-9-52) Edward Arnold, Arthur Franz, Mabel Paige
3. "National Honeymoon" (10-16-52) Dick Haymes, Diana Lynn
4. "Birth of a Hero" (10-23-52) Mark Stevens, Ellen Drew
5. "Girl in the Park" (10-30-52) Joan Caulfield, Herbert Marshall
6. "Edge of the Law" (11-6-52) Macdonald Carey, Marjorie Lord, George Macready
7. "Protect Her Honor" (11-13-52) Lloyd Nolan, Jane Wyatt
8. "Sunk" (11-20-52) Charles Bickford, Kevin McCarthy
9. "The Divided Heart" [otherwise known as "Change of Heart"] (11-27-52) Barbara Hale, Stephen McNally
10. "Something Old, Something New" (12-4-52) Barbara Lawrence, Jackie Cooper, Wanda Hendrix
11. "Crossed and Double Crossed" (12-11-52) Louis Hayward, Mercedes McCambridge
12. "So Many Things Happen" (12-18-52) Bruce Bennett, Laraine Day, Virginia Field, Virginia Bruce
13. "Heart of Gold" (12-25-52) Edmund Gwenn, Anita Louise, Tommy Rettig
14. "They Also Serve" (1-1-53) John Hodiak, Maureen O'Sullivan
15. "It Happened in a Pawn Shop" (1-8-53) Eddie Bracken, Terry Moore

16. "This Is My Heart" (1-15-53) Ruth Hussey, Mark Stevens
17. "The Sermon of the Gun" (1-22-53) Macdonald Carey, K. T. Stevens
18. "Adventure in Connecticut" (1-29-53) Osa Massen, Richard Carlson, Hugo Haas
19. "The First Born" (2-5-53) Nancy Davis, Nancy Guild, Ronald Reagan, Tommy Rettig
20. "The Old Man's Bride" (2-12-53) John Agar, Joan Leslie
21. "Margin for Fear" (2-19-53) Mari Aldon, Broderick Crawford, Robert Anderson, Harry Shannon
22. "All's Fair in Love" (2-26-53) Lynn Bari, Cesar Romero
23. "Madame 44" (3-5-53) Yvonne De Carlo, Philip Carey, Rosemary DeCamp
24. "My Daughter's Husband" (3-12-53) Gene Lockhart, Lon McAllister, Mae Clark
25. "The Bet" (3-19-53) Helmut Dantine, Viveca Lindfors, Carl Esmond
26. "Double Exposure" (3-26-53) George Brent, Dan Duryea, Marvin Kaplan
27. "To Any Soldier" (4-2-53) Edmond O'Brien, Horace MacMahon
28. "Just What the Doctor Ordered" (4-9-53) Scott Brady, Joanne Dru, Lisa Ferraday
29. "Allison, Ltd. " (4-16-53) Merle Oberon
30. "The Life of the Party" (4-23-53) Sally Forrest, Marshall Thompson
31. "The Son-in-Law" (4-30-53) Peter Lawford, Bonita Granville, Eve Miller
32. "The Lady and the Champ" (5-7-53) Preston Foster, Virginia Grey, Tom Tully
33. "Look for Tomorrow" (5-14-53) Jane Greer
34. "Sweet Talk Me, Jackson" (5-21-53) Dawn Addams, James Gleason, Dick Haymes
35. "The Jewel" (5-28-53) Paul Henreid, Marjorie Lord, Paul Langton
36. "There's No Place Like Home" (6-4-53) Walter Abel, Ann Harding, Jimmy Lydon
37. "The Trestle" (6-11-53) Philip Carey, Maureen O'Sullivan, Tim Considine
38. "Malaya Incident" (6-18-53) Ann Sheridan, Richard Egan, Steven Geray
39. "The People Versus Johnston" (6-25-53) Paul Muni, Adele Jergens, Onslow Stevens

Second Season

40. "Tangier Lady" (10-1-53) Patricia Medina, Virginia Grey, Scott Brady
41. "The Doctor's Downfall" (10-8-53) June Vincent, Richard Denning, Paulette Goddard
42. "Emergency" (10-15-53) Richard Conte, Mae Clarke, Randy Stuart
43. "The Bachelor" (10-22-53) William Lundigan, Wanda Hendrix
44. "Tomorrow's Men" (10-29-53) John Derek, Pat O'Brien, Frances Helm, Ann Doran

45. "The World's My Oyster" (11-5-53) Charles Coburn, Rosemary Bowe
46. "The Ming Lama" (11-12-53) Howard Duff, Angela Lansbury, Francis L. Sullivan
47. "As the Flame Dies" (11-19-53) Sylvia Sidney, Barry Sullivan, Richard Webb
48. "Double Bet" (11-26-53) Laraine Day, Richard Egan, Marsha Hunt
49. "Kiss and Forget" (12-3-53) Virginia Field, Willard Parker, Mark Stevens, Coleen Gray
50. "And Suddenly, You Knew" (12-10-53) Teresa Wright, Ronald Reagan, Lee Aaker
51. "Gun Job" (12-17-53) Ward Bond, Ellen Drew, Philip Carey
52. "Ever Since the Day" (12-24-53) Robert Stack, Ron Randell, Audrey Totter, Edward Arnold
53. "Alias Nora Hale" (12-31-53) Claire Trevor, Warner Anderson, Rosemary DeCamp
54. "The Fugitives" (1-7-54) Barry Sullivan, Raymond Burr, Douglas Dumbrille, Mary Beth Hughes, Anita Louise
55. "The Ardent Woodsman" (1-14-54) Gilbert Roland, Phyllis Thaxter
56. "The Happiest Day" (1-21-54) Teresa Wright, Larry Parks, Fay Bainter
57. "Mantrap" (1-28-54) Shelley Winters, William Bishop, Jerry Paris
58. "Lucky Tommy Jordan" (2-4-54) Will Rogers Jr., Kevin McCarthy, Paula Raymond
59. "For the Love of Kitty" (2-11-54) Nancy Olsen, Bruce Bennett, Robert Strauss
60. "For Value Received" (2-18-54) Peter Lawford, Regis Toomey, James Whitmore, Marie Windsor, Lee Aaker
61. "Marriageable Male" (2-25-54) Jack Lemmon, Ida Lupino
62. "The Good of His Soul" (3-4-54) Thomas Mitchell, John Beal, Jane Darwell, Rosemary DeCamp, Tommy Rettig
63. "Come On, Red" (3-11-54) Edmund Gwenn, Jay C. Flippen, Randy Stuart, Sid Tomack
64. "The Last Thirty Minutes" (3-18-54) Arthur Franz, Martha Vickers, George Macready, Eve Miller
65. "The Taming of the Shrewd" (3-25-54) David Brian, Jeff Donnell, Don Taylor, Joan Vohs
66. "Turn Back the Clock" (4-1-54) Richard Conte, Laraine Day
67. "Yours for a Dream" (4-8-54) Joanne Dru, Touch (Michael) Connors, S. Z. Sakell
68. "Sister Veronica" (4-15-54) Irene Dunne, Taylor Holmes, John Hudson
69. "Wedding March" (4-22-54) James Craig, Arlene Dahl, Larry Parks
70. "Night Visitor" (4-29-54) Arthur Kennedy, Martha Vickers, Lee J. Cobb, Ernest Borgnine
71. "A Season to Love" (5-6-54) Ida Lupino, Sara Haden, Howard Duff
72. "Wonderful Day for a Wedding" (5-13-54) Joan Leslie, Scott Brady, Spring Byington, Rita Moreno
73. "Beneath These Waters" (5-20-54) Ronald Reagan, John Baer

74. "Keep It in the Family" (5-27-54) Ellen Drew, Robert Young, Sally Forrest
75. "The Unlocked Door" [adapted from the Mary Roberts Rinehart mystery] (6-3-54) Diana Lynn, Philip Carey, Fay Bainter
76. "The Mason-Dixon Line" (6-10-54) Joanne Gilbert, Peter Lawford, Reginald Denny, Craig Stevens
77. "The Tryst" (6-17-54) William Lundigan, Vera Miles, Anne Francis, Edward Arnold
78. "Indirect Approach" (6-24-54) Corinne Calvet, William Eythe, Robert Stack, Gale Robbins

Third Season

79. "Daughter of Mine" (10-7-54) Margaret O'Brien, Maureen O'Sullivan, Pat O'Brien, Richard Jaeckel
80. "Shadow of Truth" (10-14-54) Sidney Blackmer, Keefe Brasselle, Marjorie Lord, Thomas Mitchell
81. "Segment" (10-21-54) Ward Bond, Joanne Woodward, William Bendix, Rosemary DeCamp
82. "A Trip Around the Block" (10-28-54) Steve Cochran, Jan Sterling
83. "Remember to Live" (11-4-54) Dane Clark, Barbara Hale, Judy Nugent, Cleo Moore
84. "The Road Ahead" (11-11-54) Rory Calhoun, Faith Domergue, Paul Langton
85. "The Summer Memory" (11-18-54) Richard Kiley, Claire Trevor, James Barton
86. "The Legal Beagles" (11-25-54) Laraine Day, Richard Denning, Duncan Richardson
87. "Girl in Flight" (12-2-54) Joan Leslie, John Qualen, Tom Drake, Hugo Haas
88. "Charlie C Company" (12-9-54) Kerwin Mathews, Edmond O'Brien
89. "Portrait of Lydia" [by Robert Smith and Berish Rubin] (12-16-54) Donna Reed, Robert Horton, Jonathan Hale, Nan Boardman
90. "Slide, Darling, Slide" (12-23-54) Jane Darwell, Virginia Field, Allyn Joslyn, Anthony Caruso
91. "The Unbroken Promise" (12-30-54) George Brent, Frances Dee, Gertrude Michael, Gigi Perreau
92. "Magic Formula" (1-6-55) Claudette Colbert, Patric Knowles, Ann Savage
93. "... and Son" [adapted from the I. A. R. Wylie story] (1-13-55) Edward G. Robinson, Erin O'Brien-Moore, John Baer
94. "The Stars Don't Shine" (1-20-55) Philip Carey, Horace MacMahon, Teresa Wright
95. "Letters Marked Personal" (1-27-55) Joan Bennett, Melvyn Douglas, Elisabeth Risdon
96. "Touch of Spring" (2-3-55) Gene Barry, Irene Dunne, Kathryn Grant, Frank Wilcox
97. "Pretend You're You" (2-10-55) Keith Andes, Charles Coburn, Lucy Marlowe
98. "Tomorrow We'll Love" (2-17-55) Larry Parks, Nicole Maurey

99. "Too Old for Dolls" (2-24-55) Laraine Day, Franchot Tone, Natalie Wood
100. "The Lilac Bush" (3-3-55) William Leslie, Marilyn Erskine, Ruth Roman
101. "Second Sight" (3-10-55) Jane Darwell, Merle Oberon, Philip Carey
102. "Celebrity" (3-17-55) Joanne Dru, Dennis Morgan, Richard Eyer
103. "Garrity's Sons" [by Rod Serling] (3-24-55) Rory Calhoun, May Wynn, Vince Edwards
104. "Hanrahan" (3-31-55) Cecil Kellaway, Arthur Franz, Elsa Lanchester, Kathryn Grant
105. "Deception" (4-7-55) Sylvia Sidney, John Howard, Mark Andrews
106. "The Woman at Fog Point" (4-14-55) Evelyn Rudie, Joan Chandler, Charles Bickford, Lamont Johnson
107. "Sunday Mourn" (4-21-55) Wallace Ford, Brian Keith, Marilyn Maxwell, John Bromfield
108. "While We're Young" (4-28-53) Claudette Colbert, Tab Hunter, Patric Knowles, Eilene Johnson
109. "Appointment with Destiny" (5-5-55) Lyle Bettger, Adele August, Mona Freeman, William Tannen
110. "The Policy of Joe Aladdin" (5-12-55) Brian Donlevy, Bobby Van, Gale Robbins, Kathryn Grant, Sid Melton
111. "Mimi" [by Edward and Mildred Dein] (5-19-55) Rita Gam, Paul Henreid, Rick Jason, Lawrence Dobkin, Mel Welles, Louis Mercier
112. "Cardboard Casanova" (5-26-55) Ricardo Montalban, Hillary Brooke, Lucy Marlowe, Dick Foran
113. "P. J. and the Lady" (6-2-55) Ann Harding, Vera Miles, Tristram Coffin, Thomas Mitchell, Elliott Reid
114. "One Man Missing" (6-9-55) Ellen Drew, Jane Drew, Audrey Totter, Helen Wallace
115. "Favorite Son" [adapted by Charles R. Marion from the William Scott story] (6-16-55) William Gargan, Anita Louise, Louis Torres Jr. , Sammy Ogg
116. "The Mumbys" (6-23-55) Jane Darwell, Virginia Field, Willard Parker, Edgar Buchanan

Fourth Season

117. "All That Glitters" (10-6-55) Arlene Dahl, Richard Denning
118. "Husband" (10-13-55) Mala Powers, Barry Sullivan
119. "Lady in the Wind" (10-20-55) Teresa Wright, Kerwin Mathews, Claude Dauphin
120. "Twelve to Eternity" (10-27-55) Edward Arnold, Paul Langton, Philip Carey, Barbara Britton
121. "Johnny, Where Are You?" (11-3-55) Keith Andes, Gale Storm, Frances Robinson, Alix Talton
122. "The Blue Ribbon" (11-10-55) Gene Barry, Scott Brady, Marjorie Rambeau
123. "A Smattering of Bliss" (11-17-55) Betty Garrett, Larry Parks, Vivi Janiss, Joi Lansing, Richard Deacon
124. "Passage to Yesterday" (11-24-55) Joanne Dru, Guy Madison

125. "The Fabulous Sycamores" (12-1-55) Barbara Britton, Cecil Kellaway, Joyce Holden, George Givot, Nydia Westman
126. "Bet the Queen" (12-8-55) Rory Calhoun, Donald Curtis, Gale Robbins, James Millican, William Leslie
127. "South of Sengalore" (12-15-55) Rhonda Fleming, William Talman, Patric Knowles
128. "A Kiss for Santa" (12-22-55) Gene Nelson, Virginia Field, Kathryn Grant, Bobby Clark
129. "A Set of Values" (12-29-55) Edward G. Robinson, Tommy Cook, Louise de Carlo, Ann Doran, Paul Fix
130. "Journey by Moonlight" (1-5-56) Louis Jourdan, Joy Page, Mel Welles, Steve Ritch
131. "Dear Diane" (1-12-56) Joan Bennett, John Lupton, Gene Raymond, Lucy Marlowe
132. "Never Lend Money to a Woman" (1-19-56) Anna Maria Alberghetti, Keefe Brasselle, Roger Smith, Collette Lynn, Will Wright
133. "Try Me for Size" (1-26-56) Bobby Driscoll, James Gleason, Thomas Mitchell
134. "Tin Can Skipper" (2-2-56) Phyllis Kirk, Scott Brady, John Hoyt, William Leslie
135. "The Silent Strangers" (2-9-56) Hugh Beaumont, Richard Conte, Donald Curtis, Onslow Stevens
136. "Airborne Honeymoon" (2-16-56) Jeanne Crain, John Hudson
137. "Your Other Love" (2-23-56) Joan Fontaine, Warren Stevens, June Vincent
138. "Man Without a Fear" (3-1-56) Raymond Burr, Joseph Cotten, Angela Greene
139. "All for a Man" (3-8-56) Linda Darnell, Elisabeth Risdon, Allyn Joslyn
140. "That Evil Woman" (3-15-56) Marjorie Rambeau, Robert Hutton, Stephen McNally, Mari Blanchard
141. "Double Trouble" (3-22-56) Richard Denning, Brian Donlevy, Yvette Dugay
142. "The Face" (3-29-56) Mala Powers, Dale Robertson, George Keynas
143. "Autumn Fever" (4-5-56) Virginia Field, Zsa Zsa Gabor, George Sanders
144. "On the Beach" (4-12-56) Richard Denning, Irene Dunne, Elizabeth Patterson, Jo Ann Lilliquist
145. "The Lady in His Life" (4-19-56) Ricardo Montalban, Dick Foran, Jane Nigh, Beverly Tyler, Arnold Stang
146. "The Alibi" (4-26-56) Ralph Bellamy, Patricia Medina
147. "The Payoff" (5-3-56) Janet Blair, Howard Duff
148. "Behind the Mask" (5-10-56) Dane Clark, Barbara Hale, Willy Boveley
149. "The Kill" (5-17-56) Macdonald Carey, Marilyn Erskine
150. "Sheila" (5-24-56) Elinor Donahue, Irene Dunne, Stephanie Griffin
151. "The Clay Pigeon" (5-31-56) Wayne Morris, Robert Sterling, Tom Tully
152. "Mr. Kagle and the Baby Sitter" (6-7-56) Charles Coburn, Fay Holden

153. "Panic" (6-14-56) Ruth Roman, George Macready, Philip Carey
154. "Remembrance Day" (6-21-56) Thomas Mitchell, Dan Barton, Mary Ellen Kaye
155. "A Past Remembered" (6-28-56) William Bendix, Lyle Talbot, Joan Banks

Fifth Season

156. "Catch at Straws" [directed by Ray Milland] (10-3-56) Ray Milland, Virginia Gibson, Fred Keins, Kerwin Mathews, Eddie Foy Jr.
157. "Sudden Silence" (10-10-56) Barbara Stanwyck, Jeff Morrow
158. "Paris Edition" (10-17-56) Jack Carson, John Beradino, Valerie French
159. "Measure of Faith" (10-24-56) Lew Ayres, Beverly Garland, Lee Van Cleef, Charles Evans, Nestor Paiva
160. "Black Jim Hawk" (10-31-56) John Derek, Marcia Henderson, Donald Randolph
161. "Sometimes It Happens" (11-7-56) Guy Madison, Dianne Foster
162. "The Woman Who Dared" (11-14-56) Laraine Day, Gene Barry, Kim Charney
163. "The Menace of Hasty Heights" (11-21-56) Kent Taylor, Steve Cochran, Jean Hagen
164. "Stand By to Dive" (11-28-56) Farley Granger, Roger Smith, Onslow Stevens
165. "Front Page Father" (12-5-56) Charles Bickford, Mae Clarke, Horace MacMahon
166. "The Marriage Plan" (12-12-56) Eddie Bracken, Mona Freeman
167. "Duffy's Man" (12-19-56) Walter Brennan, Philip Carey, Phyllis Kirk
168. "Model Wife" (12-20-56) Felicia Farr, Ralph Bellamy, Pat Conway
169. "Fear Has Many Faces" (1-2-57) James Whitmore, June Lockhart, Don Haggerty
170. "The Quiet Stranger" (1-9-57) George Montgomery, Forrest Tucker, Bobby Clark, Lyn Thomas, Bill Hale, Ted de Corsia
171. "Sweet Charlie" (1-16-57) Dick Foran, Frank Lovejoy
172. "The Penlands and the Poodle" (1-23-57) Betty Garrett, Larry Parks
173. "Mrs. Wane Comes to Call" (1-30-57) Phyllis Kirk, Arthur Franz, Peggy Webber, Terry Kellman
174. "The Connoisseur" (2-6-57) Paul Henreid, Kathryn Grant, Virginia Bruce
175. "Ringside Seat" (2-13-57) Hugh O'Brian, Marilyn Erskine, Billy Chapin
176. "With No Regrets" (2-20-57) Ann Sheridan
177. "The Man Who Beat Lupo" (2-27-57) Louis Jourdan, Joanna Barnes
178. "Broken Barrier" (3-6-57) Macdonald Carey, Marguerite Chapman, Dick Foran

179. "Fate Travels East" (3-13-57) Linda Darnell, Craig Stevens, Sheb Wooley
180. "The Man Across the Hall" (3-20-57) Robert Sterling, Vera-Ellen
181. "House of Glass" (3-27-57) Lyle Bettger, Joan Caulfield, Marie Windsor
182. "Exclusive" (4-3-57) Phyllis Kirk, Richard Webb, Osa Massen, Everett Sloane
183. "Moment of Decision" (4-10-57) Jane Greer, Marshall Thompson, Victor Jory
184. "Singapore" (4-17-57) Paulette Goddard, Charles Korvin, Rex Reason
185. "Footnote on a Doll" (4-24-57) Bette Davis (as Dolly Madison)
186. "Strange Disappearance" (5-1-57) Stephen McNally, June Vincent, Peggy Knudsen
187. "The Idea Man" (5-8-57) Don DeFore, Richard Denning, Jack Kelly, Don Avedon
188. "The Gentle Deceiver" (5-15-57) Keenan Wynn, Lucy Marlowe
189. "Miller's Millions" (5-22-57) Otto Kruger, Thomas Mitchell, Richard Webb
190. "Torn" (5-29-57) John Baragrey, Philip Carey, Laraine Day
191. "The Lie" (6-5-57) Cesar Romero, Betty Field, Gigi Perreau
192. "Cross Hairs" (6-12-57) James Daly, Elizabeth Patterson, Ann Sheridan
193. "Desperation" (6-19-57) Teresa Wright, Kevin McCarthy, William Bishop
194. "Adventure for Hire" (6-26-57) Brian Keith, Pat O'Brien

THE FOUR STAR PLAYHOUSE

The Regulars: Charles Boyer (with episode of 9/25/52; Dick Powell (with episode of 10/9/52); David Niven (with episode of 12/4/52); Ida Lupino (with episode of 12/31/53)

The Episodes [episodes filmed as part of the series Dante's Inferno are marked by an asterisk; see episode of 10/9/52 for explanation]:

1. "My Wife Geraldine" (9-25-52) Charles Boyer, Porter Hall, Una Merkel, Noreen Nash
2. *"Dante's Inferno" [this and subsequent episodes featuring Dick Powell as investigator Willie Dante became the basis for the 1960 series Dante's Inferno, with Howard Duff in the lead] (10-9-52) Dick Powell, Regis Toomey, Virginia Grey, Marvin Miller
3. "The Lost Silk Hat" (10-23-52) Ronald Colman
4. "Backstage" (11-6-52) Charles Boyer, Hillary Brooke, Marcia Henderson
5. "Welcome Home" (11-20-52) Dick Powell, David Holt, Claire Carleton
6. "The Island" (12-4-52) David Niven, George Macready, Dianne Foster

7. "The Officer and the Lady" (12-18-52) Allen Jenkins, Charles Boyer, Andrea King
8. "Knockout" (1-1-53) Broderick Crawford, Buddy Wright, Ted DeCorsia, Ron Hargrave, Lucille Barkley
9. "Man on a Train" (1-15-53) David Niven, Alan Napier
10. "Trail's End" (1-29-53) Dick Powell, Jean Howell, Lee Van Cleef
11. "Sound Off, My Love" (2-12-53) Merle Oberon, Barbara Billingsley, James Seay, Gordon Oliver
12. "The Man in the Box" (2-26-53) Charles Boyer, Patricia Morison
13. "No Identity" (3-12-53) David Niven, Frances Rafferty, Tommy Rettig
14. "The Man Who Walked Out on Himself" (3-26-53) Ronald Colman
15. "The Last Voyage" (4-23-53) Charles Boyer
16. "Night Ride" (5-7-53) David Niven, Rhys Williams, Christine Larson
17. "The Ladies on His Mind" [a surrealist drama by Milton Merlin] (5-21-53) Ronald Colman, Benita Hume, Patricia Morison, Hillary Brooke, Elizabeth Fraser, Alix Talton
18. "Mr. Bingham" (6-4-53) David Niven
19. "Shadowed" (6-18-53) Dick Powell, Frances Dee

Second Season

20. "Finale" (9-24-53) David Niven, John Litel, Martha Hyer
21. *"The Squeeze" (10-1-53) Dick Powell, Richard Jaeckel, Regis Toomey
22. "A Place of His Own" (10-8-53) Charles Boyer, Stacy Harris
23. "Love at Sea" (10-15-53) Merle Oberon, Stephen Bekassy
24. "The Witness" (10-22-53) Dick Powell, Charles Bronson, Marion Carr
25. "A Matter of Advice" (10-29-53) David Niven
26. "Out of the Night" (11-5-53) Frank Lovejoy, Frances Rafferty, Frank Gerstle
27. "Moorings" (11-12-53) Charles Boyer, Dorothy Malone
28. *"The Hard Way" (11-19-53) Dick Powell, Lennie Breman, Regis Toomey, Jack Elam
29. "For Art's Sake" (11-26-53) David Niven, Nancy Gates, William Forrest
30. "The Girl on a Park Bench" (12-3-53) Joan Fontaine, Craig Stevens, John Litel
31. "The Room" (12-10-53) Dick Powell, Rena Regis, Jay Novello, Charlita
32. "A Man of the World" (12-17-53) David Niven, Barbara Lawrence
33. "The Gift" [adapted from a story by Amory Hare] (12-24-53) Charles Boyer, Maureen O'Sullivan
34. "House for Sale" (12-31-53) Ida Lupino, George Macready
35. "The Test" (1-7-54) Dick Powell, Frances Rafferty
36. "The Bad Streak" (1-14-54) Charles Boyer, Robert Arthur, Virginia Grey
37. "A String of Beads" [adapted from the William Somerset Maugham

story] (1-21-54) Ronald Colman, Angela Lansbury, Nigel
Bruce

38. "Indian Taker" (1-28-54) Ida Lupino, William Ching, Gerald
Mohr

39. "Second Dawn" (2-4-54) Charles Boyer, Luis Van Rooten, Edwin Jerome, Dorothy Hart

40. "The Gun" (2-11-54) Dick Powell, Barbara Billingsley

41. "The Bomb" (2-18-54) David Niven, John Dehner, Margaret
Sullavan

42. "Meet McGraw" [the pilot for the 1957 series] (2-25-54) Frank
Lovejoy, Audrey Totter, Paul Picerni, Ellen Corby

43. "Detective's Holiday" [by Ostavus Roy Cohen] (3-4-54) Dick
Foran, Dick Powell, Joan Chandler

44. "Operation in Money" (3-11-54) David Niven, Marjorie Lord

45. "Lady of the Orchids" (3-18-54) Lili Palmer, John Howard,
Robert Paige

46. "The Book" (4-1-54) David Niven, Marguerite Chapman, Claire
du Bry

47. "A Study in Panic" [by Larry Marcus] (4-8-54) Dick Powell,
Dorothy Malone, John Harmon, Claire Carleton, King Donovan, George Eldridge

48. "Masquerade" (4-15-54) Ida Lupino, John Bryant, Carleton G.
Young

49. "Village in the City" (4-22-54) David Niven, Royal Thurston,
Leslie Lorraine

50. "The Doctor and the Countess" [adapted from a chapter of Dr.
Pygmalion, the autobiography of plastic surgeon Dr. Maxwell Maltz] (4-29-54) Charles Boyer, Paula Raymond,
Carleton Young

Third Season

51. "Man in the Cellar" (9-30-54) Charles Boyer, Mae Clarke

52. "Never Explain" (10-7-54) David Niven, Barbara Lawrence,
Chris Olsen

53. "Interlude" [by Frederick L. Lipp] (10-14-54) Dick Powell,
Daria Massey, Joanne Woodward, Dona Jo Gribble

54. "The Wallet" (10-21-54) Charles Boyer, Maria Palmer, William Campbell

55. "The Adolescent" (10-28-54) Ida Lupino, Hugh Beaumont

56. "The Contest" (11-4-54) Dick Powell, Marguerite Chapman

57. "Vote of Confidence" (11-11-54) David Niven, Amanda Blake,
Chuck Connors, Elizabeth Patterson

58. "My Own Dear Dragon" (11-18-54) Charles Boyer, Vera Miles

59. "Marked Down" (11-25-54) Ida Lupino, Hal March

60. "Meet a Lonely Man" (12-2-54) David Niven, Martha Hyer

61. "Bourbon Street" (12-9-54) Dick Powell, Beverly Garland,
William Lucester, Ed Platt

62. "A Championship Affair" (12-16-54) Charles Boyer, Vera
Miles

63. "The Answer" [this episode received a nomination for an Emmy
for its film editing] (12-23-54) David Niven, Carolyn Jones,
Nestor Paiva, Anthony Caruso

64. "Go Ahead and Jump" (12-30-54) Dick Powell, Bill Johnstone
65. "A Bag of Oranges" (1-6-55) Ida Lupino, Walter Coy, Ray Walker
66. "Stuffed Shirt" (1-13-55) Charles Boyer, Philip Ahn, Peggy Maley, Christopher Dark
67. "Breakfast in Bed" (1-20-55) David Niven, Barbara Billingsley, Gloria Talbott
68. "The Good Sister" (1-27-55) Teresa Wright, Violet Rensing, Chuck Connors
69. "A Kiss for Mr. Lincoln" (2-3-55) Joanne Dru, Dick Foran
70. "Fair Trial" (2-10-55) Dick Powell, Frank Ferguson, Ray Walker
71. "The Wild Bunch" (2-17-55) Charles Boyer, Gigi Perreau, Natalie Wood, Noreen Nash, B. G. Norman
72. "Tusitala" [David Niven portrays Robert Louis Stevenson] (2-24-55) also with John Lupton, Gertrude Michael
73. "The Returning" (3-3-55) Dick Powell, Joan Elan
74. "Eddie's Place" (3-10-55) Ida Lupino
75. "Henry and the Psychopathic Horse" (3-17-55) David Niven
76. "Night at Lark Cottage" (3-24-55) Charles Boyer, Beverly Garland, John Doucette, Mimi Gibson
77. "The Girl on the Bridge" (3-31-55) Dick Powell, Coleen Gray
78. "The Collar" [this episode received an Emmy nomination for its film editing] (4-7-55) David Niven, Barton MacLane
79. "Madeira! Madeira!" (4-14-55) Charles Boyer, Angela Lansbury
80. "With All My Heart" (4-21-55) Ida Lupino, Walter Coy
81. *"The House Always Wins" [by Richard Carr] (4-28-55) Dick Powell, Alan Mowbray, Tristram Coffin, Regis Toomey, Jack Benny, Herb Vigran
82. "Uncle Fred Flits By" [adapted from the P. G. Wodehouse story; a new adaptation of the teleplay for Hollywood Opening Night aired 3/9/53] (5-5-55) David Niven, Robert Nichols, Jennifer Raines, Alex Frazer, Norma Varden, Leon Tyler
83. "Alias Mr. Hepp" [by Laszlo Gorog] (5-12-55) Charles Boyer, Barbara Fuller, Alan Mowbray, Forrest Taylor, Morris Ankrum
84. "Trudy" [by Kenneth Higgins] (5-26-55) Joan Fontaine, Steven Geray, Hans Conried, Otto Waldis, James Flaven
85. "Broken Journey" [by Stanley Niss] (6-2-55) David Niven, Don Haggerty, William Leicester, Emory Parnell, Robert Bice
86. "The Executioner" [by Laszlo Gorog] (6-9-55) Charles Boyer, Richard Hale, Berry Kroeger
87. "The Frightened Woman" [by Jerome Grushkin] (6-23-55) Merle Oberon, Craig Stevens, Hugh Beaumont, Irene Tedrow
88. "Award" [by Leslie Stevens] (6-30-55) Franchot Tone, Ida Lupino

Fourth Season

89. "Firing Squad" (10-6-55) David Niven, Hugh Beaumont
90. "The Face of Danger" [by Richard Carr] (10-13-55) Ida Lupino, Dick Foran, Paul Picerni, Vic Reaf, Ralph Moody

91. "Let the Chips Fall" [adapted from a story by Octavus Roy Cohen] (10-20-55) Charles Boyer, Paul Langton
92. "Full Circle" [by Herman J. Epstein] (10-27-55) David Niven, Joanne Woodward, Jeanne Baird, Alvin Greenman
93. "A Spray of Bullets" [by Richard Carr] (11-3-55) Dick Powell, Raymond Hatton, Jean Howell, Robert J. Wilke
94. "The Devil to Pay" [by Mark Taylor] (11-10-55) Charles Boyer, Mary Field, Joi Lansing
95. "Here Comes the Suit" (11-17-55) David Niven, Allison Hayes, Joi Lansing, Kristine Miller
96. "Looking Glass House" [by Milton Geiger] (11-24-55) Ida Lupino, Arthur Franz, Charlotte Lawrence, Sam Flint, Olivia Blakesley
97. "Something Very Special" [by Richard Carr] (12-1-55) Charles Boyer, Mary Zita Perzel, Vale Hunter, Ginger Hall
98. "A Place of Strangers" [by Willard Weiner] (12-8-55) Dick Powell, Dina Merrill, Freida Inescourt
99. "One Way Out" (12-15-55) Ida Lupino, Scott Forbes, Gaye Kellogg, Frances Robinson
100. "Dark Meeting" [by Robert Eggenweiler] (1-5-56) Ida Lupino, Warren Stevens
101. "Magic Night" [by Laszlo Gorog] (1-12-56) Charles Boyer, Joyce Gates
102. "Tunnel of Fear" [this episode received an Emmy nomination for its film editing] (1-19-56) Sir Cedric Hardwicke, David Niven, Walter Kingsford
103. *"High Stakes" [adapted by Richard Carr from a story by Roland Winters] (1-26-56) William Powell, Frances Bergen
104. "The Listener" [adapted by Frank L. Moss from a story by Cornell Woolrich] (2-2-56) Ida Lupino, Richard Lupino, Don Rickles, Ralph Moody
105. "Safe Keeping" [by George and Gertrude Fass] (2-9-56) David Niven, Tanya Borgh
106. *"No Limit" [by Richard Carr] (2-16-56) Dick Powell, Lola Albright, Regis Toomey, Alan Mowbray
107. "Command" [adapted from a story by Roland Winters] (2-23-56) Charles Boyer, Hugh Beaumont, Richard Hale
108. "Once to Every Woman" [by Leo Trelzger] (3-1-56) Phyllis Coates, Teresa Wright, Arthur Franz
109. "Red Wine" (3-8-56) David Niven
110. "To Die at Midnight" [by Michael Fessier] (3-15-56) Dick Powell
111. "Desert Encounter" [by Marc Brandell] (3-22-56) Charles Boyer, Stuart Whitman, Susan Kohner
112. "The Case of Emily Cameron" (3-29-56) Ida Lupino, Scott Forbes
113. "The Rites of Spring" [by Elick Moll] (4-5-56) David Niven, Barbara Lawrence
114. "Autumn Carousel" (4-12-56) Beverly Washburn, Dick Powell
115. "Wall of Bamboo" [by Walter C. Brown] (4-19-56) Charles Boyer, Philip Ahn, Richard Loo, Christopher Dark
116. "Touch and Go" (4-26-56) David Niven, Beverly Garland
117. *"A Long Way from Texas" (5-3-56) Dick Powell, Regis Toomey, Alan Mowbray

118. "That Woman" (5-10-56) Ida Lupino, Frank Scannell
119. "The Other Room" [by Marc Brandell] (5-17-56) Charles
     Boyer
120. "One Forty-Two" (5-24-56) Dick Powell, Akim Tamiroff
121. "Beneath the Surface" [by Elliott West] (5-31-56) Ida Lupino,
     Craig Stevens, Christopher Dark
122. "Watch the Sunset" (6-7-56) Dick Powell, Joanne Woodward,
     Marine Cooper
123. "Second Chance" (6-14-56) David Niven, Beverly Garland
124. "Woman Afraid" [by James Bloodworth] (6-21-56) Ida Lupino,
     Madge Blake, James Seay
125. *"The Stacked Deck" (6-28-56) Dick Powell, Regis Toomey,
     Alan Mowbray, Herb Vigran
126. "Distinguished Service" (7-5-56) Charles Boyer, Dorothy
     Green
127. "Yellowbelly" (7-12-56) Frank Lovejoy
128. "The Stand-In" (7-19-56) Ida Lupino, Virginia Field, John
     Harding
129. "Success Story" (7-26-56) Dick Powell, Peggie Castle, Robert
     Burton

THE GULF PLAYHOUSE

Live; under the sponsorship of the Gulf Oil Corporation.

1. "Double By-Line" (10-3-52) Dennis O'Keefe, Nina Foch,
   Frank McHugh
2. "You Can Look It Up" (10-10-52) Ward Bond
3. "The Rose" (10-17-52) Mildred Dunnock, Gene Lockhart,
   Joseph Buloff, Margaret Hamilton
4. "Necktie Party" (10-24-52) Jack Palance
5. "Mr. Nothing" (10-31-52) Kevin McCarthy, Thomas Mitchell
6. "A Question of Rank" (11-7-52) Eddie Bracken
7. "The Duel" (11-14-52) Wendell Corey, Frederic Worlock,
   Fred Stewart, Henry Jones
8. "The Whale on the Beach" (11-21-52) Hoagy Carmichael,
   Parker Fennelly
9. "One Afternoon in Caribou" (11-28-52) Robert Alda, Gene
   Lockhart
10. "Our Two Hundred Children" (12-5-52) Dean Jagger, Irene
    Hervey, Henry Jones, Charles Dingle
11. "Scream of the Crowd" (12-12-52) Robert Sterling, Felicia
    Montealegre
12. "The Trial of Charley Christmas" (12-19-52) Paul Hartman
13. "Mr. Breger" (12-26-52) Eddie Bracken

YOUR FAVORITE STORY

Sponsored by Schaefer; produced by Frederic W. Ziv.

The Regulars: Adolphe Menjou, host and narrator.

The Episodes:

1. "How Much Land Does a Man Need?" [adapted from the Leo Tolstoy story] (1-11-53)
2. "The Magician" (1-18-53) Anita Louise, Regis Toomey
3. "The Gold Bug" [adapted from the Edgar Allan Poe story] (1-25-53)
4. "Strange Journey" (2-1-53)
5. "Phantom Rickshaw" [adapted from the Rudyard Kipling story] (2-8-53) Ann Kimbell, Edward Morris
6. "An Eye for an Eye" (2-15-53)
7. "The Crime of Sylvester Bonnard" (2-22-53) Ralph Morgan
8. "Fury" (3-1-53)
9. "Work of Art" [adapted from the Anton Chekhov story] (3-8-53)
10. "The Gambler" [adapted from the Feodor Dostoevski story; narrated by Adolphe Menjou] (3-15-53)
11. "The Strange Mr. Bartleby" [adapted from the Herman Melville classic Bartleby the Scrivener] (3-22-53)
12. "The Prison with the Open Door" (3-29-53)
13. "The Copper Penny" (4-5-53) Henry Hull
14. "Jack of Hearts" (4-12-53)
15. "The Canterville Ghost" [adapted from the Oscar Wilde story] (4-19-53)
16. "Born Unto Trouble" (4-26-53) Robert Blake
17. "The World Beyond" (5-3-53) Billy Halop
18. "Turtle Island" (5-10-53) Billy Halop
19. "Mr. Double" (5-17-53)
20. "Colonel Chabert" [adapted from the Honoré de Balzac story] (5-24-53) Gertrude Michael
21. "The Man Who Sold His Shadow" (5-31-53)
22. "Martyr of Science" (6-7-53)
23. "The Story of Two Lives" (6-14-53)
24. "The Adoption" (6-21-53)
25. "The Diamond Lens" (6-28-53)
26. "The Postmistress" (7-5-53)

Second Season

27. "High Seas" (9-14-53)
28. "The Lost Duchess" (10-12-53)
29. "God Sees the Truth" [adapted from the Leo Tolstoy story] (10-26-53)
30. "A Tale of Negative Gravity" (11-9-53)
31. "Face of Paris" (1-4-54) Suzanne Flon, Gilles Queant
32. "The Robbers" (1-18-54)
33. "Dr. Morley's Daughter" (1-25-54)
34. "Heroism" (2-1-54)
35. "The Morning Finger" (2-8-54)
36. "City Hunter" (2-15-54)
37. "The Reporter Who Made Himself King" (2-22-54)
38. "Sword of the Vagabond" (3-1-54)

39. "Transferred Ghost" (3-8-53)
40. "Unforeseen" (4-12-54)
41. "Dividing Line" (4-26-54)
42. "Strange Valley" (5-3-54)
43. "Live Forever" (5-17-54)
44. "It Couldn't Happen" (5-24-54)
45. "Man Trap" (5-31-54)
46. "Storm Center" (6-7-54)
47. "Vengeance" (6-14-54)
48. "The Magic Egg" (6-28-54)
49. "Out of Darkness" (7-12-54)
50. "Decision" (7-26-54)
51. "Inside Out" (8-2-54)
52. "Lost Message" (8-9-54)
53. "The Empty Holster" [adapted from the Stephen Crane story] (8-16-54)
54. "Sudden Impulse" (8-23-54)
55. "Brave Eyes" (9-6-54)
56. "The Crime" (9-20-54) Bill Henry
57. "Twenty-one Days" (9-27-54)

Third Season [as a syndicated series]

58. "The Unknown" (10-13-54) Evan Evanson, Peter Hansen
59. "Colonel Estaban's Duel" (11-24-54)
60. "Vacant Room" (12-1-54)
61. "The Bedford House Conspiracy" (12-8-54)
62. "Thicker Than Water" (12-22-54)
63. "Magic Fog" (12-29-54)

YOU ARE THERE [after the radio series]

Alternate weeks sponsored by the Electric Light and Power Company.

The Regulars: Walter Cronkite, host and narrator.

The Episodes:

1. "The Landing of the Hindenburg at Lakehurst, New Jersey (May 6, 1937)" (2-1-53)
2. "The Capture of Jesse James" (2-8-53) James Dean (in the title role)
3. "The Boston Tea Party (December 16, 1773)" (2-15-53) E. G. Marshall (as Samuel Adams), Robert Pastene (as John Hancock), Gene Lyons (as Francis Rotch)
4. "The Capture of John Dillinger (January 25, 1934)" (2-22-53)
5. "The Final Hours of Joan of Arc (May 30, 1431)" (3-1-53) Diana Lynn (in the title role)
6. "The Assassination of Julius Caesar (March 15, 44 B. C.)" (3-8-53) Russell Conway, Paul Newman

7. "The Hamilton-Burr Duel at Weehawken Heights (July 11, 1804)" (3-15-53)
8. "The Discovery of Anesthesia, 1842" (3-22-53)
9. "The Witch Trial at Salem, Massachusetts (August 1692)" (3-29-53)
10. "The Conquest of Mexico, 1519" (4-5-53)
11. "The Impeachment of Andrew Johnson (August 1867-May 16, 1868)" (4-12-53)
12. "The Ordeal of Galileo" (4-19-53)
13. "The Signing of the Declaration of Independence (July 4, 1776)" (4-26-53) Shepperd Strudwick
14. "The Death of Socrates (399 B.C.)" (5-3-53) Shepperd Strudwick, John Cassavetes, Philip Bourneuf, Robert Culp, Richard Kiley, E. G. Marshall
15. "The Rise of Adolph Hitler (September 9, 1938)" (5-10-53)
16. "The Conquest of Yellow Fever (June 26, 1900)" (5-17-53)
17. "The Defense of the Alamo (February 23, 1836)" (5-24-53)
18. "The Dreyfus Case (October 15, 1894-1906)" (5-31-53)
19. "The Signing of the Magna Carta (June 15, 1215)" (6-7-53)
20. "The Flight of Rudolph Hess, 1941" (6-14-53)
21. "The Treason of Benedict Arnold, 1780" (6-21-53)

Second Season

22. "The Fate of Nathan Hale (September 22, 1776)" [produced by Charles Russell and directed by Sidney Lumet] (8-30-53) Paul Newman (in the title role), Richard Kiley (as Captain John Montressor, aide-de-camp to General Howe of Britain)
23. "The Capture of John Wilkes Booth (April 26, 1865)" (9-6-53)
24. "The Louisiana Purchase (July 14, 1803)" (9-13-53)
25. "The First Moscow Purge Trials (August 24, 1936)" (9-20-53)
26. "The Birth of a National Anthem (September 1814)" (9-27-53)
27. "The Secret of Sigmund Freud" (10-4-53)
28. "Christopher Columbus Sets Foot on San Salvador" [otherwise known as "Columbus Discovers America" (October 12, 1492)] (10-11-53)
29. "The Death of Cleopatra (30 B.C.)" (10-18-53)
30. "The Triumph of Simon Bolivar, 1824" (10-25-53)
31. "Grant and Lee at Appomattox (April 9, 1865)" (11-1-53) Paul Birch, Ray Engle
32. "The Abdication of Napoleon (March 21, 1814)" (11-8-53)
33. "The Recognition of Michelangelo" (11-15-53)
34. "The Sailing of the Mayflower (September 16, 1620-December 26, 1620)" (11-22-53)
35. "The Gettysburg Address (November 19, 1863)" (11-29-53)
36. "The Attack on Pearl Harbor (December 7, 1941)" (12-6-53)
37. "The Vindication of Savonarola (February 7, 1497)" (12-13-53)
38. "The Fall of Troy (1184 B.C.)" (12-20-53)
39. "The Surrender of Cornwallis at Yorktown (October 17, 1781)" (12-27-53)
40. "Mallory's Tragedy on Mount Everest, 1924" (1-3-54)
41. "The Trial of Charles the First, 1649" (1-10-54)
42. "The Resolve of Patrick Henry (March 23, 1775)" (1-17-54)

43. "The Sacrifice of Mahatma Gandhi" (1-24-54)
44. "The Last Moment of Marie Antoinette (October 16, 1793)" (1-31-54)
45. "The Ordeal of Tom Paine" (2-7-54)
46. "The Hanging of Captain Kidd (May 23, 1701)" (2-14-54) Henry Jones (in the title role)
47. "The First Command Performance of Romeo and Juliet, 1597" (2-21-54)
48. "The Trial of Peter Zenger, 1734-35" (3-7-54)
49. "The Rescue of the Statue of Liberty, 1886" (3-14-54)
50. "Burgoyne's Surrender at Saratoga (October 17, 1777)" (3-21-54) Neva Patterson
51. "The Conspiracy of Catherine the Great, 1762" (3-28-54)
52. "The Opening of King Tut's Tomb (November 26, 1922)" (4-4-54)
53. "Paul Revere's Ride (April 8, 1775)" (4-11-54)
54. "The Execution of Mary, Queen of Scots (February 8, 1587)" (4-18-54) Carmen Mathews, Mildred Natwick
55. "The Surrender of Corregidor (May 6, 1942)" (4-25-54) De-Forest Kelley, Marshall Bradford, Tor Johnson, Harte Wayne, Paul Birch, Sammee Tong, Bob Losain, James Yagi
56. "The Death of Rasputin, 1916" (5-2-54)
57. "The Court Martial of Mata Hari" (5-9-54) Everett Sloane
58. "The Scopes Trial, 1925" (5-16-54)
59. "The Great Moment of Haile Selassie (June 30, 1936)" (5-23-54)
60. "The Rise of Genghis Khan" (5-30-54) Raymond Bramley (in the title role), Bruce Gordon (as Togrue, Khan of the Karaits)
61. "The Decision of Robert E. Lee" (6-6-54)
62. "The Fall of Parnell" (6-13-54)
63. "The Crisis of Anne Boleyn, 1536" (6-20-54) Beatrice Straight
64. "The Vote That Made Jefferson President, 1801" (6-27-54)

Third Season [George Fiala served as make-up artist]

65. "The 'Treason' of Aaron Burr, 1807" (8-29-54) Richard Waring (in the title role)
66. "The Emergence of Jazz" (9-5-54) Louis Armstrong, guest.
67. "The Oklahoma Land Run" (9-12-54)
68. "William Pitt's Last Speech to Parliament" (9-19-54)
69. "The Return of Ulysses" (9-26-54)
70. "Sutter Discovers Gold" (10-3-54)
71. "The Great Adventure of Marco Polo, 1271" (10-10-54)
72. "Edison's Miracle of Light (April 14, 1891)" (10-17-54)
73. "The Burning of Rome (July 64 A. D.)" (10-24-54)
74. "The Nomination of Abraham Lincoln (May 1860)" (10-31-54)
75. "The Surrender of Wake Island, 1945" (11-7-54)
76. "Lord Nelson at Trafalgar (October 21, 1805)" (11-14-54)
77. "The Trial of Belle Starr" (11-21-54)
78. "The Plot Against King Solomon" (11-28-54)
79. "The Battle of Gibralter (July 24, 1704)" (12-5-54)
80. "The Cabinet Crisis Over Peggy Eaton, 1831" (12-12-54)
81. "La Fitte and Jackson at New Orleans" (12-19-54)

82. "The Passage of the Bill of Rights (September 25, 1789)" (12-26-54)

83. "The Torment of Beethoven (October 6, 1802)" (1-2-55) Lorne Greene, Beatrice Straight; Jacob Lateiner, guest pianist

84. "The Death of Stonewall Jackson (May 10, 1863)" (1-9-55)

85. "The First Flight of the Wright Brothers (December 17, 1903)" (1-16-55)

86. "The Trial of Susan B. Anthony (June 18, 1873)" [otherwise known as "Susan B. Anthony Is Tried for Voting"] (1-23-55) Carmen Mathews, E. G. Marshall

87. "The Tragedy of John Milton (August 13, 1660)" (1-30-55) Richard Kiley, Biff McGuire

88. "The Tragic Hour of Dr. Semmelweis, 1852" (2-13-55) Shepperd Strudwick

89. "The Liberation of Paris (August 25, 1944)" (2-20-55)

90. "Washington's Farewell to His Officers (December 4, 1783)" (2-27-55) E. G. Marshall

91. "D-Day (June 6, 1944)" (3-6-55)

92. "The Hatfield-McCoy Feud" (3-20-55) Hurd Hatfield, Madeleine Sherwood

93. "The Triumph of Alexander the Great, 324 B.C." (3-27-55) E. G. Marshall, Neva Patterson

94. "The Completion of the First Transcontinental Railroad (May 10, 1869)" (4-3-55)

95. "P. T. Barnum Presents Jenny Lind (September 11, 1850)" (4-10-55) Ray Collins

96. "The Emancipation Proclamation (January 1, 1863)" (4-17-55) Jeff Morrow

97. "Lou Gehrig's Greatest Day (July 4, 1939)" (5-1-55)

98. "The Final Performance of Sarah Bernhardt" (5-8-55)

99. "Dewey's Victory at Manila (May 1, 1898)" (5-15-55)

100. "The Sinking of the Titanic (April 14-15, 1912)" (5-22-55)

101. "The First Major Use of Penicillin (April 1, 1943)" (6-5-55)

102. "The Birth of Modern Boxing: The John L. Sullivan-James J. Corbett Battle (September 7, 1892)" (6-12-55)

103. "Napoleon's Return from Elba (March 7, 1815)" (6-19-55)

104. "The Boston Tea Party (December 16, 1773)" [restaged from 2/15/53] (6-26-55) Herbert Rudley, Russell Conway, Noel Drayton, Denver Pyle, Michael Emmett

Fourth Season

105. "The Triumph of Louis Braille" (9-11-55)

106. "The Last Day of an English Queen [Lady Jane Grey, executed February 12, 1554]" (9-18-55)

107. "The Boston Massacre (March 5, 1770)" (10-2-55) Addison Richards, Robert Burton, Whit Bissell

108. "The Rescue of the American Prisoners from Santo Tomas" (10-9-55)

109. "Moscow Today" [an 'uncensored' commentary and narrative by Robert C. Hottelet; narrated by Walter Cronkite] (10-16-55)

110. "The Secret Message That Plunged America into World War I (March 1, 1917)" (10-23-55)

111. "The Gunfight at the O. K. Corral" (11-6-55) Robert Bray, John Larch, John Alderson
112. "The Hoax of Cardiff Giant" (11-13-55)
113. "Bannister Wins the Mile Run" (11-20-55)
114. "Eli Whitney Invents the Cotton Gin (May 27, 1793)" (11-27-55)
115. "Spindletop--The First Texas Oil Strike, 1901" (12-4-55) Robert Bray, Jean Byron, Parley Baer
116. "The Chicago Fire (October 8-9, 1871)" (12-11-55)
117. "Pierre and Marie Curie Discover Radium, 1898" (12-18-55)
118. "Washington Crosses the Delaware (December 25, 1776)" (12-25-55)
119. "Benedict Arnold's Plot Against West Point (September 23, 1780)" (1-1-56)
120. "The Heroism of Clara Barton (September 17, 1862)" (1-8-56)
121. "V-J Day (September 2, 1945)" (1-15-56)
122. "Dr. Pinel Unchains the Insane" (2-12-56)
123. "The Great Comstock Silver Strike (October 29, 1873)" (2-26-56)
124. "When Stanley Finds Livingstone (November 10, 1871)" (3-11-56)
125. "Berlin Air Lift" (3-25-56)
126. "The Lost Battalion of World War I (May 31-June 1, 1916)" (4-1-56)
127. "The Recovery of the Mona Lisa, 1913" (4-8-56)
128. "William Jennings Bryan's Presidential Nomination (July 8, 1896)" (4-15-56)
129. "The Return of Halley's Comet, 1910" (4-29-56)
130. "Benjamin Franklin's Kite Experiment (June 15, 1752)" (5-13-56)
131. "The Dolittle Raiders Take Off for Tokyo (April 18, 1942)" (5-20-56)
132. "The Vote That Defeated Andrew Johnson for President (July 1868)" (5-27-56)
133. "Cyprus Today" [a documentary narrated by Walter Cronkite] (7-1-56)

Fifth Season

134. "The Fall of Fort Sumter (April 12, 1861)" (9-2-56)
135. "The Great Diamond Fraud" (9-9-56)
136. "Decatur's Raid at Tripoli (February 16, 1804)" (9-23-56)
137. "The Scuttling of the Graf Spee (December 17, 1939)" (9-30-56)
138. "Mr. Christian Seizes the Bounty (April 28, 1789)" (10-7-56)
139. "Hitler Invades Poland (September 1, 1939)" (10-14-56)
140. "Daniel Webster's Sacrifice to Save the Union (March 7, 1850)" (10-28-56)
141. "The End of the Dalton Gang" (5-12-57) David Janssen
142. "The Overthrow of the Tweed Ring (November 19, 1874)" (5-26-57) Herbert Rudley, Sam Finn
143. "The Attempt to Assassinate Theodore Roosevelt (October 14, 1912)" (6-2-57) Roland Winters
144. "The Bank Holiday Crisis of March 6, 1933" (6-9-57)

ABC ALBUM [also known as THE PLYMOUTH PLAYHOUSE]

Sponsored by The Chrysler Corporation.

The Episodes:

1. "Justice" [by Halstead Welles; directed by Ralph Nelson; Herbert Brodkin, executive producer; settings by James McNaughton; with accolades to the Legal Aid Society; the pilot for the 1954 series] (4-12-53) Paul Douglas, Lee Grant, John Lehine
2. "Mr. Glencannon Takes All" [directed by Sir Cedric Hardwicke] (4-19-53) Robert Newton
3. "Jamie" [pilot for the 1953 series] (4-26-53) Brandon de Wilde, Ernest Truex
4. "A Tale of Two Cities" [Part I; adapted from the Charles Dickens classic; filmed at Hollywood Entertainment Headquarters with a cast of sixty extras on a twenty-three acre site] (5-3-53) Wendell Corey (as Sydney Carton), Carleton Young (as Charles Darnay), Wanda Hendrix, Judith Evelyn
5. "A Tale of Two Cities" [Part II] (5-10-53) as above.
6. "Hogan's Daughter" (5-17-53) Sheila Bond
7. "Four Stories" [Sir Cedric Hardwicke, host] a) "The Chaser" Boris Karloff, Philip Truex; b) "You Were Perfectly Fine" Kyle MacDonnell; c) "Nightmare Number Three"; d) "Reticence of Lady Anne" (5-24-53)
8. "Colonel Humphrey J. Flack" [adapted from the Saturday Evening Post series; basis for the 1953 television series] (5-31-53) Alan Mowbray, Constance Ford
9. "The Split Second" [adapted from the Daphne du Maurier story] (6-7-53) Geraldine Fitzgerald, Alan Webb
10. "Baby and Me" (6-14-53) Janis Paige, Robert Preston
11. "The Turning Point" (6-21-53) Richard Ney, Neva Patterson, Johnny Stewart
12. "Jetfighter" (6-28-53) John Granger

THE GENERAL ELECTRIC THEATRE [after the radio series]

The Regulars: Ronald Reagan, host (with episode of 9/12/54)

The Episodes:

1. "Wedding Day" (2-1-53) J. Carrol Naish, Erin O'Brien-Moore, Jerome Cowan, Gisele Werbesirk, Basil Ruysdael
2. "Ride the River" (2-8-53) Broderick Crawford, Skippy Homeier, Bob Crane
3. "Hired Mother" (2-22-53) Laraine Day, Macdonald Carey, Gigi Perreau
4. "Best Seller" (3-1-53) Sir Cedric Hardwicke, Diana Lynn
5. "Winners Never Lose" (3-15-53) Pat O'Brien, Ruth Hussey, Ward Bond

6. "Trapped" (3-22-53) Nina Foch, Dan O'Herlihy, Francis L. Sullivan

Second Season

7. "Bilshan and the Thief" (7-5-53) Aurello Galli
8. "Thirteen O'Clock" (7-19-53) Eduard Franz, John Qualen, Lurene Tuttle
9. "The Wine of St. Albans" (8-2-53) Dan O'Herlihy
10. "Test of Love" (8-16-53)
11. "The Cat with the Crimson Eyes" (8-30-53) Charles McGraw, Rita Moreno
12. "Twinkle, Twinkle, Little Star" (9-6-53) Marilyn Maxwell
13. "My Wife, Poor Wretch" (9-20-53) Frances Gifford, Allyn Joslyn
14. "Confession" (10-18-53) Robert Newton, Mark Stevens, Frances Rafferty
15. "Woman's World" (10-25-53) Virginia Bruce, Peter Lawford, Marilyn Erskine, Otto Kruger
16. "The Hunted" (11-15-53) Preston Foster, Skip Homeier, Evelyn Ankers
17. "Atomic Love" (11-22-53) Dennis Morgan, Marjorie Rambeau, Joyce Holden
18. "The Marriage Fix" (11-29-53) Jack Carson, Marvin Kaplan, Joan Shawlee, Elizabeth Patterson
19. "The Eye of the Beholder" [on the differing psychological perceptions of an artist by his associates; directed by Stuart Reynolds; filmed (25 minutes)] (12-6-53) Richard Conte, Martha Vickers, Otto Waldis, Katherine Warren, Charles Victor
20. "Walking John Stopped Here" (1-24-54) Edward Arnold, Vera Miles
21. "Foggy Night" (2-14-54) Claire Trevor
22. "Here Comes Calvin" (2-21-54) Jack Carson, Phyllis Coates, Alan Jenkins
23. "The Other Sunlight" (3-14-54) David Brian, Marjorie Lord, Martha Vickers, Sheila James
24. "Pardon My Aunt" (4-4-54) Richard Carlson, Zasu Pitts
25. "To Lift a Feather" (5-2-54) Ruth Hussey, William Lundigan
26. "Wild Luke's Boy" (5-16-54) Alan Young, Veda Ann Borg
27. "Exit for Margo" (5-23-54) June Havoc, Nancy Gates, Victor Jory
28. "You Are Young Only Once" (6-6-54) Joan Bennett, John Beal, Melinda Markey
29. "The Crime of Daphne Rutledge" (6-13-54) Angela Lansbury, Hugh Marlowe, Frieda Inescourt
30. "Desert Crossing" (6-20-54) James Dunn, Miriam Hopkins
31. "Pretending Makes It So" (9-12-54) Audrey Totter, Richard Stapley
32. "Too Old for the Girl" (9-19-54) Thomas Mitchell, Robert Hutton, Joan Evans

Third Season

33. "Nora" [adapted from Henrik Ibsen's A Doll's House] (9-26-54)
    Phyllis Thaxter, Ronald Reagan, Luther Adler
34. "The High Green Wall" [adapted by Charles Jackson from the
    Evelyn Waugh novel] (10-3-54) Joseph Cotten (in his video
    debut), Thomas Gomez
35. "The Long Way 'Round" (10-10-54) Ronald Reagan, Nancy
    Gates
36. "Edison the Man" [adapted from the 1940 film scenario by Dore
    Schary and Hugo Butler] (10-17-54) Burgess Meredith
37. "The Road to Edinburgh" (10-31-54) Joan Crawford, Chuck
    Connors, John Sutton
38. "I'm a Fool" (11-14-54) James Dean, Natalie Wood; narrated
    by Eddie Albert
39. "The Face Is Familiar" (11-21-54) Jack Benny, Otto Kruger,
    Joi Lansing, Jesse White, Jean Willes, Benny Rubin
40. "The Rider on the Pale Horse" (11-28-54) Lee Marvin, Eva
    Marie Saint
41. "Committed" [by Russell B. Hughes] (12-5-54) Alan Ladd (in
    his video debut), John Howard, Virginia Gibson, Frank Fer-
    guson
42. "Out of the Night" (12-12-54) James Dean, Ronald Reagan
43. "The White Steed" [adapted from the Paul Vincent Carroll play]
    (12-26-54) Barry Fitzgerald (repeating his stage role), Dan
    O'Herlihy, Sallie Brophy, Dennis King Jr.
44. "Amelia" (1-2-55) Jane Wyman, Bill Goodwin, Louise Beavers,
    Jarilyn Oliver
45. "D. P. " (1-9-55) James Edwards
46. "Yankee Peddler" (1-16-55) Jackie Cooper
47. "The Martyr" [adapted by Leo Davis from a story by Frank
    O'Connor on the 1922 Irish Civil War] (1-23-55) Brian
    Aherne, J. M. Kerrigan, Lee Marvin, Ronald Reagan
48. "The Big Shot" (1-30-55) Johnnie Ray (in his dramatic video
    debut), Nancy Gates
49. "The Return of Gentleman Jim" (2-6-55) Richard Greene,
    George Montgomery, Joe Louis (as "the Champ")
50. "Love Is Eternal" [adapted by Irving Stone from his own novel,
    on the love between Abraham Lincoln and Mary Todd] (2-
    13-55) Richard Boone, Teresa Wright
51. "The Bachelor's Bride" (2-20-55) Fred MacMurray, Virginia
    Field, Patricia Crowley
52. "The Blond Dog" [a psychological drama] (3-6-55) Cornel
    Wilde, Jean Wallace
53. "War and Peace on the Range" [a comedy-western version of
    Leo Tolstoy's War and Peace] (3-13-55)
54. "The Bitter Choice" (3-20-55) Madeleine Carroll, George
    Macready
55. "Clown" [adapted from the Emmett Kelly autobiography; Kelly
    plays "Willie the Tramp"] (3-27-55) Henry Fonda, Dorothy
    Malone
56. "It Gives Me Great Pleasure" (4-3-55) Myrna Loy, Zachary
    Scott, Robert Preston

57. "O, Lonely Moon" [a drama of Ireland] (4-17-55) E. G. Marshall, Neva Patterson, Margaret Wycherly
58. "The Windmill" (4-24-55) James Stewart, Barbara Hale, John McIntire, Donald MacDonald
59. "Mr. Ocean Blue" (5-1-55) Boris Karloff, Bramwell Fletcher, Susan Strasberg, Anthony Perkins, Haim Wynant
60. "Into the Night" (5-8-55) Eddie Albert, Dane Clark, Ruth Roman, Robert Armstrong
61. "A Man with a Vengeance" [by Rod Serling] (5-15-55) Luther Adler, Barry Sullivan, Neva Patterson
62. "When in France" [by Leo Davis] (5-22-55) Wally Cox, Deirdre Owens
63. "Star in the House" (6-5-55) Joan Blondell, John Sutton, Ellen Corby, Madge Kennedy, Susan Whitney
64. "The Half-Promised Land" (6-12-55) Ezio Pinza, Mike Wallace, Joan Copeland
65. "The Day He Got Fired" (6-19-55) Richard Kiley, Monica Lewis

Episodes continue with Television Drama Series Programming: A Comprehensive Chronicle, 1959-1975.

EYE WITNESS

Produced by Robert Montgomery.

The Episodes:

1. "The Cruel Clinic" (3-30-53) Mercer MacLeod
2. "Apartment 4-D" (4-6-53) Nita Talbot, Lee Bowman (also the program host), Robert Webber, Robert Keith Jr.
3. "Dilemma" (4-13-53) Dorothy Donohue, Gene Lyons
4. "Mr. Loveday's Little Outing" (4-20-53) Melville Cooper, Romney Brent
5. "Burial Plot" (4-27-53) Mary Scott, James Gregory, Larry Haines
6. "The Righteous" (5-4-53) Henry Jones, Barbara Joyce, Rusty Lane
7. "Statement of the Accused" (5-11-53) Carl Schiller
8. "Invitation" (5-18-53) Millard Mitchell, Jean Carson; Fay Bainter narrates
9. "The Three Hours" [by Quentin Reynolds] (5-25-53) Michael Evans, Peter Cappell
10. "Youth from Vienna" (6-1-53) John Newland, Eva Marie Saint, Joseph Anthony
11. "The Baby Sitter" (6-8-53) Emlyn Williams, Sally Brophy, Dennis Harrison
12. "My Father's a Murderer" (6-22-53) Janet Parker, Wesley Addy, Mary Stewart
13. "The Green Glass" (6-29-53) Vaughn Taylor, Beverly Whitney, Richard Coogan

DOUGLAS FAIRBANKS JR. PRESENTS THE RHEINGOLD THEATRE

The Regulars: Douglas Fairbanks Jr., host.

The Episodes:

1. "The Accused" (1-7-53) Clifford Evans
2. "The Scream" (1-14-53)
3. "Little Brother" (1-21-53)
4. "The Clock" (1-28-53)
5. "Dialogue with Two Faces" (2-4-53) Joan Tetzel, Scott McKay
6. "The Surgeon" (2-11-53) Basil Sydney, Elizabeth Sellars
7. "Lochinvar" [adapted from the Sir Walter Scott story] (2-18-53)
8. "Take a Number" (2-25-53) George Benson, Jay Whittaker, Rick Wise
9. "Thought to Kill" (3-4-53) James Thompson, Eileen Moore
10. "Happy Birthday" (3-11-53) Dermot Palmer, Anouk
11. "Five Pound Note" (3-18-53) Percy Manmont
12. "Destination Milan" (3-25-53) Christopher Lee, Thomas Duggan, Lorraine Clews
13. "Foolish Notions" (4-1-53) Barbara Mullens, Clifford Evans
14. "American Duet" (4-8-53) Ron Randell, June Thorburn
15. "The Last Moment" (4-15-53) Douglas Fairbanks Jr.
16. "The Parlor Trick" (4-22-53) Arthur Franz
17. "Outpost" (4-29-53)
18. "My Name Is Jones" (5-6-53) Warren Stanhope, Joan Tetzel
19. "A Lodging for the Night" [adapted from the Robert Louis Stevenson story] (5-13-53) Douglas Fairbanks Jr.
20. "A Priceless Pocket" (5-20-53) Murie George, James Hayter, Wilfrid Hyde-White
21. "Sylvia" (5-27-53) Greta Gynt, Peter Reynolds
22. "The Red Dress" (6-3-53)
23. "The Runaway Marriage" (6-10-53)
24. "The Journey" (6-17-53) Clifford Davis, Renee Asherson
25. "Lowland Fling" (6-24-53) John Laurie, Barbara Mullen
26. "Emerald Green" (7-1-53)
27. "The Genie" (7-8-53)
28. "The Heel" (7-15-53)
29. "My Favorite Aunt" (7-22-53) Lou Jacobi, Marjorie Fielding, Phil Brown

Second Season

30. "The Door" (9-9-53) Ingelborg Wells, Peter Reynolds
31. "The Great White Bird" (9-23-53) Walter Rilla
32. "Forever My Heart" (9-30-53) Douglas Fairbanks Jr.
33. "Moment of Truth" (10-7-53) Philip Friend
34. "The Silent Snow" (10-21-53) Ingelborg Wells
35. "The Bitter Heart" (11-4-53) Barbara Mullen
36. "The Death of Michael Turbin" (11-18-53)
37. "Panic" (12-9-53)
38. "The Charm" (12-30-53)
39. "The Silent Man" (1-27-54)

40. "King High" (2-3-54) Patricia Medina
41. "Gramma Bren" (2-10-54)
42. "The Ship's Doctor" (2-17-54)
43. "The Wedding Veil" (2-24-54)
44. "Pardon My Ghost" (3-3-54)
45. "The Trap" (3-10-54) Mary Parker
46. "Second Wind" (3-17-54) Michael Shepley
47. "Leave to Die" (3-24-54) Yvonne Mitchell
48. "The International Settlement" (3-31-54)
49. "Double Identity" (4-14-54)
50. "The Refugee" (4-21-54)
51. "A Lesson in Love" (4-28-54) Dulcie Gray
52. "Myra and the Moneyman" (5-5-54)
53. "The Heirloom" (5-12-54) Dame Sybil Thorndike
54. "The Witness" (5-19-54)
55. "Johnny Blue" (5-26-54) Sam Levene
56. "Street of Angels" (6-2-54)
57. "The Happy McBains" (6-9-54) Dulcie Gray, Michael Denison
58. "Rain Forest" (6-16-54) Douglas Fairbanks Jr.
59. "Provincial Lady" (6-30-54)
60. "The Awakening" (7-14-54) Buster Keaton
61. "The Apples" (7-21-54) Ron Randell
62. "Pattern for Glory" (8-4-54) Ron Randell, Anne Crawford
63. "A Line in the Snow" (8-18-54)
64. "One Way Ticket" (8-25-54) Eunice Gayson
65. "Dreamstuff" (9-8-54) Betty McDowall, Lee Patterson
66. "Four Farewells in Venice" (9-22-54) Douglas Fairbanks Jr.

Third Season

67. "Mr. Sampson" (9-29-54) Douglas Fairbanks Jr., Dame Sybil Thorndike
68. "The Man Who Heard Everything" (10-13-54) Michael Gough
69. "The Last Knife" (10-20-54) Douglas Fairbanks Jr.
70. "Rehearsal" (11-3-54) Marius Goring
71. "Face of the Law" (11-10-54)
72. "The Relative Truth" (11-24-54)
73. "The Lovely Peace" (12-8-54) Diana Dors, Ron Randell
74. "The Mixup" (12-15-54)
75. "Silent Night: The Story of the Original Christmas Carol" [filmed at the actual setting] (12-22-54)
76. "Stand By" (12-29-54)
77. "Forever Is a Long Time" (1-12-55)
78. "Border Incident" (1-26-55)
79. "The Patriarch" (2-2-55)
80. "The Hideaway" (2-9-55)
81. "The Nineteenth Day" (2-16-55)
82. "Counterfeit" (2-23-55) Douglas Fairbanks Jr.
83. "Honeymoon Deferred" (3-2-55)
84. "The Long White Line" (3-9-55)
85. "The Dark Lake" (3-16-55)
86. "Pitfall" (3-23-55)
87. "Con Gregan's Legacy" (4-6-55)

88. "Crime a la Carte" (4-13-55)
89. "Room 506" (4-20-55)
90. "The Thoroughbred" (4-27-55)
91. "While the Circus Passes" (5-4-55)
92. "The Leprechaun" (5-11-55)
93. "The Little Big Shot" [a drama of gangster Candy Nolan] (5-18-55)
94. "The Auction" (5-25-55)
95. "The Only Son" (6-1-55)
96. "Another Day" (6-15-55)
97. "Flight One-zero-one" (6-29-55)
98. "The Wedding" (7-13-55)
99. "The Enchanted Doll" (7-20-55)
100. "Tony" (8-3-55)
101. "Blue Murder" (8-24-55)
102. "The Sound of Your Voice" (8-31-55) Douglas Fairbanks Jr.
103. "Big Nick" (9-7-55) Rosanno Brazzi
104. "Milkman" (9-14-55) Leslie Duryer, Mary MacKenzie
105. "The Treasure of Urbano" (9-28-55)
106. "Atlantic Night" [a documentary drama of the Titanic incident] (10-5-55)
107. "The Hero" (10-12-55)

Fourth Season

108. "Success Train" (11-7-55) Douglas Fairbanks Jr.
109. "Guilt" (11-14-55) Joan Miller
110. "A Borderline Case" (11-21-55) Greta Gynt, Bernard Lee, Robin Bayley
111. "Heritage" (12-5-55) Robert Beatty, Betty McDowall
112. "The Immigrant" (12-12-55) Andre Morell
113. "A Fast Buck" (1-2-56)
114. "Demetrios" (1-16-56) Dermot Walsh
115. "Deadline Vienna" (1-23-56)
116. "Gabrielle" (1-30-56)
117. "Better Mousetraps" (2-6-56) Ella Raines, Paul Carpenter
118. "The Present" [by James Kenny] (2-13-56) J. Carrol Naish
119. "Jason's House" (2-20-56) Finlay Currie, Gene Anderson, Patrick Holt
120. "The Samples" (2-27-56) Betty McDowall, Ron Randell, Al Mulock
121. "A Walk in the Wilderness" (3-5-56) Douglas Fairbanks Jr., Roddy McDowall
122. "Welcome My Wife" (3-12-56) Paula Wright, Barry Keegan
123. "First Day" (3-19-56) Tom McCauley, Frances Latemore, Mary Steele
124. "A Flight of Birds" (3-26-56) Margaret McCourt, Richard Palmer
125. "The Intruder" (4-2-56)
126. "A New Life" (4-9-56) Ron Randell, Renee Asherson, June Rodney
127. "The Dunce" (4-23-56) Eva Maria Melnecks, Hellane Beland, Wolf Peterson

128. "Ship Day" (4-30-56) Cyril Cusack, Clifford Evans
129. "The Murderer" (5-7-56) Douglas Fairbanks Jr., Marianne Wischmann, Howard Vernorl
130. "Point of View" (5-14-56) Bobby Howes, Barbara Mullen, Michael Ripper
131. "Mutiny" (5-28-56) Clifford Evans, Laurence Payne
132. "The Story of Pan Yuzef" (6-4-56)
133. "A Train to the Sea" (6-11-56) Ian Hunter, Nora Swinburne
134. "A Likely Story" (6-25-56) Nicola Braithwaite, Betty McDowall
135. "Play Me a Blue Note" (7-2-56) Douglas Fairbanks Jr.
136. "The Way Home" (7-9-56) Mary Kerridge
137. "Mr. Purley's Profession" (7-23-56) Roland Culver, Jane Baxter, Leslie Perrins
138. "Treasure in Store" (8-20-56) Kathleen Harrison
139. "Beloved Stranger" (9-3-56) Douglas Fairbanks Jr., Ella Raines
140. "Guy in the Middle" (9-10-56) Robert Beatty, Yolande Donlan

Fifth Season

141. "Timmy the Shanks" (9-17-56) Richard O'Sullivan
142. "The Man Who Wouldn't Escape" (10-1-56)
143. "Winning Sequence" (10-8-56) Jean Cadell, Harold Lang, Barbara Mullen
144. "This Last Tour" (10-15-56) Charlotte Thiele
145. "Someone Outside" (10-22-56) Lois Maxwell, Maurice Kaufmann
146. "One Can't Help Feeling Sorry" (10-29-56) Douglas Fairbanks Jr., Lois Maxwell
147. "Crown of the Andes" (11-5-56) Christopher Rhodes
148. "Homecoming" (11-12-56) Barry Foster, Barbara Mullen
149. "Rendezvous at Dawn" (11-19-56) Robert Beatty
150. "Scheherezade" (11-26-56) Maya Koumani, Hugh Williams
151. "To What Great Heights" (12-3-56) Robert Beatty, Sean Barrett
152. "The Best Man" (1-14-57) Ron Randell, Betta St. John
153. "The Ludlow Affair" (1-28-57) Robert Beatty
154. "The Trouble with Destiny" (2-4-57) Douglas Fairbanks Jr.
155. "Together" (3-11-57) Lee Patterson, Luciana Paluzzi

ADVENTURE

Documentary shorts produced under the auspices of the Museum of Natural History.

The Regulars: Walter Cronkite, host and narrator.

The Episodes:

1. "The Story of the Mutiny on the Bounty and Descendants" (6-28-53)

2. "Gems, Lampreys and Antarctic Sea Expeditions" (7-5-53)
3. a) "Fish"; b) "Storms" (7-12-53)
4. "The Chicken Embryo" (7-19-53)
5. a) "From the Neck Up"; b) "Gorillas" (7-26-53)
6. a) "Who Rules the World?"; b) "Human Perception Studies"; c) "Bird Islands of the Pacific" (8-2-53)
7. a) "African Tribal Dances"; b) "Life on the Antarctic Sea Islands" (8-9-53)
8. a) "Non-Kontiki"; b) "Jaguar Hunting" (8-16-53)

BEN HECHT'S TALES OF THE CITY

Not until The Naked City were the huddled inhabitants of urbania poetically sermonized; yet the video was never without its dramatic debt to the city dweller. Though boasting teleplays by the Hollywood veteran Ben Hecht and an ardent guest cast, Tales of the City had too much the hurried look of pre-packaging to be taken seriously, and so survived a mere six episodes.

The Regulars: Ben Hecht, host.

The Episodes:

1. [unknown title] (6-25-53) Robert H. Harris, Ann Rutherford, Barry Nelson, Gary Merrill, Janis Carter
2. [unknown title] (7-9-53) Wendell Corey, Laraine Day
3. [unknown title] (7-23-53) Gary Merrill, Robert H. Harris, Madeleine Carroll
4. [unknown title] (8-6-53) Charles Coburn, Martha Scott, Patty McCormack
5. "Miracle in the Rain" (8-20-53) William Prince, Mildred Dunnock, Una Merkel, Phyllis Thaxter
6. [unknown title] (9-3-53) Hume Cronyn, Diana Douglas

FIRST PERSON PLAYHOUSE

The Episodes:

1. "I'd Rather Be a Squirrel" (7-10-53) Wally Cox
2. "Death of the Old Man" (7-17-53) Mildred Natwick, William Hanson
3. "Comeback" (7-24-53) Jessie Royce Landis
4. "One Night Stand" (7-31-53) James Dunn, Conrad Janis
5. "August Heat" [adapted from the W. F. Harvey story] (8-7-53)
6. "The Tears of My Sister" (8-14-53) Kim Stanley, Lenka Peterson
7. "Crip" (8-21-53) Evelyn Varden, Leo Penn, Kathy Nolan
8. "The Lady Looks Ahead" (8-28-53) Judith Evelyn, Shepperd Strudwick

9. [unknown title] (9-4-53)
10. "A Present from Cotton Mather" (9-11-53) Joseph Anthony,
    Mildred Dunnock

THE CAMPBELL TELEVISION SOUNDSTAGE

The Episodes:

1. "Innocent Till Proven Guilty" (7-10-53) Leora Dana, Kristine
    Miller, Paul McGrath
2. "Something for an Empty Briefcase" (7-17-53) James Dean,
    Susan Douglas
3. "No Scar" (7-24-53) Warren Stevens, Betsy Von Furstenberg
4. "One Swell Guy" (7-31-53) Jack Lemmon
5. "Run Away" (8-7-53) Cliff Hall, Ralph Lee Robertson
6. "Deception" (8-14-53) Martin Brooks, Howard Freedman
7. "The Dark Room" (8-21-53) Hildy Parks, James Gregory,
    Charles Nolte
8. "Wonder in Your Eyes" (8-28-53) Clifford Sales, Walter Matt-
    hau, Nancy Coleman
9. "The Square Hole" (9-4-53) Art Carney
10. "The Promise" (9-11-53) Jack Warden, Janet Ward
11. "Exit Laughing" (9-18-53) Patricia Breslin, Arnold Moss
12. "Believe" (9-25-53) Joseph Anthony, Joan Copeland
13. "Last Spring" (10-2-53) Claudia Morgan
14. "Darling Come Home" (10-9-53) Alice Frost, Allen Nourse

Second Season

15. "Life Sentence" (10-16-53) James Dean, Georgiann Johnson
16. "Johnny No-Name" (10-23-53) Mickey Knox, Wolfe Barzell,
    Patricia Jenkins
17. "Nemesis" (10-30-53) E. G. Marshall, Una Muson, Harry
    Townes
18. "The Meaning of Truth" (11-6-53) John Beal, Margaret Hayes
19. "Ten Little Words" (11-13-53) Melville Ruick, Carol Goodner
20. "Solitaire" (11-20-53) William Podmore, James Gregory
21. "Home Is Where Love Is" (11-27-53) Elliott Reid, Joan Potter
22. "We Wanna Get Married" (12-4-53) James Holden
23. "Too Little a Kiss" (12-11-53) Katherine Emmett, Betsy
    Palmer
24. "The Man Who Knew O. Henry" (12-18-53) Wallace Ford,
    Dorothy Peterson
25. "The Happy Headline" (12-25-53) James Costigan, Richard
    Bishop
26. "Reveille for Two Angels" (1-1-54) Robert Brown, Jo Van
    Fleet
27. "Marked Money" (1-8-54) Joseph Sweeney, Kate McComb,
    Dean Harris
28. "I Remember, I Remember" (1-15-54) Patty McCormack,
    Richard Waring

29. "The Shy One" (1-22-54) Roddy McDowall, Patricia Collinge
30. "A Time for Hope" (1-29-54) Malcolm Lee Beggs, Carmen Mathews
31. "Lost: One Friday" (2-5-54) Dennis Harrison, Mary Alice Moore
32. "The Golden Box" (2-12-54) Patty McCormack, Dorothy Donahue, John Stephen
33. "Journey to Java" (12-19-54) Brian Keith, Patricia Kirkland
34. "Break the Mirror" (2-26-54) Zachary Scott, Ruth Ford, Harry Sheppard
35. "An Eye for an Eye" (3-5-54) Margaret Hamilton, Dean Harens, Parker Fennelly
36. "The Magnificent Lie" (3-12-54) Kevin McCarthy, Kathleen McLean
37. "The Green Convertible" (3-19-54) John Baragrey, Georgann Johnson
38. "The Test Case" (3-26-54) Henry Hull, Robert Cummings, Gene Lockhart
39. "God's Children" (4-2-54) Eddie Brian, Jean Gillespie, Maurice Sehrong
40. "XXXXX Isn't Everything" (4-9-54) Darren McGavin, Barbara Bel Geddes, Elliott Reid, Maurice Sehrong
41. "A Kiss to Conquer" (4-16-54) Janice Rule, Carl Reiner
42. "The Almighty Dollar" (4-23-54) Henry Hull, Mildred Natwick, Parker Fennelly
43. "Al Toolum and His Buddy Leo" (4-30-54) Robert Preston, Leo Durocher, Van Dyke Parks
44. "Emma's Antenna" (5-7-54) Hugh Reilly, Lydia Reed, Chris White
45. "The Man of the House" (5-14-54) Don Hanmer, Barbara Baxley
46. "A Little Child Shall Lead Them" [a story of Tom Sawyer] (5-21-54) Eileen Heckart, Joey Fallon
47. "The Corner Druggist" (5-28-54) Richard Kiley, Lillian Gish

THE CHRYSLER MEDALLION THEATRE

Produced by William Spier; sponsored by the Chrysler Corporation.

The Episodes:

1. "The Decision at Arrowsmith" [adapted from the Sinclair Lewis novel Arrowsmith] (7-11-53) Henry Fonda, Diana Douglas, Juano Hernandez
2. "A Job for Jimmy Valentine" (7-18-53) Ronald Reagan, Dorothy Hart, Jack Arthur
3. "The Grand Cross of the Crescent" (7-25-53) Jack Lemmon, Ernest Truex
4. "The Man Who Liked Dickens" (8-1-53) Claude Rains
5. "Mrs. Union Station" (8-8-53) June Havoc, Scott McKay, Richard Carlyle

6. "The Consul" (8-15-53) Charles Ruggles
7. "The Quiet Village" (8-22-53) Robert Preston, Rod Steiger
8. "Columbo Discovers Italy" (8-29-53) Dane Clark
9. "The Scent of the Roses" (9-5-53) Martha Scott

Second Season

10. "The Padre of San Pablo" (9-12-53) Zachary Scott
11. "The Bartlett Desk" (9-19-53) Mildred Natwick, Edward Everett Horton
12. "The Big Bow Mystery" (9-26-53) Sir Cedric Hardwicke, Bethel Leslie
13. "The Archer Case" (10-3-53) Claude Rains
14. "The Trouble Train" (10-10-53) Jeffrey Lynn, Madge Evans, Iris Mann
15. "A Time for Heroes" (10-17-53) Victor Moore
16. "Return Match" (10-24-53) Maria Riva, Joseph Anthony, William Prince
17. "Gran'ma Rebel" (10-31-53) Beulah Bondi, Betsy Von Furstenberg, Jackie Cooper
18. "Battle Hymn" [an original drama by Norman Lessing] (11-7-53) Helen Hayes (as Harriet Beecher Stowe), Steven Courtleigh, Eric Dressler
19. "The Bishop's Candlesticks" [adapted from Victor Hugo's Les Miserables] (11-14-53) Victor Jory, Barry Jones
20. "The Canterville Ghost" [adapted from the Oscar Wilde story] (11-21-53) Edward Everett Horton
21. "Dear Cynthia" (11-28-53) Janet Gaynor, Vicki Cummings
22. "Standish Started Something" (12-5-53)
23. "A Day in Town" [restaged from the Actor's Studio episode of 1/2/49] (12-12-53) Charlton Heston
24. "Twenty-four Men in a Plane" (12-19-53) Leslie Nielsen, Jackie Cooper
25. "They Call Them Meek" (12-26-53) Thomas Gomez, Gene Raymond
26. "Suitable Marriage" (1-2-54) Otto Kruger, Roddy McDowall
27. "The Magic Touch" (1-9-54) Paul Douglas
28. "The Gentle Deception" (1-16-54) Thomas Mitchell
29. "The Blue Serge Suit" (1-23-54) Diana Lynn, Jerome Courtland
30. "Book Overdue" (1-30-54) Jan Sterling, Barry Sullivan, George Macready
31. "The Teacher" (2-6-54) Nancy Olsen, Don Taylor, Hope Emerson
32. "The Thirty-ninth Bomb" (2-13-54) Steve Cochran, Geraldine Brooks, Frederic Worlock
33. "The Voyage Back" (2-20-54) Nancy Kelly, Richard Kiley
34. "Homestead" (2-27-54) Eddie Albert
35. "Sinners" (3-6-54) Mildred Dunnock, Rhys Williams
36. "Flight to Fame" (3-13-54) Edith Fellows
37. "Contact with the West" (3-20-54) Jerome Thor, Joseph Wiseman
38. "The Alibi Kid" (3-27-54) Stephen McNally, Ben Gazzara, Sam Levene
39. "Safari" (4-3-54) Brian Donlevy, Marilyn Erskine

THE REVLON MIRROR THEATRE

The Episodes:

1. "The Little Wife" [adapted by David Shaw from the William Marik short story] (6-23-53) Eddie Albert, Georgann Johnson, Henry Jones
2. "Salt of the Earth" (6-30-53) Martha Scott, Richard Kiley
3. "Someone Like You" (7-7-53) Ralph Meeker, Hildy Parks
4. "Don't Wink at Fate" (7-14-53) Vanessa Brown, William Prince
5. "The Enormous Radio" (7-21-53) Darren McGavin, Felicia Montealegre, John Baragrey
6. "A Reputation" (7-28-53) Jackie Cooper, Peggy Ann Garner
7. "White Night" (8-4-53) Joan McCracken, Warren Stevens
8. "The Happy Tingle" (8-11-53) Ralph Meeker, Eva Marie Saint, Oliver Thorndyke
9. "The Party" [adapted from the F. Scott Fitzgerald story] (8-18-53) Patty McCormack, Shepperd Strudwick, Katherine Bard, Alan Bunce
10. "One Summer's Rain" (8-25-53) Franchot Tone, Barbara Baxley, Joseph Anthony, Rusty Lane
11. "The Bottle Party" (9-1-53) Maria Riva, Murray Hamilton

Second Season

12. "Because I Love Him" (9-19-53) Joan Crawford (her video debut), William Ching
13. "Heads or Tails" (9-26-53) John Ireland, Joanne Dru
14. "Lullaby" (10-3-53) Agnes Moorehead, Tom Drake, Betty Lynn
15. "Flight from Home" (10-10-53) Ruth Hussey, David Brian
16. "Equal Justice" (10-17-53) Dane Clark, Faith Domergue
17. "The Surprise Party" (10-24-53) Wanda Hendrix, Robert Hutton, Craig Stevens, Dorothy Malone
18. "Dreams Never Lie" (10-31-53) Michael O'Shea, Angela Lansbury, Patrick Knowles
19. "Award Performance" (11-7-53) Virginia Field, Zachary Scott
20. "Key in the Lock" (11-14-53) George Brent, Marguerite Chapman
21. "Summer Dance" (11-21-53) Jane Greer, Glen Langen, Barbara Bates
22. "Uncle Jack" (11-28-53) Jack Haley, Elizabeth Fraser
23. "Next Stop Bethlehem" (12-5-53) Charles Bickford, Ronald Reagan, Lyle Talbot

THE LORETTA YOUNG SHOW [a. k. a. A LETTER TO LORETTA]

First season episodes were titled A Letter to Loretta.

The Regulars: Loretta Young, hostess.

The Episodes:

1. "Trial Run" (9-20-53) Loretta Young
2. [unknown title] (9-27-53) Loretta Young
3. "Prisoner at One O'Clock" (10-4-53) Bruce Bennett, William Campbell
4. "Girl on a Flagpole" (10-11-53) Loretta Young, Paul Langton
5. "The Lady Killer" (10-18-53) Loretta Young
6. "Earthquake" (10-25-53) Loretta Young, Paul Langton
7. "The One That Got Away" (11-1-53) Richard Travis, Loretta Young, Mike Hathaway
8. "Kid Stuff" (11-8-53) Loretta Young, Lee Aaker, George Nader
9. "The Brontë Story" [a biographical drama of Charlotte Brontë] (11-15-53) Loretta Young
10. "Thanksgiving in Beaver Run" (11-22-53) Loretta Young, Dick Foran, William Campbell
11. "This Is a Love Story" (11-29-53) Loretta Young, Robert Strauss
12. "The Queen" (12-6-53) Alex Nicol, Loretta Young
13. "The Faith of Chata" (12-13-53) Loretta Young, Nancy Gilbert
14. "The Night My Father Came Home" [a Christmas story] (12-20-53) Loretta Young
15. "Hotel Irritant" (12-27-53) Loretta Young, George Nader
16. "Inga" (1-3-54) Loretta Young, Don Murphy, Robert E. O'Connor, Stanley Clements
17. "Secret Answer" (1-17-54) Donald Curtis, Loretta Young, Paul Langton
18. "The Mirror" (1-24-54) Loretta Young
19. "The Hollywood Story" (1-31-54) Loretta Young
20. "A Family Out of Us" [a Boy Scout tribute] (2-7-54)
21. "Act of Faith" (2-14-54) Eddie Albert, Loretta Young, Frieda Inescourt
22. "Big Little Lie" (2-21-54) Beverly Washburn
23. "New York Story" (2-28-54) Loretta Young, Billy Chapin
24. "Nobody's Boy" [produced in co-operation with the Chicago Youth Rehabilitation Center] (3-7-54) Peter Reynolds

25. "The Count of Ten" (3-14-54) Eddie Albert, Loretta Young
26. "The Clara Schumann Story" [a biographical drama] (3-21-54)
     Loretta Young, George Nader
27. "Son, This Is Your Father" (3-28-54) Alan Hale, Jr.
28. "The First Man to Ask Her" (4-4-54) Loretta Young, Jock
     Mahoney
29. "Man's Estate" (4-11-54) Bobby Ellis
30. "Forest Ranger" (4-18-54) Christopher Dark, Bruce Cowling
31. "The Enchanted Schoolteacher" (4-25-54) Loretta Young,
     George Nader, Earl Roby
32. "The Judgment" (5-2-54) Mae Clarke, Loretta Young, John
     Howard
33. "Oh, My Aching Heart" (5-9-54) George Nader, Loretta Young,
     Sally Blane
34. "Dear Midge" (5-16-54) Loretta Young, William Frawley
35. "Something Always Happens" (5-23-54) Loretta Young, Lamont
     Johnson
36. "Lady in War Paint" (5-30-54) Loretta Young
37. "Inga" (6-6-54) Loretta Young [repeat of 1/3/54 episode]

Second Season

38. "A Guest in the Night" (8-29-54) Hugh O'Brian, Loretta Young,
     Earl Roby
39. "Dr. Juliet" (9-5-54) Barbara Ruick
40. "Double Trouble" (9-12-54) Loretta Young, Hugh O'Brian
41. "The Lamp" (9-19-54) Loretta Young
42. "You're Driving Me Crazy" (9-26-54) Charles Drake, Loretta
     Young
43. "The Case for Father Darling" (10-10-54) Loretta Young
44. "The Girl Scout Story" (10-31-54) Loretta Young
45. "No Help Wanted" (11-7-54) Jock Mahoney, Loretta Young
46. [unknown title] (11-14-54) Bruce Cowling
47. "Big Jim" (12-5-54) Bobby Driscoll
48. "Evil for Evil" (12-12-54) Griff Barnett, Loretta Young
49. "Three Minutes Too Late" (12-26-54) Loretta Young, Hugh
     O'Brian
50. "The Girl Who Knew" (1-2-55) Loretta Young, Hugh Beau-
     mont, Chuck Connors
51. "The Flood" (1-9-55) William Campbell
52. "Decision" (1-16-55) Jock Mahoney, Loretta Young
53. "Something About Courage" (2-6-55) Gene Barry
54. "Dickie" (2-13-55) Richard Eyer, Bruce Cowling
55. "Option on a Wife" (2-20-55) Jock Mahoney, Loretta Young
56. "Tale of a Cayuse" (2-27-55) Jock Mahoney, Loretta Young
57. "Dateline Korea" [a documentary drama; Major General Charles
     W. Christenberry, President of the American Korean Founda-
     tion, guests] (3-13-55) Loretta Young
58. "Inga II" (3-20-55) Dennis Hopper, Loretta Young, Donald
     Murphy
59. "Mink Coat" (3-27-55) Jock Mahoney, Loretta Young
60. "Let Columbus Discover You" (4-3-55) Craig Stevens
61. "He Always Comes Home" (4-10-55) Richard Arlen, Elinor
     Donahue

62. "Feeling No Pain" (4-17-55) Hugh O'Brian
63. "The Little Teacher" [by Richard Morris] (4-24-55) John Hudson, Mimi Gibson, John Bryant
64. "I Remember the Rani" (5-1-55) Loretta Young, Edward Ashley

Third Season

65. "Fear Me Not" (8-28-55) Phyllis Thaxter, Robert Preston; Rosalind Russell, hostess
66. "Week-end in Winnetka" (9-4-55) Virginia Bruce, Gene Raymond, Elinor Donahue; Rosalind Russell, hostess
67. "Reunion" (9-11-55) Donald Curtis, Nina Foch; Joseph Cotten, host
68. "My Uncles O'More" (9-18-55) Teresa Wright, Scott Forbes; Barbara Stanwyck, hostess
69. "Gino" [by William Bruckner] (9-25-55) Ricardo Montalban, Thomas Coley
70. "Moment of Decision" (10-2-55) Diana Lynn, Merle Oberon, Liam Sullivan
71. "The Waiting Game" (10-9-55) Joanne Dru, Glen Langan; Barbara Stanwyck, hostess
72. "The Last Spring" [by Gene Levitt] (10-16-55) John Hodiak; Van Johnson, host
73. "Katy" (10-23-55) Beverly Washburn, Margaret Hayes; Van Johnson, host
74. "Slander" (10-30-55) Laraine Day, Kenneth Tobey, Corey Allen, Betty Caulfield; Irene Dunne, hostess
75. "Tropical Secretary" (11-6-55) Phyllis Kirk, Rod Cameron; Irene Dunne, hostess
76. "The Bracelet" [adapted from the Andre Maurois story] (11-13-55) Merle Oberon, Judith Evelyn
77. "Across the Piaza" [by Gene Levitt] (11-27-55) Margaret Hayes, Richard Webb, Gerald Mohr; Dinah Shore, hostess
78. "A Pattern of Deceit" (12-4-55) Laraine Day, Susan Morrow, Paul Langton, Robert Burton; Claudette Colbert, hostess
79. "Man in the Ring" (12-11-55) Scott Brady, Phyllis Thaxter; Ann Sothern, hostess
80. "A Shadow Between" (12-18-55) Stephen McNally, Mary Sinclair, Marjorie Lord; Joan Fontaine, hostess
81. "The Christmas Stopover" (12-25-55) Loretta Young
82. "Tickets for May" (1-1-56) Dorothy Malone, John Ericson
83. "Inga III" [by William Bruckner] (1-8-56) Loretta Young
84. "The Challenge" (1-15-56) Keith Andes, Barbara Hale, Regis Toomey
85. "Song of Rome" (1-22-56) Anna Maria Alberghetti, Scott Forbes
86. "The Secret" (1-29-56) John Newland
87. "The Pearl" (2-12-56) Teru Shimada
88. "Tightwad Millionaire" (2-19-56) Robert Sterling, Marilyn Erskine, Barbara Billingsley
89. "Gesundheit" (2-26-56) Loretta Young, Scott Forbes
90. "Father Happe" (3-4-56) Romney Brent, Mercedes McCambridge

91. "His Inheritance" (3-18-56) Loretta Young, John Newland
92. "The Wise One" (3-25-56) Stephen McNally, Joy Page
93. "But for God's Grace" (4-1-56) Hugh Beaumont
94. "Hapless Holiday" (4-8-56) Phyllis Thaxter, Mildred Natwick
95. "Case 258" (4-15-56) Frank Lovejoy
96. "The Cardinal's Secret" (4-22-56) Ricardo Montalban
97. "Casebook" (4-29-56) Charles Drake
98. "The Refinement of Ab" (5-13-56) Hugh Beaumont, Lee Aaker

Fourth Season

99. "Double Partners" (8-26-56) Bruce Cowling, Loretta Young, Ross Elliott
100. "Who Are You?" (9-2-56) Loretta Young, Craig Stevens
101. "Saigon" (9-9-56) Steve Forrest
102. "Little League" (9-16-56) Loretta Young
103. "Incident in Kaur" (9-23-56) Loretta Young
104. "Political Copywriter" (9-30-56) Loretta Young
105. "The Years Between" (10-7-56) Loretta Young, John Newland
106. "New Slant" (10-14-56) Lee Bowman, Rod Cameron
107. "Goodbye, Goodbye" (10-21-56) John Newland
108. "The Great Divide" (10-28-56) Loretta Young
109. "Take Care of My Child" (11-4-56) Betty Field, Hugh Beaumont, Beverly Washburn
110. "The End of the Day" (11-11-56) Loretta Young, Johnny Crawford
111. "Inga IV" (11-18-56) Donald Murphy, Loretta Young
112. "Rhubarb in Apartment 7-A" (12-2-56) Ricardo Montalban, Patricia Hardy
113. "Somebody Else's Dream" (12-9-56) Mark Roberts
114. "Three and Two Please" (12-16-56) Loretta Young
115. "Imperfect Balance" (12-30-56) Loretta Young
116. "Queen Nefertiti" (1-6-57) Loretta Young, Lawrence Dobkin, Ken Remo, Robert Warwick
117. "My Favorite Monster" (1-13-57) John Newland
118. "Miss Ashley's Demon" (1-27-57) Loretta Young
119. "The Bad Apple" (2-3-57) Lee Bowman, Regis Toomey, Bobby Diamond
120. "Tension" (2-17-57) John Newland
121. "Louise" (3-10-57) Viveca Lindfors, Herbert Marshall
122. "Emergency" (3-24-57) John Ericson, Anna Maria Alberghetti
123. "The Room Next Door" (3-31-57) Loretta Young
124. "So Bright a Light" (4-7-57) Loretta Young
125. "Rummage Sale" (4-14-57) Jan Sterling, Mark Roberts
126. "The Legacy" (4-21-57) John Newland
127. "The Man on Top" (4-28-57) Ricardo Montalban, Harry Townes
128. "Countess" (5-5-57) Loretta Young
129. "A Mind of Their Own" (5-12-57) Loretta Young
130. "Royal Partners" [Part I] (5-19-57) Loretta Young
131. "Royal Partners" [Part II] (5-26-57) as above.
132. "Son, This Is Your Father" (6-2-57) Loretta Young [repeat of 3/28/54 episode]

Fifth Season

133. "A Dollar's Worth" (10-20-57) Loretta Young
134. "The Defense" (10-27-57) Mark Stevens
135. "Innocent Conspiracy" (11-3-57) Loretta Young, Teru Shimada
136. "Understanding Heart" (11-10-57) Gary Merrill Nancy Gates
137. "The Little Witness" (11-24-57) Johnny Crawford
138. "Blizzard" (12-1-57) Patricia Crowley, Stephen McNally
139. "Friends at a Distance" (12-8-57) Charles Korvin
140. "Man in a Hurry" (12-15-57) Kim Spaulding, Laraine Day
141. "Power Play" (12-29-57) James Daly, Anita Louise
142. "The Demon and Mrs. Devon" (1-5-58) Loretta Young, Craig Stevens
143. "The Accused" (1-12-58) Ann Doran, Loretta Young, Dabbs Greer
144. "The Hidden One" (1-19-58) Dewey Martin, Julie Adams
145. "Far-Away Island" (1-26-58) Loretta Young, John Newland, George Keymas
146. "My Two Hands" (2-2-58) Gary Merrill, Nancy Gates
147. "Dear Milkman" (2-9-58) Robert Rockwell, Loretta Young
148. "The Bargain" (2-16-58) Wally Cox, Patricia Crowley, Mark Stevens
149. "A Greater Strength" (2-23-58) Loretta Young, Mae Clark
150. "Conflict" (3-2-58) Keefe Brasselle, John Newland
151. "Windfall" (3-16-58) Hume Cronyn, Veda Ann Borg
152. "Time of Decision" (3-23-58) John Newland
153. "Air Stewardess" (3-30-58) James Daly
154. "To Open a Door" (4-6-58) Tom Helmore, Loretta Young
155. "Thanks to You" (4-13-58) Hume Cronyn
156. "Dangerous Verdict" (4-20-58) Loretta Young, Barney Phillips
157. "Second Rate Citizen" (4-27-58) Dewey Martin
158. "South American Uncle" (5-4-58) Loretta Young, Regis Toomey
159. "Strange Adventure" (5-11-58) Loretta Young, Paul Picerni
160. "Day of Rest" (5-18-58) Loretta Young, Robert Rockwell, Shelley Fabares
161. "Wedding Day" (5-25-58) Loretta Young

Sixth Season

162. "The Near Unknown" (10-5-58)
163. "For Better or for Worse" (10-12-58) Edward Binns, Mark Stevens
164. "The Good Old Summertime" (10-19-58) Robert Rockwell, Loretta Young
165. "A Visit to San Paolo" (10-26-58) Loretta Young, James Philbrook, Carlo Tricoli, Mario Siletti, Vincent Paula
166. "Out of Control" (11-2-58) Frank Lovejoy, Nick Adams
167. "The Twenty-Cent Tip" (11-9-58) Loretta Young
168. "I Want to Get Married" (11-16-58) Ralph Meeker, Loretta Young
169. "The Woman Between" (11-23-58) Loretta Young, John Newland

170. "The Last Witness" (11-30-58) Eddie Albert, Helen Kleeb, George Tobias, Frank Scannell
171. "The Happy Widow" (12-7-58) Loretta Young
172. "Strange Money" (12-14-58) Ralph Meeker, Regis Toomey
173. "Operation Snowball" (12-28-58) Virginia Mayo, Lee Goodman

Episodes continued with Television Drama Series Programming: A Comprehensive Chronicle, 1959-1975.

THE UNITED STATES STEEL HOUR PRESENTS THE THEATRE GUILD OF THE AIR [after the radio series]

Episodes staged by Alex Segal, formerly affiliated with The Pulitzer Prize Playhouse.

The Episodes:

1. "P. O. W. " [by David Davidson] (10-27-53) Richard Kiley, Gary Merrill, Phyllis Kirk, Sally Forrest, Brian Keith, Johnny Stewart, Don Hanmer
2. "Hope for a Harvest" [adapted from the Sophie Treadwell play] (11-10-53) Faye Emerson, Robert Preston, Dino Di Luca
3. "The Wedding" [adapted from the 1948 play] (11-24-53) Eddie Albert, Phyllis Thaxter, Billie Worth, Audrey Christie
4. "The Man in Possession" [adapted from the H. M. Harwood play] (12-8-53) Rex Harrison
5. "The Vanishing Point" (12-22-53) Peter Lorre, Claude Dauphin, Viveca Lindfors
6. "Hedda Gabler" [adapted from the Henrik Ibsen classic] (1-5-54) Tallulah Bankhead (in her feature video debut), John Baragrey, Alan Hewitt, Luther Adler, George Tesman, Eugenia Rawls
7. "The Rise of Carthage" (1-19-54) Nina Foch, Paul Douglas
8. "Papa Is All" [adapted from the Patterson Greene play] (2-2-54) Walter Slezak, Jessie Royce Landis
9. "Highway" (2-17-54) Diana Lynn, Kevin McCarthy, Jerome Kilty
10. "Morning Star" [adapted from the Sylvia Regan play] (3-2-54) Gertrude Berg, Marilyn Erskine, Jo Van Fleet, David Winters, Oscar Karlweis, Fred Sadoff
11. "Welcome Home" [subsequently restaged for The United States Steel Hour episode of 3/22/61] (3-16-54) Helen Hayes, Charles Ruggles, Carmen Mathews
12. "The Last Notch" [western drama by Frank Gilroy] (3-30-54) Richard Jaeckel, Jeff Morrow, George Mitchell, Louisa Horton
13. "Late Date" [by William Kendall Clarke; subsequently restaged for the Matinee Theatre episode of 9/28/56] (4-13-54) Patty McCormack, Walter Matthau, Barbara Baxley, Jessie Royce Landis
14. "The Laphams of Boston" [adapted from the William Dean Howells novel] (4-27-54) Thomas Mitchell, Dorothy Gish

15. "The End of Paul Dane" [a drama of a psychiatrist and his two patients] (5-11-54) Robert Preston, Teresa Wright
16. "The Great Chair" [adapted by Eric Barnouw from the play by Leo Lieberman] (5-25-54) Gary Merrill (as a university president), Walter Hampden, Lori March
17. "Good for You" (6-8-54) Orson Bean, Kenny Delmar, Jack Klugman, Diana Lynn, Barbara Nichols
18. "The Fearful Decision" [by Cyril Hume and Richard Maibaum] (6-22-54) Sam Levene, Ralph Bellamy, Meg Mundy, Edward Binns, Joey Fallon
19. "Haven's End" [adapted from the John P. Marquand story] (7-6-54) Viveca Lindfors, Richard Hylton, Howard Lindsay
20. "A Garden in the Sea" (7-20-54) Dorothy McGuire, Mildred Natwick, Donald Murphy
21. "Oberstrasse Forty-Nine" (8-3-54) Dan O'Herlihy, Ben Astar, Tom Helmore, Margaret Phillips
22. "The Grand Tour" [adapted from the Elmer Rice play] (8-17-54) Zachary Scott, Julie Haydon
23. "Two" (8-31-54) Patricia Crowley, Jack Klugman, Jerome Courtland

Second Season

24. "The Notebook Warrior" [by Ira Levin; subsequently restaged for the Matinee Theatre episode of 3/19/56] (9-14-54) Richard Kiley, Ben Gazzara, Sidney Blackmer
25. "Baseball Blues" (9-28-54) House Jameson, Frank Lovejoy; Frankie Frisch, Lefty Gomez, guests.
26. "The Man with the Gun" (10-12-54) Gary Merrill, Leueen MacGrath
27. "The Fifth Wheel" (10-26-54) Orson Bean, Faye Emerson, Margaret Hamilton, Franchot Tone
28. "Goodbye ... But It Doesn't Go Away" [by Raphael Hayes; subsequently restaged for The United States Steel Hour episode of 12/31/58] (11-19-54) Jack Carson, June Lockhart, Geraldine Brooks
29. "King's Pawn" (11-23-54) John Forsythe, Janet Blair, Neil Hamilton
30. "One for the Road" (12-7-54) Jeff Donnell, Charles Coburn
31. "Presento" (12-21-54) Don Taylor, Jack Klugman, Patricia Crowley, Hans Conried, Shirley Yamaguchi
32. "The Thief" (1-4-55) James Dean, Mary Astor, Paul Lukas, Diana Lynn
33. "The Bogey Man" (1-18-55) Robert Preston, Celeste Holm, Ann Thomas
34. "Six O'Clock Call" [by James Yaffe] (2-1-55) Gertrude Berg, David Opatoshu, Michael Wager, Louis Sorin
35. "Freighter" (2-15-55) Thomas Mitchell, James Daly, Martin Balsam, Henry Hull, Cameron Mitchell, Jocelyn Brando
36. "Man in the Corner" (3-1-55) Jack Carson, Ernest Truex, Harold Vermilyea
37. "No Time for Sergeants" [adapted by Ira Levin from the Mac Hyman novel; filmed by Warner Brothers, 1958] (3-15-55) Andy Griffith [in his video debut; he repeated role for the film] Eddie Le Roy, Robert Emhardt, Harry Clark

38. "Scandal at Peppernut" (3-29-55) Theodore Bikel, Terry Moore, Charles Korvin, Ruth Gates, Jack Mullaney
39. "The Rack" [by Rod Serling; filmed by Metro Goldwyn Mayer, 1956] (4-12-55) Marshall Thompson, Wendell Corey (who repeated his role for the film), Keenan Wynn
40. "The Roads to Home" [by Horton Foote] (4-26-55) James Daly, Johnny Washbrook, Beatrice Straight
41. "The Fearful Decision" [by Cyril Hume and Richard Maibaum; restaged from 6/22/54] (5-10-55) Sam Levene, Ralph Bellamy, Meg Mundy, Edward Binns, Joey Fallon
42. "Big Winner" [a satire on the television quiz show by Richard Bimonte] (5-24-55) Frank Puglia, Maria Reid, Richard Morris, George Ives, Dolores Sutton
43. "Hung for a Sheep" [by Frank D. Gilroy] (6-7-55) Hugh Marlowe, George Macready, Jerome Thor
44. "Red Gulch" [adapted from the Bret Harte story] (6-21-55) Franchot Tone, Jayne Meadows, Teresa Wright

Third Season

45. "The Meanest Man in the World" [adapted from the play by Augustin MacHugh] (7-6-55) Wally Cox, Josephine Hull, Parker Fennelly, Kenny Delmar, Betsy Palmer
46. "The Gambler" [by Irving Richin] (7-20-55) Jack Carson, John McQuade, Kay Medford, Bert Freed, Robert Ellenstein
47. "The Seventh Veil" [adapted by Arthur Arent from the Broadway play] (8-3-55) Diana Lynn, Dan O'Herlihy
48. "The Bride Cried" [by Mae Cooper and George Klein] (8-17-55) Tammy Grimes, Barbara O'Neil, Janice Rule, Jamie Smith, Ruth Ford, Jayne Seymour
49. "Counterfeit" [adapted by Ellen Violett from the J. B. Priestley play Laburnum Grove] (8-31-55) Boris Karloff, John McGiver, Edna Best, Sarah Marshall, Jessie Royce Landis
50. "A Wind from the South" [by James Costigan, on an Irish country girl's first love] (9-14-55) Julie Harris, Donald Woods

Episodes continued in alternation with Television Drama Series Programming: A Comprehensive Chronicle, 1959-1975.

THE MOTOROLA TELEVISION HOUR

The Episodes:

1. "Outlaw's Reckoning" [adapted from the Ernest Haycox story] (11-3-53) Eddie Albert, Wallace Ford, Jane Wyatt, Vicki Cummings, Lee Marvin
2. "Westward the Sun" (11-17-53) Jackie Cooper, Richard Ney, Brian Keith, Brenda Bruce
3. "Brandenberg Gate" (12-1-53) Jack Palance, Maria Riva, Elisha Cook

4. "At Ease" (12-15-53) Horace MacMahon, Brian Donlevy, Madge Evans
5. "The Thirteen Clocks" [musical version of the James Thurber play] (12-29-53) Basil Rathbone, John Raitt, Sir Cedric Hardwicke, Roberta Peters, Russell Nype, Alice Pearce
6. "The Last Days of Hitler" (1-12-54) Philip Bourneuf, Martin Kosleck, Lotta Stavisky, Arnold Moss
7. "Side by Side" (1-26-54) Helen Hayes, Dennis King
8. "A Dash of Bitters" (2-9-54) Zachary Scott, Estelle Winwood, Joan Lorring
9. "The Muldoon Matter" (2-23-54) Charles Ruggles, Ed Begley, Frank McHugh, Kent Smith
10. "The Family Man" (3-9-54) Hume Cronyn, Jane Wyatt, Elaine Stritch
11. "Nightmare in Algiers" (3-23-54) Tony Randall, Francis L. Sullivan, Rita Gam, Luther Adler
12. "The Sins of the Fathers" (4-6-54) Elliott Nugent, Walter Hampden, Gene Lockhart, Betty Field
13. "Black Chiffon" [adapted from the play by Lesley Storm] (4-20-54) Leora Dana, Dame Judith Anderson, Sir Cedric Hardwicke
14. "Love Song" (5-4-54) Lisa Kirk, Oscar Homolka
15. "Atomic Attack" (5-18-54) Walter Matthau, Phyllis Thaxter, Robert Keith

THE PLAYHOUSE

The Episodes:

1. "Journey to Nowhere" (10-1-53) Eddie Albert, Lorne Greene, Constance Ford
2. "Room 203" (10-8-53) Nina Foch
3. "Crime and Punishment" [adapted from the Fedor Dostoevski classic] (10-15-53) Jean-Pierre Aumont, Blanche Yurka
4. "Temptation" (10-22-53) Franchot Tone, Louise Albritton
5. "Nightmare" (10-29-53) Jeffrey Lynn
6. "Ballet for a Stranger" (11-5-53) Vincent Price
7. "Man Versus Town" (11-12-53) Everett Sloane
8. "Beautiful World" (11-19-53) Cloris Leachman, Hurd Hatfield
9. "The Sacrifice" (11-26-53) Charles Korvin
10. "Deadline" (12-3-53)
11. "Serenade in Manhattan" (12-10-53) Miriam Hopkins, Donald Cook, Everett Sloane
12. "The Gioconda Smile" [adapted from the Aldous Huxley novel] (12-17-53) Dennis King, Leueen McGrath
13. "David's Star of Bethlehem" (12-24-53) Gene Raymond, William Prince, Louisa Horton
14. "To Love and to Cherish" (12-31-53) Jane Wyatt, John Beal, John Emery
15. "Kitty Doone" (1-7-54) Constance Bennett, Everett Sloane, Nydia Westman

16. "The Little Stone House" (1-14-54) Betty Field, Charles Castleman
17. "Make Me Happy, Make Me Sad" (1-21-54) Donald Cook, Janis Paige
18. "Taste" (1-28-54) Joseph Schildkraut, Ed Begley, Patricia Breslin
19. "Up for Parole" (2-4-54) Dane Clark, Cathy O'Donnell
20. "The Man They'd Murdered" (2-11-54) Basil Rathbone, Joan Wetmore, Francis L. Sullivan
21. "Walk in the Night" (2-18-54) Chester Morris
22. "The Murderer Who Wasn't" (2-25-54) Rod Steiger
23. "A Soldier's Return" (3-4-53) John Beal

THE PEPSI COLA PLAYHOUSE

The Regulars: Arlene Dahl, hostess; Anita Colby served as hostess as of 5/21/54; Joan Bennett served as hostess as of 10/3/54.

The Episodes:

1. "When a Lovely Woman" (10-2-53) Marguerite Chapman, Tony Randall, Ron Randell, James Millican
2. "Wait for Me Downstairs" (10-9-53) John Hudson, Allene Roberts
3. "Night Light at Vorden's" (10-16-53) Craig Stevens, Jean Byron, Myra McKinney
4. "Death Has a System" (10-23-53) Kim Spalding, Ian MacDonald
5. "The Ragged Stranger" (10-30-53) Michael Hall, Hayden Rorke, Joanne Davis
6. "Melody in Black" (11-6-53) Nancy Gates, Robert Paige
7. "The House Nobody Wanted" (11-13-53) Marilyn Erskine, Craig Stevens
8. "Claire" (11-20-53) Marguerite Chapman, Marilyn Erskine, Walter Coy
9. "Frozen Justice" (11-27-53) Morris Ankrum
10. "Vacation Wife" (12-4-53) Frances Rafferty, Robert Paige
11. "The Motive Goes Round and Round" (12-11-53) Ludwig Donath, Eve Miller
12. "Death Makes a Pass" (12-18-53) Lloyd Corrigan, Jay Novello
13. "Who Is Sylvia?" (12-25-53) Frances Rafferty, Rick Jason
14. "Miss Darkness" (1-1-54) Dee Carroll, Peter Graves
15. "Gold Thumb" (1-8-54) Jeanne Cooper, Walter Reed
16. "Account Closed" (1-15-54) George Nader, Carolyn Jones
17. "Farewell Performance" (1-22-54) Joan Shawlee, John Hoyt
18. "Too Gloomy for Private Puskin" (1-29-54) Steve Brodie, Robert Strauss
19. "The Psychophonic Nurse" [subsequently restaged for the Campbell TV Soundstage episode of 6/25/55] (2-5-54) Lee Marvin, Joanne Davis
20. "A Far, Far Better Thing" (2-12-54) Robert Lowery, Nancy Gates

21. "Live a Little" (2-19-54) Marie Windsor, Bethel Leslie, Jean Byron, Walter Coy
22. "His Brother's Girl" (2-26-54) George Nader, Nancy Gates, Keith Larsen
23. "Taps for a Hoofer" (3-5-54) Roy Roberts, Peggy Knudsen, Andrea King
24. "Don't You Remember?" (3-12-54) Philip Ober, Nancy Gates
25. "Open Season" (3-19-54) Dennis Morgan, Lee Marvin, Douglass Montgomery
26. "The Silence" (3-26-54) Rod Cameron, Carolyn Jones
27. "The Grey and Gold Dress" (4-2-54) Peggy Converse, Gerry Gaylor, Vera Miles, Jan Arvan, Gertrude Michael
28. "Borrow My Car" (4-9-54) Bill Phipps, Lola Albright, Louis Jean Heydt
29. "Hollywood, Home Sweet Home" (4-16-54) Francis X. Bushman, Frances Bavier, Lloyd Corrigan
30. "The Sound of Silence" (4-23-54) Jack Kelly, Sallie Brophy, Carl Benton Reid
31. "And the Beasts Were There" (4-30-54) William Bishop, John Bishop
32. "Girl on the Drum" (5-7-54) Jack Kelly, Lita Baron, Carleton Young
33. "The Black Purse" (5-14-54) Pat Carroll, Patrick O'Neal
34. "Fie, Fie, Fifi" (5-21-54) Lloyd Corrigan, Fifi D'Orsay
35. "Grenadine" (5-28-54) Sally Blaine, William Bishop
36. "Unfair Game" (6-4-54) Marguerite Chapman, Richard Travis
37. "Terror Train" (6-11-54) Frances Rafferty, Whit Bissell
38. "Doubled in Danger" (6-18-54) Carolyn Jones, Lawrence Dobkin, Bill Phipps
39. "When the Police Arrive" (6-25-54) Cesar Romero, Hillary Brooke

[now as a repeat series]

40. "Dear Little Fool" (7-4-54) Patrick O'Neal, Leslye Banning
41. "Uncle Charley" (7-11-54)
42. "The Whistling Room" (7-18-54) Barbara Bester
43. "Bachelor's Week-end" (7-25-54) Robert Paige
44. "Annual Honeymoon" [repeat of the Schaefer Century Theatre episode of 5/31/52] (8-1-54) Garry Moore, Bonita Granville, Alan Mowbray
45. "Long, Long Ago" (8-8-54)
46. "Mungahana" (8-15-54) John Hoyt
47. "The Perfect Gentleman" (8-22-54) Bruce Cabot
48. "Playmates" [repeat of the Schaefer Century Theatre episode of 8/20/52] (8-29-54) Natalie Wood
49. "Adopted Son" (9-5-54)
50. "A Mansion for Jimmy" [repeat of the Schaefer Century Theatre episode of 8/6/52] (9-12-54) Robert Paige
51. "One Thing Leads to Another" (9-19-54)
52. "Portrait of Tobey" [repeat of the Schaefer Century Theatre episode of 5/24/52] (9-26-54) Lynne Roberts, John Qualen

Second Season

53. "Sal" (10-3-54) Gladys George, Jean Byron, Craig Stevens
54. "Sunday in Town" [a comedy-musical revue] (10-10-54) Judy
    Holliday, Steve Allen, Dick Shawn
55. "Death the Hard Way" (10-17-54) Patrick O'Neal, William
    Gargan, Eve Miller
56. "Such a Nice Little Girl" [by Lawrence Kimball] (10-31-54)
    Marguerite Chapman, Vera Miles, Hugh Sanders, Bob Forrest
57. "Melody in Black" [restaged from 11/6/53] (11-7-54) Nancy
    Gates, Peter Graves
58. "This Man for Hire" (11-14-54) Jean Willes, Jack Kelly,
    Frank Wilcox
59. "Iron Curtain" (11-21-54)
60. "Death Rides a Wildcat" (11-28-54) Jim Thorn, Whit Bissell,
    Dorothy Green, Alan Dexter
61. "Santa's Old Suit" (12-19-54)
62. "Lost Lullaby" (12-26-54) William Gargan
63. "Midnight Chimes" (1-2-55)
64. "The Golden Flowers" (1-9-55) Vera Miles
65. "Unblushing Bride" [otherwise known as "The Bewildered Bride"]
    (1-16-55) Mala Powers, Gene Reynolds, Mary Field, Chick
    Chandler
66. "The House on Judas Street" (1-23-55) Jean Byron, Peter
    Votrian
67. "Otto and the Coat" (1-30-55) Hans Conried, Gloria Talbott,
    Liam Sullivan
68. "And Never Come Back" (2-6-55) Laura Elliott, Eve Miller
69. "Pals to the End" (2-13-55) Robert Armstrong, Brian Keith
70. "The Vanishing Suitor" (2-20-55) Irene Hervey, Karen Sharpe,
    Richard Simmons
71. "The Quiet Wife" (2-27-55) Eleanore Tanin
72. "Mr. Donald Takes a Risk" [by Richard Collins] (3-6-55) Ar-
    thur Space, Mary Field, Lee Ericson
73. "Wait for George" (3-13-55) Josephine Hutchinson, Walter
    Baldwin
74. "A Husband Appears" [by Joseph Ruscoll] (3-20-55) Sallie
    Brophy, Herbert Rudley, Dorothy Adams, Phil Teeck
75. "The Loner" (3-27-55) Peter Votrian, Anna Lee, Hayden
    Rorke
76. "Passage Home" (4-3-55) Brian Keith
77. "Peterson's Eye" (4-10-55)
78. "The House Where Time Stopped" (4-17-55) Vera Miles, Ian
    Keith, Josephine Hutchinson
79. "The Lady Challenges" (4-24-55)
80. "Longest Legs in the Show" (5-1-55)
81. "Stake My Life" (5-8-55) Lynn Bari, Hugh Beaumont
82. "The Man Nobody Wanted" (5-15-55) Tom Drake, Bruce Ben-
    nett
83. "Australian Search" (5-22-55)
84. "The Boy with the Beautiful Mother" (5-29-55) Peter Votrian
85. "The Boy and the Coach" (6-5-55) Sammy Ogg
86. "Woman in the Mine" (6-12-55) Beverly Garland, Charles
    Bronson

87. "I'll Be Waiting" (6-19-55) Judith Ames
88. "The Nightingale" (6-26-55) Bruce Bennett, Alf Kjellin, Jeanne Bates
89. "Murder Is My Business" (7-3-55)
90. "Philo Vance's Secret Mission" (7-10-55)

THE MASK

One of the earliest and most conscientious of series on criminal investigation and legal restitution. Gary Merrill and William Prince are in good form as the barrister brothers; homicidal characters and their abettors are also judiciously cast.

The Regulars: Barr. Walter Guilfoyle: Gary Merrill; Barr. Peter Guilfoyle: William Prince

The Episodes:

1. "Murder in the Burlesque House" (1-10-54) Sherry Britton
2. "Hotel Murder" (1-17-54) James Gregory
3. "Murder in the Print Shop" (1-24-54)
4. "The Will" (1-31-54) Gaby Rodgers
5. "Framed for Murder" (2-7-54) Brian Keith
6. "The Young Dancer" (2-14-54) Cloris Leachman, Steven Hill
7. "Marked for Murder" (2-21-54)
8. "Poisoned Village" (2-28-54) Joey Walsh
9. "The Visitor" (3-7-54) Luther Adler, Virginia Gilmore
10. "Sixty-five Pacific Street" (3-14-54) Peg Hillias, Don Dubbins, Daryle Grimes
11. "Fingers of Fear" (3-21-54) Mary Linn Beller
12. "The Gambler" (4-4-54) Perry Fiske
13. "Party Night" (4-11-54) Paul Newman, Patricia Breslin, Jo Van Fleet
14. "The Backyard" (4-18-54)
15. "Royal Revenge" (4-25-54) Patricia Breslin

LOVE STORY

The Episodes:

1. "Norma Loves Mike" (4-20-54) Betty Lou Holland, Perry Fiske
2. "Timmy" (4-27-54) James Gregory
3. "The Matchmaker" (5-4-54) Murray Matheson, Beatrice Straight
4. "The Arms of the Law" (5-11-54) Lee Bowman, Peggy McCay
5. "The Wedding Dress" (5-18-54) Patricia Collinge, Paul McGrath
6. "Turn Back the Clock" (5-25-54) Harry Townes, Audrey Lindley

7. "The Yo-Yo People" (6-1-54) Basil Rathbone, Beatrice Straight
8. "For All We Know" (6-8-54) Joan Lorring, James Gregory
9. "Shadow Waltz" (6-15-54) Betty Field, Arthur O'Connell
10. "The Orchard" (6-22-54) Frank McHugh, Mildred Natwick
11. "The Good Morrow" (6-29-54) Frances Starr, Leslie Nielsen, Patricia Breslin

JUSTICE

In an era in which television carried home infractions of civil liberties how refreshing it was to find among the filmed banality a champion for the legally disenfranchised. Justice, a collection of video essays on litigatory restitution, whose source is the files of the National Legal Aid Association, gently skirts courtroom rhetoric while offering perspicacious images of abject citizens. How ironic that the series premiered but nine days after the now celebrated Edward R. Murrow catechumen on McCarthy despotism.

The Regulars: Atty. Jason Tyler: Gary Merrill; Atty. Richard Adam: Dane Clark; William Prince appeared regularly as a legal aid attorney with the third season.

The Episodes:

1. "Keith's Case" (4-15-54) Richard Kiley, Phyllis Kirk, Warren Stevens
2. "Run from Honor" (4-22-54) Sidney Blackmer, Eileen Heckart, Wallace Ford
3. "Positive Identification" (4-29-54) Ed Begley, Ben Gazzara, Louisa Horton, Don Hanmer
4. "The Quiet Life" (5-6-54) Ed Begley, J. Carrol Naish
5. "Hit and Run" (5-13-54) E. G. Marshall, Ed Begley, Betty Field
6. "An Eye for an Eye" (5-20-54) Richard Kiley, Skip Homeier, Harvey Lembeck
7. "In the Deep Night" (5-27-54) Rod Steiger, Johnny Stewart, Christine Aelsmann
8. "The Eight Alien Boys" (6-3-54) James Barton, Mildred Natwick
9. "The Greedy Man" (6-10-54) Joseph Sweeney, Nancy Guild
10. "The Desperate One" (6-17-54) Madge Evans, Lorne Greene
11. "The Spinster" (6-24-54) Signe Hasso, Paul McGrath, Peter Cookson
12. "Call Me Guilty" (7-1-54) Ernest Truex
13. "The Scandal That Rocked the Town" (7-8-54) John Kerr, June Walker
14. "Murder at Red Oaks" (7-15-54) Dick Foran
15. "Ride with Terror" (7-22-54) Nina Foch, Eddie Firestone
16. "A Matter of Life and Death" (7-29-54) Ed Begley, Sylvia Field
17. "The Blackmailer" (8-5-54) Eva Gabor, George Macready

18. "Circumstantial Evidence" (8-12-54) Pamela Rivers
19. "Man on the Hunt" (8-19-54) Lenka Peterson, Patrick O'Neal
20. "The Fugitive" (8-26-54) Lamont Johnson, Lilia Skala
21. "The Quiet Prisoner" (9-2-54) features Gary Merrill
22. "The Crisis" (9-9-54) June Lockhart, Robert Cummings

Second Season

23. "The Deadly Silence" (9-16-54) Dennis O'Keefe, Mildred Dunnock
24. "Belmont Prison Break" (9-23-54) Lee Bowman, Dick Foran
25. "The Frightened Clown" (9-30-54) Geraldine Fitzgerald, Paul Hartman
26. "The Timid Thief" (10-7-54) Patricia Collins, Ben Gazzara
27. "Terror on the Tracks" (10-14-54) Gaby Rodgers, Skip Homeier
28. "The Safe-Cracker" (10-21-54) Leora Dana
29. "The Firebug" (10-28-54) Harry Townes, Janet Ward
30. "Run for Your Life" (11-4-54) features Dane Clark
31. "Gamble with Life" (11-11-54) William Prince
32. "Express to Disaster" (11-18-54) June Lockhart, James Daly
33. "The Invader" (11-25-54) Betty Field, Carmen Mathews
34. "Witness to Murder" (12-2-54) Ben Gazzara, Jeff Harris
35. "Edge of Fear" (12-9-54) Peggy Ann Garner, William Redfield
36. "Death for Sale" (12-16-54) Royal Dano
37. "Escape from Freedom" (12-23-54) Ed Begley
38. "A Dog, a Boy and a Gun" [by Jerome Ross] (12-30-54) Paul Tripp, Kevin Coughlin
39. "Cry Wolf" (1-6-55) Martin Brooks
40. "Save Me Now" (1-13-55) Gaby Rodgers, Jack Warden
41. "Out to Kill" (1-20-55) features Gary Merrill
42. "Strange Terror" (1-27-55) features Gary Merrill
43. "Fatal Friendship" (2-3-55) features Gary Merrill
44. "Witness for Death" (2-10-55) Jackie Cooper
45. "House of Hatred" (2-17-55) Glenda Farrell, Frank McHugh
46. "Violence at Stover's Corner" (2-24-55) Jeffrey Lynn
47. "Jail Break" (3-3-55) Bruce Freed, Bruce Gordon
48. "Revenge Is Mine" (3-10-55) William Prince, Meg Mundy
49. "Guilty Secret" (3-17-55) Mark Richman, Patricia Breslin
50. "Thunder on Troy Street" [dramatizing juvenile gang warfare] (3-24-55) Jarmilla Novotna
51. "Fearful Hour" (3-31-55) features Gary Merrill
52. "The Wiretap Case" (4-7-55) Joe Maross, June Lockhart
53. "Shadow of Terror" (4-14-55) Peggy Ann Garner, William Redfield
54. "Shot in the Dark" (4-21-55) Vanessa Brown
55. "Fear by Day" [by Don Ettlinger] (4-28-55) Leora Dana
56. "The Blues Kill Me" [by Newton Meltzer] (5-5-55) Kim Hunter
57. "Hard to Get" (5-12-55) Gisele MacKenzie, Murray Hamilton
58. "Badge of Dishonor" (5-19-55) Arthur Franz
59. "The Intruder" (5-26-55) Eva Gabor
60. "The Frightened" (6-2-55) William Daniels, William Lundmark
61. "Uncommon Thief" (6-16-55) Charles Coburn
62. "Edge of Disaster" (6-23-55) features Gary Merrill

63. "Pattern of Guilt" [by Alfred Brenner] (6-30-55) Joan Potter

Third Season

64. "Positive Identification" [restaged from 4/29/54] (10-2-55) Ed Begley, Don Hanmer; introduces William Prince in his continuing role
65. "The Desperate Man" (10-9-55) Robert Simon, Ruth White
66. "Flight from Fear" (10-16-55) Biff McGuire, Cameron Prud'homme, Jack Warden, Peg Feury
67. "Booby Trap" (10-23-55) Walter Matthau
68. "Decision by Panic" (10-30-55) Jason Robards Jr., Georgiann Johnson, Philip Abbott
69. "The Lonely" (11-6-55) Lee Philips, Kathleen Maguire
70. "The Big Frame" (11-13-55) George Grizzard, James Gregory, Michael Strong
71. "Shadow of Guilt" (11-20-55) Don Murray
72. "The Girl Without a Name" (11-27-55) Lois Smith
73. "Track of Fear" (12-11-55) Theodore Bikel, Maureen Stapleton
74. "Fatal Payment" [by Vance Bourjaily] (12-18-55) Dick York, Alexander Scourby
75. "End of a Chase" [by David Paduia] (12-25-55) Kevin Coughlin, Pat Hingle, Lori March
76. "Eyewitness" [by Irving Gaynor Neiman] (1-1-56) Ernest Truex
77. "Moment of Panic" (1-8-56) Joe Mantell, Larry Gates
78. "Hooked" [by Bernard Wolfe] (1-15-56) Jack Klugman, Lois Wheeler
79. "Broken Lullaby" [by Roger Hirson] (1-22-56) Polly Rowles, Alan Hewitt, Paul Tripp
80. "The Trapped" (1-29-56) Biff McGuire, Edward Binns
81. "The Guilty" [by Art Wallace] (2-5-56) Mark Rydell, J. Pat O'Malley
82. "The Bolted Door" (2-12-56) Patricia Collinge
83. "The Glory Hunter" (2-19-56) Lee Philips
84. "Sentence of Death" (2-26-56) Edward Andrews
85. "Sign Right Here" (3-4-56) Howard St. John
86. "The Willing Victim" (3-11-56) George Grizzard
87. "The Frightened Witness" (3-18-56) Jack Klugman
88. "Pattern of Love" [by Bernard Wolfe] (3-25-56) Jason Robards Jr.

CENTER STAGE

The Episodes:

1. "Chivalry at Howling Creek" (6-1-54) Henry Hull, Jack Warden, Cathy O'Donnell
2. "Grandfather Takes Off" (6-15-54) Robert Barrat, Bert Freed, Charles Taylor
3. "The Human Touch" (6-29-54) Walter Matthau, Polly Rowles
4. "Golden Anniversary" (7-13-54) Janis Carter, Otto Kruger, Frances Starr

5. "Lucky Louie" (7-27-54) Elliott Reid, Henry Jones, Joseph Buloff, Charles Dingle, Margaret Hamilton, Gaby Rodgers
6. "The Desdemona Murder Case" (8-10-54) Martha Scott, Donald Woods, Rex Thompson
7. "The Worthy Opponent" (8-24-54) Charles Coburn, Thomas Gomez, Parker Fennelly
8. "The Day Before Atlanta" (9-7-54) Lee Marvin, Luther Adler, Joan Lorring, John McQuade, Paul Stevens
9. "The Heart of a Clown" (9-21-54) Frank McHugh, Vivian Blaine, Kevin Coughlin, Lili Darvas, Barbara Nichols, Thomas Coley

THE ELGIN HOUR

1. "Flood" (10-2-54) Dorothy Gish, Janet Blair, Robert Cummings, Charles Dingle, Dorothy Sands, Richard Jaeckel
2. "Family Crisis" (10-19-54) Fay Bainter, James Daly, Betty Field
3. "High Man" (11-2-54) Ralph Bellamy, Jeffrey Lynn, John Beal, Joanne Woodward, William Redfield, Neva Patterson
4. "Warm Clay" (11-16-54) Ruth Hussey, Louis Jourdan, Margaret Hamilton
5. "Hearts and Hollywood" (11-30-54) Gertrude Berg, Mikhail Rasumny
6. "Yesterday's Magic" (12-14-54) Dame Judith Anderson, E. G. Marshall, Francis Lederer, Roddy McDowall, Herbert Marshall
7. "Falling Star" [by George Lowther] (12-28-54) Polly Bergen, Jackie Cooper, E. G. Marshall, Luella Gear, Frank McHugh
8. "The Bridge" [by Joseph Schull; directed by Don Petrie and produced by Herbert Brodkin] (1-11-55) Tonja Selwart, John Ireland, Kim Stanley, Anthony Dawson, Walter Armstrong, Jarmita Norotna, Miko Oscard, J. Pat O'Malley
9. "Family Meeting" (1-25-55) Polly Rowles, Alan Bunce, Janice Carter
10. "Days of Grace" (2-8-55) Franchot Tone, George Macready, Peggy Conklin
11. "The Sting of Death" [adapted from the novel by H. F. Heard] (2-22-55) Boris Karloff, Hermione Gingold, Martyn Green
12. "Crime in the Streets" [by Reginald Rose; directed by Sidney Lumet; settings by Fred Stover; filmed by Allied Artists, 1956] (3-8-55) John Cassavetes, Glenda Farrell, Robert Preston, Van Dyke Parks, Ivan Cury
13. "The Thousand Dollar Window" [adapted from the Mark Hellinger screenplay] (3-22-55) Sir Cedric Hardwicke, Mary Astor, Kenny Delmar, Larry Blyden
14. "Black Eagle Pass" (4-5-55) Richard Kiley, Paul Douglas, Edward Binns, Valerie Bettis, Joan Lorring, Charles Dingle
15. "Midsummer Melody" (4-19-55) June Lockhart, Ernest Truex, Kathy Nolan, Jerome Courtland
16. "Driftwood" [by Michael Dyne] (5-3-55) John Forsythe, Teresa Wright, Lorne Greene
17. "San Francisco Fracas" [by Alvin Sapinsley] (5-17-55) Orson Bean, Theodore Bikel, Polly Bergen

18. "Mind Over Momma" [by Gertrude Berg and James Yaffe] Eulabelle Moore (5-31-55) Gertrude Berg, E. G. Marshall, Frieda Altman, Norma Crane, Gene Saks
19. "Combat Medic" [by David Davidson; a tribute to the medical corps in the Korean conflict] (6-14-55) John Cassavetes, Brian Keith, John Kerr, Jack Lord, Richard Loo, Joe Maross, Mickey Shaughnessy

MEDIC

James Moser's splendid, meticulously researched medical drama, with the blessings of the American Medical Association and filmed in actual hospitals, examined cholera ("Death Rides a Wagon"), manic depression ("Break Through the Bars"), hemophilia ("A Time to be Alive"), dipsomania ("Vagrant Heart, Vagrant Cup"), and even post-partum psychosis (in the two-part "And There Was Darkness and There Was Light"). A wonderful, very literary and stylized forerunner to Moser's 1961 masterpiece Ben Casey.

The Regulars: Richard Boone as Dr. Konrad Styner, host and star.

1. "White Is the Color" (9-13-54) Beverly Garland, Richard Boone
2. "Laughter Is a Boy" (9-20-54) Peter Votrian, Bobby Driscoll, Claude Akins
3. "I Climb the Stairs" (9-27-54) Sallie Brophy
4. "Death Rides a Wagon" (10-4-54) Denver Pyle, Jaclynne Greene
5. "Vagrant Heart, Vagrant Cup" (10-11-54) Doris Dowling, Arthur Millan
6. "My Brother Joe" (10-25-54)
7. "Day 10" [episode examines the outbreak of pneumonic plague in Los Angeles in 1924] (11-1-54)
8. "After the Darkness" (11-8-54) Sean McClory
9. "With This Ring" (11-22-54) Natalie Norwick
10. "My Very Good Friend Albert" (11-29-54)
11. "The Wild Intruder" (12-6-54) Vera Miles
12. "Red Christmas" (12-20-54) June Leabow
13. "When Comes the Autumn" (12-27-54)
14. "Boy in the Storm" (1-3-55) Dennis Hopper, Evelyn Eaton
15. "White Is the Color" [repeat of episode of 9/13/54] (1-17-55)
16. "Breath of Life" (1-24-55)
17. "A Time to Be Alive" (1-31-55) Barry Curtis, Emaline Davis, David McMahon
18. "Flash of Darkness" [episode examines destruction of a major city by an H-Bomb attack; Val Peterson, Civil Defense Administrator, speaker] (2-14-55)
19. "Mercy Wears an Apron" (2-21-55) Ann Morrison, Onslow Stevens
20. "Dr. Impossible" (2-28-55) Arthur Space

21. "Break Through the Bars" (3-14-55) Lee J. Cobb
22. "Death Is a Red Balloon" (3-21-55) Susan Hart
23. "All My Mothers, All My Fathers" (3-28-55) Joann Banks, Madame Sul-Te-Wan
24. "Physician Heal Thyself" (4-11-55) Robert Bray
25. "Breath of Life" [repeat of episode of 1/24/55] (4-18-55)
26. "My Child's Keeper" (4-25-55) Linda Sterling
27. "My Child's Keeper" [repeat of episode of 4/25/55] (5-9-55)
28. "Lifeline" (5-16-55) Robert F. Simon
29. "Never Come Sunday" (5-23-55) Denver Pyle, Peggy Weber, Carol Sydes
30. "After the Darkness" [repeat of episode of 11/8/54] (6-6-55)
31. "General Practitioner" (6-13-55) Robert Strauss, Michael Ann Barrett
32. "A Time to Be Alive" [repeat of episode of 1/31/55] (6-20-55)
33. "I Climb the Stairs" [repeat of episode of 9/27/54] (7-4-55)
34. "Laughter Is a Boy" [repeat of episode of 9/20/54] (7-11-55)
35. "Break Through the Bars" [repeat of episode of 3/14/55] (7-18-55)
36. "Boy in the Storm" [repeat of episode of 1/3/55] (8-1-55)
37. "The Wild Intruder" [repeat of episode of 12/6/54] (8-8-55)
38. "Dr. Impossible" [repeat of episode of 2/28/55] (8-15-55)
39. "Flash of Darkness" [repeat of episode of 2/14/55] (8-29-55)

Second Season

40. "All The Lonely Night" (9-5-55) Karen Steele
41. "Walk with Lions" (9-12-55) John Saxon, Jacqueline May, Neadon Booth
42. "And There Was Darkness and There Was Light" [Part I] (9-26-55)
43. "And There Was Darkness and There Was Light" [Part II] (10-3-55)
44. "A Room, a Boy, and Mr. Bodine" (10-10-55) Butch Bernard, Barry Atwater
45. "When I Was Young" (10-24-55) Mae Clarke, Raymond Bailey
46. "When Mama Says Jump" (10-31-55)
47. "Candle of Hope" (11-7-55) Audrey Dineen, Peter Mamakos
48. "Black Friday" (11-21-55) Robert Vaughn, Austin Greene
49. "Glass of Fear" (11-28-55) Richard Erdman, Marilyn Nash
50. "Pray Judgment" (12-5-55) Paul Birch, Mary Ellen Kay, Elizabeth Whitney, Charles Davis
51. "Red Christmas" [repeat of episode of 12/20/54] (12-19-55)
52. "The World So High" [a tribute to army doctor William Lovelace; the story of aviation medicine] (12-26-55) Hugh Beaumont
53. "A Time for Sleep" [Dr. Eden Smith, guest] (1-2-56)
54. "The Laughter and the Weeping" (1-16-56) Michael Ansara
55. "Just Like Your Father" (1-23-56) Lewis Martin, Harvey Dunn
56. "If Tomorrow Be Sad" [by James E. Moser] (2-6-56) Cynthia Stone, Herbert Patterson
57. "The Homecoming" (2-13-56) Richard Karlan, Naomi Stevens

58. "Never Come Sunday" [repeat of episode of 5/23/55] (2-20-56)
59. "Who Search for Truth" (2-27-56) Charles Bronson
60. "The Glorious Red Gallagher" (3-12-56) Hope Emerson
61. "My Best Friend, My Guilty Friend" (3-19-56)
62. "Awake unto Spring" (3-26-56)
63. "Don't Count the Stars" (4-9-56) Richard Crenna, Henry Hunter
64. "The Glorious Red Gallagher" [repeat of episode of 3/12/56] (4-16-56)
65. "The Inconstant Heart" (4-23-56) Robin Short
66. "Someday We'll Laugh" (5-7-56) Eddie Firestone, Whitney Blake
67. "To the Great--A Most Seldom Gift" (5-14-56) Harry Townes
68. "The Good Samaritan" (5-21-56)
69. "The World So High" [repeat of episode of 12/26/56] (6-4-56)
70. "Reach for a Giant" [Part I] (6-11-56) James Martin, Diana Douglas
71. "Reach for a Giant" [Part II] (6-18-56) as above.
72. "Black Friday" [repeat of episode of 11/21/55] (7-2-56)
73. "Till the Song Is Done ... Till the Dance Is Gone" (7-9-56) Carolyn Craig
74. "Candle of Hope" [repeat of episode of 11/7/55] (7-16-56)
75. "If Tomorrow Be Sad" [repeat of episode of 2/6/56] (7-30-56)
76. "She Walks in Beauty" (8-6-56)
77. "When I Was Young" [repeat of episode of 10/24/55] (8-13-56)
78. "This Strange End" (8-27-56)
79. "Vagrant Heart, Vagrant Cup" [repeat of episode of 10/11/54] (9-3-56)
80. "The Glorious Red Gallagher" [repeat of episodes 3/12/56 and 4/16/56] (9-10-56)
81. "My Best Friend, My Guilty Friend" [repeat of episode of 3/19/56] (9-24-56)
82. "Reach for a Giant" [repeat of episode of 6/11/56] (10-1-56)
83. "Reach for a Giant" [Part II] [repeat of episode of 6/18/56] (10-8-56)
84. "The Homecoming" [repeat of episode of 2/13/56] (10-22-56)
85. "My Brother Joe" [repeat of episode of 10/25/54] (10-29-56)
86. "To the Great--A Most Seldom Gift" [repeat of episode of 5/14/56] (11-19-56)

PRODUCER'S SHOWCASE

The Episodes:

1. "Tonight at 8:30" [adapted by F. Hugh Herbert from the three Noel Coward plays; produced by Otto Preminger] [10-18-54 Monday 8-9:30 NBC] a) "The Red Peppers" Ginger Rogers, Martyn Green; b) "Still Life" Ginger Rogers, Ilka Chase, Trevor Howard; c) "Shadow Play" Ginger Rogers, Gig Young, Estelle Winwood; introduced by Gloria Vanderbilt
2. "State of the Union" [adapted by Howard Lindsay and Russell Crouse from their own play; directed by Arthur Penn and

produced by Fred Coe] [11-15-54 Monday 8-9:30 NBC]
Joseph Cotten, Margaret Sullavan, Nina Foch, John Cromwell

3. "Dateline" [a tribute to the American reporter by the Overseas
Press Club; with contributions by Robert E. Sherwood (dra-
matic vignette on Ernie Pyle), Carl Sandburg (reading dedi-
cation to newsmen); Richard Rodgers conducts the orchestra;
produced by Fred Coe] [12-13-54 Monday 8-9:30 NBC]
Marian Anderson, Bob Hope, Eddie Fisher, Perry Como,
Carl Reiner, Martha Raye, Elsa Maxwell, Bob Considine,
Hal Boyle, Sid Caesar, Milton Caniff, John Daly, Lawrence
Spivak, Henry Ford II; President Eisenhower also appeared.

4. "Yellow Jack" [adapted from the play by Sidney Howard and
Paul De Kruif concerning the pursuit of the cause for yellow
fever by Dr. Walter Reed and his Army medical colleagues;
directed by Delbert Mann and produced by Fred Coe] [1-10-
55 Monday 8-9:30 NBC] Jackie Cooper, Dane Clark, E. G.
Marshall, Raymond Massey, Wally Cox, Eva Marie Saint,
Broderick Crawford, Rod Steiger, Dennis O'Keefe, Lorne
Greene, Carlos Montalban

5. "The Women" [adapted from the play by Clare Booth Luce; settings by Paul Barnes] [2-7-55 Monday 8-9:30 NBC] Mary
Astor, Mary Boland, Paulette Goddard, Valerie Bettis,
Cathleen Nesbitt, Ruth Hussey, Nancy Olson, Shelley Winters, Pat Carroll, Nita Talbot

6. "Peter Pan" [musical version of the 1928 Sir James M. Barrie
children's classic, with music by Mark Charlap, additional
music by Jule Styne; lyrics by Carolyn Leigh; additional
lyrics by Betty Comden and Adolph Green; production staged
by Clark Jones and choreographed by Jerome Robbins; produced by Fred Coe] [3-7-55 Monday 7:30-9:30 NBC] Mary
Martin, Cyril Ritchard, Heller Halliday, Kathy Nolan, Joseph Stafford, Robert Harrington, Margalo Gillmore

7. "Reunion in Vienna" [adapted by David Shaw from the Robert
Emmett Sherwood romantic comedy; produced by Fred Coe]
[4-4-55 Monday 8-9:30 NBC] Greer Garson, Robert Flemyng, Brian Aherne, Peter Lorre, Lilli Darvas, Frederick
Worlock, Cathleen Nesbitt, Herbert Berghoff, George Voskovec

8. "Darkness at Noon" [adapted by Robert Alan Aurthur from the
stage play by Sidney Kingsley, from the Arthur Koestler
novel; directed by Delbert Mann; scenic design by Otis
Riggs; with a closing commentary by Vice President Richard
M. Nixon] [5-2-55 Monday 8-9:30 NBC] Lee J. Cobb, Jos-
eph Wiseman, Oscar Homolka, David Wayne, Keenan Wynn,
Nehemiah Persoff, Mikhail Rasumny, Ruth Roman, Henry
Silva

9. "The Petrified Forest" [adapted by Tad Mosel from the play
by Robert Emmett Sherwood; directed by Delbert Mann]
[5-30-55 Monday 8-9:30 NBC] Humphrey Bogart, Lauren
Bacall, Henry Fonda, Richard Jaeckel, Paul Hartman, Jack
Warden

10. "Wide, Wide World" [the premiere program, with Dave Garro-

way as host; features Shakespearean festival from Ontario, Canada; jazz program from Washington, D. C. ; skiing at Mt. Hood and an "Arabian Nights" at Jones Beach; produced with the co-operation of the Canadian and Mexican television stations] [6-27-55 Monday 8-9:30 NBC]

11. "The Fourposter" [adapted by Clark Jones and Hume Cronyn from the 1952 play by Jan de Hartog] [7-25-55 Monday 8-9:30 NBC] Hume Cronyn, Jessica Tandy (repeating their Broadway roles)

12. "The King and Mrs. Candle" [original musical comedy by Sumner Locke Elliott, with songs by Moose Charlap and Charles Sweeney and choreography by Tony Charmoli; directed by Arthur Penn and produced by Fred Coe] [8-22-55 Monday 8-9:30 NBC] Cyril Ritchard, Theodore Bikel, Irene Manning, Joan Greenwood, Richard Haydn, Donald Marge

Second Season

13. "Our Town" [musical version of the Thornton Wilder classic, adapted by David Shaw, with music and lyrics by Sammy Kahn and James Van Heusen; directed by Delbert Mann and produced by Fred Coe] [9-19-55 Monday 8-9:30 NBC] Frank Sinatra, Paul Newman, Eva Marie Saint, Ernest Truex, Sylvia Field, Paul Hartman, Peg Hillias

14. "Cyrano de Bergerac" [adapted by Joseph Schrank from the Brian Hooker adaptation of the Edmond Rostand classic; directed by Kirk Browning; production supervised by Donald Davis and Dorothy Mathews] [10-17-55 Monday 8-9:30 NBC] Jose Ferrer, Claire Bloom, Christopher Plummer, Jacques Aubuchon, John McQuade

15. "Dateline 2" [a salute to freedom of the press by the Overseas Press Club, with contributions by Robert E. Sherwood, Irving Berlin, Robert Frost, John Steinbeck and Donald Bevan; commentary by Vice President Richard M. Nixon] [11-14-55 Monday 8-9:30 NBC] Milton Berle, Greer Garson, William Holden, John Wayne, Martha Raye, Janet Blair, John Raitt, Darren McGavin, Peggy Lee, Jan Peerce, Buzz Martin, Patricia Benoit, Antonio and his Spanish Ballet

16. "The Sleeping Beauty" [performed by the Sadler's Wells Ballet Company under the management of Sol Hurok, directed by Clark Jones; music conducted and directed by Robert Irving; the Corps de Ballet under the direction of Ninette de Valois and Frederick Ashton (associate director); with an introductory play by John Van Druten and narrated by David Wayne; costumes by Oliver Messel] [12-12-55 Monday 8-9:30 NBC] Margot Fonteyn, Michael Somes, Rosemary Lindsay, Beryl Grey, Brian Shaw, Rowena Jackson, Pauline Clayden, Philip Chatfield, Frederick Ashton

17. "Peter Pan" [restaged by Jerome Robbins; see episode of 3/7/55] [1-9-56 Monday 7:30-9:30 NBC] Mary Martin, Cyril Ritchard, Kathy Nolan, Heller Halliday, Robert Harrington, Richard Martin, Margola Gillmore

18. "Festival of Music" [music panorama hosted by Charles Laughton [1-30-56 Monday 8-9:30 NBC]

19. "Caesar and Cleopatra" [adapted from the George Bernard Shaw play] [3-5-56 Monday 8-9:30 NBC] Claire Bloom, Judith Anderson, Farley Granger, Jack Hawkins, Cyril Ritchard, Sir Cedric Hardwicke, Anthony Quayle, Patrick MacNee, Thomas Gomez

20. "The Barretts of Wimpole Street" [adapted from the Rudolph Besier 1930 play] [4-2-56 Monday 8-9:30 NBC] Katherine Cornell, Anthony Quayle, Henry Daniell, Nancy Coleman, Margalo Gillmore

21. "Dodsworth" [adapted by David Shaw from the Sidney Howard play derived from the Sinclair Lewis novel; directed by Alex Segal] [4-30-56 Monday 8-9:30 NBC] Fredric March, Claire Trevor, Geraldine Fitzgerald, Regis Toomey

22. "Bloomer Girl" [adapted from the 1944 Broadway musical by Sig Herzig and Fred Saidy which was derived from the play by Dan and Lilith James; music by Harold Arlen and lyrics by E. Y. Harburg] [5-28-56 Monday 8-9:30 NBC] Barbara Cook, Keith Andes, Carmen Mathews, Paul Ford, Nydia Westman, Rawn Spearman

23. "Happy Birthday" [adapted from the 1946 Anita Loos Broadway comedy; directed by Alex Segal] [6-25-56 Monday 8-9:30 NBC] Betty Field, Barry Nelson, Enid Markey, Harry Bellaver, Parker McCormick, Harold Vermilyea, Luella Gear, Tina Louise, Wynn Gibson

24. "Rosalinda" [adapted from the 1942 Broadway musical by John Meehan Jr. and Gottfried Reinhardt; a Max Reinhardt version of Johann Strauss' Die Fledermaus with lyrics by Paul Kerby; production presented by the Light Opera Association of Los Angeles and San Francisco] [7-23-56 Monday 8-9·30 NBC] Cyril Ritchard, Lois Hunt, Robert Wright, Thomas Hayward, Jean Fenn, Sig Arno, Ralph Dumke, The Wiere Brothers; production directed by Bob Banner.

Third Season

25. "The Lord Don't Play Favorites" [original musical by Jo Swerling and Hal Stanley based upon the short story by Patrick Malloy] [9-17-56 Monday 8-9:30 NBC] Buster Keaton, Louis Armstrong, Kay Starr, Dick Haymes, Robert Stack

26. "The Letter" [adapted from the William Somerset Maugham short story and play of 1927; directed by Kirk Browning and produced by William Wyler] [10-15-56 Monday 8-9:30 NBC] Siobhan McKenna, Michael Rennie, John Mills, Anna May Wong, Aki Aleong

27. "Jack and the Beanstalk" [original musical with book and lyrics by Helen Deutsch and music by Jerry Livingston] [11-12-56 Monday 8-9:30 NBC] Cyril Ritchard, Joel Grey, Celeste Holm, Peggy King, Arnold Stang, Leora Dana, Billy Gilbert; narrated by Dennis King

28. "Festival of Music" [produced by Sol Hurok; narrated by Jose Ferrer] [12-10-56 Monday 8-9:30 NBC] Arthur Rubinstein, Andres Segovia, Boris Christoff, Marian Anderson; orchestra conducted by Alfred Wallenstein

29. "Call to Freedom" [an historical drama with music, produced and scripted by Henry Salomon and scored by Robert Russell Bennett from the Beethoven opera Fidelio; narrated by Alexander Scourby] [1-7-57 Monday 8-9:30 NBC] Members of the cast of Fidelio: Martha Modl, Anton Dermota, Paul Schoffler, Irmgard Seefried, Ludwig Weber, Waldemar Kmentt, Karl Kamann

30. "Mayerling" [adapted from the 1927 book Idyl's End by Claude Anet; produced and directed by Anatole Litvak] [2-4-57 Monday 8-9:30 NBC] Mel Ferrer, Audrey Hepburn, Raymond Massey, Basil Sidney, Diana Wynyard, Judith Evelyn, Nehemiah Persoff, Isobel Elsom, Lorne Greene, Sorrell Booke, David Opatoshu, Peter Donat, Nancy Marchard, Ian Wolfe, Suzy Parker, Monique Van Vooren

31. "Romeo and Juliet" [an Old Vic version of the Shakespeare classic under the management of Sol Hurok] [3-4-57 Monday 8-9:30 NBC] Claire Bloom, John Neville, Paul Rogers

32. "The Great Sebastians" [adapted from the Howard Lindsay and Russell Crouse play] [4-1-57 Monday 8-9:30 NBC] Alfred Lunt, Lynn Fontanne, Akim Tamiroff, Lisa Ferraday, Simon Oakland, Anne Francis, Arny Freeman, Stefan Schnabel

33. "Cinderella" [Frederick Ashton's ballet performed by the Royal Ballet Company with the music of Sergei Prokofiev] [4-29-57 Monday 8:30-9:30 NBC] Margot Fonteyn, Michael Somes

34. "Festival of Magic" [featuring Milbourne Christopher and his model Eva Lynd; several others; Ernie Kovacs hosted] [5-27-57 Monday 8-9:30 NBC]

STUDIO 57

The Episodes:

1. "Ring Once for Death" (9-21-54) John Howard, Keye Luke
2. "No Great Hero" (9-28-54) Craig Stevens
3. "Trap Mates" (10-5-54) Hugh Beaumont, Nancy Gates, Michael Hall, Tol Avery
4. "The Traveling Room" (10-12-54) Marguerite Chapman
5. "The Plot Against Mrs. Pomeroy" (10-19-54) Natalie Wood
6. "So False and So Fair" (10-26-54) Karen Steele, Paul Picerni, John Lupton
7. "Never Five-Thirty" (11-2-54) Lawrence Dobkin, Joanne Davis
8. "Step Lightly, Please" (11-9-54) Virginia Gibson, John Lupton
9. "The Duel" (11-16-54) Don Haggerty, Alan Wells, Claudia Barrett
10. "Cubs of the Bear" (11-23-54) James Craig
11. "Matter of Calculation" (11-30-54) Peter Van Eyck
12. "The Witness--A Case of Blackmail" (12-7-54)
13. "The Circle" (12-14-54) Remington Olmsted
14. "Christmas Every Day" (12-21-54) Craig Stevens, Jean Byron, Madge Kennedy
15. "Sauce for the Gander" (12-28-54) Marguerite Chapman, Peter Graves

16. "Human Bomb" (1-4-55) Jean-Pierre Aumont
17. "The Big Jump" (1-11-55) Nancy Gates, John Bryant
18. "The Will to Survive" (1-18-55) Marguerite Chapman, Robert Horton, Joanne Davis, Donald Curtis
19. "Miss Jeremy and the Brain Serjen" (1-25-55) Barbara Eiler
20. "The Westerner" (2-1-55) James Craig
21. "Hazel Craine" (2-8-55) Eleanor Tanin, Walter Reed
22. "The Engagement Ring" (2-15-55) K. T. Stevens, Hugh O'Brian
23. "The Haver Technique" (2-22-55) Brian Keith, Irene Hervey
24. "Bitter Rival" (3-1-55) Margaret Field, Lawrence Dobkin
25. "Center Ring" [otherwise known as "Earthbound"] (3-8-55) Jane Darwell
26. "Take My Hand" (3-15-55) Jay Novello, Olive Sturgess
27. "Sam" (3-22-55) Charles Coburn, Phyllis Love, John Harmon
28. "Call from Robert Jest" (3-29-55) Robert Horton, Carolyn Jones
29. "Rescue" (4-5-55) Brian Keith
30. "Fish Widow" (4-12-55) Pat Carroll
31. "Rainy Night" (4-19-55) Nancy Gates, Robert Cornthwaite, Tom Avera
32. "The Black Sheep's Daughter" (4-26-55) Carolyn Jones
33. "Deadly Doubt" (5-3-55) John Bryant
34. "The Last Day on Earth" (5-10-55) Walter Coy, Rod Taylor
35. "One Kiss Too Many" (5-17-55)
36. "Secret Message" (5-24-55) Bobby Clark
37. "Anytime You Need Me" (5-31-55) Irene Hervey
38. "The Battle of Dabbit Run" (6-14-55)

THE BEST OF BROADWAY

The Episodes:

1. "The Royal Family" [adapted from the play by George S. Kaufman and Edna Ferber] (9-15-54 Wednesday 10-11:00 CBS) Fredric March, Helen Hayes, Claudette Colbert, Charles Coburn, Nancy Olson, Kent Smith
2. "The Man Who Came to Dinner" [adapted from the play by George S. Kaufman and Moss Hart] (10-13-54 Wednesday 10-11:00 CBS) Reginald Gardiner, Merle Oberon, Joan Bennett, Monty Woolley, Buster Keaton, ZaSu Pitts, Margaret Hamilton, Bert Lahr
3. "Panama Hattie" [adapted from the musical play by Herbert Fields and B. G. DeSylva; music and lyrics by Cole Porter] (11-10-54 Wednesday 10-11:00 CBS) Ethel Merman, Neil Hamilton, Art Carney, Jack E. Leonard, Ray Middleton
4. "The Philadelphia Story" [adapted from the play by Philip Barry] (12-8-54 Wednesday 10-11:00 CBS) Mary Astor, Dorothy McGuire, John Payne, Dick Foran, Herbert Marshall, Neva Patterson, Richard Carlson, Charles Winninger
5. "Arsenic and Old Lace" [adapted from the play by George Kesselring] (1-5-55 Wednesday 10-11:00 CBS) Boris Karloff,

Helen Hayes, Billie Burke, Orson Bean, Peter Lorre, Edward Everett Horton, Patricia Breslin, John Alexander [Messrs. Karloff and Alexander repeated their stage roles]

6. "The Show-Off" [adapted from the play by George Kelly] (2-2-55 Wednesday 10-11:00 CBS) Jackie Gleason, Thelma Ritter, Cathy O'Donnell

7. "The Guardsman" [adapted from the play by Ferenc Molnar] (3-2-55 Wednesday 10-11:00 CBS) Franchot Tone, Claudette Colbert, Mary Boland, Reginald Gardiner, Margaret Hamilton

8. "Stage Door" [adapted by Gore Vidal from the play by George S. Kaufman and Edna Ferber; directed by Sidney Lumet and produced by Felix Jackson] (4-6-55 Wednesday 10-11:00 CBS) Diana Lynn, Dennis Morgan, Charles Drake, Rhonda Fleming, Elsa Lanchester, Victor Moore, Peggy Ann Garner, Nita Talbot

9. "Broadway" [adapted from the play by George Abbott and Philip Dunning] (5-4-55 Wednesday 10-11:00 CBS) Joseph Cotten, Gene Nelson, Keenan Wynn, Piper Laurie, Martha Hyer, Akim Tamiroff

DISNEYLAND

The Episodes:

1. "A Pictorial Salute to Mickey Mouse" [animated features: "Plane Crazy" (1928), Mickey Mouse's first film; "The Lonesome Ghosts," with Mickey, Donald Duck and Goofy; excerpts of "The Sorcerer's Apprentice" from Fantasia (1940); a story of Br'er Rabbit and his laughing place; scenes at Disney studios with Kirk Douglas, Peter Lorre, James Mason] (10-27-54)

2. "Alice in Wonderland" (1951) [feature film with the voices of Kathryn Beaumont, Ed Wynn and Richard Haydn] (11-3-54)

3. Adventureland: excerpts from Seal Island (1949) and The Vanishing Prairie (1954); story of their filming (11-10-54)

4. "The Story of Donald Duck" (11-17-54)

5. So Dear to My Heart (1949) [feature film, with Bobby Driscoll, Luana Patton, Beulah Bondi, Burl Ives] (11-24-54)

6. Fantasyland: "A Story of Dogs" [featuring "Pluto"; excerpts from animated feature The Lady and the Tramp (1955 release), with songs by Peggy Lee and Sonny Burke] (12-1-54)

7. "Operation Undersea" [story of the filming of 20,000 Leagues Under the Sea (1954)] (12-8-54)

8. Frontierland: "The Saga of Davy Crockett, Indian Fighter" (12-15-54) Fess Parker, Buddy Ebsen

9. "1954 Christmas Show" [featuring the animated characters "Pablo the Penguin" and "Jose Carioca"; guests Aurora Miranda of Brazil, Carmen Molina and Dora Luz of Mexico] (12-22-54)

10. Adventureland [features "Beaver Valley" and "2,000 Mile Safari in Africa" with photographers Alfred and Elma Milotte] (12-29-54)

11. Treasure Island [Part I; 1950 feature film] (1-5-55) Bobby
     Driscoll, Robert Newton, Walter Fitzgerald, Basil Sydney
12. Treasure Island [Part II] (1-12-55)
13. "Monsters from the Deep" [underwater photography, with guests
     Kirk Douglas and Peter Lorre; excerpts from Pinocchio
     (1940)] (1-19-55)
14. "Davy Crockett Goes to Congress" (1-26-55) Fess Parker,
     Buddy Ebsen
15. animated features The Wind in the Willows (1948) and The Re-
     luctant Dragon (1941); Kenneth Grahame, guest. (2-2-55)
16. "A Progress Report" [a guided tour of the sixteen-acre "Disney-
     land" under construction] "Nature's Half Acre" [feature]
     (2-9-55)
17. "Cavalcade of Songs" [on the composition of music for Disney
     films; excerpts from The Three Little Pigs (1932), Snow
     White and the Seven Dwarfs (1937), Song of the South (1946),
     The Lady and the Tramp (1955); composers Peggy Lee and
     Sonny Burke are featured] (2-16-55)
18. "Davy Crockett at the Alamo" (2-23-55) Fess Parker, Buddy
     Ebsen
19. "From Aesop to Hans Christian Andersen" [Academy award
     features "The Tortoise and the Hare" (1934), "The Ugly
     Duckling" (1939), and "The Lion and the Mouse," "The Frog
     and the Ox"] (3-1-55)
20. Tomorrowland: "Man in Space" [feature; guests Dr. Wernher
     von Braun, Dr. Heinz Haber and Willy Ley] (3-8-55)

Second Season

21. Fantasyland: Dumbo [1941 animated feature film, narrated by
     California columnist Paul Coates; characters include "Timothy
     Mouse," "Casey Jr.," the "Five Black Crows," the "Dowager
     Elephants," "The Ringmaster" and the "Clowns"; subsequent-
     ly telecast 12/25/57] (9-14-55)
22. Adventureland: "Behind the True Life Cameras: Olympic Elk,
     A Wildlife Tour" [on filming of The African Lion; subse-
     quently telecast 6/20/56] (9-21-55)
23. "Jiminy Crickett Presents Bongo" [a "hepcat" adaptation of the
     "Chicken Little" animated films] (9-28-55)
24. "People and Places" [a travelogue; Sardinia, Morocco, the Seri
     Indians on Tiburon Island off the Gulf of California, and an
     icebreaker bound for the polar cap are visited] (10-5-55)
25. "The Adventures of Mickey Mouse: 'The Story of Jack and the
     Beanstalk'" [with Pluto, Donald Duck and Goofy; narrated by
     Sterling Holloway] (10-12-55)
26. Fantasyland: "The Story of the Silly Symphony" [the animated
     films "The Three Orphan Kittens," "The Old Mill" and "Fer-
     dinand the Bull"; excerpts from "Plow Boy," "Flowers and
     Trees," the feature Sleeping Beauty] (10-19-55)
27. The Legend of Sleepy Hollow [1948 animated feature; narrated
     by Bing Crosby; subsequently telecast 10/30/57] (10-26-55)
28. The Story of Robin Hood [1952 feature film, Part I; subsequent-
     ly telecast 5/16/65 and 5/23/65] (11-2-55) Richard Todd,

Joan Rice, James Hayter, Martita Hunt, Peter Finch, James Robertson Justice, Bill Owen, Hubert Gregg, Michael Hordern, Elton Hayes, Patrick Barr, Reginald Tate, Hal Osmond, Clement McCallin, Louise Hampton, Anthony Eustrel, Anthony Forwood

29. The Story of Robin Hood [Part II] (11-9-55) as above.
30. Davy Crockett and the Keelboat Race (11-16-55) Fess Parker, Buddy Ebsen, Jeff York, George Lewis, Walter Catlett, Paul Newlan
31. Adventureland: "Behind the True Life Cameras, Olympic Elk" [repeat of episode of 9/21/55] (11-23-55)
32. Fantasyland: "The Story of the Animated Drawing" [excerpts from animated films] (11-30-55)
33. "The Goofy Success Story" [excerpts from four animated films] (12-7-55)
34. "Davy Crockett and the River Pirates" (12-14-55) Fess Parker, Buddy Ebsen, Jeff York, George Lewis, Walter Catlett, Paul Newlan, Frank Richards, Mort Mills, Kenneth Tobey, Clem Bevans, Irvin Ashkenazy, Troy Melton, Dick Crockett, Hank Worden
35. Fantasyland: Dumbo [1941 animated feature; repeat of episode of 9/14/55] (12-21-55)
36. "Man and the Moon" [an animated feature on the first successful rocket flight around our satellite, with a discussion by Dr. Wernher von Braun] (12-28-55)

Episodes continue with Television Drama Series Programming: A Comprehensive Chronicle, 1959-1975.

CLIMAX! [alternating with SHOWER OF STARS]

The Regulars: William Lundigan and Mary Costa, hosts.

The Episodes:

1. Shower of Stars (9-30-54) Betty Grable, Harry James, Mario Lanza
2. Climax!: "The Long Goodbye" [by Raymond Chandler] (10-7-54) Dick Powell, Cesar Romero, Teresa Wright, Tom Drake, Horace MacMahon
3. Climax!: "The Thirteenth Chair" [adapted from the play by Bayard Veiller] (10-14-54) Ethel Barrymore, Dennis O'Keefe, Joan Evans, Paul Harvey, Arthur Franz
4. Climax!: "Casino Royale" [by Ian Fleming] (10-21-54) Peter Lorre, Barry Nelson
5. Shower of Stars: "Lend an Ear" [adapted from the Broadway musical review by Charles Gaynor] (10-28-54) Mario Lanza, Gene Nelson, Edgar Bergen, Sheree North
6. Climax!: "Sorry, Wrong Number" [adapted from the Lucille Fletcher radio play and film] (11-4-54) Shelley Winters, Paul Guilfoyle, Lillian Bronson, Nestor Paiva

7. Climax!: "The Gioconda Smile" [adapted from the Aldous Huxley story] (11-11-54) Franchot Tone, Dorothy McGuire, Eduard Franz

8. Shower of Stars: "Entertainment on Wheels" (11-18-54) Betty Grable, Harry James, Ed Wynn, William Bishop, James Dunn, Michael O'Shea, Gil Stratton, Jr., Danny Thomas

9. Climax!: "The After House" [adapted from the Mary Roberts Rinehart story] (11-25-54) Steve Cochran, Patricia Medina

10. Climax!: "An Error in Chemistry" [adapted from the William Faulkner story] (12-2-54) Edmond O'Brien, Irene Manning

11. Climax!: "Epitaph for a Spy" [adapted from the book by Eric Ambler] (12-9-54) Edward G. Robinson

12. Climax!: "The White Carnation" (12-16-54) Boris Karloff, Teresa Wright, Claudette Colbert

13. Shower of Stars: "A Christmas Carol" [musical version of the Charles Dickens classic, with libretto by Maxwell Anderson and music by Bernard Herrmann] (12-23-54) Fredric March, Basil Rathbone, Ray Middleton, Bob Sweeney

14. Climax!: "Adventure in Copenhagen" (12-30-54) Vera Miles, Frank Lovejoy

15. Climax!: "The Bigger They Come" (1-6-55) Art Carney, Jane Darwell

16. Climax!: "Escape from Fear" [adapted from the A. J. Cronin story] (1-13-55) Howard Duff, Mari Blanchard

17. Shower of Stars: "Show Stoppers" [Broadway sketches] (1-20-55) Ethel Merman, Red Skelton, Bobby Van, The Kean Sisters

18. Climax!: "The Mojave Kid" [adapted from the story by Oliver Drake] (1-27-55) Ward Bond, John Lupton, Barbara Rush, Ricardo Montalban

19. Climax!: "A Leaf out of the Book" (2-3-55) Diana Lynn, George Brent, Sylvia Sidney

20. Climax!: "The Valiant Men" [adapted from the novel by Nicholas Monsarrat] (2-10-55) Robert Young, Jay C. Flippen, Skip Homeier, Tom Brown

21. Shower of Stars: "That's Life" (2-17-55) Shirley MacLaine, Larry Storch, Harry James, Johnnie Ray, Anna Maria Alberghetti

22. Climax!: "The Box of Chocolates" [adapted from the mystery story by Anthony Berkely] (2-24-55) Vanessa Brown, Robert Preston, Pat O'Brien, Victor Jory

23. Climax!: "South of the Sun" (3-3-55) Jeffrey Hunter, Margaret O'Brien, Thomas Gomez, Edward Arnold

24. Climax!: "The Great Impersonation" [adapted from the book by E. Phillips Oppenheim] (3-10-55) Michael Rennie, Zsa Zsa Gabor, Maureen O'Sullivan

25. Shower of Stars: "Burlesque" [musical version of the play by George Manker Watters and Arthur Hopkins] (3-17-55) Jack Oakie, Joan Blondell, Dan Dailey, Jimmy Burke, James Gleason, Dick Foran, Marilyn Maxwell, Helene Stanley; walk-on by Jack Benny

26. Climax!: "The Darkest Hour" (3-24-55) Zachary Scott, Joanne Dru

27. Climax!: "Champion" [adapted by Rod Serling from the short story by Ring Lardner] (3-31-55) Rory Calhoun, Wallace Ford, Ray Collins, Geraldine Brooks
28. Climax!: "Private Worlds" [adapted from the novel by Phyllis Bottome] (4-7-55) Claudette Colbert, Marguerite Chapman, Marilyn Erskine, Lorne Greene
29. Shower of Stars: "Ethel Merman's Show Stoppers" (4-14-55) Ethel Merman, Red Skelton, Peter Lind Hayes, Mary Healey, Harold Lang, Cindy Robinson
30. Climax!: "Flight 951" [by Milton Geiger] (4-21-55) Paul Douglas, Barbara Britton, Irene Hervey, Cathy O'Donnell, Lili Darvas
31. Climax!: "The First and the Last" [adapted from the John Galsworthy short story] (4-28-55) Robert Newton, John Agar, Peggy Ann Garner, John Carradine
32. Climax!: "The Deliverance of Sister Cecilia" [adapted by De-witt Bodeen from the book by William Brinkley] (5-5-55) Claudette Colbert, Judith Evelyn
33. Shower of Stars: "High Pitch" [a musical comedy] (5-12-55) Tony Martin, Vivian Vance, Mel Allen, William Frawley, Marguerite Piazza
34. Climax!: "No Stone Unturned" [by Ian Hamilton] (5-19-55) Dan O'Herlihy, Sir Cedric Hardwicke, Tom Drake, Jeff Donnell
35. Climax!: "A Farewell to Arms" [adapted by Gore Vidal from the Ernest Hemingway classic] (5-26-55) Guy Madison, Diana Lynn
36. Climax!: "The Unimportant Man" (6-2-55) Macdonald Carey, Ruth Hussey
37. Shower of Stars: (6-9-55) Betty Grable, Harry James, Char-lie McCarthy with Edgar Bergen, Jack Oakie, Marilyn Max-well, Gene Nelson, Red Skelton, Dick Foran, Ethel Merman, Tony Martin, Dan Dailey
38. Climax!: "The Dark Fleece" [adapted by Dewitt Bodeen from the story by Joseph Hergesheimer] (6-16-55) Lloyd Bridges, Joan Bennett, Phyllis Thaxter
39. Climax!: "To Wake at Midnight" [by Rod Serling] (6-23-55) George Voskovec, Wendell Corey, Maria Riva, Akim Tamir-off
40. Climax!: "The Dance" [adapted by James Cavanagh from the F. Scott Fitzgerald story] (6-30-55) Vanessa Brown, Bar-bara Baxley, Janet Blair, Richard Kiley, Frieda Inescourt, Ethel Waters
41. Climax!: "Wild Stallion" [an adaptation of William Faulkner's Knight's Gambit] (7-7-55) Mary Astor, Paul Henreid, Richard Long, Evelyn Keyes
42. Climax!: "The Escape of Mendès-France" [adapted from the article by the former French Premier on the escape from a Vichy government prison on Bastille Day, World War II; Walter Cronkite narrates] (7-14-55) Louis Jourdan, Maur-ice Marsac, Eva Wolf
43. Climax!: "The Healer" [adapted by Dewitt Bodeen from the Frank G. Slaughter novel] (7-21-55) Geraldine Fitzgerald,

       Barry Sullivan, Marguerite Chapman, Bonita Granville, Arthur Franz

44.   Climax!: "Dr. Jekyll and Mr. Hyde" [adapted by Gore Vidal from the Robert Louis Stevenson classic; directed by Allen Reisner] (7-28-55) Michael Rennie, Mary Sinclair, Sir Cedric Hardwicke, John Hoyt

45.   Climax!: "One Night Stand" [a biographical drama of the Jazz Era's Joe Sullivan and his Bobcats] (8-4-55) Bob Crosby (Sullivan's associate), John Forsythe, Cloris Leachman, Donald Buka, Bob Sweeney

46.   Climax!: "Edge of Terror" (8-11-55) Lloyd Bridges, Phyllis Kirk, Dennis O'Keefe, Tom Laughlin

47.   Climax!: "Fear Strikes Out" [a documentary drama on Boston outfielder Jimmy Piersall and the fight against mental illness] (8-18-55) Tab Hunter (as Piersall), John Conte, Mona Freeman

48.   Climax!: "Deal a Blow" [by Robert Dozier; directed by John Frankenheimer and produced by Martin Manulis; filmed by Universal as The Young Stranger, 1957] (8-25-55) James MacArthur (his acting debut; MacArthur repeated his role for the film), Macdonald Carey, Phyllis Thaxter, Margaret Hayes, Edward Arnold

49.   Climax!: "The Adventures of Huckleberry Finn" [adapted from the Mark Twain classic] (9-1-55) Charles Taylor (in the title role), John Carradine, Thomas Mitchell, Minor Watson, Walter Catlett, Catherine Warren, Elizabeth Patterson

50.   Climax!: "Public Pigeon Number One" [adapted from the story by Don Quinn and Larry Berns] (9-8-55) Red Skelton, Ann Rutherford

51.   Climax!: "Silent Decision" [adapted from the Laura Hobson story] (9-15-55) Betty Furness, Franchot Tone, Katherine Bard, John Baragrey

52.   Climax!: "Night of Execution" [adapted from the Faith Baldwin story] (9-22-55) Nina Foch, Dick Foran, Vincent Price

Second Season

53.   Climax!: "Sailor on Horseback" [adapted from the Irving Stone biographical novel of Jack London] (9-29-55) Lloyd Nolan (as London), Mary Sinclair, Mercedes McCambridge

54.   Shower of Stars: "Time Out for Ginger" [adapted from the Ronald Alexander Broadway play] (10-6-55) Ruth Hussey, Edward Everett Horton, Janet Parker, Ronnie Burns, Gary Crosby

55.   Climax!: "Thin Air" [adapted from the Howard Browne novel] (10-13-55) Robert Sterling, Marguerite Chapman, Pat O'Brien, June Vincent

56.   Climax!: "House of Shadows" (10-20-55) James Daly, Diana Lynn, Jane Darwell, Ernest Truex

57.   Climax!: "Pink Cloud" (10-27-55) Brian Donlevy, Sally Forrest, Jay C. Flippen, Doris Dowling

58.   Shower of Stars: The Jack Benny Show [a musical review] (11-3-55) Benny; Gracie Allen, Marilyn Maxwell, Frankie Laine, Gary Crosby, The Sportsmen Quartet

59. Climax!: "Scheme to Defraud" [by Marc Brandel] (11-10-55)
    Dennis O'Keefe, Marilyn Erskine, Phyllis Thaxter
60. Climax!: "A Promise to Murder" [adapted from the Oscar
    Wilde story] (11-17-55) Louis Hayward, Peter Lorre, Ann
    Harding
61. Climax!: "Portrait in Celluloid" (11-24-55) Kim Hunter, Jack
    Carson, Don Taylor, Audrey Totter
62. Climax!: "A Man of Taste" (12-1-55) Michael Rennie, Zsa
    Zsa Gabor, John Kerr
63. Climax!: "The Passport" (12-8-55) Frank Lovejoy, Viveca
    Lindfors, Charles Korvin
64. Shower of Stars: "A Christmas Carol" [a musical adaptation
    of the Dickens classic; music by Bernard Herrmann (who
    also conducted); dialogue and lyrics by Maxwell Anderson]
    (12-15-55) Fredric March (as Scrooge), Basil Rathbone,
    Ray Middleton, Bob Sweeney, Sally Fraser; the Roger Wag-
    ner Choral
65. Climax!: "The Day They Gave Babies Away" [by Dale Eunson]
    (12-22-55) Brandon de Wilde, Barbara Hale, Joan Evans
66. Climax!: "Bail Out at Forty-three Thousand" [by Paul Monash;
    filmed by United Artists in 1957] (12-9-55) Charlton Hes-
    ton, Lee Marvin, Richard Boone, Nancy Davis
67. Climax!: "The Prowler" (1-5-56) Cameron Mitchell, Wallace
    Ford, Claire Trevor, Pat O'Brien
68. Climax!: "The Hanging Judge" [by Sir Cedric Hardwicke] (1-
    12-56) Sir Cedric Hardwicke, Raymond Massey, Reginald
    Denny, Hurd Hatfield, John Carradine, John Williams
69. Shower of Stars: "The Jack Benny Show" (1-19-56)
70. Climax!: "The Secret of River Lane" [by Adrian Spies] (1-26-
    56) James Dunn, Bobby Driscoll, Beulah Bondi, Dick Foran,
    Lon Chaney Jr., Victor Jory
71. Climax!: "Gamble on a Thief" [adapted by James P. Cavanagh
    from the Frank Cameron story] (2-2-56) Macdonald Carey,
    Dewey Martin, Phyllis Kirk, Elizabeth Patterson
72. Climax!: "The Fifth Wheel" (2-9-56) Hume Cronyn, James
    Gleason, Bonita Granville, Arthur Treacher, John Lupton,
    Peter Lorre, Buddy Baer
73. Shower of Stars: "The Jack Benny Show" (2-16-56)
74. Climax!: "Nightmare by Day" [by James P. Cavanagh] (2-23-
    56) Warner Anderson, Mary Astor, Gene Nelson, Katy
    Jurado, Coleen Gray
75. Climax!: "The Sound of Silence" [by Jack DeWitt] (3-1-56)
    Lloyd Bridges, Raymond Burr, Jean-Pierre Aumont, Mary
    Sinclair
76. Climax!: "The Gay Illiterate: The Louella Parsons Story"
    (3-8-56) Teresa Wright
77. Shower of Stars: "The Jack Benny Show" (3-15-56)
78. Climax!: "Pale Horse, Pale Rider" [adapted from the Kather-
    ine Anne Porter story] (3-22-56) John Forsythe, Dorothy
    Maguire, Ann Rutherford
79. Climax!: "An Episode of Sparrows" [adapted from the Rumer
    Godden novel] (3-29-56) Lynn Bari, Brandon de Wilde,
    Patty McCormack, Jessie Royce Landis, J. Carrol Naish
80. Climax!: "Spin into Darkness" [by Hagar Wilde] (4-5-56)

Charles Drake, Ruth Roman, Virginia Grey, Vincent Price
81. Shower of Stars: "The Jack Benny Show" (4-12-56)
82. Climax!: "The Lou Gehrig Story" (4-19-56) Wendell Corey, Jean Hagen, James Gregory, Harry Carey Jr.
83. Climax!: "Sit Down with Death" (4-26-56) Ralph Bellamy, Vicki Cummings, Constance Ford, John Williams, William Talman
84. Climax!: "The Empty Room Blues" [by Adrian Spies] (5-3-56) Celeste Holm, Gerald Mohr, Peggy Webber
85. Shower of Stars: "The Jack Benny Show" (5-10-56)
86. Climax!: "Flame Out on T-6" [by George Lowther] (5-17-56) Richard Carlson, Kevin McCarthy, Shepperd Strudwick, Sidney Blackmer
87. Climax!: "The Shadow of Evil" [by Hagar Wilde] (5-24-56) Richard Boone, Raymond Burr, Jan Sterling, Elizabeth Montgomery, Eduardo Ciannelli
88. Climax!: "Figures in Clay" [by Howard Leeds and Jerry Davis] (5-31-56) Lloyd Bridges, Edmond O'Brien, Henry Hull, Georgiann Johnson
89. Climax!: "Faceless Enemy" [adapted from the Eliot Asinof story] (6-7-56) Farley Granger, Phyllis Kirk, Jay C. Flippen
90. Climax!: "To Scream at Midnight" [adapted by John McGreevey from the Patricia Highsmith suspense drama] (6-14-56) Richard Jaeckel, Diana Lynn, Dewey Martin, Karen Sharpe
91. Climax!: "The Circular Staircase" [adapted by Frank Gruber from the Mary Roberts Rinehart story] (6-21-56) Kathleen Crowley, Dame Judith Anderson, Kevin McCarthy, Rhys Williams
92. Climax!: "A Trophy for Howard Davenport" [by Gene Levitt] (6-28-56) Dennis O'Keefe, Bill Chapin, Ruth Hussey, Gale Gordon
93. Climax!: "Phone Call for Matthew Quade" (7-5-56) Arthur Franz, Mary Astor, Everett Sloane, Mona Freeman
94. Climax!: "Fear Is the Hunter" (7-12-56) Anne Bancroft, Steve Cochran, Albert Dekker
95. Climax!: "Fury at Dawn" (7-19-56) Howard Duff, Jeff Morrow, Marilyn Erskine, Henry Jones, Morey Amsterdam
96. Climax!: "The Man Who Lost His Head" [by Ellis St. Joseph] (7-26-56) John Ericson, Debra Paget, Sir Cedric Hardwicke, Peter Lorre
97. Climax!: "Child of the Wind" [adapted by Anne Chapin and Frank Glicksman from the Burgess Drake novel] (8-2-56) Agnes Moorehead, Susan Kohner, Marshall Thompson
98. Climax!: "No Right to Kill" [adapted by Victor Woolfson from Fyodor Dostoyevsky's Crime and Punishment] (8-9-56) John Cassavetes, Robert H. Harris, Terry Moore, Joe Mantell
99. Climax!: "The Seventy-eighth Floor" [by Leonard Lee] (8-16-56) Scott Brady, Patricia Crowley, Rosemary De Camp, Otto Kruger
100. Climax!: "The Dark Wall" [by John Kneubuhl] (8-30-56) William Talman, Shepperd Strudwick, Shelley Winters, Harry Townes

101. Climax!: "Bury Me Later" [adapted by Jean Holloway from the H. F. M. Prescott story] (9-6-56) Boris Karloff, Angela Lansbury, Sean McClory, Torin Thatcher, Henry Jones
102. Climax!: "Burst of Violence" [by Richard Landau and Fred Frieberger] (9-13-56) Eddie Albert, Betsy Palmer, John Baragrey, Malcolm Broderick
103. Climax!: "The Gorsten Case" (9-20-56) Warner Anderson, Judith Evelyn, Everett Sloane, Audrey Totter

Third Season

104. Climax!: "The Fog" [by Dale Wasserman] (9-27-56) Ralph Bellamy, James Whitmore, Hurd Hatfield, Mona Freeman, Wallace Ford, Beverly Garland
105. Climax!: "Island in the City" [by Adrian Spies] (10-4-56) Ricardo Montalban, Sal Mineo, James Gregory, Eduardo Ciannelli, Doris Dowling, Rafael Campos
106. Climax!: "Journey into Fear" [adapted from the Eric Ambler novel] (10-11-56) John Forsythe, Eva Gabor, Arnold Moss, Anthony Dexter
107. Climax!: "The Midas Touch" [by Robert Bloomfield] (10-18-56) Walter Abel, Robert Preston, Margaret Hayes
108. Climax!: "Night of the Heat Wave" [by Lowell Barrington] (10-25-56) Darren McGavin, Phyllis Thaxter, Kurt Kasznar, Edward Andrews
109. Shower of Stars: "The Jack Benny Show" (11-1-56)
110. Climax!: "Flight to Tomorrow" [by Al C. Ward] (11-8-56) Steve Forrest, Terry Moore, Richard Arlen, Sir Cedric Hardwicke, Yma Sumac
111. Climax!: "Night Shriek" [by Hagar Wilde] (11-15-56) Brian Aherne, Joanne Dru
112. Climax!: "The Chinese Game" [by Charles Larson] (11-22-56) Anna May Wong, Macdonald Carey, Constance Ford, Rita Moreno, Harry Townes
113. Climax!: "The Secret Thread" [by Ethel Vance] (11-29-56) Anna Maria Alberghetti, John Barrymore Jr., Richard Carlson, Elisha Cook
114. Climax!: "Savage Portrait" (12-6-56) Raymond Burr, John Cassavetes, Marie Windsor
115. Shower of Stars: "A Christmas Carol" [a repeat of episode of 12/23/54 and 12/15/55] (12-13-56)
116. Climax!: "Strange Hostage" [by Whitfield Cook] (12-20-56) Richard Eyer, Raymond Massey
117. Climax!: "Ten Minutes to Curfew" (12-27-56) Neville Brand, Dewey Martin, Susan Kohner
118. Climax!: "Carnival at Midnight" [by Leo Liberman] (1-3-57) Peter Graves, Buddy Ebsen, Debra Paget, Oscar Homolka
119. Shower of Stars: "The Jack Benny Show" (1-10-57) Benny; Liberace, William Lundigan, Jayne Mansfield
120. Climax!: "The Gold Dress" [adapted by Robert Tallman from the Stephen Vincent Benet story] (1-17-57) Sylvia Sidney, June Lockhart, Leif Erickson, Cameron Prud'homme
121. Climax!: "Circle of Destruction" (1-24-57) Dale Robertson, Skip Homeier, Beulah Bondi, Joe Mantell

122. Climax!: "The Trouble at Number Five" [adapted by Charles Larson from the Shelby Smith novel] (1-31-57) Ann Harding, Jacques Sernas, Patricia Collinge, Reginald Owen

123. Climax!: "The Stalker" [by Elizabeth McCoy] (2-7-57) Marilyn Erskine, James Whitmore, Jay C. Flippen

124. Climax!: "Stain of Honor" [by Adrian Spies] (2-14-57) Lee Marvin, Betsy Palmer, Don Taylor, Wallace Ford

125. Climax!: "The Long Count" [by John McGreevey] (2-21-57) Jacques Bergerac, John Ericson, Viveca Lindfors, Paul Stewart

126. Climax!: "Don't Ever Come Back" [by Dick Stenger] (2-28-57) Richard Boone, Everett Sloane, Gene Lockhart, Kathleen Crowley, Elizabeth Patterson

127. Climax!: "Night of a Rebel" (otherwise known as "Nine Day Wonder") (3-7-57) John Kerr, Margaret O'Brien, Harry Townes, Eduardo Ciannelli

128. Shower of Stars: "The Jack Benny Show" (3-14-57)

129. Climax!: "Let It Be Me" [by Eileen and Robert Mason Pollock] (3-21-57) Eddie Albert, Steve Forrest, Maureen O'Sullivan, Charles Ruggles, Jill Corey, Johnny Damorn

130. Climax!: "Strange Sanctuary" [by Ellis Kadison] (3-28-57) Michael Rennie, Cesar Romero, Osa Massen, Rita Moreno, Noah Beery

131. Climax!: "Don't Touch Me" [by Jerome Gruskin] (4-4-57) Shelley Winters, Henry Silva, Mildred Dunnock, Warren Stevens

132. Shower of Stars: "The Jack Benny Show" (4-11-57) Benny; Tallulah Bankhead, Ed Wynn, Julie London, Tommy Sands

133. Climax!: "The Mad Bomber" (4-18-57) Dane Clark, Jim Backus, Theodore Bikel, Anne Bancroft, Estelle Winwood

134. Climax!: "Avalanche at Devil's Pass" (4-25-57) John Ireland, Wanda Hendrix, Vincent Price, Judith Evelyn, Edgar Buchanan

135. Climax!: "Strange Death at Burnleigh" [by Charles Larsen] (5-2-57) Michael Rennie, Sir Cedric Hardwicke, Joan Tetzel

136. Shower of Stars: "The Jack Benny Show" (5-9-57) Benny; Van Johnson, Jean Durand (Haitian singer and dancer)

137. Climax!: "Bait for the Tiger" [adapted by Whitfield Cook from the Nicholas Montsarrat novel] (5-16-57) Peter Lawford, Corrine Calvet, Anna Maria Alberghetti, Carl Esmond

138. Climax!: "Hand of Evil" [adapted by Leo Liberman from the Jhan and June Robbins story] (5-23-57) John Forsythe, Vera Miles, Mary Anderson

139. Climax!: "The Disappearance of Amanda Hale" [by Dale and Katherine Eunson] (5-30-57) Carolyn Jones, Lloyd Bridges, Miriam Hopkins, Alexander Scourby

140. Climax!: "Mr. Runyon of Broadway" [by Leonard Spigelgass] (6-6-57) Ralph Bellamy, Jesse White, Joi Lansing, Jay C. Flippen, Jack Lord, Leo Fuchs

141. Climax!: "The Man Who Stole the Bible" (6-13-57) Guy Madison, Sally Forrest

142. Climax!: "A Taste for Crime" [adapted by Ellis St. Joseph] (6-20-57) Michael Rennie, Marsha Hunt, Peter Lorre, Beverly Garland

143. Climax!: "The Trial of Captain Wirz, The Andersonville Jailor" [by Saul Levitt (the basis for his 1959 Broadway play); directed by Don Medford and produced by Ralph Nelson; music composed by Jerry Goldsmith] (6-27-57) Charlton Heston, Everett Sloane, Harry Townes, William Lundigan, Mary Costa

144. Climax!: "Locked in Fear" [otherwise known as "False Witness"; adapted by John McGreevey from the Marie Baumer Broadway play Little Brown Jug] (7-4-57) Eddie Bracken, Agnes Moorehead, Dean Harens, Gloria Talbot, John Baragrey

145. Climax!: "Payment for Judas" (7-11-57) Cameron Mitchell, Phyllis Thaxter

146. Climax!: "Walk a Tightrope" [by Mann Rubin] (7-18-57) Laraine Day, Leif Erickson, Neville Brand

147. Climax!: "The High Jungle" [by Sheldon Stark] (7-25-57) Mary Astor, Charles Bickford, Alexander Scourby, Barry Atwater

148. Climax!: "The Giant Killer" [by Mann Rubin] (8-1-57) Dane Clark, Inger Stevens, Shepperd Strudwick, Jerry Colonna

149. Climax!: "Trial of Terror" [by Seeleg Lester] (8-8-57) Robert Preston, Diana Lynn, Kurt Kasznar

150. Climax!: "Murder Is a Witch" (8-15-57) Mona Freeman, Dean Stockwell, Nancy Kelly

151. Climax!: "The Stranger Within" (8-22-57) George Nader, Rita Moreno, Charles Korvin

152. Climax!: "Deadly Climate" (8-29-57) Nina Foch, Kevin McCarthy, Warren Stevens, Edgar Buchanan, Estelle Winwood

153. Climax!: "Trial by Fire" (9-5-57) Linda Darnell, Forrest Tucker, Malcolm Broderick

154. Climax!: "The Mystery of the Red Room" (9-12-57) Michael Rennie, Anna Maria Alberghetti, Judith Evelyn, Arthur Franz, Una Merkel

155. Climax!: "The Necessary Evil" (9-19-57) Dewey Martin, Victor Jory, Margaret O'Brien, Lon Chaney Jr.

Fourth Season

156. Climax!: "Along Came a Spider" [by Leonard Spigelgass] (9-26-57) John Ericson, Ruth Hussey, Don Dubbins, Natalie Trundy

157. Climax!: "Jacob and the Angel" (10-3-57) Gig Young, Eva Gabor, June Lockhart, Otto Kruger, Keye Luke

158. Climax!: "Mask for the Devil" (10-10-57) Steve Forrest, Jan Sterling, Nita Talbot, Paul Stewart

159. Climax!: "The Largest City in Captivity" (10-17-57) Franchot Tone, Viveca Lindfors, Kurt Kasznar

160. Climax!: "Tunnel of Fear" (10-24-57) Jack Carson, Leora Dana, Buddy Ebsen

161. Shower of Stars: "The Jack Benny Show" (10-31-57)

162. Climax!: "Keep Me In Mind" (11-7-57) Johnny Desmond, James Dunn, Marisa Pavan

163. Climax!: "Two Tests for Tuesday" (11-14-57) Julie Adams, John Baragrey, John Barrymore Jr., Susan Oliver

164. Climax!: "A Matter of Life and Death" (11-21-57) Bradford

Dillman, Janis Paige, Ralph Meeker, Betsy Palmer, Tina
Louise

165. Climax!: "Murder Has a Deadline" (11-28-57) Eddie Albert,
Constance Ford
166. Climax!: "The Devil's Brood" [by Al C. Ward] (12-5-57)
John Ericson, Angela Lansbury, Stephen McNally, Peter
Whitney, Torin Thatcher
167. Climax!: "Hurricane Diane" (12-12-57) Vanessa Brown,
Jeffrey Hunter, Beulah Bondi, Brian Keith, Jan Merlin
168. Climax!: "To Walk the Night" (12-19-57) Richard Boone,
Judith Evelyn, Walter Matthau
169. Climax!: "Shadow of a Memory" (12-26-57) Alex Nicol,
Marguerite Chapman, Harry Townes, Ann Todd
170. Climax!: "Scream in Silence" [by Eileen and Robert Mason
Pollock] (1-2-58) Anne Francis, Skip Homeier, Betty Field,
William Talman, Sidney Blackmer
171. Shower of Stars: "The Jack Benny Show" (1-9-58)
172. Climax!: "Thieves of Tokyo" (1-16-58) Dewey Martin, Everett Sloane, Karen Sharpe, Mickie Kobi
173. Climax!: "Sound of the Moon" (1-23-58) Ray Danton, Vera
Miles, Hoagy Carmichael, Royal Dano
174. Climax!: "Burst of Fire" (1-30-58) Sally Forrest, Dennis
Weaver, Richard Garland, Joe Mantell
175. Climax!: "Four Hours in White" (2-6-58) Dan Duryea, Steve
McQueen, Ann Rutherford, Eduard Franz, Gloria Talbot
176. Shower of Stars: "The Jack Benny Birthday Anniversary Show"
(2-13-58)
177. Climax!: "The Secret Love of Johnny Spain" (2-20-58) Terry Moore, James Best, Conrad Nagel, Gene Raymond, Audrey Totter
178. Climax!: "Albert Anastasia, His Life and Death" [adapted by
Malvin Wald and Henry F. Greenberg from the Bernard Ger-
ard story] (2-27-58) Don Ameche, Eli Wallach
179. Climax!: "The Thief with the Big Blue Eyes" (3-6-58) Lew
Ayres, Betty Furness
180. Climax!: "So Deadly My Love" (3-13-58) Kim Hunter, Scott
McKay, Ralph Meeker, Shepperd Strudwick
181. Shower of Stars: "The Jack Benny Show" (3-20-58)
182. Climax!: "The Great World and Timothy Colt" (3-27-58)
Don Taylor, Margaret Hayes, Milburn Stone, Cloris Leachman
183. Climax!: "On the Take" (4-3-58) Paul Douglas, Katherine
Bard, Nehemiah Persoff
184. Shower of Stars: "The Jack Benny Show" (4-17-58)
185. Climax!: "Shooting for the Moon" (4-24-58) John Forsythe,
Dick York, Bethel Leslie
186. Climax!: "Deadly Tarot" (5-1-58) Anna May Wong, Peter
Graves, Henry Silva, Olive Deering
187. Climax!: "The Big Success" (5-8-58) Ed Begley, Scott
Brady, Marilyn Erskine, Richard Garland, Jonathan Harris
188. Climax!: "The Disappearance of Daphne" [adapted by Robert
Blees from the magazine story by Nancy Rutledge] (5-15-58)
Mona Freeman, Elaine Stritch, Irene Papas, Ray Danton,
Eduardo Ciannelli

189. Climax!: "Time of the Hanging" (5-22-58) Marsha Hunt, Lee Marvin, William Shatner, John Litel, Harry Townes
190. Climax!: "The Push-Button Giant" [adapted by Irving Wallace from the Arnold Shaw novel] (5-29-58) Barry Nelson, Martha Hyer, Everett Sloane, Barbara Nichols
191. Climax!: "Spider Web" (6-5-58) Fernando Lamas, Dina Merrill, Rita Moreno
192. Climax!: "The Volcano Seat" (6-12-58) Michael Rennie, Albert Salmi, Michael Wilding, Margaret Phillips, James Edwards, Patricia Cutts
193. Climax!: "House of Doubt" (6-19-58) Stephen McNally, Gene Raymond, Patricia Medina, Vera Miles, Elizabeth Patterson
194. Climax!: "Cabin B-13" [by John Dickson Carr, as revised from the Suspense episode of 3/29/49] (6-26-58) Barry Sullivan, Hurd Hatfield, Kim Hunter, Alex Nicol

THE VISE

    Filmed in Great Britain. As of December 23, 1955, The Vise became the title for the British produced series Mark Saber, Private Investigator, with Donald Gray in the title role.

The Regulars: Ron Randell, host.

The Episodes:

1. "One Just Man" (10-1-54) Alexander Knox
2. "Set a Murder" (10-8-54) Clifford Evans, Martin Boddey
3. "Let Murder Be Done" (10-15-54) Dennis Price, Avis Scott, Betty Ann Davies
4. "Dr. Damon's Experiment" (10-22-54) Laurence Naismith
5. "Death Pays No Dividends" (10-29-54) Peter Reynolds, Eunice Gayson
6. "Gabriel's Choice" (11-5-54) Clifford Evans
7. "The Diamond Expert" (11-12-54) Hugh Latimer, Paul Carpenter
8. "The Secret Place" (11-19-54) Margaret Rawlings, John Stewart
9. "The Fair and the Fallen" (11-16-54) Jean Aubrey, Anthony Snell, Josephine Douglas
10. "The Eavesdropper" (12-3-54) Frederick Leister, Terrence Brook, Neila Parely
11. "The Very Silent Traveler" (12-10-54) Donald Masters, Robert O'Neill
12. "Yellow Robe" (12-17-54) Robert Raglan, Tony Pendrill
13. "Lucky Man" (12-24-54) Leslie Phillips
14. "The Gambler" (12-31-54) Thea Gregory, Martin Benson, John Witty
15. "Count of Twelve" (1-7-55) John Longden
16. "The Final Column" (1-14-55) Christopher Lee, John Longden, Kay Collard
17. "The Benevolent Burglar" (1-21-55) Peter Dynelay, James

Hayter, Pauline Olson, Joan Drummond
18. "Blind Man's Bluff" (1-28-55) Patrick Holt, Eunice Gayson, John Bentley
19. "Eighth Window" (2-4-55) Robert Arden
20. "Broken Honeymoon" (2-11-55) Adrienne Corri, Robert Ayres
21. "Death on the Boards" (2-18-55) Maureen Swanson, Robert Parker, Joan Schofield
22. "Behind the Mask" (2-25-55) Betta St. John, Philip Friend
23. "Dress Rehearsal" (3-4-55) Patrick Holt, Sandra Dorne, Kay Callard
24. "Cruel Test" (3-11-55) Mark Digman, Joyce Heron, Ian Whittaker
25. "The Deception" (3-18-55) Marjorie Stewart, Ann Stephens, Mary Parker, Roman O'Basey
26. "Week-end Guest" (3-25-55) Kenneth Haigh, Brenda Hogan
27. "Fame and the Fury" (4-1-55) Patrick Holt, Sandra Dorne, David Horne
28. "Ring of Fear" (4-8-55)
29. "The Imperfect Gentleman" (4-15-55) Jack Watling
30. "The Schemer" (4-22-55) Brian Smith
31. "Double Pay-Off" (4-29-55) Mary Scott
32. "Account Closed" (5-6-55) Dennis Price
33. "The Serpent Beneath" (5-13-55) Dennis Price
34. "The Price of Vanity" (5-20-55) Eric Lander
35. "Man in Demand" (5-27-55) Enid Lorimer, Brian Worth, Dorothy Gordon
36. "The Hosning Chinaman" (6-3-55) Colin Tapley, Ronald Adam, Michael Kelly
37. "The Rattan Trunk" (6-10-55) Anne Valery, Barry Keigan
38. "Murder of a Ham" (6-17-55) Leslie Duryer, April Olrich
39. "The Better Chance" (6-24-55) Kay Callard, Leslie Phillips
40. "Diplomatic Error" (7-1-55) Sandra Dorne, Patrick Holt, Ron Randell
41. "Stranglehold" (7-8-55) Maureen Swanson, John Bentley
42. "The Corpse in Room Thirteen" (7-15-55) Phil Brown, Margaret Anderson, Raymond Hollet
43. "Death Walks by Night" (7-22-55) Nanette Newman, Michael Ashwit, Joy Adamson, Robert Berceval
44. "The Verdict" (7-29-55) Fred Johnson, Adrienne Allen, Brian Smith
45. "The Bargain" (8-5-55) John Loder, Eunice Gayson, Bryan Forbes, Joy Adamson
46. "Death in White" (8-19-55) Ronald Leigh-Hunt, Jill Clifford
47. "The Broken Link" (8-26-55) Peter Neil, Philip Friend
48. "Never Let Me Die" (9-2-55) Kay Callard, Phil Brown, Gordon Tanner

Second Season

49. "Bond of Hate" (9-9-55) Kay Callard, Lloyd Lamble
50. "Death Mask" (9-16-55) Wanda Hudson, Richard Molinas
51. "Side Entrance" (9-23-55) John Loder, Thea Gregory, Philip Friend, Jennifer Jaine

52. "The Search for Martha Harris" (9-30-55) Jennie Laird, John Gorsley, Lloyd Lamble
53. "Money To Burn" (10-7-55) Alan Tilvern, Brenda Hogan
54. "Two of a Kind" (10-14-55) Donald Wolfit, Aleta Morrison
55. "Cross Channel" (10-21-55) Patrick Holt, Paula Byrne
56. "Death Takes No Holiday" (10-28-56) Kay Callard, Dinah Ann Rogers, Alan Owens, Ted Babcock
57. "Dead Man's Evidence" (11-4-55) John Stone, Honor Blackman, Brenda Hogan
58. "Stranger in Town" (11-11-55) Shirley Lawrence, Neil Halliett, Barry Keegan
59. "By Person Unknown" (11-18-55) Laurence Naismith, Brenda Hogan
60. "Killer at Large" (11-25-55) Roman O'Casey, Lloyd Lamble
61. "Wrong Time Murder" (12-2-55) John Loder, Peter Reynolds, Jean Aubrey
62. "Gift from Heaven" (12-9-55) Colin Craft, Mary Laura Woods, Patrick McGoohan
63. "Second Sight" (12-16-55) Jack Watling, Gene Anderson, Hugh Latimore
64. "Good Name Murder" [originally scheduled for 11/4/55] Sylvia Pemberton, Ronald Briggs
65. "Snapshot" [originally scheduled for 12/16/55] Dorothy Gordon, Rosamund Waring, Philip Friend

RHEINGOLD THEATRE

The Regulars: Henry Fonda, host.

The Episodes:

1. "Dark Stranger" (1-8-55) Edmond O'Brien, Joanne Woodward
2. "Honolulu" [adapted from the William Somerset Maugham story] (1-15-55) Frank Lovejoy
3. "The Lie" (1-22-55) Dan Duryea
4. "Ferry to Fox Island" (1-29-55) Jan Sterling
5. "Safe Journey" (2-5-55) Frank Lovejoy
6. "Brief Affair" (2-12-55) Joanne Dru
7. "Louise" [adapted from the William Somerset Maugham story] (2-19-55) Dame Judith Anderson, George Macready
8. "Total Recall" (2-26-55) William Lundigan
9. "The Back of Beyond" [adapted from the William Somerset Maugham story] (3-5-55) Alexis Smith
10. "The Great Shinin' Saucer of Paddy Faneen" (3-12-55) Edmund Gwenn
11. "The Round Dozen" [adapted from the William Somerset Maugham story] (3-19-55) Brian Aherne
12. "First Offense" (3-26-55) Howard Duff
13. "A Matter of Courage" (4-2-55) Keefe Brasselle
14. "Her Crowning Glory" (4-9-55) Teresa Wright
15. "The Unforgivable" (4-16-55) Thomas Mitchell

16. "The Lady's Game" (4-23-55) Charles Coburn
17. "Virtue" [adapted from the William Somerset Maugham story] (4-30-55) Dame Judith Anderson
18. "Hand to Hand" (5-14-55) Zachary Scott
19. "Newspaper Man" (5-21-55) Pat O'Brien
20. "The Treasure" [adapted from the William Somerset Maugham story] (5-28-55) Angela Lansbury
21. "Desert Story" (6-4-55) Jan Sterling
22. "The True Confessions of Henry Pell" (6-11-55) Howard Duff
23. "The Norther" (7-16-55) Stephen McNally

Second Season

24. "End of Flight" [adapted from the William Somerset Maugham story] (10-29-55) Edmond O'Brien
25. "The Man Who Was Dead" (11-12-55) Thomas Mitchell
26. "The Creative Impulse" [adapted from the William Somerset Maugham story] (12-3-55) Dame Judith Anderson
27. "The Blue Landscape" (12-10-55) Peter Lorre
28. "A Point of Honor" (1-7-56) Zachary Scott
29. "The Difficult Age" (1-21-56) Charles Coburn
30. "Payment in Kind" (1-28-56) Howard Duff
31. "Appearances and Reality" [adapted from the William Somerset Maugham story] (2-11-56) Brian Aherne
32. "Arab Duel" (2-18-56) Sidney Blackmer
33. "They" (3-3-56) Thomas Mitchell
34. "Act of Decision" (3-10-56) Frank Lovejoy
35. "The Force of Circumstance" [adapted from the William Somerset Maugham story] (3-24-56) Angela Lansbury
36. "The Whizzer" (3-31-56) Frank Lovejoy
37. "The Lonely Ones" (4-7-56) Teresa Wright
38. "The Señora" (4-14-56) Dame Judith Anderson

DAMON RUNYON THEATRE

The Regulars: Donald Woods, host.

The Episodes:

1. "Pick the Winner" (4-16-55) Bruce Bennett, Vivian Blaine, Robert Strauss, Gene White
2. "Dancing Dan's Christmas" (4-23-55) Broderick Crawford, Marilyn Erskine, Robert Knapp
3. "All Is Not Gold" (4-30-55) Scott Brady, Nancy Gates
4. "The Lacework Kid" (5-7-55) Steve Brodie, John Banner, Gladys Holland
5. "Numbers and Figures" (5-14-55) Paul Douglas, Allen Jenkins, June Vincent, Wally Vernon
6. "Tobias the Terrible" (5-21-55) Wallace Ford, Beverly Garland, Gil Stratton Jr.
7. "Old Em's Kentucky Home" (5-28-55) Edmond O'Brien, Gale Robbins, Raymond Greenleaf, Fay Baker

8. "Lonely Heart" (6-4-55) Ann Harding, Allen Jenkins, Steven Geray
9. "It Comes Up Money" (6-11-55) Thomas Mitchell, Jack Kruschen, Wally Vernon, Frances Bavier, Tom Daly
10. "The Big Umbrella" (6-18-55) James Gleason, Rick Jason, Adelle August, Murvyn Vye
11. "Big Shoulders" (6-25-55) Mona Freeman, Edward Brophy
12. "Teacher's Pet" (7-2-55) Fay Bainter, Adele Jergens, Gene Davis, Joseph Downing
13. "The Mink Doll" (7-9-55) Wayne Morris, Dorothy Lamour, Willis Bouchey
14. "Bunny on the Beach" (7-16-55) William Frawley, Sara Haden, Elisabeth Risdon, Douglas Fowley, Ben Waldon
15. "The Big Fix" (7-23-55) Sidney Blackmer, Sheila Ryan, Michael O'Shea
16. "A Light in France" (7-30-55) Edward Everett Horton, Hugh O'Brian, Maxie Rosenbloom
17. "A Nice Price" (8-6-55) James Dunn, Wally Vernon, James Craven, Jack Kruschen
18. "Small Town Caper" (8-13-55) Dick Foran, Irene Hervey, Charles Cantor
19. "There's No Forever" (8-20-55) John Ireland, Fay Wray, Joseph Downing
20. "Earthquake Morgan" (8-27-55) Buddy Baer, Alex Nicol, Sheila Ryan, John Beradino, Sid Melton

Second Season

21. "Bred for Battle" (10-8-55) Nancy Gates, Sheldon Leonard, Race Gentry, John Bromfield
22. "Miami Moolah" (10-15-55) Ken Murray, Marty Fain, Allyn Joslyn, Gale Robbins
23. "Situation Wanted" (10-29-55) Allen Jenkins, Horace McMahon, Anthony Caruso, Cesar Romero, Yvette Dugay
24. "A Star Lights Up" (11-5-55) Virginia Field, Carleton Young, Robert Strauss
25. "Broadway Dateline" (11-12-55) Pat Carroll, Jack Carson, Wally Vernon, Sue England
26. "A Job for the Macarone" (11-26-55) Dane Clark
27. "The Barbeque" (12-3-55) Brian Donlevy, Jean Parker
28. "Honorary Degree" (12-10-55) Jackie Coogan, Allen Jenkins, William Leslie
29. "Dog About Town" (12-31-55) James Gleason, John Hubbard, Frances Robinson
30. "Blond Mink" (1-7-56) James Whitmore, John Beradino, Coleen Gray
31. "The Good Luck Kid" (1-21-56) Gene Barry, Barbara Hale, Barry Froner
32. "Judy, the Jinx" (1-28-56) Adele Jergens, Kent Taylor, George E. Stone
33. "The Face of Johnny Dolliver" (2-4-56) Biff Elliott, Allen Jenkins, Beverly Tyler
34. "Cleo" (2-18-56) Keenan Wynn, Laurie Mitchell
35. "The Pee Wees Take Over" (2-25-56) Steve Brodie

36. "The Pigeon Gets Plucked" (3-3-56) Dick Foran, David Kasday
37. "A Tale of Two Citizens" (3-17-56) Sonny Tufts
38. "Hot Oil" (3-24-56) Charles Coburn, Robert Armstrong
39. "Miracle Jones" (4-14-56) John Carradine, Bill Williams

APPOINTMENT WITH ADVENTURE

The Episodes:

1. "Minus Three Thousand" [the pilot for the 1955 series Paris Precinct] (4-3-55) Claude Dauphin, Louis Jourdan, Mala Powers
2. "Five in Judgment" [by Douglas Taylor] (4-10-55) Henry Hull, Paul Newman, Jeff Harris, Jack Lord, Frank McHugh, Patricia Breslin
3. "The Fateful Pilgrimage" [by Rod Serling] (4-17-55) William Prince, Viveca Lindfors, George Macready, Martin Kosleck, Theodore Bikel
4. "The Quiet Gun" (4-24-55) Neville Brand, Geraldine Brooks, Macdonald Carey
5. "Rendezvous in Paris" (5-1-55) Polly Bergen, Dane Clark, Hugh Reilly
6. "Escape from Vienna" (5-8-55) James Daly, Erik Rhodes, George Voskovec, Elaine Stritch
7. "Priceless Cargo" (5-15-55) Leora Dana, Arthur Franz
8. "Forbidden Holiday" (5-22-55) Phyllis Kirk, Jerome Thor, Peter Cookson
9. "Stranger on a Plane" (5-29-55) Sheila Bond, Richard Derr, Charlotte Rae
10. "Perilous Journey" (6-5-55) Eva Gabor, Michael Evans
11. "The Secret of Juan Valdéz" (6-12-55) Robert Middleton, Betsy Palmer
12. "Race the Comet" [by Mann Rubin] (6-19-55) Kim Hunter, Gene Barry, Conrad Janis
13. "Honeymoon in Spain" [by Julian Claman] (6-26-55) Paul Newman, Monica Lewis
14. "Bridge of the Devil" [by Jerome Ross] (7-3-55)
15. "Crash Landing" [by Ian Martin] (7-10-55) William Prince, Frank Overton, Georgiann Johnson
16. "Return of the Stranger" (7-17-55) Joan Lorring, Theodore Bikel, Lyn McCarthy
17. "Desperate Game" (7-24-55) Maria Riva, Richard Derr, Patricia Englund, Gregory Morton
18. "The Snow People" [by Eileen and Robert Mason Pollock] (7-31-55) Gloria DeHaven
19. "Never to Know" (8-7-55) John Baragrey, Dennis Lor
20. "The Royal Treatment" (8-14-55) Dane Clark, Edie Adams, Don Keefer
21. "Five Star Crisis" (8-21-55) Barbara Britton, Hugh Reilly
22. "Masquerade" (8-28-55) Patrick O'Neal, Janice Rule, Robert Clary

23. "The Pirate's House" (9-4-55) Jack Klugman, Tony Randall, Gena Rowlands
24. "When in Rome" [by Newton Meitzer] (9-11-55) Geraldine Brooks, Charles Drake
25. "Dangerous Mayhem" [by Ann Howard Bailey] (9-18-55) Philip Abbott, Herbert Nelson, Luana Anders
26. "Destination Freedom" (9-25-55) Jason Robards Jr.

Second Season

27. "The Allentown Incident" (10-2-55) Pat Hingle, Lin McCarthy, Cameron Prud'homme, Bert Benson
28. "Number Seven, Hangman's Row" (10-9-55) Biff McGuire, Joyce Smight
29. "The Helping Hand" (10-16-55) Patricia Benoit, Perry Fiske, George Macready, Martin Kosleck
30. "Pattern for Thieves" (10-23-55) Neva Patterson
31. "Dark Memory" (10-30-55) Lili Darvas, Louis King
32. "State of Siege" [adapted from the Robert Louis Stevenson story] (11-6-55) Gene Lyons, Sarah Marshall
33. "Stage Fright" (11-13-55) Louise Albritton
34. "Relative Stranger" (11-20-55) Elizabeth Montgomery, Hurd Hatfield, George Voskovec
35. "Time Bomb" [by Jean-Charles Tacchella; filmed by United Artists, 1961] (11-27-55) Chester Morris
36. "Escape" [by Art Wallace] (12-4-55) George Grizzard, Philip Abbott, Jess Harris, Addison Powell
37. "A Sword Has Two Edges" (12-11-55) Patricia Collinge
38. "The Big Mistake" (12-18-55) Russell Nype, Peggy McCay
39. "A Touch of Christmas" (12-25-55) James Daly
40. "Mutiny" [by William Bruckner] (1-1-56) John Ericson, Dorothy Malone
41. "The Top of the Mountain" (1-8-56) Richard Carlyle, Geraldine Brooks
42. "Suburban Terror" (1-15-56) June Lockhart, Henry Jones, Carl Betz
43. "Betrayal" [by Irving Werstein] (1-22-56) Bramwell Fletcher
44. "The Battle of Hewitt Hill" [by Harold Gast] (1-29-56) Nancy Berg, Lin McCarthy
45. "All Through the Night" (2-5-56) John Cassavetes, Tina Louise, Betsy Von Furstenberg
46. "Till the End of Time" (2-19-56) Signe Hasso
47. "Paris Venture" (2-26-56) Patti Page, Marilyn Greene
48. "Career" (3-11-56) Margaret Phillips
49. "A Thief There Was" (3-18-56) Jason Robards Jr., Christopher Plummer, Constance Ford
50. "Two Falls for Satan" (4-1-56) Forrest Tucker

STAGE 7

The Episodes:

1. "The Deceiving Eye" (1-30-55) Frank Lovejoy
2. "Appointment in Highbridge" (2-6-55) Dan O'Herlihy, Phyllis Coates
3. "The Legacy" (2-13-55) Vanessa Brown, Elizabeth Patterson
4. "Debt of Honor" (2-20-55) Edmond O'Brien, Charles Bronson, Wendy Winkleman
5. "Tiger at Noon" [by Sidney Sheldon] (2-27-55) Stephen McNally, Jorja Curtwright
6. "To Kill a Man" [adapted from the Jack London story] (3-6-55) Alexis Smith, Scott Forbes
7. "The Greatest Man in the World" (3-13-55) Pat O'Brien, Polly Chapin
8. "The Press Conference" (3-20-55) Dennis Morgan
9. "The Long Count" (3-27-55) Frank Lovejoy, Biff Elliott, Joan Voha, Richard Deacon, Ted de Corsia, Nestor Paiva, Mel Wells
10. "Down from the Stars" (4-3-55) Diana Lynn, Lamont Johnson
11. "Young Girl in an Apple Tree" (4-10-55) Ann Harding, Regis Toomey
12. "Emergency" [by Gordon McDonnell] (4-17-55) Lee Bowman
13. "The Magic Hat" [by Irving Gaynor Neiman] (4-24-55) Kristine Miller, George Brent, Lydia Reed
14. "Armed" [by Dick Stenger] (5-1-55) Neville Brand, Robert Nichols
15. "Billy and the Bride" [by Joseph Cochran] (5-8-55) Hugh O'Brian, Claire Trevor, Dick Foran, Angela Lansbury
16. "A Note of Fear" [by Frederic Brady] (5-15-55) Jan Sterling, Don Rickles, Gordon Mills
17. "The Verdict" [by Ken Field] (5-22-55) Stephen McNally, Karen Booth
18. "The Time of Day" (5-29-55) Irene Hervey, Peggy Ann Garner, Charles Bronson
19. "Yesterday's Pawnshop" [by Robert Dozier] (6-5-55) Don Taylor, Jane Frazee, Randy Stuart
20. "The Traveling Salesman" [adaptation of the short story] (6-12-55) George Montgomery
21. "End of the Line" (6-19-55) Maria Riva, Don Haggerty, Roger De Koven
22. "Where You Loved Me" (9-4-55) Frances Rafferty, Macdonald Carey
23. "The Hayfield" [by Charles Stewart, from the characters created by Eric Hodgins] (9-18-55) Phyllis Thaxter, Macdonald Carey, Dick Foran
24. "The Fox Hunt" (9-25-55) Dennis Morgan, Harry Shannon, Paul Burke

TV READER'S DIGEST [after the radio series]

Created by Chester Erskine, who also produced; presented by the Studebaker-Packard Corporation; filmed at American National Studios.

The Regulars: Hugh Reilly, host.

The Episodes:

1. "The Last of the Old Time Shooting Sheriffs" [by Cleveland
    Amory, from the Reader's Digest article]   (1-17-55)
2. "Trouble on the Double" [adapted from the David O. Woodbury
    article; Reader's Digest July 1953, pgs. 31-34]   (1-24-55)
    Nancy Gates, Peter Graves
3. "Mrs. Robert Louis Stevenson" [adapted from the Reader's Di-
    gest article "The Treasure of Robert Louis Stevenson" by
    Donald and Louise Peattie; RD October 1952, pgs. 83-87]
    (1-31-55)   Martha Scott, Douglass Montgomery
4. "How Chance Made Mr. Lincoln President" [adapted from the
    Reader's Digest article]   (2-7-55)   Richard Gaines
5. "I'd Pick More Daisies" [adapted from the Don Herold article,
    Reader's Digest October 1953, pgs. 71-72]   (2-14-55)
    Jeanne Cagney, Richard Denning, Kim Charley
6. "Top Secret" [adapted by Frederick Hazlett from the Norbert
    Muhlen Reader's Digest article]   (2-21-55)   Fred Essler,
    Leonid Kinsky, Alfred Linder, Fritz Feld, Otto Waldis
7. "A Matter of Life or Death" [adapted from the Hodding Carter
    article; Reader's Digest October 1950, pgs. 60-62]   (2-28-
    55)   Bobby Driscoll, Minor Watson
8. "The End of Blackbeard the Pirate" [adapted from the Edwin
    Muller article; Reader's Digest October 1950, pgs. 100-104;
    article originally appeared in Esquire, September 1950]   (3-
    7-55)   Jeff Morrow, Jessica Tandy, Randy Farr, Kay Stew-
    art, Robert Knapp
9. "The American Master Counterfeiters" [adapted from the Stew-
    art Robinson article; Reader's Digest November 1947, pgs.
    61-66; article originally appeared in Harper's September
    1947]   (3-14-55)   Ralph Dumke
10. "America's First Great Lady" [adapted from the Donald Calross
    Peattie article; Reader's Digest April 1947, pgs. 91-94]
    (3-21-55)   Gloria Talbott, Richard Ney
11. "The Manufactured Clue" [adapted from the Alan Hynd article,
    Reader's Digest August 1950, pgs. 41-45; article originally
    appeared in Murder! magazine]   (3-28-55)   Chuck Connors,
    Paul Stewart, Douglas Spencer
12. "Incident on the China Coast" [adapted from the Peter Thacher
    article; Reader's Digest November 1954, pgs. 14-22]   (4-4-
    55)   Robert Bray, Dan Barton, Noel Toy, Joan Elan
13. "How Charlie Faust Won a Pennant for the Giants" [adapted
    from the Edwin Burkholder article; Reader's Digest October
    1950, pgs. 79-82; article originally appeared in Sport June
    1950]   (4-11-55)   Alan Reed, Lee Marvin, Lee Van Cleef,
    John Larch, John Cliff
14. "Honeymoon in Mexico" [adapted from the John and Peggy Wil-
    helm article; Reader's Digest December 1954, pgs. 5-9;
    article originally appeared in the Christian Herald December
    1954]   (4-18-55)   Richard Long, Merry Anders
15. "The Great Armored-Car Robbery" [adapted by David Dortort

from the Frederic Sondern Jr. article; Reader's Digest May
1948, pgs. 101-105; article originally appeared in Argosy
May 1948] (4-25-55) Alex Nicol, Dorothy Green

16. "A Million Dollar Story" [adapted from the George Kent article;
Reader's Digest May 1952, pgs. 53-57; article originally ap-
peared in Quill March 1952] (5-2-55) Bill Bouchley, James
Bell, Julie Bishop, Milburn Stone, Joyce Arling

17. "Dear Friends and Gentle Hearts" [adapted from the Alexander
Woollcott article; Reader's Digest January 1943, pgs. 47-48]
(5-9-55) Johnny Johnston (as Stephen Foster), Jerry Hauser,
Joan Camden, Harlan Warde, Napoleon Simpson, Paul Maxey

18. "France's Greatest Detective" [adapted by Wills Root from the
Irving Wallace article; Reader's Digest February 1950, pgs.
103-107; article originally appeared in True January 1950]
(5-16-55) Arthur Franz (as Alphonse Bertillon), Philip Van
Zandt, Lawrence Dobkin

19. "Around the Horn to Matrimony" [adapted by Katherine and Dale
Bunson from the Tom S. Hyland article; Reader's Digest
November 1942, pgs. 42-44; article originally appeared in
American Mercury October 1942] (5-23-55) Robert Hutton,
Emma Scofield

20. "The Anatomy of Graft" [adapted from the Joseph F. Dinneen
article; Reader's Digest December 1952, pgs. 80-85; article
originally appeared in Harper's July 1952] (5-30-55) Gene
Barry, Jaclynne Greene, Emerson Treacy

21. "Human Nature Through the Rearview Mirror" [adapted from the
Reuben Hecht book condensation of the same title; Reader's
Digest June 1950, pgs. 103-116] (6-6-55) Eddie Albert,
Herb Vigran, Jill Jarmyn, Sid Melton, Sarah Selby, William
Henry

22. "Mister Pak Takes Over" [adapted from the article by Captain
Frederick Haight II; Reader's Digest March 1953, pgs. 63-
66; article originally appeared in Kiwanis March 1953] (6-
13-55) Philip Ahn, Kenneth Tobey, James Edwards, Dan
Barton

23. "My First Bullfight" [adapted from the Sidney Franklin Reader's
Digest article] (6-20-55) Jack Kelly (as Sidney Franklin,
the "Brooklyn Bullfighter"), George Huertt, Edward Colmans, Chalo Alvarado, Nacho Galindo

24. "Comrade Lindemann's Conscience" [adapted from the article by
Frederick Sondern Jr. and Norbert Muhlen; Reader's Digest
March 1953, pgs. 21-25; article originally appeared in Freeman January 26, 1953] (6-27-55) Alf Kjellin, Maria Palmer, Kurt Katch

25. "Six Hours of Surgery That Saved a Boy's Life" [adapted from
the Earl Ubell article; Reader's Digest October 1954, pgs.
76-78; article originally appeared in the New York Herald
Tribune May 30, 1954] (7-4-55) Walter Kingsford, Jerry
Paris, Damion O'Flynn, Jean Byron, Robert Osterloh

26. "The Baron and His Uranium Killing" [adapted by Arthur E.
Orloff from the Tom Howard article; Reader's Digest February 1954, pgs. 97-101; article originally appeared in the
Saturday Evening Post November 21, 1953] (7-11-55) Marcel Dallo, Gladys Holland

Second Season

27. "Child Pioneer" [adapted from the Honore Willie Morrow Reader's Digest article] (10-17-55) Jack Kelmond
28. "Old Master Detective" [adapted from the Reader's Digest article; July 1937] (10-24-55) William Talman, Walter Kingsford, Jesse White
29. "The Archer-Shee Case" [adapted from the Alexander Woollcott article; Reader's Digest April 1939] (10-31-55) Henry Daniell, Sir Cedric Hardwicke, Christopher Cook
30. "The Brainwashing of John Hayes" [adapted from the Frederick Sondern Jr. article; Reader's Digest July 1955, pgs. 27-32] (11-7-55) Philip Ahn, Vincent Price, Steven Geray, Richard Loo
31. "The Making of a Submariner" [adapted from the John G. Hubbell article; Reader's Digest May 1955, pgs. 25-35] (11-14-55) Douglas Dick, Richard Crosson, Walter Sande, Louis Jean Heydt, Charles Smith, John Hoffman
32. "The Voyage of Captain Tom Jones, Pirate" [adapted from the Reader's Digest article; March 1934] (11-21-55) Louis Hayward, John Stephenson, John Bryant, Kathryn Beaumont, Edward Colmans, Noel Drayton
33. "If I Were Rich" [adapted from the Reader's Digest article, May 1935] (11-28-55) Jim Backus, Helen Parrish, Chick Chandler, Carol Nugent, Chet Marshall
34. "The Sad Death of a Hero" [adapted by Albert Duffy from the Reader's Digest article, August 1936, which focusses on the Scopes Monkey Trial] (12-5-55) Carl Benton Reid, Douglass Dumbrille, Rosemary De Camp
35. "Emergency Case" [adapted from the Reader's Digest article, January 1939] (12-12-55) Arthur Franz
36. "When the Wise Man Appeared" [adapted from the article by William Ashley Anderson; Reader's Digest December 1945, pgs. 1-3; article originally appeared in the Philadelphia Bulletin December 24, 1942] (12-19-55) Dick Foran, Rudy Lee, Dorothy Green
37. "Ordeals of Yuba Gap" [adapted from the J. Campbell Bruce condensation of the True magazine (January 1955) story; Reader's Digest December 1955, pgs. 143-146] (12-26-55) Margaret Lindsay, Douglas Kennedy
38. "In the Eye of the Hurricane" [adapted from the article by Captain George H. Grant; Reader's Digest August 1955, pgs. 146-150] (1-2-56) Richard Arlen, Tod Griffin, John Doucette
39. "Why the Choir Was Late" [adapted from the George H. Edeal article; Reader's Digest June 1950, pgs. 135-136; article originally appeared in Life March 27, 1950] (1-9-56) Byron R. Foulger
40. "The Man Who Beat Death" [adapted from The Man Who Beat Diabetes by David Hulburd; Reader's Digest January 1954, pgs. 51-54; article originally appeared in Life September 7, 1953] (1-16-56) William Talbert, Phyllis Coates
41. "A Bell for Okinawa" [adapted from the Bruce Bliuen condensation of the Christ Kind story of the same title; Reader's Digest August 1955, pgs. 83-86] (1-23-56) Ludwig Stossel,

Paul Cavanagh

42. "Cochise--Greatest of the Apaches" [adapted from the article by
Elliott Arnold; Reader's Digest April 1951, pgs. 69-72; article originally appeared in the Arizona Quarterly, spring
1951] (1-30-56) John Howard, Rhodes Reason

43. "The Mystery of Minnie Francis McDonald" [adapted from the
article by George F. Worts; Reader's Digest December 1950,
pgs. 23-26] (2-6-56)

44. "Texas in New York" [adapted from To Teach Is to Love by
Cordelia Baird Gross; Reader's Digest November 1955, pgs.
35-39] (2-13-56) Marilyn Erskine

45. "Return from Oblivion" [adapted from A Sick Mind Finds Itself
by Leonard Wallace Robinson; Reader's Digest November
1955, pgs. 41-45] (2-20-56) Lyle Bettger, Emerson Treacy

46. "The Case of the Uncertain Hand" [adapted from the article by
Hannah F. Sulner; Reader's Digest May 1954; pgs. 133-136]
(2-27-56) Marguerite Chapman

47. "Lost, Strayed and Lonely" [adapted from the Joseph Eckert
condensation of his novel The Practicing of Christopher;
Reader's Digest May 1947, pgs. 153-176] (3-5-56) Billy
Chapin, Philip Terry

48. "Night Court" [adapted from Your Day in Court--Will It Be
Fair? by James Finan; Reader's Digest February 1952, pgs.
5-10] (3-12-56) John Archer

49. "No Horse, No Wife, No Mustache" [adapted from the J. P.
McEvoy article; Reader's Digest November 1955, pgs. 75-
80] (3-19-56) Bobby Driscoll

50. "The Trigger Finger-Clue" [adapted from the J. Edgar Hoover
article on the solving of the Lamer, Colorado bank murders;
Reader's Digest June 1947, pgs. 65-68] (3-26-56) Elisha
Cook, Louis Jean Heydt, Gloria Marshall

51. "The Secret Weapon of Joe Smith" [adapted from the Robert
Wallace article; Reader's Digest January 1953, pgs. 15-17;
article originally appeared in Harper's September 1952]
(4-2-56) Louis Jean Heydt

52. "Courage" [adapted from the Felix Holt article; Reader's Digest
September 1952, pgs. 133-136] (4-9-56) John Howard

53. "The Woman Who Changed Her Mind" [adapted from the Fulton
Oursler article; Reader's Digest June 1952, pgs. 129-132]
(4-16-56) Marilyn Erskine, Marshall Thompson, Victor
Jory

54. "Uncle Sam's C-Men" [adapted from the Frederick Sondern Jr.
article; Reader's Digest January 1949, pgs. 111-115; article
originally appeared in the American Mercury January 1949]
(4-23-56) Roy Roberts

55. "Miss Victoria" [adapted from the Patricia Strauss article;
Reader's Digest October 1942, pgs. 123-125; article origi-
nally appeared in Vogue, May 15, 1942] (4-30-56) Judith
Evelyn

56. "The Old, Old Story" [adapted from the Adela Rogers St. Johns
article; Reader's Digest April 1951, pgs. 14-18] (5-7-56)
Rosemary De Camp, June Kenney, Martin Milner

57. "Britain's Most Baffling Murder Case" [adapted from the Anthony Abbot article on the question of the William Wallace murder charge; Reader's Digest March 1950, pgs. 88-92] (5-14-56) Anthony Evertrel

58. "Down on the Tennessee" [adapted from the Richard Pike Bissell article; Reader's Digest March 1950, pgs. 39-45; article originally appeared in the Atlantic Monthly January 1950] (5-21-56) Richard Long, Thurston Hall

59. "The Man Who Dreamt Winners" [adapted from Tell Me the Next One by John Godley; Reader's Digest December 1952, pgs. 136-140] (5-28-56) Robert Hutton, Joyce Holden

60. "The General's Escape" [adapted from Giraud's Brilliant Escape from a Nazi Prison by Frederick C. Painton; Reader's Digest September 1943, pgs. 61-64] (6-4-56) George Macready

61. "The Gigantic Blacknote Swindle" [adapted from The Great Portuguese Banknote Swindle by Frederick Sondern Jr.; Reader's Digest April 1955, pgs. 65-70] (6-11-56) Victor Jory, Paul Stewart, Carole Kelly

62. "Go Fight City Hall" [adapted from The Little Man Who Got Mad by Karl Detzer; Reader's Digest March 1948, pgs. 100-102; article originally appeared in the Kiwanis magazine] (6-18-56) Gene Raymond, Jean Byron

63. "Family Reunion, U.S.A." [adapted from the Andrew Hamilton article; Reader's Digest March 1956, pgs. 189-194; article originally appeared in Kiwanis February 1956] (6-25-56) John Bailer, Helen Mowery

64. "The Only Way Out" [adapted from the Claus Gaedemann and Robert Cittell article; Reader's Digest September 1955, pgs. 93-98] (7-2-56) Arthur Franz, Paul Stewart

65. "The Smugglers" [adapted from A Mistake Doesn't Have to Be Final by Joseph Phillips; Reader's Digest May 1956, pgs. 65-68] (7-9-56) Bobby Driscoll, Richard Loo, Keye Luke

THE MILLIONAIRE

As derived from Robert H. Andrews' If I Had a Million (first the basis for a 1932 Paramount film), these studies of nobles, fools and profligates, all recipients of a million-dollar slice of John Beresford Tipton's estate, were to prove the success formula for mid-1950's interrelated teleplays. For in the dubious Hollywood ethic inheritors not by birthright are by and large a boorish lot; herewith two hundred and five reasons upholding noblesse oblige.

The Regulars: Michael Anthony: Marvin Miller.

The Episodes:

1. "Millionaire Amy Moore" (1-19-55) Toni Gerry, Ray Galli, John Archer, Ray Gordon

2. "Millionaire Carl Nelson" (1-26-55) Arthur Franz, Beverly Garland, William Forrest, John Gallaudet
3. "Millionaire Joe Iris" (2-2-55) John Hudson, Nancy Gates, Walter Coy, Frank Richards, Robert B. Williams
4. "The Story of Dan Mulcahy" (2-9-55) James Flavin, Nora Marlowe, Jane Ficher, Olaf Hytten, Harry Tyler
5. "The Story of Emily Short" (2-16-55) Carolyn Jones
6. "The Story of Margaret Browning" (2-23-55) Fay Baker, Nan Leslie
7. "The Story of Harvey Blake" (3-2-55) Jay Novello, Joe Besser, John Dehner
8. "The Story of Nancy Marlborough" (3-9-55) Ellen Corby, Richard Jaeckel, Paul Cavanagh, Frank Scannell, Frank Marlowe
9. "The Story of Betty Jane Ryan" (3-16-55) Jean Byron, Richard Garland, John Howard
10. "The Story of Charles Lamar" (3-23-55) Lamont Johnson, Jean Howell, John Wengraf, Irene Tedrow
11. "The Story of Ken Fowler" (3-30-55) Sallie Brophy, Whitfield Connor
12. "The Story of Pev Johnson" (4-6-55) Arthur Shields, Eleanora Tannen, Lennie Freeman
13. "The Story of Quentin Harwood" (4-13-55) Robert Cornthwaite, Barbara Eller
14. "The Story of Fred Malcolm" (4-20-55) Les Tremayne, Marjorie Reynolds, Jill Jarmyn, Liam Sullivan, Herbert Heyes
15. "The Story of Luke Fortune" (4-27-55) Hugh O'Brian, Coleen Gray
16. "The Story of Jack Martin" (5-4-55) Paul Langton, Phyllis Coates, John Alvin
17. "The Story of Walter Carter" (5-11-55) Edmund Gwenn, Julie Jordan, Rand Brooks
18. "The Story of Merle Roberts" (5-18-55) Vera Miles, James Bell, Robert Quarry, Jacqueline de Witt, Charles Kane
19. "The Story of Uncle Robby" (5-25-55) Percy Helton, Barbara Bates, John Bryant
20. "The Story of Sam Donovan" (6-1-55) Robert Nichols, Barbara Bestar
21. "The Story of Vickie Lawson" (6-8-55) Phyllis Avery, Craig Stevens, Hillary Brooke, Roy Corden
22. "The Story of Cobb Marley" (6-15-55) Donald Woods, Mary Field, Lloyd Corrigan, Judith Ames, Roy Gordon
23. "The Story of Mildred Milliken" (6-22-55) Hildy Parks, Jess Barker, Del Moore, Helen Westcott, Helen Spring, James Hawley

Second Season

24. "The Story of Rita Keeley" (9-28-55) Joan Vohs
25. "The Robert Croft Story" (10-5-55) Warren Stevens, Randy Stuart, Walter Reed, Sara Haden
26. "Millionaire Joe Seaton" (10-12-55) Eddie Firestone, Thomas Browne-Henry, Joan Sudlow
27. "Millionaire Iris Miller" (10-19-55) Virginia Grey, Olive Sturgess, DeForrest Kelley, Carlyle Mitchell, Gilmore Bush

28. "The Story of Tom Bryan" (11-2-55) James Daly, Billy Chapin, Gladys Hurlbut, June Vincent
29. "The Story of Peggy Demos" (11-9-55) Virginia Gibson, Philip Pine
30. "The Story of Jerome Wilson" (11-16-55) Christopher Dark, Maxine Cooper, Fay Roope, Ross Elliott
31. "The Story of Nora Paul" (11-23-55) Katherine Bard, Olive Blakeney, Bart Burns, Clark Howat
32. "The Story of Steve Carey" (11-30-55) Gene Barry, Edna Skinner, James Seay, Maureen Stephenson
33. "The Story of Don Lewis" (12-7-55) Robert Hutton, Joan Weldon, Marian Carr, Jean G. Harvey
34. "The Story of Jeff Ellis" (12-14-55) Ed Kemmer, Carl Milletaire, Nancy Howard, Ted Jacques
35. "The Story of Wilbur Gerrold" (12-21-55) Rhys Williams, Cheerio Meredith, Michael Bryant, Evelynne Eaton
36. "The Story of Philip Sargent" (12-28-55) Elliott Reid, Marjie Miller, Norman Willis, Robert Forrest
37. "The Reverend Hardin Story" (1-11-56) Carl Benton Reid, John Craven, Marion Ross, Brad Morrow
38. "The Cindy Bowen Story" (1-18-55) Fran Bennett, Michael Emmett, Nancy Hadley, Ina Poindexter
39. "The Jean Griffith Story" (1-25-56) Marcia Henderson, Steve Dunne, Dorothy Bernard
40. "The Dr. Larry Evans Story" (2-1-56) Herbert Patterson, Darlene Fields, James Todd, Gordon Mills
41. "The Brian Hendricks Story" (2-8-56) Leif Erickson, Carole Matthews, Larry Dobkin, Jean Vaughn
42. "The Arthur Darner Story" (2-15-56) Denver Pyle, Nancy Hale, Sandy White, Jean Dante, Kay Stewart
43. "The Story of Victor Volante" (2-22-56) Touch (Michael) Connors, Richard Eyer, Adele Mara, Jack LaRue, Eleanor Moore
44. "The Candy Caldwell Story" (2-29-56) Peggie Castle, Todd Griffin, Irene Hervey, John Stephenson, Lyn Guild
45. "The Rip Matson Story" (3-7-56) Steve Brodie, Cathy Downs, Stacy Harris
46. "The Rita Hanley Story" (3-14-56) Karen Steele, Robert Lowery, Beverly Washburn, Helen Andrews, Robert Burton
47. "The Eric Vincent Story" (3-21-56) James Anderson, Carol Stone, Hurd Hatfield
48. "The Bedelia Buckley Story" (3-28-56) Ellen Corby, Robert Bray, Adrienne Marden, Sue George
49. "The Tom Mead Story" (4-4-56) John Larch, Claudia Barrett, Dorothy Patrick
50. "The Story of Lucky Swanson" (4-11-56) John Smith, Joyce Van Der Veen, Vladimir Sokoloff, Nora O'Mahony
51. "The Jane Costello Story" (4-18-56) Ann Doran, Joan Evans, Corey Allen, Hayden Roarke
52. "The Ed Murdock Story" (4-25-56) Don Haggerty, Martha Vickers, Robert Faulk, Jon Shepodd
53. "The Louise Williams Story" (5-2-56) Vanessa Brown, William Ching, Scott Forbes, Beverly Willis
54. "The Todd Burke Story" (5-9-56) Adam Williams, Gloria

Talbott, Olive Carey, Joan Sudlow
55. "The Captain Carroll Story" (5-16-56) William Hopper, Aline Towne, Bill Phipps, Nelson Leigh, Ronald Anton
56. "The Sally Delaney Story" (5-23-56) Natalie Norwick, Ann Lee, Tod Andrews, Sue Carlton
57. "The Story of Olivia Grainger" (5-30-56) Frances Rafferty, Rex Reason, Jacqueline Holt
58. "The Jill Mayfield Story" (6-6-56) Joan Camden, Peter Hanson, Gail Kobe, Barbara Fuller
59. "The Ralph McKnight Story" (6-13-56) Richard Crenna, Claude Akins, Jeanne Baird

Third Season

60. "The Kathy Munson Story" (9-12-56) Barbara Hale, Bill Williams, William Roerick
61. "The Story of Jane Carr" (9-19-56) Angie Dickinson, James Craig, Tom McKee
62. "The Story of Anna Hartley" (9-26-56) Constance Ford, Peter Graves, Maria Palmer, Reta Shaw
63. "The Story of Charlie Simpson" (10-3-56) James Gleason, John Qualen, Taylor Holmes
64. "The Story of Fred Graham" (10-10-56) Jack Kelly, Cynthia Baxter, Lyle Talbot
65. "The Story of Virginia Lennart" (10-24-56) Betty White, Jacques Bergerac, Mabel Albertson, Mimi Aguglia, Franco Corsaro
66. "The Story of Joey Diamond" (10-31-56) Vic Morrow, Judith Braun, John Vick, Aaron Spelling
67. "The Story of David Tremayne" (11-7-56) Douglas Odney, Ann Robinson, Lurene Tuttle, Douglas Spencer
68. "The Story of Waldo Francis Turner" (11-14-56) Reginald Gardiner, Kathy Nolan, John Goddard, Raymond Greenleaf
69. "The Story of Jay Powers" (11-21-56) Robert Vaughn, Merry Anders, Raymond Bailey, James Hong
70. "The Story of Harvey Borden" (11-28-56) Patrick O'Neal, Peggy Knudsen, Chris Olsen, Herbert Butterfield
71. "The Story of Valerie Hunt" (12-5-56) Annie Kimball, Marshall Thompson, Richard Shannon, Barbara Knudsen, Harry Tyler
72. "The Story of Salvatore Michaelangelo Buonarotti" (12-12-56) Frank Puglia, Penny Santon, Nestor Paiva
73. "The Story of Mildred Kester" (12-19-56) Peggy Webber, Fred Wayne, K. T. Stevens
74. "The Story of Betty Perkins" (12-26-56) Inger Stevens, Philip Reed, Amzie Strickland
75. "The Story of Nick Cannon" (1-2-57) William Campbell, Kasey Rogers, Robert Clark, Otto Waldis
76. "The Story of Nancy Wellington" (1-9-57) Anita Louise, Lisa Montell, Peter Cookson, Alberto Morin, Isobel Withers
77. "The Story of Russell Herbert" (1-16-57) Lewis Martin, Mari Aldon, Paul Dubov, Milton Parsons
78. "The Story of Anton Bohrman" (1-23-57) Charles Korvin, Kristine Miller, Morris Ankrum, John Maxwell, Dick Tretter

79. "The Story of Charles Wyatt" (1-30-57) James Bell, George Wallace, Susan Cummings, Edith Evanson
80. "The Story of Jim Driskill" (2-6-57) Jim Davis, Jody Lawrence, Bill Cassidy, Frank Gerstle
81. "The Story of Professor Amberson Adams" (2-13-57) Robert Rockwell, Gale Robbins, Alan Hale, Richard Deacon, Benny Rubin
82. "The Story of Judge William Westholme" (2-20-57) Harry Shannon, Elisha Cook, Marilyn Buferd, Will J. White
83. "The Story of Jerry Bell" (2-27-57) Charles Bronson, Georgann Johnson, Louise Lorimar, Harvey Stephens
84. "The Story of Jerry Patterson" (3-6-57) Richard Webb, Strother Martin, Marianne Stewart
85. "The Story of Jimmy Reilly" (3-13-57) John Lupton, Janice Rule
86. "The Story of Rose Russell" (3-27-57) Jane Nigh, Carl Betz, Robert Foulk, Robert Cabal
87. "Millionaire Doctor Alan March" (4-3-57) Tom Drake, Allison Hayes, Walter Baldwin, Morgan Jones, Dorothy Morris
88. "Millionaire Crystal Sands" (4-10-57) Barbara Ruick, Kim Spalding, Liam Sullivan, Lisa Davis, Nora Hayden, Dori Simmons
89. "Millionaire Maggie Sheeler" (4-17-57)
90. "Millionaire Carol Wesley" (4-24-57) Norma Crane, Michael Pate, Victoria Ward, Lillian Bronson
91. "The Hub Grimes Story" (5-1-57)
92. "The Chris Daniels Story" (5-8-57) Murray Hamilton
93. "The Josef Marton Story" (5-15-57) Helmut Dantine, Violet Rensing, Eugene Martin, John Gallaudet
94. "The Ted McAllister Story" (5-22-57) Barry Atwater, Ray Stricklyn, Marian Seldes, John Carlyle
95. "The Dan Larsen Story" (5-29-57) Don Beddoe, Christine White, Helen Spring, Jerome Courtland, Douglas Dick, Walter Woolf King
96. "The Diane Loring Story" (6-5-57) Tracey Roberts, Anthony George, Donna Martell, Billy Snyder, Jason Johnson
97. "The Bob Fielding Story" (6-12-57) Jerry Paris, Kathleen Case, Isabel Randolph, James McCallum, Henry Cordon, Stafford Repp

Fourth Season

98. "The Story of Matt Kirby" (9-18-57) Carolyn Jones, Jeff Morrow, Marie Brown, Howard Wendell
99. "The Pete Marlowe Story" (9-25-57) Regis Toomey
100. "The Roy Delbridge Story" (10-2-57) Harry Guardino, Jeanne Cooper, Celia Lovsky
101. "The Story of Carl Bronson" (10-9-57)
102. "The Laura Hunter Story" (10-16-57) Mari Blanchard, Logan Field, John Vivyan, Sid Clute, Ralph Peters
103. "The Larry Parker Story" (10-23-57) Joseph Waring, Barbara Eller, Kristie Miller, James Douglas
104. "The Ruth Ferris Story" (10-30-57) Joan Banks, Joe Maross,

Bethel Leslie
105. "The Story of Hap Connolly" (11-13-57) Malcolm Broderick, Royal Dano, Zoe Hazlett, David McMahon, Wheaton Chambers
106. "The Story of Frank Keegan" (11-20-57) Frank Jenks, Catherine McLeod, Johnny Crawford
107. "The Story of Larry Smart" (11-27-57)
108. "Millionaire Anitra Dellano" (12-4-57) Karen Sharpe, Keith Larsen, Penny Edwards, Kathleen O'Malley, Nan Boardman
109. "The Story of Hugh Waring" (12-11-57) Dick Foran, Jewel Lain, Jorja Curtwright, Sydney Smith, Denis McCarthy, Charles Evans, Larry Kerr, Pierre Watkin
110. "Millionaire Barbara Lydon" (12-18-57) Diane Brewster, George Dolenz, Louis Jean Heydt
111. "The Regina Wainwright Story" (12-25-57) Frieda Inescourt, David Janssen, Marcia Henderson
112. "The Rod Matthews Story" (1-1-58) Richard Anderson, Lee Meriwether, Larry Dobkin, Carlyle Mitchell
113. "The Marjorie Martinson Story" (1-8-58) Virginia Grey, Russ Conway, Frank Albertson, Tony Barrett, Vivi Janiss, Eleanor Audley, Norma Dehaan, Jack Herrin
114. "The Peter Barkley Story" (1-15-58) John Ericson, Jeanette Nolan, Johnny Washbrook
115. "The Jonathan Bookman Story" (1-22-58) John Baragrey
116. "The Doris Winslow Story" (1-29-58) Joanna Moore, Larry Pennell, Rebecca Welles, Roland Winters, Jo Gilbert, Dick Ryan, Tyler McVey
117. "The Michael Holm Story" (2-5-58) Gene Lyons, Elaine Edwards, Harry Bellaver
118. "The Martha Crockett Story" (2-15-58) Margaret Lindsay, Jay Novello, Ronnie Patterson
119. "The John Richards Story" (2-26-58) Patrick McVey, Linda Leighton, Steve Terrell
120. "The Johanna Judson Story" (3-5-58) June Dayton, Richard Long, Reta Shaw
121. "The Raymond Dupar Story" (3-12-58) Biff Elliott, Anita Gordon
122. "The Neal Bowers Story" (3-19-58) Peter Hanson, Martin Milner, Joyce Meadows, Roger Til
123. "The John Smith Story" (3-26-58) Richard Garland, Carole Mathews, James Griffith, John Harmon
124. "The Susan Birchard Story" (4-2-58) Luana Patten
125. "The Tony Drummond Story" (4-9-58) Tom Tryon, Fay Spain, John Eldredge, Jon Lormer
126. "The Story of the Thorne Sisters" (4-16-58) Lillian Bronson, Frances Morris, Lurene Tuttle, Howard McNear
127. "The Rafe Peterson Story" (4-23-58) Ron Randell
128. "The Story of Andrew Sterling" (4-30-58) Ernest Truex, Jackie Loughery, Sylvia Field, Dean Harens
129. "The Wally Bannister Story" (5-7-58) Skip Homeier
130. "The Jack Garrison Story" (5-14-58) Rick Jason, Joan Marshall, Carl Betz
131. "The Paul Naylor Story" (5-21-58) John Beal, Joy Hodges
132. "The Russ White Story" (5-28-58) Lee Farr

Fifth Season

133. "The Betty Hawley Story" (9-3-58) Lisa Daniels, Richard
     Jaeckel, Don Kennedy
134. "The Norman Cornover Story" (9-10-58) Leif Erickson, Mar-
     guerite Chapman, Bobby Driscoll
135. "The Fred Morgan Story" (9-17-58) James Best, Karen
     Steele, Barry Cahill, John Truex
136. "The Ken Leighton Story" (9-24-58) Dick York, Joan Vohs,
     George Neise
137. "The David Barrett Story" (10-1-58) David Janssen, Torin
     Thatcher, Dorothy Provine, K. L. Smith
138. "The Martin Scott Story" (10-8-58) Patric Knowles, Margaret
     Hayes
139. "The Ellen Curry Story" (10-15-58) Audrey Dalton, Kevin
     Del-Grande, Sheridan Comerate
140. "The William Vaugh Story" (10-22-58) Edgar Buchanan
141. "The Cat Story" (10-29-58) Del Moore, Jean Willes, Lois
     Bridge, Charles Lane, Gregory Gay, Richard Reeves
142. "The Dan Howell Story" (11-5-58) Steve Dunne, Celia Whit-
     ney, Harry Landers, James Seay, Thomas B. Henry
143. "The Newman Johnson Story" (11-12-58) Orson Bean, Sue
     Randall, Douglass Dumbrille, Amzie Strickland
144. "The Lee Randolph Story" (11-19-58) Jack Lord, Robert
     Rockwell
145. "The Frank Harrigan Story" (12-3-58) Arthur Franz, Virginia
     Leith, Joan Granville
146. "The Pete Hopper Story" (12-10-58) William Bishop, Carol
     Ohmart, Robert Eyer, Carl Milletaire, Kenneth Alton, Robert
     Nash
147. "Millionaire Eric Lodek" (12-17-58) Stephen Bekassy, Ray
     Danton, Chana Eden, Tommy Vize
148. "Millionaire William Coutney" (1-7-59) Pat Conway, Sally
     Pearce, Richard Ney, Harry Lauter, William Vaughan
149. "Millionaire Terrence Costigan" (1-14-59) Charles Winninger,
     Sue George, Skip Ward, Maudie Prickett, Frank London
150. "Millionaire Irene Marshall" (1-21-59) Jan Clayton, James
     Griffith, John Stephenson, John Hoyt, Richard Travis
151. "Millionaire Julie Conrad" (1-28-59) Robert Alda, Ellen
     Drew, Raymond Bailey
152. "Millionaire Emily Baker" (2-4-59) Sally Forrest, John Lup-
     ton, Frank Puglia, Ezelle Poule
153. "Millionaire John Rackman" (2-11-59) Don Dubbins, Gloria
     Castillo, Abraham Sofaer, David R. Cross
154. "Millionaire Father Gilhooley" (2-18-59) Cecil Kellaway,
     Lillian Powell, John Wilder, Donald Foster
155. "Millionaire Hank Butler" (2-25-59) Robert Knapp, Patricia
     Barry, Lynn Bernay, Richard Gaines, Martha Wentworth,
     Helene Hawley
156. "Millionaire Angela Temple" (3-4-59) Ruta Lee, Dennis Pat-
     rick, John Duke, William Fawcett, Robert Paquin
157. "Millionaire Charlie Weber" (3-11-59) Joe Mantell, Virginia
     Vincent, George Wallace, Ken Christy, Phil Arnold
158. "Millionaire Alicia Osante" (3-18-59) Rita Moreno, Ben

Cooper, Mary Ford, Liliane Taelemans
159. "Millionaire Marcia Forrest" (3-25-59) Nancy Gates, Gene Nelson
160. "Millionaire Henny Banning" (4-1-59) Jim Backus, Lee Aaker, Fay McKenzie, Paul Langton, Ernest Anderson, Olan Soule, Robert Burton, Sid Melton
161. "Millionaire Sally Simms" (4-8-59) Venetia Stevenson, Elisabeth Fraser, Elliott Reid, Mason Alan Dinehart, Rodney Bell, Bob Turnbull
162. "Millionaire Ann Griffin" (4-15-59) Ann Cord, Ronnie Burns, Whit Bissell, Ernestine Barrier
163. "Millionaire Karl Miller" (4-22-59) John Carradine, Jean Allison, Paul Burke
164. "Millionaire Gilbert Burton" (4-29-59) Carleton Carpenter, Dolores Donlon, Grant Williams, Sid Clute
165. "Millionaire Susan Ballard" (5-6-59) Patricia Breslin, Rhodes Reason
166. "Millionaire Bill Franklin" (5-13-59) Kent Smith, Virginia Field, John Van Dreelen, Carol Morris, Marc Platt, Monty Margetts
167. "Millionaire Louise Benson" (5-20-59) Beverly Garland, Don Gordon, Robert Boon, Greta Granstedt, Marshall Kent
168. "Millionaire Martha Halloran" (5-27-59) Pat Donahue, Bill Williams, Clifford, Stephen Roberts
169. "Millionaire Charles Bradwell" (6-10-59) Frank McHugh, Tommy Kirk, Carol Nugent, Mary La Roche

Sixth Season

170. "Millionaire Mark Fleming" (9-16-59) Martin Milner, Anna-Lisa, Celia Lovsky, Edit Angold, Robert Schiller
171. "Millionaire Harry Brown" (9-23-59) Dean Miller, Marcia Henderson, Charles Herbert, Judy Nugent, Jack Straw
172. "Millionaire Lorraine Daggett" (9-30-59) Lori Nelson, Charles Aidman, Richard Shannon, Nick Georgiade, Jack Lambert
173. "Millionaire Phillip Burnell" (10-7-59) Scott Forbes, Susan Oliver, Angela Stevens, Linda Leighton
174. "Millionaire Doctor Joseph Frye" (10-21-59) Tod Andrews, Frances Helm, Frank Gorshin, Jean Carson
175. "Millionaire Jim Hayes" (10-28-59) Tommy Noonan, Phyllis Avery
176. "Millionaire Maureen Reynolds" (11-4-59) Christine White, Robert Fortier, Marshall Thompson, Martin Garralaga
177. "Millionaire Jeff Mercer" (11-11-59) Dennis Kohler, Toni Gerry, Pete Marshall
178. "Millionaire Tom Hampton" (11-18-59) William Campbell, Ann Baker, Francis Morris
179. "Millionaire Sergeant Matthew Brogan" (11-25-59) Bert Freed, Rex Holman, Ron Ely
180. "Millionaire Mitchell Gunther" (12-2-59)
181. "Millionaire Andrew C. Cooley" (12-9-59) Andy Clyde, Joan Taylor, Edmund Penney, John Galludet, Frank Wilcox, Lee Kross, Jeff Daley

182. "Millionaire Nancy Pearson" (12-16-59) Connie Hines, Darryl Hickman, Abbey Shelton, Robert O'Connor
183. "Millionaire Jackson Greene" (12-23-59) Adam Williams, Joanna Moore, Patricia George, James Bacon, Dick Patterson, John Eldredge
184. "Millionaire Timothy Mackail" (12-30-59) William Reynolds, Suzanne Lloyd, James Coburn, William Boyett
185. "Millionaire Elizabeth Tander" (1-6-60) June Dayton, Patrick O'Neal, Vaughn Taylor
186. "Millionaire Sylvia Merrick" (1-13-60) Diane Brewster, Richard Lupino, Wayne Rogers, Robert Griffin, Janet Lord, Flip Mark
187. "Millionaire Whitney Ames" (1-20-60) Frances Bergen, Robert Paige, Anita Sands, Elvia Allman, Julie Van Zandt
188. "Millionaire Janie Harris" (1-27-60) Mary Murphy, Jeffrey Stone, Sue England, Penny Edwards
189. "Millionaire Margaret Stoneham" (2-3-60) Mona Freeman, James Franciscus, Florence Ravenal, Frances DeSales, Henry Hunter
190. "Millionaire Jerry Mitchell" (2-10-60) George Grizzard, Dan Tobin, Walter Reed, Lisa Gaye, Dani Nolan
191. "Millionaire Sandy Newell" (2-17-60) Dick York, Robert Easton, Mary Webber, Susan Dorn, Jack Chefe, Willard Sage
192. "Millionaire Larry Maxwell" (3-2-60) Larry Pennell, Patricia Barry, Don Drysdale, Fred Haney, Gregg Martell, Janet Stewart
193. "Millionaire Karen Summers" (3-9-60) Joanna Barnes, Edward Kemmer, Gertrude Flynn, Monty Margetts, Monica Keating
194. "Millionaire Jessica Marsh" (3-16-60) Rachel Ames, Sam Flint, Gregg Palmer, Frank Maxwell
195. "Millionaire Julie Sherman" (3-23-60) Barbara Lawson, Dennis Hopper, Alex Gerry, Jack Larson, Robert Gibbons
196. "Millionaire Tony Rogers" (3-30-60) Joe Cronin, Stubby Kaye, Jean Ingram, Roy Engel
197. "Millionaire Susan Johnson" (4-6-60) Sherry Jackson, John Ashley, Frank Jenks, Ann Doran, Sheila James
198. "Millionaire Nancy Cortez" (4-13-60) Whitney Blake, Gustavo Rojo, Lou Merrill, Rafael Lopez, Tom Hernandez, Joseph Sanchez
199. "Millionaire Katherine Boland" (4-20-60) Agnes Moorehead, Tuesday Weld, Jerome Cowan, Bob Newkirk
200. "Millionaire Mara Robinson" (4-27-60) Debra Paget, Rick Jason, Isabel Elsom, Edgar Barrier
201. "Millionaire Dixon Cooper" (5-4-60) Dick Sargent, Virginia Gibson, Marjorie Reynolds, Russell Pennell, John Bangert
202. "Millionaire Vance Ludlow" (5-11-60) Jock Mahoney, Louise Fletcher, Mary Tyler Moore, William A. Forester, Barbara Woodell, William Bakewell
203. "Millionaire Peter Longman" (5-25-60) Robert Harland, Susan Cummings, Paul Dubov, Emile Meyer, Harlan Warde
204. "Millionaire Maggie Dalton" (6-1-60) Joan Camden, Ron Ran-

dell, Natalie Masters, Dick Wilson, Roger Til
205. "Millionaire Patricia Collins" (6-8-60) Joan Vohs, Mark Miller, Joseph Holland, Ralph Clanton, Ben Erway

MR. CITIZEN

Suffused with McCarthyism, though the vital force had collapsed, a nation sought a redress of wrongs through homage paid the heroics of individual citizens. Here then the video laudation, where telephone pole jumper ("High Rescue") and railroad passenger ("Late for Supper") have their ministrations accorded their share of esteem.

The Episodes:

1. "Late for Supper" (4-20-55) Hal Holbrook, Cathy Wheeler, Nancy Kenyon; Senator Clifford P. Case of New Jersey, guest
2. "Seven Below at Midnight" (4-27-55) Frances Starr
3. "Second Class Citizens" [a documentary drama of Mrs. Clarice Streeyer's efforts on behalf of epileptics] (5-4-55) Anita Bayless, Sandy Horn, William Bush, Tom Reynolds
4. "Man with a Conscience" [documentary drama of Air Force Sergeant Charles Badger's efforts on behalf of a war widow] (5-11-55) Miriam Laserson, Rod Colbin, Theo Goetz
5. "A Present for Mary" [documentary drama of Bill Hennessey's efforts on behalf of an abject child] (5-18-55) William Gargan (as Hennessey)
6. "High Rescue" (5-25-55) James Daly, Ronnie Fletcher
7. "Terror on Jack Rabbit Hill" (6-1-55) Edward Binns; Harold B. Miller presents an award.
8. "The Friendly Stranger" (6-8-55) Paul Lukas, Miriam Laserson, Carl Swenson
9. "One for the Padre" [by Robert J. Shaw; Judge Samuel S. Leibowitz presents an award to Msgr. D. J. Kanaly] (6-15-55) John Gibson, Wendell Holmes
10. "The Inner Vision" (6-22-55) William Redfield; Major General Robert E. Hogaboon presents an award.
11. "Trouble in Gallery Five" (6-29-55) Lin McCarthy
12. "For My Brother" (7-6-55) Jane Rose
13. "The Door Is Always Open" (7-13-55) Anne Seymour

STAR TONIGHT

The Episodes:

1. "You Need Me" (2-3-55) Jacqueline Holt, Kevin McCarthy
2. "The Week-end" (2-10-55) Darryl Grimes, John Conte, Peg Hillias, Judy Parrish

3. "Concerning Death" [adapted from the John Collier story] (2-17-55) Edward Andrews, Jo Van Fleet
4. "How Beautiful the Shoes" [adapted from the short story by Wilbur Daniel Steele] (2-24-55) John Baragrey, Lois Smith
5. "Zone of Quiet" [adapted from the Ring Lardner short story] (3-3-55) Patricia Englund, William McGuire
6. "Ile" [adapted from the Eugene O'Neill drama] (3-10-55) Perry Wilson, Philip Kenneally, Luis Van Rooten, Bruce Gordon
7. "The Murderer" [based upon the two-character suspense drama by Joe Townsley Rogers] (3-17-55) Charles Aidman, Buster Crabbe
8. "A Matter of Life" (3-24-55) Lois Smith
9. "Death of a Stranger" [adapted from the Rupert Brooke drama Lithuania] (3-31-55) Joanne Woodward, Vaughn Taylor
10. "Treasure Trove" [adapted from the short story by Fryniwyd Tennyson Jesse] (4-7-55) Pat Sully
11. "The Lavender Kite" (4-14-55) Margaret Feury, Edward Binns
12. "The Giant's Stair" [adapted from the Wilbur Daniel Steele story] (4-21-55)
13. "Zero Hour" [adapted from the Ray Bradbury science fiction story] (4-28-55)
14. "The Dark Search" [by Jay Fresson] (5-5-55) Ruth Ford
15. "Second String" [by Chester Hadley] (5-12-55) Jeff Harris
16. "Tender Roots" [by Gilbert Braun and William Welch] (5-19-55) John A. Washbrook
17. "Golden Victory" (5-26-55) Sue Randall, Kathleen Comegys
18. "Taste" [adapted from the Roald Dahl short story] (6-2-55) Rudy Vallee, Leonard Elliott, Diana Millay, Violet Hemming
19. "Wanted--Poor Boy" [adapted from the Jerome Weidman short story] (6-9-55) Harold J. Stone
20. "Strength of Steel" [by Rod Serling] (6-16-55) Frederick Tozere, Wyatt Cooper, Jim Holden
21. "Cross-Words" (6-23-55) Ethel Remey, Kim Hunter, Dennis Patrick, Ann Dere
22. "Gallant Lady" [by Florence Ryerson and Collin Clements] (6-30-55) Virginia Kaye, Maureen Stapleton, Peter Cookson, Philip Huston
23. "Footfalls" [adapted from the short story by Wilbur Daniel Steele] (7-7-55) Theodore Bikel
24. "The Critic" [by Harry W. Junkin] (7-14-55) Philip Coolidge, James Broderick, Rebecca Sand, E. A. Krumschmidt, Shirley Grayson
25. "The Keupie Doll" [by Greer Johnson] (7-21-55) Joe Helgessen, Dorothy Peterson
26. "The Matrimony Shoppe" [by Gladys Seidelhuber] (7-28-55) Katherine Hynes, Leslie Barrie, Walter Burke
27. "Edge of Light" [by Robert J. Shaw] (8-4-55) Paul Roebling, Doreen Lang, Hugh Reilly
28. "The Ring of General Maclas" (8-1-55) Katharine Sergava, Miriam Colon, Gene Peterson
29. "The Prom" (8-11-55) Roni Dengel, David Anderson, Augusta Roeland, John Griggs

30. "Flame and Ice" (8-25-55) Jason Robards Jr., Gordon Dilworth, Joe Helgessen, Miko Oscard

Second Season

31. "Trifles" (9-1-55) Barbara Joyce, Roland Wood, Jane Seymour, Alan Nourse, Walter Klayton
32. "Success Story" [by Laurence Williams] (9-8-55) Fredrick Worlock
33. "Long Distance" (9-15-55) Neva Patterson, Ray Bramley, Frederic Downs
34. "Visitation" [adapted from the short story by James Ullman] (9-22-55) Burt Brinckerhoff, Lloyd Bochner
35. "The Terrible Woman" [adapted from the short story by Wilbur Daniel Steele] (9-29-55) Valerie Cossart, Joseph Warren, Judith Parrish
36. "Not for Me" [by Enid and Bernard Rudd] (10-6-55) Dora Weissman, Hildy Parks
37. "One Day More" [adapted from the Joseph Conrad story] (10-13-55) Scott Marlowe, Margaret Phillips, Frederic Worlock, Bramwell Fletcher
38. "The Little Wife" [adapted by David Shaw from the story by William March] (10-20-55) Joe Maross
39. "Finder's Keepers" (10-27-55) Marion Winters, Signe Hasso
40. "Night, Be Quiet" (11-3-55) Clifford David, Nancy Coleman, Buster Crabbe
41. "That Ryan Girl" [by Edmund Goulding] (11-10-55) Kay Medford, Dana White
42. "The Cage" (11-17-55) Patricia Collinge, Vaughn Taylor, Bruce Hall
43. "Have Faith in Your Agent" [by Judith Parrish] (11-24-55) Ernest Truex, Sylvia Field
44. "The Summer Road" (12-1-55) Don Dubbins, Joan Tetzel, Don Briggs
45. "Nightmare by Day" [by Anne Howard Bailey] (12-8-55) Doreen Lang, James Gregory
46. "Gang Up" [by Nicholas E. Baehr] (12-15-55) George Grizzard, Paul Carr, Polly Rowles
47. "The Selfish Giant" [adapted from the Oscar Wilde fable; narrated by Basil Rathbone] (12-22-55) George Mathews, Mia Slavenska
48. "Write Me a Love Scene" (12-29-55) Tom Middleton, Tom Helmore, Mary Boylan
49. "The Big Fifteenth" (1-5-56) Kenny Delmar, Peter Turgeon
50. "Glory with Honor" (1-12-56) Coe Norton, Kathleen Maguire
51. "A Night Visitor" (1-19-56)
52. "Early Frost" (1-26-56) Jada Rowland, Kathleen Comegys
53. "Below Average" (2-2-56) Dennis Patrick, Carl Law, Ray Brown, Robert Emhardt, Patricia Sully
54. "Happy Journey" [adapted from the Thornton Wilder play] (2-9-56) Elizabeth Wilson
55. "The Thing That Never Happened" [by Jane Barbour] (2-16-56) Nancy Malone

56. "Rite of Love" (2-23-56) Ralmonda Orsellis
57. "Three Hours Between Planes" [adapted from the F. Scott Fitz-gerald story] (3-1-56) Jack Manning, Nancy Coleman
58. "Night Escape" [by Abby Mann] (3-8-56) Frank Overton, Neva Patterson, Jerome Cowan
59. "Love Is a Lawyer" (3-15-56) Laurence Hugo, Mary Sinclair
60. "The Chevigny Man" (3-22-56) Robert Culp, Leora Dana, Leo G. Carroll
61. "Boy Crazy" (3-29-56) June Lockhart, Jason Robards Jr.
62. "Two Windows" (4-5-56) Diane Gentner, Richard Davalos
63. "A Door You Can Close" (4-12-56) Norma Crane, Signe Has-so, Margery MacDaniel
64. "An Ambulance for Jill" (4-19-56) Louise Platt, Chester Morris
65. "Tough Boy" (4-26-56) Richard Davalos
66. "Can You Coffeepot on Skates?" (5-3-56) Susan Harrison, Leo G. Carroll
67. "The Girl" (5-10-56) Patrick Macnee, Douglas Watson
68. "A Trip to Czardie" (5-17-56) Van Dyke Parks, Nancy Cole-man, Peter Lazer, Laurence Hugo
69. "Faith and Patience" (5-24-56) Horace MacMahon, Rosalind Paige
70. "Kingdom's Child" (5-31-56) Deirdre Owen
71. "A Small Glass Bottle" [by David Hill] (6-7-56) Abby Lewis, Harry Townes, Virginia Kaye
72. "The Long View" [by Kay Arthur] (6-14-56) Efrem Zimbalist Jr., Lois Holmes, Henry Hull
73. "The Ascent of P. J. O'Hara" (6-21-56) Dennis Patrick, Ed-die Dowling, Peter Lazer, Doreen Lang
74. "Mr. Bell's Creation" [adapted from the play by Stanley Rich-ards] (6-28-56) John Gibson, Virginia Vincent
75. "Shadow of Evil" (7-5-56) Charles Aidman, Lori March, John Shellie
76. "The Coffee Shop Incident" (7-12-56) Loretta Leversee, Joe Maross
77. "The Blood Call" (7-19-56) Michael Ingram, Lisa Daniels, Pamela Simpson
78. "Will Power" [by George Lowther] (7-26-56) Roy Fant, Diane Gentner
79. "The Gentleman Caller" (8-2-56) Ruth McDevitt, Don Hammer
80. "The Mirthmaker" (8-9-56) Al Hedison, Kenny Delmar

POND'S THEATRE [see also KRAFT TELEVISION THEATRE]

The Episodes:

1. "The Hickory Limb" [adapted from the John Van Druten play] (1-13-55) Mary Astor, Gene Raymond, Mildred Dunnock, Sylvia Sidney, Phyllis Love
2. "The Rugged Mountains" (1-20-55) Rex Thompson, Lori March
3. "The Cornered Man" (1-27-55) Dick Davalos, Buster Crabbe, Horace MacMahon

4. "Thirty, Honey, Thirty" (2-3-55) Charlotte Rae, Ernest Truex
5. "Prologue to Glory" [adapted from the E. P. Conkle play] (2-10-55) Del Yarnell (as Abraham Lincoln), Jane Walker, Russell Collins, Elizabeth Ross
6. "The Dover Road" [adapted from the A. A. Milne play] (2-17-55) John Cromwell, Leueen MacGrath, Larry Gates, Claudia Morgan
7. "The Second Chance" (2-24-55) Biff McGuire, Ed Begley, Jo-anne Roos
8. "Anna Christie" [adapted from the Eugene O'Neill play; directed by Fred Carney and sponsored by the J. Walter Thompson agency] (3-3-55) Constance Ford, Everett Sloane, James Daly
9. "Billy Budd" [adapted from the Herman Melville classic] (3-10-55) Geoffrey Horne, Joseph Wiseman, Luther Adler
10. "The Silver Box" [adapted from the John Galsworthy play] (3-17-55) Roddy McDowall, Tom Helmore
11. "Autumn Crocus" [adapted from the Dorothy Gladys Smith (C. L. Anthony) play] (3-24-55) Carmen Mathews, Harry Townes
12. "The Forger" [a satire on the New York theatre] (3-31-55) Kurt Kasznar, Leora Dana
13. "The Glass Parlor" [by Hal Hackady] (4-7-55) Polly Rowles
14. "No Riders" [by Wendell Mayes (the former actor's first tele-play)] (4-14-55) Jack Warden, Jose Perez
15. "Thunder Rock" [adapted from the Robert Ardrey Broadway play] (4-21-55) John Baragrey, George Voskovec, Alexander Scourby, Sally Chamberlin, June Dayton, Dan Morgan
16. "Hang Up My Guns" [by Wendell Mayes] (4-28-55) Harry Townes, Bruce Gordon, Bob Shawley
17. "Candle Light" [adapted from the Siegfried Geyer Broadway play] (5-5-55) Eva Gabor, John Baragrey, Michael Evans, Stiano Braggiotti, Rebecca Sand, Joan Wetmore
18. "Cynara" [adapted from the play and film by R. F. Gore-Browne and H. M. Harwood] (5-12-55) Joanne Woodward, E. G. Marshall, Ruth Matteson, Barbara Barrie, Patricia Englund, Murray Matheson
19. "The Ways of Courage" [by Will Lorin] (5-19-55) Philip Ab-bott, Edward Binns, Michael Gorrin, Jerome Kilty, Gene Saks, Edgar Stehli, Allen Nourse, Gena Rowlands
20. "The Kingdom of Andrew Jones" [by Robert J. Shaw] (5-26-55) George Macready, Audra Lindley, Bradford Dillman, Frances Brandt
21. "Erricka" [by Patricia Joudry] (6-2-55) Murray Matheson, Gaby Rodgers, Peter Turgeon
22. "Life and Taxes" [by Nelson Bond] (6-9-55) Alan Bunce, Pol-ly Rowles
23. "Mother Is Watching" [adapted by Patricia Joudry from a radio play] (6-16-55) Katherine Meskill, Julia Follansbee, Pa-tricia Benoit, Richard Kendrick, Lin McCarthy
24. "The Fascinating Stranger" [adapted by Elizabeth Hart from the Booth Tarkington play] (6-23-55) Larry Gates, Sidney Poi-tier, Parker McCormick, Nydia Westman
25. "Death Is a Spanish Dancer" [by Wendell Mayes; flamenco

dancing by Luis Olivares] (6-30-55) Cameron Prud'homme, Lee Grant, Luis Olivares

26. "Coquette" [adapted from the George Abbott play] (7-7-55) Joan Lorring, Cameron Prud'homme, John Cassavetes

THE CONRAD NAGEL THEATRE

The Regulars: Conrad Nagel, host.

The Episodes:

1. "The Queen of Spades" [adapted from the Alexander Pushkin story] (1-27-55) George Gonneau, Lenore Shanewise, Tom Middleton
2. "Ask Me No Questions" [adapted from the Honoré de Balzac story] (2-3-55) Sebastian Cabot, Faye Marlowe
3. "The Model Couple" (2-10-55) Peg LaCentra, Leslie Daniels
4. "A Bride for a Violin" (2-17-55) Lee Kresel, John Fostine, Judith Tutaeff
5. "The Storm" (2-24-55) Peter Trent, Mary Metcalf
6. "The Three Searchers" [adapted from the Geoffrey Chaucer story] (3-3-55) Sebastian Cabot, Adam Genette
7. "The Gypsy" (3-10-55)
8. "The House in the Sea" (3-17-55) Madelaine Chambers, Lenore Shanewise
9. "Clothes Make the Lady" (3-24-55) Gertrude Flynn, John Fostini, Dorothy Biasco
10. "The Idol" (3-31-55) Paul Campbell, Tonio Selwart
11. "To Whom It May Concern" (4-7-55)
12. "Of Pigs and Kings" (4-14-55)
13. "Contents Unlabeled" (4-17-55)
14. "The Sandman" (4-24-55) Walt Richter, Sebastian Cabot
15. "The Temple of Truth" (5-1-55) Fiorella Mari, Donald Buka
16. "Blakeman's Bottle" (5-8-55) Pat Crean, Christine Thorer
17. "In the Service of the Emperor" (5-15-55) Donald Buka, Faye Marlowe
18. "Carmen without Roses" (5-22-55) Rols Tasna, Stephen Garrett
19. "The Other Don Juan" (5-27-55) Donald Buka, Faye Marlowe
20. "Dear Evelina" (6-5-55) John Stacey, Gertrude Flynn
21. "The Jewels of Rosanna Higgins" (6-12-55) Pat Crean, Lou Bradley
22. "Guilette and Romeo" (6-19-55) Angela Carroll
23. "Tomorrow Is the Avenger" (6-26-55)
24. "Unknown Madonna" (7-6-55) Peg La Centra, Michael Tor
25. "The Visitor" [adapted by Robert Sterling from the Leo Tolstoi story] (7-13-55) Tonio Selwart, Cecil Mathews
26. "The Door to Darkness" (7-20-55) Henry Vidon, Cindy Ames, Bill Barker

SCIENCE FICTION THEATRE

The Regulars: Truman Bradley, host.

The Episodes:

1. "Beyond" (4-5-55) Tom Drake, Bruce Bennett, Ellen Drew, William Lundigan
2. "Time Is Just a Place" (4-15-55) Don DeFore, Marie Windsor
3. "No Food for Thought" (4-22-55) Otto Kruger, John Newland
4. "Out of Nowhere" (4-29-55) Richard Arlen
5. "Stranger in the Desert" (5-13-55) Marshall Thompson
6. "The Sound of Murder" (5-20-55) Howard Duff
7. "The Brain of John Emerson" (5-27-55) Ellen Drew, John Howard
8. "Spider, Incorporated" (6-3-55) Gene Barry, Audrey Totter, Ludwig Stossel
9. "Death at 2 A. M. " (6-10-55) John Qualen, Skip Homeier
10. "Conversation with an Ape" (6-17-55) Hugh Beaumont, Barbara Hale, Nancy Stanton
11. "Marked Danger" (6-24-55) Nancy Gates, Otto Kruger
12. "Hour of Nightmare" (7-1-55) Lynn Bari, William Bishop, Charles Evans
13. "The Strange Dr. Lorenz" (7-15-55) Donald Curtis, Kristine Miller, Edmund Gwenn
14. "One Hundred Years Young" (7-22-55) Ruth Hussey, John Archer, John Abbott
15. "The Frozen Sound" (7-29-55) Marshall Thompson, Marilyn Erskine, Ray Collins
16. "The Stones Began to Move" (8-12-55) Basil Rathbone
17. "The Lost Heartbeat" (8-19-55) Zachary Scott
18. "The World Below" (8-26-55) Gene Barry, Marguerite Chapman

Second Season

19. "Y. O. R. D. " (9-2-55)
20. "Barrier of Silence" (9-9-55) Adolph Menjou
21. "The Negative Man" (9-16-55) Dane Clark, Carl Switzer
22. "Dead Reckoning" (9-29-55) James Craig
23. "A Visit from Dr. Pliny" (9-30-55) Edmund Gwenn
24. "Dead Storage" (10-7-55) Virginia Bruce
25. "Strange People at Pecos" (10-14-55)
26. "The Human Equation" (10-21-55) Macdonald Carey
27. "Target: Hurricane" (10-28-55) Marshall Thompson, Ray Collins
28. "Water Maker" (11-4-55) Craig Stevens
29. "The Unexplored" (11-11-55) Kent Smith, Osa Massen
30. "The Hastings Secret" (11-18-55) Bill Williams, Barbara Hale
31. "Postcard from Barcelona" (11-25-55)
32. "Friend of a Raven" (12-2-55) Virginia Bruce
33. "Beyond Return" (12-9-55) Zachary Scott, Peter Hansen, Joan Vohs

34. "Before the Beginning" (12-16-55) Dane Clark
35. "The Long Day" (12-23-55) George Brent
36. "Project 44" (1-6-56) Bill Williams
37. "Are We Invaded?" (1-20-56) Pat O'Brien
38. "Operation: Flypaper" (2-3-56) Vincent Price
39. "The Other Side of the Moon" (2-17-56) Skip Homeier
40. "Signals from the Heart" (4-6-56) Peter Hansen, Joyce Holden, Walter Kingsford
41. "The Long Sleep" (4-13-56) Dick Foran
42. "Who Is This Man?" (4-20-56) Bruce Bennett, Harlow Wilcox, Charles Smith
43. "The Green Bomb" (4-27-56) Kenneth Tobey, Whit Bissell
44. "When a Camera Fails" (5-4-56) Gene Lockhart
45. "Bullet Proof" (5-11-56) Marshall Thompson
46. "The Flicker" (5-18-56) Victor Jory
47. "The Unguided Missile" (5-25-56) Ruth Hussey
48. "End of Tomorrow" (6-1-56) Christopher Dark, Dabbs Greer
49. "The Mind Machine" (6-8-56) Bill Williams
50. "The Missing Waveband" (6-15-56) Dick Foran
51. "The Human Experiment" (6-22-56) Marshall Thompson
52. "The Man Who Didn't Know" (6-29-56) Arthur Franz
53. "The Phantom Car" (7-20-56) Judith Ames, John Archer
54. "Beam of Fire" (7-27-56) Wayne Morris
55. "The Legend of Crater Mountain" (8-3-56) Marilyn Erskine, Brad Johnson
56. "Living Lights" (8-10-56) Skip Homeier
57. "Jupitron" (8-17-56) Bill Williams
58. "The Throwback" (8-24-56) Peter Hansen, Ed Kemmer
59. "The Miracle of Dr. Dove" (8-31-56) Gene Lockhart
60. "One Thousand Eyes" (9-7-56) Vincent Price
61. "Brain Unlimited" (9-14-56) Arthur Franz

Third Season

62. "The Sound That Kills" (9-28-56) Ludwig Stossel
63. "Survival in Box Canyon" (10-12-56) Bruce Bennett
64. "The Voice" (10-26-56) Donald Curtis
65. "Three Minute Mile" (11-9-56) Marshall Thompson, Martin Milner
66. "The Last Barrier" (11-16-56) Bill Ching, Bruce Wendell
67. "Signals from the Moon" (11-23-56) Bruce Bennett
68. "Dr. Robot" (11-30-56) Peter Hansen
69. "The Human Circuit" (12-7-56) Joyce Jameson, Marshall Thompson
70. "Sun Gold" (12-14-56) Ross Elliott, Marilyn Erskine
71. "The Miracle Hour" (12-28-56) Dick Foran, Jean Byron
72. "The Killer Tree" (1-4-57) Bill Williams, Bonita Granville
73. "Gravity Zero" (1-11-57) Percy Helton, Lisa Gaye
74. "The Magic Suitcase" (1-25-57) Charles Winninger, Judith Ames
75. "Bolt of Lightning" (2-1-57) Bruce Bennett, Kristine Miller
76. "The Strange Lodger" (2-8-57) Peter Hansen, Jan Shepard

FRONT ROW CENTER

The Episodes:

1. "Dinner at Eight (adapted from the George S. Kaufman and Edna Ferber play; produced and directed by Fletcher Markle] (6-1-55 Wednesday 10-11:00 CBS) Pat O'Brien, Mary Beth Hughes, Everett Sloane, Mary Astor, John Emery
2. "The Barretts of Wimpole Street" [adapted from the play by Rudolph Besier] (6-8-55 Wednesday 10-11:00 CBS) Geraldine Fitzgerald, Sir Cedric Hardwicke, Robert Douglas
3. "Ah, Wilderness!" [adapted from the play by Eugene O'Neill] (6-15-55 Wednesday 10-11:00 CBS) Robert Driscoll, Leon Ames, Lillian Bronson, Lyle Talbot, Olive Sturgess
4. "Three for Tonight" [adapted from the Broadway musical by Paul Gregory with the voice of Walter Schumann; Betty Benson, vocalist; directed by Bill Colleran and narrated by Hiram Sherman] (6-22-55 Wednesday 10-11:00 CBS) Marge and Gower Champion, Hiram Sherman, Harry Belafonte
5. "Johnny Belinda" [adapted from the Elmer Harris play; produced and directed by Fletcher Markle] (6-29-55 Wednesday 10-11:00 CBS) Katharine Bard, Eddie Albert, Tudor Owen, James Gavin, Maudie Prickett
6. "Kitty Foyle" [adapted from the novel by Christopher Morley] (7-13-55 Wednesday 10-11:00 CBS) Janet Blair, Elliott Reed, Dick Elliott, Nan Boardman
7. "Dark Victory" [adapted from the George Brewer Jr. and Bertram Bloch novel] (7-27-55 Wednesday 10-11:00 CBS) Kent Smith, Margaret Field
8. "Outward Bound" [adapted from the play by Sutton Vane] (8-10-55 Wednesday 10-11:00 CBS) Patricia Hitchcock, John Irving, Dorothy Bernard, Wilfred Knapp, Alan Napier
9. "Guest in the House" [by Hagar Wilde and Dale Eunson] (8-24-55 Wednesday 10-11:00 CBS) Sally Forrest, Mary Beth Hughes, Paul Langton, Louise Lewis
10. "Tender Is the Night" [adapted from the novel by F. Scott Fitzgerald] (9-7-55 Wednesday 10-11:00 CBS) Mercedes McCambridge, James Daly, John Abbott, Olive Sturgess

Second Season

11. "Meeting at Mayerling" [adapted from the story by Brainard Duffield] (9-21-55 Wednesday 10-11:00 CBS) Claude Dauphin, Marisa Pavan
12. "Finley's Fan Club" [by Robert Dozier] (1-8-56 Sunday 4-5:00 CBS) Eddie Bracken, Diana Lynn, Beulah Bondi, Lilia Skala, Mikhail Rasumny
13. "Strange Suspicion" [by Ernest Kinoy] (1-15-56 Sunday 4-5:00 CBS) James Daly, Betsy Palmer, Ann Harding, Sidney Blackmer
14. "The Challenge" [by Bernard Girard] (1-22-56 Sunday 4-5:00 CBS) James Arness, Alicia Ibanez, Ray Collins
15. "The Ainsley Case" [adapted from the Bellamy Patridge book]

(1-29-56 Sunday 4-5:00 CBS) Mona Freeman, Lloyd Bridges, Philip Bourneuf

16. "Deadlock" (2-5-56 Sunday 4-5:00 CBS) Rita Gam, John Baragrey, John Carradine, Torin Thatcher
17. "The Teacher and Hector Hodge" [by Harry W. Junkin] (2-12-56 Sunday 4-5:00 CBS) Don Taylor, Sally Forrest
18. "Winter Dreams" [adapted from the F. Scott Fitzgerald story] (2-19-56 Sunday 4-5:00 CBS) Piper Laurie, Anthony Perkins
19. "Uncle Barney" (2-26-56 Sunday 4-5:00 CBS) Irene Ryan, Tom Tully, Glenda Farrell, Jim Backus, Ronnie Burns
20. "Innocent Witness" [by Marc Brandel] (3-4-56 Sunday 4-5:00 CBS) Margaret O'Brien, Dean Stockwell, John McIntire
21. "Morals Squad" [adapted by Norman Katkov from his magazine story] (3-11-56 Sunday 4-5:00 CBS) Howard Duff, Beverly Garland, Jan Merlin, Robert Middleton, Milburn Stone
22. "Dinner Date" [adapted from the story by Hindi Brooks] (3-18-56 Sunday 4-5:00 CBS) Peggy Webber, Richard Jaeckel, Lee Marvin, Whitfield Connor
23. "Search for a Stranger" [by Adrian and Virginia Spies] (3-25-56 Sunday 4-5:00 CBS) Richard Eyer, Dewey Martin, Elizabeth Patterson
24. "Hank's Head" [adapted from the Victor Woolfson novel] (4-1-56 Sunday 4-5:00 CBS) Jan Sterling, Patricia Collinge, Judith Evelyn
25. "Instant of Truth" [by Cy Cermak] (4-8-56 Sunday 4-5:00 CBS) Angela Lansbury, Paul Kelly, Kevin McCarthy
26. "The Human Touch" [based upon an idea by Lisa Kirk] (4-15-56 Sunday 4-5:00 CBS) Lisa Kirk, James Daly, John Howard
27. "Pretend You Belong to Me" [by Gertrude Walker and Dave Lussor] (4-22-56 Sunday 4-5:00 CBS) Mercedes McCambridge, Katharine Bard

WINDOWS

The Episodes:

1. "The Love Letters of Smith" (7-29-55) Eileen Heckart
2. "A Domestic Dilemma" (8-5-55) Geraldine Page, Jason Robards Jr., Ralph Nelson Jr.
3. "The Language of the Roses" [adapted from the Mary E. Wilkins Freeman short story] (8-12-55) Judith Evelyn, Wesley Addy
4. "Arcade" [adapted from the Ray Bradbury short story] (8-19-55) Melvyn Douglas, Patricia Smith
5. "The Calliope Tree" [by Doris Frankel] (8-26-55) Henry Hull, Van Dyke Parks

THE FORD STAR JUBILEE

The Episodes:

1. "The Judy Garland Special" [a variety presentation centering around highlights of her career; produced for television by Sid Luft and directed by Paul Harris; filmed in color] (9-24-55 Saturday 9:30-11:00 CBS) Judy Garland, David Wayne; Japanese vocalist Mitsuko Sawamura; comedy quintet The Goofers; dancing chorus The Escorts

2. "Together with Music" [Mary Martin and Noel Coward in a musical revue of their careers] (10-22-55 Saturday 9:30-11:00 CBS)

3. "The Caine Mutiny Court-Martial" [adapted for television by Herman Wouk from his own Pulitzer Prize novel; directed by Franklin Schaffner and under the supervision of Charles Laughton and Paul Gregory, the latter of whom also produced] (11-19-55 Saturday 9:30-11:00 CBS) Lloyd Nolan, Barry Sullivan, Frank Lovejoy, Russell Hicks, Ainslie Pryor, Robert Gist, Charles Nolte, Herbert Anderson

4. "The Maurice Chevalier Musical Revue" [by William Friedberg and Neil Simon; a Sunday Spectacular filmed as part of the Ford Star Jubilee series] (12-4-55 Sunday 7:30-9:00 CBS) Maurice Chevalier, Marcel Marceau, Pat Carroll

5. "I Hear America Singing" [being a story of American music] (12-17-55 Saturday 9:30-11:00 CBS) Debbie Reynolds, Eddie Fisher, Nat "King" Cole, Ella Fitzgerald, Bobby Van, Red Skelton, The Floradora Sextet

6. "Blithe Spirit" [adapted from the 1941 Noel Coward play] (1-14-56 Saturday 9:30-11:00 CBS) Noel Coward, Lauren Bacall, Mildred Natwick, Claudette Colbert

7. "The Day Lincoln Was Shot" [adapted by R. Denis Sanders and Terry Sanders from the Jim Bishop book] (2-1-56 Saturday 9:30-11:00 CBS) Jack Lemmon, Raymond Massey, Lillian Gish; Charles Laughton narrated.

8. "High Tor" [a musical version of the 1937 Maxwell Anderson romantic fantasy] (3-10-56 Saturday 9:30-11:00 CBS) Everett Sloane, Julie Andrews (at twenty, her television debut), Bing Crosby, Nancy Olson, Hans Conried, Lloyd Corrigan

9. "The Twentieth Century" [adapted from the 1932 Ben Hecht and Charles MacArthur play] (4-7-56 Saturday 9:30-11:00 CBS) Orson Welles, Betty Grable, Ray Collins, Keenan Wynn

10. "This Happy Breed" [adapted by Noel Coward from his own 1943

play; directed by Ralph Nelson] (5-5-56 Saturday 9:30-11:00
CBS) Noel Coward, Edna Best
11. "A Bell for Adano" [adapted by Robert Buckner from the Paul
Osborn adaptation of the 1944 John Hersey Pulitzer Prize
novel; directed by Paul Nickell; with music and lyrics by
Arthur Schwartz and Howard Dietz] (6-2-56 Saturday 9:30-
11:00 CBS) Barry Sullivan, Anna Maria Alberghetti

Second Season

12. "You're the Top" [a salute to Cole Porter] (10-6-56 Saturday
9:30-11:00 CBS) Louis Armstrong, Dorothy Dandridge, Dolores Gray, Sally Forrest, George Sanders, Gordon MacRae
13. The Wizard of Oz [the 1939 film classic; its television debut]
(11-3-56 Saturday 9-11:00 CBS)
14. "High Button Shoes" [adapted by Arny Rosen and Coleman Jacoby
from the 1947 Broadway musical by Stephen Longstreet and
Jule Styne and with choreography by Jerome Robbins] (11-
24-56 Saturday 9-10:30 NBC) Nanette Fabray, Joey Faye,
Hal March, Janet Ward, Jack Collins, Don Ameche
15. "Holiday on Ice" (12-22-56 Saturday 9-10:30 NBC) Sonja Hen-
ie, Ernie Kovacs, Alan Jenkins, Al Kelly; "The Goofers"
and "The Nairobi Trio"

FRONTIER

The Regulars: Walter Coy, program narrator.

The Episodes:

1. "Paper Gunman" (9-25-55) John Smith, King Donovan, Scott
Forbes
2. "Tomas and the Widow" (10-2-55) Laura Elliot, Touch Connors, Sean McClory
3. "A Stillness in Wyoming" (10-16-55)
4. "The Shame of a Nation" (10-23-55)
5. "The Founding of Omaha, Nebraska" (10-30-55) Sally Brophy,
Jeff Morrow
6. "King of the Dakotas" [Part I] (11-13-55) Phyllis Coates, Tom
Tryon
7. "King of the Dakotas" [Part II] (11-20-55) as above.
8. "Cattle Drive to Casper" (11-27-55) Beverly Garland, Stuart
Randall, Ray Teal
9. "The Romance of Poker Alice" (12-11-55) Joan Vohs, Barry
Atwater
10. "Ferdinand Meyer's Army" (12-18-55) Richard Karlan
11. "Long Road to Tucson" (12-25-55) Sally Brophy
12. "The Texicans" [by Morton Fine and David Friedkin] (1-8-56)
13. "Mother of the Brave" (1-15-56)
14. "The Ten Days of John Leslie" (1-22-56) Richard Crenna
15. "The Devil and Doctor O'Hara" (2-5-56) J. M. Kerrigan

16. "The Captivity of Joe Long" (2-12-56) Jan Merlin, Tamar Cooper, John Miljan
17. "The Voyage of Captain Castle" (2-19-56) Donald Murphy, Gloria Saunders
18. "Assassin" (3-4-56) Chuck Connors, John Hoyt
19. "Hanging at Thunder Butte Creek" (3-11-56) Donald McDonald, Robert Bray, Vic Perrin
20. "The Big Dry" (3-18-56) Scott Forbes, Maura Murphy
21. "The Ballad of Pretty Polly" (4-1-56) Nancy Hadley
22. "The Well" (4-8-56) Christopher Dark, Don Kelly
23. "Salt War" (4-22-56) Richard Boone, Carol Thurston
24. "Patrol" (4-29-56)
25. "A Somewhere Voice" (5-6-56)
26. "The Hunted" (5-13-56) Jan Merlin, Joan Hotchkis
27. "Georgia Gold" (6-10-56) John Dehner, Catherine McLeod
28. "Out from Taos" (6-24-56) Ken Tobey, Ted de Corsia
29. "The Return of Jubal Dolan" (8-26-56)
30. "Hostage" (9-2-56)

MATINEE THEATRE

The Regulars: John Conte, host.

The Episodes:

1. "Beginning Now" [adapted by Frank Gilroy from the short story by John P. Marquand] (10-31-55) Louis Hayward, Addison Richards, Philip Bourneuf, Frances Reid, Julie Bennett
2. "The Make-Believe Mother" [adapted by Nicholas Baehr from the story by Ricky Zurex] (11-1-55) Augusta Dabney, Kevin McCarthy
3. "The Persistent Image" [adapted from the novel by Gladys Schmitt] (11-2-55) William Bishop
4. "I'm Straight with the World" [by Theodore Apstein] (11-3-55) James Dunn, Joe De Santis
5. "Progress Jr. and Minnie Sweeney" [by Ed Kellso] (11-4-55) Ann Harding
6. "The House on Woldwood Lane" [by George Lowther] (11-7-55) Bobby Hyatt, Adrienne Marden, Ross Elliott
7. "Beyond a Reasonable Doubt" (11-8-55) Cara Williams, DeForest Kelley, Melinda Plowman
8. "One for the Road" [by Ellis St. Joseph] (11-9-55)
9. "An Apple for Miss Myrtle" [adapted by Kathleen and Robert Howard Lindsay from the story by Margaret Cousins] (11-10-55) Geraldine Page
10. "Big-Hearted Herbert" [adapted by Kay Arthur from the story by Sophia Kerr and A. S. Richardson] (11-11-55)
11. "Jigsaw" [by Seymour Stern] (11-14-55) Judith Evelyn, Tom Laughlin
12. "She's the One with the Funny Face" [adapted by Helene Hanff from the story by Robert Barbash] (11-15-55)

13. "All the Hoffmeyers in the World" (11-16-55)
14. "The Aspern Papers" [adapted by Michael Dyne from the story by Henry James] (11-17-55)
15. "Roman Fever" [adapted by H. R. Hays from a story by Edith Wharton] (11-18-55)
16. "Midsummer" [adapted by Speed Lamkin from the story by Nancy Hale] (11-21-55) Margaret O'Brien
17. "The Lady Chooses" [by William McCleery] (11-22-55) Judith Evelyn, John Hoyt
18. "The Courtship of Miles Standish" [adapted by Ellen and Richard McCracken from the Longfellow classic] (11-23-55)
19. "The Dispossessed" [adapted by Elizabeth Hart from the novel by Nedra Tyre] (11-25-55)
20. "One for the Road" [by Ellis St. Joseph] (11-28-55) John Abbott [repeat of episode of 11-9-55]
21. "The Touchstone" (11-29-55)
22. "Wuthering Heights" [adapted from the Emily Brontë classic] (11-30-55) Richard Boone, Shelley Fabares, Peggy Weber, Natalie Norwick
23. "The Brass Ring" [by Jacqueline Rhodes] (12-1-55)
24. "Jason" [adapted by Lawrence Hazard from the Broadway play] (12-2-55) Lamont Johnson, John Hoyt, Helen Westcott
25. "Arrowsmith" [adapted from the Sinclair Lewis classic] (12-5-55) Grant Williams
26. "Passing Strange" [by E. Jack Neuman] (12-6-55) Val Dufour, Sally Brophy
27. "For These Services" [by Theodore and Matthilde Ferro] (12-7-55) Richard Jaeckel
28. "Cordially--With Bombs" (12-8-55) Arthur O'Connell
29. "The White-Oaks" [adapted by Kay Arthur from the Mayo de la Roche novel] (12-9-55) Lenore Shanewise
30. "O'Toole from Moscow" [by Rod Serling] (12-12-55) Leo Durocher, Chuck Connors
31. "The Milwaukee Rocket" (12-13-55)
32. "This One Is Different" (12-14-55) John Conte
33. "Sins of the Fathers" (12-15-55)
34. "See You on Sunday" (12-16-55) Jan Merlin, Angie Dickinson
35. "Coming of Age" [by Harold and Joanne Brodkey] (12-19-55) Madge Evans
36. "Technique" (12-20-55) Clare Luce, Shirley Ross, Hayden Rorke, Angie Dickinson
37. "Gallin--All American" (12-21-55)
38. "Santa Is No Saint" (12-22-55)
39. "The Unwelcomed" (12-23-55)
40. "The Red Sanders Story" [by Wilton Schiller] (12-26-55) Richard Arlen
41. "Elisha and the Long Knives" [by Dale Wasserman and Jack Balch] (12-27-55) Harry Carey Jr.
42. "Horns of the Dilemma" [by Harold Callen] (12-28-55)
43. "Little Girls Grow Up" [by George Baxt] (12-29-55)
44. "The Shot" [a Civil War drama] (12-30-55)
45. "Mr. Krane" [by Arthur Rodney Coneybeare] (1-3-56) Sir Cedric Hardwicke, John Hoyt, Peter Hansen
46. "Yesterday Is Gone" [by Ellen and Robert Mason Pollock] (1-4-56)

47. "Double Door" [adapted from the play by Elizabeth McFadden] (1-5-56)
48. "The Happy Rest" [by W. Richard Nash] (1-6-56)
49. "The Gate" [by Kathleen Lindsay] (1-9-56) Richard Long, Gertrude Michaels, Marcia Henderson
50. "One Left Over" [by Robert Howard Lindsay] (1-10-56)
51. "All the Trees in the Field" [by Sylvia Richards] (1-11-56) Melinda Plowman, James Bell
52. "The Century Plant" [by Theodore Apstein] (1-12-56) Ross Elliott, Anna Novarro, Constance Ford, John Dolittle
53. "Friday the Thirteenth" (1-13-56)
54. "The Old Maid" [adapted from the Pulitzer Prize play by Zoë Akins] (1-16-56) Sarah Churchill
55. "Mother Was a Bachelor" [by Irving Phillips] (1-17-56) Billie Burke
56. "Bottom of the River" [by Arnold Schulman] (1-18-56)
57. "Company Manners" [by William McCleery] (1-19-56)
58. "The Child and the Muse" [by Greer Johnson] (1-20-56)
59. "The Big Box" [by Arnold Averbach] (1-23-56)
60. "Sincerely Yours, Charlie Fisher" [by Donald Hymington and Dean Harens] (1-24-56) Dean Harens
61. "Doc" [by Betty Grove] (1-25-56) Ann Doran
62. "The Amateur" [by Mort Thaw] (1-26-56) Paul Gilbert
63. "Light and Shadow" [by Glenn and Elaine Wolfe] (1-27-56)
64. "Romney" [adapted by Lois Landauer from the story by A. L. Barker] (1-30-56)
65. "O, Promise Me" [by Greer Johnson] (1-31-56) Dick Elliott, Cheerio Meredith
66. "Hold My Hand and Run" [by Jeanette and Francis Letton] (2-1-56) Clare Luce, Paul Burke, Maxine Cooper, Lowell Gilmore
67. "Dark Possession" [by Gore Vidal; as adapted from his own drama for "Studio One," February 15, 1954] (2-2-56) Carol Stone, Karen Sharpe, Adrienne Marden
68. "The Diamond" [by David Chandler] (2-3-56)
69. "Susan and God" [adapted by Lawrence Hazard from the Rachel Crothers play] (2-6-56) Sarah Churchill, Lenore Shanewise
70. "As Young As You Feel" [adapted from the story by Virginia Faulkner] (2-7-56) Ann Harding
71. "The White Knight" [by Jack Laird] (2-8-56)
72. "The Anxious Years" [adapted by Kathleen and Robert Howard Lindsay from the play by Thyra Samter Winslow] (2-9-56)
73. "The Heart of Mary Lincoln" [adapted by Robert Howard and Kathleen Lindsay from the Mary W. Ballard play] (2-10-56) Lenore Shanewise
74. "The Middle Son" [by Nicholas Baehr] (2-13-56) Mr. and Mrs. Ernest Truex
75. "Valentine's Day" [by Virginia Rooks] (2-14-56) Frances Reid
76. "Summer Cannot Last" [by Diana Lutton] (2-15-56) Philip Bourneuf
77. "The Last Battlefield" [by Harold Callen] (2-16-56)
78. "The Catbird Seat" [adapted by Robert J. Shaw from the James Thurber story] (2-17-56)

79. "Dream House" [by Arthur Cavanaugh] (2-20-56) Virginia Vincent, Herbert Rudley
80. "The Runaways" [by Alfred Brenner] (2-21-56) John Barrymore Jr., Karen Sharpe
81. "The Ledger" [by Jack Laird] (2-22-56) Ann Doran, Lyle Talbot, Tom Brown
82. "When the Bough Breaks" [by Michelle Cousin] (2-23-56)
83. "I Want to March" [by H. R. Hays] (2-24-56)
84. "Skylark" [adapted from the play by Sampson Raphaelson] (2-27-56) Sarah Churchill, Gene Raymond
85. "Tall Dark Stranger" [by Peter Barry] (2-28-56) Hugh O'Brian, Zsa Zsa Gabor
86. "Anything But Love" [by William McCleery] (2-29-56) John Conte, Diana Lynn
87. "Robin Daw" [by Ira Avery] (3-1-56) June Havoc
88. "Letter to a Stranger" [adapted from the novel by Elswyth Thane] (3-2-56) Margaret Hayes, Jeff Morrow, Susan Kohner
89. "Dinner at Antoine's" [adapted by Samuel W. Taylor from the novel by Frances Parkinson Keyes] (3-5-56) Jean Parker
90. "The Mating of Watkins' Turtle" [adapted from the short story by Charles Dickens] (3-6-56)
91. "Her Son's Wife" [by Claire Wellis] (3-7-56) Hope Lange
92. "The Shining Palace" [by Peggy Phillips] (3-8-56)
93. "The Odd Cnes" [by Betty Ulius] (3-9-56) Marilyn Erskine, Darryl Hickman
94. "A Cowboy for Chris" [by Walter Black and William Mandrek] (3-12-56) Kim Charney, John Lupton, Ray Montgomery
95. "The Rocking Chair" [adapted by Bob Barbash] (3-13-56) Lamont Johnson, Karen Sharpe
96. "The Big Guy" [by Leonard Freeman] (3-14-56) Tom Geray, Alan Hale Jr.
97. "Statute of Limitations" [by A. J. Russell] (3-15-56) Herbert Anderson, Richard Crane
98. "The Baron and the Banshees" [adapted by Jack Laird from the Samuel White story] (3-16-56)
99. "Notebook Warrior" [by Ira Levin] (3-19-56) Ben Cooper, Richard Carlyle
100. "Temptation for a King" [adapted by Michael Dyne from the story by John H. Secondari] (3-20-56) John Conte, Onslow Stevens
101. "The Antidote" [by Richard McCracken] (3-21-56) James Bell
102. "Shadows" [by Ira and Jane Avery] (3-22-56)
103. "M Is for the Many" [by Joan Cunningham] (3-23-56) Ann Harding
104. "The Silent Partner" [by Joseph Liss] (3-26-56) Steven Geray, Lili Darvas
105. "Winter in April" [by Robert Nathan] (3-27-56) Margaret O'Brien
106. "Bread Upon the Waters" [by Ray Lukshes] (3-28-56) Marshall Thompson, Patricia Smith
107. "The Giant Killer" [by Joseph Caldwell] (3-29-56)

108. "The Book of Ruth" [adapted by Howard Rodman from the Bible] (3-30-56) Sarah Churchill, Fay Bainter
109. "Singer in the Valley" [by Dorothy Reid Stewart] (4-2-56) Beverly Tyler
110. "The Heart of a Husband" [by Margaret Culken Banning] (4-3-56) Gene Raymond, Catherine McLeod
111. "From the Desk of Margaret Tydings" [adapted by Robert Esson from the Fannie Hurst story] (4-4-56) Margaret Hayes, Johnny Crawford, Don Murphy, Peggy McCay, Craig Stevens
112. "But You Look Like Sisters" (4-5-56) Vicki Cummings
113. "The House of the Seven Gables" [adapted by Elihu Winer from the Nathaniel Hawthorne classic] (4-6-56) Marshall Thompson, John Carradine
114. "Fiddlin' Man" (4-9-56) Gene Nelson, Murvyn Vye, Betty Lynn
115. "The Hollow Woman" [by Bruce Pines] (4-10-56) Diana Lynn, Ellen Corby, Sara Haden, Otto Nesmith, Jess Barker, Robert Patten
116. "People in Glass" [by Kathleen and Robert Howard Lindsay] (4-11-56) Virginia Bruce
117. "One of the Family" [by S. S. Schweitzer] (4-12-56) Irene Ryan
118. "Young Hands, Young Feet" [by Steven Gethers] (4-13-56) Regis Toomey, Irene Hervey
119. "The Lark Shall Sing" [adapted from the novel by Elizabeth Cade] (4-16-56) Jeannie Carson
120. "Dread of Winter" [by Jess Greg] (4-17-56)
121. "The Century Plant" [repeat of episode of 1/12/56] (4-18-56)
122. "Babylonian Heart" [by Robert Arthur] (4-19-56) Zsa Zsa Gabor, Philip Reed
123. "Ask Me No Questions" [by Max Wilk] (4-20-56) Alan Young, Marcia Henderson
124. "Whom Death Hath Joined Together" [by Alvin Sapinsley] (4-23-56)
125. "The Wedding" [by Hagar Wilde and Judson O'Donnell] (4-24-56) Jane Frazee
126. "The Reckoning" [by Daniel Morgan] (4-25-56)
127. "A Woman Named Ruby" [by Christie Munro] (4-26-56)
128. "Bright Boy" [by John Boruff] (4-27-56)
129. "The Carefree Tree" [adapted by Helene Hanff from the story by Aldyth Morris] (4-30-56) Karen Sharpe, Lamont Johnson
130. "Graybeards and Witches" [by Robert Esson] (5-1-56) Agnes Moorehead, Cathy O'Donnell
131. "The Legend of Jenny Lind" [by Irve Tunick] (5-2-56) Dorothy Kristan
132. "Daughter of the Seventh Day" [by S. S. Schweitzer] (5-3-56) Leon Ames
133. "Night Must Fall" [adapted from the Emlyn Williams play] (5-4-56) Richard Jaeckel
134. "The Twenty-fifth Hour" [by James Blumgarten] (5-7-56); produced in association with the Lutheran Television Association.
135. "A Man and a Maid" [by Therese Lewis] (5-8-56) Craig Stevens

136. "Perspective" [by H. R. Hayes] (5-9-56)
137. "The Catamaran" [by J. P. Miller, as adapted from his own "Philco Television Playhouse, " telecast January 25, 1954] (5-10-56) Patrick O'Neal, Mary Astor
138. "Johnny Came Marching Home" [by Anthony Spinner] (5-11-56)
139. "A Family Affair" [by Henry Misrock] (5-14-56) Jim Backus, Lurene Tuttle, Ronnie Burns
140. "Statute of Limitations" [repeat of episode of 3/15/56] (5-15-56)
141. "Blind Date" [by Joan Cunningham] (5-16-56)
142. "To Have and to Hold" [by Irving Elman] (5-17-56)
143. "Edwina Black" [by William Dinner and William Morum] (5-18-56)
144. "The Spare Room" [adapted by Peggy Phillips from the play by Nelia Gardner White] (5-21-56)
145. "The Bottle Imp" [adapted from the story by Robert Louis Stevenson] (5-22-56)
146. "Brief Music" [by Emmet Lavery] (5-23-56)
147. "The Girl from Boro Park" [by Albert Meglin] (5-24-56)
148. "To Whom It May Concern" [by Ralph Rose] (5-25-56)
149. "Bachelor Buttons" [by Michelle Cousin] (5-28-56)
150. "The Children of Papa Juan" [adapted from the Guy de Maupassant story] (5-29-56)
151. "Herself Alone" [by Charles Mergendahl] (5-30-56)
152. "Three for the Money" [adapted from the story by James McConnaighey] (5-31-56)
153. "Taxi to the Moon" [by Sheppard Kerman] (6-1-56)
154. "The Good-Time Boys" [adapted from the short story by Ira Avery] (6-4-56) Patricia Neal, Addison Richards
155. "The American" [adapted by Michael Dyne from the Henry James classic] (6-5-56) Lili Darvas
156. "Cause for Suspicion" (6-6-56)
157. "Fight the Whole World" [by Caleb Gray] (6-7-56) Dean Stockwell, Nancy Malone, Irene Tedrow, Dayton Lummis
158. "Autumn Crocus" [adapted from the Broadway play by C. L. Anthony] (6-8-56) Margaret Truman
159. "George Has a Birthday" [by Jean Clifford Raymond] (6-11-56) Eddie Cantor, Lillian Bronson, Mae Clarke, Benny Baker, Paul Cavanagh
160. "The Serpent's Tooth" [by B. M. Atkinson Jr.] (6-12-56) Bill Goodwin, Johnny Crawford
161. "Crime at Blossoms" [adapted by Jerome Ross from the short story by Mordaunt Sharp] (6-13-56)
162. "The Luck of Amos Currie" [by Kathleen and Robert Howard Lindsay] (6-14-56) Charles Ruggles
163. "Alison's House" [adapted by Richard McCracken from the Broadway play by Susan Glaspell] (6-15-56)
164. "Safe Place" [adapted by S. S. Schweitzer from the novelette by Melba Marleitt] (6-18-56)
165. "Guest Cottage" [by William McCleery] (6-19-56)
166. "Forsaking All Others" [adapted by Peggy Phillips from the narrative poem by Alice Duer Miller] (6-20-56)
167. "Love, Honor and O'Day" [by Eileen and Robert Mason] (6-21-56) Patricia Breslin, William Taylor

168. "The Damask Cheek" [adapted from the play by John Van Druten] (6-22-56)

169. "Moon Over Manhattan" [adapted by Betty Ulius from the novel by Pearl Buck] (6-25-56)

170. "But Fear Itself" [adapted by Martin Grussmith from the story by Stuart Hawkins] (6-26-56)

171. "Birthday Present" [adapted by Andrew Rosenthal from his own stage play] (6-27-56)

172. "The Ghost of Greenwich Village" [adapted by Robert Esson from the magazine story by Elsie Milnas] (6-28-56)

173. "The Young and the Damned" [adapted by Warner Law from the play by Kenneth Phillips Britton] (6-29-56)

174. "There's Always Juliet" [adapted by Helen Hanff from the story by John Van Druten] (7-2-56) John Conte, Joan Elan

175. "Seasoned Timber" (7-3-56)

176. "The Declaration" [by John Vlahos and Stephen W. Callahan] (7-4-56)

177. "The High Place" (7-5-56) John Baragrey, Catherine McLeod

178. "Black Chiffon" [adapted by Philip Barry Jr. from the play by Lesley Storm] (7-6-56)

179. "Class of '58" [by Louis Peterson] (7-9-56) Dean Stockwell

180. "Marriage by the Millions" (7-11-56) John Baragrey, Frances Reid

181. "Backfire" [by Marc Brandel] (7-12-56)

182. "The Bishop Misbehaves" [adapted by Kay Arthur from the play by Frederick Jackson] (7-13-56)

183. "The Remittance Man" (7-16-56)

184. "Beg, Borrow or Steal" (7-17-56)

185. "The Summer Pavilion" [by Gore Vidal; as adapted from his own "Studio One" drama, telecast May 2, 1955] (7-18-56) Isabel Jewell, Richard Crane, Judith Braun

186. "The Feast" [adapted by H. R. Hays from the novel by Margaret Kennedy] (7-19-56)

187. "The Full Rich Life" [by Viña Delmar] (7-20-56)

188. "The Reverberator" [adapted by Lois Jacoby from the story by Henry James] (7-23-56)

189. "Woman at the Window" [by Nelia Gardner White] (7-24-56)

190. "Another Sky" [by Naomi Lane Babson] (7-25-56)

191. "Letter of Introduction" [by William Templeton] (7-26-56) Audrey Totter, Marshall Thompson

192. "Home at Seven" [adapted by S. S. Schweitzer from the play by R. C. Sherriff] (7-27-56)

193. "The Cypress Tree" [by Robert J. Shaw] (7-30-56) Lillian Bronson, Mae Clarke, Ann Doran

194. "Belong to Me" [adapted by Gail Ingram from the unpublished novel by Ann Pinchot] (7-31-56) David Janssen, Judith Braun, Helen Westcott

195. "Pygmalion Jones" [adapted by Gail Ingram from the story by Dorothy Kilgallen and Richard Kollmar] (8-1-56) Carol Ohmart, William Bishop

196. "Gretel" [by Vance Bourjaily] (8-2-56)

197. "Some Man Will Want You" [adapted from the novelette by Margaret Culken Banning] (8-3-56)

198. "The Fall of the House of Usher" [adapted by Robert Esson from the Edgar Allan Poe classic] (8-6-56) Tom Tryon, Eduardo Ciannelli, Marshall Thompson
199. "Cupid Rode a Horse" [by B. M. Atkinson Jr.] (8-7-56) Robert Eyer, Lloyd Corrigan, Johnny Crawford, Bill Goodwin
200. "The Old Payola" [by Abby Mann and Jack Wilson] (8-8-56) Jackie Coogan, John Conte, Jeff Donnell
201. "The Century Plant" [repeat of episode of 1/12/56] (8-9-56)
202. "Perfect Alibi" [adapted from the story by A. A. Milne] (8-10-56) Reginald Denny, Joan Elan
203. "Fiddlin' Man" [repeat of episode of 4/9/56] (8-13-56)
204. "One of the Family" [repeat of episode of 4/12/56] (8-17-56)
205. "A Family Affair" [repeat of episode of 5/14/56] (8-21-56)
206. "The House of the Seven Gables" [repeat of episode of 4/6/56] (8-22-56)
207. "The Hollow Woman" [repeat of episode of 4/10/56] (8-23-56)
208. "Ask Me No Questions" [repeat of episode of 4/20/56] (8-24-56)
209. "Dark Possession" [repeat of episode of 2/2/56] (8-27-56)

Second Season

210. "The House Off Fifth Avenue" [by Henry Misrock] (8-28-56) Karen Sharpe, Richard Crane
211. "Yankee Doodler" [by Allen Swift] (8-29-56) Kurt Kasznar
212. "The Pink Hippopotamus" (8-30-56) Lawrence Dobkin
213. "September Tide" [adapted by Richard McCracken from the play by Daphne du Maurier] (8-31-56)
214. "Are You Listening?" [by Jack Laird] (9-3-56) Conrad Janis
215. "Ladies' Maid's Bell" [adapted by Robert Esson from the story by Edith Wharton] (9-4-56)
216. "One Hundred Red Convertibles" [by Robert Garis] (9-5-56) Constance Bennett
217. "The Ivy Curtain" [by Anthony Spinner] (9-6-56) Gene Raymond, Josephine Hutchinson
218. "Grammercy Ghost" [adapted by Richard McCracken from the Broadway play by John Cecil Holm] (9-7-56) Sarah Churchill
219. "The Lovers" [by Marion C. Baker] (9-10-56) Mary Astor
220. "Reach for the Stars" [by B. L. Hunter] (9-11-56) Edgar Stehli, Brett Halsey
221. "I Like It Here" [adapted from the Broadway play by A. B. Shiffrin] (9-12-56) John Hoyt, Steven Geray, June Vincent
222. "A Question of Balance" [by Wood Fitchette and Stuart Dunham] (9-13-56) Paul Langton, Robert Karnes, Peggy Stewart, Helen Westcott
223. "Marriage Royal" [by Robert Wallsten] (9-14-56) Jacques Sernas, Franklin Paneborn, John Abbott
224. "Graybeards and Witches" [repeat of 5/1/56] (9-17-56)
225. "The Amateur" [repeat of episode of 1/26/56] (9-18-56)
226. "Mad Money" [by Max Wilk] (9-19-56) Lee Rogow, Dick Leavine
227. "A Letter from Johnny Brock" [adapted from the short story

by Sophia Kerr] (9-20-56)

228. "Uncle Harry" [by Thomas Job] (9-21-56)
229. "At Mrs. Leland's" [adapted by Elizabeth Hart from the short story by Fannie Hurst] (9-24-56)
230. "The House Next Door" [adapted by William Templeton from the story by Vera Blackwell] (9-25-56)
231. "The Alumni Reunion" [by Nicholas Baehr] (9-26-56) Constance Ford, Don Keefer
232. "Sound of Fear" [by Bill Barrett] (9-27-56) Jerry Paris, Louis Martin, Francis Helm, Bob Simon, Amanda Blake
233. "Late Date" [by William Kendall Clark] (9-28-56)
234. "Pride and Prejudice" [adapted by Helene Hanff from the Jane Austen classic] (10-1-56)
235. "Pearls of Sheba" [adapted by Henry Misrock from the novel by Vivian Connell] (10-2-56)
236. "One of the Family" [repeat of episodes 4/12/56 and 8/17/56] (10-10-56)
237. "The Hollow Woman" [repeat of episodes of 4/10/56 and 8/23/56] (10-11-56)
238. "Babylonian Heart" [repeat of episode of 4/19/56] (10-12-56)
239. "The Stamp Caddy" [by Hal Hackady] (10-15-56)
240. "The Egoist" [adapted by Richard McCracken from the novel by George Meredith] (10-16-56)
241. "The Family Man" [by William McCleery] (10-17-56)
242. "Sight Unseen" [adapted by Warner Law from the play by Law and Rosemary Foster] (10-18-56)
243. "House of Mirth" [adapted by H. R. Hays from the book by Edith Wharton] (10-19-56) Sarah Churchill
244. "Man in the Seven League Boots" [by Anthony Spinner] (10-22-56)
245. "Woman Across the Hall" (10-23-56)
246. "And Then There Were Three" (10-24-56)
247. "The House of the Seven Gables" [repeat of episodes 4/6/56 and 8/22/56] (10-25-56)
248. "I Like It Here" [repeat of episode of 9/12/56] (10-26-56)
249. "Shake Down the Stars" [adapted by Gail Ingram from the story by Pamela Franken] (10-29-56)
250. "Horsepower" [by Mona Kent and Alfred Ryder] (10-30-56) Walter Sande, Dean Stockwell, Alex Gerry
251. "Without Sanction" [adapted by Theodore Apstein from the story by Kans Kades] (10-31-56)
252. "George Has a Birthday" [repeat of episode of 6/11/56] (11-1-56)
253. "The Outing" [by Arnold Rabin] (11-2-56) Ann Doran, Tommy Kirk, Robert Karnes
254. "Thank You, Edmondo" [by Mac Shoub] (11-5-56)
255. "The Tell-Tale Heart" [adapted by William Templeton from the Edgar Allan Poe classic] (11-6-56)
256. "Strangers on a Honeymoon" (11-7-56)
257. "A Dram of Poison" [adapted from the story by Charlotte Armstrong] (11-8-56)
258. "The Shining Hour" [adapted by Richard McCracken from the story by Keith Winters] (11-9-56)

259. "Love, Marriage and Five Thousand Dollars" (11-12-56)
260. "Step into Darkness" (11-13-56)
261. "A Candle in the Dark" (11-14-56)
262. "Savrola" [adapted by Michael Dyne from the novel by Winston Churchill] (11-15-56) Victor Jory, Sarah Churchill, Lamont Johnson
263. "A Table Set at Night" (11-16-56)
264. "Madame De Treymes" [adapted from the novelette by Edith Wharton] (11-19-56)
265. "The People vs. John Tarr" (11-26-56)
266. "The Location of Roycemore College" (11-12-56)
267. "Dracula" [adapted from the novel by Bram Stoker] (11-23-56)
268. "Cease from Anger" [by Eugene Francis] (11-26-56)
269. "The Empty Nest" [adapted by Dale Ritt from the novel by Joseph Lawrence] (11-27-56)
270. "Share Your Pity" [adapted by William Templeton from the story by Stafford Dickens] (11-28-56)
271. "The House of the Seven Gables" [repeat of episodes 4/6/56, 8/27/56 and 10/25/56] (11-29-56)
272. "The Last Leaf" [by Ross Caliborne and Frances Banks] (11-30-56) Evelyn Varden, Sally Moffatt, Eve McVeagh
273. "Therese" (12-3-56) Constance Ford
274. "House of Mirth" [repeat of episode of 10/19/56] (12-4-56)
275. "Julie" [by David Davidson] (12-5-56) Dean Stockwell
276. "Refugee" [adapted by Nicholas Baehr from the story by Thelma Nurenberg] (12-6-56)
277. "Jenny Kissed Me" [adapted by Richard McCracken from the play by Jean Kerr] (12-7-56) Rudy Vallee
278. "Miracle at Carville" [adapted by William Mourne from the Betty Martin autobiography] (12-10-56)
279. "The Upper Hand" [adapted by George Lowther] (12-11-56)
280. "Love Is a Locksmith" [adapted by William McCleery from an article by Nathaniel Benchley] (12-12-56)
281. "Captain Brassbound's Conversion" [adapted from the play by George Bernard Shaw] (12-13-56)
282. "The Wisp End" [by Richard Wendley] (12-14-56) Will Hutchins, Karen Sharpe, Gene Raymond
283. "Prominent Citizen" (12-17-56)
284. "Head of the Family" [by S. S. Schweitzer] (12-18-56)
285. "The Password" [by Helen Cotton] (12-19-56)
286. "Late Love" [adapted by Gail Ingram from the play by Rosemary Casey] (12-20-56)
287. "Eugenie Grandet" [adapted by Betty Ulius from the novel by Honoré de Balzac] (12-21-56) Val Dufour, Peggy McCay, Dayton Lummis, Lillian Bronson
288. "Cold Christmas" [adapted by Theodore Apstein from the play by Anna Maria Barlowe and Brooke White] (12-24-56)
289. "Little Women" [adapted by Elaine Ryan from the Louisa May Alcott classic] (12-25-56) Diane Jergens, Irene Hervey, Judith Braun, Adrienne Ulmer, Alexander Lockwood
290. "For Sweetheart, Wife or Mother" [adapted by Helene Hanff from the magazine story by Lenora Mattingly Weber] (12-26-56)

291. "Smilin' Through" [by Alan Langdon Martin] (12-27-56)
292. "Strong Medicine" [by William Mourne] (12-28-56) Patrick O'Neal, Joe Maross, Mary Webster, Myron Healey
293. "Everything Is Relative" [by Dan Beaumont] (12-31-56)
294. "Miss Morissa" [by Mari Sandoz] (1-2-57)
295. "The Scandalous Priest" [by Frank and Doris Hursley] (1-3-57)
296. "Dark Victory" [adapted by Kathleen and Robert Howard Lindsay from the play by George Emerson Brewer Jr. and Bertram Block] (1-4-57)
297. "The Lonely Look" [by Herman Raucher] (1-7-57)
298. "The Sudden Truth" [by Charles Cagle] (1-8-57)
299. "The Man in the Half-Moon Street" [adapted by Kathleen and Robert Howard Lindsay from the story by Barre Lyndon] (1-9-57)
300. "The Hex" [by Gene Feldman] (1-10-57)
301. "If This Be Error" [adapted by William Kendall Clark from the play by Rachel Grieve] (1-11-57)
302. "On the Trial of the Kingsfeld" [by Philip Kalfus] (1-14-57)
303. "Here We Are" [by Sol Salss] (1-15-57)
304. "Arms and the Man" [adapted from the George Bernard Shaw classic] (1-16-57) Robert Burton, Peter Hansen, Marcia Henderson
305. "Home Is the Hunted" [by Howard Berk] (1-17-57)
306. "Madam Ada" [adapted by Richard McCracken from the play by Aurand Harris] (1-18-57)
307. "Night Train to Chicago" [by Franklin Barton] (1-22-57) Patrick McVey
308. "This Language Called Love" [adapted by Barbara Davidson from the short story by Hila Coleman] (1-23-57)
309. "The Thirteenth Crypt" [by Anthony Spinner] (1-24-57)
310. "Mr. Pim Passes By" [adapted by Warner Law from the play by A. A. Milne] (1-25-57)
311. "Daughter of the Seventh Day" [repeat of episode of 5/3/56] (1-28-57)
312. "Anything for a Laugh" (1-29-57) Eve Greene, Doris Gilbert
313. "The Realms of Gold" [by Howard Lawrence Davis] (1-30-57)
314. "A Deacon at Oak Ridge" [adapted by Harold Gast from the article by Harold Lang on physicist Dr. William G. Pollard] (1-31-57)
315. "Accent on Youth" [by Samson Raphaelson] (2-1-57)
316. "Three Kids" [by Martin Donovan] (2-4-57) Julius LaRosa
317. "Frankenstein" [adapted by Robert Esson from the Mary Wollstonecraft Shelley classic] (2-5-57)
318. "The Most Dangerous Man" [by Irving Riehin] (2-6-57)
319. "One" [adapted by David Karp from the comedy by Oscar Wilde] (2-7-57) Everett Sloane, Paul Langston
320. "The Importance of Being Earnest" [adapted from the Oscar Wilde classic] (2-8-57) Hermoine Gingold
321. "The Brat's House" [by Roy Hargrove and Joseph DiReda] (2-11-57) Skip Homeier, Richard Jaeckel, Dick Ray Hong
322. "The Mysterious Mr. Todd" [by George Sumner Albee] (2-12-57)
323. "A Case of Pure Fiction" [by Jerome Ross] (2-13-57)

324. "The Master Builder" [adapted from the Henrik Ibsen classic] (2-14-57) Oscar Homolka, Joan Tetzel
325. "The Others" [adapted by Michael Dyne from the Henry James classic The Turn of the Screw] (2-15-57) Sarah Churchill, Tommy Kirk, Geoffrey Tune
326. "From the Desk of Margaret Tydings" [repeat of episode of 4/4/56] (2-18-57)
327. "The Remarkable Mr. Jerome" [adapted by Helene Hanff from the biography by Anita Leslie on the romance of Jenny Jerome and Randolph Churchill] (2-19-57) Roland Winters, Vera Vague, Roger Moore
328. "Bobbie" [by Narda Stokes] (2-20-57)
329. "The Hickory Limb" [adapted by Meade Roberts from the play by John Van Druten] (2-21-57)
330. "The Bridge" [by Joseph Caldwell] (2-22-57)
331. "The Serpent's Tooth" [by B. M. Atkinson Jr.] (2-25-57) Bill Goodwin, Johnny Crawford
332. "Voyage to Mandock" [by Peter Barry] (2-26-57)
333. "The Day Before the Wedding" [by Anthony Spinner] (2-27-57)
334. "The Queen of Spades" [adapted by Michael Dyne from the story by Alexander Pushkin] (2-28-57)
335. "Shadow and Substance" [by Paul Vincent Carroll] (3-1-57) Sir Cedric Hardwicke
336. "You Touched Me" [adapted from the Tennessee Williams play] (3-4-57) Oscar Homolka, Joan Tetzel
337. "In the Hemlock Cup" [adapted by Richard McCracken from the play by Edward Hunt] (3-5-57)
338. "Papa's Wife" [adapted by Elizabeth Hart from the novel by Thyra Ferre Bjorn] (3-6-57)
339. "The Prizewinner" [by Jerome Ross] (3-7-57) Mona Freeman
340. "Dr. Jekyll and Mr. Hyde" [adapted by Robert Esson from the Robert Louis Stevenson classic] (3-8-57) Douglass Montgomery
341. "The Carefree Tree" [repeat of episode of 4/30/56] (3-11-57)
342. "Bread upon the Waters" [repeat of episode of 3/28/56] (3-12-57)
343. "The Outing" [repeat of episode of 11/2/56] (3-13-57)
344. "Yesterday's Magic" [adapted by Michael Dyne from the play by Luigi Pirandello] (3-14-57)
345. "Tongue of Silver" [by Michael Dyne] (3-15-57)
346. "The Peaceable Kingdom" [by Arthur Arent] (3-18-57)
347. "The Nineteenth Hole" [adapted by Warner Law from the play by Frank Craven] (3-19-57) Wally Cox, Betty Lynn
348. "Wedding in the Family" [adapted by Betty Ulius from the novel by Dale File] (3-20-57)
349. "Mr. Krane" [repeat of episode of 1/3/56] (3-21-57)
350. "The Last Leaf" [repeat of episode of 11/30/56] (3-22-57)
351. "The Ways of Courage" [by Will Lorn] (3-25-57)
352. "Journey into Darkness" [adapted by Theodore Apstein from the article by Selwyn James] (3-26-57) Skip Homeier, Peggy McCay
353. "Barricade on the Big Black" [adapted by Anthony Spinner from the story by Terrence Kilpatrick] (3-27-57) Andrew Duggan, Richard Crenna, Mary Laroche, George Galbreth

354. "The Vicarious Years" [adapted by Peggy Lamson from the novel by John Van Druten] (3-28-57) Roddy McDowall
355. "The First Year" [adapted from the Broadway play by Frank Craven] (3-29-57)
356. "End of the Rope" [by Sheldon Stark] (4-1-57) John Barrymore Jr., Susan Oliver, George Peppard, Norma Moore, Parley Baer
357. "We Won't Be Any Trouble" [by George Lowther] (4-2-57) Patty McCormack
358. "The Daughter of Mata Hari" (4-3-57) Rita Moreno, Anna Maria Alberghetti
359. "Talk You of Killing?" [by Joe Barry] (4-4-57) Roddy McDowall
360. "The Pursuit of Happiness" (4-5-57) Jacques Sernas
361. "Wuthering Heights" [adapted from the Emily Brontë classic; restaged] (4-8-57) Tom Tryon
362. "Long Distance" [adapted by George Lowther from the story by Reita Lambert] (4-9-57) Lili Darvas, Fenton Mayd
363. "Point of Clearing" [by Robert Thompson] (4-10-57) Tom Helmore, Elaine Riken
364. "The Sport" [by Helene Hanff] (4-11-57) Lurene Tuttle, Chet Marshall, Alvy Moore
365. "Flashing Stream" [adapted by Kathleen and Robert Howard Lindsay from the play by Charles Morgan] (4-12-57)
366. "The Thread That Runs So True" [adapted by Howard Gast from the Jesse Stuart autobiography] (4-15-57)
367. "Jamie Picks a Wife" [adapted by Peggy Phillips from the story by Gertrude Schweitzer] (4-16-57)
368. "Blind Man's Bluff" [adapted by Richard Wendley from the story by Nelia Gardner White] (4-17-57)
369. "Horsepower" [repeat of episode of 10/30/56] (4-18-57)
370. "The Story of Joseph" [adapted by Howard Rodman from the Old Testament] (4-19-57) Brett Halsey
371. "Winter in April" [repeat of episode of 3/27/56] (4-22-57)
372. "Arms and the Man" [repeat of episode of 1/16/57] (4-23-57)
373. "The Pushover" [adapted by William McCleery from the short story by Harriet Frank Jr.] (4-24-57) Marshall Thompson, Kathleen Crowley
374. "Ashes in the Wind" [by Mac Shoub] (4-25-57) Vic Morrow, Edward Binns, Russell Conway
375. "A Hat, a Coat, a Glove" [by Luther Reed and Monique Jean] (4-26-57) Donald Murphy, Elaine Aiken
376. "The Professional" [by Stan Cutler] (4-29-57)
377. "Guardians of the Temple" [by Gene Feldman] (4-30-57) Lamont Johnson
378. "The Short Safari of B'wana Ben" [adapted by Nicholas Baehr from the short story by Stanley Schneider] (5-1-57) Edward Everett Horton, Ernest Truex, Frank McHugh, Glenda Farrell
379. "Church on Monday" [by Marjorie Duhan Adler] (5-2-57) James Whitmore, Marilyn Maxwell
380. "The Gioconda Smile" [adapted from the Aldous Huxley story] (5-3-57) Tom Helmore, Maureen O'Sullivan

381. "Show of Strength" [by Herman J. Epstein] (5-6-57) Kerwin Mathews
382. "Make-Believe Affair" [adapted from the story by Robert Standish] (5-7-57) Francis Lederer, Phyllis Avery, Richard Long
383. "Hymn to the Dedicated" [by Mikhail Ryoff] (5-8-57) Jim Backus, Fay Wray, Molly Bee
384. "Thursday's Child" [adapted from the short novel by Mary George Kochos] (5-9-57) Patty McCormack, Peter Hansen
385. "Big-Hearted Herbert" [adapted by Kay Arthur from the story by Sophia Kerr and A. S. Richardson; restaged] (5-10-57) Bill Goodwin, Michael Whelan, Elinor Donahue
386. "Embattled Maiden" [adapted by Betty Ulius from the Giraud Chester biography on Anna Dickinson] (5-13-57)
387. "The Middle-Aged Freshman" [adapted by Robert J. Shaw from the short story by Samuel Raphaelson] (5-14-57)
388. "The Best Friend in Town" [by Theodore Apstein] (5-15-57)
389. "Jane Eyre" [adapted by Robert Esson from the Charlotte Brontë classic] (5-16-57) Marcia Henderson, Joan Elam, Patrick MacNee, Isobel Elsom, Tita Purdom
390. "The Starmaster" [by Will Schneider and Herman Goldberg] (5-17-57) Victor Jory, Marianne Stewart, Raymond Bailey
391. "Aftermath" [by Howard Berk] (5-20-57) Richard Jaeckel, George Peppard
392. "A Guest at the Embassy" [by Jerome Ross] (5-21-57)
393. "Second-Hand Lover" [by George Lowther] (5-22-57) Patricia Morison, Gene Raymond, Fritz Feld
394. "The Avenging of Anne Leete" [adapted by Robert Esson from the story by Marjorie Bunen] (5-23-57) Roger Moore, Lisa Daniels
395. "Lonesome Husband" [adapted from the Phyllis Duganne magazine story] (5-24-57)
396. "Puzzle in the Stars" [adapted by Harold Gast from the short story by David Eynon] (5-27-57) Lila Lee, Everett Sloane
397. "Gwendolyn Harleth's Story" [adapted by Elizabeth Hart from the novel by George Eliot] (5-28-57) Lisa Daniels
398. "The Girls Named Almaya" [adapted by George Lowther from the magazine story by Matt Taylor] (5-29-57)
399. "The Dream That Was Fixed" [by Julian Fink and Arthur Geller] (5-30-57)
400. "A Growing Wonder" [adapted by Gail Ingram from the novel by Hildegarde Dolson] (5-31-57)
401. "Bachelor Father" [adapted by Helene Hanff from the novel by Ben Stanfford] (6-3-57) John Conte
402. "The Golden Door" [by Melba Redmond] (6-4-57) Gertrude Berg
403. "Rain in the Morning" [by Paula Fox and Marjorie Kellogg] (6-5-57) Roddy McDowall, Peggy McCay, Robert Morse
404. "The Alumni Reunion" [repeat of episode of 9/26/56] (6-6-57)
405. "Eye of the Storm" [by Norman Jacob] (6-7-57) Ray Danton, Gloria Talbot, Marian Seldes
406. "Rich Man, Poor Man" (6-10-57)
407. "The Party Dress" (6-11-57)

408. "White-Headed Boy" (6-12-57) Roddy McDowall
409. "Sound of Fear" [repeat of episode of 9/27/56] (6-13-57)
410. "Night Train to Chicago" [repeat of episode of 1/22/57] (6-14-57)
411. "Liza" [adapted by Elsie Lee from the story by Faith Baldwin] (6-17-57) Marcia Henderson, Steve Dunne
412. "Three Kids" [repeat of episode of 2/4/57] (6-18-57)
413. "Pigeons and People" [adapted by Joseph Shrank from the play by George M. Cohan] (6-19-57)
414. "Things Hoped For" [adapted by Nicholas Baehr from the story by Lulu Vollmer] (6-20-57)
415. "Mr. Wendigo" [adapted by S. S. Schweitzer from the play by Charles Allen] (6-21-57) Peter Hansen, Peggy Maurer
416. "Stopover" [adapted by Richard Wendley from the story by Samson Raphaelson] (6-24-57) Paul Langton, Barbara Billingsley
417. "A Light in the Sky" [adapted by Harold Gast from the story by Jim Davis] (6-25-57)
418. "The Charmer" [by Gertrude Schweitzer] (6-26-57) Peggy McCay, Catherine McLeod, Richard Long
419. "The Wisp End" [repeat of episode of 12/14/56] (6-27-57)
420. "Brief Candle" [by Robert Powell] (6-28-57) Gladys Cooper
421. "Too Much Johnson" [by William Gillette] (7-1-57)
422. "Money in the Bank" [adapted by George Lowther from the play by Henry S. Maxfield] (7-2-57)
423. "The Trouble Traine" [by Ellen and Richard McCracken] (7-3-57) Richard Eyer, Sally Brophy, Richard Shannon
424. "The Last Voyage" [by James Truex on the Benjamin Franklin voyage to France] (7-4-57) Maurice Manson, Zsa Zsa Gabor
425. "Price of Scandal" [adapted by Theodore Apstein from the magazine novel by Harriet Frank Jr.] (7-5-57) Gene Raymond, Catherine McLeod
426. "The Remarkable Mr. Jerome" [repeat of episode of 2/19/57] (7-18-57)
427. "Strong Medicine" [repeat of episode of 12/28/56] (7-10-57)
428. "But When She Was Bad" [by Marjorie Duhan Adler] (7-11-57)
429. "The Fable of Harry" [by Frank Defelitta] (7-12-57) Ernest Truex, Molly Bee, Benay Venuta
430. "Portrait in Miniature" [by George Lowther] (7-15-57)
431. "The Cask of Amontillado" [adapted by Robert Esson from the Edgar Allan Poe classic] (7-16-57) Eduardo Ciannelli
432. "The Richest Man in the World" [by Warner Law] (7-17-57) John Abbott, Gloria Castillo
433. "The Last Hour" [adapted by Alvin Boretz from the story by Bob and Wanda Duncan] (7-18-57) Patrick McVey, Douglas Dick, Mary LaRoche
434. "The Brat's House" [repeat of episode of 2/11/57] (7-19-57)
435. "The First Captain" [by Henry Misrock] (7-22-57) Joe Maross, Ann Kimball
436. "The Nineteenth Hole" [repeat of episode of 3/19/57] (7-23-57)
437. "The Shuttered Heart" [adapted by Ellen McCracken from the

short story by Mary Jane Waldo] (7-24-57) Marcia Henderson, John Baer

438. "One for All" [adapted by Harold Gast from the story by James Skardon] (7-25-57) Robert Bray, Dina Merrill, Robert Gist

439. "Call It a Day" [adapted from the Dodie Smith London and Broadway play] (7-26-57) Tom Conway

440. "Ann Veronica" [adapted by Greer Johnson from the novel by H. G. Wells] (7-29-57) Wendy Hiller

441. "Boys Will Be Men" (7-30-57)

442. "The Forbidden Search" [adapted by William Altman from the novel by Don Stanford] (7-31-57)

443. "The Fawn with the Crooked Legs" [by Lucile Duffy] (8-1-57) Tommy Rettig, Dick Foran

444. "Sunday in Sonora" [adapted by Shelley Stark from the short story by James Dombrovski] (8-2-57) Leona Gagennes, Marshall Thompson, Les Tremayne

445. "The Rose Bush" [by Blanche Kanalis] (8-5-57)

446. "Finley's Fan Club" [by Robert James] (8-6-57)

447. "Laugh a Little Tear" [adapted by Robert Thompson from the play by Gerald Sanford] (8-7-57)

448. "The Invisible Man" [adapted by Robert Esson from the H. G. Wells classic] (8-8-57) Geoffrey Tune, Chester Stratton

449. "Where Angels Fear to Tread" [adapted by George Lowther from the story by Edwin Rutt] (8-9-57)

450. "Eugenie Grandet" [repeat of episode of 12/21/56] (8-12-57)

451. "First Love" [adapted by Ellen McCracken from the play by Gertrude Schweitzer] (8-13-57)

452. "The Lost Survivors" (8-14-57)

453. "Time for Action" [adapted by Greer Johnson from the story by David Lamson] (8-15-57)

454. "Dr. Jekyll and Mr. Hyde" [repeat of episode of 3/8/57] (8-16-57)

455. "Horsepower" [repeat of episode of 10/30/56] (8-19-57)

456. "Haven's End" [adapted from the play by John P. Marquand] (8-20-57)

457. "Heed the Falling Sparrow" [adapted by Alvin Boretz from the story by Sol Offsey] (8-21-57)

458. "The President's Child Bride" [by Leo Guild on the Teddy Roosevelt/Alice Lee marriage] (8-22-57)

459. "Now or Never" [by Martha Wilkerson] (8-23-57)

460. "Barricade on the Big Black" [repeat of episode of 3/27/57] (8-26-57)

461. "The Awakening" [by Richard Wendley] (8-27-57)

462. "Angel Face" [adapted from the play by Mary McCarthy and Melville Burke] (8-28-57)

463. "The Star Sapphire" [adapted by Alvin Boretz from the play by Ben Hecht and Charles Lederer] (8-29-57)

464. "Women Have Ways" [adapted by George Lowther from the magazine story by David Lamson] (8-30-57)

465. "The Jewel Box" [by Dick Moore] (9-2-57) John Emery

466. "Molly Morgan" [adapted by Reginald Lawrence from the book by John Steinbeck] (9-3-57)

467. "Woman Alone" (9-4-57) Miriam Hopkins

468. "Mr. Krane" [repeat of episodes 1/3/56 and 3/21/57] (9-5-57)
469. "Among Strangers" [by Carol Warner Gluck] (9-6-57)
470. "The Adjustable Mr. Willing" [adapted from the novelette by Lucy Core] (9-9-57)
471. "Freedom Comes Later" [by Sidney Paine] (9-10-57) Kurt Kasznar, Warren Berlinger
472. "In the Fog" [adapted from the short story by Richard Harding Davis] (9-11-57)
473. "Son of Thirty-seven Fathers" [by Jack Lewis] (9-12-57)
474. "Hand-Me Down" [by Helen Cotton] (9-13-57)
475. "Emma" [adapted by Helene Hanff from the Jane Austen classic] (9-16-57)
476. "The Personal Equation" [by Irving Neiman] (9-17-57)
477. "Night Cry" [adapted by Robert Thompson from the novel by William L. Stuart] (9-18-57)
478. "Mysterious Disappearance" [by Jacob Nay] (9-19-57)
479. "The Impersonal Touch" [adapted from the novelette by Oscar Shisgall] (9-20-57)
480. "The Story of Sarah" [adapted by Marjorie Duhan Adler from the Old Testament] (9-22-57) Marian Seldes
481. "The Waiting Swan" (9-24-57)
482. "One Mummy Too Many" (9-25-57)
483. "Hearthstones" (9-26-57)
484. "The Reluctant Heiress" (9-27-57)
485. "The Others" [repeat of episode of 2/15/57] (9-30-57)
486. "Eye of the Storm" [repeat of episode of 6/7/57] (10-1-57)
487. "Forbidden Search" [repeat of episode of 7/31/57] (10-4-57)
488. "Jane Eyre" [repeat of episode of 5/16/57] (10-8-57)
489. "Second-Hand Lover" [repeat of episode of 5/22/57] (10-11-57)

Third Season

490. "Father Come Home" [adapted by Warner Law from the story by Robert Carson] (10-15-57) Cesar Romero
491. "Villa of the Angels" [adapted from the story by Alec Coppel] (10-16-57)
492. "A Tone of Time" [adapted by Theodore Apstein from the story by Henry James] (10-17-57) Sarah Churchill
493. "Almost Any Man Will Do" [adapted from the story by Isabel Langis] (10-18-57)
494. "Sing for Me" (10-21-57) Ethel Waters
495. "Run for the Money" [by Frank D. Gilroy] (10-22-57)
496. "Lest We Forget" [adapted from the script by Frank Bukvic] (10-23-57)
497. "The Glass Hill" [adapted from the novel by Kenneth Evans] (10-24-57)
498. "Out of the Frying Pan" [adapted from the Broadway play by Francis Swann] (10-25-57)
499. "The Last Stop" (10-28-57)
500. "The Weak and the Strong" (10-29-57) Marian Seldes, Michael Landon, Addison Richards
501. "Nine Finger Jack" [by George Lowther] (10-30-57) Eva Gabor, Patrick MacNee

502. "Elementals" [adapted from the story by Stephen Vincent Benet] (10-31-57) Mala Powers, Tom Tryon, Conrad Nagel
503. "A Plummer in Paradise" (11-1-57)
504. "Something About a Dollar" [adapted by Harold Gast from the story by James Gould Cozzens] (11-4-57)
505. "The Fall of the House of Usher" [repeat of episode of 8/6/56] (11-5-57)
506. "The Ivy Curtain" [repeat of episode of 9/6/56] (11-6-57)
507. "Return in Winter" [adapted by S. S. Schweitzer from the story by Nathan Teitel] (11-7-57)
508. "Grandmama and the Grandfather Clock" [adapted by Warner Law from the story by Charles Robbins] (11-8-57)
509. "Aesop and Rhodope" [adapted by Helene Hanff from the legend of antiquity] (11-11-57) Lamont Johnson, Sarah Churchill
510. "All over the World" (11-12-57) Margaret O'Brien
511. "The Ransom of Sigmund Freud" [by Harold Callen] (11-13-57)
512. "Iris" [by Arnold Rubin] (11-14-57) Margaret Truman
513. "Remember Me Kindly" (11-15-57)
514. "Embassy House" (11-18-57)
515. "Witness to Murder" (11-19-57)
516. "The Johnson House" [by Donald Symington] (11-20-57)
517. "Ann Veronica" [repeat of episode of 7/29/57] (11-21-57)
518. "We Won't Be Any Trouble" [repeat of episode of 4/2/57] (11-22-57)
519. "Cadenza" [by Philip Freund and Joel Ross] (11-25-57) Susan Kohner, Steven Geray
520. "Green Shores" [adapted by Michael Dyne from the story by C. P. Breen] (11-26-57)
521. "Question of Balance" [by Wood Fitchette and Stuart Dunham; restaged] (11-27-57) Paul Langton, Helen Westcott
522. "Daniel Webster and the Sea Serpent" [adapted from the Stephen Vincent Benet classic] (11-29-57) John Carradine
523. "The Conversation Tables" [by Marjorie Worthington] (12-2-57) Estelle Winwood
524. "Out of My Darkness" [adapted from the William Shepard autobiography] (12-3-57)
525. "The Man That Corrupted Hadleyburg" [adapted by Dale Wasserman from the Mark Twain story] (12-4-57)
526. "The Broom and the Groom" [by Kurtz Gordon] (12-5-57)
527. "And Jeni" [by Mort Thaw] (12-6-57)
528. "The Consul" [adapted from the story by Richard Harding Davis] (12-9-57) Sidney Blackmer, Les Tremayne, John Litel
529. "The Old Friend" (12-10-57)
530. "Give Me a Wand" [by Robert E. Thompson] (12-11-57)
531. "The Sure Thing" [adapted by George Lowther] (12-12-57)
532. "Dark of the Moon" (12-13-57)
533. "The Giver and the Gift" [adapted from the novel by Nelia Gardner White] (12-16-57) Sylvia Sidney
534. "No Time for Comedy" [adapted from the play by S. N. Behrmann] (12-17-57) Sarah Churchill, Katharine Bard
535. "A Gentleman of Fortune" [adapted from the story by Stephen Vincent Benet] (12-18-57) Charles Ruggles, Morey Amsterdam

536. "The Gentleman Caller" [adapted from the story by Veronica Johns] (12-19-57)

537. "The Tender Leaves" [by Robert J. Shaw] (12-20-57) Neva Patterson

538. "In Twenty-five Words or Less" [adapted by Ellen McCracken from the play by George Bradshaw] (12-23-57)

539. "Sara Creive" [adapted from the novel by Frances Hodgson Burnett] (12-24-57) Reba Waters, Brenda Forbes

540. "Amahl and the Night Visitors" [the Gian-Carlo Menotti opera classic; restaged and conducted by Herbert Grossman] (12-25-57) Rosemary Kuhlmann, Andrew McKinley, Kirk Jordan, David Viken Jr., Leon Lisnek

541. "The Little Minister" [adapted by Helene Hanff from the James M. Barrie story] (12-26-57) Margaret O'Brien, Ben Cooper, Henry Daniell

542. "Fight the Whole World" [repeat of episode of 6/7/56] (12-27-57)

543. "The Invisible Man" [repeat of episode of 8/8/57] (12-30-57)

544. "Daughter of Kings" [adapted from the story by Lesley Conger] (12-31-57)

545. "Survival Kit" [adapted by S. S. Schweitzer] (1-2-58)

546. "The House with Golden Streets" [by Bob and Wanda Duncan] (1-3-58)

547. "The Europeans" [adapted from the Henry James classic] (1-6-58) Zsa Zsa Gabor, Peter Cookson, Nico Minardos

548. "The Collected Letters of Mr. Sage" (1-7-58)

549. "Two-Picture Deal" (1-8-58)

550. "Great Obstacle Courtship" (1-9-58)

551. "A Chance to Die" (1-10-58)

552. "Home on the Range" (1-13-58)

553. "The Makropoulos Secret" [adapted by Michael Dyne from the Karel Casek story] (1-14-58) Sarah Churchill

554. "More Than a Man" [by Arthur Rubin] (1-15-58) Buster Crabbe, Michael Bradford, Jeanette Nolan

555. "Something Stolen, Something Blue" [by William Mourne] (1-16-58)

556. "The Thunderbolt" [by A. W. Pinero] (1-17-58)

557. "Daisy Mayne" [adapted from the play by George Kelly] (1-20-58) Paul Hartman, Lurene Tuttle

558. "The Man Who Wanted to Hate" [adapted by Nicholas Baehr from the story by Jan Speas] (1-21-58)

559. "The Golden Fleecing" [by Mateo Lettunich] (1-22-58)

560. "Forever and Ever" [adapted by Edward S. Fox from the story by Kathleen and Robert Howard Lindsay] (1-23-58) Peter Hansen, Patricia Barry

561. "Decision" [adapted by S. S. Schweitzer from the story by Joseph Cochran] (1-24-58) Gene Raymond, Tommy Kirk, Vivi Janiss

562. "Soldier's Boy" (1-27-58)

563. "The Man with the Pointed Toes" (1-28-58) Earl Holliman, Vanessa Brown

564. "The Cask of Amontillado" [repeat of episode of 7/16/57] (1-29-58)

565. "The Awakening" [repeat of episode of 8/27/57] (1-30-58)
566. "Love out of Town" [by William McCleery] (1-31-58) Sarah Churchill
567. "Cave-In" [by Jack Cleck] (2-3-58) Paul Langton, Jeanne Cooper, Stacy Harris, Catherine McLeod
568. "The Iceman" [by Anthony Spinner] (2-4-58) Stacy Harris, Jackie Coogan, Andrew Duggan, Peggy McCay, Johnny Crawford
569. "The Long, Long Laugh" [by Bernard Slate] (2-5-58) June Lockhart, Russell Arms
570. "The Man Without a Country" [adapted by Elihu Winer from the Edward Everett Hale classic] (2-6-58) Richard Shannon, Peter Hansen, Ralph Clinton
571. "The Odd Ones" [repeat of episode of 3/9/56] (2-7-58)
572. "Charcoal Pink" (2-10-58)
573. "Monsieur Beaucaire" [adapted by S. S. Schweitzer from the story by Booth Tarkington] (2-11-58)
574. "Life upon the Wicked Stage" [adapted by Robert Wallsten from the story by George Bradshaw] (2-12-58)
575. "Without Fear or Favor" [by H. R. Hays on the New York Times help in dissolving a criminal Tweed political regime] (2-13-58)
576. "The Third Person" [adapted by Warner Law from the story by Henry James] (2-14-58) Judith Evelyn
577. "Eden End" [adapted from the play by J. B. Priestley] (2-17-58) Wendy Hiller, Tom Helmore, Margaret Phillips
578. "The Tenth Muse" [adapted by Sam Hall from the play by Edith Sherman] (2-18-58) Ann Harding
579. "Laugh a Little Tear" [repeat of episode of 8/7/57] (2-19-58)
580. "Goodbye on Thursday" [adapted by Harold Gast from the story by Mil Smith] (2-20-58)
581. "The Heart's Desire" [by Helene Hanff] (2-21-58) Kuldip Singh
582. "Marriage of Convenience" (2-24-58)
583. "The Suicide Club" [adapted by Robert Esson from the story by Robert Louis Stevenson] (2-25-58)
584. "The Sixty-fifth Floor" [adapted by Nicholas Baehr from the story by Newton Arnold] (2-26-58) Hugh Marlowe
585. "The Hickory Heart" [adapted by Greer Johnson from the story by Demma Oldham] (2-27-58)
586. "The Devil's Violin" [by Margery Finn Brown] (2-28-58) Patty McCormack
587. "Wednesday's Child" [adapted from the Leonard Atlas story] (3-3-58) Jan Clayton, Patrick Dennis, Nancy Valentine
588. "The Vigilante" (3-4-58) Leif Erickson
589. "The Prophet Hosea" [by Marjorie Duhan Adler] (3-5-58)
590. "Journey into Darkness" [repeat of episode of 3/26/57] (3-6-58)
591. "Mrs. Moonlight" (3-7-58) Margaret O'Brien
592. "The Mask of Venus" [by Nelia Gardner White] (3-10-58) Margaret Hayes
593. "With Love We Live" (3-11-58) Marilyn Erskine
594. "You and I" [adapted from the story by Philip Barry] (3-12-58) Donald Woods

595. "Career Angel" [by Gerald Murray] (3-13-58) Nita Talbot, Cecil Kellaway
596. "The Contingent Fire" (3-14-58) Paula Raymond, Paul Langton
597. "One For All" [repeat of episode of 7/25/57] (3-17-58)
598. "Anxious Night" [by David Lamson] (3-18-58) John Beal, Dale Evans, Tommy Kirk
599. "On Approval" [by Frederick Lonsdale] (3-19-58)
600. "Dandy Dick" [adapted from the play by Sir Arthur Wing Pinero] (3-20-58) Reginald Gardiner, Edward Everett Horton, Gladys Cooper
601. "Hush, Mahala, Hush" (3-21-58)
602. "End of the Rope" [by Sheldon Stark] [repeat of episode of 4/1/57] (3-24-58)
603. "O'Rourke's House" [by Tim Kelly] (3-25-58)
604. "The Alleyway" [by Robert Esson] (3-26-58)
605. "The Vagabond" [adapted by Betty Ulius from the Colette story] (3-27-58) Jacques Bergerac, Eva Gabor
606. "The Silver Spider" [by John Bloch] (3-28-58)
607. "Rain in the Morning" [repeat of episode of 6/5/57] (3-31-58)
608. "Design for Glory" [adapted by Harold Gast from the story by Maxine Wood] (4-1-58)
609. "The Inspector General" [adapted by Warner Law from the Nikolai Gogol classic] (4-2-58) Akim Tamiroff, Wally Cox
610. "The Two Mrs. Carrolls" [by Martin Vale] (4-3-58) Zsa Zsa Gabor, John Sutton, Paula Raymond
611. "The Velvet Glove" (4-4-58)
612. "The Lost Survivors" [repeat of episode of 8/14/57] (4-7-58)
613. "Death Takes a Holiday" [adapted by Michael Dyne from the play by Alberto Casella] (4-8-58) Gene Raymond, Janice Rule
614. "The Man of the House" [adapted by Rosemary Foster from the play by Carl Leo and Ben Zavin] (4-9-58) Henry Morgan, June Lockhart
615. "A Case of Fear" [by Herman Goldberg and Will Schneider; from the files of the American Cancer Society] (4-10-58) Julie Adams, Charles Aidman
616. "Walk in the Sky" [adapted by George Lowther from the story by Joss McFee] (4-11-58)
617. "From the Desk of Margaret Tydings" [repeat of episodes of 4/4/56 and 2/18/57] (4-14-58)
618. "The Canterville Ghost" [adapted by George Lowther from the Oscar Wilde classic] (4-15-58) Ernest Truex, Sylvia Field
619. "The Ivy Curtain" [repeat of episodes 9/6/56 and 11/6/57] (4-16-58)
620. "Found Money" (4-17-58)
621. "Washington Whispers Murder" (4-18-58) Donald Woods, Lynn Bari, Irene Hervey, Douglas Kennedy
622. "The Last Voyage" [repeat of episode of 7/4/57] (4-21-58)
623. "A Boy Grows Up" [by Dorothy Stewart] (4-22-58) Leo Castillo, Jane Darwell
624. "The Phony Venus" [adapted from the play by George Bradshaw] (4-13-58)
625. "Some Blessed People" [by Jean Leslie] (4-24-58)

626. "Quiet Street" [by Selda Popkin]   (4-25-58)
627. "The Fall of the House of Usher" [repeat of episodes 8/6/56
     and 11/5/57]   (4-28-58)
628. "Great Big Guy" [by Biff McGuire]   (4-29-58)
629. "It Came from Out of Town" [by Robert James]   (4-30-58)
630. "Prosper's Old Mother" [adapted from the story by Bret Harte]
     (5-1-58)
631. "End of a Sentence" [by Theodore Apstein]   (5-2-58)
632. "Elementals" [repeat of episode of 10/31/57]   (5-5-58)
633. "Top Platter" [by Warner Law]   (5-6-58)
634. "The Guest of Quesnay" [adapted by Robert Esson from the
     novel by Booth Tarkington] (5-7-58) Joanne Linville, Geor-
     gann Johnson, Dayton Lummis
635. "Good Housekeeping" [by William McCleery]   (5-8-58)
636. "Angel Street" [directed and adapted by Walter Grauman from
     the play by Patrick Hamilton] (5-9-58) Judith Evelyn,
     Vincent Price, Leo G. Carroll
637. "The Cause" [by Rod Serling]   (5-12-58) Sidney Blackmer,
     Richard Crenna, Kent Smith, Lois Smith
638. "Fight the Whole World" [repeat of episodes of 6/7/56 and
     12/27/57]   (5-13-58)
639. "The Long, Long Laugh" [repeat of episode of 2/5/58]   (5-14-
     58)
640. "The Ice Man" [repeat of episode of 2/4/58]   (5-15-58)
641. "Cave-In" [repeat of episode of 2/3/58]   (5-16-58)
642. "Nine Finger Jack" [repeat of episode of 10/30/57]   (5-19-58)
643. "Much Ado About Nothing" [adapted from the Shakespeare clas-
     sic; Part I] (5-20-58) Herschel Bernardi, Nina Foch, Rob-
     ert Hutton
644. "Much Ado About Nothing" [Part II]   (5-21-58)
645. "Day of Discoveries"   (5-22-58) Edmon Ryan, Dina Merrill,
     Peter Hansen
646. "The Young and the Fair" [adapted from the Broadway play by
     N. Richard Nash] (5-23-58) Marian Seldes, Frances Starr
647. "The Broom and the Groom" [repeat of episode of 12/5/57]
     (5-26-58)
548. "The Riddle of Mary Murphy" [by Helene Hanff]   (5-27-58)
649. "The Gardenia Bush" [by Bob and Wanda Duncan]   (5-28-58)
     Dick Foran, Martha Scott
650. "Button, Button"   (5-29-58)
651. "Hands"   (5-30-58) William Shatner, Bethel Leslie
652. "Love out of Town" [repeat of episode of 1/31/58]   (6-2-58)
653. "The End of a Sentence" [repeat of episode of 5/2/58]   (6-3-58]
654. "Look Out for John Tucker"   (6-4-58)
655. "The Road to Recovery" [by Budd Schulberg]   (6-5-58) Ed-
     ward Binns, Joe Maross
656. "The Night-bird Crying"   (6-6-58)
657. "The Sixty-fifth Floor" [repeat of episode of 2/26/58]   (6-9-58)
658. "The Story of Marcia Gordon"   (6-10-58)
659. "Town in a Turmoil"   (6-11-58)
660. "Washington Square" [adapted from the Henry James classic]
     (6-12-58) John Abbott, Lurene Tuttle, Roddy McDowall,
     Peggy McCay

661. "Course for Collision" [by Arthur Hailey] (6-13-58) Law-
     rence Dobkin, John Dehner, Dayton Lummis, Lyle Talbot,
     Addison Richards
662. "The Odd Ones" [repeat of episodes 3/9/56 and 2/7/58] (6-
     16-58)
663. "The Man with the Pointed Toes" [repeat of episode of 1/28/58]
     (6-17-58)
664. "A Question of Balance" [repeat of episode of 9/13/56] (6-18-
     58)
665. "The Heart's Desire" [repeat of episode of 2/21/58] (6-19-58)
666. "The Man Without a Country" [repeat of episode of 1/31/58]
     (6-20-58)
667. "The Prophet Hosea" [repeat of episode of 3/5/58] (6-23-58)
668. "Journey into Darkness" [repeat of episode of 3/26/57] (6-24-
     58)
669. "From the Desk of Margaret Tydings" [repeat of episodes
     4/4/56 and 2/18/57] (6-25-58)
670. "Rain in the Morning" [repeat of episode of 3/31/58] (6-26-58)
671. "End of the Rope" [repeat of episode of 4/1/57] (6-27-58)

WARNER BROTHERS PRESENTS [KING'S ROW/CHEYENNE/CASA-
   BLANCA/FEATURES]

     Cheyenne has been chronicled separately.

     This anthology of filmed dramas is principally distinguished
for its having inaugurated the series "pilot" tradition. Here studio
production is kept to an inexpensive minimum, allowing for a critical
"testing" period with the mass audience. This now notorious practice
has been attributed as a major cause in the artistic decline of the
medium. It is hard to imagine less inspired adaptations of the film
classics King's Row (Casey Robinson's screenplay of the Henry Bel-
lamann novel) and Casablanca (the Howard Koch, Julius J. Epstein
and Philip G. Epstein celebrated scenario). Now stock characters
exchange ersatz dialogue in stagnant situations; whispered reminders
of their predecessors, here indeed are the rudiments of artistic fall.

The Regulars: King's Row: Dr. Parris Mitchell: Jack Kelly; Ran-
   dy Monoghan: Nan Leslie; Drake McHugh: Robert Horton; Elise
   Sandor: Peggy Webber; Dr. Alexander Tower: Victor Jory;
   Casablanca: Rick Blaine: Charles McGraw; Ilsa Lund Laszlo:
   Anita Ekberg; Victor Laszlo: Peter Van Eyck. Gig Young served
   as the composite series host.

The Episodes:

   1. King's Row: [unknown title] (9-13-55) Lillian Bronson
   2. Casablanca: [unknown title] (9-27-55) Gig Young
   3. King's Row: "Juvenile Delinquency" (10-4-55) Wallace Ford
   4. Casablanca: "Black Market Operation" (10-18-55) Nicole
      Maurey

5. King's Row: "Possessive Love" (10-25-55) Joy Page, Kathryn Givney
6. Casablanca: "Labor Camp Escape" (11-8-55) Don Randolph, William Hopper, Maureen O'Sullivan
7. King's Row: "Mail Order Romance" (11-15-55) Lee Patrick, Rhys Williams
8. Casablanca: "Hand of Fate" (11-29-55) Dan Seymour, Michael Fox
9. King's Row: "Introduction to Erica" (12-6-55) Maria Palmer, John Alderson, Isa and Nadene Ashdown
10. Casablanca: "Family Dispute" (12-20-55) Arlene Whelan, Joe De Santis, Lydia Reed, Patty McCormack
11. King's Row: "The Wedding Gift" (12-27-55) Dennis Hopper, Natalie Wood, Lillian Bronson
12. Casablanca: "Fateful Night" (1-10-56)
13. King's Row: "Carnival" (1-17-56) Sydney Chaplin, Claire Kelly
14. Casablanca: "Satan Veil" (1-31-56) Rossanna Rory
15. Warner Brothers Presents: "Siege" (2-14-56) Paul Richards, Elizabeth Montgomery
16. Casablanca: "The Alley" (2-28-56) Marcel Dallo
17. Warner Brothers Presents: "Survival" (3-13-56) Jim Backus, Julie Bishop, Butch Bernard
18. Warner Brothers Presents: "Explosion" (3-27-56) Lyle Bettger, Joy Page
19. Casablanca: "Siren Song" (4-10-56) Mari Blanchard
20. Casablanca: "Deadlock!" (4-24-56) Olive Sturgess
21. Warner Brothers Presents: "Deep Freeze" (5-8-56) Gerald Mohr, Charles Bronson, Jon Shepodd
22. Warner Brothers Presents: "The Wife of Bath's Tale" [adapted from the Geoffrey Chaucer story] (5-22-56) Natalie Wood, Jacques Sernas, Torin Thatcher

CHEYENNE [subsequently alternating with SUGARFOOT and BRONCO]

The Regulars: Cheyenne Bodie: Clint Walker; L. Q. Jones appeared as sidekick Smitty for the duration of the first season; Diane Brewster appeared in the recurring role of Samantha Crawford with episode of 9/11/56.

The Episodes:

First Season [as part of the anthology WARNER BROTHERS PRESENTS (q. v.)]

1. "Julesburg" [introductory episode] (9-20-55)
2. "Cattle Outlaws" (10-11-55) Adele August, Ray Teal, David Albert
3. "The Mine" (11-1-55) Rodney (Rod) Taylor, Ed Andrews, Steve Conte
4. "Border Showdown" (11-22-55) Myron Healey, Lisa Montell,

Julian Rivero, Adele Mara
5. "The Outlander" (12-13-55) Leo Gordon, Doris Dowling, Onslow Stevens
6. "The Traveler" (1-3-56) James Gleason, Robert Armstrong, Dennis Hopper, Diane Brewster, Morris Ankrum
7. "The Black Hawk War" (1-24-56) Nancy Hale, Richard Denning
8. "The Storm Riders" (2-7-56) Regis Toomey, Beverly Michaels, Anne Whitfield
9. "Rendezvous at Red Rock" (2-21-56) Gerald Mohr, Leo G. Carroll
10. "The Argonauts" [adapted from the 1948 John Huston film scenario of the Ben Traven novel] (3-6-56)
11. "West of the River" (3-20-56) Stefanie Griffin, Lois Collier
12. "Quicksand" (4-3-56) Dennis Hopper, Norman Frederic
13. "Fury at Rio Hondo" (4-17-56) Ralph Moody, Peggie Castle
14. "Star in the Dust" (5-1-56) Don Megowan, Adele Mara
15. "Johnny Bravo" (5-15-56) Carlos Rivas, Harry Shannon, Penny Edwards
16. "The Last Train West" (5-29-56) Barbara Lawrence
17. "Decision" (6-5-56) Richard Denning

Second Season [alternating with CONFLICT (q. v.)]

18. "The Dark Rider" (9-11-56) Diane Brewster
19. "The Long Winter" (9-25-56) Tom Pittman, Robert J. Wilke
20. "Death Deals This Hand" (10-9-56) Pat Tierman, Arthur Hunnicutt
21. "The Bounty Killer" [an Emmy nominee for film editing, 1956] (10-23-56) Andrew Duggan, Gail Kobe
22. "The Law Man" (11-6-56) Andrea King, Grant Williams, Paul Engle
23. "The Mustang Trail" (11-20-56) Diane Brewster, Ross Elliott
24. "Lone Gun" (12-4-56) Nancy Hale, Paul Brinegar
25. "The Trap" (12-18-56) Maggie Hayes, Rhodes Reason, Sally Fraser
26. "The Iron Trail" (1-1-57) Dane Clark
27. "Land Beyond the Law" (1-15-57) Andrew Duggan
28. "Test of Courage" (1-29-57) Mary Castle, George Neise, John Archer
29. "War Party" (2-12-57) Angie Dickinson
30. "Deadline" (2-26-57) Mark Richman, John Qualen, Mark Roberts
31. "Big Ghost Basin" (3-12-57) Robert Hover, Merry Anders, Buddy Baer
32. "Born Bad" (3-26-57) Wright King, Jil Jarmyn, Robert F. Simon
33. "The Brand" (4-9-57) Edward Byrnes, Susan George
34. "Decision at Gunsight" (4-23-57) John Carradine, Patrick McVey, Marie Windsor
35. "The Spanish Grant" (5-7-57)
36. "Hard Bargain" (5-21-57) Richard Crenna, Regis Toomey
37. "The Broken Pledge" (6-4-57) John Dehner, Jean Byron, Paul Birch, Norman Frederic

Third Season [alternating with SUGARFOOT (Will Hutchins as Tom
  Brewster)]

38. Sugarfoot: "Brannigan's Boots" (9-17-57) Dennis Hopper
39. Cheyenne: "Incident at Indian Springs" (9-24-57) Dan Barton,
    Carlyle Mitchell, Bonnie Bolding, John Cliff, Chris Olsen
40. Sugarfoot: "The Strange Land" (10-1-57)
41. Cheyenne: "The Conspirators" (10-8-57) Joan Weldon, Guinn
    Williams, Tom Conway
42. Sugarfoot: "The Devil to Pay" (10-15-57) Tol Avery
43. Cheyenne: "The Mutton Puncher" (10-22-57) Robert J. Wilke,
    Marie Windsor, Billy Gray, Lauren Chapin
44. Sugarfoot: "Bunch Quitter" (10-29-57) Ray Danton
45. Cheyenne: "Traveling Princess" (11-5-57) Rhodes Reason
46. Sugarfoot: "Trail's End" (11-12-57)
47. Cheyenne: "Devil's Canyon" (11-19-57) Robert Foulk, Jack
    La Rue, Ainslie Pryor, Joanna Barnes, Mark Cavell
48. Sugarfoot: "Quicksilver" (11-26-57)
49. Cheyenne: "Town of Fear" (12-3-57) Walter Coy, Alan Wells,
    Steven Darrell
50. Sugarfoot: "Misfire" (12-10-57) Connie Stevens, Frank Al-
    bertson, Eve Brant, Pernell Roberts
51. Cheyenne: "Hired Gun" (12-17-57) Don Megowan, Alan Hale
52. Sugarfoot: "The Stallion Trail" (12-24-57) Paul Birch, Pat-
    rick Waltz, Will Wright
53. Cheyenne: "Top Hand" (12-31-57)
54. Sugarfoot: "Small War at Custer Junction" (1-7-58)
55. Cheyenne: "The Last Comanchero" (1-14-58) Harold J. Stone,
    Edward Byrnes, Virginia Aldridge
56. Sugarfoot: "Bullet Proof" (1-21-58) Joi Lansing, Gregory
    Walcott
57. Cheyenne: "The Gamble" (1-28-58) Evelyn Ankers
58. Sugarfoot: "Deadlock" (2-4-58) Herbert Heyes, John Vivyan
59. Cheyenne: "Renegades" (2-11-58) Bartlett Robinson, Peter
    Brown, Olive Sturgess, Steven Durrell
60. Sugarfoot: "Man Wanted" (2-18-58)
61. Cheyenne: "The Empty Gun" (2-25-58) Audrey Totter, John
    Russell
62. Sugarfoot: "The Dead Hills" (3-4-58) Ruta Lee
63. Cheyenne: "White Warrior" (3-11-58) Michael Landon, Peter
    Whitney
64. Sugarfoot: "A Wreath for Charity Lloyd" (3-18-58) Erin
    O'Brien
65. Cheyenne: "Ghost of Cimarron" (3-25-58) Patrick McVey,
    Peter Brown
66. Sugarfoot: "Hideout" (4-1-58) Paul Fix, Anita Gordon, Peter
    Brown
67. Cheyenne: "Wagon Tongue North" (4-8-58)
68. Sugarfoot: "Contraband Cargo" (4-15-58)
69. Cheyenne: "The Long Search" (4-22-58) Claude Akins, Nor-
    man Frederic
70. Sugarfoot: "Price on His Head" (4-29-58) Patrick McVey,
    Dorothy Green

71. Cheyenne: "Standoff" (5-6-58) Rodolfo Acosta, Richard Garland
72. Sugarfoot: "Short Range" (5-13-58)
73. Cheyenne: "Dead to Rights" (5-20-58) John Russell, Michael Connors, Joanna Barnes
74. Sugarfoot: "The Bullet and the Cross" (5-27-58) Charles Bronson
75. Cheyenne: "Noose at Noon" (6-3-58) Charles Quinlivan, Theona Bryant
76. Sugarfoot: "Mule Team" (6-10-58)
77. Cheyenne: "The Angry Sky" (6-17-58) Adele Mara, Joan Evans, Andrew Duggan

Fourth Season [SUGARFOOT alternating with BRONCO (Ty Hardin as Bronco Layne); series were collectively referred to as THE CHEYENNE SHOW]

78. Sugarfoot: "Ring of Sand" (9-16-58) John Russell
79. Bronco: "The Besieged" (9-23-58) Claude Akins, Sue Randall, Jack Elam, Allen Case
80. Sugarfoot: "Brink of Fear" (9-30-58) Jerry Paris
81. Bronco: "Quest of the Thirty Dead" (10-7-58) Beverly Tyler, Ray Danton, Jay Novello
82. Sugarfoot: "The Wizard" (10-14-58) Efrem Zimbalist Jr., John Lomer, Beverly Gowan, Norma Moore, Edward Kemmer, Oliver McGowan, Paul Keast
83. Bronco: "The Turning Point" (10-21-58) Scott Marlowe (as John Wesley Hardin), R. G. Armstrong
84. Sugarfoot: "The Ghost" (10-28-58)
85. Bronco: "Four Guns and a Prayer" (11-4-58)
86. Sugarfoot: "The Canary Kid" (11-11-58) Will Hutchins in a dual role; Frank Albertson, Louise Blackmas, Saundra Edwards
87. Bronco: "The Long Ride Back" (11-18-58) Mort Mills, Kathleen Crowley, Gerald Mohr, Paul Fix, Charles Fredericks
88. Sugarfoot: "The Hunted" (11-25-58) Michael Lane
89. Bronco: "Trail to Taos" (12-2-58) Joanne Gilbert, Edward Kemmer
90. Sugarfoot: "Yampa Crossing" (12-9-58) Harold J. Stone
91. Bronco: "The Burning Spring" (12-16-58) Rhodes Reason, Suzanne Lloyd, Berry Kroeger, Adam West
92. Sugarfoot: "The Devil To Pay" (12-23-58) [repeat of 10-15-57]
93. Bronco: "Freeze-Out" (12-30-58) Grace Raynor
94. Sugarfoot: "The Desperadoes" (1-6-59) Jack Kruschen, Anthony George
95. Bronco: "The Baron of Broken Lance" (1-13-59)
96. Sugarfoot: "The Extra Hand" (1-20-59) Karl Swenson
97. Bronco: "Payroll of the Dead" (1-27-59)
98. Sugarfoot: "The Return of the Canary Kid" (2-3-59) Will Hutchins in dual role; Wayne Preston (as Christopher Colt of Colt . 45), Saundra Edwards, Donald Barry
99. Bronco: "Riding Solo" (2-10-59) Robert Lowery, Ray Teal

100. Sugarfoot: "The Mysterious Stranger" (2-17-59) Adam West
101. Bronco: "Borrowed Glory" (2-24-59) Robert Vaughn, Andra Martin, Charles Cooper
102. Sugarfoot: "The Giant Killer" (3-3-59) R. G. Armstrong, Patricia Barry, Jay North, John Litel, Dorothy Provine
103. Bronco: "The Silent Witness" (3-10-59) Chris Alcaide, Russell Conway, Karl Davis
104. Sugarfoot: "The Royal Raiders" (3-17-59) Helmut Dantine, Jacqueline Beer, Horst Vonn Hoffstedt
105. Bronco: "The Belles of Silver Flat" (3-24-59) Pernell Roberts, Vaughn Taylor, John Beradino
106. Sugarfoot: "The Mountain" (3-31-59) Don Dubbins, Miranda Jones
107. Bronco: "Backfire" (4-7-59) Barry Kelley, Troy Donahue, Don Beddoe, Jeff York
108. Sugarfoot: "The Twister" (4-14-59) Don Dubbins, Stephen Talbot, Fred Beir, Betty Lynn
109. Bronco: "School for Cowards" (4-21-59)
110. Sugarfoot: "The Vultures" (4-28-59) Faith Domergue, Alan Marshall, Richard Long
111. Bronco: "Prairie Skipper" (5-5-59) Arlene Howell, Lorne Greene, Bing Russell, Stephen Chase
112. Sugarfoot: "The Avengers" (5-12-59) Steve London, Luana Anders, Vito Scotti, Dorothy Provine, Richard Cutting, Edgar Stehli
113. Bronco: "Shadow of a Man" (5-19-59)
114. Sugarfoot: "Small Hostage" (5-26-59) Robert Warwick, Gary Hunley
115. Bronco: "Hero of the Town" (6-2-59) Lynn Bari, Ken Mayer, Karl Weber, Stephen Coit
116. Sugarfoot: "Wolf" (6-9-59) Wright King, Judy Nugent, Virginia Gregg
117. Bronco: "Red Water North" (6-16-59) Sarah Selby, Burt Douglas, Michael Forest, Kelly Thordsen, Hugh Sanders, Dorothy Provine, Karl Swenson

Episodes continued with Television Drama Series Programming: A Comprehensive Chronicle, 1959-1975.

THE ARMSTRONG CIRCLE THEATRE/THE UNITED STATES STEEL HOUR [rotating with THE TWENTIETH CENTURY-FOX HOUR and PLAYWRIGHTS '56]

The Regulars: John Conte was host for "The Twentieth Century-Fox Hour"

The Episodes:

1. The Armstrong Circle Theatre: "The Strange War of Sergeant Krezner" [by Jerome Cameron] (9-27-55) Richard Kiley,

Betsy Palmer

2. The United States Steel Hour: "Ashton Buys a Horse" [by Norman Lessing] (9-28-55) Menasha Skulnik, Conrad Janis

3. Playwrights '56: "The Answer" [adapted from the Philip Wylie fantasy; directed by Delbert Mann] (10-4-55) Paul Douglas, Conrad Nagel, Albert Dekker, Nina Foch, Walter Abel

4. The Twentieth Century-Fox Hour: "Heart of a Woman" (a. k. a. "Cavalcade") [adapted from the Noel Coward play] (10-5-55) Merle Oberon, Michael Wilding, Marcia Henderson

5. The Armstrong Circle Theatre: "Lost $2 Billion: The Story of Hurricane Diane" [by Irve Tunick] (10-11-55) Jason Robards Jr., Silvio Minciotti, Augusta Merighi; John Cameron Swayze narrated.

6. The United States Steel Hour: "Obsession" [by Ernest Pendrell] (10-12-55) Philip Abbott, Phyllis Thaxter, Neva Patterson

7. Playwrights '56: "The Battler" [adapted by A. E. Hotchner and Sidney Carroll from the magazine story by Ernest Hemingway; directed by Arthur Penn and produced by Fred Coe] (10-18-55) Paul Newman, Dewey Martin, Phyllis Kirk, Frederick O'Neal

8. The Twentieth Century-Fox Hour: "Portrait for Murder" (a. k. a. "Laura") [adapted from the novel by Vera Caspary] (10-19-55) Dana Wynter, Robert Stack, George Sanders, Scott Forbes

9. Playwrights '56: "The Heart's a Forgotten Hotel" [by Arnold Schulman] (10-25-55) Sylvia Sidney, Edmond O'Brien, Arlene Whelan, Paul Hartman, Cliff Tatem

10. The United States Steel Hour: "Shoot It Again" [title song performed by Teresa Brewer] (10-26-55) Geraldine Page, Jerome Courtland, Kenny Delmar

11. The Armstrong Circle Theatre: "Minding Our Own Business" (11-1-55) Maureen Stapleton, Edward Andrews

12. The Twentieth Century-Fox Hour: "The Lynch Mob" (a. k. a. "The Ox-Bow Incident") [adapted from the novel by Walter Van Tilburg Clark] (11-2-55) Cameron Mitchell, E. G. Marshall, Robert Wagner, Raymond Burr, Wallace Ford, Jay Brooks

13. Playwrights '56: "Snow Job" [by Richard Turner] (11-8-55) James Gregory, Joan Blondell, Arthur Sussman, Meg Mundy, Charles Taylor

14. The United States Steel Hour: "Outcast" [adapted by Turner Bullock from the story by Frank Gabrielson] (11-9-55) Lillian Roth, Joe Maross, Barbara Baxley, Bert Thorn, Beverly Lunsford, Bert Freed

15. The Armstrong Circle Theatre: "Saturday Visit" [by Douglas Taylor from the files of the Family Service Association of America] (11-15-55) Jack Klugman, Kathleen Maguire

16. The Twentieth Century-Fox Hour: "Back Bay Romance" (a. k. a. "The Late George Apley") (11-16-55) Raymond Massey, Joanne Woodward, Ann Harding, Arthur Franz, Barbara Rush

17. Playwrights '56: "Daisy, Daisy" [by Sumner Locke Elliott; directed by Arthur Penn and produced by Fred Coe]

(11-22-55) Jane Wyatt, Tom Ewell, Edith Miser, Eloise McElhone

18. The United States Steel Hour: "Incident in an Alley" [by Rod Serling; filmed by United Artists, 1962] (11-23-55) Farley Granger, Alan Hewitt, Larry Gates, Lori March, Peg Hillias, Don Hammer

19. The Armstrong Circle Theatre: "The Town That Refused to Die" (11-29-55) Darren McGavin, Paul Tripp, Jerome Kilty, Maxine Stuart, Bert Freed

20. The Twentieth Century-Fox Hour: "Death Paints a Legacy" (a.k.a. "Christopher Bean") [adapted from the play by Sidney Howard] (11-30-55) Gene Lockhart, Thelma Ritter, Mildred Natwick, Allyn Joslyn, Kip Hamilton

21. Playwrights '56: "The Sound and the Fury" [adapted by William F. Durkee from the "Dilsey" section of the William Faulkner novel; directed by Vincent J. Donahue and produced by Fred Coe] (12-6-55) Franchot Tone, Lillian Gish, Ethel Waters, Janice Rule, Valerie Bettis, Steven Hill

22. The United States Steel Hour: "Edward, My Son" [by Robert Morley and Noel Langley; directed by Norman Felton] (12-7-55) Robert Morley, Ann Todd, Geoffrey Toone, Frederic Tozere, Sally Cooper

23. The Armstrong Circle Theatre: "I Was Accused" [by Jerome Coopersmith, based upon the story of exile of actor George Voskovec] (12-13-55) George Voskovec, Hurd Hatfield, Cameron Prud'homme, June Dayton, Luis Van Rooten, Patricia Englund

24. The Twentieth Century-Fox Hour: "Meet Mr. Kringle" (a.k.a. "Miracle on Thirty-fourth Street") [adapted from the novel by Valentine Davies] (12-14-55) Macdonald Carey, Teresa Wright, Ray Collins, Hans Conried, Dick Foran

25. Playwrights '56: "The Waiting Place" [by Tad Mosel] (12-20-55) Kim Stanley, Louis Jean Heydt

26. The United States Steel Hour: "White Gloves" [by James Costigan] (12-21-55) Joanne Woodward, Joan Blondell

27. The Armstrong Circle Theatre: ("Project 20" special) "Nightmare in Red" [how communism came to Russia; produced by Henry Salomon] (12-27-55)

28. The Twentieth Century-Fox Hour: "Man on the Ledge" (a.k.a. "Fourteen Hours") [adapted from the magazine story by Joel Sayre] (12-28-55) Cameron Mitchell, William Gargan, Sylvia Sidney, Eduard Franz, Vera Miles

Episodes continued with Television Drama Series Programming, 1959-1975.

NAVY LOG

When the ocean vastness kept dominion over a thousand imperiled crafts, Herman Melville could expound on its allegorical significance, making for literary majesty. Now the waters have been reduced to playing fields for the strategems of military men and seemingly impervious vessels circumnavigate as chessmen. Navy Log, produced with the assistance of the United States Navy Department, is a series dramatizing the moves of strategists and chessmen; they that are pilots and they that are--dubiously--left to be piloted.

The Episodes:

1. "The Frogman" (9-20-55) Ross Elliott, Robert Nichols, Harry Landers, Morgan Jones, Robert Knapp, Mike Garrett, Bill Allyn
2. "Hiya Pam" (9-27-55) Douglas Dick, James Edwards
3. "The Leave" (10-4-55) Dick Jones, Dan Barton
4. "Home Is the Sailor" (10-11-55) Wright King, Toni Gerry
5. "The Phantom of the Blue Angels" (10-18-55) Paul Picerni
6. "Sky Pilot" (10-25-55) Paul Burke, Stanley Clements, Harry Townes
7. "Operation Three-In-One" [nominated for an Emmy for its film editing, 1955] (11-1-55) Lawrence Dobkin, Francis de Sales, Henry Kulky
8. "Family Special" (11-8-55) Paul Smith, Beverly Garland, Veda Ann Borg, Clark Howat, Frank Kreig
9. "The Captain's Choice" (11-15-55) Chick Chandler, Jon Shepodd, James Dobson, Gregg Palmer
10. "The Transfer" (11-22-55) Alvy Moore, Sally Fraser, Gayle Kellogg
11. "Navy Corpsman" (11-29-55) Bobby Driscoll, Gordon Gebert, Dabbs Greer, Dick Foote
12. "The Pentagon Story" (12-6-55) Dan Barton, Kay Riehl, Carleton Young, Vernon Rich, Nelson Leigh
13. "The Pollywog of Yosu" (12-13-55) Tom Laughlin, Pat Waltz, Alan Wells, Jimmy Murphy, Alan Hale, Britt Lomond
14. "The Bishop of Bayfield" (12-20-55) Peter Whitney, Wellington Soo Hoo
15. "Of Caution and Courage" (12-27-55) Walter Sande, Joseph Downing
16. "The Bomb" (1-3-56) Wally Cassell, Howard Price
17. "Dr. Van" (1-10-56) Richard Loo, Roland Moryama, Wally Richard
18. "Operation Typewriter" (1-17-56) Les Tremayne, Philip Ahn, Benson Fong
19. "The Gimmick" (1-24-56) Richard Benedict, William Swan
20. "Demos the Grik" (1-31-56) George Conrad
21. "Little More Than a Brother" (2-7-56) Donald Murphy, Jerry Paris
22. "Lunger at Kunsan" (2-14-56) Philip Bourneuf, James Stewart
23. "The Web Feet" (2-21-56) Casey Adams, Phyllis Coates, Lyle Talbot
24. "The Helium Umbrella" (2-28-56) Robert Crosson, Peter Bourne
25. "Ninety Day Wonder" (3-6-56) Ron Hagerthy, Russell Hicks
26. "The Fatal Crest" (3-20-56) Liam Sullivan, Arthur Hanson, Virginia Hale, Nelson Leigh

27. "Not a Leg to Stand On" (3-27-56) Harry Landers, Veda Ann Borg
28. "Men from Mars" (4-3-56) Douglas Kennedy, Willis Bouchey
29. "The First Shot" (4-10-56) Herbert Rudley, Robert Boon
30. "The Beachcomber" (4-17-56) Harry Tyler, Hugh Sanders
31. "Get Back Somehow" (4-24-56) Stanley Clements
32. "Rock Break Scissors" (5-1-56) James Seay
33. "Ghost Ship" (5-8-56) Jerry Nickelson, Bill Henry
34. "Bucket of Sand" (5-15-56) Tom Laughlin, Sue Carlton
35. "Sacrifice" (5-22-56) Phil Tead, Sue Carlton, Leonard Nimoy
36. "Night Landing" (5-29-56) Dani Sue Nolan
37. "The Plebe" (6-5-56) John Wilder
38. "The Long Week-End" (6-12-56) Ed Kemmer
39. "LST-999" (6-19-56) Michael Emmet
40. "The Pirate and the Pledge" (6-26-56) Ross Elliott, Robert Nichols

Second Season

41. "The Death of Dillinger-San" (10-17-56)
42. "The Big A" (10-24-56) Rayford Barnes, Harry Harvey, Carl Milletaire, Leo Gordon, Jack Larson, Jerry Paris
43. "A Day for the Stingray" (10-31-56) Russ Conway
44. "Scratch One Hearse" (11-7-56) Harry Landers, Joseph Turkel
45. "In the Labonza" (11-14-56)
46. "Man Alone" (11-21-56) Don Hayden
47. "The Pilot" (11-28-56) Alberto Morin
48. "Incident at Formosa" (12-5-56) Martin Milner, James Lydon
49. "Peril on the Sea" (12-12-56) Robert Shayne, Robert Quarry, Art Lewis, Wayne Waylor, Chuck Courtney
50. "Destination: 1600 Pennsylvania Avenue N.W." (12-19-56) Harry Lauter, Walter Coy
51. "A Guy Called Mickey" (12-26-56) Lane Nakano, Charles R. Keane
52. "Buzzy Boy" (1-2-57) Robert Easton
53. "Operation Golden Rule" (1-9-57) Paul Richards
54. "The Countess and the Convicts" (1-16-57) Christopher Dark
55. "Thack Weaves a Trap" (1-23-57) Wright King
56. "Survive" (1-30-57) Barry Truex, Kay Kuter, Robert Dirn, Scotty Beckett
57. "Ping Happy Spit Kid" [by Rear Admiral Daniel Gallery] (2-6-57)
58. "Amscray" (2-13-57)
59. "Operation Hideout" (2-20-57) Paul Richards
60. "The Star" (3-6-57) John Carradine
61. "War of the Whaleboats" (3-13-57) Richard Jaeckel
62. "After You, Ludwig" (3-20-57) Bart Burns
63. "The U.S.S. Enrico Tazzoli" (3-27-57) Paul Richards
64. "Ito of Attu" (4-3-57) John Bryant, Harold Fong
65. "SSN-571" (4-10-57) Addison Powell, Ed Rigney, Pat Henning, Mark Rydell
66. "Assignment ... BRT" (4-17-57) Herbert Rudley, Jerry Barclay
67. "The Decoy" (4-24-57) Veda Ann Borg

68. "Nightmare Off Brooklyn" (5-1-57)
69. "Goal ... Mach Two" (5-8-57) Ross Elliott, Richard Crane
70. "The Saga of Irving Cohan" (5-15-57) George Conrad
71. "Mission to Murmansk" (5-22-57) William Lundmark, Norman Leavitt, Henry Slate
72. "The Lady and the Atom" (5-29-57) Maggie Mahoney, Ron Haggerthy, Walter Coy, Peter Hansen, Dennis McCarthy, Douglas Dick, Robert Shayne
73. "The Fighting Fig" (6-5-57) Robert Arthur
74. "The Marines Are Landing" (6-12-57)

Third Season

75. "The Ballad of the Big E" [narrated by John Carradine] (9-18-57)
76. "Call CONAD" (9-25-57)
77. "Phantom Commander" (10-2-57) Walter Sande
78. "Capture of the U-50s" (10-9-57)
79. "Lost Human Bomb" (10-24-57) Jack Larson; Ernest Borgnine, guest host.
80. "The Commander and the Kid" (10-31-57) Brenda Lee, Tristram Coffin
81. "Fire at Sea" (11-7-57) Edward Binns, Robert Rockwell
82. "The Storm Within" (11-14-57) John Zaremba
83. "P. O. W. at Forty Fathoms" (11-21-57) Don Gordon
84. "One If By Sea" (11-28-57)
85. "The Amateurs" (12-5-57) John Archer, Steven Terrell
86. "Joe Foss Devilbird" (12-12-57) Fred Eisley
87. "The Beach Pounders" (12-19-57) Cesar Romero, guest host.
88. "The Big White Albatross" (12-26-57) Alvy Moore, Richard Deacon, George Cesar
89. "The Butchers of Kapsan" (1-2-58) Robert Montgomery, guest host.
90. "The Lonely Watch" (1-9-58) Clint Eastwood; James Cagney, guest host.
91. "The Blood Line" (1-16-58) Meade Martin, Dorothy Green, George Eldridge
92. "American U-Boat III" (1-23-58) Steve Brodie
93. "The Way of the Wrangell" (1-30-58) Ken Tobey, George Breslin, Richard Foote
94. "And Then There Was None" (2-6-58) John Doucette; John Daly, narrator.
95. "Blood Alley" (2-13-58) Frank Gerstle
96. "The Draft Dodger" (2-20-58) Ron Haggerthy
97. "The Soapbox Kid" (2-27-58) John Doucette, Richard Beymer, Paul Engle; Dennis Day, guest host.
98. "Helldivers Over Greece" (3-6-58) Richard Erdman, Michael Emmet, Dale Cummings
99. "PT 109" [a documentary drama of John Fitzgerald Kennedy in World War II] (3-13-58)
100. "One Grand Marine" (3-20-58) Regis Toomey

THE SCREEN DIRECTORS' PLAYHOUSE

Teleplays chosen, directed and cast by film directors.

The Episodes:

1. "Meet the Governor" [directed by Leo McCarey] (10-5-55)
   Herb Shriner, Bobby Clark, Barbara Hale, Paul Harvey,
   Rita Lynn
2. "Day Is Done" [by William Tunberg] (10-12-55) Rory Calhoun,
   Bobby Driscoll
3. "Midsummer Daydream" [by William Saroyan; directed by John
   Brahm] (10-19-55) Keenan Wynn, Don Hamner, Kim Hunter, Don Wilson
4. "Arroyo" (10-26-55) Jack Carson, Lynn Bari, Lola Albright,
   Neville Brand, Lloyd Corrigan
5. "Want Ad Wedding" (11-2-55) Sally Forrest, James Lydon,
   Richard Webb, Leon Ames, Fred Clark
6. "The Life of Vernon Hathaway" [by Barbara Merlin and Richard
   Wormser] (11-9-55) Alan Young, Cloris Leachman, Jay
   Novello, Florenz Ames, Susan Morrow, Douglass Dumbrille
7. "The Final Tribute" (11-16-55) Dan O'Herlihy, Thomas Mitchell, Laraine Day, Joyce McCluskey, Linda Lowell, Jonathan Hale
8. "The Bush Roper" (11-23-55) Walter Brennan, Chuck Connors,
   Edgar Buchanan, Olive Carey, Lee Aaker
9. "Tom and Jerry" [by Mary McCarey] (11-30-55) Peter Lawford, Nancy Gates, Mark Windsor, Frank Fay
10. "Rookie of the Year" [directed by John Ford] (12-7-55) John
    Wayne, Patrick Wayne, Vera Miles, James Gleason, Ward
    Bond
11. "Lincoln's Doctor's Dog" [adapted from the Christopher Morley
    story] (12-14-55) Robert Ryan, Charles Bickford
12. "The Silent Partner" [an Oscar presentation] (12-21-55) Bust-
    er Keaton, Zasu Pitts, Evelyn Ankers, Joe E. Brown
13. "Titanic Incident" [by W. R. Cox] (12-28-55) Leo Genn, May
    Wynn, Philip Reed, George Leigh
14. "Hot Cargo" (1-4-56) Yvonne de Carlo, Rory Calhoun, June
    Vincent, Alan Reed, Peter Brocco
15. "It's Always Sunday" (1-11-56) Dennis O'Keefe, Fay Wray,
    Chick Chandler, Sheldon Leonard
16. "Number Five Checked Out" (1-18-56) Teresa Wright, Peter
    Lorre, Ralph Moody, William Talman
17. "Prima Donna" [by Gene Raymond] (2-1-56) Jeanette MacDon-
    ald, Alfred Calanza, Laraine Day, Leo Durocher
18. "Cry Justice" (2-15-56) Dick Haymes, Macdonald Carey,
    James Dunn, June Vincent
19. "Affair in Sumatra" (2-22-56) Ralph Bellamy, Basil Rathbone,
    Rita Gam
20. "One Against Many" (3-7-56) Lew Ayres, Wallace Ford
21. "It's a Most Unusual Day" (3-14-56) Fred MacMurray, Jimmy
    McHugh, Marilyn Erskine

22. "Sword of Villon" (4-4-56) Errol Flynn, Pamela Duncan, Murvyn Vye, Hillary Brooke
23. "Markheim" [adapted from the Robert Louis Stevenson story] (4-11-56) Ray Milland, Rod Steiger
24. "Claire" (4-25-56) George Montgomery, Angela Lansbury
25. "A Ticket for Thaddeus" (5-9-56) Edmond O'Brien, Narda Onyx, Alan Hale
26. "Dream" [adapted from the Ivan Turgenev story] (5-16-56) George Sanders, Sal Mineo, Patricia Morrison
27. "What Day Is It?" [a musical by Jean Hollont] (6-6-56) Marge and Gower Champion
28. "Every Man Had Two Wives" (6-3-56) Janet Blair, Barry Nelson, Buddy Ebsen, Mary Sinclair
29. "Partners" (7-4-56) Brandon de Wilde, Casey Tibbs
30. "White Corridors" (7-11-56) Linda Darnell, Virginia Field, Scott Forbes, Pat Hitchcock, John Bentley
31. "The Carroll Formula" (7-18-56) Michael Wilding, Henry Davenport
32. "Apples on the Lilac Tree" [directed by John Rich] (7-25-56) Joan Caulfield, Macdonald Carey
33. "Bitter Waters" [adapted by Zoë Akins from the Henry James short story Louis Pallant] (8-1-56) George Sanders, Constance Cummings
34. "The Day I Met Caruso" (9-5-56) Sandy Dencher, Lofti Mansfieri
35. "High Air" [subsequently restaged for an episode of Decision (telecast 9/7/58)] (9-12-56) William Bendix, Dennis Hopper

CROSSROADS

The Episodes:

1. "Shadow of God" (10-7-55) Paul Kelly, Strother Martin
2. "Cleanup" (10-14-55) Vincent Price, Sally Blane, Lloyd Corrigan
3. "The Unholy Trio" (10-21-55) Luther Adler, Russell Johnson, Christopher Dark, Joe Turkell
4. "With All My Love" (10-28-55) Hugh Beaumont, Ann Harding
5. "Hostage" (11-4-55) Don Taylor, Robert Armstrong, Laurence Dobkin
6. "Broadway Trust" (11-11-55) Gene Lockhart, Lloyd Bridges
7. "Mr. Liberty Bell" (11-18-55) Brian Donlevy, Adrienne Marden, Kam Tong, Ricky Marshall, Malcolm Connell, Rankin Mansfield
8. "The Good Thief" [the story of Father Emil Joseph Kapaun, chaplain in Korean conflict] (11-25-55) Philip Ahn, James Whitmore, Philip Pine, Jack Kramer, Terry Frost
9. "Mightier Than the Sword" (12-2-55) Carl Benton Reid, Kristine Miller, Tony George, Paul Sorenson, Gregory Gay
10. "The Gambler" (12-9-55) Robert Hutton, Dennis Morgan, Mark Runyon

11. "Chinese Checkers" (12-16-55) Richard Denning, Brian Aherne, Harry Shannon, Philip Ahn, Donald Randolph
12. "Vivi Shining Bright" (12-23-55) Hillary Brooke, Kent Smith, Anne Kimbell
13. "A Bell for C'Donnell" (12-30-55) Glenn Langen, Edmund Lowe
14. "Through the Window" (1-6-56) Steve Brodie, Arthur Shields, Douglas Dumbrille, Marcia Henderson, Casey Adams
15. "Cavalry in China" (1-13-56) Arthur Franz, Marya Marko, Philip Ahn, Keye Luke
16. "The Mountain Angel" [the story of Methodist missionary the Reverend Robert F. Thomas] (1-20-56) Howard Duff, Noah Beery
17. "St. George and the Dragon" (1-27-56) Richard Arlen, Gloria Blondell, Tommy Cook
18. "The Inner Light" (2-3-56) George Brent, Benson Fong
19. "The Little Herald" (2-10-56) Donald Woods
20. "Strange Bequest" (2-17-56) Pat O'Brien, Barton MacLane
21. "Pavement Pastor" (2-24-56) Jeff Morrow, Harry Antrim
22. "The Rebel" (3-2-56) Vincent Price
23. "Mother C'Brien" (3-9-56) Arthur Shields, Donald Murphy, James Lyndon, Ruth Donnelly
24. "The Sacred Trust" (3-16-56) Brian Aherne
25. "The Bowery Bishop" (3-23-56) Richard Denning, Robert Armstrong, Jean Welles
26. "Dig or Die, Brother Hyde" (3-30-56) Hugh Marlowe, John Qualen
27. "Two-Fisted Saint" (4-6-56) Paul Kelly, Walter Coy, Robert S. Carson
28. "Deadly Fear" (4-13-56) Rod Cameron, John Baer, Jeanette Nolan
29. "Anatole of the Bayous" (4-20-56) Donald Crisp, John Qualen
30. "The White Carnation" (4-27-56) J. Carrol Naish
31. "Home Is the Sailor" (5-4-56) William Leslie, David Brian
32. "Lifeline" (5-11-56) Kent Taylor, Barbara Hale, Regis Toomey, Maria English
33. "The Judge" (5-18-56) Brian Donlevy, Donald Curtis
34. "God in the Streets" (5-25-56) Jeff Morrow, Helen Parrish, Reed Hadley, Andrew Tomlin
35. "The Man on the Totem Pole" (6-1-56) Richard Erdman, Coleen Gray, Stacey Harris
36. "The Rabbi Davis Story" (6-8-56) Arthur Franz, Howard Petrie, Dayton Lummis
37. "The Singing Preacher" (6-15-56) Dick Foran, John Smith, Gloria Talbott
38. "A Holiday for Father Jim" (6-22-56) Pat O'Brien, Russell Johnson, Jonathan Hole
39. "False Prophet" (6-29-56) Bruce Bennett, Robert Horton, John Emery, Ann Baker

Second Season

40. "The Comeback" (10-5-56) Kevin Connors, Lou Brissie

41. "Circus Priest" (10-12-56) Pat O'Brien
42. "Ringside Padre" (10-19-56) Stephen McNally
43. "The Pure White Orchid" (10-26-56) Richard Denning
44. "Sky Pilot of the Cumberlands" (11-2-56) Donald Woods, Lee Van Cleef
45. "With Charity for All" (11-9-56) J. Carrol Naish, Alan Hale, Gene Reynolds
46. "Timberland Preacher" (11-16-56) David Brian, Martin Milner, Barry Kelley
47. "Thanksgiving Prayer" (11-23-56) Jeff Morrow, Douglas Dumbrille
48. "God's Healing" (11-30-56) Vincent Price, Marcia Henderson, Frieda Inescourt
49. "The Lamp of Father Cataldo" (12-7-56) Brian Aherne, Edgar Buchanan
50. "Tenement Saint" (12-14-56) Cecil Kellaway, Elizabeth Patterson
51. "Our First Christmas" (12-21-56) Don Taylor
52. "The Kid Had a Gun" (12-28-56) George Brent
53. "The Man Who Walked on Water" (1-4-57) Alan Mowbray, William Prince, Maureen O'Sullivan
54. "Week-end Minister" (1-11-57) Richard Arlen, Eduard Franz, Frank Wilcox, Ron Hargrave, Patricia Hardy
55. "The Patton Prayer" (1-18-57) Stephen McNally, Carl Benton Reid
56. "God of Kandikur" (1-25-57) Brian Donlevy, Eva Miller
57. "The Happy Gift" (2-1-57) Richard Carlson, Sue George
58. "Barbed Wire Preacher" (2-8-57) Scott Brady
59. "In God We Trust" (2-15-57) Jeff Morrow, K. T. Stevens
60. "Boomtown Padre" (2-22-57) Dick Foran
61. "Call for Help" (3-1-57) Richard Carlson
62. "The Ice Cathedral" (3-8-57) Kevin McCarthy
63. "Lone Star Preacher" (3-15-57) Victor Jory
64. "The Last Strand" (3-22-57) Conrad Nagel, Mala Powers
65. "Paratroop Padre" [Part I; the story of paratroop padre Lt. Col. Francis L. Sampson, the United States Army's most decorated captain] (3-29-57) Richard Jaeckel, Charles McGraw
66. "The Light" [Part II] as above.
67. "The Big Sombrero" (4-12-57) Cecil Kellaway
68. "Riot" (4-19-57) Pat O'Brien
69. "Jhonakehunga--Called John" (4-26-57) Hugh Marlowe, Pat Hogan
70. "The Wreath" (5-3-57) David Brian
71. "Convict 1321, Age 12" (5-10-57) Stephen McNally
72. "Half Mile Down" (5-17-57) Jeff Morrow
73. "9:30 Action" (5-24-57) Richard Arlen, Susan Oliver
74. "Coney Island Wedding" (5-31-57) Dick Foran, Robert Paige, Kathleen Crowley
75. "The Miracle of Faith" (6-7-57) Robert Hutton, Conrad Nagel, Catherine Givney
76. "The Deadline" (6-14-57) Arthur Franz, Pat Crowley
77. "Patchwork Family" (6-21-57) Stuart Erwin, Dorothy Green

78. "A Green Hill Faraway" [the story of New York chaplain, The Reverend Drury L. Patchell] (6-28-57) Lloyd Corrigan, Barbara Eden, Steve Terrell, Lumsden Hare, William Swan

STAR STAGE

The Episodes:

1. "The Toy Lady" [by Max Watson] (9-9-55) Sylvia Sidney, Lorne Greene, Will Kuluva, Ruggero Romor
2. "Cop Without a Badge" [adapted by Joel Carpenter from a story by John and Ward Hawkins] (9-16-55) Joey Walsh, James Gregory
3. "The United States Versus Alexander Holmes" [the basis for the 1956 series On Trial (q. v.)] (9-23-55) Joseph Cotten (who repeats his role for the series), Sally Blane, Robert Middleton, Ellen Corby, Robert Warwick, Frank Gerstle Sally Brophy
4. "First Date" (9-30-55) Robin Morgan, Joyce Smight, Phyllis Newman, Paula Truman
5. "Honest John and the Thirteen Uncle Sams" (10-7-55) Brian Donlevy
6. "Brands from the Burning" (10-14-55) Zachary Scott, Ruth Ford
7. "Trumpet Man" (10-21-55) Gary Merrill
8. "A Letter to Mr. Priest" [restaged from the Philco Television Playhouse episode of February 19, 1950] (10-28-55) Wendell Corey
9. "Dr. Jordan" (11-4-55) Dennis Morgan, Sidney Blackmer, Cloris Leachman, Roy Roberts, Sarah Selby
10. "Spring over Brooklyn" (11-11-55) Alan Young
11. "In Houses I Enter" (11-18-55) James Daly, Wallace Ford
12. "The Girl Who Wasn't Wanted" (11-25-55) Jeanne Crain, John Ericson
13. "The Marmalade Scandal" (12-2-55) Mildred Natwick, Rhys Williams
14. "The One Thousand Dollar Bill" (12-9-55) Eddie Bracken, Howard St. John, Hildy Parks
15. "Foreign Wife" (12-16-55) Phyllis Kirk, Stephen McNally
16. "The Recluse" [adapted from a story by Norman Katkov] (12-23-55) Don Taylor, Georgiann Johnson, Harry Townes
17. "The Knife" (12-30-55) Donald Woods, Pud Flanagan, Edward Binns
18. "The Marshal and the Mob" (1-6-56) Dan Duryea, Ward Bond, Ken Dibbs
19. "Of Missing Persons" (1-13-56) Ralph Meeker, Joan Lorring
20. "Articles of War" (1-20-56) Ralph Bellamy, Edward Binns
21. "Screen Credit" [by Hagar Wilde] (1-27-56) Cornel Wilde, Jim Backus, Carolyn Jones, Kathleen Crowley, Bruce Cowling

22. "Killer on Horseback" (2-3-56) Rod Cameron, Beverly Garland
23. "White Night" [by James R. Ullman] (2-10-56) Paul Douglas, Polly Bergen
24. "The Schoolmistress" (2-17-56) Lois Smith, Jessica Tandy, Torin Thatcher, Frieda Altman
25. "Career" [by Richard Landau] (2-24-56) Greer Garson, Patric Knowles, Linda Bennett
26. "I Am Her Nurse" (3-2-56) Mary Astor
27. "Cleopatra Collins" (3-9-56) Betty Grable, Casey Adams, Rick Jason
28. "The Man Who Was Irresistible to Women" (3-16-56) Art Carney, Carmen Mathews, Lisa Ferraday
29. "The Secret Place" (3-23-56) Kevin McCarthy, Teresa Wright
30. "Scandal on Deepside" (3-30-56) Maureen O'Sullivan
31. "The Sainted General" (4-6-56) Luther Adler, Yvonne De Carlo, John Abbott
32. "Being Nice to Emily" (4-13-56) Robert Sterling, Anne Jeffreys
33. "The Shadowy Third" [adapted by Collier Young from the Ellen Glasgow play] (4-20-56) Joan Fontaine, John Baragrey, Judith Evelyn
34. "A Place to Be Alone" (4-27-56) John Forsythe
35. "Bend to the Wind" [by Roger Lawton] (5-4-56) Brandon de Wilde
36. "The Guardian" (5-11-56) Preston Foster, Barbara Hale, Arthur Space, Beverly Washburn
37. "The Man in the Black Robe" (5-18-56) Frank McHugh, Joseph Cotten, John McIntire, Paul Douglas
38. "Foundations" (5-26-56) Polly Bergen, John Baragrey
39. "The Real Thing" [adapted by A. J. Russell from the Louis Auchincloss short story] (6-1-56) Betsy Palmer, George Macready, Nicholas Joy

TELEPHONE TIME

Historical dramas; subjects may appear in brackets.

The Regulars: John Nesbitt, host and narrator. Dr. Frank Baxter served as host and narrator with the third season.

The Episodes:

1. "The Golden Junkman" (4-8-56) Lon Chaney Jr.
2. "The Man Behind the Beard" (4-15-56) Walter Coy, William Ching, Beverly Washburn
3. "Captain from Copenick" (4-22-56) Emmett Kelly
4. "Away Boarders" (4-29-56) Scotty Beckett
5. "The Mystery of Casper Hauser" (5-6-56) Henry Daniell
6. "The Stepmother" (5-13-56) Ronnie Lee, Rita Lynn
7. "Time Bomb" (5-20-56) Steven Geray, Osa Massen, Keye Luke

8. "Emperor Norton's Bridge" (5-27-56) Edgar Stehli, Jan Merlin, Ted de Corsia
9. "The Man Who Believed in Fairy Tales" [Henrich Schliemann] (6-3-56) Robert Middleton, Kathleen Hughes
10. "Harry in Search of Himself" [Henry Bergh, founder of the ASPCA] (6-10-56) Philip Bourneuf, Edgar Buchanan
11. "Felix the Fourth" [the 1904 Olympics medalist] (6-17-56)
12. "Smith of Ecuador" [by Donald S. Sanford] (6-24-56) Kenneth Tobey, Eve Miller
13. "The Gingerbread Man" [on the Baker-General of the Continental Army] (7-1-56) Hugo Haas, Celia Lovsky, Barry Truex
14. "The Joyful Lunatic" (7-8-56) Alexander Scourby, Lowell Gilmore
15. "The Key" [Laura Bridgman, the "Helen Keller" of the 1800's] (7-15-56) Beverly Washburn, Kevin McCarthy
16. "Grandpa Changes the World" [the Peter Zenger case] (7-22-56) Thomas Mitchell, Reginald Denny, John Eldridge, Peter Hansen, Barney Phillips, Patricia Blake
17. "Again the Stars" (7-29-56) Robert Ellenstein

Second Season

18. "Keely's Wonderful Machine" (9-16-56) Melville Cooper
19. "I Am Not Alone" (9-23-56) Victor Jory
20. "Mr. and Mrs. Browning" [Elizabeth Barrett and Robert Browning] (9-30-56) Scott Forbes, Leora Dana
21. "Vicksburg, Mississippi, 5:35 P.M." (10-7-56) June Lockhart
22. "The Churchill Club" (10-14-56)
23. "She Sette Her Little Foote" (10-21-56) Barbara Baxley, Robert Rockwell
24. "Hatfield, the Rainmaker" (10-28-56)
25. [unknown title] (11-4-56) Laura La Plante
26. "Chico and the Archbishop" (11-18-56) Ricky Vera
27. "Fortunatus" (12-9-56) Jacques Sernas
28. "Scio, Ohio" (12-16-56)
29. "The Sergeant Boyd Story" (12-23-56) Patrick McVey, William Talman
30. "The Mountain That Moved" (12-30-56) Tom Tully
31. "Passport to Life" [documentary drama of the post-World War II Sopron prison camp] (1-6-57) William Campbell, Steven Geray, Stephen Bekassy, Lazio Vadnay
32. "The Jumping Parson" (1-13-57) Billy Halop
33. "Parents of a Stranger" (1-20-57) Peter Cookson, Jean Howell
34. "The Consort" [on Queen Victoria's proposal of marriage to Prince Albert] (1-27-57) Robert Vaughn
35. "The Man Who Discovered O. Henry" (2-3-57)
36. "Plot to Save a Boy" (2-17-56) Thelma Ritter, Peter Votrian
37. "The Unsinkable Mrs. Brown" [Molly Brown] (2-24-57) Cloris Leachman
38. "The Intruder" (3-3-57) Joel Grey, Phyllis Avery
39. "Fight for the Title" [former lightweight champion Benny Leonard] (3-17-57) Michael Landon, George Brenlin
40. "Escape" (3-24-57) Hugo Haas

41. "Castle Dangerous" (3-31-57)
42. "Bullet Lou Kirn" (4-11-57) Johnny Crawford, Alan Baxter
43. "Elfego Baca" (4-18-57) Manuel Rojas
44. "Rabbi on Wheels" (4-25-57) Hugo Haas
45. "Diamond Peer" ["Wild Jack" Howard, England's Earl of Suf-
folk] (5-2-57) Tom Helmore
46. "Stranded" (5-9-57)
47. "Line Chief" [by Marion Hargrove] (6-11-57) Dennis Morgan
48. "Pit-a-Pit and the Dragon" (6-18-57)
49. "The Koshetz Story" [by Zoë Akins] (6-25-57) Nina Koshetz
(as herself), Marina Koshetz (as herself), William Schallert

Third Season

50. "Revenge" (9-10-57) Greer Garson
51. "Here Lies François Gold" (9-17-57) George Tobias
52. "Campaign for Marriage" (9-24-57) Robert Sterling, Anne
Jeffreys
53. "The Gadfly" (10-1-57) Henry Daniell; narrated by Thomas
Mitchell
54. "Hole in the Wall" (10-8-57)
55. "The Man the Navy Couldn't Sink" (10-15-57) Joseph Cotten
56. "Under Seventeen" (10-22-57) Katherine Warren, Ken Osmand,
Dean Dwight
57. "The Other Van Gogh" (10-29-57) Beverly Garland
58. "Arithmetic Sailor" [Nathaniel Bowditch] (11-5-57)
59. "I Get Along Without You Very Well" (11-12-57) Hoagy Carmichael, Walter Winchell
60. "Alice's Wedding Gown" [Alice Roosevelt Longworth] (11-19-57)
Fay Wray, Norma Eberhardt
61. "Rescue" (11-26-57) Douglass Dumbrille
62. "Novel Appeal" [Mary Roberts Rinehart] (12-3-57) Claudette
Colbert, John Carradine, John Hoyt, John Dierkes, Alan
Dexter
63. "Sam Houston's Decision" (12-10-57) Don Taylor
64. "The Frying Pan" (12-17-57) Ray Farrell, Jerome Cowan
65. "A Picture of the Magi" (12-24-57)
66. "Death of a Nobody" [directed by James Mason] (12-31-57)
Jackie Cooper, Frank Faylen
67. "Abby, Julia, and the Seven Pet Cows" (1-7-58) Dame Judith
Anderson, Dorothy Stickney
68. "Cavalry Surgeon" (1-14-58) John Roberts
69. "A Stubborn Fool" (1-21-58)
70. "Flight for Life" (1-28-58) Stephen McNally
71. "The Immortal Eye" (2-4-58) Wanda Hendrix
72. "Recipe for Success" (2-11-58) Sebastian Cabot, Walter Slezak
73. "The Checkered Flag" (2-18-58) Victor Morrow, Kathy Nolan
74. "The Vestris" (2-25-58) Boris Karloff, Rita Lynn
75. "War Against War" [on the relationship between Baroness Bertha Kinsky Von Suttner and Alfred Nobel] (3-4-58) Jessica
Tandy, Hume Cronyn
76. "The Quality of Mercy" (3-11-58) Harry Townes, Ann Sargent
77. "Man of Principle" [Archimedes; principle of specific gravity]
(3-25-58) Neil Hamilton

78. "Trail Blazer" [Charles Goodnight, who pioneered cattle trail from Texas to New Mexico in 1866]   (4-1-58)

GENERAL ELECTRIC SUMMER ORIGINALS

The Episodes:

1. "It's Sunny Again"   (7-3-56)   Vivian Blaine, Jules Munshin, Shirley Mitchell
2. "Duel at Dawn"   (7-10-56)   James Mason, Pamela Kellins, Scott Forbes
3. "Country Store"   (7-17-56)   Joe E. Brown
4. "The Unwilling Witness"   (7-24-56)   Zachary Scott, Frances Rafferty
5. "Alias Mike Hercules"   (7-31-56)   Hugh Beaumont, Anne Kimbal, Ellen Corby, Reginald Denny
6. "The Green Parrot"   (8-7-56)   Claude Dauphin
7. "Blizzard Bound"   (8-28-56)   Forrest Tucker, Donna Martel, Bill Phipps
8. "Down at Damascus"   (9-4-56)   Paula Corday, Donald Murphy, Gene Raymond

COMBAT SERGEANT

Having none of the poignancy of the 1962 Combat! (graced, as it were, with some superb direction by Robert Altman), is this uncompromising tale of martinets who pushed through World War II's North African campaign.

The Regulars: Sergeant Nelson: Michael Thomas; General Harrison: Cliff Clark; Corporal Murphy: Frank Marlowe; Corporal Harbin: Mara Corday.

The Episodes:

1. "Flight to Eternity"   (6-29-56)
2. "Pass into Danger"   (7-6-56)
3. "Mission to Mademoiselle"   (7-13-56)
4. "Destined for Death"   (7-20-56)
5. "East of Algiers"   (7-27-56)
6. "Destruction at Dawn"   (8-3-56)
7. "Desert Vengeance"   (8-10-56)
8. "Fatal Hour"   (8-17-56)
9. "Dark Alleys of Algiers"   (8-24-56)
10. "All Faces East"   (8-31-56)
11. "Desert Falcon"   (9-13-56; this episode telecast Thursday, 9-9:30 P.M.)

THE BUCCANEERS

The nationalist cause mixes with the 1722 swordplay at the high seas in this typical adventure. The late Robert Shaw, now so fondly remembered as the monomaniacal but cynical Quint of Steven Spielberg's Jaws, made a purely straight-faced paraclete in this 1956 Captain Tempest.

The Regulars: Captain Dan Tempest: Robert Shaw; Lieutenant Beamish: Peter Hammond; Governor Woods Rogers: Alec Clunes

The Episodes:

1. "Blackbeard" (9-22-56) Terence Cooper
2. "The Raiders" (9-29-56)
3. "Dan Tempest" (10-6-56) Hugh David
4. "Dan Tempest's War with Spain" (10-13-56)
5. "The Wasp" (10-20-56) Wilfrid Downing
6. "Whale Gold" (10-27-56)
7. "The Slave Ship" (11-3-56)
8. "The Gunpowder Plot" (11-10-56)
9. "The Ladies" (11-17-56)
10. "The Surgeon of Sangra Rojo" (11-24-56)
11. "Dan Tempest and the Amazons" (12-1-56)
12. "The Articles of War" (12-8-56)
13. "Mr. Beamish and the Hangman's Noose" (12-15-56)
14. "The Hand of the Hawk" (12-22-56)
15. "Gentleman Jack and the Lady" (12-29-56)
16. "Dangerous Cargo" (1-5-57) Sarah Lawson, Wilfrid Downing, Ivan Craig
17. "Dead Man's Rock" (1-12-57)
18. "Blood Will Tell" (1-19-57)
19. "The Ghost Ship" (1-26-57) Bob Keeshan
20. "The Return of Calico Jack" (2-2-57)
21. "Conquistador" (2-9-57)
22. "Mother Doughty's Crew" (2-16-57)
23. "Conquest of New Providence" (2-23-57)
24. "The Hurricane" (3-2-57)
25. "The Cutlass Wedding" (3-9-57)
26. "Aztec Treasure" (3-23-57)
27. "Prize of Andalusia" (3-30-57)
28. "Dan Tempest Holds an Auction" (4-6-57)
29. "The Spy Aboard" (4-13-57)

30. "Flip and Jenny" (4-20-57) Peter Soule, Jane Asher
31. "Indian Fighters" (4-27-57)
32. "Mistress Higgins' Treasure" (5-4-57) Adrienne Corri
33. "To the Rescue" (5-11-57)
34. "The Decoy" (5-18-57)
35. "Instrument of War" (5-25-57)
36. "Pirate Honor" (6-1-57)
37. "Printer's Devil" (6-8-57)
38. "Marooned" (6-15-57)

AIR POWER

Documentary features.

The Regulars: Walter Cronkite, host and narrator.

The Episodes:

1. "Introduction" (11-11-56)
2. "The Early Days" (11-18-56)
3. "The Lost Waffe" (11-25-56)
4. "Pearl Harbor" (12-2-56)
5. "The Battle of Britain" [narrated by Sir Winston Churchill and Michael Redgrave] (12-9-56)
6. "Counterblast" (12-16-56)
7. "Fools, Daredevils and Geniuses" (12-23-56)
8. "The 1930's" [Lieutenant General James H. Doolittle, guest] (12-30-56)
9. "The Pioseti Raids" (1-6-57)
10. "Schweinfurt" (1-13-57)
11. "Conquest of the Air" (1-20-57)
12. "The Japanese Perimeter" (1-27-57)
13. "Interdiction and Blockade" (2-3-57)
14. "Strangle" (2-10-57)
15. "Pacific Patterns" (2-17-57)
16. "Advance the Bomber Line" (2-24-57)
17. "The Winning of France" (3-3-57)
18. "Superfort" (3-10-57)
19. "Victory in Europe" (3-17-57)
20. "Kamikaze" (3-24-57)
21. "The Defeat of Japan" (3-31-57)
22. "The Cold Decade--Airlift" (4-7-57)
23. "The Cold Decade--To the Yalu" (4-14-57)
24. "The Cold Decade--Korean Stalemate" (4-21-57)
25. "Starfighter" (4-28-57)
26. "New Doctrine" (5-5-57)

THE ADVENTURES OF SIR LANCELOT

Historicity was mitigated with the Sir Arthur Legend; now cavaliers and squires abound in the clumsiest of teleplays, replete with anachronistic set pieces. Here in mid-decade, five years before a real-life Camelot revival, an Arthurian sophistry found a ready audience.

The Regulars: Sir Lancelot: William Russell; King Arthur: Ronald Leigh-Hunt (subsequently replaced by Bruce Seaton); Merlin: Cyril Smith; Squire Brian: Robert Scroggins

The Episodes:

1. "The Night of the Red Plume" (9-24-56)
2. "The Ferocious Fathers" (10-1-56)
3. "The Queen's Knight" (10-8-56)
4. "The Outcast" (10-22-56)
5. "Winged Victory" (10-29-56)
6. "Sir Bliant" (11-5-56)
7. "Magic Sword" (11-19-56)
8. "Roman Wall" (11-26-56)
9. "Shepherd's War" (12-3-56)
10. "Caledon" (12-17-56)
11. "The Pirates" (12-24-56)
12. [unknown title] (12-31-56)
13. "The Black Castle" (1-14-57)
14. "Magic Book" (1-21-57)
15. "Knight Must Fall" (1-28-57)
16. "Knight Errant" (2-11-57)
17. "The Lesser Breed" (2-18-57)
18. "The Ruby of Radnor" (2-25-57)
19. "Sir Crustabread" (3-11-57)
20. "Witch's Brew" (3-18-57)
21. "The Maid of Somerset" (3-25-57)
22. "Double Identity" (4-8-57) Howard Pays
23. "The Bridge" (4-15-57)
24. "Lady Lilith" (4-22-57)
25. "The Ugly Duckling" (5-6-57)
26. "Knight's Choice" (5-13-57)
27. "The Mortaise Fair" (5-20-57)
28. "Prince of Limerick" (6-3-57)
29. "The Missing Princess" (6-10-57)
30. "The Thieves" (6-17-57)

NOAH'S ARK

Noting an absence amid the medical series, Jack Webb produced and directed this hymn to veterinary heroism. Artistically hollow, Noah's Ark, never sonorous, merely plunked the virtues of its benevolent doctors.

The Regulars: Dr. Noah McCann: Paul Burke; Dr. Sam Rinehart: Vic Rodman; Liz Clark: May Wynn; Glen White: Russell Whitney; Agnes Marshall: Natalie Masters; Davey Marshall: Paul Engel

The Episodes:

1. "Introduction" (9-18-56)
2. "The Seeing Eye Dog" (9-25-56) Virginia Vincent
3. "The Petition" (10-2-56)
4. "The Toothless Monkey" (10-9-56)
5. "Mascot" (10-23-56)
6. "Friendly Lion" (10-30-56)
7. "The Hardware Cow" (11-6-56)
8. "The Displaced Deer" (11-13-56)
9. "The Foundling" (11-20-56)
10. "Cure All" (11-27-56)
11. "Syncopated Squirrel" (12-4-56)
12. "A Girl's Best Friend" (12-11-56)
13. "Once Upon a Midnight" (12-18-56)
14. "Reluctant Reindeer" (12-25-56)
15. "Out to Pasture" (1-1-57)
16. "The Guide" (1-8-57) Lillian Powell, Paul Brinegar, Jim Horan
17. "Talking Ostrich" (1-15-57)
18. "The Psychotic Seal" (1-22-57)
19. "Vitamin Derby" (1-29-57)
20. "Gentle Peril" (2-5-57)
21. "Kangaroo's Tale" (2-12-57)
22. "Jehoshaphat" (2-19-57)
23. "The Intruder" (2-26-57)

CONFLICT

The Episodes:

1. "Shock Wave" (9-18-56) Scott Brady, Kenneth Tobey, Ted de Corsia
2. "Condemned to Glory" (10-2-56) Jorja Curtwright, Geoffrey Toone
3. "The Magic Brew" (10-16-56) Jim Backus, Will Hutchins, Fay Spain, Joi Lansing
4. "Captain Without a Country" (10-30-56) Jacques Sernas
5. "The People Against McQuade" (11-13-56) Tab Hunter, George T. Davis
6. "The Man from 1997" (11-27-56) Jacques Sernas, Charles Ruggles, Johnny Vlakoz, James Garner, Gloria Talbott
7. "Stranger on the Road" (12-11-56) Will Hutchins, Kathy Nolan, Barton MacLane
8. "Silent Journey" (12-25-56) Eugene Martin
9. "Girl on a Subway" (1-8-57) Natalie Wood, Charles Ruggles,

Joe Kearne, James Garner, Murray Hamilton
10. "Blind Drop: Warsaw" (1-22-57) Keith Andes, Raymond Bailey, Gregory Gay, Otto Waldes
11. "Passage to Maranga" (2-5-57) Rex Reason, Adele Mara
12. "The Money" (2-19-57) Charles McGraw
13. "Capital Punishment" (3-5-57) Rex Reason, Ray Teal, Edward Binns
14. "A Question of Loyalty" (4-2-57) Patrick McVey, Dennis Hopper, Gerald Mohr
15. "Anything for Money" (4-16-57) Efrem Zimbalist Jr., Richard Webb, Margaret Hayes, Barton MacLane
16. "No Man's Road" (4-30-57) Dennis Hopper
17. "Pattern for Violence" (5-14-57) Jack Lord, Karen Steele, Meg Randell
18. "Execution Night" (5-28-57) Efrem Zimbalist Jr., Virginia Mayo, Edmund Lowe, Audrey Conti

WIRE SERVICE

Of no documentary significance, and bereft of the handsome mounting of the 1962 Saints and Sinners, this was a spurious tale of international reportage.

The Regulars: reporters Dean Evans: George Brent; Katherine Wells: Mercedes McCambridge; Dan Miller: Dane Clark [the thirteen Clark segments were titled Deadline for Action]

The Episodes:

1. "Blood Rock Mine" (10-4-56) Clark; Harry Townes, Maxine Cooper
2. "Campaign Train" (10-11-56) Brent
3. "Hideout" (10-18-56) McCambridge; Murray Hamilton, Marjorie Lord
4. "The Johnny Rath Story" (10-25-56) Clark; Beverly Garland
5. "The Night of August Seventh" (11-1-56) Brent; Paul Richards, Malcolm Atterbury, Virginia Gregg, Lee Van Cleef
6. "Conspiracy" (11-8-56) McCambridge; Shepperd Strudwick, Katherine Wells
7. "The Tower" (11-15-56) Clark; Jay Robinson
8. "Deported" (11-22-56) Brent; Peter Mamakos, Anthony Caruso
9. "Until I Die" [by Gabrielle Upton] (11-29-56) McCambridge; Ralph Votrian
10. "The Avengers" (12-6-56) Clark; Philip Pine, Peter Baldwin
11. "The Deep End" (12-13-56) Brent; Margaret Hayes
12. "High Adventure" (12-20-56) McCambridge; Scott Marlowe, John Beradino, Sarah Selby, Michael Landon
13. "The Block Rock Mine" (12-27-56) Clark; Arthur Hunnicutt, John Shepodd
14. "Chicago Exclusive" (1-3-57) Brent; Vaughn Taylor, Ainslie Pryor

15. "World of the Lonely" (1-10-57) McCambridge; Robert Cornth-
      waite, Virginia Gregg, Carla Merey
16. "The Third Inevitable" (1-17-56) Clark; Steve Terrell
17. "Flowers for the General" (1-24-57) Brent; Reinaldo Rivera
18. "The Comeback" (1-31-57) McCambridge
19. "Atom at Spithead" (2-11-57) Clark; Robert Beatty
20. "El Hombre" (2-18-57) Brent; Edvardo Noriega, Rafael Al-
      cayde, Elvira Quintana
21. "Profile of Ellen Gale" (2-25-57) McCambridge; Beverly Gar-
      land
22. "Dateline Las Vegas" (3-4-57) Clark; Carolyn Jones
23. "Forbidden Ground" (3-11-57) Brent; Barton MacLane
24. "No Peace at Lo Dao" (3-18-57) McCambridge; Keye Luke
25. "A Matter of Conscience" (3-25-57) Clark
26. "Misfire" (4-1-57) Brent
27. "The Indictment" (4-8-57) McCambridge
28. "Ninety and Nine" (4-15-57) Clark
29. "The Oil Man" (4-22-57) Brent
30. "Run, Sheep, Run" (4-29-57) McCambridge
31. "The Death Merchant" (5-6-57) Clark
32. "Violence Preferred" (5-13-57) Brent
33. "The Last Laugh" (5-20-57) McCambridge
34. "Confirm or Deny" (5-27-57) Clark
35. "Four Minutes to Shot" (6-3-57) Brent
36. "The Washington Stars" (6-10-57) McCambridge
37. "A Death at Twin Pines" (6-17-57) Clark

ON TRIAL [also known as THE JOSEPH COTTEN SHOW]

   Mundane courtroom ritual making for mundane drama, it is
celebrated litigation which calls for re-enactment. By this exclu-
sivity, On Trial deriving from the telefeature "The United States
Versus Alexander Holmes" for the anthology Star Stage [q. v.], necessarily loses, as does the genre, the authenticity central to the
best documented of teleplays--as were indeed some of what follow.

The Regulars: Joseph Cotten, host, narrator and occasional performer.

The Episodes:

1. "The Trial of Edward Pritchard" (9-14-56) Cotten; Jan Chaney
2. "We Who Love Her" (9-21-56) Carl Williams, Alexis Smith
3. "The Nevada Nightingale" (9-28-56) Diana Lynn
4. "Twice in Peril" (10-19-56) Cotten; Joseph Wiseman, Chris-
      topher Dark
5. "The De Santre Affair" (10-26-56) Joan Fontaine
6. "The Law Is for Lovers" (11-9-56) Gene Lockhart, Everett
      Sloane, Craig Stevens
7. "Death in the Snow" (11-16-56) Hoagy Carmichael, Keenan Wynn
8. "The Trial of Mary Surratt" (11-23-56) Cotten; Ray Collins

9. "The Person and Property of Margery Hay" (12-7-56) Lurene Tuttle, Kim Hunter, Walter Abel
10. "The Jameson Case" (12-14-56) Everett Sloane, James Gregory
11. "The Fourth Witness" (12-21-56) Mala Powers, Dane Clark
12. "The Trial of Colonel Flood" (1-4-57) Michael Wilding
13. "Dog Versus Biddeford" (1-11-57) Cotten
14. "Libel in the Wax Museum" (1-18-57) John Baragrey, June Lockhart
15. "The Tichbourne Claimant" (2-1-57) Gladys Cooper, Robert Middleton
16. "The Case of the Girl on the Elsewhere" (2-8-57) Cotten; Kathleen Crowley
17. "The Lie Detector Case" (2-15-57) Ben Alexander
18. "The Case of the Double Trouble" (3-1-57) Cotten
19. "The Case of the Panicky Man" (3-8-57) Cotten; Philip Ober, Ralph Moody, Christopher Dark
20. "The Freeman Case" (3-15-57) Cotten
21. "The Ghost at Devil's Island" (3-29-57) Paulette Goddard, Philip Reed
22. "The Case of the Jealous Bomber" (4-5-57) John Kerr
23. "The Case of the Abandoned Horse" (4-12-57) Eva Bartok, Hugh Marlowe
24. "Alibi for Murder" (4-26-57) Macdonald Carey
25. "The Case of the Absent Man" (5-3-57) Kent Taylor, Margaret Hayes
26. "The Case of the Sudden Death" (5-10-57) Dick Foran
27. "The Gentle Voices of Murder" (5-24-57) Cotten
28. "The Secret of Polanto" (5-31-57) Eduardo Ciannelli, Paul Stewart
29. "The Deadly Chain" (6-7-57) Dan O'Herlihy, Patrick O'Neal
30. "The Fatal Charm" (6-28-57) Joan Fontaine, Eduard Franz, Geoffrey Toone, Robert Cornthwaite

THE WEST POINT STORY

The public chastisement accorded Joseph McCarthy by the princely Edward R. Murrow on March 9, 1954, and the devastating excoriation of the Wisconsin Senator by the normally quiescent Attorney Joseph Welch on the twenty-second of that month but dispelled the most obvious ideologue, for whom the movement was named. Cold War acolytes still flourished wildly as of mid-decade and their dictums permeated many media forms. One example was this parable of martinets and the soft-skinned novices they commandeer. The series more than once, if only by moral inference, argued the cause for global pre-eminence.

The Regulars: Donald May, host and narrator.

The Episodes:

1. "The Mystery of Cadet Layton" (10-5-56) Martin Milner,

Carolyn Craig, Don Eitner
2. "The Operator and the Martinet" (10-12-56) Robert Vaughn, Chet Marshall, Chuck Connors
3. "Officer's Wife" (10-19-56) Olive Sturgess, Diana Douglas
4. "The Honor Code" (10-26-56) Richard Jaeckel, Terence Kilburn
5. "Thicker Than Water" (11-2-56) Corey Allen, William Campbell
6. "The Right to Choose" (11-9-56) Bob Gothie, Gloria Talbott, Hillary Brooke
7. "His Brother's Fist" (11-16-56) John Beradino, Jeff Harris, Leonard Nimoy
8. "Decision" (11-23-56) Don Oreck, Barbara Eden
9. "His Highness and the Halfback" (11-30-56) Glen Kramer, Felix A. Blanchard
10. "Man of Action" (12-7-56) Larry Pennell
11. "Heat of Anger" (12-14-56) Henry Silva, Patricia Crowley
12. "Christmas Present" (12-21-56)
13. "Double Reverse" (12-28-56) Cynthia Baxter
14. "The Hard Task" (1-4-57) Jack Grinnage, Chet Marshall, Peter Miller, Paul Grant, Del Erickson
15. "The Army-Navy Game" (1-11-57) Chuck Connors
16. "Start Running" (1-18-57) Pat Conway, Brett Halsey, Mike Mason, Betsy Meade, Mike Garth
17. "Wrong Fight" (1-25-57) Patrick Waltz, William Traylor
18. "Operation Survival" (2-1-57)
19. "Jet Fight" (2-8-57) William Lundmark, Richard Erdman, Melville Cooper
20. "Combat Proof" (2-15-57) Jan Merlin, Race Gentry
21. "The Command" (2-22-57) Richard Jaeckel, Richard Davalos, Edward C. Platt
22. "White Fury" (3-1-57) Clint Eastwood, Bruce Bennett, Jerome Courtland
23. "Ambush" (3-8-57) Steve McQueen
24. "The Only Witness" (3-15-57) Eddie Foy III
25. "Manhunt" (3-22-57)
26. "The Dangerous Area" (3-29-57)
27. "Backfire" (4-5-57)
28. "Cold Peril" (4-12-57) Larry Pennell, Leonard Nimoy
29. "Contact" (4-19-57) Steve Terrell
30. "No Reason" (4-26-57) Martin Milner
31. "Flareup" (5-3-57)
32. "M-24" (5-10-57) Roger Smith
33. "The Benefit of Doubt" (5-17-57)
34. "The Harder Right" (5-24-57) Richard Jaeckel
35. "The Drowning of the Gun" (5-31-57)
36. "The Fight Back" (6-7-57) Patrick Waltz
37. "Duty, Honor, and Trouble" (6-14-57)
38. "The Deep End" (6-21-57) Robert Beneveds, Chris White
39. "Pressure" (6-28-57) James Dobson, Dale Hutchinson, Jo Ann Lilliquist, Maureen Cassidy, Helen Brown, Gloria Talbott, Frank Fenton
40. "Dragoon Patrol" (7-5-57)

ETHEL BARRYMORE THEATRE

The Regulars: Ethel Barrymore, hostess.

The Episodes:

1. "The Victim" (9-21-56) Arthur Kennedy, Edward Arnold, Julie Bishop
2. "The Gentle Years" (9-28-56) Walter Brennan
3. "The Daughters of Mars" (10-5-56) Ethel Barrymore, Selena Royle, Elizabeth Risden
4. "This Is Villa" (10-12-56) Akim Tamiroff, Arthur Kennedy
5. "The Peabodys" (10-19-56) Eddie Bracken, Jeff Donnell
6. "General Delivery" (10-26-56) Ethel Barrymore, Virginia Grey
7. "The Duke" (11-2-56) Patric Knowles, K. T. Stevens
8. "Mimsel's Man" (11-9-56) Michael O'Shea, Jeff Donnell
9. "Justice for All" (11-16-56) Gene Lockhart
10. "Funny Money" (11-23-56) Barbara Laurence, Marshall Thompson
11. "Lady Investigator" (11-30-56) Gene Raymond, Bonita Granville
12. "Dear Miss Lovelace" (12-7-56) Anita Louise
13. "Winter and Spring" (12-14-56) Charles Coburn

LILLI PALMER THEATRE

The Regulars: Lilli Palmer, hostess.

The Episodes:

1. "The Assassin" (9-21-56) André Morell, Brian Wilde
2. "The Game and the Onlooker" (9-28-56) Wendy Hiller, Joyce Barbour
3. "The Weakness of Frau Borkhardt" (10-5-56) Mary Clare
4. "Death Under the City" (10-12-56) Emry Jones, Michael Ripper
5. "The Brown Man's Servant" (10-19-56) David Kossoff, Harry Ross
6. "The Bride Wore an Opal Ring" (10-26-56) Ada Reeve, Joyce Barbour, Brenda Hogan
7. "The Portrait" (11-2-56) Andrew Cruikshank
8. "Bardell Vs. Pickwick" [adapted from the Charles Dickens story] (11-14-56) Donald Wolfit
9. "The No Man" (11-21-56) David Tomlinson, Valerie Miller
10. "Mister Betts Runs Away" (11-28-56) Eric Portman, Mona Washbourne
11. "The Little Black Book" (12-5-56) Flora Robson, Wilfrid Hyde-White
12. "The Suicide Club" (12-12-56) Derrick de Marney, Karel Stapanets
13. "The Ends of Justice" (12-19-56) Felix Aylmer
14. "The Great Healer" (12-26-56) Pamela Brown

THE TALES OF WELLS FARGO

Neither a substantive western nor a very offensive one, contentedly within the mold, is this salute to persevering stagecoach travel. Its ruminating hero, wandering Jim Hardie, merely substantiates Wells Fargo's base in conventionality.

The Regulars: Jim Hardie: Dale Robertson

The Episodes [untitled segments are not chronicled]:

1. "Sam Bass Episode" (3-18-57) Chuck Connors
2. "The Hasty Gun" (3-25-57) Leo Gordon, John Merrick
3. "Alder Gulch" (4-8-57) Lee Van Cleef, John Doucette
4. "The Bounty" (4-15-57)
5. "A Time to Kill" (4-22-57) Robert Rockwell
6. "Shotgun Messenger" (5-6-57) Michael Landon, Ken Dibbs
7. "The Lynching" (5-13-57) Victor Millan
8. "Renegade" (5-20-57) Francis McDonald, George Chandler, Denver Pyle, Morgan Woodward, Dan Blocker, Paul Brinegar, Rick Vallin
9. "Rio Grande" (6-3-57) Diane Brewster, Joe De Santis, Russell Johnson, Rico Alaniz, Luis Gomez, Lisa Montell
10. "Shotgun Messenger" [repeat of 5-6-57] (6-10-57) Michael Landon, John Pickard, Eilene Janssen
11. "Stage to Nowhere" (6-24-57)

Second Season

12. "Two Cartridges" (9-16-57)
13. "John Wesley Hardin" (9-30-57) Lyle Bettger, Frank Ferguson, Rand Brooks, Robert Foulk, Dick Forester
14. "Billy the Kid" (10-21-57) Robert Vaughn, Addison Richards, Aline Towne
15. "The Kid" (11-18-57) Michael Landon
16. "Barbary Coast" (11-25-57)
17. "Ride with the Killer" (12-2-57)
18. "The Inscrutable Man" (12-9-57)
19. "The General" (12-16-57) Jane Nigh
20. "The Witness" [Part I] (12-23-57)
21. "The Witness" [Part II] (12-30-57)
22. "Doc Bell" (1-6-58)
23. "Stage West" (1-13-58)
24. "Hoss Tamer" (1-20-58)
25. "Hide Jumpers" (1-27-58) Jimmy Gavin, Guy Wilkerson
26. "Walking Mountain" (2-3-58)
27. "Bill Longley" (2-10-58) Steve McQueen
28. "The Prisoner" (2-17-58)
29. "Dr. Alice" (2-24-58) Diane Brewster
30. "The Sooners" (3-3-58)
31. "Alias Jim Hardie" (3-10-58) Kent Taylor
32. "Johnny Ringo" (3-17-58)
33. "Indian Warfare" (3-31-58)

34. "The Homecoming" (4-7-58)
35. "The Reward" (4-21-58) Marcia Henderson
36. "The Renegade" (5-5-58)
37. "The Break" (5-19-58)
38. "The Sniper" (5-26-58)
39. "The Thin Rope" (6-2-58) Chuck Connors
40. "The Auction" (6-16-58)

Third Season

41. "The Manuscript" (9-15-58)
42. "White Indian" (9-22-58) Dick Evans
43. "The Golden Owl" (9-29-58)
44. "Faster Gun" (10-6-58)
45. "Butch Cassidy" (10-13-58)
46. "End of Trail" (10-20-58)
47. "A Matter of Honor" (11-3-58)
48. "The Most Dangerous Man Alive" (11-10-58) Claude Akins
49. "The Gunfighter" (11-17-58) Lyle Bettger
50. "Deserter" (11-24-58)
51. "The Killer" (12-1-58)
52. "The Counterfeiters" (12-8-58)
53. "The Dealer" (12-29-58) Vic Perrin, Jeanne Bates, Johnny
    Crawford

Episodes continued with Television Drama Series Programming: A Comprehensive Chronicle, 1959-1975.

PANIC!

The Episodes:

1. "The Priest" (3-5-57) James Whitmore
2. "The Prisoner" (3-12-57) Kenneth Tobey, Jaclynne Greene
3. "The Boy" (3-19-57) Billy Chapin
4. "The Subway" (3-26-57) Eduard Franz, Barbara Billingsley
5. "The Embezzler" (4-2-57) Whit Bissell
6. "Airline Hostess" (4-9-57) Carolyn Jones
7. "Nightmare" (4-16-57) Eduardo Ciannelli
8. "Two Martinis" (4-23-57) Kent Taylor, William Ching
9. "Marooned" (4-30-57) James, Pamela, Portland and Morgan
   Mason
10. "Courage" (5-7-57) Paul Burke
11. "Peter and the Tiger" (5-14-57) Richard Eyer, Mel Koontz
12. "The Prospector" (5-21-57)
13. "The Kidnapper" (5-28-57) Richard Erdman
14. "May Day" (6-11-57) Richard Jaeckel, Keye Luke
15. "Botulism" (6-18-57) Marshall Thompson
16. "Love Story" (6-25-57) Darryl Hickman, Mary Webster, Lila
    Lee
17. "Reincarnated" (7-2-57) June Havoc

THE O. HENRY PLAYHOUSE

The Regulars: Thomas Mitchell (as O. Henry), host and narrator

The Episodes:

1. "The Reformation of Calliope" (1-23-57) Ernest Borgnine
2. "Man About Town" (1-30-57) Thomas Mitchell, Mona Freeman
3. "Sam Plunkett's Promise" (2-6-57)
4. "Two Renegades" (2-13-57) Thomas Mitchell, John Carradine
5. "The Marionettes" (2-20-57)
6. "Fog in Sanstone" (2-27-57)
7. "Hearts and Hands" (3-6-57)
8. "The World and the Door" (3-13-57)
9. "The Guilty Party" (3-20-57)
10. "A Ramble in Aphasia" (3-27-57)
11. "After Twenty Years" (4-3-57)
12. "Trick of Nature" (4-10-57)
13. "Sisters of the Golden Circle" (4-17-57)
14. "Hygeia at the Solito" (4-27-57)
15. "Only the Horse Would Know" (5-4-57)
16. "The Atavism of John Tom Little Bear" (5-11-57)
17. "Miller's Millions" (5-18-57) Otto Kruger
18. "A Black Jack Bargainer" (5-25-57)

THE ERROL FLYNN THEATRE

The Regulars: Errol Flynn, host

The Episodes:

1. "My Infallable Luck" (3-22-57) June Havoc
2. "The Duel" (3-29-57) Errol Flynn
3. "Fortunes of War" (4-5-57) Errol Flynn
4. "The Girl in Blue Jeans" (4-12-57) Glynis Johns, Herbert Lom
5. "The Mirror" (4-19-57) Patrice Wymore, Philip Friend
6. "Mademoiselle Fifi" [adapted from the Guy de Maupassant story] (4-26-57) Paulette Goddard, Peter Reynolds
7. "All in the Family" (5-3-57) Mai Zetterling, Derek Farr
8. "Love Token" (5-10-57) Rosanna Rory, Christopher Lee
9. "Strange Auction" (5-17-57) Errol Flynn, Patrice Wymore
10. "The Kinsman" (5-24-57) Peter Reynolds, Ronald Squire
11. "Rustle of Silk" (5-31-57) Phyllis Kirk
12. [unknown title] (6-14-57) Derek Bond, Patrice Wymore
13. "Farewell Performance" (6-21-57) Patrice Roe, Ivan Craig
14. "The Red Geranium" (6-28-57) Betta St. John, Leslie Phillips
15. "Out of the Blue" (7-5-57) Rosanna Rory
16. "First Come, First Love" (7-26-57) Jean Pierre Aumont

THE GEORGE SANDERS MYSTERY THEATRE

The Regulars: George Sanders, host.

The Episodes:

1. "The Man in the Elevator" [by Leonard Lee] (6-22-57) Dan
   Haggerty, Dorothy Green, Paul Peterson, Helen Brown
2. "And the Birds Still Sing" (6-29-57) Mae Clarke John Archer
3. "The Call" (7-6-57) Tony Gerry, James Gavin,
4. "You Don't Live Here" (7-13-57) Marion Ross, Jim Hayward,
   Alex Gerry, Freeman Morse, Peter Thompson
5. "Last Will and Testament" (7-20-57) Robert Horton
6. "The Liar" (7-27-57) Sue England, Harry Lauter
7. [unknown title] (8-3-57)
8. "Try It My Way" (8-10-57) Jerry Paris, Jeanne Cooper
9. "Round Trip" (8-17-57) Elisha Cook
10. "Love Has No Alibi" (8-24-57)
11. "The Night I Died" (8-31-57) Howard McNear, Scotty Beckett,
    Eve McVeagh

RICHARD DIAMOND, PRIVATE DETECTIVE

Within the decade's throng of youthful detection experts with
seemingly inexhaustible private incomes was one Richard Diamond,
claiming as his diadem the always preferred assistance of a whispering telephone operator. Her sighs were presumably genuine;
viewers, however, merely sighed with discomfort produced by spurious thrills.

The Regulars: Richard Diamond: David Janssen; "Sam" (telephone
operator): Mary Tyler Moore (alternately played by Roxanne
Brooks); Regis Toomey plays a friend

The Episodes:

1. "The Mickey Farmer Case" (7-1-57)
2. "Custody" (7-8-57) Cheryll Callaway
3. "Escape from Oak Lane" (7-15-57) Christine White, Jeanette
   Nolan, Burt Masters
4. "The Homicide Habit" (7-22-57) Osa Massen
5. "The Picture of Fear" (7-29-57)
6. "Hit and Run" (8-5-57) Hershel Bernardi
7. "The Big Score" (8-12-57)
8. "The Chess Player" (8-19-57)
9. "The Torch Carriers" (8-26-57) Phyllis Avery
10. "The Peter Rocco Case" (9-9-57) Charles Bronson
11. "Venus of Park Avenue" (9-16-57)
12. "The Percentage Takers" (9-23-57)

Second Season

13. "The Space Society" (1-2-58)
14. "The Bungalow Murder" (1-9-58) Marguerite Chapman
15. "The Payoff" (1-16-58)
16. "The Botticelli Miniatures" (1-23-58)
17. "Lost Testament" (1-30-58) Jocelyn Brando
18. "The Ed Church Case" (2-6-58) Roscoe Karns
19. "Chinese Honeymoon" (2-13-58) Keye Luke
20. "A Cup of Black Coffee" (2-27-58)
21. "Juvenile Jacket" (3-13-58) Nick Adams
22. "Pension Plan" (3-27-58)
23. "The Purple Penguin" (4-24-58)
24. "The Fine Art of Murder" (5-24-59) Hillary Brooke, Bethel Leslie
25. "Dead to the World" (1-11-60) Geraldine Brooks

MEET McGRAW

Perhaps the most disgruntled and least compromising of video detectives was McGraw, an outcast of his choosing in his relative anonymity (there was no reference to his first name), indefatigable through no less than thirty-nine conundrums. Meet McGraw was, indeed, a stigmatic addition to the era's law and order air.

The Regulars: McGraw: Frank Lovejoy

The Episodes:

1. "The New Orleans Story" (7-2-57) Judith Braun, James Edwards
2. "Tycoon" (7-9-57) Grant Richards, Joe Barry, Angie Dickinson
3. "The Girl from Molina" (7-16-57) Kathy Nolan, Michael Pate
4. "Border City" (7-23-57) Hugh Beaumont
5. "The Torn Map" (7-30-57)
6. "The Florentine Shield" (8-6-57) Marcia Henderson
7. "The Cheat" (8-13-57)
8. "Ballerina" (8-20-57)
9. "Acapulco" (8-27-57)
10. "Wild Autumn" (9-3-57)
11. "The Good Doctor" (9-10-57)
12. "Texas Story" (9-17-57) Robert Rockwell, Craig Stevens

Second Season

13. "King's Ransom" (9-24-57)
14. "The Funeral" (10-1-57) Joan Banks, Carl Benton Reid
15. "The Fighter" (10-8-57) Perry Lopez
16. "Lucky's Dinner" (10-15-57) Nancy Gates, Bartlett Robinson, Anthony Letter, Sam Buffington

17. "Mojave" (10-22-57)
18. "Kiss of Death" (10-29-57) Hillary Brooke, Valerie French
19. "Lady in Limbo" (11-12-57) Marcia Henderson
20. "Keys of the City" (11-19-57)
21. "The Brief Case" (11-26-57)
22. "McGraw in Reno" (12-3-57) Angie Dickinson, Harry Landers, Charles Gray, Paul Bryar, Kenneth MacDonald, Jack Hogan
23. "The White Rose" (12-10-57)
24. "The Joshua Tree" (12-17-57) Marie Windsor
25. "In Memoriam" (12-24-57)
26. "The Snow Job" (12-31-57)
27. "McGraw Meets McGinley" (1-7-58) Roy Thinnes
28. "Vivian" (1-14-58) Sebastian Cabot
29. "A Time for Dying" (1-21-58)
30. "The Island" (1-28-58)
31. "The Diploma" (2-4-58) Kathryn Givney, James McCallion
32. "Face of Death" (3-25-58)
33. "The Lie That Came True" (4-1-58) Ray Teal, John Bryant, Ann McCrea

THE WEB

Mystery anthology.

The Episodes:

1. "A Matter of Degree" (7-7-57) Dan Barton, Robert Burton
2. "After the Fact" (7-14-57) Keith Larsen, Philip Ober, Tina Carver
3. "The Gambler" (7-21-57) Alexander Scourby
4. "Hurricane Coming" (7-28-57) Beverly Garland, Mark Roberts, Jacques Aubuchon
5. "Added Attraction" (8-4-57)
6. "Kill and Run" (8-11-57) James Darren
7. "The Puppeteer" (8-18-57) John Hudson, Bert Remsen
8. "A Time for Dying" (8-25-57) Jerry Paris, Paul Richards, Ann Robinson
9. "Last Chance" (9-1-57) John Larch, Rebecca Welles
10. "The Man Below" (9-8-57) Robert F. Simon
11. "Easy Money" (9-15-57) Joe Mantell, Ned Glass, Ken Lynch
12. "Dead Silence" (9-22-57) Joe Maross, Fay Spain, Christopher Dark
13. "Fatal Alibi" (9-29-57) Rex Reason, George Neise
14. "Man with a Choice" (10-6-57) Jeff Richards

HAVE GUN--WILL TRAVEL

Perhaps the most innovative of television westerns, an enigmatic, thematically unpredictable (there were teleplays on the mentally aberrant, Eastern mystics and humorous oldsters) series on the wanderings of nomistic marksman Paladin. Highly conscientious in an age of maligning stereotypes, Indians, Chinese and the nonconforming were now accorded a dignified expression.

The Regulars: Paladin: Richard Boone; Hey Girl: Lisa Lu (with episode of 10/1/60); Hey Boy: Kam Tong (with episode of 4/12/58 through the third season and again for the episode of 11/26/60 and with fifth season); June Lockhart is twice featured as Dr. Phyllis Thackeray; Patricia Medina is twice featured as Diana Coulter; Martin Gabel and Roxanne Berard are twice featured as Nathan and Rivka Shotness.

The Episodes:

1. "Three Bells to Perdido" (9-14-57) Janice Rule, Jack Lord
2. "The Outlaw" (9-21-57) Charles Bronson, Grant Withers
3. "The Great Mojave Chase" (9-28-57)
4. "Winchester Quarantine" (10-5-57)
5. "A Matter of Ethics" (10-12-57) Harold J. Stone, Roy Barcroft, Steven Terrell
6. "The Bride" (10-19-57) Bruce Gordon, Michael Connors, Marian Seldes, Barry Cahill
7. "Strange Vendetta" (10-26-57) June Vincent, Michael Pate
8. "High Wire" (11-2-57) Strother Martin, John Dehner, Buddy Baer, Fay Spain
9. "Show of Force" (11-9-57) Vic Perrin, Peter Coe, Rudolfo Acosta
10. "The Long Night" (11-16-57) Kent Smith, James Best, William Schallert
11. "The Colonel and the Lady" (11-23-57) Robert F. Simon
12. "No Visitors" (11-30-57) June Lockhart; Grant Withers, Peg Hillias, Whit Bissell, Ruth Storey, Johnny Western, John Anderson
13. "The Englishman" (12-7-57)
14. "The Yuma Treasure" (12-14-57) Warren Stevens, Henry Brandon, Harry Landers
15. "The Hanging Cross" (12-21-57)

16. "Helen of Abajnian" (12-28-57) Harold J. Stone, Lisa Gaye, Wright King, Vladimir Sokoloff, Nick Dennis, Naomi Stevens
17. "Ella West" (1-4-58) Norma Crane, Earle Hodgens, William Swan, Mike Mazurki
18. "The Reasonable Man" (1-11-58) Barry Atwater
19. "The High Graders" (1-18-58) Susan Cabot, Robert Steele
20. "The Last Laugh" (1-25-58) Stuart Whitman, Jean Allison, Gil Borden
21. "The Bostonian" (2-1-58) Harry Townes, Chris Alcaide, Constance Ford, Joe De Santis, Louis Gomez
22. "The Singer" (2-8-58)
23. "Bitter Wine" (2-15-58) Eduardo Ciannelli, Richard Shannon, Rita Lynn
24. "The Girl from Piccadilly" (2-22-58) Betsy Von Furstenberg, Fenton Meyler
25. "The O'Hare Story" (3-1-58) Victor McLaglen, John Doucette, Herbert Rudley, Christine White
26. "Birds of a Feather" (3-8-58) Robert H. Harris, James Craig
27. "The Teacher" (3-15-58) Carl Benson, Marian Seldes
28. "Killer's Widow" (3-22-58) Barbara Baxley
29. "Gun Shy" (3-29-58)
30. "The Prize Fight Story" (4-5-58) Hal Baylor, Don Megowan, King Calder, George E. Stone, Gage Clarke
31. "Hey Boy's Revenge" (4-12-58) features Kam Tong
32. "The Five Books of Owen Beaver" (4-26-58) Lurene Tuttle, James Olsen, Paul Lukather, Tyler McVey, Walter Barnes
33. "The Silver Queen" (5-3-58) Lita Milan, Earle Hodgins, Whit Bissell
34. "Three Sons" (5-10-58) Parker Fennelly, Paul Jasmin, Jacqueline Mayo, S. John Launer, Kevin Hagen
35. "Twenty-four Hours to North Fork" (5-17-58) June Lockhart; Charles Aidman, Grant Withers, Johnny Western
36. "Deliver the Body" (5-24-58)
37. "Silver Convoy" (5-31-58) Donald Randolph
38. "The Manhunter" (6-7-58) James Franciscus, R. G. Armstrong, Robert Gist
39. "The Statue of San Sebastian" (6-14-58) Judson Pratt, Bart Bradley, John Carradine, Simon Oakland

Second Season

40. "In an Evil Time" (9-13-58) Joseph Calleia, David Whorff, Steve Coit, Martin Newman, Roy Poole
41. "The Man Who Wouldn't Talk" (9-20-58) Hank Patterson, William Stevens, Charles Horvath
42. "The Gentleman" (9-27-58) Charles Bronson
43. "The Hanging of Roy Carter" (10-4-58) Scott Marlowe, Robert Armstrong, John Larch, Paul Birch
44. "Duel at Florence" (10-11-58) Dean Harens
45. "The Protégé" (10-18-58) Peter Breck, George Mitchell, Ken Mayer, William Meigs, Mel Welles
46. "The Road to Wickenberg" (10-25-58) Christine White, Harry Carey Jr., Rayford Barnes, Ed Faulkner

47. "A Sense of Justice" (11-1-58) Barrie Chase
48. "Young Gun" (11-8-58) Paul Carr, Dick Foran, Robert Simon, Meg Wylie, Abby Dalton, Frederick Miller
49. "The Lady" (11-15-58) Patricia Medina, Robert Karnes, George Richardson, Earl Parker
50. "A Share for Murder" (11-22-58) Harry Morgan
51. "The Ballad of Oscar Wilde" (12-6-58) John O'Malley, David Lewis, Chet Stratton, Richard Shannon, Roy Engel, Jack Hogan
52. "The Solid Gold Patrol" (12-13-58) Sean McClory, Don Keefer, Michael Hagen, Robert Cabal, Jim Kline
53. "Something to Live For" (12-20-58) Rayford Barnes, John Anderson, Tom Brown, Vaughn Taylor, Don Megowan, Nancy Hadley
54. "The Moor's Revenge" (12-27-58) Vincent Price, Patricia Morison, Morey Amsterdam, Richard Shannon, Joe Perry
55. "The Wager" (1-3-59) Denver Pyle, Jacqueline Scott, Steve Gravers, Ken Lynch
56. "The Taffeta Mayor" (1-10-59) Edward Platt, Robert Karnes, Norma Crane, Jeanne Bates
57. "Lady on the Stagecoach" (1-17-59) Dolores Vitina, Fay Baker, Raymond Bailey, Ward Wood, Mark Dana
58. "Treasure Trail" (1-24-59) Henry Brandon, Bruce Gordon, Dean Stanton, Willard Sage
59. "Juliet" (1-31-59) Miranda Jones, John Beradino, Allen Case, Earle Hodgins, Ronald Green
60. "The Man Who Lost" (a. k. a. "The Avengers") (2-7-59) Robert J. Wilke, James Drury, Madlyn Rhue, Vic Rodman, Mark Tapscott, Ralph Reed
61. "The Scorched Feather" (2-14-59) Lon Chaney Jr., Mario Alcalde, Sy Malis, Mike Steele
62. "The Return of the Lady" (2-21-59) Patricia Medina, Gene Nelson, Theodore Marcuse, Pilar del Rey
63. "The Monster of Moon Ridge" (2-28-59) Barney Phillips, Natalie Norwick, Walter Coy, Ralph Moody, Robert Forster
64. "The Long Hunt" (3-7-59) Stephen Roberts, Lane Bradbury, Anne Barton, Anthony Caruso
65. "Death of a Gunfighter" (3-14-59) Suzanne Pleshette, Russell Arms, Christopher Dark, I. Stanford Jolley, Joe Bassett, Larkin Ford, Tom Greenway
66. "Incident at Borasca Band" (3-21-59) Jacques Aubuchon, Perry Cook, Ben Wright, Ted Markland
67. "Maggie O'Bannion" (4-4-59) Marion Marshall, Peggy Rea, Paul Sorensen, Mickey Simpson, George Cesar, Don Haggerty
68. "The Chase" (4-11-59) Olive Sturgess, Paul Birch, Adam Williams, Paul Richards, Wright King
69. "Alaska" (4-18-59) Richard Shannon, Karl Swenson, Elizabeth York, Allen Case, Paye Roope
70. "Hunt the Man Down" [directed by Ida Lupino] (4-25-59) Mort Mills, Ed Nelson, Rudolfo Acosta, Jack Elam, Marilyn Hanold
71. "The Return of Roy Carter" (5-2-59) Clu Gulager, Larry

Blake, Brad Von Beltz, Diana Crawford, Craig Duncan
72. "The Sons of Aaron Murdock" (5-9-59) Philip Coolidge, Lee Kinsolving, Elizabeth York, Wesley Lau, Bill Shaw
73. "Commanche" (5-16-59) Shirley O'Hara, Larry Pennell, Susan Cabot, Roy Barcroft, Robert Anderson
74. "Homecoming" (5-23-59) Lewis Martin, Ed Nelson, Don Megowan, Dick Rich
75. "The Fifth Man" (5-30-59) John Emery, Ward Wood, Leo Gordon, Clarke Alexander
76. "Heritage of Anger" (6-6-59) Carol Hill, Ricky Vera, Peter Coe, James Gavin, Carol Thurston, Roberto Contreras
77. "The Haunted Trees" (6-13-59) Doris Dowling, Roy Barcroft, Jane Chang, Duane Grey, Brad Trumbull
78. "Gold and Brimstone" (6-20-59) Eduardo Ciannelli, Philip Pine, Alan Reed, William Vaughan

Third Season

79. "First, Catch a Tiger" (9-12-59) Harry Bartel, John Anderson, King Calder, Don Megowan, Pamela Lincoln
80. "Episode in Laredo" (9-19-59) Eugene Lyons, Norma Crane, J. Pat O'Malley, Johnny Eimen
81. "Les Girls" (9-26-59) Roxanne Berard, Danielle De Metz
82. "The Posse" (10-3-59) Perry Cook, Harry Carey Jr., Denver Pyle, Ken Curtis
83. "Shot by Request" (10-10-59) John Abbott, Malcolm Atterbury, Sue Randall, John Holland, Robert Gist, Greg Dunne
84. "Pancho" (10-24-59) Rafael Campos, Rico Alaniz, Luis Montell, Edward Colmans
85. "Fragile" (10-31-59) Warner Klemperer, Jacqueline Scott, Alan Caillou
86. "The Unforgiven" (11-7-59) David White, Hampton Fancher, Luicana Paluzzi, William Phipps, Paul Burke
87. "The Black Handerchief" (11-14-59) Ed Nelson, Joe Perry, Terrence De Marney, Svea Grunveld
88. "The Gold Toad" (11-21-59) Lorna Thayer, David White, Bill Wellman Jr., Kevin Hagen, Paul Sorensen
89. "Tiger" (11-28-59) Parley Baer, Elsa Cardenas, Paul Clark
90. "Champaigne Safari" (12-5-59) Bill Mims, Patric Knowles, Valerie French, Lou Krugman, Gilman Rankin, Vic Perrin
91. "Charley Red Dog" (12-12-59) Scott Marlowe, Raymond Bailey, Kelton Garwood, Edmund Glover, William Bryant
92. "The Naked Gun" (12-19-59) Robert J. Wilke, Ken Curtis, Lane Chandler, Dallas Mitchell, Hal Needham
93. "One Came Back" (12-26-59) James Coburn, Tommy Cook, Strother Martin, George Mathews, Robert Dorough
94. "The Prophet" (1-2-60) Shepperd Strudwick, Barney Phillips, Florence Martin, Lorna Thayer, Eddie Little Sky, Brad Von Beltz
95. "The Day of the Bad Man" (1-9-60) William Joyce, Eleanor Audley, Harry Fleer, Norman Shelly, Sue Randall, Tony Haig, Hal Needham
96. "The Pledge" (1-16-60) Robert Gist, Charles Gray, Brad Weston, Susan Davis

97. "Jenny" (1-23-60) Ellen Clark, Peter Leeds, Phil Chambers, Quentin Sondergaard, Trevor Bardette, Ben Brogan, Olan Soule, Bud Osborne, Hal Needham

98. "Return to Fort Benjamin" (1-30-60) Anthony Caruso, Herbert Patterson, Charles Aidman, Robert J. Wilke

99. "The Night the Town Died" (2-6-60) Barry Cahill, Robert J. Stevenson, Mary Gregory, Arthur Space, Barney Phillips, Sally Singer, Vic Perrin

100. "The Ledge" (2-13-60) Richard Shannon, Don Beddoe, John Hoyt, Richard Rust

101. "The Lady on the Wall" (2-20-60) Howard Petrie, Ralph Clanton, Hank Patterson, James Stone, Barry Ivins, William Bronson

102. "The Misguided Father" (2-27-60) Harry Carey Jr., Douglas Kennedy, Hampton Fancher, Gregg Palmer, Lee Sands

103. "The Hatchet Man" (3-5-60) Lisa Lu, Allen Jung, Nolan Leary, Benson Fong, Fuji

104. "Fight at Adobe Wells" (3-12-60) Ken Lynch, Miranda Jones, Sandy Kenyon, Dorothy Dells, Brad Weston, Gregg Palmer

105. "The Gladiators" (3-19-60) Dolores Donlon, Paul Cavanagh, George Neise, James Coburn, Chet Stratton

106. "Love and a Bad Woman" (3-26-60) Geraldine Brooks, Lawrence Dobkin, Bob Hopkins, Ed Faulkner, Sherwood Keith, Edwin Mills, Harry Landers, Mitchell Kowal, Franz Roehn

107. "An International Affair" (4-2-60) Ziva Rodann, Fenton Meyler, David Janti, Harry Corden, Oscar Beregi

108. "Lady with a Gun" (4-9-60) Jack Weston, Paula Raymond, Jean Eager, Ron Soble

109. "Never Help the Devil" (4-16-60) Jack Lambert, Kelton Garwood, Lewis Martin, Bill Wellman Jr., Dick Rich

110. "Ambush" [directed by Richard Boone] (4-23-60) Alan Dexter, Michael Ferris, Natalie Norwick, George Macready, Dan Barton, Ed Nelson, Hal Needham

111. "Black Sheep" (4-30-60) Pat Wayne, Stacy Harris, June Vincent, Suzanne Lloyd, Ed Faulkner, Ross Strulin

112. "Full Circle" (5-14-60) Adam Williams, Barbara Baxley, Stewart Bradley, Raymond Hatton, Howard Dayton, Bobby Rose, Hal Needham

113. "The Twins" (5-21-60) Brian Hutton, Jennifer Lea, Lane Chandler, Tony Reagan, Sonia Warren

114. "The Campaign of Billy Banjo" (5-28-60) Jacques Aubuchon, Rita Lynn, Charles Davis, Dorothy Dells, Stewart East, Brad Von Beltz, Vic Perrin, Chuck Robertson, Denise Myers, Hal Needham

115. "Ransom" (6-4-60) Valerie French, Gene Roth, Robert H. Harris, Denver Pyle, Tom Palmer, Alex Davion

116. "The Trial" (6-11-60) Robert F. Simon, Bud Slater, Raymond Hatton, Hal Smith, John Thye, Harry Antrum, Tom Jackson, James Bell, Bill Hunt, Rick Silver, Angela Stevens

117. "The Search" (6-18-60) Wright King, Earl Hodgins, Perry Cook, Peggy Rae, Tex Lambert, Charles Aidman, William Bronson

Fourth Season

118. "The Fatalist" (9-10-60) Martin Gabel, Roxanne Berard; Regina Gleason, Robert Blake, John Close, Lee Sands
119. "Love's Young Dream" (9-17-60) Ken Curtis, Lorna Thayer, Mike Mazurki
120. "A Head of Hair" (9-24-60) Ben Johnson, George Kennedy, Donna Brooks
121. "Out at the Old Ball Park" (10-1-60) John Larch, J. Pat O'Malley, Jack Albertson, Ted Hamilton, Sandy Kenyon, Perry Cook
122. "Saturday Night" (10-8-60) Martin Balsam, Joanne Linville, Wesley Lau, Denny Miller, Rudy Solari, Terence De Marney, Raoul De Leon
123. "The Calf" (10-15-60) Denver Pyle, Parker Fennelly, Don Grady, Carl Henry, Hal Needham
124. "The Tender Gun" (10-22-60) Jeanette Nolan, Don Keefer, Tony Reese, Herb Patterson, Lou Antonio
125. "The Shooting of Jesse May" (10-29-60) Robert Blake, William Talman, Hari Rhodes, Rayford Barnes, Barney Phillips, John Milford
126. "The Poker Friend" (11-12-60) Jack Weston, Betsy Jones-Moreland, Warren Oates, Peter Falk, Brett Sommers, Leo Penn, Tony Haig, James Boles
127. "Crowbait" (11-19-60) Russell Collins, Jacqueline Scott, Gordon Polk, Eddie Little Sky
128. "The Marshal's Boy" (11-26-60) Ken Lynch, Andrew Prine, Harry Carey Jr., Hal Needham
129. "Fogg Bound" [a variation on the western adventures of the Jules Verne character Phileas Fogg] (12-3-60) Patric Knowles, Peter Whitney, Arlene McQuade, Jon Silo
130. "The Legacy" (12-10-60) George Kennedy, Harry Carey Jr., Chuck Roberson, Harry Lauter
131. "The Prisoner" (12-17-60) Buzz Martin, Barry Kelley, George Mitchell, Liam Sullivan, Narda Onyx, Howard McNear
132. "The Puppeteer" (12-24-60) Crahan Denton, Natalie Norwick, Peter Boone (son of actor Richard, in his acting debut), Denver Pyle
133. "Vernon Good" (12-31-60) John Mauldin, James Anderson, Albert Salmi, Leo Gordon, Oscar Beregi
134. "A Quiet Night in Town" [Part I] (1-7-61) Robert Carricart, Robert Emhardt, Phyllis Love, James Best, Sydney Pollock, Fredd Wayne, Kavin Hagen, William Challee
135. "A Quiet Night in Town" [Part II] (1-14-61) as above
136. "The Princess and the Gunfighter" (1-21-61) Arline Sax, Ben Wright, Shirley O'Hara, Earl Parker, Barry Cahill
137. "Shadow of a Man" (1-28-61) Kent Smith, Dianne Foster, Walter Burke, Mike Kellin, Robert Karnes
138. "Long Way Home" (2-4-61) William Talman, Ivan Dixon, Rayford Barnes, John Milford
139. "The Tax Gatherer" (2-11-61) Roy Barcroft, Harry Carey Jr., Raymond Hatton, Stewart East, John Hopkins, Bob Woodward, Hal Needham

140. "The Fatal Flaw" (2-25-61) Allyn Joslyn, Royal Dano, Jena Engstrom, Miguel de Anda
141. "Fandango" (3-4-61) Robert Gist, Karl Swenson, Andrew Prine, Jerry Summers, Rudolfo Acosta
142. "The Last Judgment" (3-11-61) James Anderson, Harold J. Stone, Donald Randolph, Leo Gordon, Robert J. Stevenson
143. "The Gold Bar" (3-18-61) John Fiedler, Jena Engstrom, Val Avery, Chet Stratton
144. "Everyman" (3-25-61) Barry Kelley, David White, Vic Perrin, June Vincent, Don Engel, Suzi Carnel
145. "The Siege" (4-1-61) Mike Kellin, Perry Lopez, David J. Stewart, Brad Weston, Robert Karnes, Russ Bender
146. "The Long Weekend" (4-8-61) Roy Barcroft, Ralph Moody, Paige Adams, Clegg Hoyt, Stephen Roberts, Ned Glass
147. "El Paso Stage" (4-15-61) Buddy Ebsen, Karl Swenson, Jeremy Slate, Hank Patterson, Mary Mundy
148. "Duke of Texas" (4-22-61) Scott Marlowe, Eduard Franz, Robert Carricart, Albert Cavens, Roberto Contreras
149. "Broken Image" (4-29-61) Kenneth Tobey, June Vincent, Johnny Eiman, Bob Woodward, Rick Silver, Stewart East, Joan Dupuis, Hal Needham
150. "My Brother's Keeper" (5-6-61) Wright King, Ben Wright, Karl Swenson, Betsy Jones-Moreland, Ed Nelson, Otto Waldis, Allen Wood
151. "Bear Bait" (5-13-61) Judi Meredith, Richard Rust, Martin West, Ralph Reed, Stephen Roberts, Frank Ferguson, Ollie O'Toole, Jack Tesler
152. "The Cure" (5-20-61) Norma Crane, Jerry Wayne, Jeanne Vaughn, Craig Duncan, Olan Soule
153. "The Road" (5-27-61) Ben Wright, George Kennedy, Gene Lyons, Trevor Bardette, Perry Cook, Joel Crothers
154. "The Uneasy Grave" (6-3-61) Pippa Scott, Werner Klemperer, Lillian Bronson, Steve Warren, Wolfe Barzell, Don Beddoe
155. "Soledad Crossing" (6-10-61) Ed Faulkner, Ken Curtis, Natalie Norwick, Chuck Roberson, Walter Edmiston

Fifth Season

156. "The Vigil" (9-16-61) Mary Fickett, George Kennedy, Dan Stafford
157. "The Education of Sara Jane" (9-23-61) Jena Engstrom, Duane Eddy
158. "The Revenger" (9-30-61) Anthony Caruso, Janet Lake, Russell Arms, Shug Fisher, Harry Carey Jr., Rayford Barnes
159. "Odds for a Big Red" (10-7-61) Richard Ney, Hope Holiday, Virginia Capers, Ollie O'Toole, Robert Karnes, Perry Cook
160. "A Proof of Love" (10-14-61) Charles Bronson, George Kennedy, Shirley O'Hara, Chana Eden
161. "The Gospel Singer" (10-21-61) Suzi Carnell, John McLiam, Ed Peck, Noah Keen, Brad Weston, Roy Engel
162. "The Race" (10-28-61) Ben Johnson, Michael Pate, Stu East
163. "The Hanging of Aaron Gibbs" (11-4-61) Rupert Crosse,

Odetta, Barry Cahill, Ed Faulkner, Hal Needham

164. "The Piano" (11-11-61) Keith Andes, Antoinette Bower, Richard Reeves, Gertrude Flynn, Arny Freeman

165. "Ben Jalisco" (11-18-61) Charles Bronson, Coleen Gray, Chuck Roberson, Rick Silver, Lane Chandler, John Litel

166. "The Brothers" (11-25-61) Buddy Ebsen, Paul Hartman, Stu East, Peggy Stewart, Edward Faulkner, Hal Needham

167. "A Drop of Blood" (12-2-61) Martin Gabel, Roxanne Berard; Mike Kellin, Regina Gleason, Noah Keen

168. "A Knight to Remember" (12-9-61) Hans Conried, Robert Carricart, Dolores Donlon, Wright King

169. "Blind Circle" (12-16-61) Susan Davis, Gerald Gordon, Hank Patterson, Ellen Atterbury, Harrison Lewis, Bob Jellison

170. "Squatter's Rights" [a.k.a. "The Kid"] (12-23-61) Flip Mark, Jacques Aubuchon, Roy Engel, Eleanor Audley

171. "Justice in Hell" (1-6-62) Strother Martin, Dabbs Greer, Chris Alcaide, L. Q. Jones, Gaylord Cavellero, Gerald Gordon

172. "The Mark of Cain" (1-13-62) Betsy Hale, Don Beddoe, William Schallert, Alan Carney, John Alderson, Larry Brightman

173. "Lazarus" (1-20-62) Phil Collidge, Roy Barcroft, Iphigenie Castiglioni

174. "The Exiles" (1-27-62) Gerald Price, Jay Novello, Vivi Janiss, Richard Bermudez, Bob Hopkins, Joan Tabor

175. "The Hunt" (2-3-62) Joan Elan, Hank Patterson, Edward Faulkner, John Mitchum, Leonid Kinskey

176. "Dream Girl" (2-10-62) Peggy Ann Garner, Joseph Dimmitt, Fred Hakim, Chuck Couch, Hal Needham

177. "One, Two, Three" (2-17-62) Robert F. Simon, Jack Elam, Lloyd Corrigan, Eve McVeagh, Barbara Pepper, Dorothy Dells, William Woodson, Dean Smith

178. "The Waiting Room" (2-24-62) James Griffith, Dean Stanton, George Cesar, Byron Foulger

179. "The Trap" (3-3-62) Jeanette Nolan, Frank Sutton, Crahan Denton, Ed Peck

180. "Don't Shoot the Piano Player" (3-10-62) George Kennedy, James Callahan, Fenton Meyler, Virginia Gregg, Mike Mazurki

181. "Alive" (3-17-62) Jena Engstrom, Jeanette Nolan, Richard Shannon, Mary Gregory, William Stevens, Perry Cook

182. "The Man Who Struck Moonshine" (3-24-62) William Conrad, Phyllis Avery

183. "Silent Death" (3-31-62) Robert Emhardt, John Holland, Michael Pate

184. "Hobson's Choice" [a drama on Alfred Nobel] (4-7-62) Milton Selzer, Parley Baer, Olan Soule, Titus Moede, Harrison Lewis, Jan Peters

185. "Coming of the Tiger" (4-14-62) Marc Marno, Teru Shimada, James Hong, Fuji, Bob Okazaki, Beulah Quo

186. "Darwin's Man" (4-21-62) Kent Smith, Richard Rust, Buzz Martin, Bud Osborne

187. "Invasion" (4-28-62) Robert Gist, Lew Brown, Douglas Lambert, Roy Roberts, Robert Gibbons, Vicki Benet

188. "Cream of the Jest" (5-5-62) Stanley Adams, Jeff Davis, Catherine McLeod, Peter Brocco, Naomi Stevens
189. "Bandit" (5-12-62) Natalie Norwick, Robert Adler, Charles Couch, Bob Woodward, Jerry Gatlin, Hal Needham
190. "Pandora's Box" (5-19-62) Martin West, Lorna Thayer, Ken Curtis, Lewis Martin, Mary Mundy, Robert J. Stevenson, Jamie Brothers
191. "The Jonah" (5-26-62) Crahan Denton, Richard Shannon, Harry Carey Jr., Dorothy Dells
192. "The Knight" (6-2-62) Jay Novello, Will Corey, Charles Kuenstle, Jean Inness

Sixth Season

193. "Genesis" [a biographical drama of Paladin, with Richard Boone in three roles] (9-15-62) James Mitchum, William Conrad, Parley Baer, Ann Morrison
194. "Taylor's Woman" (9-22-62) Kathie Browne, Harry Carey Jr., Tom Hennessey, Olan Soule
195. "The Fifth Bullet" (9-29-62) Ben Johnson, Shug Fisher, Peter Boone, Dorothy Dells
196. "A Place for Abel Hix" (10-6-62) Kevin Hagen, Robert Blake, Paul Tripp, Jean Engstrom
197. "Beau Geste" (10-13-62) Paul Richards, Faith Domergue, Henry Beckman, Ray Guth
198. "The Bird of Time" (10-20-62) George Mathews, John Hoyt
199. "Memories of Monica" (10-27-62) Judi Meredith, Bing Russell, Larry Ward, Hal Needham
200. "The Predators" (11-3-62) Richard Jaeckel, Ellen Willard, Lester Maxwell
201. "Shootout at Hogtooth" (11-10-62) Patrick McVey, Les Damon, Doodles Weaver
202. "A Miracle for St. Francis" (11-17-62) Rafael Campos, David Garner, Miriam Goldyn
203. "Marshal of Sweetwater" (11-24-62) David White, Kathie Browne, Gordon Jones
204. "Man in an Hourglass" (12-1-62) Edgar Buchanan, Jim Stacy, Morgan Woodward, Alan Baxter, Dan White, Jerry Gatlin
205. "Penelope" (12-8-62) Joanna Barnes, Lawrence Dobkin, Ivan Bonar, Jack Doner
206. "Trial at Tablerock" (12-15-62) Sherwood Price, Barry Kelley, William Mims, Gregg Palmer, John Damier, Joey Higgins
207. "Be Not Forgetful to Strangers" [a Christmas story by Sarno Jr.; directed by Richard Boone] (12-22-62) Duane Eddy, Josie Lloyd, Roy Barcroft, Pat Newby, Robert J. Stevenson, Ed Faulkner, Hal Needham
208. "The Treasure" (12-29-62) Jeanne Cooper, Jim Davis, DeForest Kelley, Lee Van Cleef, Bob Woodward
209. "Brotherhood" (1-5-63) Charles Bronson, Michael Keep, Max Mellinger, Shug Fisher, Dawn Eiulesky, Warren Joslin
210. "Bob Wire" (1-12-63) Woodrow Parfrey, Irish McCalla, Chris King, James Bell, Hal Baylor

211. "The Debutante" (1-19-63) Robert Emhardt, Wayne Rogers, Eleanor Audley
212. "Unforgiving Minute" (1-26-63) Patricia Medina, Al Ruscio
213. "American Primitive" (2-2-63) Harry Morgan, Robert J. Wilke, Pitt Herbert, Peggy Rea
214. "The Burning Tree" (2-9-63) Elinor Donahue, Whit Bissell, Paul Fix
215. "Cage at McNaab" (2-16-63) Lon Chaney, Jacqueline Scott, Christopher Dark, John Harmon
216. "Caravan" (2-23-63) Miriam Colon, Dolores Faith, John Alderson, Cliff Osmond, Hal Needham
217. "The Walking Years" [directed by Richard Boone] (3-2-63) Elen Willard, Jacqueline Wilson, Satenio Donigan, Fred Hakim, Stewart East, Hal Needham
218. "Sweet Lady of the Moon" (3-9-63) Crahan Denton, Richard Shannon, Dorothy Dells, Harry Carey Jr., Robert J. Stevenson
219. "The Savages" (3-16-63) Patric Knowles, Judi Meredith, James Griffith
220. "The Eve of St. Elmo" (3-23-63) Warren Stevens, Brett Sommers, George Kennedy, Chris Alcaide, P. L. Smith
221. "The Lady of the Fifth Moon" (3-30-63) Bethel Leslie, William Schallert
222. "Two Plus One" (4-6-63) Susan Silo, Gail Kobe, Rex Holman, Ken Hudgins
223. "The Black Bull" (4-13-63) Carlos Romero, Faith Domergue, Lita Marsell
224. "Face of a Shadow" (4-20-63) Enid Jaynes, Lee Van Cleef, Nestor Paiva, Richard Reed, Harry Carey Jr., Rayford Barnes, Roy Barcroft, William Woodson, Laurindo Almeida
225. "The Sanctuary" (6-22-63) Harry Carey Jr., Hank Patterson, Jerry Summers
226. "The Mountebank" (8-3-63) Warren Stevens, Robert J. Stevenson, Natalie Norwick, Carlos Romero, Sandy Kenyon

MAVERICK

Few westerns have been as ingratiating as Roy Huggins' satire of fraternal poker-playing rogues. With teleplays by Marion Hargrove and Leo Townsend, Maverick celebrated a West that never was--or could have been. Still, one watches jubilantly, as the production team of John Ewing (art director), David Butolphe (musical accompanist) and Paul Frances Webster (composer of the title ballad) make an immeasurable contribution to the carnival.

The Regulars: Bret Maverick: James Garner; Bart Maverick: Jack Kelly; Beau Maverick: Roger Moore (with episode of 9/18/60); Brent Maverick: Robert Colbert (with episode of 3/26/61); Dandy Jim: Efrem Zimbalist Jr. (recurring guest role); Samantha Crawford: Diane Brewster (recurring guest role).

The Episodes:

1. "The War of the Silver Kings" (9-22-57) Edmund Lowe, John Litel, Leo Gordon, Paul Baxley
2. "Point Blank" (9-29-57) Michael Connors, Karen Steele
3. "According to Hoyle" (10-6-57) Kathleen Crowley
4. "Ghost Rider" (10-13-57) Joanna Barnes, Rhodes Reason, Willard Sage, Stacy Keach
5. "The Long Hunt" (10-20-57) Richard Webb
6. "Stage West" (10-27-57) Erin O'Brien
7. "Relic of Fort Tejon" (11-3-57) Sheb Wooley, Dan Tobin, Maxine Cooper
8. "Hostage" (11-10-57) Laurie Carroll, Stephen BeKassy, Mickel Simpson
9. "Stampede" (11-17-57) Efrem Zimbalist Jr.
10. "The Jeweled Gun" (11-24-57) Kathleen Crowley, Stephen Coit, Miguel Landau
11. "The Wrecker" [adapted from the Robert Louis Stevenson story] (12-1-57) Patric Knowles, Lloyd Osbourne
12. "The Quick and the Dead" (12-8-57) Gerald Mohr, Marie Windsor
13. "Naked Gallows" (12-15-57) Michael Connors, Sherry Jackson, Morris Ankrum, Fay Spain, Jeanne Cooper
14. "Comstock Conspiracy" (12-29-57) Werner Klemperer
15. "The Third Rider" (1-5-58) Dick Foran, Barbara Nichols, Frank Faylen, Michael Dante, Casey Rodgers
16. "A Rage for Vengeance" (1-12-58) John Russell, Catherine McCleod, Gage Clark
17. "Rope of Cards" (1-19-58) Tol Avery, Frank Cody, Joan Marshall, William Reynolds, Will Wright
18. "Diamond in the Rough" (1-26-58) William Forrest, Jacqueline Beer, Fred Wayne, Lilli Valenti, Otto Waldis
19. "Day of Reckoning" (2-2-58) Russell Thorsen
20. "The Savage Hills" (2-9-58) Diane Brewster, Peter Whitney, Thurston Hall
21. "Trail West to Fury" (2-16-58) Efrem Zimbalist Jr., Gene Nelson, Aline Towne, Charles Fredericks
22. "The Burning Sky" (2-23-58) Gerald Mohr, Joanna Barnes, Whitney Blake
23. "The Seventh Hand" (3-2-58)
24. "Plunder of Paradise" ["Seed of Deception"] (3-9-58) Joi Lansing, Adele Mara, Myron Healey, Gerald Mohr, Bing Russell, Frank Ferguson
25. "Black Fire" (3-16-58) Hans Conried, Jane Darwell, Will Wright, Theoni Bryant, Charles Bateman, Dan Sheridan

Episodes continued with Television Drama Series Programming: A Comprehensive Chronicle, 1959-1975.

THE SEVEN LIVELY ARTS

The Regulars: John Crosby, television critic for the New York Herald Tribune, host. Series conceived and developed by John Houseman.

The Episodes:

1. "The Changing Ways of Love" [a review of American romantic patterns from the 1920's to the present, by S. J. Perelman; Perelman, Crosby and Mike Wallace narrate] (11-3-57) Jason Robards Jr., Piper Laurie, Dick York, Rip Torn
2. "The World of Nick Adams" [a dramatization by A. E. Hotchner of the Ernest Hemingway stories "The Battler," "The End of Something," "Now I Lay Me," "Three-Day Blow" and "Light of the World"; directed by Robert Mulligan] (11-10-57) Eli Wallach, Steven Hill, William Marshall
3. "The Revivalists" [analyzing the methods of the Reverend Dr. Billy Graham, Billy Sunday, Aimee Semple McPherson, Oral Roberts and Mahalia Jackson] (11-17-57)
4. "The Sound of Jazz" [a musical salute, with Count Basie, Pee Wee Russell, Red Allen, Jo Jones, Billie Holiday, Vic Dickenson, Roy Eldridge, Gerry Mulligan, Big Bill Broonzy, The Jimmy Guiffre Three and Coleman Hawkins] (12-8-57)
5. "Here Is New York" [by E. B. White; narrated by E. G. Marshall] (12-15-57)
6. "The Nutcracker" [staged by George Balanchine to the music of Tchaikovsky] (12-22-57 at 3-4:00)
7. "Hollywood Around the World" (12-29-57)
8. "Blast in Centralia No. 5" [adapted by Loring Mandel from the magazine story by John Bartlow Martin; directed by George Roy Hill] (1-26-58) Maureen Stapleton
9. "Gold Rush" [musical choreographed by Agnes de Mille to the score of "Paint Your Wagon" by Alan Jay Lerner and Frederick Loewe] (2-9-58) James Mitchell, Gamye de Lappe, John Reardon, Sono Osato, Beatrice Arthur
10. "Profile of a Composer: Norman Dello Joio" (2-16-58)

A TURN OF FATE [THE ALCOA-GOODYEAR THEATRE]

The Regulars: Robert Ryan, David Niven, Jack Lemmon, Jane Powell, Charles Boyer, featured performers.

The Episodes:

1. The Goodyear Theatre: "Silhouette of a Killer" [adapted by Palmer Thompson from a story by Tita Brooks] (9-30-57) Robert Ryan
2. The Alcoa Theatre: "Circumstantial" (10-7-57) David Niven, Angie Dickinson
3. The Goodyear Theatre: "Lost and Found" (10-14-57) Jack Lemmon, Joanna Moore

4. The Alcoa Theatre: "Encounter on a Second-Class Coach"
    (10-21-57) Jane Powell, Stuart Whitman
5. The Goodyear Theatre: "The Danger by Night" (10-28-57)
    David Niven, Katherine Bard
6. The Alcoa Theatre: "Guests for Dinner" (11-4-57) Charles
    Boyer
7. The Goodyear Theatre: "Voices in the Fog" (11-11-57) Jack
    Lemmon
8. The Alcoa Theatre: "On Edge" (11-18-57) Robert Ryan
9. The Goodyear Theatre: "Hurricane" (11-25-57) Jane Powell
10. The Alcoa Theatre: "Souvenir" (12-2-57) Jack Lemmon,
    Douglas Dumbrille, Gloria Talbott, Grant Richards, Bill
    Kendis
11. The Goodyear Theatre: "The Crowd Pleaser" (12-9-57) Rob-
    ert Ryan
12. The Alcoa Theatre: "Cupid Wore a Badge" (12-16-57) Jane
    Powell, David Janssen
13. The Goodyear Theatre: "The Tinhorn" [received an Emmy
    nomination for its film editing, 1957] (12-23-57) David
    Niven, Michael Pate
14. The Alcoa Theatre: "The Face of Truth" (12-30-57) Robert
    Ryan
15. The Goodyear Theatre: "The Victim" (1-6-58) Jack Lemmon
16. The Alcoa Theatre: "In the Dark" (1-13-58) David Niven,
    Richard Long, Barbara Lawrence, Keye Luke
17. The Alcoa Theatre: "Hidden Witness" (1-27-58) Robert Ryan,
    Ann Palmer
18. The Goodyear Theatre: "Music in the Night" (2-3-58) Jane
    Powell, Maggie Mahoney, Peter Hansen
19. The Alcoa Theatre: "Night Caller" (2-10-58) David Niven,
    Henry Daniell
20. The Goodyear Theatre: "White Flag" (2-17-58) Robert Ryan,
    Whit Bissell
21. The Alcoa Theatre: "The Days of November" (2-24-58) Jack
    Lemmon, Richard Jaeckel
22. The Goodyear Theatre: "The Fatal Charm" (3-3-58) David
    Niven
23. The Alcoa Theatre: "Even a Thief Can Dream" (3-10-58)
    Charles Boyer
24. The Goodyear Theatre: "The Seventh Letter" (3-17-58) Rob-
    ert Ryan
25. The Goodyear Theatre: "Taps for Jeffrey" (3-31-58) David
    Niven, Virginia Grey
26. The Alcoa Theatre: "Loudmouth" (4-7-58) Jack Lemmon,
    Harold J. Stone, Penny Edwards
27. The Goodyear Theatre: "Fix a Frame for Mourning" (4-14-58)
    Jane Powell, John Baragrey
28. The Alcoa Theatre: "My Wife's Next Husband" (4-21-58)
    David Niven, James Daly
29. The Goodyear Theatre: "The Giant Step" (4-28-58) Robert
    Ryan
30. The Alcoa Theatre: "Most Likely to Succeed" (5-5-58) Jack
    Lemmon
31. The Goodyear Theatre: "The Lady Takes the Stand" (5-12-58)

Jane Powell, Keith Andes
32. The Alcoa Theatre: "Mr. Perfectionist" (5-19-58) Robert Ryan, Frances Rafferty
33. The Goodyear Theatre: "Decision by Terror" (5-26-58) David Niven
34. The Alcoa Theatre: "The Clock Struck Twelve" (6-2-58) Charles Boyer
35. The Goodyear Theatre: "Disappearance" (6-9-58) Jack Lemmon
36. The Alcoa Theatre: "Johnny Risk" (6-16-58) Lew Ayres, Michael Landon
37. The Goodyear Theatre: "Three Dark Years" (6-23-58) Barbara Stanwyck, Gerald Mohr, Russell Conway
38. The Alcoa Theatre: "Decoy Duck" (6-30-58) Jane Powell, David Janssen

SUSPICION

The Regulars: Dennis O'Keefe, host. Walter Abel host as of episode of May 12, 1958.

The Episodes:

1. "Four O'Clock" [adapted by Francis Cockrell from the story by Cornell Woolrich; produced and directed by Alfred Hitchcock] (9-30-57) E. G. Marshall, Nancy Kelly, Richard Long
2. "Murder Me Gently" (10-7-57) Kurst Kasznar, Jessica Tandy, Reginald Gardiner
3. "The Other Side of the Curtain" [adapted from the Helen McClay story] (10-14-57) Donna Reed, Jeff Richards
4. "Hand in Glove" (10-21-57) Burgess Meredith, Cathleen Nesbitt
5. "The Story of Margery Reardon" [adapted by John Kneubuhl from the story by Susan Seavy] (10-28-57) Margaret O'Brien, Rod Taylor, Henry Silva, Sara Haden
6. "Diary for Death" (11-4-57) Macdonald Carey, Jack Klugman, Everett Sloane, Julie Wilson
7. "Heartbeat" (11-11-57) David Wayne, Pat Hingle, Barbara Turner, Warren Beatty, Raymond Bramley
8. "The Sparkle of Diamonds" (11-18-57) Margaret Leighton, Enid Markey, Ralph Bellamy
9. "Flight" (11-25-57) Audie Murphy, Susan Kohner, Jack Warden
10. "Rainy Day" [adapted from the William Somerset Maugham story by William Pertwee] (12-2-57) Robert Flemyng, George Cole, John Williams, Tom Conway, Martin Wilkins, A. E. Gould-Porter
11. "The Deadly Game" (12-9-57) Gary Merrill, Boris Karloff, Joseph Wiseman, Harry Townes
12. "Doomsday" [by Sy Bartlett] (12-16-57) Robert Middleton, Edward Binns, Dan Duryea
13. "The Dark Stairway" (12-23-57) Phyllis Thaxter, Jack Klugman, Marian Seldes

14. "Someone Is After Me" [by Robert Soderberg] (1-6-58) Patricia Neal, Lee Bowman, Edward Andrews, Joanne Linville
15. "Lord Arthur Savile's Crime" [adapted from the Oscar Wilde story; produced by Alfred Hitchcock] (1-13-58) Ronald Howard, Gladys Cooper, Rosemary Harris, May Forbes, Sebastian Cabot, Melville Cooper
16. "End in Violence" [adapted by Harold Gast from the novel by Lorenz Heller] (1-20-58) John Ireland, Lisa Kirk
17. "Comfort for the Grave" [adapted by Adrian Spies and Halsey Malone from the story by Richard Deming] (1-27-58) Jan Sterling, Paul Douglas, Anthony Caruso, Mrs. Paul Douglas
18. "Meeting in Paris" [produced by Alfred Hitchcock] (2-10-58) Walter Abel, Rory Calhoun, Jane Greer, Maurice Marsac
19. "A Touch of Evil" [adapted by Halstead Welles from the magazine article by E. J. Kahn] (2-17-58) Audrey Totter, Harry Guardino, John Carradine, Bethel Leslie
20. "If I Die Before I Live" [by James P. Davis] (2-24-58) Edith Adams, James Gregory
21. "The Hollow Man" [by George Lefferts] (3-3-58) Dane Clark, Georgiann Johnson
22. "A World Full of Strangers" [by James Yaffe and William Wise] (3-10-58) Janice Rule, John Baragrey, Katharine Sergava
23. "The Eye of Truth" [adapted by Eric Ambler from his own story] (3-17-58) Joseph Cotten, Leora Dana, George Peppard, Philip Van Zandt
24. "Diagnosis: Death" [by Ernest Kinoy] (3-31-58) Larry Parks, Anne Meacham, Nancy Wickwire
25. "The Bull Skinner" [by Ernest Kinoy] (4-7-58) Rod Steiger, John Beal, Sallie Brophy
26. "The Girl Upstairs" [adapted from the Patrick Hamilton play] (4-14-58) Denholm Elliott, Douglas Campbell
27. "Fraction of a Second" [adapted by Kathleen Hite from the Daphne du Maurier story] (4-21-58) Bette Davis
28. "The Way to Heaven" (4-28-58) Marion Lorne, Patricia Smith, Tony Maxwell, Albert Carrier, Sebastian Cabot
29. "The Woman with Red Hair" [by Sam Lock] (5-5-58) Dennis O'Keefe, Roddy McDowall, Marian Seldes
30. "Protégée" (5-12-58) Agnes Moorehead, Phyllis Love, William Shatner, Jack Klugman
31. "The Velvet Vault" (5-19-58) Carmen Mathews, Elizabeth Montgomery
32. "The Voice in the Night" [adapted from the William Hope Hodgson classic] (5-26-58) James Donald, Patrick Macnee, James Coburn, Barbara Rush
33. "Death Watch" (6-2-58) Edmond O'Brien, Janice Rule
34. "The Man with the Gun" [adapted from the N. B. Stone Jr. and Richard Wilson scenario] (6-9-58) Anthony Quayle, Maureen Hurley
35. "The Woman Turned to Salt" (6-16-58) Michael Rennie, Susan Oliver, Pamela Brown
36. "Eye for Eye" [adapted by John Kneubuhl from the story by Leigh Brackett] (6-23-58) Macdonald Carey, Kathleen Crowley, Andrew Duggan, Ray Milland

37. "Return from Darkness" (6-30-58) Lorne Greene, Phyllis
    Thaxter, John Baragrey
38. "The Devil Makes Three" [by Marc Brandel] (7-7-58) Dennis
    O'Keefe, James Daly, Dolores Dorn-Heft
39. "The Imposter" [by Theodore Apstein] (7-14-58) Kent Smith,
    Roddy McDowall, Joanna Moore
40. "The Death of Paul Dane" [by Morton Wishengrad and Virginia
    Mazer] (7-21-58) Eli Wallach, Warren Stevens, Janice
    Rule

THE WALTER WINCHELL FILE

    One among the strident entries, echoing an inquisitorial time,
was this dramatized collection of the syndicated columnist's investi-
gative reports. The actual appearance of Winchell as performer in
these pedagogic accounts only further diluted any claims to plausi-
bility.

The Regulars: Walter Winchell, host, narrator and performer

The Episodes:

1. "Country Boy" (10-2-57)
2. "Thou Shalt Not Kill" (10-9-57) Karl Swenson, Joe Lo Presti
3. "A Day in the Sun" (10-16-57) Harry Bartell
4. "Where Is Louise Milk?" (10-23-57) Robert Ellenstein, Maggie
    Mahoney
5. "The Boy from Mason City" (10-30-57) Tom Laughlin
6. "The Decision" (11-6-57) Harry Landers
7. "The Candlestick" (11-13-57) Tol Avery, Peggy Webber
8. "The Fallen Idol" (11-20-57)
9. "The Semi-Windup" (11-27-57)
10. "Cup Cake" (12-4-57) John Wengraf, Anna Maria Nanasi, Anna
    Sten
11. "The Law and Aaron Benjamin" (12-11-57) Robert Middleton
12. "Act of Folly" (12-18-57)
13. "The Steep Hill" (12-25-57)
14. "Terror" (1-3-58) Hershel Bernardi
15. "A Good Address" (1-10-58)
16. "The High Window" (1-17-58) James Westerfield
17. "Night People" (1-24-58)
18. "David and Goliath" (1-31-58) William Phipps, Jim Hyland
19. "The Bargain" (2-7-58) Brian Hutton, Anita Gordon
20. "Hot Night in Manhattan" (2-14-58) Denise Alexander, Ray
    Foster, Kevin Hagen, George Brenlin
21. "Frame-Up" (2-21-58)

ZORRO

As adapted from Johnston McCulley's The Mark of Zorro, which had inspired numerous motion pictures, including that of the same title with Tyrone Power in 1940, the cavaliero romance now flashed across the home screen courtesy of Disney studios. A specious adventure, even to the knowing eyes of children, Zorro cereminiously enjoins its swordsman hero to dispel maleficent magistradoes and conquistadors. Secure in his anonymity (an indication of what audiences were asked to believe, for a narrow mask across the eyes made Don Diego impervious to detection), "Zorro" transversed his largely fictional countryside, and so quelled the fantastic appetite of post-McCarthy era audiences.

The Regulars: Don Diego (alias "Zorro"): Guy Williams; Bernardo: Gene Sheldon; Captain Monasterio: Britt Lomand; Sergeant Garcia: Henry Calvin; Torres: Jan Arvan; Elina: Eugenia Paul; Anita Cobrillo: Annette Funicello; Ricardo del Amo: Richard Anderson; Anna Maria: Jolene Brand; Don Alejandro: George Lewis; Galindo: Vinton Hayworth; "The Eagle": Charles Korvin (continuing guest role); Corporal Reyes: Don Diamond

The Episodes [chronicled from the ninth teleplay]:

1. "A Fair Trial" (12-5-57)
2. "Garcia's Sweet Mission" (12-12-57)
3. "Double Trouble for Zorro" (12-19-57) Tony Russo
4. "The Luckiest Swordsman Alive" (12-26-57)
5. "The Fall of Monasterio" (1-2-58) John Dehner
6. "Shadow of Doubt" (1-9-58)
7. "Garcia Stands Accused" (1-16-58)
8. "Slaves of the Eagle" (1-23-58)
9. "Sweet Face of Danger" (1-30-58)
10. "Zorro Fights His Father" (2-6-58)
11. "Death Stacks the Deck" (2-13-58) Jim Bannon
12. "Agent of the Eagle" (2-20-58) Anthony Caruso
13. "Zorro Springs a Trap" (2-27-58)
14. "The Unmasking of Zorro" (3-6-58)
15. "The Secret of the Sierra" (3-13-58) Laurie Carroll
16. "The New Commandants" (3-20-58)
17. "The Fox and the Coyote" (3-27-58)
18. "Adios Señor Magistrado" (4-3-58)
19. "The Eagle's Brood" (4-10-58)
20. "Zorro by Proxy" (4-17-58)
21. "Quintana Makes a Choice" (4-24-58)
22. "Conspiracy" (5-1-58)
23. "The Man with the Whip" (5-8-58) Kent Taylor
24. "The Cross of the Andes" (5-15-58)
25. "The Missing Jewels" (5-22-58)
26. "The Well of Death" (5-29-58)
27. "The Tightening Noose" (6-5-58)
28. "The Sergeant Regrets" (6-12-58)

29. "The Eagle Leaves Nest" (6-19-58)
30. "Bernardo Faces Death" (6-26-58)
31. "Day of Decision" (7-3-58)

Second Season

32. "Welcome to Monterey" (10-9-58)
33. "Zorro Rides Alone" (10-16-58)
34. "Horse of Another Color" (10-23-58)
35. "The Señorita Makes a Choice" (10-30-58) Eduard Franz
36. "Rendezvous at Sundown" (11-6-58)
37. "The New Order" (11-13-58)
38. "An Eye for an Eye" (11-20-58) Barbara Luna
39. "The Flag of Truce" (11-27-58)
40. "Ambush" (12-4-58)
41. "Practical Joker" (12-11-58)
42. "The Flaming Arrow" (12-18-58) Yvette Dugay
43. "Zorro Fights a Duel" (12-25-58)
44. "Amnesty for Zorro" (1-1-59)
45. "The Runaways" (1-8-59)
46. "The Iron Box" (1-15-59)
47. "The Gay Caballero" (1-22-59) Cesar Romero
48. "Tornado Is Missing" (1-29-59) Cesar Romero
49. "Zorro Versus Cupid" (2-5-59)
50. "The Legend of Zorro" (2-12-59)
51. "Spark of Revenge" (2-19-59)
52. "The Missing Father" (2-26-59)
53. "Please Believe Me" (3-5-59)
54. "The Brooch" (3-12-59)
55. "The Mountain Man" (3-19-59)
56. "The Hound of the Sierras" (3-26-59)
57. "Manhunt" (4-2-59)
58. "The Man from Spain" (4-9-59)
59. "Treasure for the King" (4-16-59)
60. "Exposing the Tyrant" (4-23-59)
61. "Zorro Takes a Dare" (4-30-59)
62. "An Affair of Honor" (5-7-59)
63. "The Sergeant Sees Red" (5-14-59)
64. "Invitation to Death" (5-21-59)
65. "The Captain Regrets" (5-28-59)
66. "Masquerade for Murder" (6-4-59)
67. "Long Live the Governor" (6-11-59)
68. "The Fortune Teller" (6-18-59)
69. "Señor China Boy" (6-25-59) James Hong
70. "Finders Keepers" (7-2-59)

JEFFERSON DRUM

This innocuous western (it couldn't be taken seriously) involves an editor's pugilistic efforts to bring to a mid-nineteenth century town of coal miners some properly balanced reportage. Teleplays are expectedly infused with editor Jeff's patriarchal dictums for his idolizing son.

The Regulars: Jefferson Drum: Jeff Richards; Joey Drum: Eugene Martin; Lucius Coin: Cyril Delevanti; Big Ed: Robert J. Stevenson

The Episodes:

1. "The Bounty Man" (4-25-58)
2. "Law and Order" (5-2-58)
3. "The Hanging of Joe Lavetti" (5-9-58)
4. "Bad Day for a Tinhorn" (5-16-58)
5. "The Cheater" (5-23-58) Andrew Duggan, Philip Ahn
6. "A Very Deadly Game" (5-30-58)
7. "Madame Faro" (6-6-58)
8. "Bandidos" (6-13-58)
9. "The Outlaw" (6-20-58)
10. "Wheel of Fortune" (6-27-58) Richard Webb
11. "The Poet" (7-4-58)
12. "A Matter of Murder" (7-11-58)
13. "The Lawless" (7-18-58)

Second Season

14. "Showdown" (9-26-58)
15. "The Keeney Gang" (10-3-58) Brad Dexter
16. "Stagecoach Episode" (10-10-58) Dan Blocker
17. "Obituary" (10-16-58)
18. "Band of Iron" (10-23-58)
19. "Return" (10-30-58)
20. "Mistaken" (11-6-58)
21. "The Captive" (11-13-58)
22. "Maltreated" (11-20-58)
23. "Thicker Than Water" (11-27-58)
24. "Prison Hill" (12-4-58)
25. "Simon Pitt" (12-11-58)
26. "Arrival" (12-18-58) John Ashley, Hal Smith, Harry Hickox

NO WARNING

The Episodes:

1. "Emergency" (4-6-58) Elisha Cook Jr.
2. "Hear No Evil" (4-13-58) Mercedes McCambridge
3. "Fire Lookout Post" (4-20-58) Ann Rutherford
4. "Ashley and Son" (4-27-58) Everett Sloane, Alfred Toigo
5. "Stranded" (5-4-58) Marsha Hunt
6. "Patrol" (5-11-58) Richard Bakalyan, Mark Damon, Richard Bull
7. "Survivors" (5-18-58) Bruce Bennett, Robert Fuller
8. "The Amnesiac" (5-25-58) Leon Ames

9. "Double Identity" (6-1-58) Ronnie Burns
10. "Flight" (6-8-58) Richard Jaeckel
11. "Parole" (6-15-58) Whit Bissell
12. "Fingerprints" (6-22-58) Paul Stewart, Lola Albright
13. "Nightmare" (6-29-58) Eduardo Ciannelli

CIMARRON CITY

One of the most appealing of western dramas, in both its capitalizing on the psychological interaction of the Cimarron nomads, and in its comparative diminution of the theme that roguish might makes right. Here disgruntled juveniles (of "To Become a Man"), monomaniac (of "I, the People"), the dissipated (of "The Beauty and the Sorrow") and unseen predator ("The Beast of Cimarron") cross daggers of the mind, and not merely pistols and fists, with the stalwart Mayor Rockford.

The Regulars: Mayor Matt Rockford: George Montgomery; Beth Purcell: Audrey Totter; Lane Temple: John Smith

The Episodes:

1. "I, the People" (10-11-58) Fred MacMurray
2. "Terror Town" (10-18-58) Dan Duryea, Barbara Lawrence
3. "To Become a Man" (10-25-58) Robin Riley, William Talman
4. "Twelve Guns" (11-1-58) Nick Adams
5. "Medicine Man" (11-8-58) Gary Merrill, June Lockhart
6. "Hired Hand" (11-15-58) Michael Connors, Elizabeth Montgomery
7. "Kid on a Calico Horse" (11-22-58) Linda Darnell, Dean Stockwell
8. "The Beast of Cimarron" (11-29-58)
9. "A Respectable Girl" (12-6-58) Dorothy Malone, Glenda Farrell
10. "The Bloodline" (12-13-58) J. Carrol Naish
11. "Cimarron Holiday" (12-20-58) Tim Hovey, Dinah Shore
12. "McGowan's Debt" (12-27-58)
13. "The Unaccepted" (1-3-59) Judith Ames, Peter Graves
14. "A Legacy for Ozzie Harper" (1-10-59) Carlton Carpenter, Judi Meredith, James Seay
15. "Child of Fear" (1-17-59) Luana Anders, Tom Pittman
16. "Bore the Town Down" (1-24-59)
17. "Runaway Train" (1-31-59) Diane Brewster
18. "The Beauty and the Sorrow" (2-7-59) Debra Paget, George Hamilton
19. "Return of the Dead" (2-14-59) Brad Dexter, Tom Drake
20. "Blind Is the Killer" (2-21-59) Robert Fuller
21. [unknown title] (2-28-59)
22. "The Ratman" (3-7-59) Everett Sloane, Dennis McCarthy

23. "Have Sword, Will Duel" (3-14-59) John Baragrey
24. "Chinese Invasion" (3-21-59)
25. "The Town Is a Prisoner" (3-28-59) Rita Moreno
26. "The Evil One" (4-4-59) Eduard Franz, Olive Carey

NORTHWEST PASSAGE

Adapted from the Kenneth Roberts novel and the Laurence Stallings and Talbot Jennings 1940 film scenario, although not the calibre of either, is this tale of the comradeship among the "Rogers' Rangers," who trek insouciantly in search of the legendary Northwest Passage. Yet if one sets aside the derring-do and stock dialogue, there are some well-intended historical teleplays, of which those on bought servitude ("The Bound Women") and the French Huguenots ("Trial by Fire") are two.

The Regulars: Major Robert Rogers: Keith Larsen; Langdon Towne: Don Burnett; Hunk Marriner: Buddy Ebsen; General Amherst: Philip Tonge; Elizabeth Browne: Lisa Davis; Black Wolf: Larry Chance; Jonas: Jim Hayward; Rivas: Pat Hogan; Natula: Lisa Gaye

The Episodes:

1. "Vengeance Trail" (9-14-58) Paul Fix
2. "The Counterfeiters" (9-21-58)
3. "The Gunsmith" (9-28-58)
4. "Surprise Attack" (10-5-58)
5. "The Bound Women" (10-12-58) Angie Dickinson, Rebecca Welles
6. "Break Out" (10-19-58)
7. "Court Martial" (10-26-58)
8. "The Hostage" (11-2-58)
9. "Sorrow Song" (11-9-58)
10. "The Assassin" (11-16-58)
11. "The Long Rifle" (11-23-58) Dean Harens
12. "War Sign" (11-30-58)
13. "The Traitor" (12-7-58)
14. "The Redcoat" (12-14-58)
15. "Fight at the River" (12-21-58)
16. "The Vulture" (12-28-58)
17. "The Secret of the Cliff" (1-9-59) Taina Elg
18. "Death Rides the Wind" (1-16-59)
19. "Dead Reckoning" (1-23-59)
20. "The Fourth Brother" (1-30-59) Gene Nelson, Marcia Henderson
21. "Ambush" (2-6-59)
22. "Witchcraft" (2-13-59)
23. "Stab in the Back" (2-20-59)
24. "Deserter" (2-27-59)
25. "Trial by Fire" (3-6-59) Peter Whitney
26. "The Killers" (3-13-59) John Russell

ENCOUNTER

[Telecast live from Toronto, Canada.

The Episodes:

1. "Breakthrough" (10-5-58)
2. "End of Summer" [a modern version of the Ivan Turgenev short story "First Love"] (10-12-58) Hildegarde Rossi, Donald Pope
3. "The Flower in the Rock" (10-19-58) Frances Hyland, William Needles, Douglas Rain
4. "Depth Three-hundred" [by Maurice Gagnon] (10-26-58) Barry Morse, Patrick Macnee
5. "Men Don't Make Passes" (11-2-58) Ray Hawtrey, Ruth Springford

THE NAKED CITY

Mark Hellinger's poetic excursion through workaday life in the most claustrophobic megalopolis inspired as little else on the subject had before. Serialized now in half-hour installments (and in 1960 with a splendid full hour four-year series (q. v.), filmed on sweltering New York City afternoons, it remained a testament to the polity. Note just one full hour example: "The King of Venus Will Take Care of You," in which a child consistently hides amid the tenements, pondering the confines of life in the big city and of dreams forever unfulfilled.

The Regulars: Detective James Halloran: James Franciscus; Lieutenant Dan Muldoon: John McIntire (subsequently displaced by Horace MacMahon as Lieutenant Mike Parker with episode of 3/17/59)

The Episodes:

1. "Meridian" (9-30-58)
2. "Nickel Ride" (10-7-58)
3. "Line of Duty" (10-14-58) Diane Ladd, Eugenie Leontovich
4. "Sidewalk Fisherman" (10-21-58) Jay Novello
5. "The Violent Circle" (10-28-58) Suzanne Storrs
6. "Stakeout" (11-4-58)
7. "No More Rumbles" (11-11-58) David Winters
8. "Belvedere Tower" (11-18-58)
9. "The Bird Guard" (11-25-58) Diana Van Der Vlis
10. "The Other Face of Goodness" (12-2-58) Arnold Merritt, Loretta Leversee
11. "Lady Bug, Lady Bug" (12-9-58) Leon B. Stevens, Peter Falk
12. "Susquehanna 4-7598" (12-16-58) Sandy Robinson
13. "And Merry Christmas to the Force on Patrol" (12-23-58)
14. "The Explosive Heart" (12-30-58) Barbara Lord

15. "Manhole" (1-6-59) George Maharis, Will Kuluva
16. "Even Crows Sing Good" (1-13-59)
17. "Burst of Passion" (1-20-59)
18. "Goodbye, My Lady Love" (1-27-59) James Barton
19. "The Shield" (2-3-59) Jack Klugman, Vic Morrow
20. "One to Get Lost" (2-10-59) Kent Smith, Harry Bellaver
21. "Hey, Teach!" (2-17-59) Jose Alcarez, Jean Muir, Robert
    Morris, Lawrence Tierney
22. "Ticker Tape" (2-24-59) Ernest Sarracino
23. "Fire Island" (3-3-59) Henry Hull, George Maharis
24. "Ten Cent Dreams" (3-10-59) Ross Martin, Richard X. Slat-
    tery
25. "The Bumper" (3-17-59) introduces Horace MacMahon as Lt.
    Parker
26. "A Running of Bulls" (3-24-59) Michael Ansara
27. "Fallen Star" (3-31-59) Robert Alda, Rocky Graziano
28. "Beyond Truth" (4-7-59) Martin Balsam, Suzanne Storrs
29. "Baker's Dozen" (4-14-59) Joseph Ruskin, Vincent Gardenia
30. "The Rebirth" (4-21-59)
31. "Four Street Corners" (4-28-59) George Maharis, Irene Dailey
32. "Sandman" (5-5-59) Will Kuluva, Mike Kellin
33. "Turn of Events" (5-12-59)
34. "A Little of the Action" (5-19-59) James Barton
35. "The Bloodhounds" (5-26-59) Louis Nye
36. "The Scorpion Sting" (6-2-59) Nehemiah Persoff
37. "Saw My Baby There" (6-9-59) Harold J. Stone, Rochelle
    Oliver
38. "The Canvas City" (6-16-59) Harry Guardino, Rocky Grazi-
    ano, Diane Ladd, Clem Fowler
39. "A Wood of Thorne" (6-23-59) Cara Williams

PURSUIT

The pilot episode, "The Lady Died at Midnight," was composed by Charles Lanson and directed by Paul Nickell and aired as a special February 23, 1958, with Paul Douglas, Gary Merrill and Earl Holliman as the lead performers. This program was subsequently replayed via the Studio One episode of September 1, 1958.

The Episodes:

1. "The Vengeance" [by Adrian Spies] (10-22-58) Sal Mineo,
    Macdonald Carey, Stuart Erwin, Robert H. Harris, Carol
    Lynley, Vivian Nathan
2. "Free Ride" (10-29-58) Keenan Wynn, Ralph Meeker, Linda
    Darnell, Jackie Cooper, Sidney Blackmer
3. "Ticket to Tangier" [by Irwin and Gwen Gielgud] (11-5-58)
    Barry Sullivan, Nina Foch, Zachary Scott, William Gargan,
    Martin Balsam
4. "Tiger on a Bicycle" (11-12-58) Neville Brand, Laraine Day,
    Dan Duryea, Chester Morris

5. "Kiss Me Again, Stranger" [adapted by Leonard Kantor from a
    story by Daphne du Maurier] (11-10-58) Jeffrey Hunter,
    Margaret O'Brien, Myron McCormick, Mort Saul, Mary Beth
    Hughes
6. "The House at Malibu" (11-26-58) Jan Sterling, Dane Clark,
    Mervyn Vye, Warren Stevens, James Gregory, Marie Wind-
    sor
7. "Eagle in a Cage" [by Robert Bloomfield] (12-3-58) Fernando
    Lamas, Robert Alda, Robert Middleton, Joan Caulfield, Lyle
    Talbot, Marguerite Chapman
8. "Calculated Risk" (12-10-58) John Cassavetes, E. G. Mar-
    shall, Warner Anderson, Mona Freeman, Conrad Nagel
9. "Last Night in August" [by Rod Serling] (12-17-58) Dennis
    Hopper, Cameron Mitchell, Franchot Tone
10. "The Silent Night" (12-24-58) Victor Jory
11. "The Dark Cloud" [by Joseph Landon] (12-31-58) Gary Mer-
    rill, Ann Sheridan, Eduardo Ciannelli, Darryl Hickman, Fay
    Spain, James Westerfield
12. "Epitaph for a Golden Girl" (1-14-59) Michael Rennie, Joan
    Bennett

BAT MASTERSON

    Historicity may fall to the wayside--owing to the genre--but
Gene Barry's Bat Masterson embodies all the astuteness, all the
gentility that the marshal yet connotes. For Bat Masterson is that
sublime discordant; a polished figure in the very western dust.

The Regulars: Bat Masterson: Gene Barry

The Episodes:

1. "Double Showdown" (10-8-58) Elisha Cook
2. "Two Graves for Swan Valley" (10-15-58) Broderick Crawford
3. "Dynamite Blows Two Ways" (10-22-58)
4. "Stampede at Tent City" (11-5-58)
5. "Bear Bait" (11-12-58)
6. "A Noose Fits Anybody" (11-19-58)
7. "Dude's Folly" (11-26-58)
8. "The Treasure of Worry Hill" (12-3-58) Audrey Dalton, Ross
    Martin, Harvey Stephens
9. "Promised Land" (12-17-58) Gerald Mohr
10. "Trail Pirate" (12-31-58) Gloria Talbott, Barry Atwater,
    James Bannon
11. "Double Trouble in Trinidad" (1-7-59) Lance Fuller
12. "Election Day" (1-14-59) Peter Hansen
13. "One Bullet from Broken Bow" (1-21-59) H. M. Wynant, Joan
    O'Brien
14. "A Personal Matter" (1-28-59) Alan Hale
15. "License to Cheat" (2-4-59) Douglas Kennedy
16. "Sharpshooter" (2-11-59) Conrad Nagel, Lisa Gaye

17. "River Boat" (2-18-59) Jacques Aubuchon
18. "Battle of the Pass" (2-25-59) Wayne Morris
19. "Marked Deck" (3-11-59)
20. "Incident in Leadville" (3-18-59)
21. "The Tumbleweed Wagon" (3-25-59) John Carradine
22. "Brunette Bombshell" (4-1-59) Gene Nelson
23. "Deadline" (4-8-59)
24. "Man of Action" (4-22-59)
25. "A Matter of Honor" (4-29-59) Paula Raymond
26. "Lottery of Death" (5-13-59) Warren Oates
27. "The Death of Bat Masterson" (5-20-59)
28. "The Secret Is Death" (5-27-59)
29. "The Conspiracy" [Part I; a biographical drama of John Surratt, the only exonerated man in the Abraham Lincoln assassination conspiracy; the teleplay begins fifteen years after the exoneration] (6-17-59) Arthur Shields (as Surratt)
30. "The Conspiracy" [Part II] (6-24-59) as above.
31. "The Black Pearls" (7-1-59)

Episodes concluded with Television Drama Series Programming: A Comprehensive Chronicle, 1959-1975.

BEHIND CLOSED DOORS

As if the series itself were conceived within the confines of Intelligence committee rooms, this case for counterespionage, as derived from the files of Rear Admiral Ellis M. Zacharias, becomes an iconolatry for Cold Warriors. Here "subversives" creep ever so perniciously out of international shadows, to be methodically castigated.

The Regulars: Bruce Gordon (as Commander Matson), host and narrator.

The Episodes:

1. "The Cape Canaveral Story" (10-2-58)
2. "Flight to Freedom" (10-9-58) Francis Lederer
3. "Double Jeopardy" (10-16-58) Reginald Gardiner
4. "Fleeing" (10-23-58) Kenneth Tobey
5. "Trouble in Test Cell Nineteen" [by Richard Tregaskis] (10-30-58) Jacques Aubuchon
6. "Man in the Moon" (11-6-58) Judith Evelyn
7. "The Nike" (11-13-58)
8. "Hidden Bomb" (11-27-58)
9. "The Enemy on the Flank" (12-4-58) Bruce Gordon, James Best
10. "A Cover of Art" (12-11-58)
11. "The Middle East Story" (12-18-58) Ziva Rodann, Richard Webb
12. "The Brioni Story" (12-25-58) Shelton Laurence, Jeannette Sterke
13. "The Obelisk" (1-1-59) Robert Ayres, Richard Shaw, Edwin Richfield, Richard Caldicot, Dermot Walsh, Walter Gotell

14. "The Germany Story" (1-8-59)
15. "The Alkaloid Angel" (1-22-59) Biff Elliott, Natalia Daryll
16. "Crypto 40" (1-29-59) William Bishop, Osa Massen
17. "The Alaskan Story" (2-5-59) Brad Dexter, Don Haggerty,
       Frank Wilcox, Claudia Barrett, James Bell, Milton Frome
18. "The Quemoy Story" (2-12-59) Robert H. Harris
19. "The Espionage Students" (2-19-59)
20. "The Geneva Story" (2-26-59)
21. "The Meeting" (3-5-59) Ray Danton, David Opatoshu
22. "Mightier Than the Sword" (3-12-59)
23. "The Gamble" (3-19-59) Peter Votrian, Nyra Monsour
24. "Double Agent" (3-26-59)
25. "The Antidote" (4-2-59) John Lupton
26. "Assignment Prague" (4-9-59) Warren Stevens, Sue England,
       Berry Kroeger, Patricia Huston

THE FURTHER ADVENTURES OF ELLERY QUEEN

As inaugurated by the master craftsman Albert McCleery, this
video adaptation of the cases of Manfred Lee's and Frederic Dannay's
celebrated detective sustains the tongue-in-cheek style while providing
for a stellar guest cast basking jubilantly through the whimsy. This
being the right combination, of course, it was a formula nevertheless
not followed by either of the two previous Ellery Queen television
series (with Lee Bowman and Hugh Marlowe, respectively, as the
lead character). Nor could the much more recent (1975) entry, with
the late Jim Hutton as the supersleuth, qualitatively compare. There
the audience asides and labyrinthine plots were pretensions too great
to withstand.

The Regulars: Ellery Queen: George Nader (through the first nine-
    teen teleplays; thereafter, with episode of 2/27/59, Queen was
    played by Lee Philips)

The Episodes:

1. "The Glass Village" (9-26-58)
2. "The King Is Dead" (10-3-58) Ilona Massey, Torin Thatcher,
       Les Tremayne
3. "Ten Days Wonder" (10-10-58) Otto Kruger, Virginia Gibson,
       John Lupton, John Dehner
4. "The Door Between" [by Michael Dyne] (10-17-58) Robert
       Lowery, Adrienne Marden
5. "The Eighth Mrs. Bluebeard" (10-24-58) Jeanne Cooper, Gene
       Raymond
6. "Cat of Many Tails" (10-31-58) John Abbott, Paul Langton
7. "Death Before Bedtime" (11-7-58) Neil Hamilton, Heather
       Angel
8. "Double, Double" (11-14-58) Luana Anders, Rhys Williams
9. "So Rich, So Lovely, So Dead" (11-28-58) Eva Gabor, Thom-
       as Gomez
10. "Diamond Studded Typewriter" (12-5-58) James Gavin, Olive

Sturgess
11. "Four and Twenty to Live" (12-12-58)
12. "The Hollow Man" (12-26-58) Frank Silvera
13. "Bury Me Deep" [adapted by William Mourne from the novel by
     Harold Q. Masur] (1-2-59) Patrick McVey, Richard Long,
     Joanne Linville
14. "The Hinnlity Story" (1-9-59) Peggy Castle, Vanessa Brown,
     Brian Keith, James Bell
15. "Revolution" (1-16-59) Gusti Huber, Kurt Kasznar, Scott
     Forbes
16. "The Murder of Whistler's Brother" (1-23-59) Shepperd Strud-
     wick, Eduardo Ciannelli
17. "Death Likes It Hot" (1-30-59) Kent Smith, Anna Lee, Julie
     Bennett, Vivi Janis
18. "Margin of Terror" (2-13-59)
19. "Chauffeur Disguise" (2-20-59) Frankie Darro, Joan Hackett
20. "Shadow of the Past" (2-27-59) introduces Lee Philips; George
     Voskovec, Lili Darvas, Georgiann Johnson
21. "The Chemistry Set" (3-6-59) Ruth Warrick, Conrad Nagel,
     Jeff Donnell
22. "Cartel for Murder" (3-20-59) Martin Balsam
23. "A Girl Named Daisy" (3-27-59) Shelley Berman, Sherry
     Britton
24. "The Paper Tiger" (4-3-59) Doretta Morrow, Nancy Carroll,
     Paul Hartman, Alvin Epstein
25. "The Lecture" (4-10-59) Edna Best, Judith Evelyn, Edward
     Andrews
26. "Confession of Murder" (4-17-59) Scott Marlowe, Glenda Far-
     rell, Wayne Morris, Kay Medford
27. "Castaway on a Nearby Island" (4-24-59) Leueen MacGrath,
     Lloyd Bochner
28. "The Curse of Aden" (5-1-59) Julie Adams, Hurd Hatfield
29. "Dance into Death" (5-15-59) Martin Balsam, Tamara Geva,
     Morey Amsterdam
30. "Body of the Crime" (5-29-59) Gloria De Haven, Ruth Warrick
31. "This Murder Comes to You Live" (6-5-59) Buster Crabbe,
     Geraldine Fitzgerald, Ben Hecht

PETE KELLY'S BLUES

     Jack Webb's adaptation of his own 1955 film of Richard L.
Breen's story of Kansas City jazz musicians bears the characteristic
stamp: stilted dialogue, contrived situations, protracted use of documentary technique. And whereas the motion picture was occasionally distinguished by some fine acting, here the solitary saving grace
is vocalist Connee Boswell's being essentially herself.

The Regulars: Peter Kelly: William Reynolds; Savannah Brown:
    Connee Boswell; George Lupo: Philip Gordon; Johnny Casino:
    Anthony Eisley; band members included Johnny Silver, Than Wyenn,
    Fred Beams, Rocky Allen and Vic Cathcart

The Episodes:

1. "The Steve Porter Story" (4-5-59)
2. "The June Gould Story" (4-12-59)
3. "The Envelope Story" (4-19-59) Ricky Allen, William Tracy
4. "Poor Butterfly" (4-26-59)
5. "The Lex Bigelow Story" (5-10-59)
6. "The Baby Ray Story" (5-17-59)
7. "The Mike Reegan Story" (5-24-59)
8. "The Rompy Thompson Story" (5-31-59)
9. "The Gus Trudo Story" (6-7-59)
10. "The Emory Cussack Story" (6-14-59)
11. "The Fitzhugh Story" (6-21-59)
12. "The Joe Attevekian Story" (6-28-59)
13. "The Sixteen Bar Facet" (7-5-59)

THE DAVID NIVEN SHOW

The Regulars: David Niven, host.

The Episodes:

1. "Fortune's Folly" (4-7-59) Cameron Mitchell
2. "Life Line" (4-14-59) Don Taylor, Barry Nelson, Chris White
3. "Backtrack" (4-21-59) Frank Lovejoy
4. "The Promise" (5-5-59) Eddie Albert, Fay Wray
5. "The Twist of the Key" (5-12-59) Anne Francis, John Dehner
6. "A Day of Small Miracles" (5-19-59) Eddie Bracken
7. "The Lady from Winnetka" (5-26-59) Joanne Dru, Jacques Bergerac
8. "The Last Room" (6-2-59) David Niven
9. "Maggie Malone" (6-9-59) Julie London, Scott Brady
10. "Portrait" (6-16-59) Carolyn Jones
11. "Sticks and Stones" (6-23-59) John Ericson
12. "The Vengeance" (6-30-59) Dan Duryea
13. "The Good Deed" (7-7-59) Keefe Brasselle, Jay C. Flippen, Virginia Grey

THE OLDSMOBILE MUSIC THEATRE

Dramas interspersed with standard songs.

The Regulars: Bill Hayes and Florence Henderson, hosts.

The Episodes:

1. "A Nice Place to Hide" (3-26-59) Geneviève, Jackie Cooper
2. "An Almost Perfect Plan" (4-2-59) James Shigeta, Michi Kobi, Richard Loo

3. "Too Bad About Sheila Troy" [Part I] (4-16-59) Carol Lawrence, Roddy McDowall, Hurd Hatfield, Chester Morris
4. "Too Bad About Sheila Troy" [Part II] (4-23-59)
5. "The Magic Eighty-eight" (4-30-59) Bill Hayes, Florence
   Henderson
6. "Sound of Murder" (5-7-59) Dorothy Collins, Ralph Meeker,
   Cameron Prud'homme

BRENNER

There was no pause in the pistol fire of proliferating law-
and-order programs by decade's end. Claiming a share in the corrections was this tandem of New York detectives, a father (Edward
Binns) and son (James Broderick), more genial, perhaps, than their
pugnacious comrades.

The Regulars: Detective Roy Brenner: Edward Binns; Ernie Bren-
    ner: James Broderick; Captain Laney: Joseph Sullivan

The Episodes:

1. "False Witness" (6-6-59)
2. "Record of Arrest" (6-13-59)
3. "Family Man" (6-20-59)
4. "Blind Spot" (6-27-59) Gerald S. O'Loughlin, Crahan Denton
5. "Loan Shark" (7-4-59)
6. "Word of Honor" (7-11-59)
7. "I, Executioner" (7-18-59)
8. "The Buff" (7-25-59)
9. "Small Take" (8-1-59)
10. "One of Our Own" (8-8-59) Lois Nettleton, Steven Shaw
11. "Man in the Middle" (8-15-59) Lee Grant, William Daniels
12. "Thin Ice" (8-22-59) Stanley Beck, Berta Gersten
13. "Crime Wave" (8-29-59) Warren Stevens, Woodrow Parfrey
14. "Monopoly on Fear" (9-19-59) Milton Selzer, Walter Greaza
15. "The Thin Line" (6-19-61)

SECTION IV

Dramatic Programming Previously Not Chronicled,
fall, 1959-1978

THE PLAY OF THE WEEK

Telecast via PBS New York channel 13; 8-10:00 first season
and 8:30-10:30 the second; episodes repeated weeknights and Saturdays
at 10:30.

The Episodes:

1. "Medea" [adapted from the 1920 Robinson Jeffers adaptation of
   the Euripedes classic; directed for television by José Quin-
   tero] (10-12-59) Dame Judith Anderson, Aline MacMahon,
   Morris Carnovsky, Henry Brandon, Jacqueline Brooks, Betty
   Miller, Colleen Dewhurst
2. "The Power and the Glory" [adapted from the Graham Greene
   novel as dramatized by Denis Cannan and Pierre Bost; staged
   by Carmen Capalbo] (10-19-59) James Donald, Peter Falk,
   Scotty McGregor, Alfred Ryder, David J. Stewart, Rudy
   Bond, Val Avery
3. "Burning Bright" [adapted from the John Steinbeck 1950 play]
   (10-26-59) Myron McCormick, Colleen Dewhurst, Donald
   Madden, Crahan Denton
4. "Back to Back" [two original plays by John Mortimer] a) "The
   Dock Brief"; b) "What Shall We Tell Caroline?" Michael
   Hordern, George Rose, Leueen McGrath, Jean Marsh (11-
   2-59)
5. "A Month in the Country" [adapted from the 1850 Ivan Turgenev
   play as adapted and translated by Emlyn Williams] (11-9-59)
   Luther Adler, Uta Hagen
6. "The Waltz of the Toreadors" [adapted from the 1951 Jean
   Anouilh play as translated by Lucienne Hill] (11-16-59)
   Hugh Griffith, Beatrice Straight, Mildred Natwick
7. "The White Steed" [adapted from the 1938 Paul Vincent Carroll
   play] (11-23-59) Frank Conroy, Dermot McNamara, Helena
   Carroll, Tim O'Connor
8. "Crime of Passion" [adapted from the Jean-Paul Sartre play]
   (11-30-59) Claude Dauphin, Donald Harron, Horace Mac-
   Mahon, Betsy Von Furstenberg
9. "Simply Heavenly" [adapted from the 1957 play by David Martin
   and Langston Hughes] (12-7-59) Claudia McNeil, Frederick
   O'Neal
10. "The World of Sholom Aleichem" [adapted from his stories]
    (12-14-59) Gertrude Berg, Jack Gilford, Nancy Walker,

Charlotte Rae, Lee Grant, Zero Mostel, Morris Carnovsky, Sam Levene

11. "Thieves' Carnival" [adapted from the 1938 Jean Anouilh play as translated by Lucienne Hill] (12-21-59) Kurt Kasznar, Larry Blyden, Cathleen Nesbitt, Robert Morse, Frances Sternhagen, Pat Stanley, Tom Bosley

12. "The Cherry Orchard" [adapted from the 1904 Anton P. Chekhov play as translated by George Calderon] (12-28-59) E. G. Marshall, Helen Hayes, Susan Strasberg, Salome Jens

13. "The Closing Door" [adapted from the 1949 Alexander Knox play] (1-4-60) Kim Hunter, Dane Clark, George Segal, Kevin Coughlin, Arthur Hill

14. "The Emperor's Clothes" [adapted from the 1953 George Tabori play] (1-11-60) George Voskovec, Viveca Lindfors, Jules Munshin

15. "Lullaby" [adapted from the 1954 Don Appell play] (1-18-60) Anne Jackson, Eli Wallach

16. "Two Plays by Strindberg": a) "Miss Julie" Lois Smith, Robert Loggia, Madeleine Sherwood; b) "The Stronger" Patricia Neal, Nancy Wickwire [both plays adapted from the August Strindberg as dramatized by George Tabori; produced for television by Lewis Freedman and directed by Henry Kaplan] (1-25-60)

17. "Juno and the Paycock" [adapted from the 1924 Sean O'Casey play; staged for television by Paul Shyre; James Elson, camera planner] (2-1-60) Hume Cronyn, Walter Matthau, Pauline Flanagan, Liam Clancy, Evans Evans, Luella Gear, James Kenny, Thomas A. Carlin

18. "Tiger at the Gates" [adapted from the 1935 Christopher Fry play which was adapted from Jean Giraudoux's The Trojan War Shall Not Take Place; produced for television by Robert L. Joseph and directed by Harold Clurman] (2-8-60) Martin Gabel, Nina Foch, Leueen McGrath, Arthur Treacher, Cathleen Nesbitt, Donald Davis, Bramwell Fletcher, Patricia Cutts

19. "Don Juan in Hell" [adapted from the George Bernard Shaw 1905 play Man and Superman, Act III] (2-15-60) George C. Scott, Siobhan McKenna, Hurd Hatfield, Dennis King

20. "A Very Special Baby" [adapted from the 1956 Robert Alan Aurthur play; produced for television by David Susskind and directed by Marc Daniels] (2-22-60) Oscar Homolka, Larry Blyden, Marion Winters

21. "The Climate of Eden" [adapted from the 1952 Moss Hart play which was adapted from Edgar Mittelholzer's Shadows Move Them Away] (2-29-60) Kevin Coughlin, Diana Hyland, Roland Culver, Donald Harron, Lynn Loring

22. "Volpone" [adapted by Stefan Sweig from the 1606 Ben Jonson classic; directed for television by Gene Frankel and J. Robert Blum] (3-7-60) Kurt Kasznar, Jo Van Fleet, Alfred Drake, Lou Jacobi, Ludwig Donath, Evans Evans

23. "The Rope Dancers" [adapted from the 1957 play by Morton Wishengrad] (3-14-60) Jacob Ben-Ami, Walter Matthau, Siobhan McKenna

24. "The Master Builder" [adapted from the 1907 Henrik Ibsen play
    as translated by Eva LeGallienne; produced for television by
    Lewis Freedman and directed by John Stix] (3-21-60) E.
    G. Marshall, Lois Smith, Joanna Roos, Fred J. Stewart,
    James Patterson, Phyllis Love, Victor Kilian
25. "The Grass Harp" [adapted from the 1952 play by Truman Ca-
    pote and Virgil Thomson; produced for television by Jack
    Kuney and directed by Word Baker, with an intermission
    feature by The Saturday Review drama critic Henry Hewes]
    (3-28-60) Lillian Gish, Carmen Mathews, Nick Hyams,
    Russell Collins
26. "A Palm Tree in a Rose Garden" [adapted from the 1957 play
    by Meade Roberts] (4-4-60) Glenda Farrell, Robert Web-
    ber, Barbara Baxley
27. "The Enchanted" [adapted from 1958 Maurice Valency adaptation
    of the Jean Giraudoux play] (4-11-60) Walter Abel, Arthur
    Treacher, Tom Poston
28. "The Girls in 509" [adapted from the 1958 Howard Teuhmann
    play] (4-18-60) Margalo Gillmore, Nancy Walker, Larry
    Blyden, Parker Fennelly, Paul Ford
29. "Morning's at Seven" [adapted from the 1939 Paul Osborn play;
    restaged from The Alcoa Hour of November 4, 1956] (4-
    25-60) Beulah Bondi, Chester Morris, Dorothy Gish, Eileen
    Heckart
30. "Night of the Auk" [adapted from the 1956 verse play by Arch
    Oboler] (5-2-60) William Shatner, Warner Anderson, James
    MacArthur, Shepperd Strudwick
31. "A Piece of Blue Sky" [an original play by Frank Corsaro]
    (5-9-60) Roland Winters, Nancy Marchand, Marian Seldes,
    Morgan Sterns
32. "archy and mehitabel" [a comedy with music by Joe Darion and
    Mel Brooks, as adapted from the stories of Don Marquis on
    the cockroach and the cat] (5-16-60) Eddie Bracken, Tam-
    my Grimes, Jules Munshin
33. "Mary Stuart" [adapted from the 1957 Jean Stock Goldstone
    adaptation of the Johann Christoph Friedrich von Schiller
    1800 play; directed for television by Dennis Vance] (5-23-
    60) Signe Hasso, Muriel Kirkland, Eva LeGallienne, Staats
    Cotsworth, Patrick Waddington, Paul Ballantyn, John Tolitos
34. "The Grand Tour" [adapted from the 1951 Elmer Rice play;
    staged for television by William A. Graham] (5-30-60)
    Scott McKay, Audrey Meadows
35. "The House of Bernarda Alba" [adapted from the 1936 play by
    Federico Garcia Lorca, as translated by J. Graham-Lujan]
    (6-6-60) Cathleen Nesbitt, Ann Revere, Eileen Heckart,
    Lee Grant, Nancy Marchand, Suzanne Pleshette

Second Season

36. "Henry IV, Part I" [The Phoenix Theatre production of the
    Shakespeare classic, as staged by Stuart Vaughan; settings
    by Will Steve Armstrong; produced for television by David
    Susskind; Worthington Miner, executive producer] (9-26-60)

Eric Berry, Donald Madden, Stephen Joyce, Nan Martin, Dran Seitz, Donald Davis

37. "The Dybbuk" [adapted by Joseph Liss from the 1920 S. Ansky play; settings by Jack Venza and original music by John Gruen; directed for television by Sidney Lumet] (10-3-60) Michael Tolan, Carol Lawrence, Eli Mintz, Ludwig Donath, Michael Shillo

38. "Legend of Lovers" [adapted from the 1951 Jean Anouilh play as translated by Kitty Black (a modern version of the Orpheus and Eurydice legend; produced for television by Jack Kuney and directed by Ralph Nelson] (10-10-60) Piper Laurie, Robert Loggia, Sam Jaffe, Michael Constantine, Polly Rowles

39. "The Velvet Glove" [adapted from the 1949 Rosemary Casey play] (10-17-60) Helen Hayes, Larry Gates, Robert Morse, Jean Dixon, Arthur Shields

40. "Duet for Two Hands" [adapted from the 1947 play by Mary Hayley Bell] (10-24-60) Signe Hasso, Eric Portman, Lois Nettleton

41. "Seven Times Monday" [an original drama by Ernest Pendrell] (10-31-60) Ruby Dee, Ossie Davis, Warren Berlinger, Judson Laire, Milt Kamen

42. "Two by Saroyan": a) "Once Around the Block" Walter Matthau, Orson Bean, Larry Hagman, Nina Wilcox; b) "My Heart's in the Highlands" Walter Matthau, Kevin Coughlin, Myron McCormick, Eddie Hodges [adapted from the 1950 and 1937 William Saroyan plays, respectively] (11-7-60)

43. "The Iceman Cometh" [adapted from the Eugene O'Neill 1946 play; directed for television by Sidney Lumet (this episode and the concluding segment aired at 10:30-12:30 in recognition of the "adult" nature)] (Part I; 11-14-60) Jason Robards Jr., Myron McCormick, Roland Winters, Robert Redford, Farrell Pelly

44. "The Iceman Cometh" (Part II; 11-21-60) as above.

45. "Highlights of New Faces" [sketches and musical numbers from the 1952 through 1956 versions of the Leonard Sillman Broadway productions] (11-28-60) Alice Ghostley, Ronny Graham, Robert Clary, Paul Lynde, June Carroll, Virginia DeLuce, Inga Swenson

46. "Uncle Harry" [adapted from the 1942 Thomas Job play] (12-5-60) Ray Walston, Betty Field, Jeff Donnell

47. "Rashomon" [adapted from the 1959 Fay and Michael Kanin adaptation of the stories of Akutagawa] (12-12-60) Ricardo Montalban, Oscar Homolka, Carol Lawrence, James Mitchell

48. "Emmanuel" [adapted from the 1960 Christmas play of the journey to Bethlehem and the birth of Jesus; directed for television by Kirk Browning] (12-19-60) Mark Richman, Lois Nettleton, Earle Hyman, Albert Dekker

49. "The Closing Door" [repeat of episode of 1/4/60] (12-26-60)

50. "A Clearing in the Woods" [adapted from the 1957 Arthur Laurents play] (1-2-61) Celeste Holm, Arthur Hill, J. D. Cannon, Nancy Malone, Gerald S. O'Loughlin

51. "The Potting Shed" [adapted from the 1957 Graham Greene play]

(1-9-61) Fritz Weaver, Ann Harding, Ludwig Donath, Nancy Wickwire, Frank Conroy

52. "Black Monday" [adapted from the 1962 Reginald Rose play; directed for television by Ralph Nelson] (1-16-61) Myron McCormick, William Prince, Pat Hingle, Ruby Dee, Juano Hernandez, Nancy Coleman, Robert Redford, House Jameson, Marc Connelly

53. "New York Scrapbook" [a revue by Tom Jones and Harvey Schmidt] (1-23-61) Kaye Ballard, Orson Bean, Jane Connell

54. "He Who Gets Slapped" [adapted from the 1915 play by Leonid N. Andreev] (1-30-61) Richard Basehart, Carroll O'Connor, Julie Harris, David Opatoshu

55. "Four by Tennessee Williams": a) "I Rise in Flame, Cried the Phoenix"; b) "Hello from Bertha"; c) "The Lady of Larkspur Lotion"; d) "The Purification" [adapted from the 1959, 1954, 1949 and 1959 Tennessee Williams plays, respectively] (2-6-61) Jo Van Fleet, Eileen Heckart, Ann Revere, Maureen Stapleton, Mike Kellin, Alfred Ryder, Vivian Nathan, Leueen McGrath, Thomas Chalmers

56. "The Sound of Murder" [adapted from the British mystery by William Fairchild] (2-13-61) Kim Hunter, Felicia Montealegre, Donald Davis

57. "The Magic and the Loss" [adapted from the 1954 play by Julian Funt; produced for television by Jack Kuney and directed by Richard Dunlap] (2-20-61) Patricia Neal, Jeffrey Lynn, Patrick O'Neal, Vicki Cummings, Tommy White, Frederick Clark

58. a) "No Exit" [adapted from the 1936 play by Jean-Paul Sartre, as translated by Paul Bowles; directed for television by Silvio Narizzano] Colleen Dewhurst, Dane Clark, Diana Hyland; b) "The Indifferent Lover" [adapted from the Jean Cocteau monologue] Miriam Hopkins (2-27-61)

59. "The Old Foolishness" [adapted from the 1940 Paul Vincent Carroll play] (3-6-61) Fred Gwynne, Albert Salmi

60. "Thérèse Raquin" [adapted from the 1873 Emile Zola play, as translated by Kathleen Boutall] (3-13-61) Eva LeGallienne, Mark Richman, Anne Meacham

61. "The Wooden Dish" [adapted from the 1954 Edmund Morris play] (3-20-61) Henry Hull, Martha Scott

62. "A Cool Wind over the Living" [an original drama by Joseph LeSueur] (3-27-61) Diana Hyland, Carmen Mathews, J. D. Cannon, James Patterson

63. "Waiting for Godot" [adapted from the 1954 Samuel Beckett translation of his own 1953 play] (4-3-61) Zero Mostel, Burgess Meredith, Kurt Kasznar

64. "In a Garden" [adapted from the 1925 Philip Barry play] (4-10-61) Roddy McDowall, George Grizzard, Barbara Cook, Laurie Main

65. "The Wingless Victory" [adapted from the 1936 Maxwell Anderson play] (4-17-61) Hugh O'Brian, Eartha Kitt, Michael Tolan, Jane Wyatt, Cathleen Nesbitt

66. "Close Quarters" [adapted from the 1937 Gilbert Lennox

        adaptation of the W. O. Simins play] (4-24-61) Richard
        Kiley, Patricia Jessel
67. "All Summer Long" [adapted from the 1954 Robert Anderson
        play which was adapted from the Donald Wetzel novel] (5-
        1-61) Keir Dullea, Betty Field, Henderson Forsythe

F. D. R.

    This especially penetrating documentary encomium to the yet
most luminous of America's twentieth-century presidents rather over-
shadowed James Costigan's adaptation of Joseph P. Lash's biography
Eleanor and Franklin (telecast January 11 and 12, 1976). That gen-
erally excellent special's concluding teleplay Eleanor and Franklin:
The White House Years, telecast the following year, concludes--like
this documentary concludes--with the richly evocative funeral dirge
"Going Home" as unforgettably intoned by Ed Clark over the fore-
boding procession. Mrs. Roosevelt was a series consultant. Alex
North composed and conducted the background theme.

The Regulars: Arthur Kennedy, narrator. Charlton Heston reads
    from the writings of Roosevelt.

The Episodes:

1.   "The Making of a Man [Part I]" (1-8-65) the pre-presidential
     years.
2.   "The Making of a Man [Part II]" (1-15-65) his career to 1928.
3.   "I Like to Win" (1-22-65) 1932 presidential campaign
4.   "Nothing to Fear But Fear" (1-29-65) campaign, election and
     the period to 1933 Inaugural speech
5.   "Forgotten Men" (2-12-65) The Great Depression
6.   "The Hundred Days" (2-19-65) The New Deal legislation
7.   "The Stricken Land" (2-26-65) mounting farm crisis, 1933
8.   "Strife!" (3-5-65) labor-management hostilities of the Thirties
9.   "The Blue Eagle" (3-12-65) The National Recovery Adminis-
     tration
10. "That Man in the White House" (3-19-65) the 1936 presidential
     campaign
11. "Rendezvous with Destiny" (3-26-65) focuses on the court-
     packing plan to redesign the Supreme Court; Hitler and Mus-
     solini plan world aggression.
12. "Distant Thunder" (4-2-65) on the approaching Second World
     War
13. "The Face of Danger" (4-16-65) the isolation versus interven-
     tion debate
14. "The Rising Sun" (4-23-65) the Japanese Empire and Far East
     involvement
15. "Dark Days" (4-30-65) the months before Pearl Harbor
16. "Germany First" (5-7-65) the defeat of Germany takes primacy
17. "The Road to Rome" (5-14-65) focuses on the Casablanca
     meeting

18. "The Great Assault" (5-21-65) D-Day
19. "Fury in the East" (5-28-65) the attack on Japanese island strongholds
20. "The Vital Force" (6-4-65) Dewey versus Roosevelt, 1944
21. "Victory in Sight" (6-11-65) The Battle of the Bulge
22. "The Eagle and the Lion" (6-25-65) The United States-U. S. S. R. relations to conclude the War.
23. "Brothers in Arms" (7-2-65) focuses on the wartime friendship between Roosevelt and Churchill
24. "The Good Neighbor" (7-9-65) foreign policy
25. "Mr. and Mrs. Roosevelt" (7-16-65) the First Lady as political aide
26. "Going Home" (7-23-65) the Roosevelt death and funeral

THE HOLLYWOOD TELEVISION THEATRE

The Episodes:

1. "The Andersonville Trial" [adapted from the Saul Levitt play on 1865 war crimes; directed by George C. Scott (his directorial debut)] (5-17-70 8:30-11:00 PBS) William Shatner, Jack Cassidy, Buddy Ebsen, Richard Basehart, Martin Sheen, Albert Salmi, Michael Burns, Harry Townes, Cameron Mitchell, John Anderson, Whit Bissell, Wright King

Second Season

2. "Big Fish, Little Fish" [adapted from the 1961 Hugh Wheeler Broadway play; directed for television by Daniel Petrie] (1-5-71 Tuesday 10-11:30 PBS) William Windom, Martine Bartlett, Louis Gossett, Bill Bixby, Severn Dardern, Ann B. Davis, Jeff Corey
3. "The Front Page" [adapted from the Ben Hecht and Charles MacArthur play] (1-30-71 Saturday 9-11:00 PBS) Helen Hayes, Robert Ryan, Estelle Parsons
4. "Montserrat" [the Lillian Hellman adaptation of the Emanuel Robles play on political terror in Spanish occupied Venezuela, 1812] (3-2-71 Tuesday 9-11:00 PBS) Keir Dullea, Rip Torn, Earl Holliman, Jack Albertson, Geraldine Page, Hurd Hatfield, Jess Walton, Scott Colomby, Michael Baseleon, Paul Stevens, Martin Sheen
5. "Poet Game" [an original drama by Anthony Terpiloff] (4-6-71 Tuesday 9-11:00 PBS) Anthony Hopkins, Billie Whitelaw, Cyril Cusack, Barry Morse, Susan Clark, Paul Hennen, Al Mancini, Stacey Gregg
6. "U. S. A. " [adapted from the off-Broadway play by John Dos Passos and Paul Shyre dramatizing Passos' The 42nd Parallel, 1919, and The Big Money, covering the period from World War I to the Depression; George Schaefer directed; Edward G. Robinson reads the prologue] (5-4-71 Tuesday 9-11:00 PBS) Peter Bonerz, John Davidson, James Faren-

tino, Joan Hackett, Shirley Knight, Michele Lee

Third Season

7. "The Typists" [adapted from the Murray Schisgal 1963 Broadway
    play] (10-7-71 Thursday 9-10:00 PBS) Eli Wallach, Anne
    Jackson
8. "The Police" [by Slawomir Mrozek; directed by Fielder Cook]
    (10-14-71 Thursday 9-10:00 PBS) Bob Dishy, Fred Gwynne,
    Murray Hamilton, John McGiver, Neva Patterson, Steve
    Pringle
9. "Lemonade" [an original teleplay] (10-21-71 Thursday 9-10:00
    PBS) Eileen Herlie, Martha Scott
10. "Birdbath" [by Leonard Melfi; directed by Lamont Johnson]
    (10-28-71 Thursday 9-10:00 PBS) James Farentino, Patty
    Duke
11. "Beginning to End" [readings of Samuel Beckett, with Jack Mac-
    Gowran in a virtuoso] (11-4-71 Thursday 9-10:00 PBS)
12. "The Enemies" [by Arkady Leokum; directed by Fielder Cook]
    (11-11-71 Thursday 9-10:00 PBS) Sam Jaffe, Ned Glass
13. "Neighbors" [adapted from the Arkady Leokum 1963 drama; di-
    rected by Fielder Cook] (11-18-71 Thursday 9-10:00 PBS)
    Andrew Duggan, Jane Wyatt, Raymond St. Jacques, Cicely
    Tyson
14. "The Standwells: About Love" [the puppets in scenes from
    plays] (11-25-71 Thursday 9-10:00 PBS)
15. "Bread and Puppet Theatre: The Dread Man Rises" [three
    Schumann plays; The Peter Schumann troupe of puppets and
    actors] (12-2-71 Thursday 9-10:00 PBS)
16. "Young Married at Play" [by Jerome Kass]   9-9-71 Thursday
    9-10:00 PBS) Arlene Golonka
17. "The Picture" [adapted from the Eugene Ionesco play] (12-16-
    71 Thursday 9-10:00 PBS) Jacques Aubuchon, Gar Camp-
    bell, Candace Laughlin
18. "Day of Absence" [adapted from the 1965 Douglas Turner Ward
    play with members of the Negro Ensemble Company; first
    telecast via PBS in 1967] (12-30-71 Thursday 9-10:00 PBS)
    Robert Hooks, Lonne Elder, Arthur French, Judyann John-
    son, Moses Gunn, Richard Pyatt, William Jay
19. "Two Anton Chekhov Plays" [staged and narrated by Rip Torn;
    a live telecast] a) "A Marriage Proposal"; b) "The Bear"
    (originally titled "The Boor") (1-6-72 Thursday 9-10:00
    PBS) Geraldine Page, Rip Torn, Muni Seroff
20. "The Scarecrow" [adapted from the Percy MacKaye 1910 clas-
    sic] (1-10-72 Monday 8-10:00 PBS) Gene Wilder, Sian
    Barbara Allen, Nina Foch, Will Geer, Blythe Danner, Peter
    Deuel, Norman Lloyd, Peter Kastner, Tom Helmore, Joan
    Tompkins
21. "Awake and Sing" [adapted from the Clifford Odets play; direct-
    ed by Norman Lloyd] (3-6-72 Monday 8-10:00 PBS) Walter
    Matthau, Ron Rifkin, Felicia Farr
22. "Invitation to a March" [adapted from the Arthur Laurents 1960
    satire; produced and directed by Norman Lloyd] (5-29-72

Monday 8-10:00 PBS) Blythe Danner, Cliff Potts, Pat Quinn, Louise Latham, Rosemary Murphy, Michael Sacks, Gordon Pinsent, Danny Bonaduce

Fourth Season [as part of the SPECIAL OF THE WEEK format]

23. "Another Part of the Forest" [adapted from the Lillian Hellman play; directed by Daniel Mann] (10-2-72 Monday 8-10:30 PBS) Barry Sullivan, Dorothy McGuire, Tiffany Bolling, Robert Foxworth, Andrew Prine, Patricia Sterling, William H. Bassett, Maidie Norman, Bill Walker, Jack Manning, Peter Brocco, Kent Smith

24. "The Shadow of a Gunman" [adapted from the Sean O'Casey play; directed by Joseph Hardy] (12-4-72 Monday 8-9:30 PBS) Jack MacGowran, Frank Converse, Sandra Morgan, Brendan Dillon, Richard Dreyfuss, Nora Marlowe, William Glover, Allyn Ann McLerie

25. "Carola" [adapted from the Jean Renoir play; directed by Norman Lloyd] (2-5-73 Monday 8-10:00 PBS) Leslie Caron, Mel Ferrer, Michael Sacks, Anthony Zerbe, Carmen Zapata, Albert Paulsen, Douglas Anderson

26. "Winesburg, Ohio" [adapted from the Sherwood Anderson novel] (3-5-73 Monday 8-9:30 PBS) Jean Peters, William Windom, Albert Salmi, Joseph Bottoms, Laurette Spang, Norman Foster

27. "Steambath" [adapted from the Bruce Jay Friedman 1971 play] (4-30-73 Monday 8-9:30 PBS) Bill Bixby, José Perez, Valerie Perrine

Fifth Season [now under the title CONFLICTS]

28. "The Man of Destiny" [adapted from the George Bernard Shaw play] (11-21-73 Wednesday 8:30-9:30 PBS) Stacy Keach, Samantha Eggar, William H. Bassett

29. "Me" [written and directed by Gardner McKay] (11-28-73 Wednesday 8:30-9:30 PBS) Geraldine Fitzgerald, Richard Dreyfuss, Richard Basehart

30. "Incident at Vichy" [adapted from the Arthur Miller play; directed by Stacy Keach] (12-8-73 Sunday 10-11:30 PBS) Alan Garfield, Harris Yulin, Richard Jordan, Barry Primus, Rene Auberjonois, Bert Freed, Andy Robinson, Ed Bakey, Sean Kelly

31. "The Carpenters" [by Steve Tesich] (12-19-73 Wednesday 8:30-9:45 PBS) Vincent Gardenia, Marge Redmond, Joseph Hindy, Kitty Wynn, Jan Korkes

32. "Gondola" [by Alfred Hayes; produced and directed by Norman Lloyd] (1-9-74 Wednesday 8-9:00 PBS) Norman Lloyd, Sondra Locke, Bo Hopkins

33. "Double Solitaire" [by Robert Anderson] (1-16-74 Wednesday 8:30-10:00 PBS) Richard Crenna, Susan Clark, Irene Tedrow, Norman Foster, Norma Crane, Harold Gould, Nicholas Hammond

Sixth Season

34. "The Chinese Prime Minister" (10-23-74 Wednesday 9-10:30
     PBS) Dame Judith Anderson, Peter Coffield, Don McHenry,
     Elayne Heilveil, Stephen Elliott, Richard Clarke
35. "The Lady's Not for Burning" [adapted from the Christopher
     Fry play] (11-18-74 Monday 8-10:00 PBS) Richard Cham-
     berlain, Eileen Atkins, Keene Curtis, John Carradine
36. "For the Use of the Hall" [by Oliver Hailey] (1-2-75 Thursday
     9-10:30 PBS) Aline MacMahon, Barbara Barrie, David Hed-
     ison, George Furth, Susan Anspach, Joyce Van Patten, John
     Barbour
37. "Requiem for a Nun" [adapted by Ruth Ford from the William
     Faulkner novel] (2-10-75 Monday 9-10:30 PBS) Sarah Miles,
     Mary Alice, Lester Rawlins, Sam Edwards, Lawrence Press-
     man
38. "The Ladies of the Corridor" [adapted from the Dorothy Parker
     and Arnaud d'Usseau play] (4-10-75 Thursday 9-11:00 PBS)
     Cloris Leachman, Jane Wyatt, Zohra Lampert, Barbara
     Baxley, Mabel Albertson, Neva Patterson, Mike Farrell,
     Richard Long, Chris Stone
39. "Knuckle" [adapted from the David Hare mystery] (6-4-75 Wed-
     nesday 9-11:00 PBS) Michael Christofer, Jack Cassidy, Jack
     Colvin, Eileen Brennan, Gretchen Corbett
40. "The Chicago Conspiracy Trial" [abridged from the 1970 BBC
     production written, produced and directed by Christopher
     Burstal from transcripts of the case] (7-10-75 Thursday
     9-11:30 PBS) Morris Carnovsky, James Patterson, Neil
     McCallum, Cliff Gormon, Ronny Cox, Al Freeman Jr.,
     Robert Loggia, Peter Jobin, Barton Heyman, Douglas Lam-
     bert, Shane Rimmer, Paul Arlington
41. "Wanda" [the 1970 film written and directed by Barbara Loden]
     (8-28-75 Thursday 9-10:30 PBS) Barbara Loden, Michael
     Higgins
42. "Nourish the Beast" [by Steve Tesich] (9-11-75 Thursday 9-
     10:30 PBS) Eileen Brennan, John Randolph, Will Lee, Pam-
     ela Bellwood, John Beck, Randy Kim, Geoffrey Scott

Seventh Season

43. "The Ashes of Mrs. Reasoner" (1-22-76 Thursday 9-10:30
     PBS) Cara Williams, Charles Durning, Herb Edelman,
     Barbara Colby, E. J. Andre
44. "The Hemingway Play" [a drama examining the Ernest Heming-
     way character at different stages] (3-11-76 Thursday 9-10:30
     PBS) Mitchell Ryan, Perry King, Tim Matheson, Samantha
     Eggar, Biff McGuire

Eighth Season

45. "The Last of Mrs. Lincoln" [adapted by James Prideaux from
     his 1972 play] (9-16-76 Thursday 9-11:00 PBS) Julie Har-
     ris (repeating her Tony award-winning performance), Michael

Christofer, Robby Benson, Denver Pyle, Ford Rainey, Priscella Morrill, Patrick Duffy, Linda Kelsey, Kate Wilkinson, Royce Wallace, Billy Simpson

46. "Six Characters in Search of an Author" [adapted from the Luigi Pirandello classic] (9-23-76 Thursday 9-10:30 PBS) John Houseman, Julie Adams, Andy Griffith, Madlyn Rhue

47. "The Fatal Weakness" [adapted from the George Kelly play, with a discussion by the author's niece, Princess Grace] (9-30-76 Thursday 9-11:00 PBS) Eva Marie Saint, John McMartin, Gretchen Corbett, Charlotte Moore, Dennis Dugan

48. "Philemon" [the 1975 musical by Tom Jones and Harvey Schmidt] (10-7-76 Thursday 9-10:45 PBS) Dick Latessa, Michael Glenn-Smith, Howard Ross, Kathrin King Segal, Charles Blackburn, Lelia Martin

Ninth Season

49. "The Ascent of Mt. Fuji" [adapted from the 1973 contemporary drama by Chingiz Aitmatov and Kaltai Mukhamedzhanov] (1-10-78 Tuesday 8-10:00 PBS) Joseph Campanella, Jeanette Nolan, Stefan Gierasch, Joanne Linville, Andrea Marcovicci, Avery Schreiber, Diane Shallet, Michael Strong, Allan Migicovski

[Continuing]

CIVILISATION

Sir Kenneth Clark's richly crafted mosaic of art through the ages, a highly literate collection of recitations, proved to be among the most durable of television properties. Accolades are most certainly due the work of photographers and editors whose poetic filming was a recitation in itself.

The Regulars: Sir Kenneth Clark, host and narrator

The Episodes [first telecast for the BBC in 1969; subsequently aired on the days below via PBS at 7-8:00 P.M. Sundays]:

1. "The Frozen World" (10-3-71)
2. "The Great Thaw" (10-10-71)
3. "Romance and Reality" (10-17-71)
4. "Man--The Measure of All Things" (10-24-71)
5. "The Hero as Artist" (10-31-71)
6. "Protest and Communication" (11-7-71)
7. "Grandeur and Obedience" (11-14-71)
8. "The Light of Experience" (11-21-71)
9. "The Pursuit of Happiness" (11-28-71)
10. "The Smile of Reason" (12-5-71)
11. "The Worship of Nature" (12-12-71)
12. "The Fallacies of Hope" (12-19-71)
13. "Heroic Materialism" (12-26-71)

AMERICA

Alistair Cooke's opulent and optimistic panorama of American history flows through thirteen hour episodes, each of which is marinated in the Cooke patrician wit. Meticulous in detail, these 1972 recitations, whether the subject be the military-industrial complex or the question of culpability at Kent State, were embarrassingly of sterner stuff than that put forth by most American born historians.

The Regulars: Alistair Cooke, host and narrator.

The Episodes [first telecast via NBC on alternate Tuesdays, 10-11:00 P. M.]:

1. "The New Found Land" (11-14-72)
2. "Home from Home" (11-28-72)
3. "Making a Revolution" (12-12-72)
4. "Inventing a Nation" (12-26-72)
5. "Gone West" (1-9-73)
6. "A Fireball in the Night" (1-23-73)
7. "Domesticating a Wilderness" (2-13-73)
8. "Money on the Land" (2-27-73)
9. "The Huddled Masses" (3-13-73)
10. "The Promise Fulfilled and the Promise Broken" (3-27-73)
11. "The Arsenal" (4-10-53)
12. "The First Impact" (4-24-73)
13. "The More Abundant Life" (5-8-73)

THEATRE IN AMERICA

The Regulars: Hal Holbrook, host

The Episodes:

1. "Enemies" [adapted from the Maxim Gorky play; co-directed by Ellis Rabb and Kirk Browning; performed by the Lincoln Center Repertory Company] (1-23-74 Wednesday 8:30-10:30 PBS) Carrie Nye, Frances Sternhagen, Kate Reid, Peter Donat, Ellis Rabb, Joseph Sommer, Richard Woods
2. "June Moon" [adapted from the George S. Kaufman and Ring Lardner play] (1-30-74 Wednesday 8:30-10:00 PBS) Jack Cassidy, Tom Fitzsimmons, Estelle Parsons, Barbara Dana, Stephen Sondheim (in his acting debut), Austin Pendleton, Kevin McCarthy, Susan Sarandon, Marshall Efron, Lee Meredith
3. "Cyrano de Bergerac" [adapted from the Edmond Rostand play; performed by the San Francisco Conservatory Theatre] (2-6-74 Wednesday 8-10:30 PBS) Marsha Mason, Marc Singer, Earl Boen, Paul Shenar, Robert Mooney, Elizabeth Huddie, Roger Aaron Brown
4. "Antigone" [adapted from the Jean Anouilh version of the

Sophocles tragedy; a repeat of the N. E. T. Playhouse episode of 10/7/72] (2-13-74 Wednesday 8:30-10:00 PBS) Genevieve Bujold, Fritz Weaver, Stacy Keach, Aline MacMahon, James Naughton, Leah Chandler

5. "King Lear" [the New York Shakespeare Festival production of the Shakespeare play, under the auspices of Joseph Papp] (2-20-74 Wednesday 8:30-11:30 PBS) James Earl Jones, Douglas Watson, Paul Sorvino, Raul Julia, Rosalind Cash, Lee Chamberlin, Ellen Holly, Rene Auberjonois, Tom Aldredge, Robert Lanchester, Frederick Coffin

6. "Mass" [the Leonard Bernstein and Stephen Schwartz "theatre piece"; a Yale University Student Production, the music conducted by John Mouceri; taped at the Vienna Konzerthaus, 1973] (2-27-74 Wednesday 8:30-10:30 PBS)

7. "Paradise Lost" [adapted from the Clifford Odets play; a repeat of N. E. T. Playhouse episodes of 2/25/71 and 3/4/71] (3-6-74 Wednesday 8:30-11:30 PBS) Eli Wallach, Jo Van Fleet, Biff McGuire, George Voskovec, Cliff Gormon, Sam Groom, Bernadette Peters, Mike Kellin, Fred Gwynne, Jay Garner, David Hurst

8. "In Fashion" [a musical comedy adapted from George Feydeau's Tailleurs pour Dames; music by Jerry Blatt and lyrics by Lonnie Burstein] (3-13-74 Wednesday 8:30-10:00 PBS) Daniel Davis, Susan Kaslow, Pamela Hall, Charlotte Rae

9. "The Rimers of Eldritch" [adapted from the Lanford Wilson play; a repeat of the N. E. T. Playhouse production] (3-20-74 Wednesday 8:30-10:00 PBS) Frances Sternhagen, Will Hare, Rue McClanahan

10. "Feasting with Panthers" [based on the Oscar Wilde incarceration at Reading Gaol; written and performed by the Trinity Squire Repertory Company of Providence, Rhode Island] (3-27-74 Wednesday 8:30-10:00 PBS) Richard Kneeland (as Oscar Wilde), George Martin (as Isaacson)

11. "A Memory of Two Mondays" [adapted from the Arthur Miller comedy-drama; a repeat of the N. E. T. Playhouse episode of 1/28/71] (4-3-74 Wednesday 8:30-10:00 PBS) Kristoffer Tabori, Tony Lo Bianco, Estelle Parsons, Cathy Burns, Jack Warden, George Grizzard, J. D. Cannon, Dan Hamilton, Barnard Hughes, Dick Van Patten, Jerry Stiller

12. "The Contractor" [adapted from the David Storey play; performed by the New York Chelsea Theatre Center; a repeat of the N. E. T. Playhouse drama] (4-10-74 Wednesday 8:30-10:00 PBS) John Wardell, Joseph Maher, Kevin O'Connor, Michael Finn, Reid Shelton, George Taylor, John Raddick

13. "The Ceremony of Innocence" [adapted from the Ronald Ribman drama; a repeat of the N. E. T. Playhouse episode of 10/29/70] (4-17-74 Wednesday 8:30-10:00 PBS) Richard Kiley, James Broderick, Larry Gates, Jessie Royce Landis, Elizabeth Hubbard, Gilmer McCormick

14. "A Touch of the Poet" [adapted from the Eugene O'Neill play] (4-24-74 Wednesday 9-11:30 PBS) Fritz Weaver, Nancy Marchand, Roberta Maxwell, Donald Moffat, John Kellerman, Carrie Nye

15. "To Be Young, Gifted and Black" [adapted from the works of Lorraine Hansberry by her husband Robert Nemiroff; a repeat of the N.E.T. Playhouse episode of 1/22/72] (5-1-74 Wednesday 8:30-10:00 PBS) Claudia McNeil, Blythe Danner, Ruby Dee, Barbara Barrie, Al Freeman Jr., Roy Scheider, Lauren Jones

16. "The Widowing of Mrs. Holroyd" [adapted from the D. H. Lawrence play; performed by the Long Wharf Theatre of New Haven, Connecticut] (5-8-74 Wednesday 8:30-10:45 PBS) Geraldine Fitzgerald, Frank Converse, Joyce Ebert, Rex Robbins

17. "Hogan's Goat" [adapted from the William Alfred play; a repeat of the N.E.T. Playhouse special of 10/16/71] (5-15-74 Wednesday 8:30-10:00 PBS) Robert Foxworth, Faye Dunaway, George Rose

18. "Monkey, Monkey, Bottle of Beer, How Many Monkeys Have We Here?" [by Marsha Sheiness] (5-22-74 Wednesday 8:30-10:00 PBS) Dolores Gaskins, Peggy Kirkpatrick, Jean De Baer, Diane Danzi, Rosemary DeAngelis

19. "The Sty of the Blind Pig" [by Philip Hayes Dean] (5-29-74 Wednesday 8:30-10:30 PBS) Sherman "Scatman" Crothers

Second Season

20. "Zalmen, or the Madness of God" [by Elie Wiesel] (1-8-75 Wednesday 9-11:00 PBS) Joseph Wiseman, Richard Bauer, Robert Prosky, Mark Hammer, Howard Witt, Dianne Wiest, Gary Bayer, John Koch Jr., Sanford Seeger

21. "The Year of the Dragon" [by Frank Chin] (1-15-75 Wednesday 9-10:30 PBS) George Takei, Conrad Yama, Tina Cheng, Pat Suzuki, Doug Higgins, Keenan Shimizu

22. "The Seagull" [adapted from the Anton Chekhov play; performed by the Williamstown Festival Theatre] (1-29-75 Wednesday 9-11:00 PBS) Frank Langella, Lee Grant, Blythe Danner, Kevin McCarthy, Marian Mercer, Louis Zorich, William Sevetland, George Ede, Olympia Dukakis, David Clennon

23. "Brother to Dragons" [adapted from the Robert Penn Warren poetic drama; performed by the Trinity Square Repertory Company of Providence, Rhode Island] (2-19-75 Wednesday 9-10:30 PBS)

24. "Forget-Me-Not-Lane" [adapted from the Peter Nichols comedy; performed by the Long Wharf Theatre of New Haven, Connecticut] (3-12-75 Wednesday 9-11:15 PBS) Joseph Maher (who also narrates), Geraldine Fitzgerald, Donald Moffat, Joyce Ebert

25. "The School for Scandal" [adapted from the Richard Brinsley Sheridan classic; performed by the Minneapolis Guthrie Theatre Company] (4-2-75 Wednesday 9-11:00 PBS) Patricia Conolly, Nicolas Kepros, Kenneth Welsh, Larry Gates, Bernard Behrens, Blair Brown, Barbara Bryne

26. "The Rules of the Game" [adapted from the Luigi Pirandello play; performed by the New Phoenix Repertory Company of New York] (4-30-75 Wednesday 9-10:30 PBS) John McMartin, Joan Van Ark

27. "Who's Happy Now?" [by Oliver Hailey; directed by Gordon
Davidson; performed by the Mark Taper Forum of Los An-
geles] (5-7-75 Wednesday 9-10:30 PBS) Albert Salmi, Betty
Garrett, Rue McClanahan, John Ritter, Guy Raymond, John
Fiedler, Kirby Furlong

Third Season

28. "Beyond the Horizon" [adapted from the Eugene O'Neill play]
(1-14-76 Wednesday 9-11:00 PBS) Richard Backus, Kate
Wilkinson, James Broderick, John Houseman, Geraldine
Fitzgerald (who also introduces)
29. "The First Breeze of Summer" [by Leslie Lee; presented by the
Negro Ensemble Company] (1-28-76 Wednesday 9-10:30 PBS)
Frances Foster, Janet League, Moses Gunn
30. "The Mound Builders" [by Lanford Wilson; performed by the
New York Circle Repertory Company] (2-11-76 Wednesday
9-10:30 PBS) Tanya Berezin, Brad Dourif, Trish Hawkins,
Jonathan Hogan, Rob Thirkeld, Lorin Jacobs, Stephanie Gordon
31. "The Time of Your Life" [adapted from the William Saroyan
Pulitzer Prize play] (3-10-76 Wednesday 9-11:00 PBS)
Nicholas Surovy
32. "All Over" [adapted by Edward Albee (who discusses the production) from his 1971 play; performed by the Hartford,
Connecticut Stage Company] (4-28-76 Wednesday 9-11:00
PBS) Anne Shropshire, Myra Carter, William Prince, Anne
Lynn, Pirie MacDonald, David O. Peterson
33. "Sea Marks" [written and directed by Gardner McKay] (5-12-
76 Wednesday 9-11:00 PBS) George Kearn, Veronica Castang
34. "The Patriots" [adapted from the Sidney Kingsley play; performed
by the Florida Asolo State Theatre] (5-26-76 Wednesday
9-11:00 PBS) Robert Murch, Philip Le Strange, Ralph Clanton, William Jay, Stephen Johnson, Bradford Wallace, Katherine Rao

Fourth Season

35. "Ah, Wilderness!" [adapted from the Eugene O'Neill comedy;
staged by the Connecticut Long Wharf Theatre] (10-14-76
Thursday 8:30-10:30 PBS) Richard Backus, William Swet-
land, Geraldine Fitzgerald, John Braden, Joyce Ebert, Suzanne Lederer, Swoosie Kurtz, Victor Garber, Christina
Whitmore, Anthony Petrillo, Linda Hunt, Ralph Drischell
36. "The Taming of the Shrew" [the Shakespeare classic in comedia
dell'arte, directed by William Ball (who is afterwards interviewed) and performed by the American Conservatory Theatre
of San Francisco] (11-10-76 Wednesday 9-11:00 PBS) Marc
Singer, Fredi Ostler, Stephen St. Paul, Sandra Shotwell,
William Peterson, James R. Winker, Ronald Boussom, Rick
Hamilton
37. "Eccentricities of a Nightingale" [adapted from the 1948 Tennessee Williams play; a repeat of the N. E. T. Playhouse produc-
tion] (12-1-76 Wednesday 9-11:00 PBS) Blythe Danner (as
Alma Winemiller), Frank Langella (as John Buchanan)

38. "The Prince of Homburg" [adapted from the 1811 Heinrich von Kleist play] (4-27-77 Wednesday 9-11:00 PBS) Frank Langella, Randy Duncan, K. Lype O'Dell
39. "End of Summer" [adapted from the S. N. Behrman 1936 play] (6-15-77 Wednesday 9-11:00 PBS) Helen Hayes, Lois Nettleton, Dennis Michael, Pamela Lewis, Paul Shenar, Paul Rudd, Alan Mixon
40. "Waiting for Godot" [adapted from the Samuel Beckett 1953 play] (6-29-77 Wednesday 9-11:30 PBS) Dana Elcar, Donald Moffat, Ralph Waite, Bruce French

Fifth Season

41. "Uncommon Women and Others" [the initial play of Wendy Wasserstein] (5-24-78 Wednesday 9-10:30 PBS) Jill Eikenberry, Swoozie Kurtz, Alma Cuervo, Ellen Parker, Ann McDonough
42. "Tartuffe" [adapted from the Molière classic; staged by New York's Circle in the Square] (5-31-78 Wednesday 9-11:00 PBS) Donald Moffat, Tammy Grimes, Stefan Gierasch, Geraldine Fitzgerald, Patricia Ellicott, Victor Garber, Johanna Leister

[Continuing]

ANYONE FOR TENNYSON?

The Regulars: "The First Poetry Quartet"; Jill Tanner, Cynthia Herman, George Backman, Paul Hecht (subsequently Norman Snow)

The Episodes:

First Season [telecast via PBS Mondays 7-7:30 P.M.]

1. "Poems of the Sea" (1-5-76) Stuart Gillespie, guest
2. "The Restoration Wits" (1-12-76) Cyril Ritchard, guest; readings of Charles Sackville, Earl of Dorset; Sir Charles Sedley; John Dryden; William Cavendish, Duke of Newcastle; Aphra Behn; Thomas D'Urfey
3. "The Heroic Tradition" (1-19-76) readings of Sir Walter Scott; Alfred Lord Tennyson's Lochinvar, "The Charge of the Light Brigade," "In Memoriam"; Rudyard Kipling's "Gunga Din."
4. "Limericks, Epigrams and Occasional Verse" (2-2-76) George Plimpton, guest; readings of Dorothy Parker, Hilaire Belloc, Edward Lear and "Anonymous"
5. "The First Poetry Quartet on the Battlefield at Gettysburg" (2-9-76) Richard Kiley, guest; readings of Walt Whitman's "Drum Taps"
6. "A Program of Satire" (2-16-76) readings of Dorothy Parker; e. e. cummings, Jonathan Swift, Ogden Nash, Alexander Pope, Dame Edith Sitwell

7. "Voices from the South" (2-23-76) Ruby Dee, guest; readings of Southern authors, including Tennessee Williams' "Crepe de Chine"
8. "Tales of a Wayside Inn" (3-1-76) Will Geer, guest; readings of Henry Wadsworth Longfellow, title poems: "Evangeline, " "The Village Blacksmith, " "The Rainy Day"
9. "Pulitzer Prize Poets: 1922-1950 [Part I]" (3-15-76) readings of Edwin Arlington Robinson, W. H. Auden, Gwendolyn Brooks, Mark Van Doren, Robert Frost, Amy Lowell, Marya Zaturenska, Leonard Bacon, Karl Shapiro, Conrad Aiken, Archibald MacLeish, Robert Hillyer, Leonard Speyer, George Dillon, John Gould Fletcher, Stephen Vincent Benet, William Rose Benet, Peter Viereck, Robert P. Tristram Coffin
10. "Pulitzer Prize Poets: 1951-1975 [Part II]" (3-22-76) readings of Robert Lowell, Marianne Moore, Theodore Roethke, Carl Sandburg, Archibald MacLeish, Wallace Stevens, Richard Wilbur, Elizabeth Bishop, Robert Penn Warren, Stanley Kunitz, W. D. Snodgrass, Phyllis McGinley, Alan Dugan, William Carlos Williams, Louis Simpson, John Berryman, Richard Eberhart, Anne Sexton, Anthony Hecht, George Oppen, Richard Howard, William S. Merwin, James Wright
11. "An Invitation to Romance" (4-5-76) selections from twenty love poems including Shakespeare's "If Music Be the Food of Love" and Dorothy Parker's "One Perfect Rose"
12. "Edna St. Vincent Millay (1892-1950)" (4-12-76) Valerie Harper, guest
13. "A Quiet Evening with Mother Goose" (4-19-76) readings of A. A. Milne, Robert Louis Stevenson, Ogden Nash, Edward Lear
14. "The Growth of a Poet: Sylvia Plath (1932-1963)" (4-26-76)
15. "A Poetic Feast" (5-3-76) Vincent Price, guest; selections include the Witches' scene from Macbeth
16. "An American Original: e. e. cummings" (5-10-76) readings include "Buffalo Bill's Defunct" and "anyone lived in a pretty how town"
17. "A View of Four Centuries" (5-17-76) selections from Shakespeare, Ben Jonson, W. H. Auden and Dylan Thomas

Second Season [telecast via PBS Wednesdays, 11-11:30 P.M.]

18. "New England in Autumn: The Poetry of Robert Frost" (2-9-77) readings from "Mending Wall, " "The Pasture, " "Birches"
19. "William Shakespeare: A Poet for All Times" (2-16-77) readings from Macbeth, Romeo and Juliet, others.
20. "The Poetical Art of William Blake" (2-23-77) readings include "The Tyger, " "Jerusalem, " "The Chimney Sweeper" and other selections from Songs of Innocence and Songs of Experience
21. "Thomas Hardy's Wessex" (3-2-77) Roger Hammond, guest; readings include "Great Things"
22. "World War I Soldiers and Poets" (3-9-77) Darren McGavin, guest; readings include John McCrae's "In Flanders Fields, " Alan Seeger's "I Have a Rendezvous with Death" and Rupert

Brooke's "The Soldier"

23. "Contemporary English Poets" (3-16-77) Sir John Betjeman, poet laureate of England, guest.

24. "Poetry in Translation [Part I]" (3-23-77) readings from Horace, Homer, other Roman and Greek, plus French and Spanish works

25. "Poetry in Translation [Part II]" (3-30-77) readings from Omar Khayyam's The Rubaiyat, other Oriental verse including Japanese haiku; plus Russian works

26. "The Brontë Sisters" (4-6-77) readings include Charlotte Brontë's "Rochester's Song to Jane Eyre"; Emily Brontë's "To Imagination" and works by Anne Brontë

27. "A Poetic Portrait Gallery" (4-13-77) William Shatner, guest; American poetry readings

28. "The Lowell Family" (4-27-77) readings from poetry by James Russell, Amy and Robert Lowell

29. "A Tribute to Anonymous Poets" (5-4-77) Fred Gwynne, guest; selections include "Cuckoo Song," "Groovy, Man, Groovy" and "Lord Randall"

30. "Poets on Campus" (5-11-77) readings from works by Ezra Pound, Stephen Spender, Theodore Roethke, W. D. Snodgrass, others

31. "So That's Where It Came From!" (5-18-77) readings include Ernest Dowson's "Non Sum Qualis Eram Bonae Sub Regno Cynarae" (from which derived Margaret Mitchell's title Gone with the Wind) and Dowson's "Vitae Summa Brevis Spem Nos Vetat Incohare Longam" (from which derived J. P. Miller's drama title The Days of Wine and Roses)

Third Season [telecast via PBS Mondays, 10:30-11:00 P.M.]

32. "A Zooful of Poetry" (2-6-78) readings at the San Diego Wild Animal Park include Hilaire Belloc's "The Big Baboon"

33. "The Glorious Romantics [Part I]" (2-13-78) guests Jean Marsh (as Jenny Weston), Neil Hunt (as Lord Byron), John Neville-Andrews (as Leigh Hunt), Rachel Gurney (as Lady Bessborough)

34. "The Glorious Romantics [Part II]" (2-20-78) guests Nicholas Woodeson (as John Keats), Ginni Ness (as Fanny Brawne); John Neville-Andrews and Jean Marsh

35. "The Glorious Romantics [Part III]" (2-27-78) guests Stephen Lang (as Percy Bysshe Shelley), Marilyn Meyers (as Mary Shelley), Jean Marsh and John Neville-Andrews

36. "Thomas Hardy's Wessex" [repeat of episode of 3/2/77] (3-6-78)

37. "A Zooful of Poetry" [repeat of episode of 2/6/78] (3-13-78)

38. "In Praise of the Lord" (3-20-78) poetry readings in commemoration of Holy Week

39. "William Butler Yeats: The Heart of Ireland" (3-27-78) Irene Worth (as Maud Gonne), guest; readings include "Never Give All the Heart," "Easter 1916," "An Acre of Grass," "When You Are Old"

40. "William Shakespeare: A Poet for All Times" [repeat of episode

of 2/16/77] (4-3-78)

41. "D. H. Lawrence: A Restless Spirit" (4-10-78) Robert Culp, guest; readings include "Autumn at Taos," "Song of a Man Who Is Not Loved," "Mountain Lion"

42. "Poetry of the Occult" (4-17-78) readings include Edgar Allan Poe's "Ulalume," selections from Shakespeare, J. R. R. Tolkien, Kingsley Amis

43. "The Poetry of Roger McGough" (4-24-78) Jim Dale, guest; readings from the contemporary Liverpool-born poet

44. "The Poetical Art of William Blake" [repeat of episode of 2/23/77] (5-1-78)

45. "A Salute to Contemporary Poets" (5-8-78) finalists in the Scholastic Writing Awards competition; LeVar Burton, guest

46. "A Salute to the Brownings" (5-15-78) readings of Robert and Elizabeth Barrett Browning by Jill Tanner and guests Nicholas Woodeson and Jack Gwillim

47. "American Indian Poetry" (5-22-78) poet-teacher John Twobirds Arbuckle, guest; readings include "Bear Man"

48. "The Pleasure of Poetry" (6-5-78) an appreciation, with James Whitmore, guest.

THE ADAMS CHRONICLES

Although thoroughly researched and impeccably cast, Virginia Kassel's production of Adams family history sometimes proves a cumbersome encomium. For despite some clandestine revelations, the founding father's progeny walk through American history as if it were waiting for them, the proverbial godsends. Ed Wittstein designed the PBS production, which spawned the best-selling Jack Shepherd book The Adams Chronicles: Four Generations of Greatness (Boston: Little, Brown & Co., 1975).

The Regulars: John Adams: George Grizzard; Abigail Smith Adams: Kathryn Walker; Benjamin Franklin: Robert Symonds; Samuel Adams: W. B. Brydon; Justice Gridley: John Houseman; Mrs. Smith: Nancy Marchand; John Hancock: Curt Dawson; Abigail Adams II ("Nabby"): Katherine Houghton; John Quincy Adams: Mark Winkworth; Louise Catherine Johnson Adams: Pamela Peyton-Wright; John Quincy Adams (matured): David Birney; Thomas Jefferson: Albert Stratton; Colonel William Stephens Smith: Richard Cox; King George III: John Tillinger; Abigail Adams (matured): Leora Dana; Charles Francis Adams (as a boy): Philip Anglim; Thomas Boyeston: V. V. Tammi; Charles Francis Adams (matured): Thomas A. Stewart; John Quincy Adams (as president): William Daniels; Henry Clay: George Hearn; Alexis de Tocqueville: Jean-Pierre Stewart; Tappan: Jerome Dempsey; Roger Baldwin: Bernie McInerney; Cinque (West African slave): Norman Bush; Henry Laurens Pinckney: Roger Allan Brown; Charles Francis Adams II: John Beal; Abigail Brooks: Nancy Coleman; Henry Adams: Peter Brandon; Brooks Adams: Dai Stockton; Mary Adams: Sandra Gartner; Charles Francis Adams Jr.: Ron

Siebert; Abraham Lincoln: Stephen D. Newman; Lord John Russell: Emery Battis; Marian Hooper: Gilmer McCormick; John Quincy Adams II: Nicholas Pryor; Ames: Alan Hewitt; Jay Gould: Paul Hecht

The Episodes [first telecast via PBS Tuesdays, 9-10:00]:

1. "John Adams--Lawyer (1758-1770)" (1-20-76)
2. "John Adams--Revolutionary" (1-27-76)
3. "John Adams--Diplomat" (2-3-76)
4. "John Adams--Minister to England" (2-10-76)
5. "John Adams--Vice President" (2-17-76)
6. "John Adams--President" (2-24-76)
7. "John Quincy Adams--Minister to Russia" (3-2-76)
8. "John Quincy Adams--Secretary of State" (3-9-76)
9. "John Quincy Adams--President" (3-16-76)
10. "John Quincy Adams--Congressman" (3-23-76)
11. "Charles Francis Adams--Minister to Great Britain" (3-30-76)
12. "Henry Adams--Historian" (4-6-76)
13. "Charles Francis Adams II--Industrialist" (4-13-76)

MEETING OF MINDS

Steve Allen's brilliant vision--of anachronistic luminaries gathered together for round-table polemics--has surely prompted a renewed interest in historical affairs. For no less than Mr. Allen, having mastered the usages of the video, could have conceived of a way in which historicity could be served so palatably. The mind accepts this Meeting of Minds, attuned to their shouting, bantering and introspection, first conditioned by an Allen signature: the melodious theme he himself composed.

The Regulars: Steve Allen, host and moderator

The Episodes [first season telecast via PBS Mondays, 8-9:00 P.M.]:

1. "Cleopatra/Thomas Paine/Theodore Roosevelt/Thomas Aquinas" [Part I] (1-10-77) Jayne Meadows Allen, Joe Sirola, Joe Earley, Peter Bromilow
2. "Cleopatra/Thomas Paine/Theodore Roosevelt/Thomas Aquinas" [Part II] (1-17-77) as above.
3. "Marie Antoinette/Sir Thomas More/Karl Marx/Ulysses S. Grant" [Part I] (1-24-77) Jayne Meadows Allen, Bernard Behrens, Leon Askin, Joe Earley
4. "Marie Antoinette/Sir Thomas More/Karl Marx/Ulysses S. Grant" [Part II] (1-31-77) as above.
5. "Emily Dickinson/Attila the Hun/Charles Darwin/Galileo" [Part I] (2-7-77) Katherine Helmond, Khigh Dheigh, Murray Matheson, Alexander Scourby
6. "Emily Dickinson/Attila the Hun/Charles Darwin/Galileo" [Part II] (2-14-77) as above.

Second Season [telecast via PBS Mondays, 9-10:00 P. M.]

7. "Florence Nightingale/Plato/Martin Luther/Voltaire" [Part I]
    (3-6-78) Jayne Meadows Allen, David Hooks, Leon Askin,
    John Hoyt
8. "Florence Nightingale/Plato/Martin Luther/Voltaire" [Part II]
    (3-13-78) as above.
9. "Dowager Empress Tz'u-hsi/Cesare Beccaria/Frederick Doug-
    lass/The Marquis de Sade" [Part I] (3-20-78) Beulah Quo,
    Robert Carricart, Roscoe Lee Browne, Stefan Gierasch
10. "Dowager Empress Tz'u-hsi/Cesare Beccaria/Frederick Doug-
    lass/The Marquis de Sade" [Part II] (3-27-78) as above.
11. "Susan B. Anthony/Socrates/Sir Francis Bacon/Emiliano Zapata"
    [Part I] (4-3-78) Jayne Meadows Allen, Alexander Scourby,
    James Booth, Julio Medina
12. "Susan B. Anthony/Socrates/Sir Francis Bacon/Emiliano Zapata"
    [Part II] (4-10-78) as above.

Third Season [telecast via PBS Saturdays, 8-9:00 P. M.]

13. "Elizabeth Barrett Browning/Aristotle/Niccolo Machiavelli/Sun
    Yat-sen" [Part I] (5-26-79) Jayne Meadows Allen, Bernard
    Behrens, Alfred Ryder, Keye Luke
14. "Elizabeth Barrett Browning/Aristotle/Niccolo Machiavelli/Sun
    Yat-sen" [Part II] (6-2-79) as above.
15. "Shakespeare on Love" [Part I] (6-9-79) Harris Yulin (as
    Shakespeare), Jayne Meadows Allen (as the Dark Lady of
    the Sonnetts), Anthony Caruso (as Hamlet), William Marshall
    (as Othello), Charles Lanyer (as Romeo), Fred Sadoff (as
    Iago)
16. "Shakespeare on Love" [Part II] (6-16-79) as above.
17. "Empress Theodora/Bertrand Russell/Saint Augustine/Thomas
    Jefferson" [Part I] (6-23-79) Salome Jens, John Hoyt
18. "Empress Theodora/Bertrand Russell/Saint Augustine/Thomas
    Jefferson" [Part II] (6-30-79) as above.

[Continuing]

ADDENDA

Thanks to the gracious assistance of some readers, Television Drama Series Programming: A Comprehensive Chronicle, 1959-1975, which had had numerous title and cast omissions, has been amended by way of the list below. For this the author is particularly indebted to Tise Vahimagi, Jay Goldstein and Kay Anderson. Series are in chronological sequence.

THE TWENTIETH CENTURY-FOX HOUR [video adaptations of studio productions]: "Yacht on the High Sea" also starred Casey Adams; "In Times Like These" adapted from the 1943 film The Happy Land also starred Johnny Washbrook; "Deception," adapted from the 1946 film, also starred John Williams; "Gun in His Hand" also starred Robert Wagner and Royal Dano; "Mr. Belvedere," adapted from the 1949 film, also referred to as "The Genius"; "Broken Arrow," adapted from the 1950 film, also referred to as "Apache Uprising"; "The Hefferan Family," adapted from the 1956 film, also starred Mark Damon; "Child of the Regiment" also starred Canada Lee; "The Money Maker," adapted from the 1950 film Mr. Eight Eighty, also starred James "Rusty" Lane; "Smoke Jumpers" adapted from the 1952 film Red Skies of Montana; "The Last Patriarch," adapted from the 1949 film House of Strangers, also starred Alexander Scourby; "Operation Cicero" adapted from the 1952 film Five Fingers; "End of a Gun" adapted from the 1950 film The Gunfighter; "False Witness" adapted from the 1948 film Call Northside 777; "Young Man from Kentucky" also starred Alan Hale; "City in Flames" adapted from the 1938 film In Old Chicago; "The Man Who Couldn't Wait" also referred to as "Deadline Decision"; "The Still Trumpet," adapted from the 1950 film Two Flags West, also starred Regis Toomey; "The Men in Her Life" adapted from the 1941 film Remember the Day; "The Great American Hoax" adapted from the 1951 film As Young as You Feel; "The Marriage Broker," adapted from the 1952 film The Model and the Marriage Broker, also starred Lee Patrick; "Deep Water," also referred to as "Heroes of the Deep," also starred Barry Coe.

PLAYHOUSE 90: #13, "Massacre at Sand Creek" also starred Halm Winant, Ken Mayer, William Schallert, Roy Roberts, Rick Vallin, William Bryant, Anthony Lawrence; #39, "The Fabulous Irishman" was composed by Elick Moll; #52, "The Galvanized Yankee" also starred Chuck Courtney, William Boyett, Bartlett Robinson, Sheridan Comerate, Dan Sheridan, Lynn Piper, Teddy Rooney;

#50, "The Plot to Kill Stalin" also starred Marian Seldes; #92, "Face of a Hero" also starred Rip Torn

THE LORETTA YOUNG SHOW: #25, "Ten Men and a Girl" with Regis Toomey

77 SUNSET STRIP: #12, "The Court Martial of Johnny Murdo"

RAWHIDE: #102, "Deserter's Patrol"; #169, "Incident of the Banker"

CHEYENNE (as listed): #2, "Reprieve" also with Don Megowan; #11, "Gold, Glory and Custer" also with Barry Atwater, Edward Kemmer; #15, "Riot at Arroyo Seco" also with Willis Bouchey, James Bell; #16, "Apache Blood" also with Lisa Montel; #47, "Two Trails to Santa Fe" also with Robert Carricart; #57, "The Return of Mr. Grimm" also with Stephen Roberts, Maurice Manson, Orville Sherman, Sherwood Price, Myron Healey; #68, "Massacre at Gunsight Pass" also with Pat Michan; #71, "Winchester Quarantine" also with I. Stanford Jolley, Rory Mallimson, John Allonzo; #72, "Trouble Street" also with Patrick McVey, Anna Capri, Gilman Ranken; #73, "Cross Purpose" also with Edmon Ryan, Frank De Kova; #79, "Storm Center" also with Harry Shannon, Dorothy Green, Don Megowan; #92, "One Way Ticket" also with Maureen Leeds; #110, "Pocketful of Stars" also with Robert Foulk, Frank De Kova; #111, "The Vanishing Breed" also with Roy Roberts, Vaughn Taylor; #112, "Vengeance Is Mine" also with Jean Willes; #114, "Wanted for the Murder of Cheyenne Bodie" also with Dick Foran, Robert Knapp; #115, "Showdown at Oxbend" also with Andrew Duggan

SUGARFOOT (chronicled under the SUGARFOOT/BRONCO HOUR): #37, "Funeral at Forty Mile" also with Louise Fletcher

BRONCO (as part of the SUGARFOOT/BRONCO HOUR): #30, "Montana Passage" also with Charles Cooper, Rex Reason; #32, "Legacy of Twisted Creek" also with John Anderson, Richard Hale, Randy Stuart, Henry Brandon; #34, "Tangled Trail" also with Arch Johnson; (as part of THE CHEYENNE SHOW): #42, "The Mustangers" also with Robert Ridgely; #54, "The Invaders" also with Joan Marshall, Gary Vinson; #61, "Yankee Tornado" also with Whitney Blake, John Alvin, Don Haggerty, Lee Van Cleef; #80, "One Came Back" also with John Ramondetta; #83, "The Equalizer" also with Sheldon Allman; #85, "Beginner's Luck" also with Keith Richards, Buzz Martin; #90, "Trail of Hatred" also with Nina Shipman; #94, "The Last Letter" also with Jean Allison, Arthur Space, Vito Scotti, Ken Lynch

THE WITNESS: #9, "Al Capone"

THE NAKED CITY: An omitted episode was "Prince of Life" with Murray Hamilton, telecast February 13, 1963.

ACAPULCO: #4, "Death Is a Smiling Man"

EMPIRE: #24, "Down There, the World"; #28 should be corrected to "Nobody Dies on Saturday"

REDIGO: #41, "Horns of Hate"; #45 should be corrected to "The Black Rainbow"

THE VIRGINIAN: #146, "The Welcoming Town"

THE TRAVELS OF JAIMIE MCPHEETERS: #19, "The Day of the Haunted Trail"

TEMPLE HOUSTON: #10, "Billy Hart"; #19 should be corrected to "Tend Rounds for Baby"; #22, "Last Full Moon"; #25 should be corrected to "The Town That Trespassed"; #26, "Miss Katherina"

MR. BROADWAY: An omitted episode was "Take a Walk Through a Cemetery," telecast October 3, 1964.

THE REPORTER: An omitted episode was "Rachel's Mother," telecast October 23, 1964; title to the (therefore) sixth segment should read "He Stuck in His Thumb"

BRANDED: #4, "The Rules of the Game"

THE WACKIEST SHIP IN THE ARMY: #3, "Gold Snitchers"; #24, "Voyage to Never Never"

I SPY: #45, "Tonia"

SHANE: #8, "The Other Image"; #13, "The Big Fifty"

JERICHO: #11, "Four O'Clock Bomb to London"; #13, "Both Ends Against the Ridelle"; #14, "Jackal of Diamonds"; #15, "A Switch in Time"; #16, "The Loot of All Evil"

MISSION: IMPOSSIBLE: #111, "My Friend, My Enemy"; #116, "The Statue"; #117, "Orpheus"

THE SAINT: #6, "Flight Plan"

CORONET BLUE: #5, "Faces"

MANNIX: #2, "Skid Marks on a Dry Run"; #3, "Nothing Ever Works Twice"; #4, "The Many Deaths of Saint Christofer"; #5, "Make It Like It Never Happened"; #6, "The Cost of a Vacation"; #9, "Huntdown"; #10, "Coffin for a Clown"; #12, "Turn Every Stone"; #13, "Run, Sheep, Run"; #14, "Then the Drink Takes the Man"; #20, "Another Final Exit"; #23, "To Kill a Writer"; #26, "Comes Up Rose"; #28, "To the Swiftest, Death"; #32, "Who Will Dig the Graves?"; #35, "A View of Nowhere"; #39, "Only Giants Can Play"; #49, "To Catch a Rabbit"; #50, "Eagles Sometimes Don't Fly"; #51, "Color Her Missing"; #54 "A Question of Midnight"; #57, "Memory: Zero"; #65, "A Chance at the Roses"; #67, "Harlequin's Gold"; #83, "Sunburst"; #102, "Wine from These Grapes"; #105, "Run Till Dark"; #112, "To Save a Dead Man"; #113, "Nightshade"; #114, "Babe in the Woods"; #115, "The Sound of Murder"; #118, "A Walk in the Shadows"; #119, "Lifeline"; #120, "To Draw the Lightning"; #121, "Scapegoat"; #123, "The Open Web"; #124, "Cry Silence"; #126, "Broken Mirror"; #128, "The Inside Man"; #129, "To Kill a Memory"; #130, "The Upside Down Penny"; #131, "One Step to Midnight"; #132, "Harvest of Death"; #134, "Lost Sunday"; #136, "Light and Shadow"; #137, "A Game of Shadows"; #139, "A Matter of Principle"; #140, "Out of the Night"; #141, "Carol Lockwood, Past Tense"; #143, #Search for a Whisper"; #144, "To Quote a Dead Man"; #145, "A Problem of Innocence"; #146, "The Danford File"; #154, "A World Without Sundays"; #155, "Sing a Song for Murder"; #183, "Man in a Trap"; #186, "A Ransom for Yesterday"; #191, "Design for Dying"; "Portrait in Blues," telecast September 22, 1974, was omitted; the last season should be re-numbered accordingly.

THE HIGH CHAPARRAL: #2, "The Ghost of Chaparral"

CUSTER: #1, "Sabres in the Sun"; #9, "Desperate Mission"

CIMARRON STRIP: #2, "The Legend of Jud Star"; #6, "The Battle of Bloody Stone"; #7, "The Beast That Walks Like a Man"; #11, "Nobody"; #12, "The Last Wolf"; #13, "The Deputy"; #17, "Heller"; #20, "Big Jessie"

HONDO: #6, "The Apache Kid"

THE OUTCASTS: #1, "The Outcasts" (pilot)

THE IMMORTAL: An omitted episode was "The Return" telecast December 17, 1970.

SARGE: #2, "Ring Out, Ring In"; #4, "Identity Crisis"

CANNON: #8, "Dead Pigeon"; #11, "Stone, Cold Dead"; #12, "Death Is a Double Cross"; #14, "Flight Plan"; #15, "Devil's Playground"; #16, "Treasure of San Ignacio"; #19, "The Island Caper"; #22, "The Torch"; #23, "Cain's Mark"; #24, "Murder by Moonlight"; #25, "Bold Cats and Sudden Death"; #26, "Sky Above, Death Below"; #27, "Bitter Legion"; #28, "That Was No Lady"; #29, "Stakeout"; #31, "A Long Way Down"; #32, "The Rip-Off"; #33, "Child of Fear"; #34, "The Shadow Man"; #35, "Hear No Evil"; #36, "The Endangered Species"; #37, "Nobody Beats the House"; #38, "Hard Rock Roller Coaster"; #39, "The Dead Samaritan"; #40, "Death of a Stone Seahorse"; #41, "Moving Target"; #42, "Murder for Murder"; #43, "To Ride a Tiger"; #45, "The Seventh Grave"; #48, "Deadly Heritage"

THE WALTONS: #1, "The Foundling"; #2, "The Carnival, #3, "The Calf"; #4, "The Hunt"; #5, "The Typewriter"; #6, "The Star";

#7, "The Sinner"; #8, "The Boy from the C.C.C."; #9, "The Ceremony"; #10, "The Legend"; #11, "The Literary Man"; #12, "The Dustbowl Cousins"; #13, "The Reunion"; #15, "The Actress"; #17, "The Love Story"; #18, "The Courtship"; #19, "The Gypsies"; #20, "The Deed"; #21, "The Scholar"; #22, "The Bicycle"; #23, "The Townie"; #34, "The Substitute"; #66, "The Statue"

THE MAGICIAN: #5, "Ovation for Murder"

POLICE STORY: #14, "Cop in the Middle"

BORN FREE: #1, "The Wild Land"

GET CHRISTY LOVE!: #20, "A High Fashion Heist"

LUCAS TANNER: #19, "Requiem for a Son"

PLANET OF THE APES: #7, "The Surgeon"

BARETTA: #3, "Woman in the Harbor"

THE HALLMARK HALL OF FAME (additional material): "Born Yesterday" was adapted and directed by Garson Kanin from his own 1946 play; "Man and Superman" also starred Sylvia Short and Edith King; the initial "The Green Pastures" was aired Thursday evening from 7:30 unto 9:00; "On Borrowed Time" was adapted by James Costigan from the Paul Osborn play; "Twelfth Night" was adapted by William Nichols from the Shakespeare classic and also featured Dennis King; "Hans Brinker or the Silver Skates" was adapted by Sally Benson from the Mary Mapes Dodge story, with music and lyrics by Hugh Martin, directed by Sidney Lumet and produced by Mildred Freed Alberg and Paul Feigay; James Costigan's "Little Moon of Alban" takes its title from John Millington Synge's "Dierdre of the Sorrows"; "Kiss Me, Kate" was adapted for television by Samuel and Bella Spewack, who had composed the libretto for the Cole Porter score; the musical aired Thursday evening from 9:00 to 10:30; "Arsenic and Old Lace" was adapted by Robert Hartung from the Joseph Kesselring play; "Abe Lincoln in Illinois" was adapted by Robert Emmett Sherwood from his own play; "The Hands of Cormac Joyce" was adapted by S. S. Schweitzer from the Leonard Wibberly novel and directed by Fielder Cook, commemorating the one hundredth telecast of the Hallmark Hall of Fame specials series; "The Small Miracle" also starred Marco Della Cava. An omitted segment was "The Borrowers," adapted from the Mary Norton children's classic, airing December 14, 1973, Friday evening between 8:30 and 10:00 via NBC, with featured performers Eddie Albert, Tammy Grimes and Dame Judith Anderson

THE DUPONT SHOW OF THE MONTH: "Treasure Island" also starred Max Adrian, Michael Gough, Barry Morse, Douglas Campbell, George Rose, John Colicos, George Mathews, Tim O'Connor, Tom Clancy, Betty Sinclair, Woodrow Parfrey

INDEX OF SERIES TITLES

("Book II" refers to the pre-existing volume Television Drama
Series Programming: A Comprehensive Chronicle, 1959-1975.)